Processing of

D1074106

# PROCESSING OF VISIBLE LANGUAGE 2

# NATO CONFERENCE SERIES

I Ecology
II Systems Science
III Human Factors
IV Marine Sciences
V Air—Sea Interactions
VI Materials Science

## III HUMAN FACTORS

# PROCESSING OF VISIBLE LANGUAGE 2

Edited by

## Paul A. Kolers
*University of Toronto*
*Toronto, Ontario, Canada*

## Merald E. Wrolstad
*Visible Language Journal*
*Cleveland, Ohio*

## and

## Herman Bouma
*Institute for Perception Research*
*Eindhoven, The Netherlands*

Published in cooperation with NATO Scientific Affairs Division

**PLENUM PRESS · NEW YORK AND LONDON**

Library of Congress Cataloging in Publication Data

Main entry under title:

Processing of visible language 2.

(NATO conference series: III, Human factors; v. 13)
Rev. papers presented at a conference held at Niagara-on-the-Lake, Ontario, Sept. 3-7, 1979, sponsored by the University of Toronto and the Ontario Institute for Studies in Education.
Includes index.
1. Reading, Psychology of—Congresses. I. Kolers, Paul A. II. Wrolstad, Merald Ernest. III. Bouma, H. IV. University of Toronto. V. Ontario Institute for Studies in Education. VI. Series.
BF456.R2P792                         153.6                         80-22602
ISBN 0-306-40576-8

Proceedings of the second conference on Processing of Visible Language —
sponsored by the University of Toronto and the Ontario Institute for Studies
in Education, and supported principally by the NATO Scientific Affairs
Division and also by the International Reading Association and Communications
Canada — held September 3—7, 1979, at Niagara-on-the-Lake, Ontario, Canada.

© 1980 Plenum Press, New York
A Division of Plenum Publishing Corporation
227 West 17th Street, New York, N.Y. 10011

Printed in the United States of America

## Introduction

The second symposium on processing visible language constituted a different "mix" of participants from the first. Greater emphasis was given to the design of language, both in its historical development and in its current display; and to practical questions associated with machine-implementation of language, in the interactions of person and computer, and in the characteristics of the physical and environmental objects that affect the interaction. Another change was that a special session on theory capped the proceedings. Psychologists remained heavily involved, however, both as contributors to and as discussants of the work presented.

The motivation of the conferences remains one of bringing together graphic designers, engineers, and psychologists concerned with the display and acquisition of visible language. The papers separately tended to emphasize the one of the three disciplines that mark their authors' field of endeavor, but are constructed to be general rather than parochial. Moreover, within the three disciplines, papers emphasized either the textual or the more pictorial aspects. For example, a session on writing systems ranged from principles that seem to characterize all such systems to specific papers on ancient Egyptian writing, modern Korean, and English shorthand. The complementary session on the nontextual media opened with a discussion of general principles of pictorial communication and included papers on communicating instructions, general information, or religious belief through designs and other pictorial forms, as well as a discussion of misrepresentation.

Another session was devoted to textual technology, including comprehensive reviews of the state of the art in presenting language by computer-driven machines and in optimizing the person-machine interaction. Its complementary session discussed person-machine interactions in terms of computer graphics, the Telidon system for using the home TV as something more than a source of occasional diversion, and, regarding human factors, systems for enabling the deaf to follow speech on TV and for the blind to draw. This interaction between technology and human factors remains a strong concern for the conference at the level of the environment where the interaction takes place and in the nature of the medium that allows for electronic journals.

Other forms of display and processing of information are described in the ways that maps, texts, graphs, and tables may aid or hinder understanding; the issues were discussed both at the practical level of conveying information to people of varied degrees of literacy and at the theoretical level of principles that guide good design, linguistic and pictorial.

We continue to believe that interaction among engineers, designers, and psychologists concerned with display and acquisition of visible language must work for the common good of creating systems designed for optimal human use. In time, we trust, that interaction will result in studies on which members of all three disciplines collaborated.

The conference was held at Niagara-on-the-Lake, Ontario, from September 3-7, 1979, supported principally by the Scientific Affairs Division of NATO and also by the International Reading Association and Communications Canada. It was sponsored by the University of Toronto and the Ontario Institute for Studies in Education. To all of these institutions we are grateful for support and encouragement. We thank too the Conference Office of O.I.S.E., particularly Christine Sylvester of that office, who handled the numerous details that go into making a conference.

First drafts of papers were distributed several weeks ahead and so presentations at the conference were interactive, the authors communicating their messages in a give-and-take with the audience rather than merely by reading them. The papers were revised on the basis of that interaction and then edited for some uniformity of style by Barbara Sutton; consistent with the international character of the symposium, national styles were preserved in some usages. The book was designed by Fernand Baudin. It was composed at the Computer Centre of the University of Toronto largely by Dale Wright, Rita Poon, and Vera Cabanus and at the University of Toronto Press, in a system organized by Frank Spitzer and co-ordinated by Kenneth Allen. Nancy Eveleigh aided considerably by reading proof and Diane Egerton composed the index. To all of these contributors, to both the conference and the published volume, we extend our thanks.

P. A. Kolers
M. E. Wrolstad
H. Bouma

## Participants

Ronald Baecker (Human-computer interactive systems: A state of the art review, p. 423) is associate professor of computer science and electrical engineering and director of the dynamic graphics project at the University of Toronto. Address: Computer Systems Research Group, University of Toronto, Toronto M5S 1A1, Canada.

Adrian Baer (Text enhancement and structuring in computer conferencing, p. 387) is assistant professor of computer science at New Jersey Institute of Technology. He is principally interested in interactive computer systems and modeling human spatial behavior. Address: Department of Computer Science, New Jersey Institute of Technology, 323 High Street, Newark, New Jersey 07102, U.S.A.

Robert G. Baker (Simultaneous speech transcription and TV captions for the deaf, p. 445) is now a research fellow in electronics, working on television subtitling. His training was in linguistics and human communications, and his interest is in the cognitive processes of reading and spelling. Address: Department of Electronics, University of Southampton, Southampton SO9 5NH, England.

Jacques Bertin (The basic test of the graph: A matrix theory of graph construction and cartography, p. 585) founded the laboratory for cartography and is director of the laboratory of graphics at the Ecole des Hautes Etudes en Sciences Sociales, Paris. He is the author of several volumes on the theory of optimal representation of pictorial data. Address: Laboratoire de Graphique, Ecole des Hautes Etudes, 131 Boulevard St. Michel, 75005 Paris, France.

Herbert G. Brown (Telidon Videotex and user-related issues, p. 473) is director of Data Systems and Networks at the Communications Research Centre, in Ottawa. An electrical engineer, he has worked on a number of projects in communications. Address: Communications Research Centre, Department of Communications, Ottawa, K2H 8S2 Canada.

Herman Bouma was trained in physics and medicine, a combination exercised by his interest in human factors aspects of complex behavior. He is director of the institute at which he works. Address: Institute for Perception Research IPO, Eindhoven, The Netherlands.

Ahmet Çakir (Human factors and VDU-design, p. 481) was trained in human factors research (the psychology of work) and pursues these interests by teaching and conducting research in the field. A native of Turkey, he lives now in West Germany. Address: Institut für Arbeitswissenschaft, Technische Universität Berlin, 1000 Berlin 10, F.R.G.

John Chapman (Some features affecting the text processing ability of older children, p. 219) is on the faculty of educational studies at England's Open University, where he also directs a research project on textual cohesion. Address: Faculty of Educational Studies, The Open University, Milton Keynes MK7 6AA, England.

John J. Dever (Human performance in computer aided writing and documentation, p. 405) is supervisor of Design and Documentation of Work Procedures group at Bell Laboratories. His research interests are in design of technical manuals to optimize communicative efficiency and in computer aids for writing. Address: Bell Laboratories, Piscataway, New Jersey 08854, U.S.A.

Andrew C. Downton (Simultaneous speech transcription and TV captions for the deaf, p. 445) is a lecturer in electronics at the University of Southampton, where he has also worked for some time on the development of a speech transcription system. Address: Department of Electronics, University of Southampton, Southampton S09 5NH, England.

Jay Doblin (A structure for nontextual visual communications, p. 89) studied industrial design at Pratt Institute, and worked in industry for several years before becoming director of the institute of design at Illinois Institute of Technology. He has since returned to industry on a full time basis, but continues to lecture at various universities on aspects of design and visual communication. Address: 233 East Ontario St., Chicago, Illinois 60611, U.S.A.

Michael W. Dobson (The acquisition and processing of cartographic information: Some preliminary experimentation, p. 291) is a cartographer by training but has become as interested in the reading of maps as in their making. Address: Department of Geography, State University of New York, Albany, New York 12222, U.S.A.

Julia To Dutka (Anaphoric relations, comprehension, and readability, p. 537) teaches and carries out research on reading, especially the processes that mediate comprehension of text, a subject she studied at Columbia University. Address: The Reading Centre, Montclair State College, Upper Montclair, New Jersey 07043, U.S.A.

Howard E. Egeth (Interpreting direction from graphic displays: North-south superiority in the judgment of relative location, p. 315) is a professor of psychology and carries out research chiefly in the areas of perceiving, attending, learning, and remembering. Address: Department of Psychology, The Johns Hopkins University, Baltimore, Maryland 21218, U.S.A.

Lawrence T. Frase (Human performance in computer aided writing and documentation, p. 405) is on the technical staff of Bell Laboratories where, alternating with university appointments, he conducts research

on reading, reasoning, and writing, especially now on the use of computers to support literacy. Address: Bell Laboratories, Piscataway, New
Jersey 08854, U.S.A.

Ignace J. Gelb (Principles of writing systems within the frame of visual communication, p. 7) is F.P. Hixon Distinguished Service Professor at the
University of Chicago, which his extensive scholarship has graced since
1929. Address: Oriental Institute, The University of Chicago, Chicago,
Illinois 60637, U.S.A.

Leslie Henderson (Wholistic models of feature analysis in word recognition: A
critical examination, p. 207) is on the faculty of the Hatfield Polytechnic
to which he went after a stint of scholarship and teaching in Canada. He is
concerned largely with psychological aspects of literacy. Address: School
of Natural Sciences, The Hatfield Polytechnic, Hatfield, Hertfordshire
AL10 9AB, England.

Vernon A. Howard (Theory of representation: Three questions, p. 501) has
taught in departments of philosophy and schools of education in
Canada, England, and the United States. A gifted singer and dedicated
runner, he has been especially interested in applying philosophical aspects of theory of knowledge to skilled cognitive performances, including reading and writing. Address: Graduate School of Education, Harvard University, Cambridge, Massachusetts 02138, U.S.A.

Stacey A. Keenan (Human performance in computer aided writing and
documentation, p. 405) works with Frase and Dever on optimizing the
presentation of information in text and on computer aids to writing.
Address: Bell Laboratories, Piscataway, New Jersey 08854, U.S.A.

Paul A. Kolers is an experimental psychologist who has carried out research on
several aspects of mental function, perception, and use of language.
Address: Department of Psychology, University of Toronto, Toronto,
M5S 1A1 Canada.

Edmund S. Meltzer (Remarks on ancient Egyptian writing, with emphasis on its
mnemonic aspects, p. 43) earned his doctoral degree in Egyptology at
the University of Toronto and has published widely on the subject. He
and his wife are spending the current year in Egypt studying ancient
inscriptions. Address: Egyptian Department, Royal Ontario Museum,
Toronto M5S 2C6, Canada.

Neville Moray (Towards an electronic journal, p. 401) is particularly interested in
human factors aspects of the man-machine interface, and especially the
measurement of mental workload. He has taught psychology in England,
Canada, the United States, and now Scotland. Address: Department of
Psychology, University of Stirling, Stirling FK9 4LA, Scotland.

Robert A. Myers (The presentation of text and graphics, p. 337) is senior manager
of the Terminal Technologies department at IBM, where he is responsi-

ble for research on printing, facsimile, optical communications, semiconductor lasers, and image processing. Address: IBM Thomas J. Watson Research Center, Yorktown Heights, New York 10598, U.S.A.

Alan F. Newell (Simultaneous speech transcription and TV captions for the deaf, p. 445) is lecturer in electronics at Southampton and actively engaged in the development of the speech transcription system there. Address: Department of Electronics, University of Southampton, Southampton S09 5NH, England.

Georges Noizet (Optimal segmentation for sentences displayed on a video-screen, p. 375) created the laboratory of experimental psychology at the Université de Provence before becoming professor and head in Paris. Address: Laboratoire de Psychologie Experimentale, Université René Descartes, 28, rue Serpente, 75006 Paris, France.

C. Douglas O'Brien (Telidon Videotex and user-related issues, p. 473) is a research engineer and member of the team working on the Telidon project. Address: Communications Research Centre, Department of Communications, Ottawa, K2H 8S2 Canada.

Howard E. Paine (Some problems of illustration, p. 143) is art director of *National Geographic Magazine*. In addition, he lectures on design at George Washington University, and is a member of a number of national and international committees related to design and the arts. Before joining the magazine, he worked for several years in the printing and advertising industries. Address: National Geographic Magazine, Washington, D.C. 20036, U.S.A.

Helen M. Pattison (The structure of writing systems as evidence for the psychological processes involved in perception, p. 25) did her advanced studies in mathematical psychology and is at present investigating the development of literacy in deaf children. Address: Department of Psychology, University of Reading, Earley Gate, Whiteknights, Reading RG6 2AL, England.

David N. Perkins (Pictures and the real thing, p. 259) trained in mathematics and psychology and is now co-director of Project Zero investigating human use of symbols. In 1976 he received a Guggenheim Fellowship to pursue studies of creative processes, and at present actively investigates picture perception, reasoning, and other aspects of cognition and learning. Address: Project Zero, Harvard Graduate School of Education, Cambridge, Massachusetts 02138, U.S.A.

Lynne A. Price (Communicating with computers, p. 551) studied computer science and is currently engaged in research on online documentation, exercising her interests thereby in linguistics and in user-oriented computing. Address: BNR INC., 3174 Porter Drive, Palo Alto, California 94304, U.S.A.

Joël Pynte (Optimal segmentation for sentences displayed on a video-screen, p. 375) has worked for several years at the psychology laboratory maintained by the Centre National de la Recherche Scientifique in Provence, especially in psycholinguistics and the study of reading. Address: Département de Psychologie, Université de Provence, 13621 Aix-en-Provence, France.

Nathan Relles (Communicating with computers, p. 551) received his degrees in computer sciences as preparation for his work on improving the ease with which people can learn to use computers. Address: Software Research Department, Sperry Univac, Blue Bell, Pennsylvania 19424, U.S.A.

Beverly van Orden Roller (Graph reading abilities of seventh grade students, p. 305) has taught at almost all levels of the public school system and university. She is a reading specialist. She acknowledges the advice and help of William Eller in carrying out the research she reports. Address: Wheat Ridge Senior High School, Jefferson, Colorado, U.S.A.

William Sawchuk (Telidon Videotex and user-related issues, p. 473) did his advanced training in physics, and is now program manager for Image Communications at the Communications Research Centre. Address: Communications Research Centre, Department of Communications, Ottawa, Canada K2H 8S2.

Wayne L. Shebilske (Structuring an internal representation of text: A basis of literacy, p. 227) is a psychologist who has carried out research on various aspects of literacy, from movements of the eyes to understanding paragraphs. Address: Department of Psychology, University of Virginia, Charlottesville, Virginia 22901, U.S.A.

M. Jeanne Sholl (Interpreting direction from graphic displays: North-south superiority in the judgment of relative location, p. 315) at the time of writing was a graduate student in experimental psychology interested in cognitive processes. Address: Department of Psychology, The Johns Hopkins University, Baltimore, Maryland 21218, U.S.A.

Philip T. Smith (The structure of writing systems as evidence for the psychological processes involved in perception, p. 25) trained in mathematics and psychology and pursues both interests still in research on scaling and on reading and writing. Address: Department of Psychology, University of Stirling, Stirling FK9 4LA, Scotland.

Joan Gay Snodgrass (Toward a model for picture and word processing, p. 565) went to the psychology department at New York University after completing her training at the University of Pennsylvania. She is especially interested in mathematical models of memory, an aspect of pattern recognition. Address: Department of Psychology, New York University, New York, New York 10003, U.S.A.

Alan Stokes (Some features affecting the text processing ability of older children, p. 219) is a research fellow in the Faculty of Educational Studies at the Open University, where he went after several years of teaching history and modern languages, and where he now carries out research aimed at improving comprehensibility of school books. Address: Faculty of Educational Studies, The Open University, Milton Keynes MK7 6AA, England.

John R. Storey (Telidon Videotex and user-related issues, p. 473) is Head, Terminal Research, at the Communications Research Centre, where he has worked for several years on aspects of electronic communications. Address: Communications Research Centre, Department of Communications, Ottawa, Canada K2H 8S2.

Karol P. Szlichcinski (The syntax of pictorial instructions, p. 113) became interested in human factors research while at Cambridge University and joined the British Post Office Research Department on his graduation. He is concerned with the behavioral aspects of communication and especially with the way best to present instructions in written materials. Address: Post Office Long Range Studies Division, Cambridge CB2 1PE, England.

Insup Taylor (The Korean writing system. An alphabet? A syllabary? A logography?, p. 67) born in Korea, is fluent in several languages, Oriental and Occidental, a fact of some consequence for her research in psycholinguistics. Address: Division of Life Sciences, Scarborough College, University of Toronto, West Hill, Ontario M1C 1A4, Canada.

William C. Treurniet (Spacing of characters on a television display, p. 365) is a research psychologist at the Communications Research Centre, an activity he took up after first studying physics. He concentrates his research on the human factors aspects of electronic communication systems. Address: Communications Research Centre, Department of Communications, Ottawa, Canada K2H 8S2.

Murray Turoff (Text enhancement and structuring in computer conferencing, p. 387) is professor of computer science at N.J.I.T. and director of its computerized conferencing and communications center. Address: Department of Computer Science, New Jersey Institute of Technology, 323 High Street, Newark, New Jersey 07102, U.S.A.

Jean D.M. Underwood (The influence of texture gradients on relief interpretation from isopleth maps, p. 279) trained as a geographer but is particularly interested in how maps are read. Address: Matlock College of Education, Matlock, Derbyshire DE4 3FW, England.

Richard L. Venezky (Communicating with computers, p. 551) is both a computer scientist and a linguist. In addition to English orthography, his research has explored man-machine communication and computer-based education. Address: Department of Educational Studies, University of Delaware, Newark, Delaware 19711, U.S.A.

Christopher N. Vincent (Pictorial recognition and teaching the blind to draw, p. 459) has worked in industry, for government, and in schools as designer, illustrator, consultant, and teacher. He is a member of the executive council of the Institute of Scientific and Technical Communicators, and a member of the Institute of Patentees and Inventors. Address: Production Illustration Division, Bournville School of Arts and Crafts, Bristol Road South, Birmingham B31, England.

Howard Wainer (Making newspaper graphs fit to print, p. 125) studied mathematics and psychology before first joining the faculty at the University of Chicago and then concentrating his skills upon a full time research effort as Senior Research Associate at BSSR. Address: Bureau of Social Science Research, Inc., 1990 M Street, N.W., Washington, D.C. 20036, U.S.A.

Robert H.W. Waller (Graphic aspects of complex texts, p. 241) is a lecturer in textual communications. Trained as a typographer, he carries out research in conjunction with psychologists on problems of text design and evaluation. Address: Institute of Educational Technology, The Open University, Milton Keynes MK7 6AA, England.

Anthony Welch (Symbolic use of calligraphy in Islamic texts, p. 157) is a specialist in the art and architectural history of the Muslim world and has conducted research in a number of Middle Eastern and Asian countries as well as on major collections of Islamic art in Europe and North America. Address: Department of History in Art, University of Victoria, Victoria, B.C. V8W 2Y2, Canada.

Patricia Wright (Usability: The criterion for designing written information, p. 183; and Textual literacy: An outline sketch of psychological research on reading and writing, p. 517) is a member of the scientific staff of MRC where she has done research on various aspects of the perception and optimal production of written information as well as as lecturing at Churchill College, Cambridge. Address: MRC Applied Psychology Unit, 15 Chaucer Road, Cambridge CB2 2EF, England.

Merald E. Wrolstad has a long and deep interest in written languages, expressed as editor and publisher of the journal *Visible Language* and by his work in designing and editing the publications of the museum. Address: Cleveland Museum of Art, Cleveland, Ohio 44106, U.S.A.

# Contents

## Graphic literacy

## Textual technology

## Graphic technology

## Theory of representation

# Contents

# Writing systems

# Introduction

Merald E. Wrolstad

How can it be that written language, which has been since time immemorial man's basic tool for organizing his most complicated thinking, should itself still be in need of organization? Written language per se has been accomplished over millennia in strange and wonderful ways. It is our understanding of the organization of written language that is in need of attention. It is our lack of common research principles and practices after these millennia that is a little disconcerting.

Can we hope that these conferences on the processing of visible language will be able to sort things out, once and for all? Even to think in terms of a comprehensive theory of written language is a tall order. Perhaps what we need most is the confidence of the kindergarten child who, having announced his intention of drawing a picture of God, was told, "But we don't know what God looks like." "Well," he said, "we will when I get this done."

What, we might ask, does written language look like? The authors of the following papers suggest that we look again at systems and structures and principles and features and definitions. We are reminded several times that because of current priorities linguistic research will probably be of little help in our organizational efforts. Yet surely if we examine the language literature over the past decade, we have to admit that things are looking up. Is the study of language, in fact, at the apogee of a pendulum swing away from earlier priority to written language? It just may be that the pendulum is beginning its fall back again. Although lack of attention within linguistics may frustrate us at times, it should certainly not deter us from sorting things out on our own—which may be the best way after all. If leadership is needed, it was in evidence at the second conference on the processing of visible language.

More than anyone, perhaps, I. J. Gelb has been concerned about the lack of adequate consideration for the broad aspects of written language. In his tutorial paper he outlines the central topics to be addressed if we are to begin laying the foundations for "a full science of writing."

Gelb insists that we see written language in context. We must realize, first of all, that human intercommunication and personal expression are so closely intertwined that it is impossible not to consider them together. We are forced, in other words, to see written language in terms of communication. Writing is preeminently another system of signs.

In actual practice, Gelb reminds us, in any act of communication we are dealing with signs from a mixture of systems. Nowhere is this better demonstrated than in the story we can piece together of the emergence of written language. Gelb sees, for example, no sharp divisions between early artistic and communicative graphics. He discusses the influences of notational objects. He stresses the importance of a systematic correlation between "sign and sound." But written language for Gelb remains essentially "a system of visual communication." All writing is pictorial in origin, and any future research must continue to stress the relation of sign and sight.

Philip Smith and Helen Pattison are interested in the psychological processes involved in perception but their immediate research area is specialized writing-systems: shorthands for English. They theorize that an examination of the way people write when under pressure—either very quickly or using a minimum of space ("abbreviatory" systems such as classified advertising)—may reveal psychologically natural ways of representing language because only the essential infomation will be represented.

Looking at both historic and current shorthands, Smith and Pattison are interested most in the fit between written systems and spoken systems at both the abstract and surface levels of language. The fit, it turns out, is complex and unsystematic. No transcription system is pure, none being either entirely phonemic or entirely graphemic. As with any successful writing-system, shorthands provide the essential links between two or more linguistic levels, from superficial acoustic cues to the most abstract forms of comprehension and inference. Writing-systems work this way, Smith and Pattison suggest, because that is the way our perception processes probably work: by integration and interaction of diverse sources of perceptual information.

Our realization of these processes is not enhanced, they contend, by the too neatly boxed and labeled models we find worked out for us on the printed page. What these models fail to show, for example, is our processing of several levels of linguistic information at the same time. It is the gaps *between* the boxes that contain the more important and more complicated relationships.

How can these relationships be shown? Is our lack of adequate visual presentation part of our misunderstanding about language processes, for writer and reader alike? Have our most sophisticated graphic techniques been enlisted, as, for example, the introduction of a third dimension to the page (as Wim Crouwel demonstrated at the first conference in Eindhoven) or the adaptation of new computer graphic techniques for showing movement? The graphic designer has not been given the problem; the psychologist has not yet realized the range of tools he has at hand; and that is why we have brought the psychologist and the graphic designer together!

There are few graphic displays as intriguing as Egyptian hieroglyphics. Edmund Meltzer insists that we approach them visually as "word pictures." He is interested in the processes by which Egyptian writing works and the way in which it grew as a composite of mutually complementary elements—semantic, representational, phonetic. But the Egyptians are a very visual people, and the thread running through the evolution of hieroglyphic writing for over 3500 years was the pervasiveness of "the word picture as a mnenomic unit."

Meltzer is interested also in the fit of our written and spoken expressions of language but, in Egyptian, "vocalic structure" was subordinated to other priorities. Hieroglyphic script is not syllable-oriented; symmetry of the word picture took precedence over the "right" order of consonants. Phonetic complementation was but one of multiple determinatives used in a variety of ways.

Meltzer reminds us of the determining influences of the skilled scribe. The word groups provided great potential for manipulation in cryptography and inventive uses of the script. Not least among the scribes' accomplishments was the incorporation of foreign words and phrases, a continuing modification of the written languages of the early civilizations and, indeed, of our own as well. The scribes developed the cursive scripts—hieratic and demotic—as hieroglyphics were adapted to pen and ink on papyrus. Writing became increasingly simple and abstract but the composite nature of the written language remained intact, "boiled down" into a more cursive, ligatured form.

Meltzer reminds us of our biases and questions our assumptions about the undisputed superiority of alphabetic writing. If we see in the various ancient systems of writing and, indeed, in contemporary logographic systems, only unrealized graphic expression struggling towards phonetization, we have failed to grasp the essential vitality that holds these sophisticated systems together. Egyptian hieroglyphic writing must be seen as a set of conventions, as "a semiologic complex unsurpassed by any other writing system."

Insup Taylor reports on the phonetization of a writing system par excellence. Hangul was invented in the fifteenth century by a committee of scholars to enable the Korean people to write King Sejong about their problems. Taylor discusses the Korean system of writing as an optimal phonetic system with selected advantages as an alphabet, a syllabary, and a logography.

Perhaps the most interesting aspect of Hangul as a system of writing is its use of spatial units (or letters) of varying visual/syllabic complexity. We are becoming increasingly aware of the importance of spatial processing of language (some of the glue between the information-processing boxes!), and the relationship of Hangul's unique pattern of symbols to other Far Eastern languages and, indeed, to alphabetic systems, is an area in need of research. Taylor, however, is reception-oriented (which is fair enough), and she adds to our appreciation of the many approaches man has taken in evolving our systems of written language.

The authors of the following papers, then, explore ancient systems and modern systems, natural systems and contrived systems, general systems and specialized systems. Each of these systems, we discover, is a mixed bag. And, in sum, our approach to writing-systems and the world's systems of writing can be no different. We color in squares and connect dots according to our individual research predispositions.

What does written language look like? At this stage our answer can only be an echo of St. Augustine, "I knew what time was—until somebody asked me."

# Principles of writing systems within the frame of visual communication

I. J. Gelb

*In this paper principles and concepts governing systems of signs, generally, and visual communication, specifically, are discussed first. Then the definition and view of the structure and typology of writing given in* A study of writing *and subsequent studies is dealt with. Finally my new view of writing is presented.*

In order to understand the function of writing as a communicative system, it is necessary to look at it within the framework of other communicative systems or systems of signs.

### Animal communication

Ever since Pavlov's findings, the possibility has been seriously entertained that the differences between human and animal communication may be quantitative rather than qualitative. The various communicatory modes observed among animals are visual (gestures, postures, facial expressions, discrete wiggle-and-dance signals of the bees), auditory (calls, whistles), olfactory (scent signals, odor trails), and tactile (touching with paws, nose, etc.). The use of visual markings by human beings may find its functional analogue in the use of urine by dogs for signaling purposes. (I believe Julian Huxley estimated that only about 10 percent of animal communication is achieved by the usual sensory modes, leaving a great deal still to be accounted for.)

### Systems of signs

Like animals, man interacts communicatively by means of conventional signs. A system of signs is an assemblage of organically related signs. A sign may be a word in oral language or a written mark in writing. The most common systems of signs among human beings are oral language, received aurally, gesture language, received visually, and writing, including drawing, painting, scratching, or incising markings on objects or on any other more or less durable material, also received visually.

There is no good term to cover all the conventional means of communication through signs. French scholars at times use *le langage* in this sense, while calling the oral language *langage parlé*, *langage articulé*, or simply *la langue*. In English, "language" may be used for all means of communication through signs, and "speech" for the oral language alone.

*Definition of visual communication*
Visual communication may be defined as a system or device using conventional
signs which are emitted by one or more individuals by any means possible—
natural or artificial—and are received visually by one or more individuals.

*Meaning of system of signs and devices*
Communication may be achieved either by signs, such as a grin or a memorial
cross, which do not form part of a well-organized system, or by signs forming part
of a system, such as an alphabet. The term "device" is used for various kinds of
communicative behavior that cannot easily be organized into a system, such as the
body and hand motions of Neapolitans, as opposed to the gesture language of
deafmutes.
        Because of innumerable types, sub-types, and inter-types of communi-
cative behavior, it is impossible to separate clearly systems of signs from devices.

*Meaning of "conventional"*
The term "conventionally," used in the description of communicative behavior,
implies that the signs used by some individuals can be understood and reacted to
by others. Any outward expression that is not understandable is not a sign and is
not part of a communicative system. Some examples are meaningless scribblings
on paper by a child or "nonsense words" in the language.

*Process of communication*
The process of communication is composed of three elements: emission, reception, and such intervening physical features as sound or light waves. The emission
of communication may be achieved by any means possible, natural (gesture, body
motion) or artificial (fire, smoke, light, electronic). Because the means of emitting
communication are too varied and too numerous to permit any systematic
classification, the discussion of the systems must start from the point of reception,
mainly visual, auditory, and, to a much more limited extent, tactile. Olfactory and
gustatory signs led to no fully developed systems of signs.

*Communication versus expression*
Man, as a social being, finds himself or visualizes himself to be at all times in
situations in which he can express himself artistically only by communicating.
And, conversely, all forms of human communication serve or may serve at the
same time the aim of personal artistic-esthetic expression. It seems, therefore, that
the aims of communication and expression are so closely intertwined in all forms
of human behavior that normally it is impossible to discuss one without being
forced to consider the other as well.
        The two elements, artistic expression and communication, may be
exemplified in a single painting, such as Picasso's "Guernica," or in a series of

sequential pictures, such as the narrative representation on Trajan's Column,
Lynd Ward's novels in woodcuts, or comic strips such as *Peanuts* or *Dick Tracy*.

*Bilateral communication*
As implied from the etymology of the first syllable in "communication" (from the
Latin *cum*, "with"), communication involves the presence of two agents, the emittor and the receptor. Bilateral agents may be either personal (man) or impersonal
(animal), or any combination of the two. Even a communication from ego to ego
(memory aids, private notes) involves the presence of two agents, the first ego as
the emittor and the second ego as the receptor. The question of animate (man,
animal) or inanimate (smell of a flower, lightning) and of terrestrial (man, animal,
flower) or extraterrestrial (lightning) is beyond the scope of this paper.

*Sequential versus non-sequential order*
The order of the elements of a communication may be either sequential, as in oral
language, old calendar notations, or narrative representations, or non-sequential,
as in a primitive drawing on a rock or a modern map, where communication is
achieved by the totality of visual markings of various types given in a non-
sequential order. The sequential order of markings is characteristic mainly of the
phonographic stage of writing. The non-sequential order is found mainly in pre-
and proto-stages of writing and para- or meta-devices of writing. See below.

Our standard English writing which is mainly sequential, has some non-
sequential features as well, as in the writing of 22, $2^3$, $\sqrt[3]{27}$, £1, 1 lb., an icebox, a
nice box, and so on.

*Momentary versus stable communication (or recording)*
Some systems of signs, such as oral language, gesture language, or drum or fire
signals, are restricted in terms of time and space: in time because as soon as the
communication is made it is gone and cannot be revived except by repetition; in
space because it can be achieved only between individuals standing in relative
proximity to each other. Only visual systems based on the use of objects (quipu
"writing," for example) or markings on objects (writing proper) are not restricted
by the bounds of time and space and serve the purpose of stable communication or
recording.

*Concept of broad versus narrow*
Henry Sweet's very fruitful contrast of "broad" versus "narrow" is a fundamental
part of my research on writing. That concept may be illustrated by broad sounds
that we call "phones" (no limit) versus narrow sounds that we call "phonemes"
(limited number), "Saxons" versus "Saxony," "land of the Slavs" versus "Slovakia"
or "Slovenia." This concept is stressed here because of a misunderstanding of my
use of the term "forerunners," which led some scholars to infer that forerunners

of writing were excluded from my definition of writing. The use of "forerunners" for a subdivision of the broad class of writing should have been no more baffling than the general use of the term "prehistory," for a subdivision of history.

## Full versus limited systems

A system of signs may be either full, as in spoken language or writing proper, or limited, as in signaling by means of drums, whistles, or bugles, signaling by means of fire, smoke, or light, counting with the help of objects such as strings or knots, flower and gem "languages," musical notation, and mimetic-dance notation.

### Conjoint systems and devices

Pure systems may be reconstructed by scholars but in reality communication is achieved, more often than not, by the use of signs derived from more than one system. A formalized combination of language, hand gesture, and body motion has played an important role in the ritual proceedings of all times and places. A preacher may restrict himself to oral language in delivering his sermon (and perhaps put his congregation to sleep). A more effective one will accompany his speech by hand gestures, body motions, and facial expressions. There are some primitive people who can count only up to ten and only by uttering the numerals and indicating them at the same time on their fingers. Maps and charts often exhibit a combination of full writing in black plus color plus special diagrammatic devices.

Conjoint types are recognizable also within one system of signs, such as writing, and even within one kind of writing, such as our alphabet. Thus we find *pictorial* forms, such as † for the cross beside *linear* signs in "cross," or *logographic* or word signs, such as 7 or †, for the *alphabetic* "seven" or "dead."

### Primary systems versus secondary transfers

In classifying the various means or systems of human intercommunication, it is necessary to distinguish between primary and secondary means of communication or between primary and secondary systems. When a father signals a command to his son by whistling, he expresses his command directly in the whistle without the intermediary of spoken language. This is a primary means of communication. If the father calls his son by whistling two tones in imitation of the falling and rising tones in the word "son" in his language (as in the case of some African tone languages), he is calling by means of a linguistic transfer. His call, conveyed through the means of linguistic elements, represents a secondary means of communication. Similarly, the spoken word, "son," is a sign in the primary system of signs called "language." In the written word, "son," there is a secondary transfer of the language sign into three written letters of our alphabet. If the three written letters are then transmitted by means of three flashlight signals, the resulting flashes are signs of signs or tertiary signs. There is no limit to such transfers.

*Writing and oral language*
The degree of correlation between primary systems and secondary transfers may vary from very close to very loose. The correlation between the three phonemes of the spoken word, "son," of the primary system called language and the three written letters for the word, "son," of the secondary system called writing is very close. The correlation between writing and oral language is close to very close in what I call phonographic systems of writing but even in those systems the correlation is never full because, generally, they fail to indicate adequately the prosodic features of the oral language, such as quantity, stress, pitch, and so on. Within phonographic systems, the correlation is stronger in alphabetic and syllabic writings than in word-syllabic writings. It is also stronger in the earlier stages of a certain system of writing than in its later stages because a writing system, when first introduced, usually reproduces rather faithfully the underlying phonemic structure of the language. Writing, more conservative than language, generally does not keep up with the continuous changes in language and eventually diverges more and more from its linguistic counterpart. A good example is the old Latin alphabet, with its relatively good fit between graphemes and phonemes, compared to current French or English writings, with their tremendous divergencies between graphemes and phonemes. In some cases, spelling reforms have helped to remedy the situation. The best fit between phonemes and graphemes has been achieved in the Korean writing of the sixteenth century and in the modern Finnish and Czech systems.

The correlation between writing and oral language varies from loose to very loose in the pre- and proto-stages of writing and in para- or meta-devices of writing (Gelb, 1968, pp. 198-199; 1974, p.1041b; 1975, pp. 64-65).

*A previous definition of writing*
As discussed and defined in *A study of writing*, writing in the broadest sense is a system of human intercommunication by means of visual markings used conventionally. Crucial in this definition are "visual markings" (or "marks," or "signs," or "letters") — not objects or shape of objects but markings on objects or on any more or less solid material. Writing in the broadest sense includes semasiography, phonography, and para-graphy.

In semasiography (sometimes called "ideography") visual markings are used to express meaning but not necessarily linguistic elements. The semasiographic stage is best represented by the various pre- and proto-aspects of writing which I included under forerunners of writing, with their descriptive-representational and identifying-mnemonic devices. Examples are drawings on a rock (non-sequential) or a primitive lunar calendar on a cut stone (sequential) (Gelb, 1963, pp. 1, 6 ff., 11, 13, 24-51, 190-194).

In phonography, or full writing, visual markings express linguistic elements, generally in a sequential order. Examples are Sumerian logo-syllabic writing, Cherokee syllabary, or the English alphabet (Gelb, 1963, pp. 60-189, 194-198).

Para-graphy comprises various devices used within or in addition to writing proper. As in the proto- and pre-aspects of writing, there is only a loose correlation between visual markings and oral language, and the order of the elements of the various devices is generally non-sequential. Examples are statistical charts or ledgers inserted within the running text or maps with their diagrammatic and color devices (Gelb, 1963, pp. 15-20).

We can subsume the three types under two classes: first, the phonographic class, with the full type of writing, characterized by a close correlation between signs of writing and oral language, and, second, the semasiographic class, including both the pre- and proto-type as well as the para- or meta-type, in which there is only a very loose correlation between visual markings and linguistic elements.

### Typology and structure of writing
This topic has been discussed exhaustively (Gelb, 1963) and a lengthy discussion here is unnecessary. What follows is a brief outline of the various types, presented in a more or less historical order of development.

### Pictorial and diagrammatic signs
All writing is basically pictorial, "representational" in origin. There is, however, a small number of diagrammatic, non-representational signs that do not go back to original pictures, but are simple geometric forms, such as strokes, circles, triangles, or squares. Such diagrammatic signs are used mainly to express numbers.

### Forerunners of writing
The unifying characteristic of all the primitive attempts at visual communication is the lack of a systematic correlation between visual markings and linguistic elements. All employ devices and conventions relating to the meaning or meanings of certain visual marks; none has developed a set of signs with a fully established correspondence between sign and sound.

There are two main types of forerunners of writing. One is descriptive-representational devices which utilize means similar to those used in drawings produced as a result of an artistic-esthetic urge, but differ in that they may contain only those elements that are necessary for the transmission of the communication and may lack the embellishments that form part of an artistic picture. No sharp division between artistic and communicative pictures can be established. The best examples are found on rock drawings in both the Old and New Worlds, dating from the oldest paleolithic down to modern times. The other forerunner is identifying-mnemonic devices, in which the individual pictures or signs are used not to paint or describe an event but to identify or record a person, an animal, an object, a song, a proverb, and so on. Thus a drawing of a threaded needle among the African Ewe suggests the proverb, "The thread follows the needle" (our "chip off the old block"). Here an individual picture does not reproduce the whole verse or proverb, but gives only a suggestion of it.

*Development from forerunners of writing to full writing*

By using pictures to identify objects or beings a complete correspondence is established and gradually conventionalized between the pictures of objects and beings and their names in the oral language. Once people discovered that words can be expressed in written signs, a new and much improved method of communication was firmly established. It was no longer necessary to express a sentence such as "man killed lion" by a composite drawing depicting a man, spear or bow in hand, in the process of killing a lion, as in the descriptive-representational device. The three words could now be written by means of three sequential signs representing man, spear or bow (killing), and lion.

A device in which individual signs can express individual words should naturally lead to the development of a complete system of word signs, that is, word writing or logography. However, to create and memorize thousands of signs for the thousands of words and names existing in a language is so impractical that logographic writing would need to be adapted in some new way to develop into a useful system.

A primitive logographic writing can develop into a full system only if it succeeds in attaching a phonetic value to a sign independent of its meaning as a word. This process is called "phonetization" and is the most important single step in the history of writing. In modern usage, the device is called "rebus writing" as, for example, in the drawings of an eye and a saw for "I saw."

With the introduction of phonetization and the subsequent systematization of spelling rules and writing conventions, complete systems were established which made possible the expression of all linguistic elements by means of two kinds of signs: logograms or word signs and syllabograms or syllabic signs. Such systems are called "logo-syllabic."

*Logo-syllabic writing*

There are seven original and fully developed logo-syllabic systems: Sumerian (and Akkadian or Assyro-Babylonian) in Mesopotamia, 3100 B.C. to A.D. 75, Egyptian hieroglyphic in Egypt, 3000 B.C. to A.D. 400, Proto-Elamite in Elam, 3000 B. C. to 2200 B.C., Proto-Indic in the Indus Valley, around 2200 B.C., Cretan around 2000 B.C., Hittite hieroglyphic in Anatolia and Syria, 1600 B.C. to 800 B.C., and Chinese in China, 1300 B.C. to the present. Of the seven systems, three—Proto-Elamite, Proto-Indic, and Cretan—are as yet undeciphered.

The system of the Mayas does not represent a full logo-syllabic writing, because, even in its most advanced stage, it did not attain the level of phonographic development that the other systems had in their early stages.

### Syllabic writing

Out of four logo-syllabic systems four syllabaries, showing various degrees of simplification, were developed: cuneiform syllabaries (Elamite, Hurrian, etc.) from Akkadian cuneiform, West Semitic syllabaries (Ugaritic, Phoenician, Old Aramaic, Old Hebrew, etc.) from Egyptian hieroglyphic, Aegean syllabaries (Linear A, Linear B, Cypriot, etc.) from Cretan, and the Japanese syllabary from Chinese.

The term "West Semitic syllabaries" is used to express my firm conviction that these writings are syllabaries and not alphabets as is often assumed. The West Semitic writings follow exactly the pattern of their Egyptian prototype which cannot be anything else but a syllabary from the point of structure and typology of writing.

### Alphabetic writing

If by the word alphabet we understand a writing that expresses single phonemes of a language, then the first alphabet was formed by the Greeks. It was the Greeks who, having accepted in full the forms of the West Semitic syllabary, evolved a system of vowel signs which, attached to the old syllabic signs, reduced the values of the syllabic signs to simple consonantal signs, thus creating for the first time a full alphabetic system of writing. It was from the Greeks that the Semites in turn learned the use of vowel marks and created their own alphabets.

In the past three thousand years the alphabet has conquered all of civilization but no reforms have taken place in the principles of writing. Hundreds of alphabets throughout the world, different as they may be in outer form, all use the principles established in Greek writing.

### Para-graphy

Trager (1958, especially p. 8) assumed that certain communication devices which set a background for language proper (such as voice set) or serve as accompaniments of language proper (such as voice qualities and vocalizations) fall into the class of para-language. Hamp (1959) pointed out the existence of parallel features in writing and called the study of these features "paragraphemics." This field is still very obscure and its relation to both semasiography and full writing needs elaboration.

Various devices that are used within or in addition to writing proper may be called para-writing, para-graphy, meta-writing, or meta-graphy. Among the various para- or meta-devices are the following: punctuation marks to denote word, phrase, and sentence boundaries; shapes of signs, such as two forms of sigma in Greek to denote its initial, middle, or final position in a word; letterforms, such as majuscules and minuscules; type style and typography, such as roman and italic; and various conventions, including color on maps or ledgers; and statistical and instrumental graphs (Gelb, 1968, pp. 195, 198; Gelb, 1974a, pp. 1037ff., 1042).

*Fields of study*
Semiotics (or semiotic, semiology, semasiology) is the general science dealing with the various systems of signs. Semiotics covers a much broader area than the term "semantics," which is restricted to the meaning of linguistic elements. (Gelb, 1968, 1974a, 1975; Sebeok, Hayes, Bateson, 1964; Sebeok, 1974, 1976).

   Grammatology is the field of study of writing in its broadest sense.

   Graphemics, a subdivision of grammatology, deals, as an *emic* discipline, with the relation of full writing to language.

   Epigraphy and paleography, subdivisions of grammatology, deal with the formal aspects of writing.

   Linguistics is concerned with the study of the linguistic systems as reconstructed mainly from oral sources. Pursued less than the study of oral language, the study of written language, that is, of the language as it is used in written sources, is also a matter of linguistics.

   Philology is involved mainly in the study of the linguistic sources of a people or a group of peoples, especially their literature (whatever the exact meaning of that term may be). It deals less with oral sources than with written sources.

   Kinesics is concerned with the analysis of body motion and gesture and chirology (cheirology) is limited to the study of gesture sign language (Birdwhistell 1952, 1970; Stokoe 1960, 1972; Sebeok and Umiker-Sebeok 1978).

   Ethology is the term used by scholars for the study of the behavior of animals and the pertinent scientific discipline is called "zoösemiotic(s)" or "bionomics" (Gelb, 1974a, p. 1043b; Sebeok 1968, 1972; Sebeok & Ramsey, 1969).

*A reconsideration of the old definition of writing*
As discussed above, writing in its "broad" sense may be treated under the phonographic class, in which there is a close correlation between signs of writing and linguistic elements, or the semasiographic class, including forerunners of writing and all kinds of visual devices that are used side by side with phonographic writing, in which there is a loose correlation between visual markings and linguistic elements. I have considered the difference between the phonographic and semasiographic classes so crucial in the development of writing that I have called the former "full writing" and relegated the latter to pre-, proto-, and para- or meta- aspects of writing. All this is subjective, of course, and open to debate for the simple reason that the question of the broader aspects of writing has never been treated *in toto*.

I believe that I have done justice to the forerunners of writing in their pre- and proto-aspects and have succeeded in establishing a workable typology. I have not, however, studied systematically or attempted to analyze structurally and typologically the various para- or meta-devices that occur within or in addition to writing proper. The matter is very difficult. Note that linguists, who speak at times of voice qualities or vocalizations (such as a cowering or commanding voice), have never succeeded in providing a full treatment of the various aspects of language that they include under "para-language" or "meta-language."

Some scholars have criticized my emphasizing full writing in *A study of writing*, at the expense of writing in its broader sense. Let me point out that it was only natural for a philologist to treat extensively of sources written in fully developed systems. Still, Chapter II (Forerunners of Writing) is longer than chapter V (The Alphabet) and contains proportionally more information than is found in other standard books on writing.

Nevertheless, the time seems proper for a reconsideration. More than ten years ago I began to be interested in the communicative behavior of animals and, at the same time, in the broader aspects of writing and how both related to visual communication among humans.

The impetus to reconsider the broader aspects of writing came from various directions. In the spring of 1972 I gave some talks on writing at the University of Arizona. From fruitful comments following the talks (especially from Keith Basso), I learned about new types of recording used among American Indians, especially the Apaches. I was forced to consider how these most primitive types of Indian recording compared with similar types elsewhere and if they could all be made to fit my definition of writing in its broadest aspects.

Two important contributions (Marshack, 1972; Schmandt-Besserat, 1977, 1979) have shown not only how man counted in prehistorical times but also that the recording of counting formed an integral part of his abilities long before writing systems were formalized. Marshack's articles and his book published in 1972 caused no little commotion in the scholarly world. A microscopic study of the strokes, dots, or images appearing on movable objects and walls of caves, from the beginning of the Upper Paleolithic era some 30,000 years ago, helped Marshack to improve considerably the reading and interpretation of these markings. He concluded that they were not purely ornamental but dealt with the reckoning of time, such as the passage of days or lunations, or with seasonal phenomena, such as the migration of fish. I am convinced that Marshack has proved that from the beginning of the Upper Paleolithic man kept track of the sequential phases of the moon by means of sequential markings on stone. Similar notation is attested by findings not only from all over Europe, but also, from Mesolithic times, in Africa. It is interesting to note that, without being aware of Marshack's earlier contributions, Frolov (1977, 1978) stressed the role of numbers in paleolithic remains.

Schmandt-Besserat (1977, 1979) has shown that hundreds and even thousands of small clay tokens in the form of spheres, discs, cones, cubes, cylinders, and so on, have been found in excavations of different sites throughout the Near East, in Iran, Iraq, Syria, Israel, Jordan, Anatolia, and Egypt, and beyond, in Greece and West Turkestan. According to her, these tokens date from the 9th to the 2nd millennium B.C. Very rarely, other materials, such as stone or bone, were used for tokens. Tokens of various shapes may be either plain or covered with various kinds of incised markings. A small number of clay tokens was found still contained in the original hollow clay balls. The purpose of the tokens is said to be the indication of numbers and of certain types of commodities, such as grain or oil.

Schmandt-Besserat presents a very simple picture of the evolution of writing from plain clay tokens beginning in the 9th millennium B.C. to markings on tokens beginning around 3100 B.C. to the earliest Sumerian writing. It must be noted that nothing is known about the function of the tokens dating from the 9th to the first half of the 4th millennium B.C. Their function may be surmised, however, from tokens attested from the second half of the 4th millennium B.C. on. The clearest example, dated to the middle of the 2nd millennium B.C., was found at Nuzi and consists of a clay ball which originally contained 48 pebbles (now lost) and whose surface was covered by a cuneiform inscription listing 48 different sheep and goats under the custody of a certain shepherd. Functionally, the role of the pebbles would be the same as that of the various devices that illiterate shepherds (who may not be able to count orally above five or ten) have always used to keep track of the number and kind of animals in their custody—sheep and goats, male and female, old, mature, or young. One way to keep a record of the animals is by means of different kinds of pebbles in a sack, another is by means of different markings on a stick (the so-called counting sticks). We may conclude that the differentiating *shapes* of the pebbles (or any other objects) have the same function as the differentiating *markings*.

Similar in function is the quipu system of the Peruvian Incas, in which simple accounts of commodities and beings were recorded by means of strings and knots of different shapes and colors. (I discussed the shepherds' notational devices and other conventions based on the use of objects in Gelb, 1963, pp. 2-6.) The universal distribution of shepherds' counting devices makes implausible Schmandt-Besserat's assumption of one general system limited to the time between the 9th and 2nd millennium B.C. and to the Near East and some adjacent areas. It would, indeed, not be surprising if similar devices were discovered in some prehistorical or historical levels in India or China.

The dating of the tokens with representational markings is not fully established, as they may be either older than the earliest Sumerian writing or more or less contemporary with it. Even if it turns out that a token such as the one with the marking for "barley" is older than the Sumerian writing, the derivation of a Sumerian sign from a token system would not be proved as the shape of both the

Sumerian sign and of the marking on the token may have been drawn from the common repertory of markings existing for thousands of years in pictorial art and communication. In the long run it does not matter because the derivation of some Sumerian signs from a token system is just as possible as the derivation of some writing signs from gesture signs.

There is little doubt that the shapes of a number of tokens and markings on tokens, perhaps as many as a dozen, correspond or may correspond to the shapes of a number of signs, especially numbers, in the Sumerian writing system. But Schmandt-Besserat's claim that the whole Sumerian writing system, including the signary and the use of tablets, is derived from the prehistorical token system appears to be as unfounded as the claims of other scholars who have contended that writing is derived from seal iconography, gesture language, or symbolic representations. The truth is that the very rich sign inventory of early writing was drawn not from one of these devices but from all of them.

In a recent article, Forbes and Crowder (1979) deal mainly with markings occurring in the Franco-Cantabrian art around 15,000 B.C. but also point out that similar markings are attested earlier, in the Mousterian period around 45,000 B.C. and even in the Acheulian of some 150,000 to 300,000 years ago. In place of the standard classification of these as mobiliary markings on small objects and parietal markings on walls of caves and rock shelters, the authors prefer, justifiably, to classify the markings as representational (mainly animals and humans) and non-representational (abstract signs in the form of dots, lines, etc.). In a number of cases the authors indicate the importance of the sequential order of the non-representational markings. The formal connections they draw between the non-representational markings of many thousands of years ago and the signs of full writings in the Mediterranean area of historical times cannot possibly be true. Based on their interpretations of markings in prehistorical periods, the authors' contention is that the common assumption that reckoning precedes writing may not necessarily be true. In a personal communication Forbes writes: "Both these investigators [Marshack and Schmandt-Besserat] believe that counting precedes writing, an assumption that seems to have prevailed for a long time. The paper that I am sending you tentatively suggests that this may not be the case, and that writing may have preceded or be coeval with counting."

Various types of prehistorical markings that do not necessarily deal with reckoning are discussed in several fruitful articles by the Russian authors Stoliar, Zhurov, Formozov, Arutiunov, and Ivanov, all of which have been translated in *Soviet Anthropology and Archeology* (1977-78, *16*).

The above discussion has been concerned with writing in proto- and prehistorical times. The articles published in *Visible Language* provide completely different kinds of sources which illuminate the para- or meta- aspects of writing—typographical, artistic, calligraphic and related aspects of communication and recording (Wrolstad, 1971, 1976).

The different approaches discussed above force us to take a new look at the structure, typology, and definition of writing in its broadest aspects.

*A new definition of writing*
The various visual systems and devices available to human beings are listed below. The listing covers all the main types in accordance with the previous and following discussions.

(a) Momentary

> A grin, smile, gesture
> Gesture language
> Mimicry
> Mimetic dancing
> Signaling by means of fire, smoke,
> > light, or semaphore

(b) Stable

> (1) Semasiographic devices or forerunners of writing, by means of markings on objects or on any more or less durable material or by means of shapes or color of objects, both characterized by loose correlation with oral language
>
> (i) Descriptive-representational devices
>
> By means of markings on objects or on any more or less durable material:
> > pictorial communication
> > magico-religious representation
> > pictorial art
> > narrative representation
> > seal iconography
>
> By means of shape or color of objects or of any more or less durable material:
> > sculptural commemoration
> > sculptural art
>
> (ii) Identifying-mnemonic devices
>
> By means of markings on objects or on any more or less durable material:
> > recording of number, time, commodities,
> > > names,    proverbs, songs, etc.
> > property marks
> > heraldic signs
> > messenger staffs
> > mason's and potter's marks
> > wampum belts
> > branding and tattooing

By means of shape or color of objects or of any more or less
durable material:
  memory aids
  recording of number, commodities etc. by
      pebbles, clay tokens, strings and knots (quipu)
  "flower language"
  "gem language"
(2) Phonographic systems or full writing, by means of markings charac-
    terized by close correlation with oral language:
      logo-syllabic systems
      syllabic systems
      alphabetic systems
(3) Para-graphic devices or systems, by means of markings occurring
    within and in addition to writing proper and characterized by loose
    correlation with oral language:
      cartographic devices
      ledgers, charts, and graphs
      notations in mathematics, symbolic
        logic, and other sciences
      cryptography (codes and ciphers)
      shorthand systems
      musical notation
      mimetic-dance notation
      comic strips and cartoons
      calligraphic devices

Many systems and devices developed secondarily or tertiarily from our
standard alphabet, such as the Morse alphabet (visual, momentary, and stable, but
also auditory, momentary), flashlight signals using the Morse alphabet (visual,
momentary), Braille alphabet (mainly tactile, stable, but also visual, stable), and
skywriting (visual, momentary), have not been considered. There is no limit to
such transfers especially if various mechanical or electronic devices are included.

It is possible to establish the following features that characterize visual
systems of signs, generally, as contrasted with writing, specifically:

| *Visual systems of signs, generally* | *Writing, specifically* |
|---|---|
| momentary or stable | stable |
| expression or communication | communication |
| execution by any means | by motor action of the hand |

A distinction has been made above between communication of the
momentary and stable types. A momentary communication is a grin or smile, a
gesture, or fire or smoke signals; a stable communication is the quipu string-and-
knot writing and our alphabet.

If we assume, in accordance with the above discussion, that writing is

visual communication with stable, lasting effect, then all the momentary systems
and devices that are restricted in time and space, mainly gesture language and
signaling by means of fire, smoke, light, and semaphore, should be eliminated
from our definition of writing. That leaves only devices and systems based on
objects or markings on objects. Only they have the function of recording and, in
other words, writing is recording.

The widespread application of shepherds' notational devices has been
discussed in connection with the devices newly discovered on clay tokens in the
ancient Near East and some adjacent areas. In *A study of writing*, pp. 2-6, this
so-called object writing (an ad hoc translation of German *Sachschrift* or
*Gegenstandschrift*) was treated under visual communication, generally, rather than
under writing, specifically. I concluded then that writing is expressed not by the
objects themselves but by markings on objects because the meaning and etymology
of the word "to write" in many different languages indicate that written symbols
are normally executed by means of motor action of the hand in drawing, painting,
scratching, or incising. Contrary to my previous classification, shepherds' notations and other devices based on the use of objects should now be included to
account for the parallelism between the *shape or color* of objects and *markings* on
objects.

In primitive societies, the most natural way of communicating visually is
by means of markings in the form of pictures. A picture or a group of pictures
crudely fulfills the needs met in modern times by writing. In the course of time, the
pictures develop in one of two directions: either pictorial art, in which pictures
resulting from an artistic-esthetic urge continue to reproduce more or less faithfully the objects and events of the surrounding world in a form independent of
language, or writing, in which written shapes, whether they retain their pictorial
form or not, serve the purpose of communication and ultimately become signs for
linguistic elements. Like pictorial art, sculptural art and other forms of visual
expression resulting from an artistic-esthetic urge should be eliminated from
considerations of writing.

As noted earlier, communication may be achieved by any means possible:
natural (gesture, body motion, etc.) or artificial (fire, smoke, light, electronic, etc.).
In contrast, if the secondary transfers referred to above are excluded, writing is
executed solely by the motor action of the hand.

If we include, under the broad aspects of writing, systems and devices
with a stable, lasting function, namely those based not only on markings on objects
but also on the shape or color of objects, then my previous definition of writing
which is that writing in the broadest sense is a system of human intercommunication by means of visual markings used conventionally, should be changed to read:
"Writing in its broadest sense is a system of visual intercommunication by means of
markings on objects or shapes or color of objects, used conventionally." Re-
phrased more sharply in accordance with the previous discussion, the proposed

new definition of writing is as follows: Writing in its broadest sense is a recording system or device by means of conventional markings or shapes or color of objects, achieved by the motor action of the hand of an individual and received visually by another.

The concept of broad and narrow was discussed above and has been applied in the writing of this article. The following features characterize writing in its broadest aspects, generally, and full writing or writing proper, specifically:

| *Writing in its broadest aspects* | *Full writing* |
|---|---|
| (Semasiography, phonography, and para-graphy) | (Phonography) |
| loose or close correlation with oral language | close correlation with oral language |
| markings on objects or shape or color of objects | markings on objects |
| sequential or non-sequential order | sequential order |

*A future study of writing*

Approximately 25 years ago, the first edition of *A study of writing* was published. Its original subtitle, *The foundations of grammatology*, was changed in later years (by the editors) to a general description: "A discussion of the general principles governing the use and evolution of writing." The use of the indeterminate article indicated not modesty but the hope that this first study might soon be superseded by a more adequate and more thorough treatment, as was clearly expressed on p. 23: "The aim of this book is to lay a foundation for a full science of writing, yet to be written." Unfortunately, that hope has not been realized. This is not so much to the credit of the author, an old-fashioned philologist of the ancient Near East, as it is to the discredit of those linguists who are apt to generalize about writing as if it were limited in its use to the English-speaking countries.

A future study of writing must start with a thorough investigation of all the various types of visual communication, old and new, broad and narrow, full and limited, primary and secondary, with the aim of establishing their structure and exact typology. It is necessary to extend our horizons both vertically and horizontally: vertically, back in time, as far back as the Upper Paleolithic, some 30,000 years ago, even farther back to the Acheulian some 150,000 to 300,000 years ago and horizontally, to all kinds of para- and meta-aspects of writing which occur within or in addition to writing proper in modern times and earlier. Theoretically, there is almost no limit: a child drawing pictures in the sand or a bear scratching his back on a tree all leave visual markings that must be taken into consideration. *Ars longa, vita brevis*: the job is big and difficult and life is short. It is big because of the tremendous amount of data and it is difficult because it requires not merely cataloguing the data but exact typological thinking in structuring it. My fervent hope is that some enterprising person will take the suggestions offered here and use them as a basis for a new and better *Study of writing*.

I am grateful to Peter T. Daniels for reading this manuscript and offering a number of valuable comments.

## References

Birdwhistell, R. L. *Introduction to kinesics: An annotation system for analysis of body motion and gesture*. Louisville, Ky.: University of Louisville, 1952.

Birdwhistell, R. L. *Kinesics and context: Essays on body motion and communication*. Philadelphia: University of Pennsylvania Press, 1970.

Forbes, Jr., A. & Crowder, T. R. The problem of Franco-Cantabrian abstract signs: agenda for a new approach. *World Archaeology*, 1979, *10*, 350-366.

Frolov, B. A. Numbers in paleolithic graphic art and the initial stages in the development of mathematics. *Soviet Anthropology and Archeology*, 1977, *16* (3-4), 142-166; and 1978, *17* (1), 73-93 (Translation of portions of a book published in Russian, 1974).

Gelb, I. J. *A study of writing: The foundations of grammatology*. London: Routledge & Kegan Paul, and Chicago: University of Chicago Press, 1952; rev. ed., Chicago: University of Chicago Press, 1963.

Gelb, I. J. Grammatology and graphemics. In B. J. Darden, C.-J. N. Bailey, & A. Davison (Eds.), *Papers from the fourth regional meeting, Chicago Linguistic Society*. Chicago: University of Chicago, 1968.

Gelb, I. J. Written records and decipherment. In T. A. Sebeok (Ed.), *Current trends in linguistics* (Vol. 2). The Hague: Mouton, 1973.

Gelb, I. J. Writing. In *Encyclopaedia Britannica*, 15th ed., 1974, 1033-1045. (a)

Gelb, I. J. Records, writing, and decipherment. In H. H. Paper (Ed.), *Language and texts: The nature of linguistic evidence*. Ann Arbor, Mich: Center for Coördination of Ancient and Modern Studies, University of Michigan, 1975 (a slightly revised version of the article published in *Visible Language*, 1974, 7, 293-318). (b)

Hamp, E. P. Graphemics and paragraphemics. *Studies in Linguistics*, 1959, *14*, 1-5.

Marshack, A. *The roots of civilization: The cognitive beginnings of man's first art, symbol, and notation*. New York: McGraw-Hill, 1972.

Schmandt-Besserat, D. An archaic recording system and the origin of writing. *Syro-Mesopotamian Studies*, 1977, *1* (2), 1-32.

Schmandt-Besserat, D. An archaic recording system in the Uruk-Jemdet Nasr period. *American Journal of Archaeology*, 1979, *83*, 19-48.

Sebeok, T. A. (Ed.), *Animal communication: Techniques of study and results of research.* Bloomington, Ind.: Indiana University Press, 1968.

Sebeok, T. A. *Perspectives in zoosemiotics.* The Hague: Mouton, 1972.

Sebeok, T. A. Semiotics: A survey of the state of art. In T. A. Sebeok (Ed.), *Current trends in linguistics* (Vol. 12). The Hague: Mouton, 1974.

Sebeok, T. A. Contributions to the doctrine of signs. Indiana University Publications. *Studies in semiotics* (Vol. 5) Bloomington, Ind.: Indiana University Press, 1976.

Sebeok, T. A., Hayes, A. S., & Bateson, M. C. (Eds.), *Approaches to semiotics: Cultural anthropology, education, linguistics, psychiatry, psychology.* The Hague: Mouton, 1964.

Sebeok, T. A., & Ramsay, A. (Eds.), *Approaches to animal communication.* The Hague: Mouton, 1969.

Sebeok, T. A., & Umiker-Sebeok, D. J. (Eds.), *Aboriginal sign languages: Gesture systems among native peoples of the Americas and Australia.* 2 Vols. New York: Plenum Press, 1978.

Stokoe, W. C. Sign language structure: An outline of the visual communication systems of the American deaf. *Studies in linguistics, occasional papers* (Vol. 8). Buffalo, N.Y.: University of Buffalo, 1960.

Stokoe, W. C. Semiotics and human sign languages. *Approaches to semiotics* (Vol. 21). The Hague: Mouton, 1972.

Trager, G. L. Paralanguage: A first approximation. *Studies in Linguistics* 1958, *13*, 11-16.

Wrolstad, M. E. Visible language: The journal for research on the visual media of language expression. *Visible Language*, 1971, *5*, 5-12.

Wrolstad, M. E. A manifesto for visible language. *Visible Language*, 1976. *10*, 5-40.

# English shorthand systems and abbreviatory conventions: A psychological perspective

Philip T. Smith and Helen M. Pattison

*In this paper an attempt is made to suggest the psychological processes involved in perception by examining the structure of writing systems that have been developed for use when the writer is under pressure. The paper presents an historical survey of English shorthand systems and a more detailed account of two of the fastest systems in current use (Pitman New Era and Gregg Simplified). These systems are compared with the abbreviatory conventions common in newspaper advertisements. A general conclusion is that all the systems examined make use of abstract linguistic information and combine information from several distinct linguistic levels. Such systems, it is argued, are particularly appropriate for someone attempting to form an integrated percept from many different sources of information.*

The pervading medium of explanation in much contemporary experimental psychology could be called "information-processing." The prevailing model, often represented in graphical form, is one where external information undergoes a series of transformations that convert physical features into abstract structures. These transformations are hierarchically organized, low-level information at one level being used as a basis for computation of higher level information at a subsequent level, with little of the low-level information being fed forward further into the system. Perhaps the most explicit statement of this position is in attention (Treisman, 1969), but similarly organized systems can be seen in letter identification (Posner, Boies, Eichelman & Taylor, 1969), memory (Craik & Lockhart, 1972), word identification (Meyer & Schvaneveldt, 1971), and speech production (Garrett, 1975). This hierarchical organization also influences research strategy in that most experimental psychologists interested in reading, for example, carry out experiments on letter and word identification in the confident expectation that the results will provide a secure basis for studying "higher level" (syntactic and semantic) processes.

Of course, few psychologists are so naïve as to propose a strict hierarchical bottom-up process and several attempts have been made to handle contextual influences in perception and memory: perhaps the best known are analysis-by-synthesis (Neisser, 1967) and Morton's logogen model (Morton, 1970). Nonetheless, we feel that theorizing in psychology is firmly and unnecessarily constrained by what we call the *levels of processing principle*: that is, that information is processed and stored in a system consisting of a discrete number of levels, each level containing information only of one particular kind. For example, a model of speech perception might have levels corresponding to purely phonemic information, purely syntactic information, purely semantic information, and so on. There is no level, for example, where phonemic and semantic information are both partially represented. Such a principle certainly makes for tidier presentation on the printed page: a theory can be represented as a series of boxes, one labelled "phonemic," one labelled "syntactic," one labelled "semantic," and so on. If, as is argued in this paper, linguistic perception (both auditory and visual) consists of processing several different types of linguistic information at the same time, and of exploiting interactions among different linguistic levels, then it will be impossible to draw conceptually simple diagrams of the sort implied by the levels of processing principle. That, of course, would be no reason to reject the approach proposed.

Evidence against a strictly hierarchical information-processing model is of three kinds. First, there is the evidence that in certain experimental paradigms a subject can identify the meaning of a word with better than chance accuracy, even though he is able to report little about the word's graphemic or phonemic form (Allport, 1977; Marcel & Patterson, 1978). Second, there is the demonstration that some sort of parallel processing of phonemic, syntactic, and semantic information takes place when subjects shadow prose. Subjects shadowing a stimulus tape, on which the experimenter has deliberately included errors, fluently correct these errors, often with remarkably short latency which is the same whether the errors are of phonemic, syntactic, or semantic origin (Marslen-Wilson, 1975). Third, there is evidence that readers are able to integrate a large amount of heterogeneous linguistic information when they decide how to pronounce a nonsense word (in particular how to assign an appropriate stress pattern). It is not so much that graphemic information enters at a stage in the process when the subject wishes to convert graphemes to phonemes, but that graphemic information interacts with lexical, morphemic, and phonological information in a complex way to influence the final output: no hierarchical order of levels is apparent (Smith & Baker, 1976; Smith, 1980).

The point is not simply that reading and listening are parallel rather than serial processes. As Allport (1979) pointed out, parallel processing by itself does not provide a full explanation of perceptual skills. What is needed further is some account of perceptual integration, that is, how diverse sources of perceptual information interact and can be fused into a single integrated percept.

This paper does not provide an account of perceptual integration but, rather, some graphical systems that have received little formal study from psychologists. These systems are used when the writer is under pressure because he wishes either to write quickly (usually to keep pace with rapid dictation) or to occupy the minimum of space with his message (when space is at a premium, as in the advertisement columns of newspapers). These systems will be called *shorthand* and *abbreviatory* respectively. They are of interest because they may reveal psychologically natural ways of representing language: only the essential information is represented. (The aim of Sir Isaac Pitman, one of the central figures in

English shorthand systems, was to give the English language "its briefest possible form.") Conventional orthographies are much more difficult to interpret because, although they undoubtedly contain much that is psycholinguistically relevant, they are also full of historical flotsam and jetsam owing to the restrictive practices of scribes, false etymologies, printers' errors, and so on, and bound together by a deep-rooted conservatism that resists all spelling changes no matter what their origin. One or two attempts have been made to study orthographic systems that do not have a long history as, for example, Faröese orthography which was invented in the mid-nineteenth century (O'Neill, 1972), but such orthographies reflect too strongly the prejudices of their inventors, prejudices shaped partly by the non-psychological aspects of orthographies already existing.

Ideally, shorthand systems should not suffer from such drawbacks. Conservative pressures are weaker, there is a clear criterion of success (the rate at which speech can be transcribed accurately), in English alone hundreds of systems have been invented (though most have not survived their inventors) and those which have survived have been subject to successive revisions to meet the needs of their users. In short, a sort of Darwinian evolution occurs, with only the fittest shorthand systems, those adapted to the special psychological characteristics of their users, surviving. One might, therefore, expect an examination of successful modern shorthand systems to provide the best evidence for the most natural psychologically relevant way to transcribe speech.

Some qualifications must be made, however. The inventors of shorthand systems brought their own prejudices about linguistic representation to their inventions. Moreover, the criterion for a successful shorthand system is not straightforward (the system should allow rapid accurate transcription *and* it should be easy to learn: the two demands often conflict and, although the older systems emphasize speed at the expense of ease of learning, the reverse can be observed in several recent systems). It would be naïve to suppose that the most widely used systems are indeed the best (successful inventors of shorthand systems were also very good promoters). Nonetheless, there are sufficient important psychological factors at work in the structure of shorthand systems to make further examination useful.

*Early shorthand systems*
This review is restricted to English shorthand systems dating from the end of the sixteenth century. Shorthand has a long history (in Cicero's time an elaborate system was in use in the Roman Senate) and, of course, in a sense all transcription systems are examples of shorthand because there is simply too much information in the speech signal for all significant details to be recorded. Indeed, some standard orthographies use abbreviatory devices characteristic of many shorthand systems (for example, the semitic orthographies which omit almost all the vowels). However, our observations can be made with reference to English systems

and it is to these that we confine ourselves.

Almost without exception early shorthand systems were either of a simple stenographic nature (one-to-one correspondence between the shorthand signs and the letters of the alphabet) or of a simple phonographic nature (one-to-one correspondence between the shorthand signs and the phonemes of the language), usually with a few of the more common words and morphemes (*the*, *-ing*) receiving special signs. The stenographic/phonographic distinction has always been blurred, as several writers have pointed out (for example, Pocknell [1884] "stenography or 'short-writing' has always been written by *sound*, and phonography, or 'sound-writing', has always partaken of the *brief orthographic methods* found in stenography" [p. xiv].) Examples are provided later; it is sufficient now to point out a recurrent theme of this paper which is that no transcription system is pure because all seem to use several transcription principles at the same time.

Anderson (1882) summarizes 103 systems dating from 1588 to 1882. All but three could be described as stenographic/phonographic. The exceptions are instructive. Timothy Bright's *Characterie* (1588) was the first English shorthand system and had many characteristics which might be called lexigraphical. The details of its description are from Duthie (1949). Bright's system consisted of 18 basic symbols standing for letters of the alphabet (for example, $\mathsf{I} = a$) and 12 variants of each of these symbols (for example, $\mathsf{J}, \mathsf{\lfloor}, \mathsf{\sqrt{}}$, are variants of *a*). Each of the variants can appear in one of four orientations differing by 90 deg rotations from each other (for example, $\mathsf{J} \mathsf{\neg\backslash} \mathsf{\lceil} \mathsf{\backslash\lrcorner}$). There are thus potentially $18 \times 12 \times 4 = 864$ different signs. Actually Bright uses only 536 different signs, probably because some symmetrical signs do not have four distinct orientations associated with them. These 536 signs stand for 536 *characteriall* words, each word beginning with the same letter of the alphabet as the sign that symbolizes it (for example, $\mathsf{J}$ is *abound*, $\mathsf{\lfloor}$ is *about*, and so on). Words that are not among the 536 characteriall words are expressed by association with a characteriall word, together with a small sign indicating the initial letter of the target word. Thus *abandon* is expressed by the sign for the characteriall word *forsake* (ʔ) preceded by a small sign for *a* (ʔ). This ordering is used for words that are roughly synonyms of the characteriall word; for antonyms the order is reversed, the characteriall sign coming first. Thus *forget* is the sign for *remember* followed by a small sign for *f*. There is a similarity between this system and classical Chinese, where the bulk of the characters are so-called *phonetic compounds* consisting of a radical that hints at the meaning and a phonetic that hints at the sound.

How widely Bright's system was used is not clear. His contemporaries found it difficult, Willis (1618) writing that it "did necessarily require such understanding and memory, as that few of the ordinary sort of men could attain to the knowledge thereof." There are technical difficulties which limit its speed of transcription (it was written in columns) but its basic failing derives from the nature of its lexical representation, not, as some shorthand authorities might argue, because no transcription system can be fast if it does not stay close to the sound of the word but because Bright's system is not productive: there is a limit to the number of new words that can be accommodated in the system. Bright introduces 16 different articles of clothing as derivations of the characteriall word *apparel*, but there is no room to add further items as fashions change.

Another lexigraphic shorthand system is Bales' (1590) *Brachygraphie* which is similar in its basic principles to Bright's system to the point of plagiarism, and will not be discussed separately.

The third early system that departed from the usual stenographic/phonographic structure is Fancutt's (1840) *Stenography remodeled* "having for its object, the contraction of language on the same principles as those on which it is formed" (quoted in Pitman, c. 1918). This is the sort of shorthand system for which we are looking: a system which uses linguistic principles to motivate its design. Unfortunately, Fancutt does not dig very deeply. He distinguishes two sorts of words, *definitives* and *connectives* (roughly, content and function words). Definitives are transcribed in a conventional stenographic way, connectives are represented by special signs. As with Bright's system, Fancutt's subsystem for connectives is non-productive, and groups of words have to be treated as synonyms (for example, *because, therefore, nevertheless, notwithstanding* are given the same sign). Pitman (1918) notes that Fancutt's can be regarded "as nothing more than a writing riddle that might serve very well to occupy an hour at a Christmas party, but which is eminently unfit for everyday use" (p.142). (Note, however, that Levy [1862] concludes that Pitman's "is one of the most ill-constructed and deficient systems ever invented" [p.168].)

The true ancestor of all English shorthand systems is Willis's (1602) *Stenographie*. Willis seems to be the first to have emphasised the importance of phonemics in transcription: "this art prescribeth the writing of words, not according to their orthographie as they are written, but according to their sound as they are pronounced" (quoted in Pocknell [1884]). Willis's system is summarised in Table 1. From the beginning shorthand systems made inconsistent use of phonemic information. Willis uses the same sign for /s/, whether spelled with an *s* or a *c*, but he also uses a single sign for the letter *a*, no matter how it is pronounced. Again an affinity with Chinese can be identified. Willis has a small number of "illiterals" (signs standing for numerals and astronomical symbols), for example, unitary symbols for *sun, moon,* and *fish*. These symbols are then used in words that sound similar, for example, *reason = r + sun, money = moon + i, fishmonger = fish + moon + g*. A similar strategy can be observed in classical Chinese (Martin, 1972).

In summary, early shorthand systems in English displayed many of the devices found in conventional orthographies, even those as distant as Chinese, but none appears to be a linguistically "pure" system (entirely phonemic or entirely graphemic) and the vast majority keep a close correspondence between the signs

Table 1. Willis's (1602) system of signs adapted from Duthie (1949).

| ∧ | a | ∩ | b | ⌐ | d | < | e |
|---|---|---|---|---|---|---|---|
| ∟ | f | ⌐ | g | + | h | ∝ | i |
| > | j | ⌐ | k | ⊃ | l | ∪ | m |
| \ | n | ( | o | / | p | ⌣ | q |
| — | r | ∣ | s | ⊂ | t | ⌢ | u |
| V | v | ) | w | ℘ | x | ૪ | y |
| Z | z | X | č | | | | |

Most of the characters are phonemic, that is, > stands both for *j* in *jam* and *g* in *gem*. Note, however, the absence of separate signs for /š/, /ž/, /θ/, /ð/, and /ɔ/, and the very limited representation of the vowels (5 signs only).

they use and conventional graphemes or phonemes. Because none of these systems is in general use today, we cannot go much further in examining their psycholinguistic properties. Accordingly we turn next to two systems invented in the nineteenth century but still widely used, namely, those of Pitman and Gregg.

*Some theoretical considerations*
Before examining the details of these systems, consider some of the theoretical possibilities for alphabetic systems suggested by generative phonology. First, it is possible to have a system based on surface phonemes, a sort of phonetic representation from which minor phonetic details have been omitted. This system would spell *dogs* as *dogz*, *risked* as *riskt*, *eclipse* as *eklips* in contrast to one based on morphophonemic representations, which would spell each of those words exactly as they are spelled in current English orthography (because, for example, the phonemic variants of *-s* and *-ed* are predicted by straightforward rules, and so need not be marked in the orthography, and the unusual stress pattern for *eclipse* is marked by the presence of a "silent" final *e*: this is the sort of argument Chomsky and Halle [1968] use to support the claim of the "near optimality" of English orthography). Klima (1972) considers several other systems, one of which is even more abstract than current English orthography: he notes that there are several phonological

processes in English which depend on formative boundaries *within* a word. Thus *singer* = *sing* + *er* contains no audible /g/, whereas *finger*, which cannot be broken up into smaller morphemic components, contains such a /g/. This phenomenon is of some generality (contrast *singer*, *ringer*, *banger*, *hanger*, *longer* [one who longs] with *finger*, *linger*, *anger*, *longer* [distance]). English orthography is not able to make this distinction but, as Klima suggests, it is easy to add an appropriate convention such as using an inverted comma to mark a boundary within a word (*singer* = *sing'er*, but *finger* = *finger*). It may be asked what level of phonological abstractness shorthand systems mark, from the superficial phonemic form to the underlying morpho-phonemic form, with or without additional boundary markers.

A related issue is the definition of a word. Kean (1977) has shown that some useful insights into Broca's aphasia can be obtained from the notion of a *phonological word*. A phonological word in English is a string of phonemes marked by boundaries within but not across which stress assignment rules operate. When a suffix such as *-ness* is added to a word it does not affect the stress pattern of that word (*définite-définiteness*): the word *definite* in *definiteness* remains a phonological word, separated from the *-ness* suffix by a full word boundary. On the other hand, the suffix *-ive* can alter the stress pattern of the word to which it is added (*définite-definitive*): the *definit-* in *definitive* is not a phonological word, and the *-ive* suffix is separated from the rest of the word only by a "formative" boundary not strong enough to block the application of stress assignment rules to the entire word.

Though the data (and Kean's theory) are more complex, Kean essentially claims that a Broca's aphasic shows a strong tendency to produce only phonological words, leaving out function words and many affixes which do not qualify as phonological words. We examine shorthand systems to see if the systems operate with units other than words, if orthographic words that are or are not also phonological words receive different treatment, and if affixes and the different types of boundary separating affix from root have any discernible effects on the design of the system.

*Modern shorthand systems*
Pitman's shorthand first appeared in 1837 and has been revised several times, notably in 1840, 1857, 1922, and 1975. The principles, however, have not changed. The "New Era" version of 1922, to which we confine our attention, has many ways of making distinctions: the basic unit is the stroke, which stands for a consonant or group of consonants, and may be straight or curved and vary in thickness, orientation, length, and height above a reference line. To either end of this stroke may be added a variety of hooks and loops to indicate consonants or groups of consonants. Vowels are represented by dots, dashes, and arrow heads beside the strokes but are often omitted (being retained only to avoid ambiguity). Even when the vowels are omitted, however, information about the first vowel in

the word is transmitted by the height of the first consonant stroke.

Although Pitman's system is firmly based on sound, the representation involved is of a relatively abstract phonological nature: for example, a skilled phonetician who knew no English would not be able to use Pitman's system to transcribe it because so many linguistic distinctions other than the purely phonetic are made in the system. The system does have many appealing features of a surface phonemic character: light strokes are used for unvoiced consonants, heavy strokes are used for voiced consonants; light dots and dashes are used for lax vowels, heavy dots and dashes for tense vowels; straight strokes are used for stop consonants, curved strokes for fricatives; loops are used for consonant clusters beginning with /s/, hooks are used for clusters beginning with other consonants. These distinctions are not fully systematic: for example, light curves represent the nasals /m/ and /n/ and a heavy curve the nasal /ɔ/, but the difference between /n/ (*sin*) and /ɔ/ (*sing*) is one of place of articulation, not voicing; similarly, the homophones *to* and *too* are distinguished by thickness of stroke, although there is no phonetic difference whatsoever.

Gregg's shorthand system dates from 1888 and is claimed to be the most widely used. It was simplified in 1950 and in this paper we refer to the second edition of the simplified version (Gregg *et al.*, 1960). Most of the points made with respect to Pitman can be made also for Gregg. The system is phonemic in so far as it is based largely on the phonemic, not the orthographic, form of the word, but there is a lack of the phonemic systematicity found in Pitman. One or two features are phonetically fussy (the glides /y/ and /w/ are represented by the signs of the vowels /i/ and/u/, with different forms of /y/ appearing with different following vowels) and there is a major concession to English orthography in that the same sign is used for a lax vowel and its corresponding tense equivalent in English orthography, that is, *mat* and *mate* are spelled the same, as are *met* and *mete*, *mit* and *mite*, *not* and *note*, *run* and *rune*; these pairings are far from natural phonetically and in a phonological sense the connections are relatively abstract. As in Pitman, the basic unit in Gregg is the consonant stroke which can be straight or curved and vary in orientation and length. Vowels are added to the ends of the stroke in the form of hooks and loops. Voicing is the only consonantal feature that is systematically coded, the longer of a pair of signs being the voiced member of a voiced/unvoiced pair.

Both systems are more abstract than the surface phonemic in several respects. First, voicing is often neutralized: in Pitman a series of loops represent both /s/ and /z/ (*ass* or *as*), both /səz/ and /zəz/ (*prices* and *prizes*), and both /šən/ and /žən/ (*Confucian* or *confusion*); in Gregg the /s/ - /z/ and /š/ - /ž/ distinctions are not made in any context, and voicing neutralization occurs for stop consonants when they are part of a cluster (/nd/ and /nt/ are represented by the same sign).

Second, word boundaries and word length interact with many of the phonemic representations: in Pitman the symbol that stands for /s/ or /z/ in word medial or final positions stands only for /s/ in word initial position; many conventions for consonant clusters can be used only at the beginnings and ends of words (this can lead to words of similar sound and meaning being spelled differently: /s/ is not represented in the same way in *sleep* and *asleep*, or in *honest* and *honesty*); in polysyllables a stroke can be halved to indicate either a following /t/ or a following /d/, in monosyllables a light stroke is halved to indicate a following /t/, a heavy stroke is halved to indicate a following /d/ (the extra restriction on monosyllables being made, presumably, to avoid an excessive number of homographs). In Gregg with monosyllables ending in /st/, the sign for /t/ should be omitted only with seven high frequency words (*best*, *cost*, and so on), but with polysyllables ending in /st/ the sign for /t/ is always omitted, unless the morphemes *-ist* or *-est* are being added to a word ending in a vowel or abbreviated so that the final consonant is missing, in which case the sign for *-st* is written disjoined from the rest of the word (for example, *latest*: all phonemes present, therefore final *t* sign omitted; *happiest*: happy ends in a vowel, therefore *st* written disjoined from *happy*; *shortest*: *short* is abbreviated to the sign for /š/, therefore *st* written disjoined).

Third, some simple phonological processes such as assimilation of voicing are sometimes economically expressed: in Pitman the halving rule for monosyllables is roughly an abbreviatory convention to be used when two voiced or two unvoiced consonants follow one after the other (the phonologically more complex sequence of unvoiced consonant following voiced consonant, or vice versa, requires a more elaborate transcription).

Fourth, many of the abbreviatory conventions operate only after vowels have been deleted: thus, in Pitman, words such as *spring* and *separate* have similar initial segments (representing s-p-r) even though in one case we are dealing with a single consonant cluster and in the other case with the initial phonemes of three separate syllables. In Gregg the common syllables *ded*, *det*, *dit*, *ted* receive the same abbreviation, a combination of the *d* and *t* signs.

Despite its phonological complexity, little attempt is made in Pitman at morphemic regularity. Inevitably, having special signs for /s/ or /z/ and /šən/ or /žən/ means that morphemes such as *-s* or *-tion* often receive distinctive outlines, but phonemic demands dominate: *laps* and *lapse* would receive the same transcription, as would *axes* and *access*. An interesting example of an interaction between morphemics and representation is provided by the prefix *in-*, which always must be represented by an *n* stroke when its meaning is negative (*inaccurate*, *incredible*), but can be represented in other ways (for example, by halving the stroke to indicate a following *d*, as in *index* and *induction* if the prefix is not negative. This principle is not easy to follow, because some negative uses of *in-* are buried deep in a word's etymology (for example, *integral*), and Pitman's shorthand dictionary itself is inconsistent in applying it. Higher level linguistic information is sporadically present: the articles *the* and *a* receive similar representations, the homophone pair *to* and *too* are discriminated, and the tendency to abbreviate words occurring frequently means that function words are more likely to receive brief distinctive forms. Occasionally pressure to avoid homographs leads to breaking a rule: unlike *paused* which uses a single sign (the standard contraction in these contexts), *caused* (kɔ̃zd) is spelled with separate signs for /z/ and /d/ to avoid confusion between *caused* and the near homograph *cost*, which uses the contracted form for *-st*. The basic transcription principles of the system remain phonological: it is not a surface form, however, because information about consonantal voicing and syllabic structure may be omitted and word position and word length interact with purely phonemic processes. In terms of Klima's orthographic classification, the system is of comparable abstractness to conventional English orthography, emphasising some abstract phonological features that English neglects, but omitting much of the morphemic information characteristic of standard English orthography. The same conclusions can be drawn about the Gregg system, though the range of phonological processes it expresses is more limited.

In the context of Kean's (1977) ideas about phonological words, we investigate to what extent the Pitman and Gregg systems use units that are not identical with orthographic words. In many cases the units are identical: the boundaries of shorthand words and of orthographic words occur in the same positions. However, both Pitman and Gregg make extensive use of *disjoining*. There is low-level disjoining, chiefly for graphic clarity, in Pitman, for example, where two parts of a word are disjoined if the word contains many *d*'s and *t*'s; in Gregg certain morphemes (*-ed*, *-er*, *-or*) are detached from the main part of the word, but only if the final consonant of the root word has been omitted. High-level disjoining, where parts of a word are separated for purely morphemic or lexical reasons, is present in both, though it is more frequent and thoroughgoing in Gregg. In accordance with linguistic predictions about the nature of phonological words, affixes which are separated from the root of the word by a full word boundary are often written in Pitman and Gregg as disjoined from the root word (for example, in Pitman: *self-*, *-fulness* (always), *-ly*, *-ing* (sometimes); in Gregg: *-ing*, *under-*, *-hood*, *-ward* and many others). There are many exceptions however: Pitman disjoins *magn-* (as in *magnificent*) and Gregg disjoins *incl-* and *-ulate*, none of which is an affix, and Pitman fails to disjoin such a clearly separable affix as *un-* as Gregg fails to disjoin *-ly*. The conclusion is that there is only a weak correlation between the linguistic concept of a phonological word and the transcription principles used in these shorthand systems.

Finally it can be asked to what extent the systems group words together and what principles govern the groupings. Pitman and Gregg both make use of "phrasing," that is, joining several orthographic words. Criteria for phrasing are vague: "outlines should be phrased only when they join easily and naturally" (Pitman, 1938). Typical phrasing is as follows (hyphens indicate those words that are to be joined together in shorthand):

I-believe-that I-have-the necessary qualifications and experience, and-I-enclose a summary of-them for-your information. (Pitman, 1938, p. 155.)

Two characteristics of phrasing are apparent. One is the non-coincidence of phrasing boundaries with surface structure syntactic boundaries (typically *the* is joined to the previous word, not to the following word with which it belongs syntactically). This fits rather well with modern ideas about sentence production (Butterworth and Beattie, 1978; Kempen, 1978) where junctures are predicted at points where one idea is completed and the next needs to be formulated: *I-believe-that* constitutes one idea in the sense that the writer must now formulate a particular type of clause to follow it, and joining *the* to the previous word (as in *I-have-the*) is often natural because little additional reflection on the part of the writer is required, the real cognitive work beginning with the choice of the next content word (the pauses that occur in spontaneous speech more often follow an article than precede it). The other feature of both Pitman and Gregg phrasing is that no more than one phonological word appears in each unit. This suggests that, despite there being little room for morphological and lexical processes in the basic elements of these shorthand systems, such factors are influential in the final groupings of words. These aspects of phrasing are in a way accidental features of the system: in a Pitman shorthand course phrasing is purely a matter of calligraphic convenience (join words if the strokes fit easily together). Linguistic factors exert a significant influence, however.

A summary of this section is presented in Table 2.

Table 2. Comparison of the two major shorthand systems discussed in this paper.

|  | Pitman | Gregg |
|---|---|---|
| Surface phonemics | Voicing and manner of articulation of consonants and length of vowels often systematically coded. | Only consonant voicing systematically coded. Lax-tense pairing of vowels are made on English *orthographic* distinctions, not on phonetic distinctions. |
|  | Consonant clusters grouped by phonemic similarity. | Consonant clusters are smooth blends of individual signs. |
|  | Some voicing assimilation in consonant clusters. |  |

| Other phonemic characteristics | Voicing neutralization, especially in fricatives. | Widespread voicing neutralization. |
|---|---|---|
| | Vowels deleted except when ambiguity would arise. | Frequent vowel deletion. |
| | Position in word and word length affect application of abbreviatory devices. | As Pitman. |
| | Abbreviatory devices applied after deletion of vowels. | Different rules for adding syllables to abbreviated and non-abbreviated forms. |
| Morphemic information | Little more than would be expected of a system that by and large preserves phonemic form, but the morpheme *in-* is constrained when it has a negative meaning. | More morphemic than Pitman, because (a) relatively more morphemes receive abbreviations (Pitman tends to abbreviate *all* frequent words, irrespective of morphemic structure): (b) there is a greater tendency to disjoin morphemes that are separated from the rest of the word by a (phonological) word boundary. |
| Lexical information | Sporadic discrimination of homographs or near homographs. | As Pitman. |
| Phrasing | Groups of words joined together roughly have the characteristics (a) junctures occur at "cognitive" not syntactic boundaries; (b) not more than one content word per phrase. | As Pitman. |

*Abbreviatory systems*

Although both Pitman and Gregg apply general principles to enable any word to be written in an abbreviated form, both systems use idiosyncratic brief forms for dozens of high frequency words. In this respect they can be compared with the type of abbreviation common in newspaper advertisements, where the writer uses a small repertoire of abbreviations to save space as in:

JERSEY. incl. hols. Spring
'79 & all yr. ABTA

We have examined the abbreviatory conventions used in the London *Evening Standard*. First we excluded abbreviations consisting of special symbols (£,&) or composed purely of initial letters which are often rather arbitrary, requiring specialised knowledge (not many non-British readers are likely to know that ABTA stands for the Association of British Travel Agents). Of the remaining abbreviations, 90 percent could be grouped into one of three classes:

(i)      *First Few Symbols:* only the first few letters are retained (*incl.* for *inclusive*, *tel.* for *telephone*)

(ii)      *Initial and Final*: only the first and last letters are given: (*Mr.* for *Mister*, *St.* for *Saint*)

(iii)      *Vowel Deletion*: all the vowels are deleted (*wknd* for *weekend*, *Gtwck* for *Gatwick*)

In addition, a small number of final morphemes may be added to the forms already abbreviated, for example, *mins* for *minutes*, *hrs* for *hours*, *agy* for *agency*. The First Few Symbols are easily the most numerous in advertisements, and Pitman, Gregg, and advertisements have been compared to see if, when First Few Symbols abbreviations are used, there are common principles in the three systems. The Pitman system primarily transcribes *consonants* only, Gregg principally transcribes *phonemes*, and newspaper advertisements use *letters*. The three systems are, therefore, compared looking at abbreviations in consonant sequences for Pitman, phoneme sequences for Gregg, and letter sequences for advertisements. The results are shown in Table 3. We examined where the break occurred in a First Few Symbols abbreviation by looking at the last symbol to be retained and the first to be omitted (for example, in *incl.* for *inclusive*, *l* is the last symbol retained and *u* is the first symbol omitted). These symbols were then classified phonemically as shown in Table 3: clearly, the point where a break occurs is not random and the underlying principle seems straightforward: the more consonantal a phoneme, the more likely it is to precede a break and the more vocalic a phoneme, the more likely it is to follow a break, that is, highly consonantal phonemes are more likely to be retained than highly vocalic ones. (The rows of Table 3 are ordered on an intuitive basis from most consonantal [unvoiced consonants] to most vocalic [vowels].) There are, of course, differences among the three systems, mainly where the crossover from highly consonantal to highly vocalic occurs, but it is reassuring to see that all three systems converge on the same general principle, supporting the notion that, although Pitman and Gregg are highly contrived systems, they are not so far removed from psycholinguistic reality that they do not follow what appear to be psychologically natural ways of constructing their abbreviations.

Table 3. Phonemic analysis of "first few symbols" abbreviations.

| | E.S. (letters) | | Gregg (phonemes) | | Pitman (consonants) | |
|---|---|---|---|---|---|---|
| | Last ret. | First omit. | Last ret. | First omit. | Last ret. | First omit. |
| Unvoiced consonants | 14 | 0 | 12 | 9 | 32 | 22 |
| Voiced non-nasals | 3 | 3 | 11 | 8 | 21 | 10 |
| Nasals | 4 | 4 | 8 | 2 | 6 | 19 |
| Glides and liquids | 5 | 3 | 7 | 5 | 16 | 24 |
| Vowels | 4 | 20 | 18 | 32 | | |

Comparison of a sample of *Evening Standard* advertisements (E.S.) and all the frequent brief forms in Gregg and Pitman. The table examines the last symbol retained in the abbreviation (last ret. column, for example, the *l* of *incl.*) and the first symbol present in the full form of the word but omitted from the abbreviation (first omit. column, for example, the *u* of *inclusive*, when the abbreviation is *incl.*). The figures in the matrix show the actual numbers of abbreviations falling into each category.

*Conclusions*
Given the complex and unsystematic nature of many parts of the transcription systems discussed, the only conclusion might appear to be that a human being can learn almost anything if sufficiently motivated. More positive conclusions can be drawn, however. Shorthand systems fail to be "pure" linguistic systems (representing only one level of linguistic information) not because their inventors were incompetent or inconsistent but for a more profound psychological reason. The essential quality of good orthographies, including shorthand systems, is that they provide *links* between two or more linguistic levels. By providing systems of rules

that represent phonemes differently as a function of phonemic, morphemic, lexical, and syntactic context, Pitman and Gregg allow us to use their sequences of signs to relate "low"-level information (surface phonemics) and higher level syntactic and semantic information. The psychological phenomenon of perceptual integration maintains links from superficial acoustic cues to the most abstract forms of comprehension and inference. Thus, the characteristic of a good orthography is that it provides transcriptions which are closer to psychologically natural percepts and the information simultaneously relates several different levels.

Our conclusion then is that shorthand systems regarded seriously as psychologically natural ways of representing speech support a view of perception as a heterarchical and integrative process, not as a hierarchical and serial one.

This paper was written while Smith was visiting the Max-Planck-Gesellschaft, Projektgruppe für Psycholinguistik, Nijmegen, The Netherlands, and while Pattison was in receipt of a Science Research Council studentship. We thank both these institutions for their support and also the staff of the Canterbury Public Library for their assistance in making their collection of books on shorthand available to us.

## References

Allport, D. A. On knowing the meaning of words we are unable to report: The effects of visual masking. In S. Dornic (Ed.), *Attention and performance VI*. Hillsdale, N.J.: Lawrence Erlbaum Associates, 1977.

Allport, D. A. Word recognition in reading. In P. A. Kolers, M. E. Wrolstad, & H. Bouma (Eds.), *Processing of visible language 1*. New York: Plenum Press, 1979.

Anderson, T. *History of shorthand*. London: W. H. Allen, 1882.

Bales, P. Brachygraphie. In *The writing schoolmaster*. London: Thomas Orwin, 1590.

Bright, T. *Characterie: An arte of shorte, swifte and secrete writing by character*. London: I. Windet, 1588.

Butterworth, B., & Beattie, G. Gesture and silence as indicators of planning in speech. In R. N. Campbell & P. T. Smith (Eds.), *Recent advances in the psychology of language* (Vol. 4b). New York: Plenum Press, 1978.

Chomsky, N., & Halle, M. *The sound pattern of English*. New York: Harper & Row, 1968.

Craik, F. I. M., & Lockhart, R. S. Levels of processing: A framework for memory research. *Journal of Verbal Learning and Verbal Behavior*, 1972, *11*, 671-684.

Duthie, G. I. *Elizabethan shorthand and the first quarto of King Lear*. Oxford: Basil Blackwell, 1949.

Fancutt, J. *Stenography remodeled*. London: Sherwood, Gilbert & Piper, 1840.

Garrett, M. The analysis of sentence production. In G. H. Bower (Ed.), *The psychology of learning and motivation* (Vol. 9). New York: Academic Press, 1975.

Gregg, J. R., Leslie, L. A., Zoubek, C. E., & Crockett, E. W. *Gregg shorthand manual simplified* (2nd ed.). London: McGraw-Hill, 1960.

Kean, M.-L. The linguistic interpretation of asphasic syndromes: agrammatism in Broca's aphasia, an example. *Cognition*, 1977, *5*, 9-46.

Kempen, G. Sentence construction by a psychologically plausible formulator. In R. N. Campbell & P. T. Smith (Eds.), *Recent advances in the psychology of language* (Vol. 4b). New York: Plenum Press, 1978.

Klima, E. S. How alphabets might reflect language. In J. F. Kavanagh & I. G. Mattingly (Eds.), *Language by ear and by eye*. Cambridge, Mass.: MIT Press, 1972.

Levy, M. *History of shorthand writing*. London: Truber, 1862.

Marcel, A. J. & Patterson, K. E. Word recognition and production: reciprocity in clinical and normal studies. In J. Requin (Ed.), *Attention and performance VII*. Hillsdale, N.J.: Lawrence Erlbaum Associates, 1978.

Marslen-Wilson, W. D. Sentence perception as an interactive parallel process. *Science*, 1975, *189*, 226-228.

Martin, S. E. Nonalphabetic writing systems: some observations. In J. F. Kavanagh & I. G. Mattingly (Eds.), *Language by ear and by eye*. Cambridge, Mass.: MIT Press, 1972.

Meyer, D. E., & Schvaneveldt, R. W. Facilitation in recognizing pairs of words: Evidence of a dependence between retrieval operations. *Journal of Experimental Psychology*, 1971, *90*, 227-234.

Morton, J. A functional model of memory. In D. A. Norman (Ed.), *Models of human memory*. New York: Academic Press, 1970.

Neisser, U. *Cognitive psychology*. Englewood Cliffs, N.J.: Prentice-Hall, 1967.

O'Neill, W. Our collective phonological illusions: young and old. In J. F. Kavanagh & I. G. Mattingly (Eds.), *Language by ear and by eye*. Cambridge, Mass.: MIT Press, 1972.

Pitman, I. *A history of shorthand* (4th ed.). 1918.

*Pitman shorthand. New course new era edition*. London: Pitman Publishing, 1938.

Pocknell, E. *Legible shorthand* (2nd. ed.). London: the author, 1884.

Posner, M. I., Boies, S. J., Eichelman, W. H., & Taylor, R. L. Retention of visual and name codes of single letters. *Journal of Experimental Psychology*, 1969, *79*, 1-16.

Smith, P. T. Linguistic information in spelling. In U. Frith (Ed.), *Cognitive processes in spelling*. London: Academic Press, 1980.

Smith, P. T. & Baker, R. G. The influence of English spelling patterns on pronunciation. *Journal of Verbal Learning and Verbal Behavior*, 1976, *15*, 267-285.

Treisman, A. M. Strategies and models of selective attention. *Psychological Review*, 1969, *76*, 282-299.

Willis, E. *An abbreviation of writing by character*. London: George Purslow, 1618.

Willis, J. *Stenographie*. London: Cuthbert Burby, 1602.

# Remarks on ancient Egyptian writing with emphasis on its mnemonic aspects

Edmund S. Meltzer

*In ancient Egyptian writing the ideographic and phonetic elements are closely intertwined; various orthographic conventions are governed by the central importance of a recognizable word-picture and the mnemonic principle. The essential unity of hieroglyphic writing, and the importance of context, must be stressed in the origin as well as in the use of the script. These points are important in the study of the cursive (hieratic and demotic) scripts as well. Egyptian writing (and education) emphasized word-recognition and multifaceted word characterization in which an incomplete phonetic representation was supplemented by (and even subordinated to) visual and mnemonic priorities.*

Only in the writing of Coptic, the most recent stage of the language, did the ancient Egyptians adopt a purely alphabetic script (the Greek alphabet, supplemented by a few signs from demotic for phonemes absent from Greek). This alphabet was a foreign script (except for the few demotic letters which provided a direct link with native Egyptian writing), and, moreover, was widely adopted only when Pharaonic culture was virtually defunct. The earlier Egyptian scripts—hieroglyphic, hieratic, and demotic, which altogether cover a history of about 3500 years and continue into the beginning of the Coptic period—were of a very different character. In the present survey, we shall concentrate on the hieroglyphs, which are the most accessible and offer the most obvious possibilities for the study of visible language, but we shall not restrict ourselves to them. Hieroglyphic orthography and scribal conventions changed over the course of time; the majority of the writings discussed here are most characteristic of the period extending from the beginning of the Middle Kingdom through the Eighteenth Dynasty (c. 2000-1320 B.C., when Middle or Classical Egyptian was the literary language), and are typical of the *modus operandi* of the hieroglyphic script in general. Examples referring to specific periods will be so designated.

Elaborate typologies of hieroglyphic signs have been presented in recent years (Hodge, 1975; Kaplony, 1966; Schenkel, 1976), and they will not be duplicated here. The ancient Egyptians' approach to taxonomy was quite different from ours and so, rather than concentrate on the typology of individual signs, we shall examine some of the processes by which ancient Egyptian writing works. We shall, however, begin with a typology of sorts: a very simple (and simplistic) inventory of the types of signs as often presented in elementary instruction. Hieroglyphs comprise both ideograms and phonograms.

*Ideograms* are of two main types: *logograms* (word-signs) and *determinatives*, the latter being placed at the end of words spelled out with *phonograms*. Moreover, there are two types of determinatives: *generic* which label a class (motion, physical

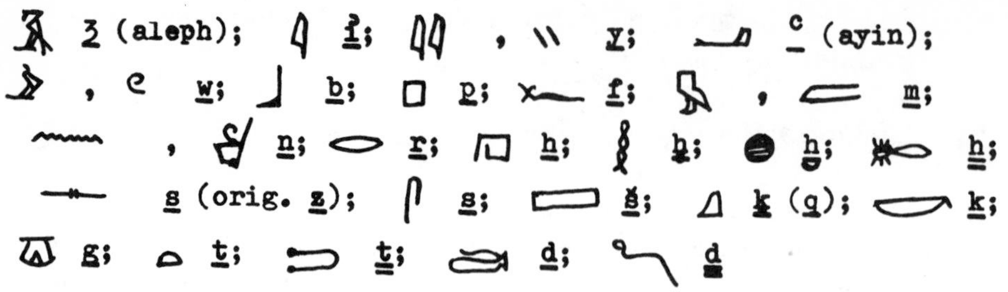

Figure 1. Uniliteral ("alphabetic") signs.

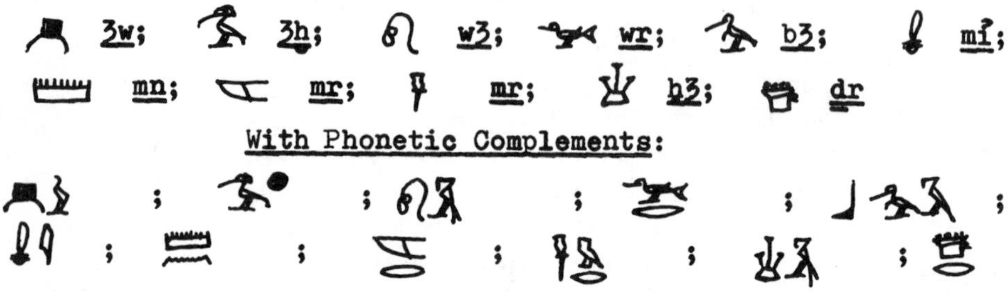

**With Phonetic Complements:**

Figure 2. Biliteral signs (including some which function as "root-signs").

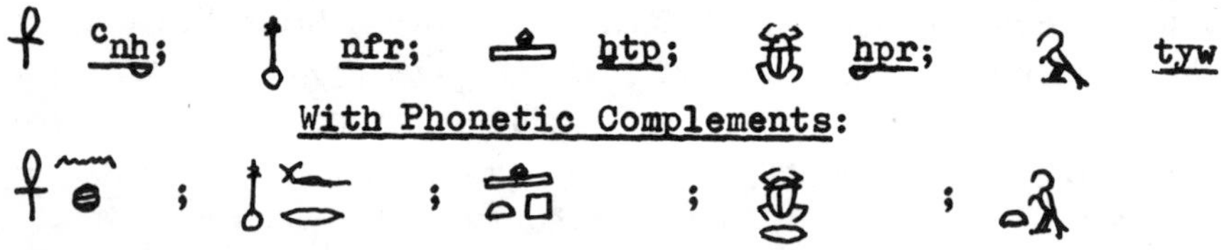

**With Phonetic Complements:**

Figure 3. Triliteral signs (mostly "root-signs").

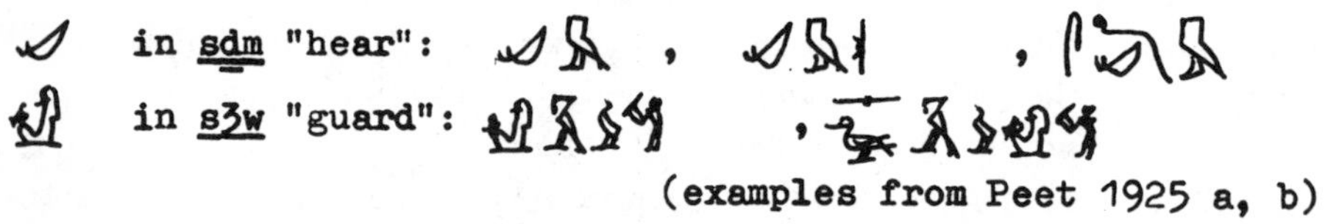

in **sḏm** "hear":

in **sꜣw** "guard":

**(examples from Peet 1925 a, b)**

Figure 4. "Semi-phonetic" signs and uses.

force, actions having to do with the mouth or speech, animals, abstractions, and so on) and *specific* which label a particular object or action. The same word can often be written with a specific or a generic determinative (for example, that for dog or that for animals in general) and many specific (as well as some generic) determinatives can also be used as logograms. Many words take more than one determinative (Figures 5-7).

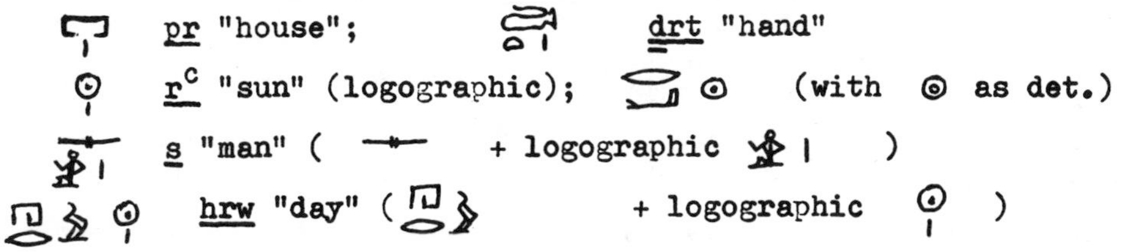

pr "house";       drt "hand"

r$^c$ "sun" (logographic);    ⊙   (with ⊙ as det.)

s "man" ( —— + logographic | )

hrw "day" ( + logographic )

Figure 5. Logograms and determinatives.

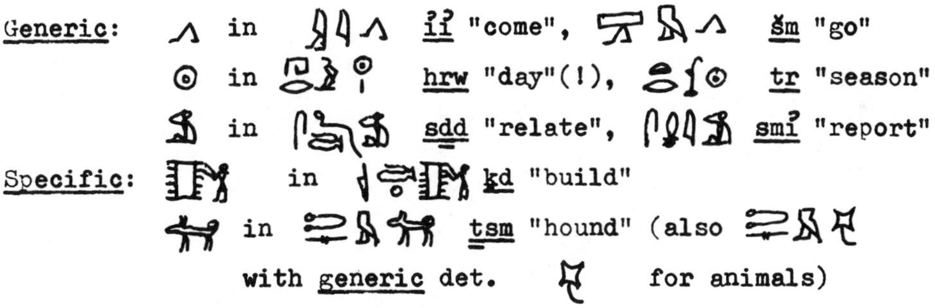

Generic: ∧ in ii "come", šm "go"

⊙ in hrw "day"(!), tr "season"

in sdd "relate", smi "report"

Specific: in ḳd "build"

in tsm "hound" (also

with generic det. for animals)

Figure 6. Generic and specific determinatives.

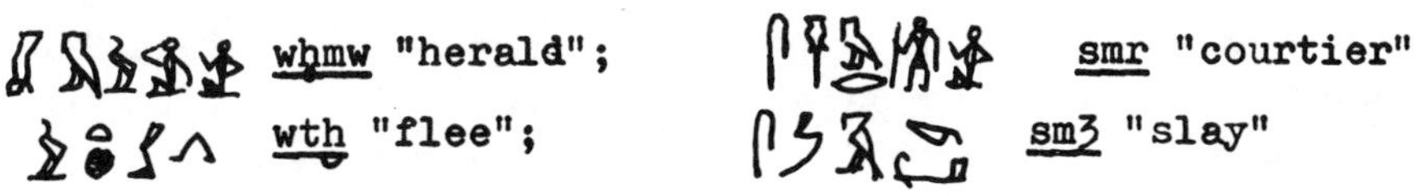

wḥmw "herald";      smr "courtier"

wtḫ "flee";      sm3 "slay"

Figure 7. Multiple determinatives.

*Phonograms* are of three types: *uniliteral* or "alphabetic" (representing a single consonant; Figure 1), *biliteral* (representing a sequence of two consonants; Figure 2), and *triliteral* (representing a sequence of three consonants; Figure 3). Bi- and triliteral signs are often accompanied by uniliteral signs which give one or more of their component consonants and are known as *phonetic complements* (Figures 2-3).

It should be emphasized that the phonetic and ideographic aspects of the script are very closely intertwined; this is basic for an appreciation of the hieroglyphs in both synchronic and diachronic terms. Gardiner (1957, p. 440) notes "the impossibility of a hard and fast classification of the uses of signs. Ideographic uses shade off into phonetic...." Perhaps this close intermingling of the phonetic and the ideographic is one reason why Egyptologists have always employed a purely phonetic (now consonantal) transliteration, rather than using upper case for ideographic writings, superscripts for determinatives, and so on, as in the cuneiform disciplines. (Edgerton [1947] is perhaps the only Egyptologist who developed such a system; Wiedemann advocated the use of hieroglyphic fount

pr "house";               ,            prw "houses"

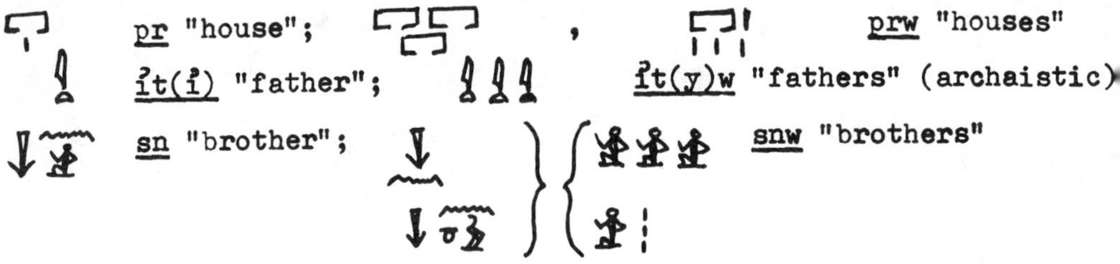

it(i) "father";            it(y)w "fathers" (archaistic)

sn "brother";                  snw "brothers"

Figure 8. Singular and plural.

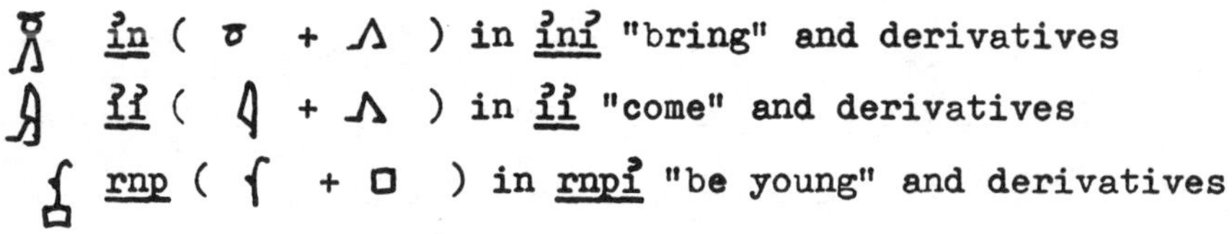

in ( σ + Λ ) in ini "bring" and derivatives

ii ( ̫ + Λ ) in ii "come" and derivatives

rnp ( ̫ + □ ) in rnpi "be young" and derivatives

Figure 9. Composite signs ("monograms").

numbers as a compromise between rival systems of transliteration but did not, apparently, ever use them himself.) The type of transliteration used by Egyptologists provides an interesting sidelight on their approach to visible language: surely it is relevant to the fact that deciphering was made possible by the realization that there are phonetic hieroglyphs, and it may even be seen as a reaction to the "symbolic" interpretation of the hieroglyphs current from Classical times to the early nineteenth century. In any case, Egyptologists do not employ a transliteration which itself makes possible a visual reconstruction of the text.

It is pertinent to discuss whether the phonograms are purely consonantal or syllabic. The early Egyptologists, who considered the *aleph* (now transliterated *ꜣ*), *ayin* (*ᶜ*), "reed-leaf" (*i*), *y*, and *w* to be vowels, regarded bi- and triliterals as "syllabic" signs and the term was perpetuated uncritically by several Egyptologists simply as a label for multiconsonantal signs (in which usage it can still be found, for example, in Bakir [1978, § 11]). More recently, Gelb (1963, pp. 72-81) has asserted that *all* the phonograms are to be seen as syllabic, that is, as sequences of CV... where C is a consonant and V is any vowel *including* φ. Callender (1975) has given qualified approval to this view, writing of "the likelihood that the Egyptians were at least aware of syllable structure if not the notion of vowels, and at least sporadically attempted to represent it" (p. 3). The following points should be noted, however.

First, the hieroglyphic orthography disregards inferrable changes in syllabification; accordingly, in many cases a biliteral would end one syllable and begin the next with no orthographic change deemed necessary.

Second, although highly speculative (especially for the early period in which the hieroglyphs were developed), what we can infer about the syllable structure of Egyptian does not suggest that words ended with open syllables; thus, especially in the case of the multiliteral signs, the concept of a grapheme for CV, CVCV, or CVCVCV should perhaps be only cautiously attributed to the Egyptians. However, it can be countered that certain final consonants such as *r*, the feminine ending *t*, the semivowels *w* and *ỉ/y*, and probably *aleph* quiesced at an early date. There are also apparently monoconsonantal words (for example, *t*, "bread"; *c*, "arm") the original consonantal structure of which is moot. (The secondary development of a possible CV notation which is specialized and limited in its use is discussed below but it may be the exception that proves the rule.)

Third, Schenkel (1976) rightly observes that, for the syllabic hypothesis to be maintained for Egyptian writing, "The syllables of the hieroglyphic script cannot be those of Egyptian language, but must be somthing like 'orthographic syllables'" (p. 4). Moreover, and more significantly a thorough study of the hieroglyphic script suggests that it is not syllable-oriented: it does not have the representation of syllables as a priority. One of the basic points which will be discussed is that one of the guiding principles of ancient Egyptian writing is the maintaining of a consistent and recognizable word-group (or, as I would like to call it, "word-picture"). As Schenkel (1967) writes:

> The most important factor in the development of the script's structure is probably the reluctance to give up sign groups, especially groups used for writing complete words, once they had been introduced; this can be observed at all periods. As the language changed, but the script did not follow these changes fast enough, historical writings developed. These are sign groups whose constituent elements no longer directly supply information about the linguistic forms they encode. If the greater complexity of the hieroglyphic script is disregarded, this results in an orthography whose relationship to the spoken language is very similar to that of contemporary English. (p. 7.)

In addition, it will be seen not only that a number of the scribal conventions and orthographic traits have a mnemonic importance but also that the mnemonic emphasis goes along with the central role of the word-picture.

*The interplay of ideographic and phonetic aspects*
Some clarification of the intertwined ideographic and phonetic aspects of the hieroglyphs is in order.

*Phonetic writings and determinatives* (Figures 4-6). As mentioned above, a (usually "specific") determinative can often be used for the logographic writing of a word. Moreover, as Gardiner (1957,§23 Obs. 25 Obs. 2) notes, in many cases the logogram was probably the earlier writing and the phonograms were added in effect to "determine" it by indicating its phonetic reading.

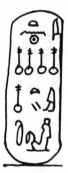

Figure 10. Long name of Nefertiti.

Figure 11. Pictogram on the Naᶜrmer palette.

*Multiliteral phonograms and word- (or root-) signs* (Figures 4, 12). Particularly in the case of the triliteral signs, the choice of multiliteral signs in the writing of most words is far from arbitrary. Gardiner (1957) notes that: "In the case of the triliterals the distinction between phonograms and ideograms becomes particularly precarious" (§ 42 Obs.; *cf.* p. 40); Gelb (1963) has denied the existence of a triliteral class of phonograms outside the domain of word-signs (but it has been pointed out that the bird *tyw* is apparently always used phonetically). The Egyptians seem to have used a given triliteral in a group of words which they regarded as being related or as having something in common regardless of whether or not the words were actually related etymologically (Gardiner, 1957, § 42 Obs., p. 440; Hodge, 1975). This is easy to understand as the Egyptian language abounds in triliteral roots, and the number of longer unrelated or unassociable words sharing the same three-consonant sequence would in most cases be quite limited. The same phenomenon is found in the use of biliteral signs in words consisting of or derived from biliteral roots.

*Phonetic complements and phonetic writings: the cart before the horse?* (Figures 4-7). As mentioned above, multiliteral signs are often accompanied by one or more of their component consonants. This has both a mnemonic and an aesthetic motivation:

the first to remind the reader of the value of the sign, the second, to form a symmetrical square or rectangular group. Many of the signs that take phonetic complements are not ambiguous in their reading in any case, but a mnemonic device is not thereby precluded. Phonetic complementation applies to root-signs; thus, in a given case it is often a matter of habit to consider a sign a "triliteral (phonogram)," and Gardiner often uses the term "semi-phonetic." Moreover, phonetic complementation is essentially the same phenomenon as the addition of phonetic writings to logograms which then become "determinatives." When the phonetic complements follow an ideogram or root-sign, it has been easiest to see them as "phonetic complements," and when they precede it, it is easiest to take them as a "phonetic writing" and the ideogram as a "determinative." Of course, once hieroglyphic writing was standardized, the Egyptians too must have accepted them that way to some extent; root-signs with phonetic complements are often followed by determinatives, and ideograms preceded by a phonetic writing (thus becoming determinatives) are often followed by additional determinatives. Thus a good many words can have multiple determinatives. It is also worth noting that some logograms are used as generic determinatives; for instance, the sun-disk can be a logographic writing for $r^c$ "sun" as well as for $hrw$ "day," and is the determinative for periods of time. At some point the writing $hrw$ + sun-disk + stroke, originally $hrw$ prefixed to the logographic writing of the word, seems to have been "reanalyzed" and the sun-disk parsed, as it were, as a determinative.

In this regard, consider "defective" or summary writings, in which a word is habitually written without its full consonantal value being (ostensibly) specified (Figure 13). Sometimes this is motivated by symmetry but sometimes it illustrates the principle that "the Egyptian was under no obligation to prefix to an ideogram more phonetic signs than were needed to remove obscurity" (Gardiner, 1957, § 59). This again is similar to other cases of phonetic complementation because only in a fairly limited number of cases (and hardly ever with a triliteral) are *all* the consonants of a multiliteral sign given in the phonetic complements. (Defective writings are probably a good deal more common than the few oft-cited examples would lead one to believe, especially writings which ignore the semivowels $w$ and $i/y$, although some examples depend on the inference or reconstruction of these consonants in a given root. (See Gardiner, 1957, § 63, 1916, p. 52, and Callender, 1975, p. 21.)

*Feminine .t in logographic writings of feminine words* (Figure 5). The separate writing of the feminine ending with logographic writings does not simply indicate that the Egyptians felt it to be an ending rather than part of the root. It is really a special case of the phonetic complementation of ideograms and testifies once again to the intermeshing of the phonetic and ideographic.

*The writing of the plural* (Figure 8). Here the close relationship of phonetic and ideographic aspects is extremely prominent (Gardiner, 1957, § § 72-4; Faulkner, 1929). There are several ways of writing a plural noun. A logogram or determinative can be repeated three times; in the latter case the plural ending can be written phonetically (optional). A logographic writing or determinative can be followed by three strokes which serve as a "plural determinative"; again, the phonetically-written plural ending is optional. Far more rarely, a brief word written entirely in phonograms can be repeated three times. The second method is the most usual in Middle Egyptian; after the Old Kingdom the third is extremely rare and limited to religious texts or archaic contexts. The first method is generally found more in hieroglyphic inscriptions than in hieratic manuscripts (though even in the latter there are words such as *ntrw*, "gods," which are most typically written with three logograms or word-signs). What has been said about the plural applies with some qualifications to the dual.

*The dual strokes and -y.* Two strokes, the marker of the dual, become a phonogram for -y at the end of words. The dual endings are .*wy* (masc.) and .*ty* (fem.) and we can see the two strokes passing from the ideographic to the phonetic as their use is extended beyond dual words (Gardiner, 1957, § 73.4).

*Composite signs* (Figure 9). Of the "monograms" (two hieroglyphs combined into a single sign, [Gardiner, 1957, § 58; Fischer 1977a, pp. 1193-94d]), there are some which combine a phonogram with an ideogram.

*The emergence of Egyptian writing and the representational context*
The situation described above is a natural outgrowth of the historical development of the hieroglyphic writing, and of the contexts in which it arose. The most essential point is that, as Fischer (1977a) writes: "The Eg. system of phonetic hieroglyphs was devised at the beginning of the First Dynasty in conjunction with a new style of art that is closely related to it in form and function; in the earliest pharaonic reliefs pictographic hieroglyphs and larger-scale representations form a complementary unity" (col. 1189). In some of the earliest examples of hieroglyphs—the palettes and maceheads of the terminal predynastic and incipient dynastic period—we see hieroglyphs (pictographic or otherwise) labeling figures or objects in a scene. In effect, the phonetic or other explicit hieroglyphs are added to gloss the representations and prepare for the complementary or intertwined relationship of ideographic and phonetic elements. When the hieroglyphs are removed from the original context of pictorial art and used to write texts, the representation is transplanted in the purely written context as a logogram or determinative. The complementation of writing and art persists after the initial period of hieroglyphic writing (Gardiner, 1957, § 5; Fischer, 1977b, § 2). Especially in the Old Kingdom, representations of people, animals, objects, or actions in a scene are accompanied by phonetic writings, as the representations

themselves supply the determinatives; similarly, a man's name written on his statue will have no determinative, as the statue itself is the determinative. After the Old Kingdom there are more and more exceptions ("redundant" determinatives) as if "the old complementary relationship between hieroglyphs and representations was never abandoned, it was gradually respected to a lesser degree" (Fischer, 1977 (a), col. 1194). But the Egyptians were always aware of it and could exploit it; they never lost sight of the suitability of the hieroglyphic script for integration into artistic and decorative contexts.

In considering the relationship of the hieroglyphs to a representational context, mention should be made of their orientation, a subject which has been investigated most exhaustively by Fischer (1977 (a), cols. 1192-93, 1977b). Hieroglyphs normally face the beginning of the line (or text, or written unit): one reads from the direction towards which the hieroglyphs face. Thus, if the signs face to the right, the text is read right to left (the most common direction), and vice versa. Parts of the same hieroglyphic text or body of writing can be oriented in different ways to fit in with certain decorative contexts or the formats of certain inscribed surfaces (borders, the two sides of a doorway, and so on). More significantly for the present survey, "the mixing of directions of writing" is an aspect of "exploitation of the script's pictorial character in order to convey pictorial information additional to the linguistic text" (Schenkel, 1976, p. 6). One example will suffice (from the late Eighteenth Dynasty, long after the Old Kingdom): the reversed writing of the word *itn* (Aten, the sun-disk) in the long form of Nefertiti's cartouche. *Nfr-nfrw-itn Nfrt-ii.ti* (Figure 10). "Aten," designating the sun-god, appears at the head of the cartouche because of honorific transposition (Gardiner, 1957,§ 57) and is oriented the opposite way from the rest of the name below it. As Tawfik has explained (1973), a parallel with the accompanying representation is expressed. Just as in the scene the sun-disk hands Nefertiti the emblems of life and dominion and accepts the offerings which she presents, in the writing of the name the word for the sun-disk is oriented so that in effect it faces the rest of Nefertiti's name.

In addition to the unity of the representations and the hieroglyphs in the early development of Egyptian writing, the organic unity of the scene itself must be considered. Gardiner (1915) asserts that, although the earliest hieroglyphs were probably "confined to the ticketing of depicted objects and the like," and accordingly were probably "phonetic, and not ideographic in character" (p. 74), we cannot approach the further development of hieroglyphic writing in terms of renderings of individual words, but must see the scene as a whole, with its hieroglyphic glosses or "labels," condensed as it were into a linguistically more explicit text. The "hieroglyphic sentence," with its composite of complementary signs, would be "developed directly from the composite picture...traced back to the complex scenes in which the Egyptians sought to record their actions" rather than to an aggregation of disembodied signs or even disembodied words (Gardiner, 1915, p. 75). He notes the parallel between this approach and the idea "that in language the ultimate unit is not the word but the sentence" (Gardiner, 1915, p. 75), a notion which has received a great deal of attention in current linguistic theory. He discusses at length (Gardiner, 1915, pp. 72 ff.) the complex pictographic group on the Naᶜrmer palette in which the Horus-falcon brings the papyrus-land captive (taking the papyrus-clump as six lotus plants or the numeral 6000), considers it "intermediate between picture and writing" (Figure 11). Perhaps this group provides some corroboration for his view of the "hieroglyphic sentence."

Hodge (1975) suggests that hieroglyphic writing arose in a ritual context, taking much impetus from word-plays and other such associations. He emphasizes the improbability of a gradual development beginning with logograms and culminating in alphabetic signs and points out the magical use of puns and the likelihood that prehistoric art had magical significance, noting "the association of magic with mnemonic symbols of various sorts" and "the recitation of formulae associated with such symbols" (Hodge, 1975, p. 334) and stressing the magical importance and function of writing throughout Egyptian history. For Hodge, hieroglyphs "were part of a symbolic system involving representation by sculpture and painting" (p. 5), and the Naᶜrmer palette "is part of the history of Egyptian symbolic art, including hieroglyphs" (p. 3). In summation, he writes: "The word plays and other phenomena discussed above are precisely the kinds of factors which must have been involved in the development of writing and which are reflected in the usage of the hieroglyphs by the Egyptians.... It would thus have been among the priests who composed and recited such spells, full of constant linguistic manipulation, that writing arose, reflecting the same associations made verbally" (p. 346). Hodge recognizes the link with representational art but seems to present the origin of hieroglyphic writing as a more abstract process, at one remove from the representational context. His formulation embodies dubious views of the antiquity of the Pyramid Texts, and the observed context of the earliest recognizable hieroglyphs is ambiguous with respect to his suggestion. Regardless of the ultimate validity of his suggestion, however, he makes extremely cogent comments on the features and principles of the hieroglyphic script. Most important, his view of the development of the hieroglyphs recognizes and emphasizes their emergence in an organic context, their complementary relationship to it, and the unity formed by the various features of the hieroglyphs themselves.

It is difficult if not impossible to derive convincingly a piecemeal origin of the script. The writer's opinion is that the script grew as a composite, a unity of mutually complementary parts. The subsequent great step would have been the adaptation of writing as a medium for recording the language in an accurate and connected fashion, independent of the original representational framework. This development, while permitting the continued complementation of writing and representations, would have given rise to a script incorporating the representational context.

An historical note is important to understanding not only the beginning writing in Egypt but also the centralization of the Egyptian state and bureaucracy and the standardization of the scribal tradition. Whatever the precise chronology, the emergence of writing accompanied the unification of Egypt at the end of the Predynastic period, the foundation of the united monarchy. While that unification is often seen as a military conquest of Lower Egypt by Upper Egypt, it more essentially represents the realization that centralization was necessary for Egypt.

*Hieroglyphic orthography: The "word-picture"*
Before proceeding to a detailed consideration of the word-picture, and of the mnemonic aspects of ancient Egyptian writing, the mnemonic principle itself should be clarified. What is meant by *mnemonic* is not the complete and accurate representation of the utterances of language, but a representation which provides enough information to bring an item unambiguously to mind and which depends to a large extent on a consistent one-to-one association between the item and the representation, which is learned and remembered even if the representation is neither complete nor accurate. In some cases completeness and accuracy must be subordinated to the main criterion of recognition; in others they can be subordinated to other considerations (for example, symmetrical grouping) because completeness and accuracy are not essential to the effective operation of the mnemonic principle. Two closely related demonstrations are phonetic complements, which seldom repeat all of the component consonants of the sign they accompany, but which remind the reader of its entire value, and the summary or defective writings of words. Another parallel example is the most elementary— the unvocalized nature of the script itself, in which the vowels and vocalic structure were subordinated to other priorities but were, of course, supplied by the ancient Egyptian reader. In that sense, the script as a whole is an incomplete mnemonic representation of the language (but a more complete representation than many other scripts). In some respects, the scribal habits of the Old Kingdom evince this to a greater degree: the first person singular suffix-pronoun .*i*, for instance, is regularly ignored (as is also the case, interestingly enough, in early demotic). As the various scribal conventions are examined, it will be seen how, even when the Egyptians attempted to increase the accuracy of the representation, they did so in a way which shows the primary importance of the word-picture.

*The standard orthography: generalities* (Figure 12). The prevalence of a consistent, standard orthography certainly owes much to the centralized training of scribes and the high degree of standardization of the literary language. Though there are variant writings of words and preferred orthographies change over the course of time, the degree of standardization is remarkable (Dévaud, 1924). The choice of signs is far from arbitrary and the total of possible combinations for spelling a word is not exploited (except for Ptolemaic inscriptions which belong to a very late period and are specialized phenomena). This standardized choice of signs does

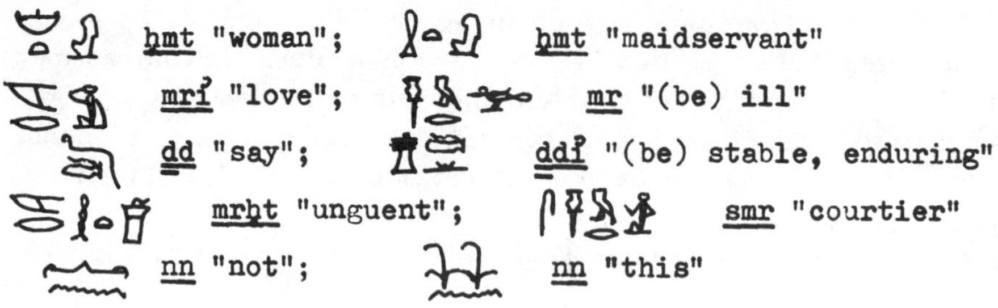

ḥmt "woman";  ẖmt "maidservant"

mri "love";  mr "(be) ill"

ḏd "say";  ḏdi "(be) stable, enduring"

mrḥt "unguent";  smr "courtier"

nn "not";  nn "this"

Figure 12. Standard orthography.

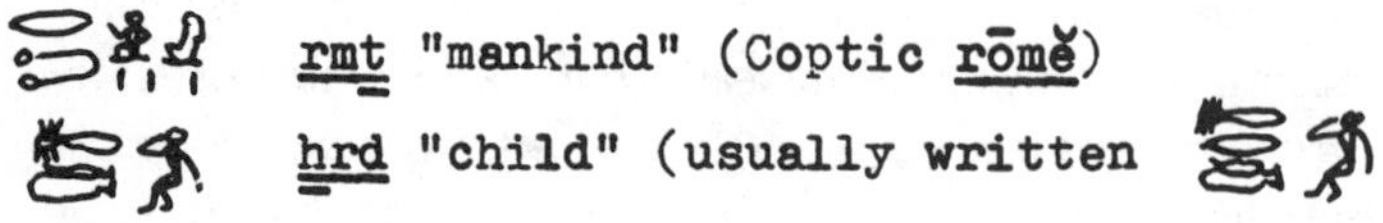

rmṯ "mankind" (Coptic rōmě)

ẖrd "child" (usually written ____)

Figure 13. Defective/summary writings.

ḫft "opposite";  ḫfty "enemy"

 ḫftyw "enemies"

Figure 14. Symmetrical misspellings.

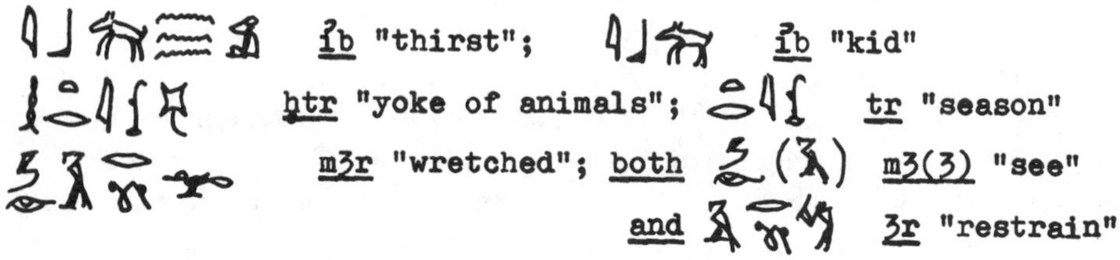

ib "thirst";  ib "kid"

ḥtr "yoke of animals";  tr "season"

m3r "wretched"; both  m3(3) "see"

and  3r "restrain"

Figure 15. Embedded homophones ("phonetic determinatives").

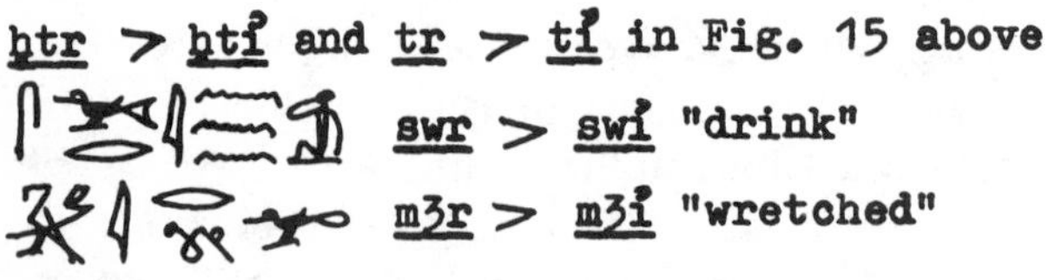

ḥtr > ḥti and tr > ti in Fig. 15 above

swr > swi "drink"

m3r > m3i "wretched"

Figure 16. Mixed spellings.

not apply only to those bi- and triliterals that serve as root-signs in groups of related or associated words. As Schenkel (1976) writes: "The strictness of this sort of orthographic convention is clearly of an altogether lesser order than that of an alphabetic script with fixed spellings, but it still constitutes a significant restriction in comparison with the range of possibilities offered by the huge repertory of signs" (p. 6). Fischer (1977a) agrees that, "Despite the overall irregularity of structure, the orthography of a given word at a given period was almost always sufficiently distinctive and consistent so as to eliminate any ambiguity" (col. 1190). Thus, the standard orthography serves both to write a given word in a consistent and recognizable way and to prevent the confusion of different words on grounds of either homophony (or near-homophony) or synonymy (that is, having the ideographic element in common). Callender (1975) draws attention to the non-interchangeability of homophonous biliterals (such as the hoe and chisel for *mr*), whether or not used as root-signs, concluding that: "This points to the likelihood that the Egyptians were at least aware of syllable structure if not the notion of vowels, and at least sporadically tried to represent it" (p. 3). The writer's opinion is that this characteristic testifies to the desideratum of maintaining distinct and consistent word-pictures; the observation that the sign in question remains constant as the word is taken through its grammatical permutations would seem to indicate that, as suggested above, syllable structure is not central to the hieroglyphic orthography. (Callender [1975] realizes that many features of the orthography are used "in order to remove any ambiguity whatsoever" [p. 3].)

The choice of a combination of signs for "spelling" the word is only one aspect of the word-picture and far from the only way in which it is established. As Schenkel (1976) notes, the convention of ending words with determinatives or terminal ideograms "provides a good criterion for dividing the continuous stream of the script into individual words. The resulting 'word images' contribute much to the legibility of hieroglyphic texts. They do, however, have the disadvantage that they prepare the way for an erosion of the values of individual phonograms, as those which belong to a 'word image' adapt to phonetic change fitfully, if at all" (p. 6). Also to be included among orthographic means of delineating a word-picture is the convention of accompanying a logographic sign with a stroke, showing at a glance that the logogram is the writing of a word rather than part of a larger unit (although this stroke is not confined to logographic writings and to some extent is used for symmetry and because of what Schenkel calls the Egyptian scribes' *horror vacui*). At the same time, it should be noted that a number of words of primarily grammatical function (prepositions, particles, demonstratives) are written purely with phonograms (in a number of cases alphabetic signs). Altogether the use of the mixed script provides the maximum opportunity for word-recognition.

We can begin to appreciate the multifaceted nature of the word-picture and what it conveys to the scribe and the reader. "Morphemes or words were identified as having many things in common, not just one or more consonants" (Hodge, 1975, p. 5), and the recognition of "various degrees of phonologic similarity and of semantic grouping" (p. 18) goes along with "differentiation of graphically [consonantally] homophonous forms" (p. 17). The central role of the standard orthography in establishing and maintaining these word-pictures is made all the more obvious by the observation that the obscurity of so-called cryptographic or enigmatic writing depends to a large extent on changing these accustomed pictures in certain ways: "by the use of abnormal phonograms (obtained, however, in the normal manner...), by the invention of new semograms [ideograms], and by the use of abnormal selections of phonograms and semograms for writing words (words generally written with phonograms are written with semograms, and *vice versa*), etc." (Schenkel, 1976, p. 6). Cryptography and "sportive" writings attest to the fact that, despite the unity of the script and the strong orientation towards word-groups, it always remained "manipulable" (Hodge, 1975, p. 16) in the hands of the erudite. This type of manipulation might seem surprising in the light of our emphasis on the organic nature of the hieroglyphic script and our avoidance of an overly typological approach to individual signs. However, it seems that the very fluidity of the categories, their ability to shift according to the individual point of view, and the apparent ability of a word-sign to grow in either or both directions provided great potential for manipulation by those scribes with a better than superficial understanding of the script.

*Defective writings and symmetrical misspellings* (Figures 13-14). It has been noted that some of the defective or summary writings are at least partially motivated by the maintaining of a symmetrical group. The same holds true for other words which, although not written defectively, are not written with the consonants in the "right" order. Thus, the preposition *ḥft*, "opposite," appears as if it were read *\*ḫtf*. Though here the decisive factor has been regarded as symmetry, the predominance of symmetry in this manner would be impossible without the primary importance of the recognizable word-picture. In fact, the "incorrect" spelling of *ḥft* can be carried over to related or derived words such as *ḫfty*, "enemy," and *ḫftyw* "enemies." In effect, we see the "phonetic" writing of a stem carrying the word-picture just as a word-sign or root-sign would. (Other graphic transpositions, treated in Gardiner [1957, § 56], belong under the same general heading.)

*"Phonetic determinatives" or embedded homophones* (Figure 15). What Gardiner (1957, § 54) calls "phonetic determinatives" are, from one point of view, determinatives of (consonantally) homophonous words, for example, the kid in *ib* "thirst," from the homophonous *ib* "kid." But it is more illuminating to see such orthographies as embedded homophones; as Gardiner recognizes, "the entire word ⟨ ⟩ *ib* 'kid' enters bodily into the writing of the etymologically unrelated verb for 'thirst.'" Such embedded homophones or transplanted words testify to the pervasiveness of the word-picture in Egyptian orthography. Moreover, in

some cases the embedded homophone is homophonous only with a part of the word into which it is transplanted; thus *tr* "season" appears in *ḥtr*, "pair of horses; yoke of animals." Instances can even be found in which one word has two "phonetic determinatives": *m3r*, "wretched," can be written as if it were compounded of *m3(3)* "see" and *3r* "restrain." As a general rule it is not as productive to see an individual sign introduced as a "phonetic determinative" than as part of a transplanted or partially coinciding word although in some cases, of course, it may have happened that way.

*Mixed spellings* (Figure 16). Mixed spellings are a convention for indicating phonetic change while keeping the original word-picture intact. The writing of "pair of horses" which one would naturally transliterate as *ḥtrỉ* actually indicates that *ḥtr* changed to *ḥtỉ* (Gardiner, 1957, p. 447, § 279); the mixed spelling provides the original word-picture and indicates the particular which has changed. This somewhat roundabout device shares the same general approach as phonetic complementation. Gardiner (1957) does not devote much attention to mixed spellings; he writes (his italics):

*"The method of this book is largely based upon the view that beginners, once having mastered the main principles of the writing, should not inquire too curiously into the nature of individual spellings, but should learn both the hieroglyphic groups and their transliterations mechanically"* (§ 54).

(Note that there is no universally accepted Egyptological convention for transliterating mixed spellings.)

*Group-writing* (Figure 17). Before leaving the fundamentals of hieroglyphic orthography, mention must be made of another device: "group-writing" or the "syllabic orthography" (Gardiner 1957, § 60). A word or name in group-writing is not written with most of the usual building-blocks of the script (apart from determinatives), but with biliterals whose second consonant is a semivowel or *3*, or pairs of alphabetic signs the second of which is a semivowel or *3*. Sometimes the writing of a monosyllabic word such as *t*, "bread", can be used as a grapheme in group-writing. Schenkel (1976) summarizes the prevailing view of this orthography:

> In the New Kingdom syllabic or "group" writing was evolved under the influence of cuneiform.... The new system was mostly used to write western Asiatic words. It employs groups of signs to encode syllables consisting of consonant + vowel.... There is still controversy among egyptologists over the interpretation of these groups as a syllabic script. Extreme views are, on the one hand, that group writing is a fully developed syllabic script, and, on the other hand, that it cannot be termed syllabic at all, as the notation of vowels is totally confused. The truth probably lies midway between the two. (pp. 5-6)

Group-writing has been attested before the New Kingdom and it can be found in native Egyptian words (Ward, 1957). Ward challenges the oft-repeated statement that Egyptian words and names in group-writing are "etymologically obscure" (Gardiner, 1957, § 60). It is certainly true that in Late Egyptian many more native words appear in group-writing but there is much ambiguity in such writings as, for instance, any biliteral ending with 3 could be used purely consonantally because of the quiescence of 3, the two-stroke *y* (and often a meaningless *w*) could be added ubiquitously as space-fillers, and so on. Moreover, although the hieroglyphic inscriptions of the Ramesside period tend to be more cluttered in appearance than most earlier ones, the influence and consequences of this "group-writing" trend are seen primarily in late hieratic and demotic orthography, not hieroglyphic. Schenkel (1976) writes: "In the New Kingdom an attempt was made to form a genuinely syllabic script. But by this time the use of the script seems to have been determined to such an extent by tradition—by the 'word images' evolved over the centuries—that an innovation as radical as this could not succeed in the long run." (p. 6.)

Group-writing is the Egyptian orthographic convention that does least to embody or convey a word-picture. Thus, it makes very good sense that it was used predominantly to write foreign words or words of obscure etymology which would be least associated with a word-picture. Not surprisingly, it was occasionally used to render familiar Egyptian words (as perhaps being more phonetically explicit, but at the expense of the word-picture); moreover, its use proliferated in Late Egyptian (in conjunction with developments in Egyptian phonology and tendencies in New Kingdom hieratic briefly alluded to above). It is not at all surprising that the word-picture prevailed. Indeed, the Egyptian attachment to word-pictures can be observed even in that form of notation which fundamentally ignored them.

*The cursive scripts (and remarks on the development of the scribal tradition in late times)*
Having illustrated the role of the word-picture and various mnemonic devices in hieroglyphic orthography, it is necessary to discuss the cursive scripts, hieratic and demotic, in so far as they offer independent considerations and do not simply

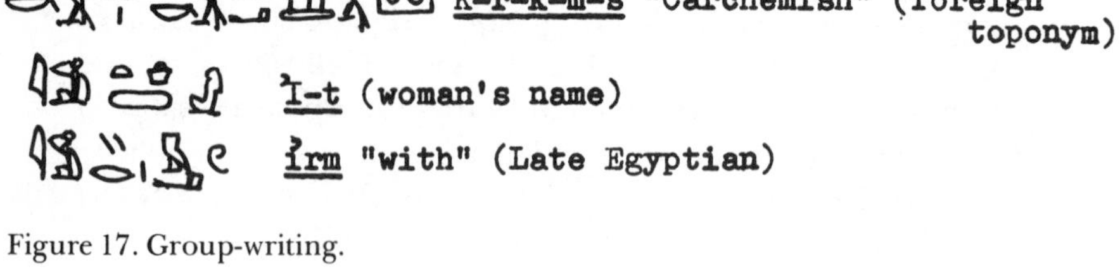

Figure 17. Group-writing.

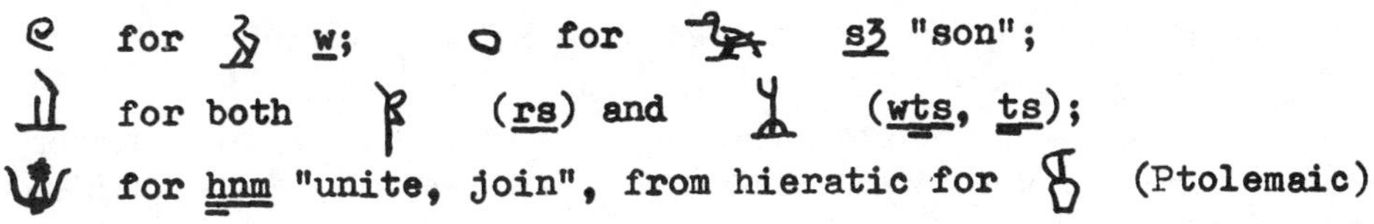

℮  for ⅄  w;      ○  for 🦆  s3 "son";

⊥  for both  ⅄  (rs) and  ⅄  (wts, ts);

𝖶  for hnm "unite, join", from hieratic for  ⅄  (Ptolemaic)

Figure 18. Hieroglyphs derived from hieratic.

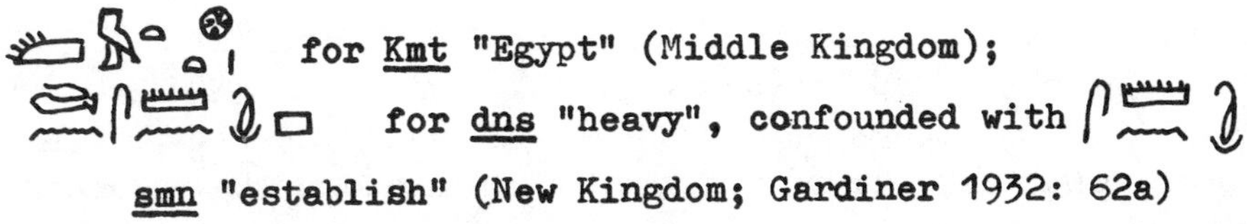

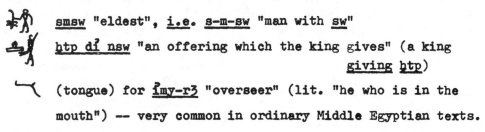

for Kmt "Egypt" (Middle Kingdom);

for dns "heavy", confounded with ⟡ smn "establish" (New Kingdom; Gardiner 1932: 62a)

Figure 19. Spelled-out determinatives (hieratic).

smsw "eldest", i.e. s-m-sw "man with sw"

htp di nsw "an offering which the king gives" (a king

giving htp)

(tongue) for imy-r3 "overseer" (lit. "he who is in the

mouth") -- very common in ordinary Middle Egyptian texts.

Figure 20. Cryptography and sportive writings.

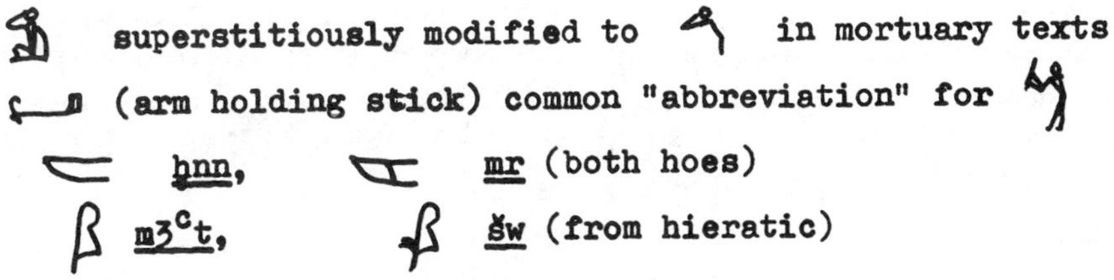

superstitiously modified to  ⅄  in mortuary texts

(arm holding stick) common "abbreviation" for  ⅄

⊂  hnn,      ⊂  mr (both hoes)

ß  m3ᶜt,      ⅄  šw (from hieratic)

Figure 21. Structure of individual signs.

reflect what is found in the hieroglyphs. As Fischer (1977a) notes: "the hiero-glyphs were supplemented, from the very beginning, by more cursive forms of the same signs, better adapted to the use of pen and ink on papyrus, and these cursive forms became increasingly simple and abstract (hieratic, and finally demotic...)" (col. 1189). Whereas hieratic was a cursive rendition of the hieroglyphs, demotic (starting about the seventh century B.C.) was a further cursive reduction of cursive hieratic (not returning to a hieroglyphic model). Moreover, neither cursive form makes any attempt to simplify the composite nature of the script; the entire script is condensed into more cursive, ligatured forms. The successive cursive scripts are derived with the same unity which characterized the emergence of the hieroglyphic writing in the first place. It should also be noted that the introduction of each successive cursive script results in a certain division of labor among the scripts; none of them entirely superseded its predecessors or put them out of use. Rather, the new script took over the more utilitarian, everyday uses of writing. The hieroglyphs always remained the monumental script, the form of writing found in artistic, architectural, decorative contexts, the script whose pictorial and aesthetic potential was greatest. Because the cursive forms are less accessible to non-Egyptologists and Egyptologists publish the mass of hieratic literary texts, letters, and documents in hieroglyphic transcription, the non-Egyptologist may not realize that the vast majority of everyday writing in ancient Egypt was not in hieroglyphs.

Though the earliest hieratic which we study as an entity dates to the Old Kingdom, the cursive writings in ink on jars and other objects from the first two dynasties must also be considered hieratic, and we know that papyrus was used as a writing material in the Archaic Period. The introduction of a cursive form of writing for everyday, utilitarian use was one of the most important steps in extending the sphere of writing, enabling it to grow as a linguistic tool and to be used independently of the original representational context. Hieratic acquired its own orthographic peculiarities (Gardiner, 1957, § 63A, pp. 422-423), dictated by differences in function and medium from the hieroglyphs; hieratic was less explicitly pictorial. Nonetheless, the purely visual element remains important. All of the components of the hieroglyphic word-picture are carried over into the hieratic. Though intricate determinatives can be replaced by an oblique stroke, hieratic determinatives and word-signs are often recognizable and can be vivid examples of calligraphy when done by a skilled scribe. Moreover, hieratic always retains a close link with the hieroglyphs. Many hieroglyphic inscriptions—on stelae, in temples, and in tombs—were composed in hieratic; inscriptions of different periods have scribal errors which result from the incorrect transcription of a hieratic original. There are also a number of signs which work their way back into the hieroglyphs from the hieratic (Figure 18).

Hieratic texts are the source of one of the most striking indications of the mnemonic principle of Egyptian writing and the pervasiveness of the word-picture: the "spelling out" of determinatives.

The hieroglyph   ⊗   is both the word-sign for "city" and the determinative for many toponyms. In Middle Kingdom hieratic the determinative is often written out   ⊗   (the writing of the word *niwt* "city"), perhaps to avoid confusing the city-sign with other circular signs in simplified hieratic form. In New Kingdom manuscripts, there are a number of cases of what Gardiner (1932) calls "prefixing to a determinative its more usual phonetic writing"—the inclusion, along with the determinative, of another word in which it is a central part, a kind of phonetic determinative in reverse (Figure 19). The pervasiveness of the word-picture as a mnemonic unit provides evidence that word-recognition, rather than a sign-by-sign spelling or analysis, was typical of the way in which writing was taught. It is also significant that, judging from the many school texts which we have, students were taught to write in hieratic before they learned hieroglyphs. Williams (1972) writes: "It is significant that the first steps in writing began with the more commonly used hieratic rather than hieroglyphic. Because of the frequent use of ligatures in this cursive hand, the pupils were taught to write complete words or phrases without analyzing the component signs. By this means they gradually learned to recognize individual words" (p. 219).

In demotic, the link with hieroglyphs is more remote, as the script is not derived directly from the hieroglyphs. It is possible to transcribe demotic into hieroglyphs but the exercise is of dubious value and the result looks very strange next to hieroglyphic spellings, largely because many of the late hieratic writings of words which directly give rise to demotic writings are like the group-writing orthographies mentioned earlier. Thus, the scribal fad described above has somewhat paradoxically given rise to new word-pictures for many words in late hieratic and demotic but not in hieroglyphic texts. This development is the logical result of the division of labor among the scripts: the scribal tradition of writing used for everyday purposes or general literacy parts company with that of the hieroglyphs, which are increasingly relegated to an academic tradition and further and further moved from utilitarian communication. (Another facet relates to language rather than writing: while late hieratic documents and demotic texts write an approximation of the language spoken at the time, late hieroglyphic texts often have as their model the literary language of the Old and Middle Kingdoms.) The academic tradition of the hieroglyphs reaches its zenith in the inscriptions of the Ptolemaic period (particularly in the temples), which embody a mixture of self-conscious scholarly manipulation of the script, sometimes of a markedly obfuscatory nature, and new values, signs, and confusions which have come about because of phonetic change and the inconsistencies arising from the incongruity between phonetic change and the archaic language which the texts attempt to reproduce (Fairman, 1943, 1945). In these inscriptions, certain tendencies of the hieroglyphic script can be exploited and exaggerated to the extent that they become counterproductive in terms of communication, consistency and recognizability being virtually neglected as guiding principles. Certain aspects of Ptolemaic orthography are the culmination of the cryptographic writings.

In demotic, ligatures abound and the pictorial element is much reduced even from hieratic. The mnemonic principle remains at least as important, however; as every student of demotic knows, the reading of the script depends to a considerable extent on the recognition of fixed word-groups. Though there are of course many readable signs, phonetic and otherwise, a number are ambiguous outside the context of particular word-groups and many have contextual variants. Demotic illustrates the following aspect of the mnemonic principle: the recognition or association of a grapheme or graphemic complex as representing an object to which it no longer bears a visual resemblance, a development well known in many of the ideograms of cuneiform and Chinese. (Note that some late demotic magical texts use an entirely alphabetic writing, with *matres lectionis*, to ensure the precise pronunciation of the text: phonetic explicitness at the expense of the word-picture once again. During the same period—and sometimes in the same text, as in the Demotic Magical Papyrus of London and Leyden—there appears "Old Coptic," written in the Greek alphabet for the same reason.)

*Remarks on sportive and cryptographic writings* (Figure 20)
Selected aspects of cryptographic writing can illuminate our investigation from another direction. As has been mentioned earlier, cryptography shows the Egyptians' ability to manipulate their own script, to exploit its potential for juggling and reshuffling its components, sometimes for deliberate obfuscation. One of the major mechanisms of cryptography is changing the word-picture around (Schenkel, 1976).

Some cryptographic writings are extremely interesting in conjunction with our discussion of the origins of the hieroglyphic script and Gardiner's "hieroglyphic sentence" because they show that the "hieroglyphic sentence," as in the Naᶜrmer palette, remained part of the repertoire or potential of the script, but was used peripherally rather than centrally in writing.

A standing man holding the biliteral sign *sw* can be found as a cryptographic writing of the word *smsw*, "eldest," the group being read as *s-m-sw* "man with *sw*" (Drioton, 1935, 1940). In effect, the word is broken down into its component consonants (or sequences featuring one strong consonant) and "spelled" or analyzed as a "sentence" or, in any case, a sequence of words which its component consonants make up. Likewise, the phrase beginning the standard offering-formula, *ḥtp dỉ nsw*, "an offering which the king gives," although usually written out in individual words, can be found written by the figure of a king holding out the *ḥtp*-sign (Faulkner, 1962, p. 179), that is, a king giving *ḥtp* (the word for offering). Here a sequence of words is written as a single group combining more than one hieroglyph but constructed essentially as a single figure. Many additional examples could be noted.

Both groups have two features worth noting. A word in the sentence or group is not directly represented or spelled out by a hieroglyph but is implicit in the figure or action represented (man *with sw*, king *giving ḥtp*), and one of the component hieroglyphs (*sw* in the first, *ḥtp* in the second) is treated quite self-consciously as a grapheme, a hieroglyph. Such groups suggest the "hieroglyphic sentence" of nascent writing but are utilized as sophisticated devices by experienced practitioners of writing. Thus, cryptographic use of the hieroglyphs embodies features of the earliest emergence of writing while still influencing the latest period of hieroglyphic inscriptions.

*Some characteristics of individual signs* (Figure 21)

Though this paper is concerned primarily with the writing of words and with the principles governing the use of signs as they function in words (and other contexts, for example, representations), the characteristics and structure of individual hieroglyphs must be mentioned. (For more comprehensive remarks see Fischer 1977 (a); Kaplony, 1966, 1973; and Schenkel, 1976.) Composite signs have already been mentioned. The repertoire of hieroglyphic signs embraces both the natural and the man-made objects of the Egyptian environment, as well as the inhabitants of the spiritual world, the gods. The rendition of a given sign is in accord with the principles governing two-dimensional art. A class of signs may consist of variations of the same basic figure in one essential feature (for instance, the seated or standing human figure with a wide variety of gestures). An interesting ramification can be observed in the magical significance of hieroglyphs. In mortuary texts it is common to avoid, or to represent in a mutilated or partial fashion, signs (especially human and animal figures) which might threaten the deceased (Lacau, 1913). In human figures, the head and hands showing a distinctive gesture are often represented, the superstitious modification resulting in the writing of the essential part of the sign only.

An important manifestation of the mnemonic principle in the structure of individual hieroglyphs is what might be termed the diacritical differentiation between signs, the establishment of an apparently arbitrary distinction between two signs which represent similar objects but have different values. Thus, the hoe without a crossbar (or rope) has the value *ḥnn*, while that with the additional feature has the value *mr*. Sometimes such a distinction arises secondarily in order to differentiate two different values of the same sign. The ostrich feather can be used as a logogram, root-sign, or determinative in *m3ʿt*, "truth, justice, universal order," and can also have the value *šw*. In hieratic, an innovation adds two ticks to the feather when it has the value *šw*.

*Conclusion*

A short-lived innovation of very late times provides the proof of the pudding. There are a very few hieroglyphic inscriptions written out entirely in alphabetic signs, notably the Naukratis stela of Nectanebo II in the middle of the fourth century B.C. (Lichtheim, 1976). This mode of writing was probably stimulated by Greek influence (Williams, 1976). It is hardly surprising that these inscriptions have presented difficulties to Egyptologists. This innovation was not widely used apparently because when the Egyptians had finished writing such a text, it was difficult for them to read it! Hodge (1975) gives an overall appraisal of hieroglyphic writing and, in particular, a comparison with purely alphabetic scripts as follows:

> It is generally acknowledged that the Egyptians were, very early, on the verge of one of the greatest of all discoveries: the alphabet. It is just as generally deplored that they did not take this logical next step.... This criticism, voiced by many scholars, assumes the undisputed superiority of alphabetic writing. These same authors, however, go on to describe some of the advantages of the cumbersome hieroglyphic system.... It is only recently, as we have been attempting to see language as a whole, that we appreciate the nature of the Egyptian hieroglyphs. To call such a manner of writing a "system" is to mislead. It is rather a set of conventions reflecting in a non-systematic fashion a number of facets of language structure.... As a semiologic complex it is unsurpassed by any other writing system. (pp. 347-348.)

Moreover, it will be noted that purely alphabetic scripts have often been eked out by various extra-alphabetic devices to enhance intelligibility: word-division, capitalization, punctuation (to say nothing of additional visual devices such as italics). In addition, various languages which use alphabetic scripts do not use a phonemic orphonetic spelling but have historical and morphophonemic spellings which reinforce the recognition of a word or root. In that sense, Schenkel's comparison (1976) of Egyptian and contemporary English orthography is apt; various attempts at spelling reform have gone the way of the Naukratis stela.

Very little (and that cursory) has been said about sportive writings and cryptography, the special characteristics of the orthography and palaeography of the cursive scripts, the hieroglyphic inscriptions of Ptolemaic times, and the structure of individual signs (as well as the inventory of the hieroglyphic repertoire as a whole); and certain graphic conventions such as honorific transposition, the colors of hieroglyphs, visual aspects of the format of written texts, and the relationship between writing and the spoken language have been omitted entirely. The emergence of Egyptian writing has been considered but not the inscriptions of the Archaic Period. The transition from the hieroglyphic sentence posited by Gardiner to the strong emphasis on the *word-picture* has not been elucidated. Nonetheless, by focussing on a few aspects, some indication has been given of the contribution which Egyptian writing can make to the study of visible language and the contribution which the study of visible language can make to understanding the ancient Egyptian scripts and the scribes who wrote them.

## References

Bakir, A.M. *An introduction to the study of the Egyptian language. A Semitic approach (Vol. I). Middle Egyptian.* Cairo: General Egyptian Book Organization, 1978.

Callender, J. B. *Middle Egyptian (Afroasiatic Dialects* 2). Malibu: Undena Publications, 1975.

Dévaud, E. *L'âge des papyrus hiératiques d'après les graphies de certains mots.* Paris: P. Geuthner, 1924.

Drioton, E. Notes sur le cryptogramme de Montouemhêt. *Annuaire de l'Institut de Philologie et d'Histoire Orientales*, 1935, *3* (Fs. J. Capart), 133-140.

Drioton, E. Recueil de cryptographie monumentale. *Annales du Service des Antiquités de l'Egypte*, 1940, *40*, 305-429.

Edgerton, W. F. Egyptian phonetic writing, from its invention to the close of the nineteenth dynasty. *Journal of the American Oriental Society*, 1940, *60*, 473-506.

Edgerton, W. F. Vowel quantity and syllable division in Egyptian. *Journal of Near Eastern Studies*, 1947, *6*, 1-17.

Fairman, H. W. Notes on the alphabetic signs employed in the hieroglyphic inscriptions of the temple of Edfu. *Annales du Service des Antiquités de l'Egypte*, 1943, *43*, 191-310.

Fairman, H. W. An introduction to the study of Ptolemaic signs and their values. *Bulletin de l'Institut français d'archéologie orientale*, 1945, *43*, 51-138.

Faulkner, R. O. *The plural and dual in Old Egyptian.* Brussels: Fondation Egyptologique Reine Elisabeth, 1929.

Faulkner, R. O. *A concise dictionary of Middle Egyptian.* Oxford: Oxford University Press, 1962.

Fischer, H. G. Hieroglyphen. *Lexikon der Ägyptologie*, Lief. *16* (Bd. II, Lief. *8*), cols. 1189-99. Wiesbaden: Otto Harrassowitz, 1977. (a)

Fischer, H. G. *Egyptian studies II: The orientation of hieroglyphs.* Pt. 1. *Reversals.* New York: Metropolitan Museum of Art, 1977. (b)

Gardiner, A. H. The nature and development of the Egyptian hieroglyphic writing. *Journal of Egyptian Archaeology*, 1915, *2*, 61-75.

Gardiner, A. H. *Notes on the story of Sinuhe.* Paris: 1916.

Gardiner, A. H. *Late-Egyptian stories (Bibliotheca Aegyptiaca* 1). Brussels: Fondation Egyptologique Reine Elisabeth, 1932.

Gardiner, A. H. *Egyptian grammar* (3rd ed.). Oxford: Oxford University Press, 1957.

Gelb, I. J. *A study of writing* (2nd ed.). Chicago: University of Chicago Press, 1963.

Hodge, C. T. Ritual and writing: An inquiry into the origin of Egyptian script. In M. D. Kinkade, K. L. Hale, & O. Werner (Eds.), *Linguistics and anthropology: In Honor of C. F. Voegelin.* Lisse: Peter Rider Press, 1975.

Kaplony, P. Strukturprobleme der Hieroglyphenschrift. *Chronique d'Egypte*, 1966, *41*, 60-99.

Kaplony, P. Die Prinzipien der Hieroglyphenschrift. *Textes et langages de l'Egypte pharaonique* 1. (*Institut français d'archéologie orientale. Biliothèque d'Étude* 64/1). Cairo: 1973.

Lacau, P. Suppressions et modifications de signes dans les textes funéraires. *Zeitschrift für ägyptische Sprache und Altertumskunde*, 1913, *51*, 1-64.

Lichtheim, M. The Naucratis stela once again. *Studies in honor of George R. Hughes* (*Studies in Ancient Oriental Civilization* No. 39). Chicago: University of Chicago Press, 1976.

Peet, T. E. Review of Dévaud 1924. *Journal of Egyptian Archaeology*, 1925, *11*, 119-120. (a)

Peet, T. E. Review of H. Sottas and Drioton. *Introduction à l'étude des hiéroglyphes*. *Journal of Egyptian Archaeology*, 1925, *11*, 122. (b)

Schenkel, W. The structure of hieroglyphic script. *Royal Anthropological Institute News*, 1976, *15* (August), 4-7.

Tawfik, S. 1973. Aton studies 2. *Mitteilungen des Deutschen Archäologischen Instituts Kairo*, 1973, *29*, 82-86.

Ward, W. A. Notes on Egyptian group-writing. *Journal of Near Eastern Studies*, 1957, *16*, 198-203.

Williams, R. J. Scribal training in ancient Egypt. *Journal of the American Oriental Society*, 1972, *92*, 214-221.

Williams, R. J. The interplay of Egyptian and Hellenic cultures. In *The Mediterranean World: Papers Presented in Honour of Gilbert Bagnani*. Peterborough, Ontario: Trent University, 1976.

# The Korean writing system: An alphabet? A syllabary? a logography?

Insup Taylor

*The Korean writing system, Hangul, is an "alphabetic syllabary" which employs many of the good and few of the bad features of an alphabet, a syllabary, and a logography. An alphabet can represent any word in the language, one phoneme at a time, but the phoneme-grapheme correspondence may be imperfect, and a single word may require a long array of letters. A syllable is a more stable unit of language than a phoneme, but a simple syllabary is practical only for a language with few different syllables. A logography, with a unique symbol for each morpheme, requires more complex and more numerous symbols. Korean text uses Hangul mixed with Chinese characters in a manner which aids reading.*

"The bright can learn the system [Hangul] in a single morning." (*a Hangul scholar, circa 1446*)

## The writing system

Hangul—the Great Letters of Korea—is regarded by some scholars as the most perfect phonetic system devised to withstand the tests of time and use (Diringer, 1968). Jensen (1970) states: "I would fully and wholly endorse the praise which H. F. J. Junker bestows on the Korean script.... One cannot describe the script-system ... as other than brilliant, so deliberately does it fit the language like a glove" (p. 215). Martin (1972) comments that "the Korean script is remarkable for its internal structure and for its graphic origin" (p. 82). Despite such praise, the Korean script is little known in the western world.

Hangul was invented in the middle of the fifteenth century by King Sejong and his committee of scholars. The King's noble aim was to provide a script that could be easily learned so that the ordinary people would be able to communicate with him in writing. The scholars made a careful study of other writing systems, went on numerous trips to consult experts in various systems, and after several years of work produced their own alphabet.

The writing systems of the world can be divided into three broad types: logographies, syllabaries, and alphabets (Diringer, 1968; Gelb, 1963; Jensen, 1970). In the first part of this paper, Hangul will be discussed as an alphabet, a syllabary, and a logography. The use of Chinese characters in the Korean writing system will be examined also. In the second part, some experiments which have used the Korean writing system will be described.

### Hangul as an alphabet

*English alphabet vs. Hangul.* In an alphabet, one letter can represent one phoneme. English is the most familiar, if not the most rational, alphabet. Because it has 26 letters to represent approximately 40 phonemes, the relation between phonemes and graphemes is irregular and complex. The single letter "a" represents several different vowels in such words as "about, fat, farm, face, fall, hurrah, fare." On the other hand, the sound /f/ is represented by a variety of different letters, as in "fat, photo, laugh, cough." Some letters have no sounds, as in *psa*lm, indi*c*t. Sometimes double letters are used for one phoneme, as in "butt, sheath." "Pontefract" will stump many readers.

In Hangul the ideal of one symbol for one phoneme is almost realized. Only 10 basic vowel symbols and 14 basic consonant symbols are needed to represent unambiguously any phoneme in the language. One symbol represents one phoneme and vice versa. Apart from a few minor exceptions, the phonemic value of each symbol is invariant. Thus, any letter string, even if unfamiliar or nonsensical, can be sounded out instantly and accurately and there is no need ever to consult a dictionary for sounds or spellings of words.

Each consonant character symbolizes its sound at both initial and final positions as, for example, in "giog, biub, niun, mium" for "g, b, n, m." The symbol for "l" is appropriately named "riul," reflecting the fact that the symbol is pro-nounced as /r/ at the initial and as /l/ at the final position of a word. In contrast, the English "doubleyou," "wai," and "aitch" have no relation to the sounds of those letters.

*Shapes of symbols*. Hangul appears to be the only alphabet, indeed the only writing system, in which the shapes of symbols reflect the articulations of sounds. For instance, for the two basic symbols representing the two consonants /g, n/ the articulatory organs—the mouth opening, the tongue shape and position—will look like (g) and (n) in Figure 1.

Especially interesting is the way symbols for related sounds are formed. A symbol for an aspirated consonant is formed by adding a stroke to its unaspi-rated counterpart, and a symbol for a tense consonant is formed by repeating its non-tense counterpart, as is shown in Figure 1.

Vowel symbols start with either a vertical bar or a horizontal bar, repre-senting /i/ and /ŭ/ (a tongue high, medial vowel) respectively. A short marker on either of the bars creates a different vowel. For example, putting the marker above a horizontal bar gives /o/ ( ⊥ ); adding another similar marker creates /jo/ ( ⊥ ). A marker to the right of the vertical bar is the symbol for /a/ ( ├ ); adding another marker makes /ja/ ( ├ ). If the two symbols for /o/ and /a/ are combined, we have the symbol for /oa/ ( ⊥ ). In this manner 16 simple vowels and diphthongs are created.

Finally, the shapes of consonants and vowels are distinct: consonant symbols are simple geometric forms and vowel symbols are combinations of horizontal or vertical straight lines. This is not the case in English where such letters as C, G, and O are easily confused (Kinney, Marsetta, & Showman, Note 1). There is only one form for symbols in Hangul and there is nothing comparable to the uppercase and lowercase letters in English or to the two Japanese syllabaries.

ㄱ   /g/: the root of the tongue as it closes the throat passage and touches the soft palate; also used in /k/ and /gg/. (see Fig. 1B)

ㄴ   /n/: the shape of the point of the tongue as it touches the ridge behind the teeth; also used in /d/, /t/, /dd/, and /r, l/.

ㅅ   /s/: the molar tooth; also used in /dz/, /t ʃ/, and their tense form/.

ㅇ   /h/: with added strokes: unobstructed throat passage

ㅁ   /m/: the shape of the closed mouth; also used in /b/, /p/, and the tense form/.

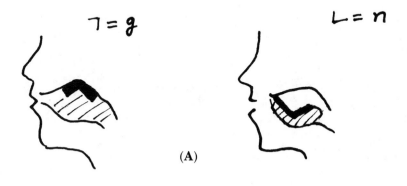

(A)

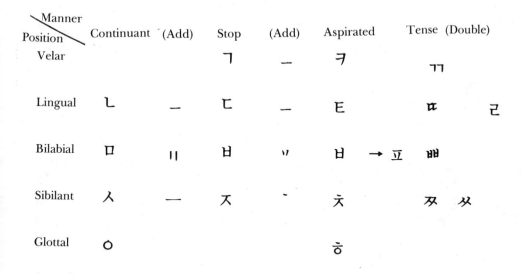

| Manner / Position | Continuant | (Add) | Stop | (Add) | Aspirated | Tense (Double) | |
|---|---|---|---|---|---|---|---|
| Velar | | | ㄱ | — | ㅋ | ㄲ | |
| Lingual | ㄴ | — | ㄷ | — | ㅌ | ㄸ | ㄹ |
| Bilabial | ㅁ | ‖ | ㅂ | ⁄⁄ | ㅂ → ㅍ | ㅃ | |
| Sibilant | ㅅ | — | ㅈ | ˙ | ㅊ | ㅉ ㅆ | |
| Glottal | ㅇ | | | | ㅎ | | |

(B)

Figure 1. Creating Hangul consonant symbols.

*Hangul as a syllabary*
*Hangul letters.* In a syllabary each letter represents a syllable. Hangul can be considered a syllabary because a visual object, seen as a letter, represents a syllable, not a phoneme. An alphabetic symbol is never used alone but always in combination with other symbols to form a single complex or block, which is a letter. A letter represents a syllable, which may be any combination of vowel and consonant, such as V, VC, CV, CVC, or CVCC. Thus Hangul may be called an "alphabetic syllabary," each syllable being represented by one letter formed by combining two to four alphabetic symbols.

Table 1 shows how alphabetic symbols can be combined to form letters of varying visual-syllabic complexity. Note that each letter is the same size and shape though the internal structures of the different letters vary in complexity.

Table 1. Hangul letters in three complexity levels.([a])

| Complexity level ([b]) | Linear Arrangement | | | | Letter([c]) | Syllable | Morpheme |
|---|---|---|---|---|---|---|---|
| | C | V | C | C | | | |
| I | | ㅏ | | | 아 | V/a/ | (suffix);ah |
| I | ㄷ | ㅏ | | | 다 | CV/da/ | all |
| II | | ㅏ | ㄹ | | 말 | VC/al/ | egg |
| II | ㄷ | ㅏ | ㄹ | | 달 | CVC/dal/ | moon;sweet |
| III | ㄷ | ㅏ | ㄹ | ㄱ | 닭 | CVCC/dalg/ | hen |

*a* All the letters in Table 1 except those in level III can represent both native morphemes and Chinese loan morphemes; only the native ones are given here.
*b* Visual complexity is partly confounded with syllable complexity.
*c* In V and VC letters, the empty circle shows that a vowel is alone in a syllable, and depicts the shape of the throat in vowel production—empty and wide open.

In forming a V or CV letter, the horizontal vowel symbol comes under a consonant symbol (/ku,ko/ in Table 2), and the vertical symbol comes to the right-hand side of a consonant symbol (/ka,ki,ke/ in Table 2). In a VC or CVC letter, the V or CV part goes over the final consonant symbol; in a CVCC letter, the CV again goes over the final consonant cluster. The pattern can be read from left to right, top to bottom, regardless of the number of constituent parts, thus utilizing both horizontal and vertical visual fields. Perhaps more important, C and V symbols are distinguishable not only by their shapes but also by their characteristic positions in letters.

The various levels of complexity of letters may be easy to read but they are difficult to type. Korean typing is possible but cumbersome. For the 304 simple V and CV letters, individual keys are available. A CVC or CVCC letter is typed in two stages: first the CV is typed and then a key from another set representing the final C or CC puts the final cluster under the initial part.

*Syllabary vs. alphabet.* Each Korean letter represents a syllable and therefore an equivalent number of sounds is coded in a more visually compact form than in an alphabetic system. A quick example is /dalg/(see Table 1), which in English requires four linearly arranged letters but one complex letter in Korean. The Korean way of arranging letters is particularly advantageous for long words: for example, "ungentlemanliness" is transcribed "phonetically" in Japanese, English, and Korean as follows:

(Japanese, 11 letters) アンゼントルマンリネス

(English, 17 letters) u n g e n t l e m a n l i n e s s

(Korean, 7 letters) 언젠틀먼리네스

Sequencing and grouping sounds and letters can be stages in word identification. Problems associated with these stages are minimized in a syllabary where the syllabic breaks within a word are immediately apparent and a word requires only a short array of letters. In Korean, a word—including its grammatical endings—seldom has more than five letters and is separated from the next word by an extra space, as in English but not in Japanese or Chinese.

Still another advantage of a syllabary is that a syllable is a concrete and stable unit to compare with a phoneme. Often a consonant phoneme by itself cannot be pronounced or described until it is paired with a vowel or vowels to form a syllable. Not surprisingly, a syllabary is easier to develop and to learn than an alphabet. Young children find it easier to segment words into syllables than into phonemes (Liberman, Shankweiler, Fisher, & Carter, 1974) and some psychologists (Gleitman & Rozin, 1973) advocate the use of some form of a syllabary in teaching reading to English-speaking children.

*Hangul vs. Kana.* The best known modern syllabaries are the two Japanese Kana: cursive Hiragana and squarish Katakana. Unlike the Japanese syllable signs, a Hangul syllable sign expresses its constituent phonemes. Table 2 compares an alphabet, an alphabetic syllabary, and a syllabary. Only the Hangul letters reflect the same consonant in the syllables /ka, ki/ and the same vowel in /ka, ma/. In Japanese secondary syllable, however, the phonetic relation between voiceless and voiced sounds is reflected in the letter shapes, the two sharing the same letter but the voiced sound having a diacritic mark.

Table 2. Three phonetic writing systems

| Alphabet | | Alphabetic Syllabary | | | Syllabary |
|---|---|---|---|---|---|
| Roman | | Hangul | | | Kana([a]) |
| CV | CV | CV<br>C= ㄱ | ㅡCV<br>C= ㅁ | V | |
| ka | ma | 가 | 마 | ㅏ | |
| ki | mi | 기 | 미 | ㅣ | |
| ku | mu | 구 | 무 | ㅜ | |
| ke | me | 게 | 메 | ㅔ | |
| ko | mo | 고 | 모 | ㅗ | |

*a* The Kana characters cannot be analyzed into a vowel and consonant.

The two Japanese syllabaries are true syllabaries and Hangul is a pseudo-syllabary, an alphabetic syllabary. Japanese can have a true syllabary because it uses only about 100 syllables. The Korean language uses a few thousand syllables, and for it an alphabetic syllabary is the only system incorporating the good features of a syllabary without requiring a few thousand different syllable signs.

Japanese readers have to learn 46 basic, 25 secondary, and approximately 35 modified syllable signs in duplicate, Hiragana and Katakana, to read slightly over 100 varied CV and V syllables (the only allowed CVC is CV-ng). Korean readers, on the other hand, learn far fewer alphabetic signs (24) plus simple rules for combining them, and then are able to read a few thousand syllables of not two but five different structures.

*Reading Hangul.* Because of the simplicity and rationality of its design, Hangul can be learned painlessly and rapidly. In English, learning the alphabet has little to do with reading and writing; one must learn its complex orthography. In Korean, learning Hangul is the only process required for mechanical reading.

The illiteracy rate in South Korea is negligible and confined largely to the mentally retarded and those too old to have benefitted from modern compulsory education. As in Japan (Makita, 1968) and Taiwan (Kuo, 1978), there are virtually no "disabled" readers in Korea. The three Asian nations may have different writing systems but they share one important item: disciplined behavior in the classroom.

Korean text can be and often is written completely in Hangul without using any Kanji (Chinese characters). Once mastered, all-Hangul script is not as difficult to read as all-Hiragana text in Japanese because Korean letters come in different levels of visual complexity and spaces are left between words. Moreover, many native Korean concepts can be written only in Hangul.

Hangul, like Japanese and Chinese writing, can be written either vertically, following the Chinese tradition, or horizontally, following the western tradition.

### Hangul as a logography

*Hangul vs. Chinese characters.* In a logography, a letter or character represents a morpheme or a word. Some letters in Hangul represent morphemes: 닭 by itself represents "hen," as does the Chinese character 鶏 . Hangul might therefore be classed as a logography as well as an alphabet and a syllabary.

In a proper logography like the Chinese system all characters, except the few used as grammatical particles, are logographs; that is, each has a meaning, usually unique. In Hangul, the likelihood of a syllable-letter representing a morpheme increases with its complexity. For example, each letter of complexity level III almost always represents one unique meaning, but a letter of level I often does not. Many level II letters represent morphemes though not necessarily unique ones. (See Table 1.)

There is only a limited number of logographic letters and they contain up to a dozen strokes. Chinese characters, on the other hand, which number several thousands, contain from one to over 50 strokes, although the current trend in China is to simplify many common characters.

Some Chinese characters can be separated into phonetic and semantic (radical) components. Phonetic components, however, merely suggest, not indicate, how characters are to be sounded. Note how the same phonetic component suggests a different syllable to the following characters.

工 /kung/; 功 /kung/; 紅 /hung/; 杠 kang/; 江 /kiang/. The characters mean: "work" (a picture of a carpenter's square), "merit," "red," "bench," and "river." Sound changes appear to be minor. But in view of the fact that, in a monosyllabic language like Chinese, a great many unrelated character-morphemes already share the same or similar monosyllable, a phonetic component is not a reliable clue to the sound of a character. A Hangul letter, in contrast, will always code its sounds precisely and fully. Hangul was, of course, designed primarily to code sounds though sometimes a Hangul letter singly can represent a morpheme.

Chinese characters are superior to Hangul in expressing semantic relations among characters. The syllable signs to the Hangul letter for "hen" have no semantic relation to "hen," as can be seen in Table 1. But the right-hand component of the Chinese character for "hen" represents "bird" and is related to "hen" semantically.

*Kanji in Korea*. Before Hangul was invented Koreans used Kanji exclusively and with considerable inconvenience. After World War II, North Korea stopped using Kanji characters and South Korea now uses only 1,300 of them. Korean pronunciation of Kanji is closer to Chinese pronunciation (one kind of monosyllabic reading) than to Japanese pronunciation (multiple readings, either mono- or polysyllabic.)

The use of Kanji in text is, however, similar in Japanese and Korean. Both have a similar syntax requiring similar kinds of grammatical items: postpositions after nouns and a rich variety of endings for verbs and adjectives. In both texts Kanji are used for roots of key words, with phonetic signs added for grammatical endings (see Figure 2).

1. 私は車に乗ります。

2. ゆたくしはくるまにのります。

3. 나는 車를 탑니다.

Figure 2. Japanese and Korean mixed scripts
1. Hiragana + 3 Kanji (I, car, ride)
2. Hiragana only
3. Hangul + 1 Kanji (car)
English translation: i am RIDEing the CAR.

The use of two types of script seems to make reading easy. Because the semantically important words are in Kanji, which are visually distinct and prominent (dark, compact, complex, slightly larger objects), a reader may attend mainly to Kanji; Kanji are figures and phonetic signs are backgrounds. In Japanese, the material to be processed visually is shorter in (1) than (2) in Figure 2. Japanese and Korean readers accustomed to mixed texts find pure phonetic text hard to read (Gray, 1956; Sakamoto, Note 2).

A number of recent studies show that skilled readers in English process unimportant function words scantily or not at all (Drewnowski & Healy, 1977; O'Regan, 1979, Rayner, 1977, Schindler, 1978). This is so even when visual distinction between function words (which tend to be short) and content words is not as prominent as that between Kanji and Kana or Hangul. In Figure 2, the differences between the function words and the content words have been exaggerated by capitalizing the latter.

An optimal text for efficient visual and semantic processing may be one that uses mixed scripts to enhance visual distinction of semantically important and unimportant words.

## Experiments on the Korean writing system

Not many experiments have been carried out using the Korean writing system. Park and Arbuckle (1977) compared Kanji and Hangul in recognition and recall, and I have carried out a few exploratory experiments with Hangul and Kanji.

*Levels of letter complexity*

As shown in Table 1, Hangul letters have three levels of visual-syllabic complexity. To see if three levels are better than one level for letter recognition and discrimination, Korean readers (in Toronto, Canada) were asked to cancel one type of target letter among other letters, cancelling as many instances of a target letter as they could in a given time. There were two experimental conditions: first, in a homogeneous background, the subjects had to recognize and discriminate a target letter among other letters of the same complexity level; and second, in a mixed background, the subjects had to recognize the same target letter among other letters of all three complexity levels. The target letters could come from any of the three complexity levels.

The subjects recognized and discriminated a target letter better in the mixed than in the homogeneous background, and the simpler target letters of level I were better recognized than the more complex letters of level III. The results were less clear for level II target letters.

*Linear vs. packaged arrangement*

A unique feature of Hangul syllabary is that two to four alphabetic symbols are packaged in one syllabic sign or letter. As mentioned earlier, packaging shortens a word's horizontal length, at the same time allowing a reader to use both horizontal and vertical dimensions of the visual field.

*Brooks' glyphs*. Brooks (1977), using an artifical alphabet, compared discrete stimuli to "glyphic" stimuli. In his experiment, an English word was written either in sequentially (and horizontally) arranged, discrete letters (IUV∞) or in a glyph ( 💥 )—the same discrete letters packaged in one compact, integrated form.

Brooks' glyphs appear to be similar to Hangul syllable-letters in that both package several alphabetic symbols in a single form. There are, however, several differences between glyphs and Hangul letters. In some of Brooks' glyphs, four discrete symbols appear to be arranged vertically rather than packaged, one symbol after another. Even in the packaged glyph above, the symbols are arranged vertically, but two of the symbols, I and U, are first packaged and then put inside a wide V. It is not clear whether this packaged glyph is to be read I and then U, or U and then I. These factors should make glyphs more difficult than Hangul.

On the other hand, the four-letter test words used by Brooks are English words familiar to his English-speaking subjects. Each of the test words requires only one glyph. The words are monosyllables (CVC or CVCC), and each subject learned only six. These factors should make Brooks' material far easier than the Hangul material described below and, in fact, Brooks' subjects read the glyphs faster than discrete letters throughout 300 trials.

*Hangul: linear vs. packaged.* Saunders and I (unpublished) recently compared linear arrangements of Hangul symbols. The test material consisted of six Hangul alphabet symbols: four basic consonants /g, n, b, m/ and two simple vowels /a, o/. The symbols were combined to form four CVCV words and four CVCCVC words. Note that, in the packaged arrangement, a word has two letters whether it consists of CVCV or CVCCVC ( 가노  or   남목  ). Interest lay in studying Hangul directly, and abstract writing principles indirectly; the words therefore reflect the Korean syllable and word structures, though they are meaningless here.

The words were presented to subjects in two experimental conditions: a packaged arrangement, in which a few symbols are packaged to form a syllable-letter, as in Hangul, and a linear arrangement (see Table 1), in which one symbol follows the other linearly as in English.

The subjects—5 males and 5 females—were English-speaking college students who did not know either the Korean language or its script. The same subjects read the eight test words in both experimental conditions, half reading the linear and then the packaged letters, the other half, the packaged and then the linear letters.

The subjects were given a 5-min explanation of how each symbol is pronounced and how they are combined systematically into CV, which are then used to form CVCV words, and then CVCCVC words. There was no practice. The words (written on index cards, one on each card), were presented to each subject one at a time, the time to pronounce it being measured as soon as the card was presented. (A small number of errors in pronunciation will be ignored in further discussion.)

The first session consisted of 6 trials, the second session one week later of 12. Each session lasted for about 45 minutes. As Figure 3 shows, the time to pronounce the test words decreases over trials within each session as well as across the two sessions.

Set I (CVCV) has a shorter pronunciation time than Set II (CVCCVC) in both the linear and the packaged conditions. However, the difference gradually narrows over the trials. In the packaged condition, it is 7 sec on trial 1, but 1 sec on 18, the last trial. In the linear condition, the difference in time is 4 sec on trial 1 and less than 1 sec on trial 18.

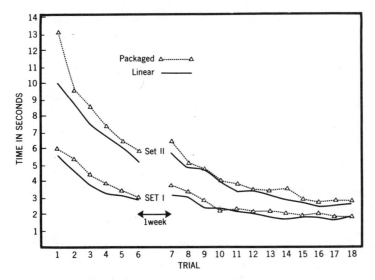

Figure 3. Pronunciation time for set 1 and set 2 words in packaged and linear arrangements.

The linear arrangement shows a shorter pronunciation time than the packaged arrangement throughout the trials but, again, the difference narrows over the trials. On trial 1, the difference is 3 sec and .4 for Sets II and I respectively; on trial 18, it decreased to .4 sec and 0 sec respectively.

Would the packaged arrangement be read faster than the linear arrangement after more trials and, if so, after how many more? Perhaps the research should be carried out with Korean children learning Hangul for the first time who would not, unlike our English-speaking subjects, have to overcome a long-established habit of linear reading. For Korean children the test words, although pseudowords, have familiar sound structures, and for them pronouncing CVCCVC words may be no more difficult than pronouncing CVCV words.

*Logography vs. phonetic scripts*
*Kanji vs. Kana or Hangul.* Whether people process—perceive, read, remember—logographs and phonetic signs differently is an interesting question and both the Japanese and the Korean systems provide effective means to study it. In Japan, the question has inspired a flurry of research activity (Hatta, 1978; Sasanuma, 1975; Taylor, in press). Very briefly, aphasic patients can develop selective impairments of Kanji and Kana so that they may retain Kanji but not Kana, or vice versa, depending on type of brain damage. A single Kanji is usually processed holistically as one integral visual pattern by the right hemisphere, but Kana or a few Kanji forming a word are processed sequentially as a phonetic pattern by the left hemisphere.

Park and Arbuckle (1977) tested Korean speakers in Canada for differences in processing Kanji and Hangul. They found that Kanji words were better recalled and recognized than the same words written in Hangul. Their Hangul words, however, appear to be transcriptions of Kanji words. Hence, their Kanji words were in customary scripts but some of their Hangul words may have been Chinese loan words written in uncustomary Hangul. (In Korean, some words are customarily written in Hangul, others in Kanji.) Their results are equivocal: if a Hangul word is less well remembered than its Kanji version, is it because the Hangul word is in an uncustomary script or because it is intrinsically less memorable than the Kanji version? Moreover, Park and Arbuckle do not discuss the complexity levels of their Hangul test words. As Table 1 shows, Hangul letters in complexity level III are almost like logographs but those in level I are not.

*Kanji vs. English words.* Kanji are logographs representing meanings primarily and sounds secondarily, whereas alphabetic signs represent sounds primarily. Is perception of meaning therefore direct in logographs but mediated by sounds in an alphabetic script?

To answer the question, two lists were prepared, one consisting of Kanji triads for Korean readers, the other of English-word triads for English readers. Figure 4 gives examples of the test material. The subjects were asked to "read" each Kanji or English-word triad and quickly circle the two items which went together. I wondered if the Korean subjects would circle two Kanji with the same or related meanings while the English-speaking subjects circle two homophones or rhyming words. Most subjects tended to connect two items on the basis of semantic rather than phonetic similarities. Unexpectedly, this tendency

| SEMANTIC RESPONSE | PHONETIC RESPONSE | WRONG RESPONSE |
|---|---|---|
| raise | trained | duo |
| rise   rays | taut   taught | two   too |

Figure 4. English-word and Chinese-character triads. The sounds and meanings of the characters, from the top, left, and right of a triad, are:
/mok, t∫ ŭk, mok/ (tree, bamboo, eye)
/ak, san, san/ (hill, mountain, produce)
/dʒ ən, ke, dʒ ən/ (total, all, field)

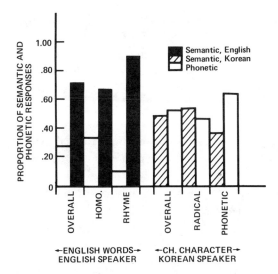

Figure 5. Proportion of semantic and phonetic responses in three categories of "overall, homophones, and rhyming words" in English (English speakers); of "overall, semantic components, and phonetic components" in Chinese characters (Koreans).

was more prevalent with the English-speaking subjects responding to the English words than with the Korean subjects responding to the Kanji. In short, the Koreans responding to Kanji showed more phonetic bias (see Figure 5).

To explain these unexpected results it should be pointed out that, in the English alphabet, individual letters code individual phonemes. However, when several letters form a (content) word, the prominent property of that word is its meaning and it was to this that the English-speaking subjects responded. They were not totally indifferent to sounds, however: as Figure 5 shows, the rhyming words, which are less similar in sounds than homophones, produced fewer phonetic responses than did the homophones.

To explain the strong phonetic bias in the Korean results, it should be pointed out that the sounds of Kanji are unambiguous and simple in Korean: unlike Japanese, a single Kanji in Korean usually has only one reading, which is monosyllabic. To explain the weak semantic bias, remember that the stimuli were individual Kanji, each representing a morpheme, not necessarily a word. Kitao, Hatta, Ishida, and Babazono (1977) observed that each Kanji with a high rating on concreteness by itself expresses one meaning, but each Kanji with a low rating does not. Each Kanji with a low rating on concreteness requires pairing with another Kanji to stabilize its meaning.

Words often have two or more Kanji, which may well be synonyms. Synonym-compounds may have arisen in China because in pronunciation many characters share the same simple monosyllable, one of a very limited variety, and hence characters may be ambiguous when spoken singly. For example, the character for "road" combines with another synonymous character for "route" to form a compound word  道路  /doro/, which means "road" unambiguously. According to Karlgren (1962), such synonym-compounds number in the thousands and have even crept into Anglo-Chinese pidgin English "look-see" for "see").

In the experiment both semantic and phonetic components influenced Kanji reading. There was a slight tendency for two Kanji sharing a radical to be judged semantically, a strong tendency for two Kanji sharing a phonetic to be judged phonetically.

This study shows that under certain conditions Kanji's sound, once learned, is an important part of Kanji processing. It also shows that a single Kanji tends to be semantically unstable until joined with other Kanji to form a word.

## Conclusion

As Kolers (1970) points out, the advantage of the alphabetic system is that a small number of symbols can be permuted to represent the entire vocabulary of a language. Letters of an alphabet can also be very simple. An alphabetic system saves greatly on memory and ensures that even unfamiliar words can be pronounced with relative ease. It does, however, require a great array on the printed page. Such an array presents not only more material to be processed visually but also poses potential difficulties in sequencing and grouping letters and sounds. Moreover, in alphabets such as the English one, letter-sound correspondence is irregular and complex.

A syllabary has advantages over an alphabet because a syllable seems to be an easier unit to encode and remember, and is more stable than a phoneme (Taylor, in press). One limitation of a syllabary is that it can be constructed only for a language with a limited variety and number of syllables.

Hangul enjoys all the advantages of the alphabetic system. In addition, the shapes of its symbols reflect the articulation of the phonemes they represent. By being not merely an alphabet but an *alphabetic syllabary*, Hangul suffers neither from some of the disadvantages of the alphabetic system nor from the limitations of a syllabary.

Hangul is a logography only to a limited degree. Only letters of level III complexity are truly logographic; letters of level II are less so; and letters of level I even less. Nonetheless, Hangul logographs have two advantages over the Chinese system: their number and complexity are not excessive and their sounds are precisely coded. Hangul logographs are not, however, as good as Chinese characters in expressing semantic relations.

Hangul is sometimes used with Kanji to express grammatical items and content words of native origin, Kanji being used to write Chinese loan words.

In sum, Hangul enjoys simultaneously the advantages of an alphabet, a syllabary, and a logography without suffering unduly from some of their disadvantages. Korean text using Hangul and Kanji in judicious mixture is optimal for reading.

This work was supported by Grant A6400 from National Science and Engineering Research Council Canada and by the Connaught Development Grant to Scarborough College.

## Reference notes

1. Kinney, G. C., Marsetta, M., & Showman, D. J. Studies in display symbol legibility. Part XII. *The legibility of alphanumeric symbols for digitized television*. Bedford, Mass.: The Mitre Corporation, ESD-TR-66,117, 1966.
2. Sakamoto, T. On reading skills of vertical versus horizontal sentences. Paper read at the 3rd Annual Congress of the Japanese Association of Educational Psychology, Nagoya, 1961.

## References

Brooks, L. Visual pattern in fluent word identification. In A. S. Reber & D. L. Scarborough (Eds.), *Toward a psychology of reading*. Hillsdale, N. J.: Erlbaum, 1977.

Diringer, D. *The alphabet*. New York: Funk & Wagnalls, 1968.

Drewnowski, A., & Healy, A. Detection errors on "the" and "and": Evidence for reading units larger than the word. *Memory & Cognition*, 1977, *5*, 636-647.

Gelb, I. J. *A study of writing* (2nd ed.). Chicago: University of Chicago Press, 1963.

Gleitman, L. R., & Rozin, P. Teaching reading by use of a syllabary. *Reading Research Quarterly*, 1973, *8*, 447-483.

Gray, W. S. *The teaching of reading and writing*. Paris: UNESCO, 1956.

Hatta, T. Recognition of Japanese Kanji and Hirakana in the left and right visual fields. *Japanese Psychological Research*, 1978, *20*, 51-59.

Jensen, H. *Sign, symbol and script*. London: George Allen & Unwin, 1970.

Karlgren, B. *Sound and symbol in Chinese*. Hong Kong: Hong Kong University Press, 1962.

Kitao, N., Hatta, T., Ishida, M., & Babazono, Y. Concreteness, hieroglyphicity and familiarity of Kanji. *Japanese Journal of Psychology*, 1977, *48*, 105-111 (in Japanese with English abstract).

Kolers, P. A. Three stages of reading. In H. Levin & J. P. Williams (Eds.), *Basic studies on reading*. New York: Basic Books, 1970.

Kuo, W. F. A preliminary study of reading disabilities in the Republic of China. *Collection of papers by National Taiwan University*, 1978, *20*, 57-78.

Lee, J.-H. *Hun-min jeoung eum* [*Correct pronunciation of letters for teaching people*]: *An explanation and translation*. Seoul, Korea: Korean Library Science Research Institute, 1972 (in English and Korean).

Liberman, I. Y., Shankweiler, D., Fisher, F. W., & Carter, B. Explicit syllable and phoneme segmentation in the young child. *Journal of Experimental Child Psychology*, 1974, *18*, 201-212.

Makita, K. The rarity of reading disability in Japanese children. *American Journal of Orthopsychiatry*, 1968, *38*, 599-614.

Martin, S. E. Nonalphabetic writing systems: Some observations. In J. F. Kavanagh & I. G. Mattingly (Eds.), *Language by ear and by eye*. Cambridge, Mass.: MIT Press, 1972.

O'Regan, K. Saccade size control in reading: Evidence for the linguistic control hypothesis. *Perception & Psychophysics*, 1979, *25*, 501-509.

Park, S., & Arbuckle, T. Y. Ideograms versus alphabets: Effects of script on memory in "biscriptual" Korean subjects. *Journal of Experimental Psychology: Human Learning and Memory*, 1977, *3*, 631-642.

Rayner, K. Visual attention in reading: Eye movements reflect cognitive processes. *Memory & Cognition*, 1977, *5*, 443-448.

Sasanuma, S. Kana and Kanji processing in Japanese aphasics. *Brain and Language*, 1975, *2*, 369-383.

Schindler, R. M. The effect of prose content on visual search for letter. *Memory & Cognition*, 1978, *6*, 124-130.

Taylor, I. Writing systems and reading. In T. G. Waller & G. E. MacKinnon (Eds.), *Reading research: Advances in theory and practice* (Vol. II). New York: Academic Press (in press).

# Graphic systems

## Introduction

Merald E. Wrolstad

Many people find it useful to locate the domain of visible language at the intersection of graphic communication and linguistic communication. We must remember, in other words, that what we are dealing with is both *visible* and *language*. Further, our approaches to written language from the two directions are equally valuable. The more usual approach has been to interpret written language solely in terms of language, in the abstract and, more particularly, in terms of spoken language. One of the things that makes the Processing of Visible Language Conference unique is the equal attention given to the visual dimension. But in doing so, we should be continually mindful of the distinction between visible language and visual communication. Visible language is written language in the strict linguistic sense, not visual "language" as in the "language" of design or the "language" of photography.

In his tutorial paper Jay Doblin makes this clear in his initial distinction between orthographic (alphanumeric) and iconographic (pictures and diagrams) visual messages. He is interested in relationships, stressing, for example, the need for clearer definition of terms, but his major concern here is with structuring iconographic communication.

Doblin is a practical man. He makes his living in the corporate business world. When he suggests how we might generalize the kinds of information we process visually, he is demonstrating how these ideas are working out in practice in the mass media and in the mass marketplace. Classification is useful, he suggests, but it is more important to see how information flows, "to structure how messages work."

He outlines the kinds of information we process visually, using a ladder of six levels of abstraction to describe their information content. For him the design process is a combination of analysis (abstracting) and synthesis (de-abstracting). The information content is overlaid with layers of persuasion and stimulation. The most valuable working tool for the graphic designer is his grasp of a message's effectiveness.

What Doblin hopes to do is put visible language in perspective for us as part of the interconnected evolution of all graphic media. More important, perhaps, his models of message flow demonstrate the unique role and properties of written language as the graphic dimension of our linguistic communication.

Karol Szlichcinski takes a closer look at the way we process graphic material. He is interested in factors affecting the comprehensibility and communicative power of pictorial information. Rather than emphasize the unique properties of purely visual communication (Doblin's "iconographic"), however, he relates his research to linguistic structures. Specifically, he wants to get at the rules which govern "the syntax of pictorial instruction."

A larger issue here, and one of continuing interest to this conference, is the applicability of a linguistic yardstick to non-linguistic visual communication. Doblin, I suspect, would be quick to point out equal and separate visual structuring! And, of course, the visual literacy movement in the United States is essentially a search for possible parallels in our processing of verbal and non-verbal visual material.

Specifically, Szlichcinski suggests that a comparison with written instructions may throw some light on the structure of pictorial ones. To study this, he used a production experiment: he asked people to draw pictorially, and then describe, how various switches operate. His general results indicate that the visual symbols most used and easiest to draw are usually among the easiest to understand. Much depends on the nature of the task.

Szlichcinski, too, is a practical man. Working for the British Post Office, he has to be interested in almost universal understanding of basic operating procedures, for native Englishman and foreigner alike. The increase in world travel and international communication systems has made this a growing area of research, especially in England. Not only must our understanding of the principles of pictorial communication be extended, Szlichcinski concludes, but also the graphic designer's very practical ability to provide materials appropriate to specific instructional requirements has to be given a more logical theoretical foundation.

Howard Wainer is also concerned about the quality of visual information. He documents the misuse of one of our most powerful visual communication tools: the statistical graph.

The conflict, Wainer suggests, is between effective, accurate communication and the designer's urge to enliven the appearance of the page. Liveliness too often wins and, as a result, many of the charts and graphs we see only obscure or distort the data which generated them. He cites examples of recurring errors in perspective, in scale, and in the clutter of "chartjunk and graphos." The solution: hire newspaper "graphers" trained in the creation of appropriate, natural visual metaphors as well as in the rules of good graphic presentation.

One of the added controls on the manifestation of written language in print is the art director. Howard Paine refers to himself as a choreographer. His concern is the printed page, both visible language and graphics, and he sees his job as making his pages "communicate complicated information effectively": to help us see how a seed sprouts or how a glacier moves.

Paine develops some of the ideas through sketches, working layouts, and final pages in all their full-color, multi-layered glory. You will recognize at once the problem we are faced with here: to demonstrate within the limitations of these black and white pages the dimensions both of Paine's challenges (to show motion, growth, dynamic process, interaction, scale) and of the solutions he has found. Dig into your past copies of *National Geographic*, therefore, and follow along as he goes over some of the problems and documents his search for creative steps with the author/artist/editor/art director ensemble.

As sophisticated as the graphic techniques of *National Geographic* are, we enter a different dimension of visual communication when we confront the genius of Muslim calligraphy. Anthony Welch reminds us that the rapid transformation of Arabic script from a simple tool into the major visual expression of Islamic culture is one of the most impressive cultural achievements of historic times.

While we can marvel at the beauty inherent in this centuries-old tradition of visualizing text, Welch rightly focusses our attention on the power of the script as foremost symbol of the Muslim world—for literate and illiterate alike. The effect may have been even greater for the illiterate, in fact, because it was calligraphic symbol and not visual image (as in the West) that depicted Islam's concept of the divine. And the pen, the first of Allah's creations (Allah be praised!), continues to be the prime instrument for transmitting Islamic culture.

Welch relates the various ways in which calligraphers have created a visual medium worthy of this role. An impressive assortment of different styles were developed. Script adorns objects of all kinds, often as the only visual element. Letters become illustrations—an identifying trademark for any believer, for example. Script is given talismanic power, sometimes being incised inside medicinal vessels.

Most importantly, Welch shows us the powerful visual impact that visible language can have as "symbolic affirmation." There is, surely, no more appropriate illustration to remind us again that what we are dealing with is both visible and language.

# A structure for nontextual communications

Jay Doblin

*Communication is the production, transmission, and consumption of messages. Messages, discrete units of content, can be as simple as a wink or as complex as the* Encyclopedia Britannica. *To prepare ourselves to function effectively in this new era requires structuring communications. We begin by identifying and defining key terms. Whereas engineers know the precise meanings of the terms they use (such as torsion, moment, velocity, and so on) the terms communicators use are ambiguous. For example, communicators still argue about the meaning of the elementary term "writing"; a final decision must be made if it means the actual marks on the page which people read or an activity carried on by writers as they conceive content. Once the key terms are defined, they must be related using diagrammatic models. This paper provides a classification and description of various pictorial and linguistic communicative techniques.*

Our capacity to receive messages is limited by our sensory apparatus. Estimates say that about 85 percent of all the messages we receive are visual, 10 percent audible, and the rest we receive by other modalities (Figure 1). Visual messages are of two kinds: orthography (writing words according to standard usage) and iconography (representations by pictures or diagrams). As a teacher-designer of iconography, my task is to try to produce a structure of what are usually called non-verbal messages. Naturally, I dislike this negative description which degrades a message form at least the equal of orthography.

Although much has been written about iconographic messages—especially about art—most is ambiguous, little is structured. This is why iconographic languages are so poorly understood and taught. Only professional artists, designers, or architects are taught to use iconography fluently as language. The vast majority are taught only the three R's which comprise only one of the two major forms of communication. The result is that most people fail to develop half their ability to communicate, think, and solve problems. As Joseph Albers is reputed to have said: "One in a hundred thinks, one in a thousand sees." Iconographic language can be structured and taught but, until it is, the public will remain half illiterate.

*Three forms of information messages*
Orthography is the visual form of alphanumeric messages and can be divided into verbal and numerical; rather than use the unwieldy term *iconographic*, this form will be called *visual* (even though orthography is also visual). Three message forms

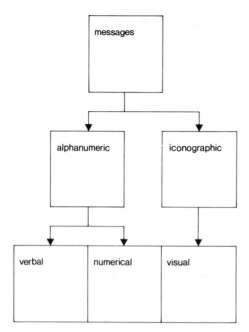

Figure 1. Tree of forms of information.

will be used: verbal, numerical, and visual. Every message has form and content which are independently variable. One message content may be encoded into three message forms; for example, the time is three o'clock, 3:00, or ⊕ . Similarly, one message form, like │ , can have three different contents: myself, one, or an image of a pole.

*Three types of information content*
There are three types of information content: nominal, noumenal, and phenomenal. Webster's offers the following definitions:
*nominal*, names or terms given for identification or classification;
*noumenal*, conceived by reason, but not knowable through the senses;
*phenomenal*, known through experience rather than thought or intuition.

*The matrix of information messages*
Matrixing the three types of message form (verbal, numerical, visual) with the three types of information content (nominal, noumenal, and phenomenal) produces nine kinds of information (Figure 2):
*verbal nominal information*, called *lexic*, is words (the definitions of which appear in lexicons).
*verbal noumenal information*, called *logic*, is words used for definition, classification, and reasoning.

|  | VERBAL | NUMERICAL | VISUAL |
|---|---|---|---|
| NOMINAL | lexic | numeric | ideogrammatic |
| NOUMENAL | logic | mathematic | diagrammatic |
| PHENOMENAL | prosaic | arithmetic | isogrammatic |

Figure 2. Matrix of information messages.

*verbal phenomenal information*, called *prosaic*, is words used to describe reality as in reports or descriptions of persons, objects, or events.

*numerical nominal information*, called *numeric*, is numbers used for identification (license plates, telephone numbers, football players, route markings, and so on). Such numbers are not used for calculation.

*numerical noumenal information*, called *mathematic*, is numbers and symbols used for complex calculations.

*numerical phenomenal information*, called *arithmetic*, is the "real world" encoded into numbers by instrumentation. These numbers are used to subtract, multiply, or divide for ordinary purposes.

*visual nominal information*, called *ideogrammatic*, is visual "words" that convey a single meaning. Included are trademarks, ideographs (Chinese characters are one form), roadway signs, flags, and so on.

*visual noumenal information*, called *diagrammatic*, includes charts and graphs used for visualizing processes that are otherwise difficult to comprehend.

*visual phenomenal information*, called *isogrammatic*, is visual representation of reality. Isogrammatic techniques include drawing, drafting, model making, sketching, photography, portraiture, illustration, and so forth.

The column of visual information messages can be conceived of as three levels of abstraction. Phenomenal messages are the most realistic, noumenal messages (images of processes, not objects) are more abstract than phenomenal messages, and nominal messages are the most abstract because of their all-or-nothing character (failure to know that a red disc on a white rectangular field means Japan is a total loss of information). These three levels are too esoteric and encompas-

| | VERBAL | NUMERICAL | VISUAL |
|---|---|---|---|
| NOMINAL | names | numbers | marks |
| NOUMENAL | theories | formulas | charts & graphs |
| PHENOMENAL | descriptions | measurements | drafting & maps |
| | | | drawings |
| | | | photographs |
| | signals | counting | models |

Figure 3. Restructured matrix of information messages.

sing, however; for practical purposes they must be subdivided into finer increments and given practical names.

Isograms are divided into four: models (isoforms), photographs, drawings, and drafting. Diagrams (usually called charts and graphs) are considered as one level. There is only one level of ideograms which designers usually call marks. These six levels form a scale from real to abstract (Figure 3):

*models*, which are three dimensional, are the most realistic type of visual messages;
*photographs* mechanically collapse the three-dimensional world into two dimensions;
*drawing*, the oldest form of isograms, are hand (or machine) drawn perspectives;
*drafting*, the most technical form of isograms, is higher on the level of abstraction than drawing;
*charts* include matrices, trees, Venn diagrams, flow charts, and so on;
*graphs* are diagrams of numerical interactions such as bell curves, bar graphs, nomographs, instrumentations, and so on;
*marks* are highest on the scale of abstraction.

These six practical levels of visual messages replace isograms, diagrams, and ideograms in the matrix. Models, the most realistic level of visual information messages, has no verbal or numerical equivalent and might be represented by calls or gestures. Numerical messages have no realistic equivalent to models but elementary forms of counting, like using the fingers or dropping stones, are closer to real than are written numbers.

*The ladder of abstraction*

This ladder of six levels of visual abstraction can be removed from the matrix and respaced to give even emphasis to the six types of visual messages (Figure 4). *Real* is

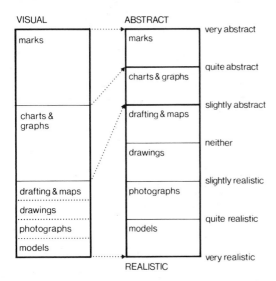

Figure 4. The ladder of abstraction.

added to the realistic end of the scale and *abstract* to the abstract end. Real is the immediate, multisensory, tangible world of space, time, and objects. Abstract comprises totally non-conventional visual messages that mean whatever maker or viewer wish them to mean.

An object can be abstracted into all eight types of visual messages. Real Chicago can be walked around in, felt, sat down in, heard, smelled, and so on; models of Chicago are frequently built for study purposes; photographs of the city can be taken; drawings can be made of it; plans or maps can be drawn; its political organization can be charted and its rate of growth can be graphed; one mark is a flag that stands for it; and an artist can abstract it into a jagged, gray lump of a painting.

The ladder also shows how visual messages can be translated from one level of abstraction to another. If an artist draws a portrait from life, it is abstraction from real to drawing (Figure 5); similarly, if Dad takes a photograph of Grandma, the input is real Grandma, the output is a photograph, a shorter jump of abstraction. Conversely, it is possible to begin with a message, a photograph of Lincoln, for example, and produce a sculptured figure, a reduction of abstraction (Figure 6). A model built from mechanical drawings involves three steps of de-abstraction. We all use this process constantly and designers use it professionally, abstraction being called analysis, de-abstraction called synthesis.

*The model of visual information messages*
The purpose of the ladder is to produce a model of visual information messages. The ladder becomes a right-angled triangle divided into six horizontal cells. Verticals are drawn from the hypotenuse to produce a semi-matrix of cells,

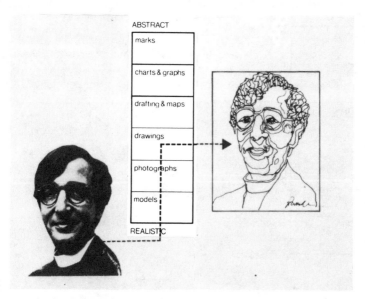

Figure 5. Increase of abstraction of messages (analysis).

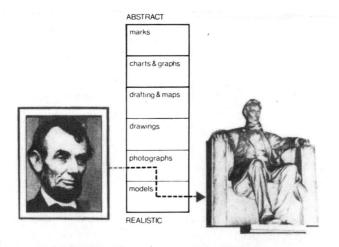

Figure 6. Reduction of abstraction of messages (synthesis).

locating and relating every type of visual information message. The lower left corner is *realistic*. The vertical right side of the triangle is *abstraction*; as messages approach this line they gradually become more abstract (Figure 7).

Note the six cells in the row called *models*. The most realistic model, in the corner, comprises working prototypes indistinguishable from production prod-

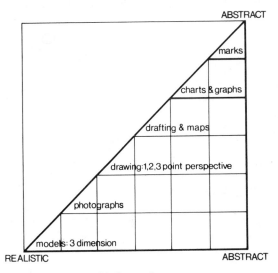

Figure 7. Model of information messages.

ucts. Cell two is fairly realistic, a store mannequin, for example. The third cell is somewhat real, perhaps being reduced in scale or having lost one dimension, like a diorama or a well-detailed scale model. The fourth cell has models with some abstraction, a marble bust or a clay model of a product, for instance. The fifth cell would be fairly abstract, a sculpture by Moore or an Origami bird, for example. The sixth cell is very abstract, content is gone, only a feeling remains.

The most realistic photograph, in the cell at the hypotenuse, is a color movie which is still less realistic than a working prototype. Photography's second cell would be color stills. The third cell is realistic black and white. Fourth cell photographs would be fairly abstract, with recognizable content but demanding a lot of interpretation. The fifth cell is fully abstract photography, content is gone.

The most realistic form of drawing, illustration, is nearly as realistic as color photographs, but not nearly as realistic as prototype models. The most abstract form of drawing is abstract painting.

Charts and graphs are two higher level cells. Marks, at the top, have only one level of abstraction: geometricized symobls with ascribed meaning.

To familiarize students with this model and the abstraction process, one exercise is to take a realistic photograph and then produce three abstractions of it to fit given locations on the model (Figures 8 and 9).

Another exercise is to produce six visual messages of one content: a photograph, a drawing, a drafting, a diagram, a mark, and an abstract (Figures 10 and 11).

These (and many more) exercises quickly produce the ability to recognize the type of visual information message, its level of abstraction, and how it operates.

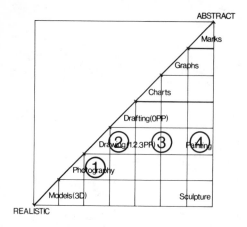

Figure 8. Distribution of three levels of abstraction of drawings.

Figure 9. Three levels of abstraction of drawing (from photograph).

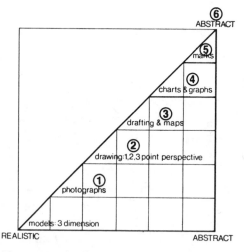

Figure 10. Distribution of six visual messages of one topic.

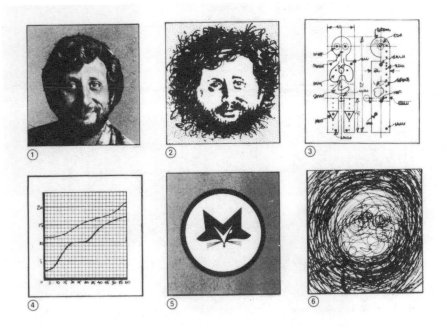

Figure 11. Six visual messages of one topic.

It would be fine if information were all that was communicated in messages, but persuasion and stimulation are involved as well and must be added as two more rows to the matrix of information messages.

*The matrix of messages*
Information must be true; if it is not, it is misinformation. Persuasion does not have to be true; it uses that part of the truth needed to convince. Whereas information opens minds so that they can function rationally, persuasion is calculated to close minds to all other messages except those favorable to the sender. Stimulation messages affect behavior without informing or persuading. Visual stimulation involves content (sex, violence, humor, and so on) and form (color, texture, size, shape, and so on). As verbal, numerical, and visual are matrixed with persuasion and stimulation, six more message types are added (Figure 12).
*Rhetoric*, originally "the art of expressive speech or discourse," is best summed up today as "selling."
*Nusuasic*, an ungainly word, describes the few instances of numerical persuasion such as the pseudoscientific XL100 used on products, the license plate number 1, or the superstitious numbers 7, 11, or 13.
*Visuasic*, a coined word, describes visual persuasion. Visuasion has always been important for maintaining social differences, separating the élite from

|              | VERBAL   | NUMERICAL  | VISUAL       |
|--------------|----------|------------|--------------|
| INFORMATION  | lexic    | numeric    | ideogrammatic |
|              | logic    | mathematic | diagrammatic |
|              | prosaic  | arithmetic | isogrammatic |
| PERSUASION   | rhetoric | nusuasic   | visuasic     |
| STIMULATION  | poetic   | music      | artistic     |

Figure 12. The matrix of messages.

the hoi polloi. In our society we are subjected through all media of promotion to thousands of visuasion messages daily about our cars, clothes, furnishings, and so on.

*Poetic* is the skilled manipulation of the meaning, sound, and rhythm of words.

*Music* comprises numbers that "incorporate expressive sounds into compositions having definite structure and continuity"; this is clearly shown on printed music.

*Artistic* describes what art schools produce: visual messages that stimulate emotional responses.

Although classification and identification are useful, more important is the structure of how messages work to affect behavior by informing, persuading, and stimulating. Obviously, one message can do all three simultaneously, for example, a TV special on killing baby seals. Diagramming how messages work to deliver information, persuasion, and stimulation requires another model.

*The model of message flow*

A conceptual model of message flow can be produced using a three-step process. The first step is to make a list of statements that begin *message must*. Each statement describes a requirement a message must fulfil or else it may fail. The second step is to compare every statement to every other statement on an interaction matrix (Figure 13). The interacting relationships are tabbed according to their strength; strong relationships by a big dot, weaker ones by smaller dots. The third step uses the interactions to produce a network model that most closely links the statements with strongest relationships (Figure 14).

This process will not be explained here but is a widely used modeling procedure. The model of message flow has the following twelve *message must* statement.

|              | reach | perceptible | time | decodable | crafted | congruent | prepare decoder | hierarchical | power | exciting | credible | integrity |
|--------------|-------|-------------|------|-----------|---------|-----------|-----------------|--------------|-------|----------|----------|-----------|
| reach        |       | ●           | •    |           |         |           |                 |              | ●     |          |          |           |
| perceptible  | ●     |             | ●    | ●         | ●       |           | •               |              | ●     | •        |          |           |
| time         | •     | ●           |      | ●         |         |           | •               | •            | •     |          |          |           |
| decodable    |       | ●           | ●    |           |         | •         | ●               | ●            | •     |          |          | •         |
| crafted      |       | ●           |      | •         |         | ●         |                 |              | •     | ●        | ●        |           |
| congruent    |       |             |      |           | ●       |           | •               |              |       |          | ●        |           |
| prepare decoder |    | •           | •    | ●         |         | •         |                 | •            |       |          | •        | •         |
| hierarchical |       |             | •    | ●         |         |           | •               |              |       |          |          | ●         |
| power        | •     | ●           | •    | •         | •       | ●         |                 |              |       | •        |          |           |
| exciting     |       | •           |      |           | ●       |           |                 |              | •     |          |          |           |
| credible     |       |             |      |           | ●       | ●         | •               |              |       |          |          | •         |
| integrity    |       |             |      | •         |         |           | •               | ●            |       |          | •        |           |

Figure 13. Interaction matrix of message statements.

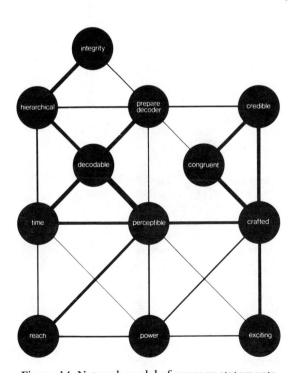

Figure 14. Network model of message statements.

*Message must reach decoders.* Reach, a term used in advertising, describes the effectiveness of a medium in getting the message to a selected segment of decoders at the right time. An example of well-planned reach is an anti-smoking campaign which begins with a 10-second TV commercial in which cigarette butts fall on a black background; as they hit, they form a smoking skull. The same skull appears inside matchbooks which later *reach* the right people with the right message at precisely the right moment (Figure 15).

*Message must be powerful.* A message must be strong enough to punch through a noisy environment to gain a decoder's attention and unique enough so that it is not confused with other similar messages. Controlled background, increased size, dramatic contrasts, strong lighting or color, and strong, simple design are some ways to increase message power. For this reason flags, trademarks, highway signs, and so on are geometric and use primary colors. Using a double-page newspaper spread is an example of an attempt to generate great message power.

*Message must have sufficient time. Every message requires time to be decoded. A single word may be perceived in a fraction of a second but it may take a week to read War and Peace.* Some messages, such as posters, packages, signs, and so on, have very limited time to deliver their meaning. Overly long messages can become boring; decoders will not invest the time and effort required to extract the meaning. This is why STOP is used (Figure 16) rather than a sign which reads:

> Chicago Statute 3413R requires all motorists to come to a full halt at designated intersections. This is one such intersection. Violators are subject to a $15 fine. Repeated offenders can lose their license.

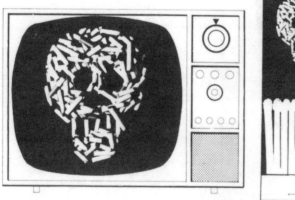

Figure 15. Anti-smoking commercial and matchbook.

Figure 16. Standard stop sign communicates quickly.

*Message must be perceptible*. Decoders must see or hear the message or they will not be able to decode it. A message must not be too small; there must be sufficient contrast between the foreground and background; letter form, thickness, spacing, leading, serifs, and so on all contribute to legibility and readability. The Snellen Eye Chart, used to test vision, determines the point at which letters become too small to read (Figure 17). We all have perception problems, for example, trying to read road maps or the menu in a dimly lit restaurant.

Figure 17. Snellen Eye Chart.

*Message must be decodable.* The message must use language that can be decoded. Foreign phrases, jargon, or big words can destroy meaning. Messages must also be "staged" to fit the decoder's capacities. Staging, a psychological concept, divides people into well-defined developmental levels of decoding ability. In wartime, messages can be intentionally coded so that they cannot be read. An example of an uncodable message which is reaching you and has sufficient power and time to be easily perceptible, but is unreadable is the page from the Gutenberg Bible shown in Figure 18.

*Message must have proper hierarchy.* Decoders can be helped to decode the message if it is organized hierarchically as is done in newspaper copy (head, subhead, body), advertisements, packages, posters, and so on. One typical mistake is to allow some irrelevant (often arty) feature to dominate the essential message, a mistake frequently made by students when designing posters.

*Message must have decoder prepared.* Decoders must be given the meaning of the symbols used before a message can be delivered successfully. Preparation can be

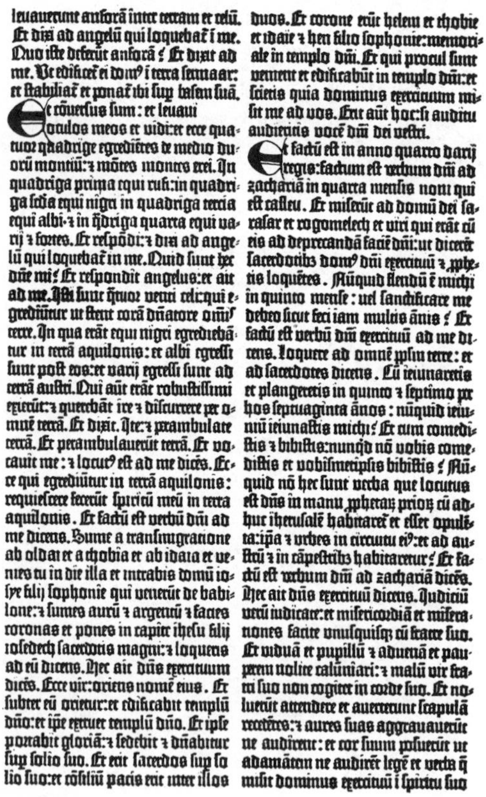

Figure 18. Page from the Gutenberg Bible.

by education, experience, or promotion. This is especially true for flags, trademarks, signs, and most packages as well. Repetition of a message can soften decoder's biases and very well prepared decoders may react automatically. When a symbol has very great penetration, such as that for Coca-Cola, it is recognized, not read (Figure 19).

Figure 19. Coca-Cola symbol (misspelled).

*Message must have integrity.* To operate efficiently, a machine must have integrity, that is, it must have the right assortment of parts which must be properly assembled. A message with integrity flaws (a mathematical formula with its parts transposed, a telephone book bound incorrectly, an out-of-perspective drawing, a grammatically wrong statement) may have its information transmitting capacity destroyed. An example of loss of integrity is when the picture and word do not match, as in the "one-way" sign in Figure 20.

Figure 20. One way sign lacks integrity.

*Message must be properly crafted.* Good craftsmanship gives a message authority. A trite song can become art when sung by a talented performer. Conversely, a squeaky voice can ruin the best speech. For this reason, advertising agencies use skilled art directors. The main objective of good craftsmanship is to permit the meaning to come through unimpeded by conscious stylisms or inept presentation. To see poor craftsmanship destroy a message, have a child (or even a beginning student) make a sign or letterhead for a well-known company (Figure 21).

Figure 21. Poorly crafted message.

*Message must be credible.* The goal of credibility, to persuade, leads to intended behavior such as voting, buying, loving, giving, and so forth. A message that is not believed cannot persuade. A crude presentation (like a typewritten letterhead) or a hucksterish presentation (like the TV ads of auto dealers) may not be believed. Careful presentation may be required to overcome prejudices held by decoders. One visual ploy to gain credibility is to use elaborate borders, similar to those on bonds or banknotes, for other displays (Figure 22).

**FORTUNE**
**SAVINGS CERTIFICATE**

A special opportunity for new subscribers to get to know FORTUNE: the world's most respected business biweekly. Use this card to save 51.7% on your introductory subscription.

**Send me 30 issues for $21.75**
**(about 73¢ each) and bill me later.**
**FORTUNE's cover price is $1.50—you save 51.7%.**
30 issues of FORTUNE cost $27.70 by regular subscription and $45 at the cover price

Mr./Ms.
Name

Address                                                                                          Apt. No

City                                              State                                              Zip
This rate is valid only in the U.S., U.S. Possessions and Canada.                    F34156

Figure 22. Attempt to increase persuasion using banknote motif.

*Message must have congruity.* Because the form of a message can project such meanings as strong, authoritative, feminine, formal, expensive, contemporary, and many others, its form must be congruent with its content. Blatant incongruity is so obvious as to be comic, but slight incongruity is difficult for the unrefined to appreciate and it is here that many errors in taste and credibility occur. An example of gross incongruity is to send a sympathy card with Mickey Mouse in bright colors (Figure 23). Organizations that emphasize precision of measurement and technical achievement would not be likely to use the emblems of Figure 24.

Figure 23. Incongruity of form and content.

Figure 24. Incongruity of form and content.

*Message must be exciting.* To arouse the emotions of laughter, joy, fear, anger, tranquillity, and so on, is the primary goal of art and entertainment such as music, painting, the theatre, poetry, novels, and so forth. Emotion is important to information and persuasion as well: a boring lecture will lose its audience. Sex, violence, and humor are typical ways to arouse emotion through content. Exciting form uses noise, color, motion, contrast, and so on. The Siné drawing of Napoleon in Figure 25 combines humor and vulgarity to stimulate.

Figure 25. Siné drawing of Napoleon.

Examination of the twelve statement network model shows three clusters of statements. One cluster includes four technical statements: reach, time, power, and perceptible. Reach is completely successful or totally unsuccessful: the decoder does or does not get the message. Perceptible, power, and time all have thresholds, failing at a point that is determinable by measurement. The second cluster has five semantic statements: decodability, hierarchy, prepare decoders, craft, and congruity. These can be evaluated only by determining the meanings that decoders derive from them. The third cluster has three effectiveness statements: integrity, credibility, and excitement. The three clusters are shown in Figure 26.

The three clusters of statements parallel three levels described by Shannon and Weaver (1947):

*Level A*. The accuracy with which the symbols of communication are transmitted (a technical problem).

*Level B*. The precision with which the transmitted symbols convey the desired meaning (a semantic problem).

*Level C*. The effectiveness with which the received meaning affects conduct in the desired way (the effectiveness problem).

Shannon and Weaver point out that the effectiveness of a message depends upon a succession of events. If the decoders cannot perceive the message at Level A, it fails. If decoders can perceive the message, but cannot decode it at Level B, then the message fails. If the message causes undesirable behavior at Level C, it fails.

Each of the three effectiveness statements is the reason for producing a message: to inform, persuade, or stimulate. Integrity delivers information; if

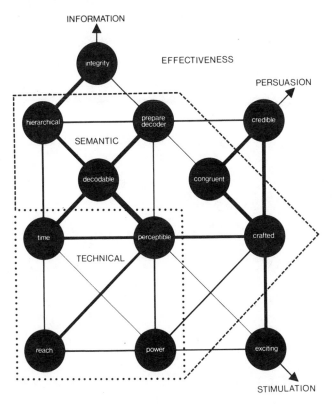

Figure 26. Three clusters of the twelve statements.

there is no integrity, it is misinformation. Credibility is the basis of a message's persuasiveness. Excitement is how stimulating a message is. The model can be broken into three parts, one each for information, persuasion, and stimulation (Figures 27, 28, 29). The purpose for producing the model of message flow can now be appreciated. If a message is found to be ineffective, it can be evaluated by tracing back through the model to determine which statement or cluster of statements is causing the problem. The process of evaluation simply changes the statements to questions. If a message is supposed to inform, but does not, the first question is, "Does the message have integrity?" If it does, the next question is, "Have the decoders been prepared?" This process continues until the trouble is located. The three models (the matrix of messages, with its derived model of visual information messages and the model of message flow) set the stage for a presentation of how iconographic messages operate. Messages are only the entities of communication, however; there is also the task of transmitting them and this leads to an analysis of media.

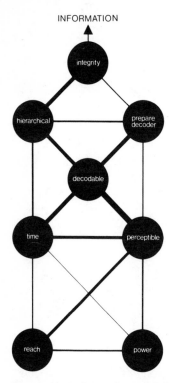

Figure 27. Information model.

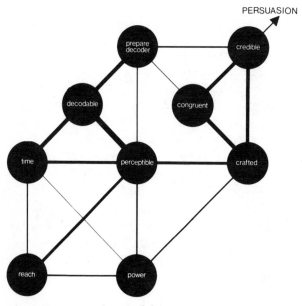

Figure 28. Persuasion model

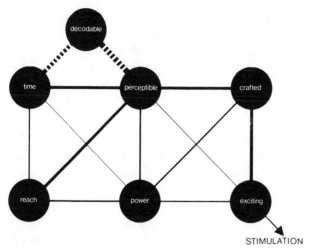

Figure 29. Stimulation model.

## The model of media

As McLuhan said, "The medium is the message," a provocative but flimsy idea that has taken hold so well perhaps because it is both alliterative and ambiguous, qualities shared by many similar wildfire statements (form follows function). The matrix of messages takes care of structuring half of the statement; the model of media, which takes care of the other half, is constructed by listing 10 principal means of communication and matrixing them (Figure 30). A network model is produced which clusters those most similar (the same process used to construct the model of message flow) and in turn produces a model which is also a chronology, a sort of Darwinian evolution where one medium leads to the next.

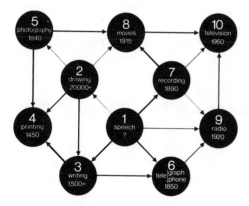

Figure 30. Matrix of media types.

The model shows a network of media in which one leads to the next. Two beginnings (speech and drawing) and two end points (print and television) are shown, leading to a consideration of two types of media: presentational and (linear) sequential. Presentational (a photograph, for example) is seen all at once, giving a total impression which the eye tracks over, picking up details in order of their perceived importance. Sequential (reading a book, for example) is a string of meaning units in time or space which are perceived and matched to stored meaning units in our memories and then accumulated into a total message. Presentational and sequential messages work in exactly opposite ways, presentational being seen all at once and reduced to details, sequential being received as details which are accumulated into meaning.

Two additional basic media must be described: static and dynamic. The messages of static media are tangible, as permanent as the materials used, and need only ambient light to operate. The messages of dynamic media are transient and require three simultaneous conditions: program, equipment, and power. Program is the content: slide, film, broadcast, record, tape, and so on. Equipment used must be in good operating condition to play the program: projector, radio, TV set, tape player, and so on. Power must flow to drive the equipment. In showing movies, for example, a film must be loaded into a working projector which must be plugged in; remove any condition and there is no message.

If the two pairs of media, presentational and sequential, and static and dynamic are matrixed, the four media types produced are as shown in Figure 31.

|  | STATIC (eye) | DYNAMIC (eye or ear) |
|---|---|---|
| PRESENTATIONAL (eye) | drawing photography | movies television |
| SEQUENTIAL (eye or ear) | writing printing | speech telegraph–telephone recording radio |

Figure 31. Ten media cluster into four types.

The model of media clusters the 10 media into these four types (Figure 32). Telegraph and telephone might perhaps be split to accomodate eye-ear division and, similarly, print might straddle the division between presentational and sequential because it is a medium for both pictures and words. Recording has lately expanded from words to pictures (with video tape); perhaps it should straddle the line between presentational and sequential.

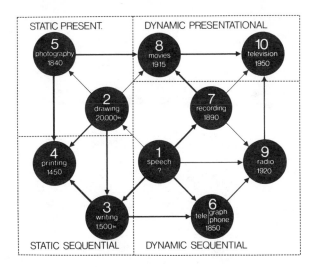

Figure 32. Clustered matrix of media.

The model of media shows the evolution of media. It appears that each of these media is thriving (even the ancient telegraphy now has exotic electronic terminals and the demise of print has been greatly exaggerated). Each medium has grown in place. For example, photography, which began with wet glass plates, progressed to film, then to miniature roll film, cartridges, color, stereo, instant developing, holography, and soon we shall have digitized electronic stills stored on chips. Ultimately, electronics (with digitized storage, satellites, interactive terminals, computers, and so on) will erase the distinctions between the discrete media and there will be an implosion into one all-purpose communications network.

**Reference**

Shannon, C. E., & Weaver, W. *The mathematical theory of communication*. Urbana: University of Illinois Press, 1949.

# The syntax of pictorial instructions

K. P. Szlichcinski

*Describing an action and co-ordinating representational and non-representational elements to express an idea are two of the most important tasks facing the designer of pictorial instructions. Previous attempts to describe a syntax for the organization of graphic materials are discussed. An experiment in which subjects drew their own pictorial instructions showed how people represent actions pictorially, the syntactic categories of elements with which they operate, and the variety of syntactic forms which can be used to express a pictorial instruction. Care must be taken, however, in generalizing conclusions from the production exercise to the design of easily comprehensible instructions.*

Pictures and graphic materials have played a role in communicating information which has occasionally been underestimated compared with that taken by the written word (Ivins, 1953), and their importance appears, if anything, to be increasing. Whereas the factors determining how effectively text communicates have been studied intensively by psychologists, those affecting the comprehensibility and communicative power of pictorial materials have received relatively little attention. In this study a group of people without special technical or artistic training was asked to draw instructions to explain how to operate each of a series of controls mounted on a panel to someone unfamiliar with them. The objective was to learn how actions should be represented and pictorial elements organized to express a complete instruction, that is, to distinguish the syntax of pictorial instructions. Both questions have been recognized as important to the success of pictorial instructions (Kolers, 1969). This study was part of a research programme aimed at determining the effectiveness of pictorial instructions for the operation of electro-mechanical equipment and establishing guidelines for their design. Other parts of the research programme, in particular, studies of the comprehension of pictorial instructions and comparisons of various instruction formats, have been reported elsewhere (Szlichcinski, 1979b, Note 6, 1980).

Conveying the nature of the action to be performed is the crucial function of an instruction. The pictorial representation of actions is also of interest in relation to the semantic organization of concepts of motion (Miller, 1972). Previous research into the representation of actions has concentrated on the designs of arrows for road signs (Rutley and Christie, Note 5) and has been concerned with perceptual rather than semantic factors.

Searches for syntaxes of some pictorial or graphic materials have already been successful. Syntaxes have been written to describe the formation of individual Chinese characters (Nagao, 1972; Rankin, cited in Watt, Note 8; Rankin,

Sillars, & Hsu, 1965), Nevada cattle brands (Watt, Note 8), and the pitch, key, and rhythm notation of music (Longuet-Higgins & Steedman, 1971). None of these materials, however, contains elements intended to depict objects or events.

Watt (Note 8) has emphasised that graphic communications may be analysed at several hierarchically organized levels and that structural principles operate only within a level of the hierarchy. For example, his cattle brand syntax describes the formation of brands only at the level of combinations and transformations of letters and numerals and functions independently of the syntax defining the formation of letters and numerals from individual lines. Similarly, the syntax of pictorial instructions can be considered at the level of the formation of individual pictorial elements depicting objects or abstract symbols, at the level of the assembly of these elements into scenes, at the level of the combination of elements and scenes into a complete instruction to perform a single action, or at the level of combining instructional units to describe a sequence of operations (Szlichcinski, 1979b, in press).

A quasi-linguistic syntactic approach to analysing the way lines compose objects and scenes has already been attempted by researchers in artificial intelligence (Clowes, 1972). Photographs and line drawings undeniably possess intrinsic structure, implying first a degree of redundancy, so that parts of a display can be predicted at better-than-chance levels given the other parts present (Harmon and Julesz, 1973) and, second, that the relationships between pictorial elements convey meaning, that is, that the meaning of the display as a whole is more than the sum of the meanings of its parts.

There is no evidence, however, that structure at this level of analysis has any psychological reality (Tweney, Heiman, & Hoemann, 1977). Moreover, scene analysis based on the assumption that pictures have a structure or syntax (defined at the level of line junctions), independent of the nature of the objects represented, has proved unsuccessful. The grouping of line junctions into discrete syntactic categories and the meaning of the categories depend on the types of object present and the viewpoint of the observer (Clowes, 1972). In photographs or illustrations the relationships among pictorial elements are not arbitrary, as are the relationships among linguistic elements, but depend on the relationships among the components of the real scene and hence on the physical laws governing the relationships among the parts of objects, on the nature of the objects concerned and the states they can adopt in situations of the kind depicted, and the nature of the mapping from the real world to the picture. For example, the rules of realistic, perspective drawing specify the relationships among objects and their representations precisely (Gregory, 1970). The increasing dependance of scene analysis on non-pictorial inference (Clowes, 1972) can be regarded as more sophisticated exploitation of picture syntax if a definition of syntax in terms of structural constraints, not necessarily independent of semantics, is accepted.

Structural analysis guided by semantic hypotheses has been applied in computer analysis of cartoon scenes (Adler, Note 1) and appears far more fruitful than a purely structure-oriented approach.

At the level of the complete instruction, the questions are whether or not elements which do not represent objects are syntactically differentiated and how they should be combined with elements which do represent objects to form an instruction. One analysis of the links among perception, semantics, and language has led to the conclusion that perception requires four primitive cognitive categories (objects, attributes, states, and events), which are likely to be reflected in communications about perceived events (Miller & Johnson-Laird, 1976). It might well be expected that pictorial instructions would show some syntactic differentiation among their component elements if they are to communicate effectively. Barnard and Marcel (in press) point out that, although conventional representations of actions and states may be widely understood, there may be little agreement on how they should be combined in an instruction and, furthermore, written language offers many alternative ways of expressing the same logical relationships. They concede, however, that the choice among alternative syntactic structures may affect performance.

A comparison with written instructions may help to reveal the structure of pictorial ones. In English the imperative is most simply expressed by omitting the subject and starting with the uninflected verb, for example, "Press the button" (Brown, 1973). Under certain circumstances, the force of the spoken imperative can be increased by stating the subject ("You press that button") but, in written instructions, including the subject can have the opposite effect, conveying a conversational or descriptive tone. It is not as important to soften the tone of written imperatives as of spoken ones although occasionally statements from which the imperative has to be inferred ("The knob should be turned to the left") are used.

Miller and Johnson-Laird (1976) argue that if a reader is to execute a written instruction he must translate it into the form "achieve $(F(x,y...))$," where $F$ is a pointer to a routine controlling the execution of the action concerned and $x, y,...$ are pointers to the values of the parameters defining the circumstances of the action. The first pointer, $x$, is to the agent; if the reader assumes the instruction is addressed to him, then it is implicit that the agent is the reader himself. If the action requires an object it will be indicated by the second pointer, and further pointers will indicate the values of other parameters governing the execution of the action. Because the need to translate an instruction into a routine for execution does not depend on the modality of the instruction, it follows that a similar routine would have to be generated from a pictorial instruction, although its components might have to be inferred rather than being explicitly indicated by syntactically differentiated elements.

*The production technique*

The technique of asking people to draw their own graphics (the "production" technique) has been used extensively as a means of discovering the kinds of representations people use and are, therefore, likely to understand most easily (Brainard, Campbell, & Elkin, 1961; Howell & Fuchs, 1968; Krampen, 1969; Mudd & Karsh, Note 3; Szlichcinski, 1979a). In the studies cited a symbol was sought for each of a set of referents. In the present study the subjects had not only to represent an object or concept but also to communicate the nature of an action relating to an object; it was the way in which they represented the action (if they did so at all) and organized the elements comprising their instructions which was of interest as well as their choice of symbols to represent the controls.

Production is not the mirror image of comprehension; symbols drawn most frequently in production experiments are not always those interpreted most easily and correctly (although they frequently are, of course) and experimenters working with complex referents have sometimes found little agreement among their subjects on the appropriate symbol (Howell & Fuchs 1968; Karsh & Mudd, Note 2). Lack of drawing skills may prevent people from drawing what they would like to. Furthermore, it has been found that, in relatively complex instructional displays, the graphic techniques used to emphasize the important parts of the display are at least as important as the choice of elements to represent objects and actions (Szlichcinski, in press). A production experiment could, however, be expected to indicate the extent to which people conceive of pictorial instructions as having a syntactic structure, that is, as comprising elements performing different syntactic functions organized in a systematic way, the nature of that structure, and how they might expect actions to be represented and related to depictions of the objects they affect.

Pictures, especially if drawn by people without training in graphic skills, can pose problems of interpretation. To avoid ambiguity, a technique was adapted from Watt (Note 8) and subjects were asked to describe their completed drawings. Their descriptions also indicated the appropriate level of analysis for the pictures.

*Procedure*

There were 82 volunteer subjects, all participating in their first psychological experiment. Each was asked to sit facing a sloping panel on which the controls were mounted, each control on a separate detachable strip with a light-emitting diode (LED) directly above it and a distinguishing number below; the LED lit up when the control was operated. The controls were: a potentiometer which had to be turned clockwise through 180 deg; a rotary switch requiring a 20 deg clockwise movement; a three-position rocker switch with an off position at the centre; a pull switch, with a knob which had to be pulled out to light the LED; a touch-sensitive switch; two push buttons, one sprung to return to the off position as soon as it was released, the other having to be pressed a second time to be switched off; and two toggle switches, one spring-loaded to return to the off position on release, the other having to be turned off.

The subject was provided with a sheet of paper, a pencil, and a rubber, and given the following instructions:

> Please draw pictures to explain how to operate the switches in front of you. Each of the switches can be operated to make the light above it glow. The pictorial instructions you produce should enable people to distinguish between the switches and between the different ways in which they are operated. You may operate each switch as many times as you like.

When the subject had finished, he or she was asked to describe each of his or her diagrams. For the first 43 subjects the experimenter noted any points from the description which were not obvious; the descriptions by the remaining 39 subjects were tape-recorded. The order of the switches on the panel was changed randomly after each subject.

Two of the subjects could not perform the task without assistance and their drawings had to be omitted from the analysis. The remaining subjects had no trouble describing their diagrams and all did so in terms of elements like switches, arrows, and hands which formed perceptually separate units in their diagrams.

The elements making up each diagram were listed by the experimenter in two different ways: in the first all elements which the subject had called by the same name were classified together, while in the second they were grouped together only if they were perceptually similar as well. The diagrams of nine of the subjects were analysed independently by a second judge and the agreement between the two judges assessed from an information measure calculated for each subject. For the classification on the basis of labels alone the agreement ranged between 71 and 95 percent (median 87) and when perceptual similarity was included agreement ranged from 81 to 97 percent (median 88).

*Results and discussion*

The communicative effectiveness of many of the instructions depended critically on the elements chosen to represent actions. Seventy-seven of the 80 subjects used arrows to represent actions in at least some of their drawings. Thirty-nine used arrows to indicate actions in some of their diagrams and fingers or hands in others, suggesting that they regarded these symbols as interchangeable, and 16 of the 39 (20 percent of all subjects) used both arrows and fingers or hands in the same diagram, as well as on their own. The fingers and hands occurred most frequently in instructions for the three controls requiring a finger held on the control to keep the LED illuminated.

The arrows representing actions came in a great variety of shapes and forms, straight, curved, or with right-angle bends, with a single head or one at each end, thin, thick, or dotted, to express different nuances of meaning (see

Figure 1). Thirty-seven subjects (46 percent) positioned and dimensioned at least some arrows to give a precise spatial description of the direction and extent of the movement required, not merely a general indication of direction. Subjects did not appear to treat arrows as discrete symbols but as symbols selected from a continuum of possibilities; the partitioning of the semantic field into discrete categories was thereby largely avoided.

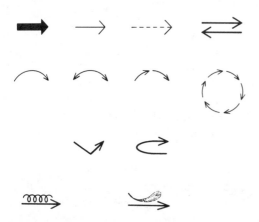

Figure 1. Some arrows representing actions drawn in the production experiment, the bottom two using additional modifier elements.

There were marked variations in the way in which the subjects combined pictorial elements to convey an instruction and also in the separate instructions produced by a single subject. There were greater similarities among the more elaborate and sophisticated drawings which appeared to follow definite patterns than among those by people who found the task difficult and whose drawings consisted of only one or two elements. Certain characteristics appeared to be common to almost all the instructions, however, including a basic differentiation of the pictorial elements in a few syntactic types.

It has been suggested that elements performing similar syntactic functions occur in similar contexts and that recognition of the recurrence of contextual patterns forms the basis of the learning of syntactic forms (Hayes-Roth, 1978). Interchangeability should, therefore, indicate which elements are treated as belonging to the same syntactic category; if two elements occur in the same context, it is probable that they are performing the same syntactic function. Drawings of controls are one obvious example, especially in instructions which consist of only two elements, an arrow and a control. A grammar was written for each subject which described his or her drawings and specified which elements appeared to be mandatory (appearing in every diagram), interchangeable (appearing in the same context), or optional (appearing in some diagrams but not in others and not apparently replaced by other elements). These grammars enabled a range of syntactic functions to be identified and the nature and relative popularity of different syntactic forms to be assessed.

Subjects drew three kinds of elements which were not used interchangeably with representations of either switches or actions: those indicating the state of a control (− and + or filled and open circles to represent the LED off and on respectively); those always associated with either an object or an action element and defining the characteristics of the operation more precisely, like linguistic "function modifiers" (Reichenbach, 1975) (pictures of springs or feathers); and, finally, those appearing to have no intrinsic meaning of their own but accentuating the relationship among other elements (lines linking elements to be interpreted together, like an arrow and a switch, or arrows marking the progression from one view to the next). None of these elements occurred often enough for an unequivocal distinction among them to be made. State indicators, however, were fundamental in one of the syntactic structures chosen by the subjects.

Figure 2. A representation of a switch and an action element.

Figure 3. The switch in its on and off positions.

Figure 4. The switch with state indicating elements marking its on and off positions.

Despite the variations it was possible to classify most of the instructions into a few categories. Elements from the object, action, and state indicator categories were combined in three different ways to convey information about the mode of operation of the controls. The operation of a control was described by drawing an element representing it and an action element (Figure 2), or by two views of the control, one in its starting position and one in its finishing position

(Figure 3), or by a view of the control and a state indicator marking the on position and usually one marking the off position as well (Figure 4). These alternative ways of describing the operation of a control were not mutually exclusive; many subjects combined two or even all three. In addition the basic "switch; action element" and "switch, off position; switch, on position" units could be linked into longer chains, a device which some subjects used to show how to switch the LED off again. The number of subjects who used the three basic conventions and their various combinations are shown in Table 1. Most based their drawings on the "switch; action element" unit: 74 out of the 80 subjects used it, 43 basing all their drawings on it either alone or in combination with other elements.

Table 1. Percentage of subjects using each syntactic construction in some or all of their drawings ($N = 80$).

| Syntax | Some of their drawings | All of their drawings |
|---|---|---|
| switch; action element | 80 | 19 |
| switch, initial position; switch, final   position | 10 | — |
| switch; state indicator | 6 | — |
| switch, initial position; action element; switch, final   position | 20 | — |
| switch; action element; state indicator | 26 | — |
| switch, initial position; switch, final   position; state   indicators | 8 | — |
| switch, initial position; action element; switch, final   position; state   indicators | 15 | — |

In many of the drawings using the basic "switch; action element" it was possible to determine the state of the switch; 66 subjects drew it in its initial position, 14 in its final position (Figure 5). By comparison, in the "switch, off position; action element; switch, on position" syntax the action element was paired with the diagram of the switch in its final position (Figure 7) by 14 subjects and with the switch in its initial position (Figure 6) by only one. It seems unlikely then that preferences for pairing action elements with diagrams of controls in a particular state reflect the way in which actions are conceptualized and, moreover, they do not correlate with the results of experiments on the comprehension of instructions (Marcel & Barnard, 1979; Szlichcinski, 1979b). Marcel and Barnard (1979) were concerned with the way people relate their actions to equipment states and how these relationships should be represented in instructions. They compared instructions in which a diagram describing each action was paired with one showing the prior state of the equipment (as in Figure 6, although their apparatus and the format of their instructions were different) or with one showing its subsequent state (Figure 7) but found no clear advantage for either presentation.

Where subjects drew instructions with more than one diagram of a control, they were equally divided between arranging successive pictures horizontally from left to right or vertically from top to bottom. A few indicated the

Figure 5. A control switch in its initial position (left) and in its final position (right).

Figure 6. Two views of the control with the arrow by the on position.

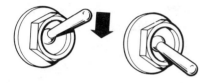

Figure 7. Two views of the control with the arrow by the off position.

order in which the diagrams were to be read, four assigning them consecutive letters or numerals and three drawing arrows to indicate the progression.

The most widely used pictorial instruction syntax, an element representing the action and an element depicting the object, is an exact analogue of its written equivalent. Drawings of hands appeared to be used interchangeably with arrows but the action to be performed is not shown explicitly and has to be inferred from the line of approach and attitude of the hand or finger. The fact that they were drawn predominantly for controls which had to be held down suggests that their purpose was to indicate a different kind of action to the arrows.

The other structures used, the representation of a control in its on and off positions and the representation of the control in its off position with a state-indicating element by its on position, require that the action be deduced rather than showing it explicitly. Neither has a written analogue because the verb is the fundamental component of a written instruction. It is, therefore, important to consider the use of pictorial instructions as one form of problem solving (Simon & Hayes 1976; Szlichcinski, 1979b), and Miller and Johnson-Laird's (1976) assertion that a reader wishing to execute a written instruction must translate it into the form "achieve $(F(x, y ...))$" is misleading when applied to pictorial instructions because it ignores almost all the important and difficult components of the process of following them (for example, breaking down the task into subtasks and testing and evaluating intermediate steps on the way to a solution).

It has been found that the symbols drawn most frequently in production experiments are usually among the easiest to understand. The evidence suggests that the same may be true of the main syntactic forms as well. When some of the syntactic forms obtained in the production experiment were compared for ease of comprehension (Szlichcinski, Note 7), subjects found it easier to operate a sequence of controls when the operations required were shown explicitly by arrows rather than having to be inferred from illustrations of the successive states of the equipment. In general, it appears that performance is worse with those presentations requiring inferences (Coppen, 1970), but the nature of the task to be performed influences the optimal instruction syntax (Szlichcinski, 1979b).

The question of whether an arrow should describe the precise spatial co-ordinates of an action, or merely indicate its general nature and direction, reveals some of the differences between production and comprehension. The strategies used to follow instructions are not uniform but vary according to the context (Szlichcinski, in press), and still other strategies govern production. The results of the production experiment should be applied with care, but insofar as they are of value they should extend the designer's knowledge of the principles of pictorial communication and improve his ability to produce instructions appropriate to specific situations.

Acknowledgement is made to the Director of Research of the British Post Office for permission to publish this paper. The author thanks Mr. D. Owens and the other members of the staff of the Human Factors Research Section for their assistance, and Dr. S. Jones of University College London for her helpful comments on the work.

## Reference notes

1. Adler, M. Understanding Peanuts cartoons. In J. A. M. Howe & B. Meltzer (Eds.), *Progress in perception* (Research Report No. 13). Edinburgh: Edinburgh University Department of Artificial Intelligence, 1975.

2. Karsh, R., & Mudd, S. A. *Design of a picture language to identify vehicle controls: III. A comparative evaluation of selected picture-symbol designs.* (Technical Memorandum 15-62, AD No. 289544). Aberdeen, Md.: U.S. Army Human Engineering Laboratories, 1962.

3. Mudd, S. A., & Karsh, R. *Design of a picture language to identify vehicle controls. I. General method and II. Investigation of population stereotypes.* (Technical Memorandum No. 22-61, AD No. 272263). Aberdeen, Md.: U.S. Army Human Engineering Laboratory, 1961.

4. Rankin, B. K., III, Sillars, W. A., & Hsu, R. W. *On the pictorial structure of the Chinese character* (Technical Note 254). Washington, D.C.: National Bureau of Standards, 1965.

5. Rutley, K. S., & Christie, A. W. *A comparison of the varieties of traffic signal filter arrow* (RRL Report No. 33). Crowthorne: Ministry of Transport, 1966.

6. Szlichcinski, K.P. *The language of pictorial instructions: A production experiment.* Martlesham: British Post Office Research Department Report, 1980.

7. Szlichcinski, K.P. *Understanding pictorial instructions: Five experiments.* Martlesham: British Post Office Research Department Report, 1980.

8. Watt, W. C. *Morphology of the Nevada cattlebrands and their blazons, Part One* (Report No. 9050). Washington, D.C.: National Bureau of Standards, 1966.

## References

Barnard, P., & Marcel, T. Representation and understanding in the use of symbols and pictograms. In R. Easterby & H. Zwaga (Eds.), *The visual presentation of information*. Chichester: Wiley, in press.

Brainard, R. W., Campbell, R. J., & Elkin, E. H. Design and interpretability of road signs. *Journal of Applied Psychology*, 1961, *45*, 130-136.

Brown, R. *A first language*. Cambridge, Mass.: Harvard University Press, 1973.

Clowes, M. B. Scene analysis and picture grammars. In F. Nake & A. Rosenfeld (Eds.), *Graphic languages*. Amsterdam: North-Holland, 1972.

Coppen, H. *Visual perception: a review of the literature relating to studies relevant to the development of teaching materials in the Commonwealth*. London: Commonwealth Secretariat, 1970.

Gregory, R. L. *The intelligent eye*. London: Weidenfeld & Nicholson, 1970.

Harmon, L. D., & Julesz, B. Masking in visual recognition: effects of two-dimensional filtered noise. *Science*, 1973, *180*, 1194-1197.

Hayes-Roth, F. Learning by example. In A. M. Lesgold, J. W. Pellegrino, F. D. Fokkema, & R. M. Glaser (Eds.), *Cognitive psychology and instruction*. New York: Plenum Press, 1978.

Howell, W. C., & Fuchs, A. H. Population stereotypy in code design. *Organizational Behaviour and Human Performance*, 1968, *3*, 310-339.

Ivins, W. M. *Prints and visual communication*. London: Routledge & Kegan Paul, 1953.

Kolers, P. A. Some formal characteristics of pictograms. *American Scientist*, 1969, *57*, 348-363.

Krampen, M. The production method in sign design research. *Print*, 1969, *23*, 59-63.

Longuet-Higgins, H. C., & Steedman, M. J. On interpreting Bach. In B. Meltzer & D. Michie (Eds.), *Machine intelligence 6*. Edinburgh: Edinburgh University Press, 1971.

Marcel, T., & Barnard, P. Paragraphs of pictographs: the use of non-verbal instructions for equipment. In P. A. Kolers, M. E. Wrolstad, & H. Bouma (Eds.), *Processing of visible language 1*. New York and London: Plenum Press, 1979.

Miller, G. A. English verbs of motion: A case study in semantics and lexical memory. In A. W. Melton & E. Martin (Eds.), *Coding processes in human memory*. Washington: Winston, 1972.

Miller, G. A., & Johnson-Laird, P. *Language and perception*. Cambridge: Cambridge University Press, 1976.

Nagao, M. Picture recognition and data structure. In F. Nake & A. Rosenfeld (Eds.), *Graphic languages*. Amsterdam: North-Holland, 1972.

Rankin, B. K., III. *A linguistic study of the formation of Chinese characters*. Unpublished doctoral dissertation, University of Pennsylvania, 1965.

Reichenbach, H. Elements of symbolic logic. In D. Davidson & G. Harman (Eds.), *The logic of grammar*. Encino, Cal.: Dickenson, 1975.

Simon, H. A., & Hayes, J. R. Understanding complex task instructions. In D. Klahr (Ed.), *Cognition and instruction*. Potomac: Erlbaum, 1976.

Szlichcinski, K. P. The art of describing sounds. *Applied Ergonomics*, 1979, *10*, 131-138. (a)

Szlichcinski, K. P. Diagrams and illustrations as aids to problem solving. *Instructional Science*, 1979, *8*, 253-274. (b)

Szlichcinski, K. P. Factors affecting the comprehension of pictographic instructions. In R. Easterby & H. Zwaga (Eds.), *The visual presentation of information*. Chichester: Wiley, in press.

Tweney, R. D., Heiman, G. W., & Hoemann, H. W. Psychological processing of sign language: effects of visual disruption on sign intelligibility. *Journal of Experimental Psychology: General*, 1977, *106*, 255-278.

# Making newspaper graphs fit to print

Howard Wainer

*Errors in the design of common newspaper graphs used to display statistical information make those graphs hard to read or, worse, misleading. Several general errors are illustrated and corrected. Several institutional changes are suggested which would help to eliminate these problems.*

Since their development by Playfair in 1786, statistical graphs have been widely used to communicate statistical information. The news media have adopted these techniques for a variety of reasons, including the following:

(1) They can often display complex data simply.

(2) They can provide an evocative image which is readily remembered.

(3) They lend seemingly scientific confirmatory evidence to the contentions of a story.

(4) They are often "eye-catching," enlivening the layout of the page and enticing the viewer to finish the story.

The last reason appears to be the primary motivator for at least one major newspaper, *The New York Times* (Silverstein, Note 3). Unfortunately, this purpose is often at odds with that of effective and accurate communication in that, by making a statistical graph "flashy," the artist often obscures or, worse, distorts the data which generated the graph.

To give examples of a common fault, consider the graphs in Figures 1 and 2.

Figure 1, using the image of shrinking dollar bills bearing the appropriate presidential faces, is misleading. A more conventional line chart (Figure 2) tells the story more correctly but, apparently, was not considered to be as eye-catching. The problem with the graph in Figure 1 is what Tufte (Note 4) has called the "old goosing up the effect by squaring the eye-ball trick." That is, the variable being displayed is conveyed by the length of the dollar bill, but it is the total area that dominates perception. Thus, when the value of the dollar shrinks, say by half, the area shrinks $(1/2)^2$, or to one-quarter the size. The presidential faces are meant to convey time intervals, but they do not denote the relation of the change during each president's term to the length of that term as the standard line chart does. This conveys an erroneous causal relationship between presidential administrations and inflation rates.

Often the errors which appear in the graphic are not present in the associated story, although the evocative image of the graphic may be the source of

Figure 1. Example of Tufte's "Goosing up the effect by squaring the eye-ball trick." ©1978 by *The Washington Post*. Reprinted by permission.

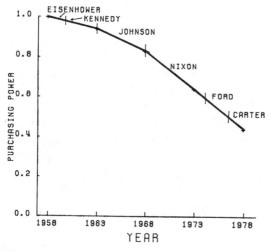

Figure 2. Graphical representation of data of Figure 1.

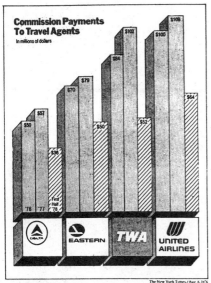

Complex web of discount fares and airlines' telephone delays are raising
travel agents' overhead, offsetting revenue gains from higher volume.

Figure 3. "Fare Cuts Lower Fees": Using a graph to corroborate a false statement.
©1978-79 by The New York Times Company.

the impression that remains with the reader/viewer. Also, the fact that a graph is so
eye-catching may have the unfortunate result that many people look at the graph
and never read the story. Sometimes one finds a misleading graph that has
apparently misled the author of the story as well. Or, alternatively, the author has
wanted to distort the data, and both word and image conspire to do so.

For example, consider the plot in Figure 3. The story argues that decreased fares have hurt the travel agent business, and the plot seems to bear this
out, giving much shorter "bars" for 1978 than for the previous two years. Small
type is used to note that the figures for 1978 are for only half a year. To see the true
picture one would have to at least double the 1978 bar. Moreover, the first half of
1978 does not include such heavy travel periods as the late summer, Labor Day,
Thanksgiving, and Christmas, so that one suspects that the doubled 1978 bar is
still an underestimate of reality. Nevertheless, the resulting picture (Figure 4)
indicates exactly the opposite of what the original picture *and the associated story*
said. It appears that the travel agents had a banner year, and that the author has
read *How to Lie with Statistics* (Huff, 1954).

Thus, although the use of statistical graphs can be a very powerful tool
for journalistic communication, they can misinform either by design or by poor
design. Sadly, from our experience with current usage, it appears that graphs are
at least as often misused as used correctly in the popular media.

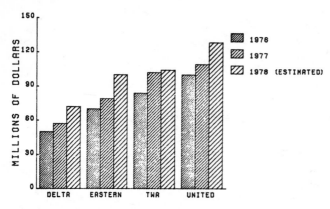

Figure 4. Same data as Figure 3.

*Unnecessary use of perspective plots*
Throughout this paper we use several terms to describe the person who actually makes the graph. Each has a slightly different meaning. *Graphician* is a pejorative term (credited to Bertin, 1973) implying someone more concerned with providing something decorative than communicative. *Grapher* is a generic term applying to anyone making graphs when we have no knowledge of their intentions or abilities. An *artist* is the person who holds the pen, but is not responsible for the drawing, being directed by the grapher.

Most plots that appear in newspapers seem to be placed to gather attention. As such they are made as flashy as possible through whatever means are at the graphician's disposal. Unfortunately this often means adding an unnecessary dimension. We have seen in Figures 1 and 2 that the addition of a second dimension caused confusion between area and length, and in Figures 3 and 4 an inconsistent third dimension added confusion to what was already a poor chart. The unnecessary use of perspective plots is very common and sometimes confuses the graphician as well as the reader. In Figure 5 we see a typical two-pronged tri-tined Blivet. This is clearly a graphical form not generally suitable for unambiguous data presentation. The same logic which generated this seems to underlie

Figure 5. Cocktail napkin.

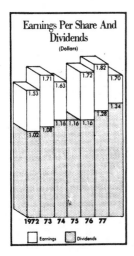

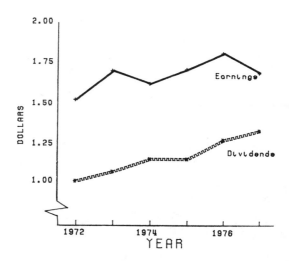

Figure 6. The improper
use of perspective
confuses both viewer and
artist. ©1979 by
*The Washington Post.*
Reprinted by permission.

Figure 7. Same data as Figure 6.

Figure 6. For example, 1975 starts as a bar and ends up nowhere. We suspect that
the perspective plot confused the (unnamed) graphician and so what is labeled
1976 is really the missing 1975 and the unlabeled bar is probably 1977. A simple
line chart with this interpretation is shown in Figure 7.

It does not require careful experimentation to confirm that for communication the line chart works quite well. It seems clear that, when newspapers
are interested in accurate communication (rather than flash) because of the innate
interest of the readers in the data to be communicated, they rely on conventional
graphic forms rather than these sorts of "boutique graphics" (Tufte, Note 5).

*Inconsistent/unwise choice of scale*
The choice of scale to be used in a plot is often critical to the impression that is
conveyed. If the scale is too large, real differences are not visible (looking at the
phenomena from too great a range). If it is too small, insignificant meanderings
loom large and ominous. If it is inconsistent the structure of the data can be
distorted to suit the aims of the grapher. To illustrate these points let us first
consider the *y*-axis.

The basis of choosing a proper scale on the *y*-axis is a knowledge of the
range of the phenomena. There are some rules that can be followed (do not
choose a scale either so small that meanderings catch the viewer's eye that are only
as large as the error of measurement or so large that significant changes are
invisible). There is no escape, however, from heavy reliance on the knowledge and

honesty of the grapher.

Consider the plot in Figure 8. This graph conveys the impression that the unemployment rate for the 14 months shown was virtually unchanged. This impression runs counter to the banner headline just above it that proclaims "Jobless Rate Dips." What is the reader to believe? The headline or the evidence that he sees with his own eyes? This plot combines the problems of scale with another problem—that of choosing a starting point. If October 1977 were chosen as the starting point, and a scale used that allowed the reader to see the data, a very different picture emerges (Figure 9). Once again a line graph is used to show these data.

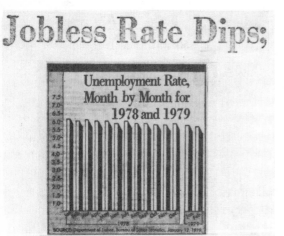

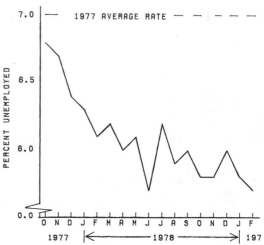

Figure 8. Choosing a scale unwisely can hide the effect of interest. By Milton Clipper. ©1979 by *The Washington Post.* Reprinted by permission.

Figure 9. Same data as Figure 8.

In Figure 9 the point is clear that the jobless rate does indeed dip. This dip is not an accident partially caused by choosing October 1977 as a start. Note that the average unemployment rate for 1977 is higher still (and the rate for 1976 was 7.7 percent). The readers' perception is affected by the starting point, but the grapher is obligated to choose a starting point which reflects the reality of the data accurately. We can only speculate why the particular scale was chosen; often it is because of unthinking adherence to the convention requiring for honesty that a scale start at zero, but this one starts at .5. One good point in favor of this plot is that its author is not anonymous. Perhaps by giving credit for good graphics and criticizing poor ones accuracy can be improved. Note that the travel agent plot from *The Times* had no such information.

    Errors of scale on the *y*-axis tend to be relatively venial, whereas errors on the *x*-axis can be very serious indeed. Consider Kresse's plot of physicians' incomes where the time axis is stretched in more recent times so that the data being represented are distorted. Thus the increase in incomes from the first data entry to the second (a difference of $5,482) spans eight years, the last two entries (a difference of $4,359) spans only one. Thus with time compressed it appears that in each time period the increase in physicians' incomes is constant (linear). It might be stated that, "Income increases are linear but time changes as a negative exponential!" Such a message is not one that would be clearly understood by the mass audience of *The Washington Post*. It seems sensible that the time ought to be held to some regular pattern, letting the dependent variable, income, vary as it might. If this is done and simultaneously the various pieces of graphic flotsam and jetsam (Tufte's "chartjunk") are eliminated, the image seen in Figure 11 results. Admittedly, this version has less pizzaz than Figure 10, but the truth is certainly clear: physicians' incomes are skyrocketing! Another interesting point, completely invisible in Figure 10, is that a strong acceleration in physicians' incomes seems to

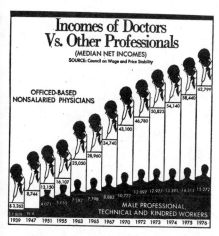

Figure 10. Varying the scale on the horizontal axis arbitrarily allows the data to assume any shape the graphician wishes. Here an exponential increase in physicians' incomes is made to look linear. By Alice Kuesse. ©by *The Washington Post*. Reprinted by permission.

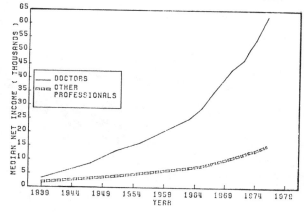

Figure 11. Same data as Figure 10.

have occurred around 1964, the year MEDICARE went into effect. (This finding points out the truth in Tukey's (1977) comment that, "A good plot forces us to see what we weren't expecting." Kresse, however, follows the precept that, "If you can't impress them with facts, wow them with flash.")

The next example (Figure 12) of odd spacing along the x-axis occurs because of the graphician's attempt to use three dimensions, as well as the usual overabundance of chartjunk. The total beer sales in the United States is represented by the height of the barrel; to read it the viewer must ignore the areal and volume cues. Whether one is supposed to read the front of the barrel or the highest point is uncertain; we shall proceed as if the front is the proper place. The varying width of the barrels causes a change in the spacing along the time axis which tends to diminish the changes at the end. The Schlitz insert is quite readable, however, and using the logo is evocative. Why it was thought necessary to slant the beginning and end lines is puzzling. The text of the story discussed how Schlitz's share of the market had been slipping, despite the increase in consumption of beer. Thus a sensible display to illustrate this point would have been one which depicts the increase in beer sales clearly, and then superimposes a plot of Schlitz's percentage share of the market as is shown in Figure 13.

### U.S. Beer Sales and Schlitz' Share

Figure 12. Using tricks of scale and false perspective here convey a very different impression from that justified by the data. By Bill Perkins. ©by *The Washington Post.* Reprinted by permission.

Figure 13. Same data as Figure 12.

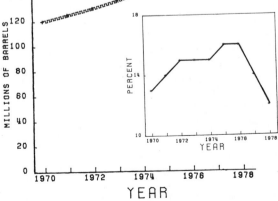

This example is one in which the choice of scale along the y-axis needs considerable thought. One could scale from zero, yielding a perception of a steady increase over the course of the past eight years. Alternatively, one could stretch the scale so that it extended just over the range of the data (say from 110 to 160 million barrels), which would give the impression of a rather steep increase in sales. In this instance, we have chosen the former approach, because it seems that the perception of a slow but steady increase suits a product which has grown steadily at 4 percent a year for eight years. Thus our choice of scale resulted from a careful consideration of the data and how best to communicate it. This same interpretation was not used for the unemployment data (Figures 8 and 9) because "steady change" does not suit this more volatile variable.

*Using area inappropriately*

As illustrated in Figure 1 by the declining size of the dollar, the use of area when length is the variable of interest is often visually confusing. The same problem was apparent in the beer barrel as well. This problem occurs often but is occasionally compounded by an inconsistency of graphical metaphor in which area sometimes is representing the variable and sometimes not. Consider the size of the pipes in Figure 14.

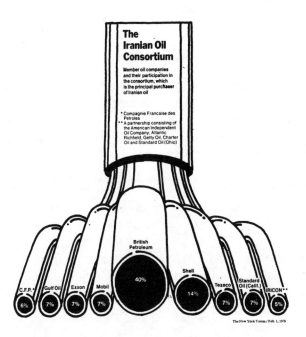

Figure 14. The visual metaphor employed here varies between using the diameters of the pipes and their areas in a haphazard fashion. ©1979 by The New York Times Company.

A careful examination of this plot led William Kruskal to write to Louis Silverstein of *The New York Times* as follows:

> Yet Iranian oil continues to bring out the devil in everyone. The ... figure ... is bewildering because it vacillates like a middle east policy statement. Consider the largest pipe and the two just to its right; I read and measure thus,

| % Shown | Diameter (mm) | Diameter squared (mm²) |
|---------|---------------|------------------------|
| 40      | 3.2           | 10.24                  |
| 14      | 1.9           | 3.61                   |
| 7       | 1.0           | 1.00                   |

> Now $40/14 = 2.86$, $3.2/1.9 = 1.68$, and $10.24/3.61 = 2.84$. "Aha!," I said at first, "the artist is using relative areas, not an unreasonable approach."

> But alas, $14/7 = 2$, $1.9/1.0 = 1.9$, and $3.61/1.00 = 3.61$ so *that* ratio is one of diameters, *not* areas.

> There must be an applicable passage in the Koran. (Letter of February, 1979)

*Using a natural visual metaphor correctly*

Playfair's contribution is noteworthy because of his use of space to represent something which is not spatial. The making of maps antedates Playfair considerably, but the notion of using the plane of the paper to represent the plane of the Earth is natural and certainly represents no great intellectual insight. Playfair, on the other hand, used space to represent variables like "value of goods imported." Using space as a representation of empirical, but non-spatial data does not appear to have been done before, and even though the visual metaphor of a rising and falling line representing rising and falling imports seems natural to us, it was quite a breakthrough.

It is a retreat if the "natural" metaphors which exist visually are ignored or, worse, misused. For example, a bar in a bar chart can be of any length and still correctly communicate the amount it represents, if that amount is inscribed. But what a waste of effort if the length of the bar does not represent that amount reasonably accurately! It seems sensible that the visual metaphor "bigger means more" ought to be followed. If we consider the anonymous display in Figure 15 we see that the bar-segment representing coal use in 1977 (14.1) is longer than the projected use in plan 2000-A (18)—the natural metaphor has been violated.

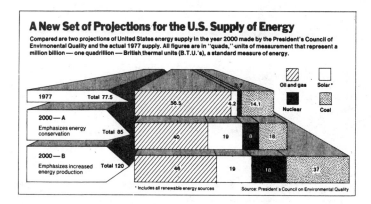

Figure 15. The natural visual metaphor is violated when a longer bar (representing 14.1 BTU) is used for a lesser amount (compare with the bar for 18 BTU's). ©1979 by The New York Times Company.

The error in Figure 15 is probably just a grapho (the graphical equivalent of a typo), yet the misuse of natural visual metaphors is common, particularly with maps. For instance, the map of the United States shown in Figure 16 is shaded according to a scheme which reflects a variety of results for the D.C. voting rights amendment. The legend indicates no particular order for the various shadings. Yet there is a natural order of both shadings and outcomes. For shadings the natural metaphor is "darker=more," and the various results can be ordered along the continuum from "ratified" to "rejected" passing through "in progress," "no action," and "stalled" along the way. If this is done and the shading is ordered so that each category becomes successively darker, the alternative shown in Figure 17 results.

*Good graphs and serious graphs found in newspapers*
Thus far errors in newspaper graphs have been stressed to the exclusion of any praise. Such a one-sided view is not entirely justified. One regularly finds good graphs in newspapers, and their structure can help us to understand what makes newspaper graphs what they are. We have found that good newspaper graphs fall into one of two categories. In the first category are those graphs done routinely for an audience that doesn't have to be enticed into looking. This type is characterized as "serious."

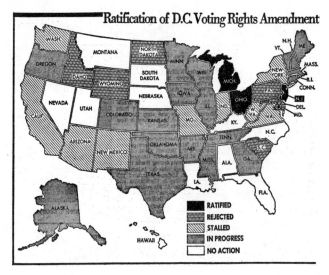

Figure 16. Map showing the status of the D.C. voting rights amendment in each of the 50 state legislatures. By Dave Cook. ©by *The Washington Post*.

The least appealing, but most carefully read, sections of the newspaper are the stock market pages and the sports' statistics and the graphs on these pages are refreshingly free from chartjunk and graphos.

In Figure 18 is the most common graph in the newspaper, which is so routinely printed *and read* that labels are almost redundant. The viewer has seen one just like it yesterday and will see another tomorrow. All that is required is a glance to see the current situation before moving along to the details.

Figure 19 is somewhat different. It reports data with which most readers are already familiar, but in a new way. Thus the point of the data (and hence the

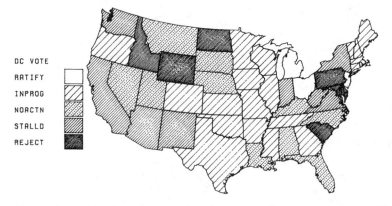

Figure 17. Ratification of D.C. voting rights amendment; same data as Figure 16.

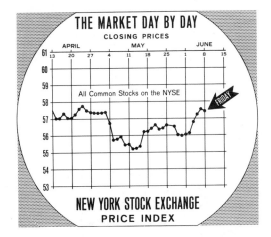

Figure 18. Daily stock market chart. Reprinted by permission, Stock Market Graphic Features, Fort Worth, Texas.

point of the graph) is made clearly. Moreover, the interest of the readers is assured so that there is no necessity to resort to baroque additions to attract their attention. We contend, of course, that "adorning" a graph with chartjunk may contribute to its being read, but opens the way to its being misunderstood as well. Our earlier illustrations have shown how the reader has to search through chartjunk to determine which features express the data quantities and which are merely ornaments and the possibilities open to him for mistaking junk for data. To quote Will Rogers: "What we don't know won't hurt us. It's what we do know that ain't."

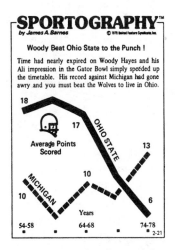

Figure 19. A simple graph intermingled with a textual explanation tells the whole story. ©1979 United Feature Syndicate, Inc. Reprinted by permission.

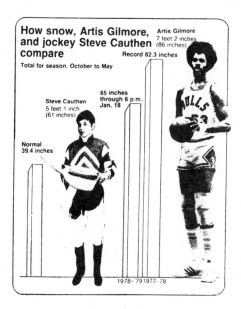

Figure 20. Overlaying a reasonable statistical graphic with other figures can yield an evocative and memorable image. ©by *The Chicago Tribune*. Reprinted by permission.

In the second category are graphs which are good not because they conform to any pattern, but more because of good luck. Sometimes the grapher produces a graph that is good, apparently more by accident than by intent. Two examples are shown in Figures 20 and 21. Figure 20 is a bar chart showing the snowfall in Chicago which is adorned with pictures of two individuals of well known height. The resulting plot yields an image that is evocative, and a memory trace that will survive for a long time.

The plot in Figure 21 is similarly evocative. Showing the sun of Japan rising before Old Glory is an image that will last and it also conveys the meaning well. It is unfortunate that the floor of the plot seems to start at -10 percent; Clipper could just as easily have started at zero.

*Paths towards making newspaper graphs fit to print*
Some of the major errors that we have found in newspaper graphs have been described. A student of the history of graphic presentation would have an extreme sense of *déjà vu* from this commentary because these same faults have been pointed out repeatedly for the past 50 years or more (Funkhouser, 1937; Macdonald-Ross, 1977; Schmid, 1954). Furthermore, it is striking to note how the alternatives offered here share so many attributes, even though the graphs they replace are quite different. The simple line chart seems very satisfactory (although

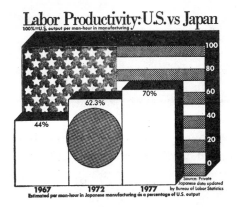

Figure 21. A graph can still be useful and yield an evocative image even when technically flawed in several ways. By Milton Clipper. ©by *The Washington Post*. Reprinted by permission.

there is some evidence [Wainer, Groves & Lono, Note 6; Wainer & Reiser, 1976] that other elementary forms would work almost as well). Indeed, the two examples of good newspaper graphs (that were not simple forms or routinized presentations) had as their basis some simple form with an iconic overlay to aid recognition or memory.

The message for clear graphic presentation is obvious: do not depart from accepted standards, or accepted formats without good reason. These standards and formats are well specified in a variety of sources (Schmid and Schmid, 1978) and they ought to be followed. It is difficult to know why these same errors are being repeated. In Playfair's original work these kinds of mistakes were not made; moreover, these errors were not as widespread in the 1930's as they are now. Perhaps the reason is an increase in the perceived need for graphs, mentioned earlier, without a concomitant increase in training in their construction. Evidence gathered by the committee on graphics of the American Statistical Association indicates that formal training in graphic presentation has had a marked decline at all levels of education over the last few decades.

How can these errors be corrected given this reduction of formal training and the pressure under which newspapers are often produced? There seem to be three levels of procedure which would correct these problems. The most optimistic would be to try to convince newspaper editors to have their graphers trained in the rudimentary rules of good graphic presentation. Kruskal (Note 2) feels that this solution is "the only long run hope." As mentioned previously, there are several careful statements of good graphical standards (Bertin, 1973; Schmid & Schmid, 1978) which, if followed, will prevent any grievous errors. Indeed, there are some simple rules and principles which, if followed, will tend to steer the grapher away from problems. I have tried to illustrate some in this paper and, as was noted earlier, all the solutions have one thing in common. They are all much simpler than the graphs they replace. The lesson is clear: "less is more." This principle has been incorporated into Tufte's (Note 5) measure of graph quality, the "Data-Ink ratio," which determines how much ink was used to plot the data, and divides that by the amount of ink used for the entire picture. In general, the larger the ratio the better the plot. As is easily seen, chartjunk tends to diminish the D-I ratio whereas simple plots tend to increase it. Following Tufte's rule will not solve all graphical problems but it is a very helpful orientative attitude.

At a somewhat lower level of optimism newspapers may perhaps be convinced to have a "graph editor" (called a *Transformierer* by Neurath [cited in Kinross, 1978]) who serves as an intermediary between the reporter who writes the story and the artist who draws the graph. This person would transform the data provided by the reporter into a sketch to guide the artist and would also check the final result to assure that it met graphical standards. It would no longer be necessary to train everyone in standards for clear graphical presentation, only the Transformierer.

I am not sanguine about the chances of either of these two solutions being implemented. The last hope, I believe, rests in technological evolution. Increasingly graphics are being prepared with the aid of a computer. It appears that it is feasible to incorporate into the systems already in use by writers and editors, a sequence of software decision-tree prompts that will allow editorial staff members to clarify and specify the quantitative elements of a story they think worthy of graphic illustration and to display schematically various diagrammatic options for graphing the desired data and relationships. Similar but more refined programs for use by chart designers might also be developed, along with features in computergraphic chart-generating software sequences which would preclude, or at least make more difficult, various errors of graphic representation. Thus, an artist attempting to execute Figure 1 with a computergraphic program might be halted by the program, which would register on his display device a query such as the following: BAR DIMENSIONS INTERPRETABLE AS AREAS, RATIOS OF ASSIGNED VALUES ARE LINEAR. DO YOU WISH BARS RESCALED TO AREA RATIOS? Similarly, in Figure 10, the program would note that the scale intervals are unequal and could prompt the designer as follows: INTERVALS ARE UNEQUAL. THE FOLLOWING DESIGN OPTIONS ARE AVAILABLE FOR DEALING WITH UNEQUAL INTERVALS IN THIS FORM OF CHART. In conventional print form, Bowman (1968) has developed a system that appears to us directly applicable to such programmed application. Bertin (1973, 1977) affords more comprehensively elaborated logical systems of graphic representation of data on which we could draw for such developments.

Although the system just described does not, to my knowledge, yet exist, there are systems for the routine production of graphics that will do a tolerably good job with their current set of default options. Most of the alternative plots produced in this paper were done with only minor changes from default on the Michigan graphical system GIST (Barge, Marks, & Schneider, Note 1). Other packages like DISPLAA and TEL-A-GRAF (two well-known computergraphic packages developed by Integrated Software Systems Corporation of San Diego) could be modified to conform more closely to established standards of good practice and their use encouraged as a floor on which newspaper artists and graphers could build to add on those baroque images that they consider suitable to make the graph more attractive. With such a system the basic form and structure of the graph will be accurate and the additions, as long as they do not mask the underlying plot, would not severely harm the perception of the graph.

Using a system like that proposed, newspapers could properly claim that their graphs were fit to print instead of producing, as in current practice, graphs that more often obscure the darkness of their topic than illuminate it.

This work was funded in part by NSF Grant (SOC 76-17768) to the Bureau of Social Science Research, Inc. I thank Albert D. Biderman and William Kruskal for their help with this project.

## Reference notes

1. Barge, J., Marks, G. A., & Schneider, E. J. *Graphical interpretation of statistical tables*. Ann Arbor: Institute for Social Research, The University of Michigan, 1979.
2. Kruskal, W. Personal communication to A. D. Biderman, March 11, 1979.
3. Silverstein, L. Graphs at *The New York Times*. Talk given at the First General Conference on Social Graphics, Leesburg, Virginia, October 1978.
4. Tufte, E. Improving conventional graphics for statistical data. Talk given at the Department of Statistics, University of Chicago, January 1977.
5. Tufte, E. Data graphics. Talk given at the First General Conference on Social Graphics, Leesburg, Virginia, October 1978.
6. Wainer, H., Groves, C., & Lono, M. On the display of data: Some empirical findings. Talk given at the First General Conference on Social Graphics, Leesburg, Virginia, October 1978.

## References

Bertin, J. *Semiologie graphique*. The Hague: Gautier-Mouton, 1973.
Bertin, J. *La graphique et le traitement graphique de l'information*. Paris: Flamarion, 1977.
Bowman, W. J. *Graphic communication*. New York: John Wiley & Sons, 1968.

Funkhouser, H. G. Historical development of the graphical representation of statistical data. *Osiris*, 1937, *3*, 269-404.

Huff, D. *How to lie with statistics*. New York: Norton, 1954.

Kinross, R. Otto Neurath und die Humanisierung des Wissens mit Hilfe der Bildpädogogik. *Kultur und Technik: Zeitschrift des Deutschen Museums München*, 1978, 32-35.

Macdonald-Ross, M. How numbers are shown: a review of research on the presentation of quantitative data in texts. *Audio-Visual Communication Review*, 1977, *25*, 359-409.

Playfair, W. *The commercial and political atlas*. London: Corry, 1786.

Schmid, C. F. *Handbook of graphic presentation*. New York: Ronald Press, 1954.

Schmid, C. F., & Schmid, S. E. *Handbook of graphic presentation* (2nd ed.). New York: Ronald Press, 1978.

Tukey, J. W. *Exploratory data analysis*. Reading, Mass.: Addison-Wesley, 1977.

Wainer, H., & Reiser, M. Assessing the efficacy of graphical displays. *Proceedings of the American Statistical Association (Social Science Section)*, Boston, 1976.

# Some problems of illustration

Howard E. Paine

*The designer of scientific illustrations for the printed page must find ways to show motion, growth, the passage of time, comparative scale, and internal structure. He must decide how much of a complicated subject can be shown in one illustration and when to break it into separate parts or to do a schematic diagram. Cut-away views, exploded views, transparent views each pose special problems. A wide variety of labeling and numbering systems are available. Designing maps requires a thorough understanding of global projections and careful use of color, line weight, and positioning of symbols and type. From coarse woodblock to slick airbrush, printed diagrams have improved through the years. What new techniques can be developed? Will they include 3-D or the elusive hologram?*

As Art Director, I spend a good part of the day at *National Geographic* attempting to give shape and direction to the artwork used to illustrate scientific and historical articles (Figure 1).

Because *National Geographic* has a circulation of ten million, I have the awesome responsibility of trying to make each of those illustrations clear, informative, imaginative, perhaps even entertaining. In other words, we are trying to make the printed page communicate complicated information effectively.

Although television and the fleeting images of film have become forceful tools of communication, we feel that the printed page is still a valuable place to portray, with some degrees of permanence, the complex world around us.

Obviously, the printed page is a superb place for visual catalogs of flora and fauna, fossils and furniture, automobiles and architecture (Figure 2). Those detailed, definitive portraits stand as ready reference for one who is classifying or comparing differing forms.

But how, on a printed page, do we show motion, dynamic processes, interactions, change? How a seed sprouts. How a glacier moves. How a space vehicle intersects with the orbit of Jupiter.

To show motion, even in a simple illustration of a man walking, the artist can use a variety of symbols. He can exaggerate the man's step. He can use speedlines, or a strobe effect, as in Marcel Duchamp's famous painting, "Nude Descending a Staircase." He can show footprints or a dotted line to suggest where the man has been. He can break the action down into a storyboard or a cartoon sequence. When all else fails, he can reach into a quiver full of all sorts of arrows.

Figure 1. Historic paintings attempt to put artifacts into an active context, to bring back to life ancient peoples and events, to recreate lost moments in a modern journalistic style of art or in a primitive style that suggests the early culture.

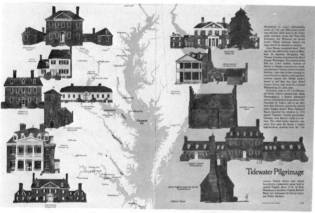

Figure 2. Catalogues of flora and fauna, fossils and furniture, automobiles and architecture give the reader a convenient reference point to classify or compare different forms.

I once put a northbound arrow west of a fault line, and a southbound arrow east of it. But then I realized that the land east of the line was not actually moving south. A split arrow, straddling the fault line, with both sides pointing north, resolved the conflict and, in fact, clearly demonstrated the shearing effect.

A man walking is infinitely simpler to portray than the complicated choreography of motion inside an engine, or inside a wave breaking against the shore, or the invisible dynamics of weather. The jet stream high above us varies in speed and altitude and size and direction and temperature. It cannot be seen. When Sir Luke Howard first identified and named the clouds, cirrus, nimbus, cumulus, he was simply one more eighteenth-century classifier of shapes. He left the invisible dynamics for us to wrestle with.

Motion, whether simple or complex, is but one test of the designer's skills. How is one to show growth, a sort of three-dimensional motion often involving enormous structural changes—as in the changing proportions from fetus to infant to adult, from seedling to mature tree?

Or how are we to portray on a printed page the endless vastness of geological time (Figure 3) or, for that matter, the handful of remembered millenia we know as history? Placing fossils and artifacts in a cross-section of strata suggests only timidly the passing of centuries.

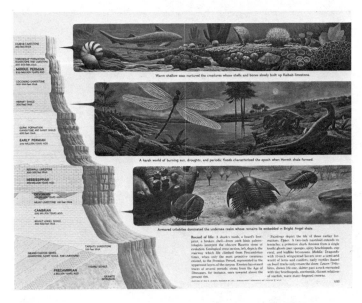

Figure 3. The passage of time can only be suggested. Here the flora and fauna of three different eras are located in their geological strata.

Scale presents still another problem. Small things like molecular structure, or the circulatory system of a tiny insect can with some difficulty be diagrammed (Figure 4). Large things, like the eccentric, elliptical orbits of the planets, or the positioning in three-dimensional space of the distant galaxies, are far more difficult to confine to a printed page but, with varying degrees of success, we continue to try.

One aspect of the problem is scale. We can show the insects a bird eats.

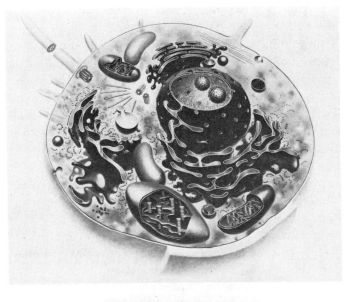

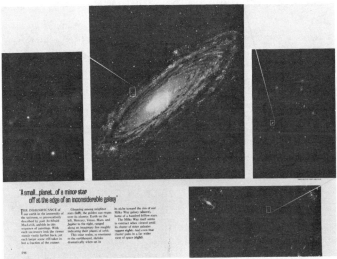

Figure 4. Scale, whether it is the submicroscopic parts of a human cell or the three-dimensional positioning of our galaxy in a universe of galaxies, is often difficult to commit to the printed page.

And we can show that bird on the back of a hippopotamus. But we cannot, in one picture, show the insect and the bird and the hippopotamus. That is why diagrams of the food chain from plankton to whale often look pedantic and dull. Or a diagram of the hydrological cycle, which tries to include everything from the respiration of a leaf to the enormous power of a thunderstorm. Or a diagram placing our little backwater solar system in its huge galaxy of 200 billion stars and our galaxy, the Milky Way, in the universe which is made up of probably 10 billion galaxies. It is not possible to see a continent and a grain of sand in the same picture.

Another test of our graphic skills is to see within, to dissect visually the muscles and organs of life, or to take the roof off the underworld labyrinth of a mine, or to see inside a spacecraft with its unnatural juxtapositions of fuels, engines, instruments, and life-support systems.

To show a man walking, the artist uses a variety of symbols. To see within, we call up whole systems of symbols. Certain subjects, such as architecture, lend themselves to cutaway views. Others, such as engines, to exploded views. Yet others, to airbrushed, transparent views. The cutaway requires surgical skills as to what is to be left in or taken out (Figure 5). The exploded view requires that pieces and sections "explode" along coherent axes. The airbrushed, transparent view, like others, demands careful editing so that the "insideness" of the subject isn't lost altogether. Of course, the trick is to know when to use which system, or indeed which combination of systems. In some situations, we might try to print on acetate overlays, or even consider making pop-up cardboard models.

We have quickly covered some of the graphic problems facing the designer of scientific illustrations: how to show motion, growth, the passage of time, comparative scale, and how to see within.

Still other questions worry us: How much of a complex subject can be shown in one illustration or should it be divided into several parts (Figure 6)? When should separate parts be synthesized? When do we depart from realism and do a schematic diagram? Does such a diagram provide fresh insight into a complex subject or does it further obscure it from the reader (Figure 7)? An awesome responsibility indeed.

The television filmmaker has all the power tools: sound effects, music, color, voice-over narration, and motion (whether normal action, or time-lapse, or freeze-frame). But when the power is off, his power tools fail.

The typographer, working with ink and paper on a static page, has a different set of tools: the 26 letters of the alphabet which, in all their myriad variations and sizes, can be used with brilliant effect to establish mood, to gain emphasis, to give order, to direct the reader. The selection of typeface, the use of punctuation, the size, and sometimes color, and the placement in the grid, all become part of the message communicated.

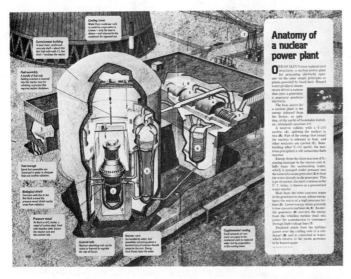

Figure 5. Cutaway views let the reader see what cannot be photographed. For some subjects an exploded view, or a transparent view, carefully airbrushed, works better. Some subjects require subtle combinations of cutaway, transparent, and exploded techniques.

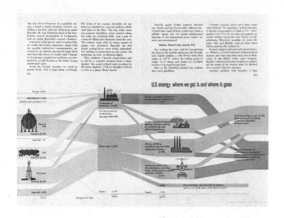

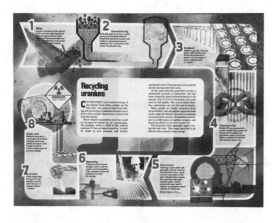

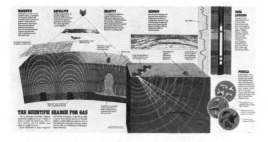

Figure 6. Schematic diagrams, flow charts, and maps help to synthesize complex subjects.

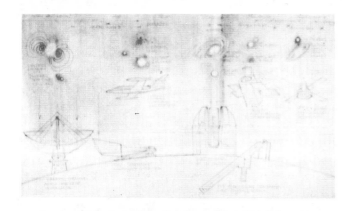

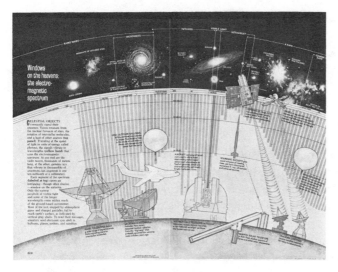

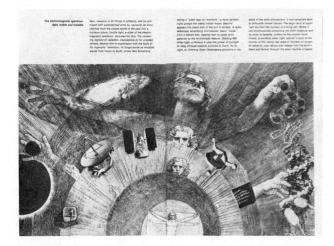

Figure 7. The electromagnetic spectrum bathes earth with radiation. Here is shown the sources of the radiation, the instruments which detect it, and the penetration into the atmosphere made by different wave lengths. At top is a rough sketch; in the center is finished art; at bottom is a more allegorical presentation of the same subject.

When we diagram something like a nuclear power plant (whose parts need labeling) we have to choose between using simple name labels or more explanatory captions. We can put labels right on the art or in the margin with arrows to the art. We can number the parts and put a list in the margin, or use differently-colored parts with a color-key in the margin. Obviously, the placement of the labels must be part of the design so that they fit comfortably, are readable against background detail, and are in some kind of logical order.

The cartographer has a tool box full of precision tools and instruments. I do not mean surveying instruments or drafting equipment but symbols and systems of symbols.

First of all, the earth is a sphere. And any map on flat paper has to be the result of some accepted system of distortion called a map projection, such as Mercator, or Mollweide, or equal-area, or azimuthal-equidistant (Figure 8).

Second, a map is not simply an aerial view. It is a schematic abstraction of relief and drainage, of political boundaries and place-names, all severely edited to fit the scale of the map, and even further edited if the map is one of topical emphasis (Figure 9). (Place-names are not found on a weather map, or mountain ranges on a population map.)

The map designer must ask himself a wide assortment of questions. And each answer depends upon other questions. What area is to be covered? What is the maximum scale that will fit on the page? What projection will be most appropriate? Must north be at the top? Would a perspective view be useful? How many printing inks? What place-names are essential? What system of showing relief—contour lines, hachures, shading, color tints, or a combination? How much vertical exaggeration? Should highways be single lines or double? What system of dots and symbols will represent city populations? What size type in crowded areas? Should type align horizontally with the page or bend with the lines of latitude?

These are but a few of the design decisions we face when planning a map. Some questions answer themselves, others have to be worked out with each map.

When the drainage and the boundaries and the transportation are scribed, and all the screened negatives for each tint are combined, and all the type is specified and set into place, we may have a readable, useful map. But sometimes the mountains, or the battle zone, or the caribou range come up too strong, or in the wrong color, and the careful balance of the map is lost.

Television has been mentioned several times as though we fashion our work in response to that all-pervasive medium. Not so. What we are trying to do is to make the printed page as effective a communicator as is editorially and technically possible. For some designers it is a great temptation to slip over into filmmaking where the range of tools is so varied and so powerful. Television has both whetted and sated our visual appetites. It may be that the illustrator's wide use of collage techniques (Figure 10) is his answer to the film techniques of fades and dissolves, quick cuts, and multiple images. For those designers still in love with the printed page and its quietly powerful effectiveness, it is a challenge to discover new techniques of exposition.

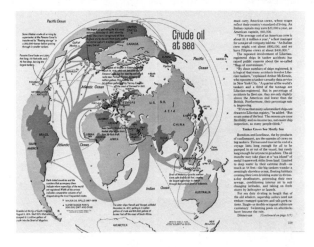

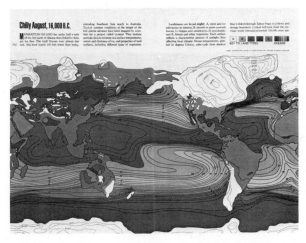

Figure 8. All map projections are flat distortions of spherical reality, but can help the designer communicate important facts. Top, the easily recognizable land masses are important. Center, land is more distorted in order to show ocean routes more clearly. Bottom, a Mercator projection is used to help the reader locate continents with very different Ice Age configurations.

154

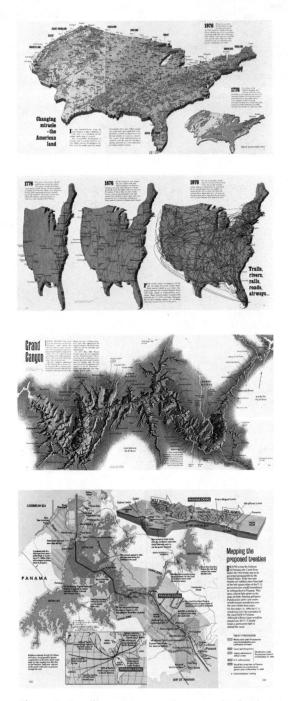

Figure 9. Familiar maps sometimes need a fresh approach to call attention to special features. More art than map, they help dramatize topical material.

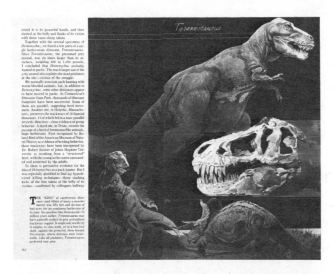

Figure 10. Collages dramatically combine various aspects of a subject, exciting the eye and the mind. Television's many images have whetted the reader's visual appetite. Collages needn't be clutter. Carefully crafted, they help the reader see "around" a subject.

The early printers used coarse woodblocks to illustrate their books. Then came delicately hand-tooled copperplate engravings. Then in rapid succession photography, the half-tone dot, four-color process printing. Today, high-speed presses, printing on magnificently coated papers, fill our eyes with sometimes startling photographic realism.

I keep looking for something more, however, and wondering who will find some innovative and exciting new forms of illustration. We have come from crude woodblock to slick airbrush. We print on acetate overlays. What is the next step? Is it the dramatic effect of 3-D or the still elusive hologram?

For me the challenge will be met not in some long-awaited technological breakthrough but in the minds of the editor and the artist whose combined talents will create imaginative new symbols, and systems of symbols, with which to portray this world around us.

# Islamic calligraphy: Meaning and symbol

Anthony Welch

*For most of Islam's fourteen centuries of history Arabic script has been the foremost symbol of the Muslim world. The 28 letters of the Arabic alphabet have served a multitude of purposes: direct conveyors of content, decorative forms, symbols of belief, talismans, esoteric signs, and poetic metaphors. In either religious or secular context the forms of the Arabic script, rendered in many different styles, have permeated almost all areas of the culture despite the fact that until modern times illiteracy was the norm in Muslim societies. The Muslim calligrapher has thus not only made the forms of visible language but also created the central forms of Islam's visual culture.*

> *Thy Lord is the Most Bounteous,*
> *Who teacheth by the pen,*
> *Teacheth man that which he knew not.*

These three lines come from chapter 96, verses 3-5, of the *Holy Qur'an* (Pickthall, 1976), Islam's central scripture, and speak of Allah's gift of knowledge to humanity. To Muslims the foremost instrument for the transmission of knowledge has always been the *qalam* or pen, according to Islamic tradition the first of Allah's creations. Throughout the fourteen hundred years of Islamic culture the *qalam* and the letters that flowed from it have been incisive symbols and have occupied the primary position in the visual culture of the faith. Human beings in fulfilling the destiny ordained for them have often been likened to so many pens writing what Allah wills. The slender form of the reed pen—the *qalam* has frequently been compared to the thin, vertical stroke of the *alif* (Figure 1), the first letter of the Arabic alphabet and therefore the beginning of transmitted knowledge. But this form has varied content: being also the initial letter of the divine name, Allah (Figure 2), with whom knowledge commences and from whom knowledge comes, it ranks as the foremost letter. In the system known as *abdjad*, in which each of the alphabet's letters has a specific, fixed numerical equivalent, the letter *alif* is also equal to the number 1, not only the first number but also the numerical sign of *tauhid*, the fundamental unity that is the basis of Islam's monotheism. On yet another level *alif* serves in love poetry as a metaphor of the slender beloved whose form inspires the lover's soul. Because much love poetry in the Muslim world expresses mystical verities as well, the lover's passion for his early *alif* mirrors his soul's yearning for the divine.

These remarks can be expanded. The fact that the visual rendering of the word Allah reveals a succession of ascending letters was early noted by

Figure 1. The letter *alif* in *muhaqqaq* style. A. Welch.

Figure 2. The word *Allah* in *muhaqqaq* style. A. Welch.

Muslims and taken as one of the proofs of Islam's truth, as was the fact that most of the letters of the *shahada*, Islam's fundamental creed, are also heaven-oriented (Figure 3). Conversely, Muslims perceived in the form of the Prophet Muhammad's name (Figure 4) the shape of a worshipper's body bent in prayer.

**Faith and script**

That letters have such complexities is, of course, not accidental, and there is a close relationship between Islam and the Arabic script. Derived from the Aramaic Nabataean alphabet in use in the Near East in the early centuries of the Christian era, Arabic script before Islam was a utilitarian vehicle and served a minor role in Arabic culture. Pre-Islamic Arabs did not richly develop their script, and two basic distinctions in writing style were made between an angular style (*Kufic*) derived from the technical necessities of stone-cut inscriptions and a cursive style (*naskhi*) suitable for handwriting. Following revelation of the *Qur'an* in the early decades of the seventh century A.D. this situation changed, and the rapid transformation of Arabic script from a simple tool into the major visual expression of Islamic culture is one of the most impressive cultural achievements of historic times. (In the twentieth century the Arabic alphabet is second only to the roman in world-wide use.) After the Prophet's death in 632 A.D. the Arabic language, its script, and the *Qur'an* accompanied Arab armies in the expansion of Islam. It was now not only necessary to transmit the *Qur'an* throughout Islam's widening empire but also

Figure 3. The *shahada* in *thuluth* style. A. Welch.

Figure 4. The word *Muhammad* in *thuluth* style. A. Welch

incumbent upon believers to create a visual medium worthy of the task of preserving and teaching Allah's Revelation. The use of Arabic script developed with the increase in power and the spread of the faith: during his 20-year reign (685-705 A.D.) the caliph 'Abd al-Malik established Arabic as the first language of the empire and ordered the construction of the Dome of the Rock in Jerusalem, the first major religious monument in which Arabic calligraphy played a fundamental role. He also revolutionized official coinage, the coin shown in Figure 5 being representative of the new type. There is no image of ruler, holy figure, or deity; instead both sides bear Arabic script, written in a straightforward, legible *Kufic*, beginning with the essential statement, "There is no god but Allah," continuing with other affirmations of religious belief, and telling place and date of issue. Coinage is the most frequently seen and used art in any state, and it is a measure of calligraphy's importance that from the late seventh century until modern times it should be the basic visual means of affirming official convictions on Islam.

Figure 5. Tenth century Muslim gold coin. American Numismatic Society.

There is another factor to be considered in the rise of Arabic script to this position of eminence. Muslims regard the *Qur'an* neither as literature nor as poetry nor as the product of Muhammad's mind moved by inspiration. Instead, the *Qur'an* is considered to be the direct words of Allah, revealed in Arabic through Muhammad, who was only a man and had no role in the making of the Book itself. Because Islam regards Allah as non-corporeal and intangible, the written *Qur'an* becomes the closest equivalent to a visible divine manifestation on earth. Hence the *Qur'an* occupies a place in Islam and Islamic art remarkably similar to that of Christ within Christianity and Christian art: where Christian arts make use of the *figural* image of Christ as the central vehicle for Christian teaching, Islam employs the *witten Qur'an* as the fundamental visual symbol of belief. Visible language and not image depicted Islam's concept of the divine.

Orthodox Muslims have often regarded the representation of living, mobile creatures as potentially idolatrous, and this attitude, established relatively early in Islam's existence, also affected the arts. Calligraphy, geometric abstractions, and other non-figural forms were favored in official and sacred arts; figural arts were restricted largely to the secular world and rarely used for illustrating religious life, history, or doctrine. On a visual level Islam was easily differentiated from other faiths like Christianity and Hinduism, where figural arts flourished and provided icons for religious worship. In Islam it was the written word that supplied forms for religious contemplation and conveyed the content of religious devotion.

The *Qur'an* is therefore never illustrated, and the written words of the text are the vehicles not only of content but also of visual aesthetics, sometimes to such a degree that aesthetic considerations weigh more heavily than simple legibility. In a ninth-century Kufic *Qur'an* page from Iran or Iraq (Figure 6), for example, letters have been extended or compressed or even dramatically changed in form for aesthetic reasons. The canons of this art are often not consistent in this early period. Words are sometimes whole and sometimes split, apparently in answer to visual needs, and letter forms are not always predictable. In this case style results in obfuscation in terms of legibility and beautification in terms of decoration. To deal with such a text has always been to some extent a problem of decipherment: fluent reading was possible only for those who already knew the text by heart. Word recognition came through visual clues and prior knowledge of the text.

The use of Arabic script extended far beyond the *Qur'an*, and calligraphy

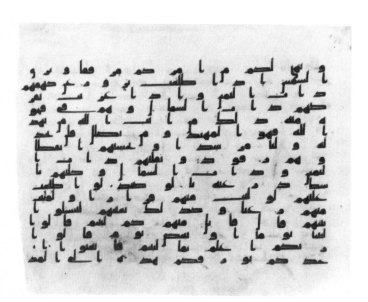

Figure 6. Ninth century *Qur'an* page. The Cincinnati Art Museum.

was used for classics of Islamic literature composed in Arabic, Turkish, Persian, or other languages using the Arabic script. Script also adorned objects: ceramics, metalworks, textiles, ivories, wood carvings, and fine stone were only some of the materials on which script was used, often as the sole visual element, though more often complemented by abstract ornament or figural design. Not all inscriptions had religious content, many conveying more mundane information about patrons and their titles. The Yemeni sultan al-Malik al-Mujahid (1321-1363 A.D.) commissioned a large bronze tray (Figure 7) from an Egyptian metalworker. Its inscriptions follow basic contemporary patterns: "Glory to our lord, our king, the ruler of our age and our time, the sultan al-Malik al-Mujahid, Sayf al-Dunya wa al-Din 'Ali, the son of the sultan al-Malik al-Mu'ayyad Mubarriz al-Dunya wa al-Din Da'ud, endowed with the glory of the two masteries, of the sword and of the pen." The Arabic incription is divided into three parts, separated by three large roundels. The key factor in setting the points of division was not the sense of the text but the goal of a nearly equal distribution of ascending letters. The total inscription contains 56 letters with tall vertical stems. The designer chose to have 18 verticals in the first section, 19 in the second, and 19 third. In order to do so, he had to delete one letter from the third section and add it to the second section. Again for compositional reasons several words were superimposed across the vertical stems of other words so that in some places the inscription runs on three levels. A "reader" finds himself deciphering the aesthetic complexities of this inscription. The designer's choices, however, were not arbitrary. The style of script he chose was *thuluth*, tall and stately and often used for monumental inscriptions. He chose to accentuate vertical elements in order to emphasize aesthetic movement towards the tray's central medallion and to intensify the sense of roundness. In addition, he was dealing with a visual similitude. The letters of the *shahada*, the Muslim creed, were predominantly vertical and by stressing this aesthetic aspect he was relating the form of the ruler's epithets to one of the central visual symbols of Islam.

### Script as power

It is clear that the close association of Arabic script with Islam as faith gave added visual force to epigraphs dealing with Islam as power. Whatever the content, the epigraphs had Islamic form. Buildings were supplied with finely written inscriptions, and the use of impressive epigraphs on both interior and exterior surfaces is one of the most distinctive features of Islamic architecture. There the central role of the written word as the vehicle for official religious and state convictions is dramatically illustrated. In the late twelfth century Muslim armies conquered Delhi and much of northern India and began to establish a Muslim state that endured until supplanted by the British in the eighteenth century. Soon after the occupation of Delhi in 1191 Qutb al-Din Aybak, the Muslim governor of northern India, ordered the construction of a great mosque which served as the principal

Figure 7. Fourteenth-century bronze tray from the Yemen. Musée du Louvre, Paris.

religious center of Islam in India until the fourteenth century. Though now a ruin (Figure 8), the mosque still reveals much about the social and religious condition of early medieval India. In its interior a huge arched screen formed the *qiblah*, the prayer wall facing toward Mecca. Its surfaces were richly inscribed with *Qur'anic* verses and Sayings (*Hadith*) of Muhammad stressing the principles of Islam, the obligations of believers, the importance of remaining true to the faith, and the benefits a believer incurred by building a mosque or participating in its maintenance. These epigraphs were intended for the Muslims who worshipped in the mosque's interior; non-believers would not have been able to enter.

Dominating the mosque's vertical dimensions is a minaret more than 73 meters high. It too was inscribed. Its *Qur'anic* verses had a different import, however, for they emphasized not so much the obligations and benefits of belief as the disasters of unbelief, and they reiterated grave admonitions against those who did not accept Islam. In keeping with the minaret's architectural function as the symbol of Islam's might in a land almost entirely non-Muslim the epigraphs refer not simply to unbelievers but far more explicitly to polytheists and idolators, image-worship being for Muslims one of the gravest sins. Epigraphs functioned here to clarify Islam's position and to stand as the faith's warning to India's Hindus and Jains not to persist in their unbelief because it would bring only the eternal grief of hell. Notably, these warnings are inscribed on the minaret which could, of course, be seen from outside the mosque; in fact, the most powerful and direct of these admonitions are placed on the lower part of the minaret where they could easily be read.

Figure 8. The Quwwat al-Islam mosque and minaret, Delhi.

It is unlikely that very many of the unbelievers could read these messages, though they might have been informed of their meaning. Probably only a small minority of the Muslims themselves were literate, and even an educated Muslim could have had trouble deciphering some of the ornate script styles used on the minaret. But literacy of the viewer and legibility of the inscription are not the sole factors to be considered. Script had many dimensions. It expressed content of a specific sort, in this case obviously selected by educated theologians who had a clear idea of their special social and political situation and who sought a logical relationship between inscriptional theme and architectural location, for the minaret's message is different from that of the mosque. Script was also beautiful form and decoration, instrumental here in creating a lively pattern over the building's stone surfaces. To literate and illiterate alike, it could be appreciated in terms of line and rhythm. Further, and perhaps most important, script was a trademark, identifying the monument as Muslim. Key words, like Allah and Muhammad, could be recognized by any believer, for their presence was pervasive in the Islamic context. Moreover, Arabic script also functioned as Islam's sacred symbol: visually, it was the earthly form of Allah's word.

The role of the written word is also indicated by the process by which a building originally used by another faith was made Muslim. When Constantinople was captured by Ottoman Turks in 1453, the great sixth-century Christian basilica of Hagia Sophia was converted into a mosque. To help mark the building as Muslim and to testify that the city was now part of Islam, towering minarets were erected on the outside. But in the building's interior the written word shaped the new religious environment. Mosaics with Christian figural themes were covered and the new surfaces were inscribed with Qur'anic verses, while large roundels, similar to Figure 9 (which shows the name of the first Muslim caliph, Abu Bakr), were hung in key locations. Provided with names central to Islam's belief and history, they functioned like Christian icons. A roundel with the name "Allah" hung just to the right of the *mihrab* (the prayer niche indicating the direction of Mecca) while Muhammad's name hung to the left. The names of Abu Bakr and 'Umar, the second caliph, were next in proximity to the *mihrab*, while the names of 'Uthman and 'Ali, the third and fourth caliphs, came further on. Chronological order was demonstrated by spatial precedence.

Figure 9. Roundel with name of Abu Bakr, eighteenth century. Ottoman Turkey, AXIA.

It is worth noting that Islam in 1453 was no longer a unity. The Ottomans were staunch upholders of Sunni Islam, the branch of the faith that included the majority of Muslims, and they were strongly opposed to the Shi'as, the other substantial branch. In some parts of the Ottoman state and in other areas of the Muslim world, like Iran, Shi'ah populations constituted a real threat to Sunni and Ottoman authority. The use in the mosque of the names of the first three Muslim caliphs, Abu Bakr (632-634), 'Umar (634-644), and 'Uthman (644-656), whom Shi'as regarded as usurpers, was, therefore, a pious statement with distinct political overtones. Arabic inscriptions reinforced then not only faith but also state.

Thus the inscriptions on an Ottoman mosque lamp are a means of proclaiming Sunni convictions as well as decorating a surface with a fluid *thuluth* style of script (Figure 10). The vessel is divided into two sections by a dark red line just above the handles. On the neck and body of the lamp the same message is repeated: "Allah, Muhammad, Abu Bakr, ʻUmar, ʻUthman, ʻAli." The lamp's form has been carefully considered by the calligrapher, for the handles form dividers between the names, and the inscription on the top has been "turned" 180 degrees so that from any angle the entire message can be read by combining top and bottom halves. In this reproduction the letter "ha" appears immediately below the handle facing us; not used as part of the message, it indicates the beginning (and the end) of the circular inscription.

Figure 10. Sixteen-century Ottoman Turkish mosque lamp. Walters Art Gallery, Baltimore.

A different variation on Islamic state and faith is shown in a page from a Mughal Indian album (Figure 11) that once belonged to Shah Jahan (1627-1657). In each corner is a *simurgh*, a mythical bird in Iranian lore often associated with mystical wisdom and fulfillment. The central area is dominated by a large *shamsa*, a "sunburst" of brilliant color: in Islam, as in most other faiths, light was widely used as a metaphor of divine illumination. In the very center of this *shamsa* is a flowing inscription written in white letters on a gold ground: "Allah preserve his sovereignty and his authority—Muhammad Shihab al-Din Jahanshah Padshah the Ghazi." Suitably pious, Shah Jahan's name is located at the bottom of the medallion, and the divine name appears at the top, while the intervening space is occupied by the emperor's titles and a plea for divine support. From Shah Jahan's name and titles originate three figure eights, strung out from vertical letters, which bind the whole inscription together. Barely legible, it is an epigraphic

Figure 11. Seventeenth-century Mulghal Indian *ex libris* to an album made for Shah Jahan. Metropolitan Museum of Art, New York.

triumph that visually links the imperial and divine names in a manner befitting the Mughal concept of the semi-divine monarch.

### The talismanic role of script

In their content and intricate patterns these examples reflect religious and political themes pertinent to particular periods and regions. Other religious inscriptions reflected Islam's underlying unity and were extremely common throughout the Muslim world. Not only the words Allah and Muhammad, but also the *shahada* and the *bismillah* ("In the name of God, the merciful, the compassionate...") could be seen on buildings and objects from Spain to Indonesia, and they constituted some of the basic "icons" of the faith. Other key epigraphs were also used with great frequency. Perhaps most notable among them was the *Quar'an's* celebrated throne verse, the *ayat al-kursi* (ch. 2:255), a fundamental statement of divine power:

> Allah! There is no God save Him, the Alive, the Eternal. Neither slumber nor sleep overtaketh Him. Unto Him belongeth whatsoever is in the heavens and whatsoever is in the earth. Who is he that intercedeth with Him save by His leave? He knoweth that which is in front of them and that which is behind them, while they encompass nothing of His knowledge save what He will. His throne includeth the heavens and the earth, and He is never weary of preserving them. He is the Sublime, the Tremendous.

The *ayat al-kursi* performs a highly significant role in Muslim life, and its widespread visual use hints at still another dimension of Arabic script within Islam. The verse is usually recited after each of the five daily prayers, and one of the most well-known *hadith* reports that Muhammad said, "That person who repeats the *ayat al-kursi* after each prayer will gain sure entrance into paradise, and that person who says the *ayat al-kursi* as he goes to bed will earn Allah's protection for himself, his house, and his neighbor's house." The verse is also often recited as a defense against fear. Its use then would suggest that it was regarded as having talismanic quality: in fact, the verse is sometimes incised on small amulets worn around the neck.

Thus the strong, proud stallion in Figure 12 is a talisman, because its whole form—outline and interior—is composed of the *ayat al-kursi*. The verse begins at the horse's nose and proceeds along its back, hindquarters, and stomach to end at its raised right forefoot. Bridle, saddlecloth, saddle, and rider are extraneous elements, figural and not calligraphic, forming no part of the verse. But they complement it and in a way explicate its meaning: the words are turned to form a mighty stallion so that this mighty verse supports a tiny man, as Allah's

Figure 12. Stallion composed of the *Qur'an*'s *ayat al-kursi*. India. Private collection.

power upholds the lives of human beings. Orthodox Muslims might regard such a combination of figural image and religious text with disapproval but the symbolic content of this animated calligraphy is wholly appropriate.

Another instance of the talismanic power attributed to inscribed verses can be noted in the use of the *Qur'an*'s chapter *Ya Sin* (ch. 36), which particularly emphasizes Allah's power as the sole giver and preserver of life. Often recited for those who were fasting, troubled, sick, dying, or dead, its presence on a number of brass bowls from seventeenth-century India defines the objects as medicinal vessels (Figure 13). Although the verse was recited during medical treatment of those who were ill, its visual presence was also deemed efficacious, for it rendered more potent the drugs that touched it: as a result it occupies the inner surface of this vessel. On the inside are also eight lines of numbers mixed with letters and words to form compounds with cabalistic significance and presumed efficacy in restoring the sick to health. Different elements are also combined on the exterior: 12 zodiac figures; the *asma' al-husna* (or 99 beautiful names of God), the *ayat al-kursi* (and other selections from the *Qur'an*), and several popular prayers requesting divine aid. Though the incised *naskhi* style of script is not aesthetically impressive, the talismanic power of writing here functions on a more directly physical level than in Figure 12.

Figure 13. Medicinal bowl from seventeenth-century India. Private collection.

Both the *ayat al-kursi* and the chapter *Ya Sin* belong to a large body of Qur'anic and other Arabic sacred evocations known as *fada'il*, statements endowed with special virtues that brought particular blessings to those who recited them in prescribed ways. Such *fada'il* also functioned visually and tactilely: to see or touch such verses was as valuable as hearing or saying them. Spoken and written repetition was important as is demonstrated in an object from eighteenth-century India, a single sheet of paper on which is written twice the *Qur'an*'s last chapter (Figure 14):

> Say: I seek refuge in the Lord of mankind,
> The King of mankind,
> The God of mankind,
> From the evil of the sneaking whisperer,
> Who whispereth in the hearts of mankind,
> Of the jinn and of mankind.

The page is divided into five horizontal frames. In frames 1 and 5 is recorded chapter 114 in *musalsal* (linked) style, a particularly flowing and ornamental manner lending the appearance of an arabesque border. Frames 2, 3, and 4 are written in *thuluth*, a stately, monumental style. Neither is used for whole *Qur'ans*; hence this page is complete in its present form, and the chapter's inherent *fada'il* were enhanced through repetition. Here again the use of the written word in Islam parallels that of figural images of saints or deities in other faiths where icons were regarded as similarly efficacious. It should be noted, however, that many Muslims, like their Christian counterparts, regarded such uses as superstitious and improper. Ibn Khaldun, the greatest of Muslim historians, delineated with great care the talismanic ways in which words, letters, and numbers were used in fourteenth-century society but was also careful to point out that such usages ran counter to Islamic law (Rosenthal, 1967, pp. 171-227).

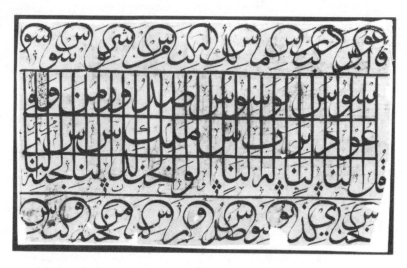

Figure 14. The *Qur'an*'s surah 114, India, eighteenth century. Private collection.


A similar kind of talismanic power was attributed to the repetition, whether written or spoken, of the *asma' al-husna*, the 99 beautiful names of God. Although not strictly icons, they served a function essentially identical to devotional images in other faiths (Welch, 1977, pp. 63-74). Literacy of the reader and legibility of the script were important but not exclusive factors, and the particular import of inscriptions was not as vital as their actual presence. Some inscriptions were, in fact, so highly ornamental that only specialists in epigraphy could read them, but any Muslim could recognize that the convoluted forms were script. Script served therefore to demonstrate the presence of Islam, making an object or a building Muslim, and establishing a sense of religious and cultural cohesiveness from North Africa to Indonesia. The strength of the written word as symbolic affirmation (Ettinghausen, 1974, pp. 297-317) is indicated by some summary information about the history of the Arabic alphabet in the twentieth century. In 1928, only four years after its creation, the Turkish republic abandoned the Arabic script, in which Turkish had been written since the Turks accepted Islam, for the roman alphabet. This move was only one part of Kemal Ataturk's determined program to separate Turkey from its Ottoman (and Islamic) past and link it more with Europe than with its Muslim neighbors. A similar awareness of the symbolic content and religious associations of Arabic script is evident in the Soviet Union which was equally interested in weakening Islam within its borders. Under the pressure of state policy Cyrillic has displaced Arabic script in the four Muslim republics of the Soviet Union. The visual symbol most central to Islam has thus been removed and, as in Turkey, only scholars and clerics use it. Because most of these languages are Turkic (of the major tongues only Tadjik is Iranian), the shift within the Turkic language group is dramatic. Until the 1920s almost every

Turkic language was written in Arabic script; 50 years later the script is used only by Turkish-speaking minorities in China, Iran, and several Arab countries. A similar shift, the result of colonialism and nationalism, can be noted in Southeast Asia where Malay and several other languages, written in Arabic script until the twentieth century, are now recorded in roman letters.

### The styles of Arabic script

Occupying the central place in Islam's visual culture before the twentieth century, Arabic script naturally developed an impressive assortment of different styles. In the hands of a master the 28 Arabic letters are a rhythmic blend of slender verticals, restful horizontals, sweeping curves, and graceful knots that can transmute script into linear music in which the balance of linguistic and pictorial cadences was a calligrapher's highest goal. As in any great art, stylistic variations abounded. Within a basic division into angular and cursive types are dozens of different styles in which specific canons detail letters' thickness, size, and curves and, allowing for the exercise of individual gifts, delineate internal relationships, proportions, and balance. Thorough command of different styles was a measure of a scribe's abilities, and knowledge of varied styles and the individual hands of their famous practitioners was a source of pride among connoisseurs. Some styles were national or regional while others were determined by the purpose that an inscription or text served. *Kufic* is a loose term, much in need of greater precision, denoting the earliest monumental style, that still carries conservative and sacrosanct associations today. It is angular, structured around straight lines and abrupt turns, as in Figure 6. It is not a flowing script, nor is it easily written, and it indicates its origins in epigraphs incised in stone. It was, however, a monumental script and apparently because of its weighty associations was used as the earliest *Qur'anic* style of script. Until the tenth century every *Qur'an* was composed in this style. It could also be used for important state inscriptions but its use was restricted almost entirely to state and faith: it would have been improper to use it for penning a love poem or for writing a mundane message. Originating in the Arab heartland and dominating early *Qur'anic* calligraphy, *Kufic* was in essence restricted to the Arabic language. With one exception in Afghanistan, neither Persian nor any other Islamic language was rendered in the Kufic style.

*Naskhi* (Figure 13) did not develop out of *Kufic* but grew simultaneously with it in a sensible dichotomy between a slowly executed monumental style and a necessarily more rapid style for use on papyrus or paper (*naskhi* in fact means "the copyist's style"). Initially *naskhi* was considered a chancery script, unsuitable for rendering *Qur'ans*. But by the tenth century attitudes had changed, and from that time *Kufic* was gradually, though never entirely, supplanted by *naskhi* and other cursive styles both for copies of the *Qur'an* and for monumental inscriptions. This major aesthetic shift was probably occasioned by the fact that the cursive forms could provide a much wider and more easily recognized series of stylistic variants.

As Islam spread and became wealthier and more sophisticated, its patrons must have desired more variety in their visual world, and *naskhi* had far more potential than *Kufic*. More than 50 cursive styles are known, and the preservation of past styles and creation of new ones was a major task for Islam's scribes.

To one of these cursive styles, *thuluth*, devolved many of the functions *Kufic* had performed. Based on a fixed proportion and moving with a slow, steady speed, its letters were used for *Qur'an* chapter headings, princely titles (Figure 7), and impressive religious epigraphs (Figures 9 and 10), as well as for architectural inscriptions. *Muhaqqaq* was a more swiftly moving style, frequently used to write entire *Qur'ans*. Some other styles were deemed unsuitable for writing scripture, however. Among them was *nasta'liq*, a fluid style of writing often likened in its forms to water currents in a stream and used for many of the finest renderings of Persian poetry after the fourteenth century. A later derivation, *shikastah*, created nervous, highly agitated letters, frequently compared to clouds broken by strong winds. Used mainly in Iran and India, it was largely restricted to poetry, letters, and documents. Special styles, like *diwani*, were developed for bureaucratic use, while the imperial *tughra* was a calligraphic form employed only for the names of rulers, particularly in the Ottoman empire. There were also regional styles, their use determined by geographic area rather than by function. Among them were *Maghribi*, restricted to North Africa, and *Bihari*, widely used in northern India (Safadi, 1978; Schimmel, 1970; Welch, 1979).

## Symbol and meaning

Script was not influenced merely by the compositional requirements of the surface on which it was written, or by the region in which it was used, or by its content and its aesthetics. It also functioned in a world of special, even esoteric, meaning. As the letter *alif* was a symbol of divine unity, so other letters acquired religious and worldly meanings. To poets the alphabet supplied appropriate metaphors (Figure 15). The roundness of the letter *mim* was like the beloved's mouth, while the combined letters *lam* and *alif* seemed to show a couple united in love. The curve of the beloved's ringlet was compared to both the *lam* and the *waw*. Thus Abu Ishaq al-Husri used the dark *lam* written on pale paper to underscore the gripping power of love: "The *lam* of that ringlet has caused my heart to drink of death. It is dark as night upon [a skin] as clear as day" (Haq, 1961, pp. 37-38). And the poet Ibn al-Khazin darkly pondered life's inequities through a comparison of the letters *alif* and *nun*: "He who acts uprightly is disappointed in his wishes, and he who acts crookedly is successful and attains his end. See the letter *alif*, it held itself up straight and missed gaining the diacritical point, which the *nun* obtained by its crookedness" (Haq, 1961, p. 212). The slender *alif* is a metaphor of the lover, upright but disappointed; the diacritical dot of the *nun* probably represents the beauty spot on the beloved's face and hence stands for the whole person of the beloved.

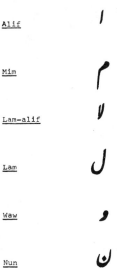

Alif

Mim

Lam-alif

Lam

Waw

Nun

Figure 15. Six letters of the Arabic alphabet in the *tal'liq* style of script. A. Welch.

Letters had more than poetic potency. Belief in their magical efficacy was as widespread as faith in the talismanic power of whole inscriptions. This attitude found its most dramatic expression in the immense body of cabalistic lore of the *Hurufis*, a mystical group that in its *'Ilm al-Huruf* (Science of Letters) gave systematic form to far earlier occult uses of the alphabet. They divided the 28 letters of the Arabic alphabet into four groups of seven letters each, corresponding to the elements of fire, air, earth, and water. Letters were combined for specific purposes: the "water" group could reduce fever, and "fire" letters increased discord or conflict. According to the *hurufis* (and other Muslims as well), the letters *alif*, *lam*, and *mim*, which begin the *Qur'an*'s chapter 2, were deemed to have healing powers. Their position at the beginning of this chapter, the longest in the *Qur'an* and the one that encapsulates most of its essential teaching, lent itself to this interpretation, and it is likely that this place of honor, as well as *hurufi* teaching, contributed to the extensive poetic use of these letters.

In the *abdjad* system researchers analyzed words (most notably those of the *asma' al-husna*) for the numerical value of their individual letters, and the numbers derived were used for magical purposes. Mystics noted that the words *Ahmad* (a common male name) and *Ahad* (divine unity) differed by only one letter, the *mim*, and thus deduced that that letter's value of 40 denoted the number of steps of mystical ascension from the human to the divine worlds. Similarly, it was perceived that the name of the most perfect of human beings, Muhammad, began with the *mim*, while the divine name, Allah, began with *alif*, the first letter of the alphabet and the equivalent of the number 1.

Figure 16. Steel plaque from the door of a tomb, Iran, seventeenth century. The Art Institute of Chicago.

From these special meanings it is apparent that script served not only this world but also the next. In tombs throughout the Muslim world the *Qur'an*'s descriptions of Paradise abound, invoking blessing and providing linguistic and pictorial images to elevate the soul. Figure 16 illustrates a steel plaque from the door of a seventeenth-century tomb in Iran. Enclosed within a curving frame and written against a delicate arabesque background is a single verse from chapter 76 of the *Qur'an*: "Reclining there upon couches, they will find there neither [heat of] a sun nor bitter cold." The short text of ten Arabic words has been divided to suit the plaque's shape and not to facilitate reading which proceeds from the upper section to the lower right, the bottom, the upper center, the middle center, and the lower left. Legibility was less important than aesthetic quality, itself closely allied to the striving for spiritual perfection. Thus teachers of calligraphy like Sultan 'Ali al-Mashhadi, emphasized that moral rectitude was an essential part of writing (Ahmad, 1959, p. 122):

> Only he who of trickery, intrigues, and hypocrisy
> Has cleansed himself, has become master in writing.
> He who knows the soul, knows that
> Purity of writing proceeds from purity of heart.
> Writing is the distinction of the pure.

By extension technical refinement of the written word could also be a patron's statement of his own soul's longing for purity and paradise.

While words or verses could serve in this way through an elegant, but

Figure 17. Silk tomb cloth, Iran, eighteenth century. Musée des Tissus, Lyon.

reasonably straightforward, rendering, they were sometimes more intricately interwoven in complex patterns based on apposite mirror images of a basic inscription. This kind of mirror-writing, known as the *muthanna* style, was frequently used for tomb covers (Figure 17), where it was considered to have special talismanic powers. Six rectangular panels on each side contain verse 13 of chapter 61 of the *Qur'an*: "Help from Allah and present victory." In each panel these six words are written in normal fashion from right to left and, facing them, the same words written in mirror-script from left to right. In the larger, pale script panels occupying the major part of the cloth is another *Qur'anic* verse (48: 1): "Lo! We have given thee a signal victory." The words "We have given" and "victory" are derived from the same root and differ here in only one, small, horizontal letter; thus their appearance is virtually identical. It is on this essential visual identity that the complexity of this calligraphy depends. Each of the segments is bounded on one side by the words "We have given" and on the other by "victory," but the latter word goes in the opposite direction so that its final vertical letter turns back towards "We have given." Thus the inscription is so composed that normally vertical letters form the very frame enclosing the other words and letters. And both opposite and above each complete segment is its mirror-image. In this central design there are, in fact, no non-calligraphic elements at all, and the letters seem to form a sturdy ladder, a metaphor of the soul's desired ascension. It is a *tour-de-force* of calligraphic complexity and brilliantly exemplifies the association of form and content central to Islamic use of the Arabic script.

## References

Ettinghausen, R. Arabic epigraphy: communication or symbolic affirmation. In D. K. Kouymjian (Ed.), *Near Eastern numismatics, iconography, epigraphy, and history*. Beirut: American University, 1974.

Moinul al-Haq, S. (Ed.), *Wafayat al-A'yan* (of Ibn Khallikan). (M. de Slane, trans.) Karachi: Pakistan Historical Society, 1961.

Pickthall, M. M. (Trans.), *The glorious Koran*. London: George Allen & Unwin, 1976.

Qadi Ahmad *Calligraphers and painters*. (V. Minorsky, trans.) Washington: Freer Gallery of Art, 1959.

Rosenthal, F. (Trans.), *The Muqadimmah* (of Ibn Khaldun). Princeton: Princeton University Press, 1967.

Safadi, Y. H. *Islamic calligraphy*. London: Thames & Hudson, 1978.

Schimmel, A. *Islamic calligraphy*. Leiden: E. J. Brill, 1970.

Welch, A. Epigraphs as icons: the role of the written word in Islamic art. In J. Gutmann (Ed.), *The image and the word: Confrontations in Judaism, Christianity, and Islam*. American Academy of Religion and the Society of Biblical Literature, Religion and the Arts Series, No. 4. Missoula: Scholars Press, 1977.

Welch A. *Calligraphy in the arts of the Muslim world*. Austin: University of Texas Press, 1979.

# Textual literacy

## Introduction

Paul A. Kolers

Patricia Wright is on the staff of the Applied Psychology Research Unit of England's Medical Research Council, and her work over the years has been a mix of theory and basic research or, better, basic research directed at and interacting with applied research. Her tutorial paper admirably emphasizes the practical applications that literacy may be designed to serve and the way that practical problems can feed back as stimulus and goad to the development of theory.

Of course, printed language serves multiple purposes. Poetry, fiction, historical descriptions, instructions—these are some of the ways that print may advise and inform the reader. Passing time, searching for information, seeking diversion, studying language—these are some of the ways that readers may relate to print. The reader's attitudes and strategies will differ markedly with the circumstances of reading even as the writer's style and craft will express themselves differently with purpose. Reading is not a monolithic process that is always executed in the same way. Wright's emphasis is upon the fact that text is used for a purpose and, therefore, that the organization and presentation of the text should reflect that purpose; moreover, she proposes usability as a new way of studying literacy and may well be right to do so.

The theme is illustrated by a study of instructional manuals designed for third world nations where literacy levels are not often very high and technical skills are equally limited. Manuals designed to show how to construct a windmill or how to make a corn-sheller are important documents, novel experiences in village life. They have not always been successful in fulfilling their role, however. Training manuals are, of course, in wide use in industrialized societies and so the principles illustrated by Wright's article should not be thought to apply only to conveying information in the special circumstances she describes. And, if not with training manuals, we are all likely to have tried to follow a list of instructions for assembling a bicycle or a chair or some other object and know well that writing good instructions is indeed a high art. Wright examines some of the components that might go into a deliberate study of usability, concentrating upon characteristics of the reader, the reader's cognitive purposes and resources, and the constraints the intended task imposes. Perhaps the practical observation she makes surprises by the need of making it in the circumstances; her analysis "has suggested that written materials are used more easily if they are designed to be compatible with the perceptual strategies, conceptual knowledge, and the information processing resources of the user." In a word, if text is to be used, it is useful to make it usable. But what makes it so is not always known.

Perception of the words making up the text is surely an important component. A classic problem in the perception of text is the means by which words are apprehended by the reader and a classic claim is that they are not apprehended letter by letter. J. M. Cattell, who supported the claim with experimental evidence about one hundred years ago, went on to say that not only were words not apprehended letter by letter, they were not apprehended piecemeal either, for he showed that a short sentence required no more time for its perception than any one of the words making it up when they were presented singly, and less time than the same sentence anagrammatized. Leslie Henderson's scholarly analysis of some of the issues surrounding the notion of "wholism" as a factor in perception of text suggests that Cattell's conclusion was premature. His claim that words were perceived as whole units fails as a strong hypothesis because it lacks a clear sense of the meaning of "whole." Henderson describes three ways that wholism might be interpreted; his conclusions about what constitutes a correct interpretation of word perception makes of reading more a task of synthesis than one in which deliberate analysis is directed at physical marks.

At a more elaborate linguistic level are the complementary papers by Shebilske and Chapman and Stokes. In both, the emphasis is upon the coherence of text, not the coherence of individual words or even of sentences, but of texts as wholes. John Chapman and Alan Stokes approached the matter by studying the influence of some parts of speech upon the interpretation students could give to texts; the main finding was a greater sensitivity (or flexibility in response) to language as age increased through the school years. The writer, who has to be much more explicit with younger children, can allow for more filling in and inference in older ones.

Wayne Shebilske studied the processes in connection with an interest—shared with Chapman and Stokes—in designing more informative and more useful textbooks. His paper reports on the use of formal behavioral measures applied to texts and shows that the behavioral are more useful than the formal. Indeed, lacking a coherent theory of readability, it would be difficult to know except by behavioral correlations which formal measures might be used appropriately. Work along the lines described, related to the usability of texts, might actually lead to such a theory.

On a different line, but clearly related to usability, is the topic of layout. Robert Waller, professionally concerned with typography, discusses some aspects of the way that layout and, particularly, punctuation, work to make a text accessible. Linguists and psychologists have not often concerned themselves with punctuation, concentrating more on the syntactic and semantic aspects of words rather independently of their punctuation. How important it is and how it can function to create syntactic and semantic realities is shown by the schoolboy puzzle of trying to make sense of "John where James had had had had had had had had had had been preferred." Proper use of commas, quotation marks, and semicolon are required to transform this gothic string into a statement about the relative merits of using the past or past perfect tenses of *to have*. So, from the smallest mark on the page to the text considered as a whole, everything seems to play a role in the interpretations made and hence to the uses to which a text can be put. Usability is what a text is about.

# Usability: The criterion for designing written information

Patricia Wright

*Usability is a function of the diverse cognitive activities involved when people use documents. Analysis of these activities can facilitate designers' decisions about the language and presentation of written, factual information. Such analysis necessarily incorporates contextual factors which will influence the interpretation of text. Analysis of usability can also provide a framework for research. The practical relevance of such research is illustrated by health manuals designed for the third world. Analysing usability has several advantages over other research and design approaches such as psycholinguistic models of comprehension and models of the reading process.*

It is being recognised more and more that there must be an improvement in the design and thereby in the comprehensibility of many kinds of written factual information (Chapanis, 1965; Ellis, 1978; Hampson, 1979). The comprehension of fiction is certainly an interesting area and one in which valuable theories are being developed (Kintsch, 1976; Mandler & Johnson, 1977). Nevertheless, the psychological processes governing the reader's interaction with factual documents may be quite different from those involved in understanding a short story. Krugg and Reddish (Note 1) give one indication of this difference by replacing the terms *readers* and *writers* by *users* and *producers*. The connotations of the conventional terms were felt to be too narrow because producing a document involves much more than merely writing it. Production includes integrating decisions about language and layout with logistic constraints such as budget limitations, deadlines, and distribution procedures. In the same way, the user of written factual information draws on a broad range of psychological resources of which "reading" is only one.

## Context, comprehension and usability

A detailed task analysis is a familiar human factors approach to equipment design (Easterby, in press). Recognition that such an analysis of cognitive demands is a necessary approach to information design is increasing only slowly (Pettu, 1979). However, exploring what cognitive resources users draw upon will lead to design improvements only if it is known how the written information can be made compatible with these cognitive requirements. The evaluation of the concept of "usability" has two components, therefore. The first is research: is the analysis of usability valuable as a research framework and does it generate research into issues which might otherwise have been overlooked? The second is design: is the concept of usability viable as an heuristic method during the production of written information?

Analyses of usability have been proposed elsewhere. For example, Clark and Clark (1977) have suggested that three stages enable a listener to utilise a spoken message: identification of the meaning of the message, integration with memory for other relevant information, and performance of an appropriate act. Although all three apply to reading factual materials, each stage is influenced by such variables as the characteristics of the readers themselves, the purpose for reading, the task constraints, and the characteristics of the text. A satisfactory design of usable written materials must deal with these contextual factors.

*Readers' characteristics*. Readers vary in reading fluency, familiarity with the subject matter, and range of cognitive abilities. Such variables influence word-identification processes, as is shown by the differences between good and poor readers in detecting letters in text (Drewnowski, 1978). Fillenbaum (1974) has shown that expectations may dominate interpretation of statements about impro-bable events. The user of written factual information often has to integrate the message in the text with information in memory. Rothkopf (1978) has proposed a mathematical model of the relation between a reader's previous knowledge of a topic and the amount learned from an instructional text. One effect of previous knowledge is to provide readers with a variety of different strategies for inte-grating the meanings of sentences as has been illustrated in studies of verbal reasoning (Quinton & Fellows, 1975). Because of the range of individual differences among readers, information about them is needed by authors.

*Reading purpose*. The tacit assumption that, apart from major variations such as skimming or reviewing, all reading is virtually the same process, is now known to be incorrect. Aaronson and Scarborough (1976) showed that people distribute their pauses differently within a sentence when reading for verbatim retention and when reading for a subsequent quiz. Samuels and Dahl (1975) demonstrated that different types of quiz also influence reading speed. People read faster when their purpose is a general overview than when it is to pick up specific factual details. Readers pause longer at material thought to be relevant to a subsequent quiz (Rothkopf & Billington, 1979). Such data imply that purpose is a major determinant of the cognitive activities in reading. Producers of written informa-tion thus need to have some idea of the user's purpose.

*Task constraints* are related to reading purposes. The constraints imposed by the task itself are related to the task reading purposes. For example, the purpose in reading a manual may be to find out how to change the brake linings of a car or how to lay out the pieces of a dress pattern on a fabric. Often the course on which the user embarks requires modification as the task progresses, however. The user may interact with the text in a pattern of question and answer ("I was going to do this, but I can't, so can I do that?"). The task may also impose constraints on the way the information is used. For example, while processing film in the darkroom it may not be possible to re-read the instructions and if hands are covered with dough it may not be easy to turn the pages of the recipe book. Clearly, an analysis of what the user is doing while reading may have an important bearing on design.

The temporal contingencies within a task can have an important bearing on how information is encoded. For example, in a sentence-picture verification task the sequence Sentence-Picture has different behavioural consequences from the sequence Picture-Sentence (Clark & Chase, 1972). Expectations about the task, particularly about what events are unlikely, is another determining factor (Wason, 1965; Wright & Threlfall, 1980). The instructions given for the task can also change the way information is encoded (Jones, 1968).

*Characterization of the text.* Texts differ in length, subject matter, density of ideas, abstractness of concepts, logical sequence, and fluency of expression, to list but a few of the more obvious factors. Gilliland (1972) schematizes twelve types of paragraph structure. There may well be others. These structures influence the reader's performance in a variety of ways. For example, the apparent length of a text may reduce people's willingness to start reading it at all. Yet fewer ideas are remembered from a précis than from an expanded text (Wason, Note 3). Materials with higher scores on readability formulae are read more slowly (Coke, 1974). This is a variation in reading speed resulting from a change in reading strategy because when the passage becomes easier the slower rate of reading continues (Rothkopf & Coatney, 1974). Lack of thematic organisation within a paragraph also slows readers down (Kieras, 1978). There are many other psycholinguistic factors which influence reading. Some of the implications of psycholinguistic research for designers of written materials have been summarized elsewhere (Broadbent, 1977; Wright, in press).

The characterization of a text is not complete if only the linguistic structure is considered. The reader's ability to use written material depends on the overall presentation and layout of the text as well. Variables range from the legibility of the print (Poulton, 1965; Tinker, 1965; Spencer, 1969) and other typographic factors (Foster, 1977; Hartley, 1978) to such adjuncts of the text as headings and summaries (Kozminsky, 1977; Hartley, Goldie, & Stein, 1979). Radical departures from prose have sometimes been found advantageous (Wason, Note 3) although the research literature has not yet clarified when and in which directions these departures should occur (Blaiwes, 1974; Kamman, 1975; Srivastava, 1978a). Waller (1977-1978) has stressed the importance of providing readers with the means of locating specific information within a text. Clearly a considerable number of presentation factors must be borne in mind when designing text.

*Coping with context.* Few people would deny that comprehension is influenced by contextual factors such as those outlined above, but the problem is how to incorporate such disparate factors within a conceptual framework which can be used to guide both design and research. By considering the psychological factors which contribute to the usability of written materials, however, it is possible to integrate contextual variables so that findings of the consequent research have strong implications for the design of written information.

*Analysing usability*

Reading begins with processes of perception and attention which may result from the user's past experience (knowing where to look) or from the specification of the reading purpose (knowing what to look for). These will be top-down, conceptually-driven cognitive processes (Bobrow & Norman, 1975). The user's perception and attention will also be influenced by bottom-up or data-driven processes generated by the text and the task environment. An analysis of the user's perceptual and attentional activities inevitably incorporates a wide range of contextual variables. They do not have to be dealt with as separate factors because they are integrated by the user's cognitive activities.

This is true also if the analysis of usability continues through other cognitive processes such as making decisions, memory (both working memory and general knowledge of the world), the linguistic processes themselves, of course, and, finally, the generation of the performance necessary to use the material successfully. The order in which readers draw upon the various cognitive processes varies from task to task and perhaps from user to user within the same task. Nevertheless, by considering these multiple cognitive processes it becomes possible to explore the cognitive demands of a wide variety of written materials. The interest in such an exploration lies in determining how successfully the usability approach generates research findings which can help predict and solve potential problems in designing written information.

*Perceptual and attentional processes.* Perceptual processes are affected by factors which can be grouped under three headings: legibility, language, and layout. Summaries are available of the research within each of these groups. Legibility research has been reviewed by Tinker (1965) and Spencer (1969); the perceptual strategies influencing the interpretation of sentences have been discussed by Bever (1970) and Clark and Clark (1977); research on various aspects of spatial layout has been summarised by Hartley (1978) who has also shown that appropriate changes to the page layout can improve the usability of documents as diverse as a college prospectus (Burnhill, Hartley, Young, & Fraser, 1975) and the motions to be taken at a Special General Meeting (Hartley & Burnhill, 1976). Similar improvements have been found with tabular materials when appropriate typographic cuing and spatial groupings are used (Wright, 1970).

These groups of factors will also affect the user's attention but there has been little research on the subject. One exception is the study by Whalley and Flemming (1975) who found that only when an illustrative figure occurs soon after being mentioned do people bother to look at it. This was true even if the illustration was on the same page or at the top of the next column and even if some of the information illustrated was provided nowhere else in the text. There is an urgent need for other research studies on presentation factors influencing the user's attention to various parts of a text.

*Decision processes.* Users of written information may make a variety of decisions while reading. The first decision may well be to ignore the instruction manual altogether and ask somebody instead (Sticht, 1972). Although technical writers understandably assume that their material will be read as intended, they may be mistaken. There is no research dealing systematically with the issue of when instructions are likely to be read and followed but some informal data suggest that the majority of users of domestic appliances fall into one of two categories. Either they feel that the equipment is so familiar that there is no need to read any accompanying instructions or they feel that misuse of the appliance could have such dire consequences that they would prefer to be "trained" by someone else rather than learn from an instruction booklet (Wright, in press).

Decisions are important when tabulated arrays are being used. Here the location of a specific cell requires that decisions be made about the information in the row or column headings of the table. Wright (1977) has shown that for a table with a given number of cells, the more decisions which must be made, the slower is the locating of a specific cell. Making a series of four binary decisions takes longer than making two decisions each among four alternatives. For some subject matters the number of decisions may be fixed. For others, the designer may be able to provide higher order groupings within the table to reduce the number of decisions that the user need make.

In completing a form, decisions must often be made about what information is really wanted. It may be linguistically a simple task to understand that the question concerns last week's income. The problem is whether or not to include the winnings from the office sweepstake, the money from selling vegetables from the garden, or the insurance annuity which fell due. Design solutions might include rephrasing the question or amplifying it elsewhere. There seems to be no research available on making such decisions and it is a frequent source of difficulty (Krugg & Reddish, Note 1). Decisions about which question to complete next may even have to be made. The dividing lines between decision processes and other cognitive activities are not always clear. When the user of a document decides to represent the negative rather than the positive attributes of an array (Wason, 1965) or decides to accept a command instruction verbatim rather than generating a simpler paraphrase (Jones, 1968) it is perhaps a moot point if these decisions are really separable from perceptual or linguistic processes. The label is probably far less important than an awareness of the cognitive requirements of the user, however.

*Memory processes*. Three aspects of memory can influence the user's interaction with written information. One is the user's general knowledge on which he or she will base suppositions about both the structure and the content of written material. There are advantages in presenting written information in a format compatible with the user's conceptual structures. For example, Barnard, Morton, Long, and Ottley (1977) showed that, if a list is subdivided into familiar categories such as fish, flowers, fruit, items are found faster than when presented in a single alpha-beticised list. Research on the user's conceptual structures is, therefore, a necessary prerequisite for designers.

A second aspect is working memory (Baddeley, 1976). The interpretation both of language and of layout may be subject to its limitations. Syntactically complex constructions such as disjunctions (either ... or) may make heavy demands on working memory (Trabasso, Rollins, & Shaughnessy, 1971), as may certain kinds of questions on forms, particularly when presented in a matrix where the queries in the column headings apply to a variety of items listed on the left of the page. People tend to work along each row in turn, dealing with the entire series of questions on every row and inevitably trying to remember the questions rather than re-reading them each time. Errors result, of course, twice as many in fact as when the row and column information is interchanged (Wright & Barnard, 1978). With a revised spatial layout each question was interpreted once only and then applied to all the items along the row.

Working memory is involved when people use matrix structures, even when simply looking up information in a table. The user must remember which column has been selected while finding the appropriate row. The memory load is reduced if the selections are nested within one spatial dimension and the table is then easier to use (Wright, 1977).

The third aspect is that of getting new material into long-term memory. Although there is a sizable research literature on verbal learning, very little seems to have direct implications for the design of memorable written materials. The contrast between performance in laboratory studies and in reality is illustrated in a study of compliance with examination rubrics. Psycholinguistic studies suggest that instructions which are easy to understand are easy to remember but it seems that in some practical contexts they may be just as easy to forget. With the instruction to "Answer ten of the following questions" more attempted the wrong number of questions than with the linguistically more complex: "Answer ten of the following questions doing not more than three from any one section." These findings can be seen as consistent with predictions made from a depth of processing model of retention (Craik & Lockhart, 1972) but, as Baddeley (1978) has pointed out, the absence of a metric for depth of processing often makes it difficult to generate firm predictions from this model.

*Response processes.* The analysis of usability inevitably continues to the point at which users achieve their objectives in consulting the written material. For example, the user's cognitive activity relating to some tabular displays will continue beyond the location of a cell value. If the user is trying to find out if it is cheaper to fly to Toronto with airline A rather than airline B, comparative judgments among cell values will be involved. Psycholinguistic research has shown an asymmetric difficulty of many comparatives (Clark, 1969). A similar difficulty is found in interpreting numerical tables. It is possible to decide more accurately if critical values are "more than" tabulated amounts than if they are "less than" (Wright & Barnard, 1975). Here the analysis of usability draws attention to the existence of psycholinguistic factors in what appears superficially to be a purely numerical task.

When the user's objective is the completion of a form, there is considerable evidence that constraints on how the answers are recorded can impair performance (Wright, 1979). For example, in one study it was found that people could cope with a complex response code when the questions were easy. They could also answer difficult questions if the response requirements were simple. But the combination of difficult questions and complex response codes produced errors (Wright, Aldrich, & Wilcox, 1977). Even the familiar instruction to delete what does not apply is cognitively more demanding than responding to the item which does apply (Barnard, Wright, & Wilcox, 1979).

To answer questions sucessfully depends also on the relationship between the way the information is expressed in the question and the way it is represented in the mind of the respondent. For example, passive questions are usually more difficult to answer than active, although not if the information being queried has been represented with greater focus on the object than on the agent (Wright, 1969). Such representations may result from task instructions, the temporal characteristics of the task, or the thematic structure of the text.

Compatibility factors are also important when verbal instructions are being followed. For example, when the event requiring some action has been explicitly mentioned in the instruction, responses are faster than when inferential processes are necessary. In some tasks in which an event $X$ occurred, an instruction having a double negative (do not ... unless $X$) received a faster response than an instruction with only one negative (do not ... if $Y$) (Wright, 1977). When the critical event was $Y$, response to the double negative was slower than to a single negative, as would be expected from psycholinguistic theories of sentence complexity (Carpenter & Just, 1975).

There is nothing new in these notions of compatibility with information in memory and with other presented information. They are closely related to such concepts as "congruence" (Clark, 1969). Their relevance to answering questions or following instructions is pointed out here in order to illustrate the way in which an analysis of usability will force a consideration of contextual variables without which it can be difficult to draw valid inferences from the research literature. Research generated by a usability analysis is much more likely to retain its validity when applied to practical problems.

*Achieving usability*

The analysis of usability has suggested that written materials are used more easily if they are designed to be compatible with the perceptual strategies, the conceptual knowledge, and the information processing resources of the user. The problem is how to achieve such design, how to convince producers of written materials to consider in detail the usability of those materials.

The production of a specific category of documents illustrates one way in which usability can assist designers. Manuals and instructional texts are particularly suitable for discussion because they encompass a diversity of types of communication—explanations, instructions, tables, and sometimes questions. Although the points raised are intended to illustrate the general application of usability as a design heuristic, the discussion will focus on health manuals produced for the third world. Some are concerned with intermediate technology, others with primary health care. Often the two are related because certain equipment may be necessary to provide adequate medical aid. Health care increasingly is involving part-time workers from the village level (Arole, 1977; Morley, 1977). Such workers receive little formal training, probably less than 100 hours (Jelliffe & Jelliffe, 1977), but may be given manuals to supplement the training.

The design of such manuals needs to satisfy a number of potentially conflicting criteria. The information must be medically sound yet comprehensible to someone with a limited education. Moreover, the language of the text may not be the first language of the health worker (King, King, & Martodipoero, 1977). It seems essential to give adequate consideration to the needs of such users but the limitations of both time and budget often necessitate a compromise between the ideal and the barely adequate. To achieve satisfactory compromises, the producers of written materials need to have at least three different classes of information about readers, textual presentation, and the adequacy of the draft text.

*Finding out about the readers.* The general characteristics of village health workers are often known. For example, the workers described by Morley (1977) were chosen by the community for their willingness to serve the village group rather than on the basis of education. Usually they have gained the respect of the village through their skills as farmers or parents, and their remuneration as health workers will depend on decisions of the villagers. The manual writer needs to know much more about the readers, however, because health manuals can serve a variety of different functions. Godwin (1977) defines three kinds of manual: a *work* manual which comprises procedures to be followed by the health worker, a *reference* manual which is a repository of medical information which the health worker consults from time to time when problems arise, and a *training* manual. Srivastava (1978a) subdivides the last into manuals intended to "self-train" the reader and those to assist the health worker in teaching fellow villagers about primary health care.

Different texts are best suited to these different functions. For example, the conventional medical grouping by diseases may be satisfactory for the reference manual but the work manual is more helpful if it groups by symptoms because symptoms are what confront the health worker. A work manual may need to be smaller and more portable than a reference manual and a training manual may need to have much larger illustrations if it is to be used when talking to groups of villagers.

Techniques for discovering what the users want from a manual range from informal conversations to formal surveys. Where comparable manuals already exist they may be surveyed as well. Survey techniques can also be used to establish if certain words are understood and if the worker's previous experience in health care has led to any presuppositions which may need explicit correction in the manual or, alternatively, can be used constructively by the writer. Srivastava (1978a) comments that one Indian health manual does not take sufficient account of the indigenous systems of medicine. In the end, however, if the village health workers feel that consulting a manual in front of the patient undermines the patient's confidence and lessens their own status, they will not use the manual no matter how carefully it has been designed.

*Finding out how to present the text.* Decisions about the order of sections within a manual can be made in the light of information obtained about readers and their intended use of the text. Other design considerations emerge when anticipated cognitive interaction with the text is examined. A first consideration is that the user will want to find things in the manual. The designer must, therefore, provide adequate access structures such as headings, coloured pages, indexes, or reference keys in the margins of the page. The choice may depend on the user's familiarity with the alternative schemes.

A work manual needs to use presentation factors in such a way that there will be only a minimal risk of users losing their place in the procedural sequence and inadvertently missing a step. Figure 1 illustrates how changing the layout can make instructions easier to follow. There are a number of other solutions to the problem of re-sequencing (linking arrows, for example) but no research data to assist the designer.

A reference manual may need an appropriate cross-referencing system and it certainly needs a well-designed contents page. Guidelines sometimes recommend that the distance between titles and page numbers should be small to

192

EXPERIMENT TO SHOW THAT AIR CAN SUPPORT A COLUMN OF WATER

Air can support things. You can
carry out an experiment to show that
air can support a column of water.
You will need a tumbler, a piece
of cardboard and water.

Method

1 Fill a glass tumbler with water
right up to the brim.

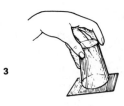

2 Slide a piece of cardboard over
the top of the glass so that it
touches the water. Do not allow
any bubbles of air to creep in.

3 Turn the tumbler upside down
holding the card against the glass.
Take your hand away from the card.
If you do this carefully, the water
will remain in the tumbler. It will
not fall out because it is supported
by the air pressure below.

EXPERIMENT TO SHOW THAT AIR CAN SUPPORT A COLUMN OF WATER

Air can support things.   You can
carry out an experiment to show that
air can support a column of water.
You will need a tumbler, a piece
of cardboard and water.

Method

1  Fill a tumbler with water up to the brim.

2  Slide a piece of card over the top of the glass
so that it touches the water.
Do not allow air bubbles to creep in.

3  Turn the tumbler upside down holding the card against the glass.
Take your hand away from the card.
If you do this carefully, the water will remain in the tumbler.
It will not fall out because it is supported by
the air pressure below.

Figure 1. Variations in the spatial layout of procedural instructions. At the top are the
original instructions; below is a revision proposed by Hartley. (Courtesy James Hartley,
1978.)

| | |
|---|---|
| 3 | General Rules for Copy Preparation |
| 3.1 | General instructions |
| 3.2 | Standard page |
| 3.2.1 | Size |
| 3.2.2 | Typing |
| 3.3 | Headings |
| 3.4 | Sections, sub-sections |
| 3.5 | Footnotes |
| 3.6 | Cross references |
| 3.7 | Quotations |
| 3.8 | Figures and tables |
| 3.8.1 | Artwork |
| 3.8.2 | Tables |
| 3.8.3 | Captions |
| 3.9 | Spelling |
| 3.9.1 | ize/ise |
| 3.9.2 | Spellings to note |
| 3.9.3 | Ampersand (&) |
| 3.9.4 | Hyphens |
| 3.10 | Punctuation |
| 3.10.1 | Full stop (full point)/abbreviations |
| 3.10.2 | Parentheses |
| 3.10.3 | Comma |
| 3.10.4 | Quotation marks |
| 3.10.5 | Dash (em rule) |
| 3.10.6 | Omissions (ellipsis) |
| 3.11 | Capitals |
| 3.12 | Numerals |
| 3.12.1 | Decimal point |
| 3.12.2 | Dates |
| 3.12.3 | Time |
| 3.12.4 | Percentage in descriptive text |
| 3.12.5 | Page references |
| 3.13 | Italics/bold type |
| 3.13.1 | Titles |
| 3.13.2 | Foreign words and phrases |
| 3.14 | References |
| 3.14.1 | Text reference |
| 3.14.2 | Book |
| 3.14.3 | Journal |
| 3.14.4 | Government document |
| 3.14.5 | Open University references |
| 3.15 | SI units (The International System of Units) |

Figure 2. A contents page where the layout obscures the most important section headings (Courtesy Robert Waller, 1977.)

reduce errors in reading. The need for sensitive interpretation of such advice is illustrated in Figure 2 where, to reduce the gap between section numbers and page numbers, the section numbers have been vertically aligned on the right. Prominence is thus given to the sections with the longest section numbers (3.8.1) although they are the minor subsections within the chapter. The user has to work to discover where and what the major subdivisions are. Considering what the user does with the written information creates an awareness which avoids such problems. There is no substitute for careful evaluation of design options.

If a working manual is being used as a diagnostic tool it may require pictures or algorithms which may well differ from the illustrations needed in a training manual. Srivastava (1978a) reports that, when a passage from an Indian health manual was presented as a tabular array, the information was used more accurately than when it was presented either in flow-chart form or in the prose of the original text. It is not known if this was due to some special characteristics of the subject matter or to the particular details of the flow-chart. The issues relating to selection among such alternatives have had very little research.

Writers sometimes describe procedures with little consideration for the limitations under which users are working, as is illustrated by the corn-sheller in

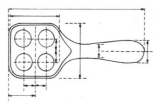

(a) The detailed specification (measurements have been omitted)

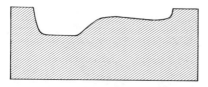

(b) The template accompanying the instruction manual

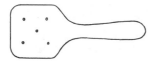

(c) An alternative template showing entire shape and centre
     points for drilling

Figure 3. Alternative approaches to presenting technical information. Sections (a) and (b) require much greater conceptual understanding by the user than does section (c). (Courtesy G. S. Pinson, Note 8.)

Figure 3. During construction of the corn-sheller the user must make decisions about the overall size and thickness of wood to use, where to make the holes (which involves many further decisions about taking measurements and marking the wood), shaping the handle, and what to do if the completed sheller seems to be the wrong size. It would obviously help if the user were assisted in making such decisions. The booklet provides the technical specifications in section (a) and a plastic silhouette of the shape in section (b), but how much more usable might the information have been if the template shown in section (c) had been provided. Again it would seem that a lack of awareness of the user's cognitive activity has meant that a problem in design has been overlooked. Jenkins (1976) has pointed out that textbook writers often use a formal, impersonal style when a friendly, personal approach would be more helpful to the reader. In some cultures the variation in style, or linguistic code, may produce a distinct separation between the language used by villagers and that used by qualified medical practitioners to talk about the same health problems (Srivastava, 1978a). One advantage of recruiting village health workers is that they may translate. But the problem of what language to use in the health manual remains. An ingenious solution has been put forward by Godwin (personal communication) who suggests that cartoon dialogue might be introduced into a health manual to create a plausible context for the local language. In this way a health worker would know what questions to ask the mother of a sick infant. The instruction to "enquire about nutritional habits" may require too much translation by the health worker to be practical.

Authors of manuals may be able to draw on the findings of psycholinguistic research if they are readily available through summaries or guidelines (Hartley, 1978). Unfortunately, this research has often studied reaction only to single sentences, but problems of comprehension arise at the level of the relationships among propositions within and across paragraphs. Srivastava (1978b) found logically invalid relationships which may have occurred in part because the manual had been translated from English into Hindi. In some places it appeared that Hindi words and phrases had been fitted into the sentence pattern of English in violation of Hindi syntax. To avoid such problems it is generally recommended that translators should translate into their native language.

In a training manual, it is often helpful to provide the reader with an explicit statement of the objectives in each section of the text. They may be presented in a formal list or in a more informal discursive style (Jenkins, 1976). They may be supplemented by questions, thereby enabling the reader to monitor his own progress through the manual. Jenkins lists several advantages in the judicious use of self-assessment questions, ranging from checking that readers have fully grasped a new concept to dividing the material into small manageable sections to encourage readers by showing them that they can use their knowledge. King et al. (1977) has reported that the draft of a health manual distributed in Indonesia was ignored by health workers until an associated set of multiple choice questions was circulated.

Retention of the information in training manuals can be improved by various mnemonic techniques. The provision of mnemonic retrieval cues, for the retinal location and chromatic function of rod and cone receptors, in an introductory psychology text is one instance (Lindsay & Norman, 1972). Hendrickse (1977) commented that even though medical students may forget the biochemistry involved in fluid and electrolyte therapy they remember how to treat diarrhoea and vomiting once they have heard this doggerel:

> Babies who have D. and V.
> Shrivel up and fail to wee.
> When this happens, then we oughta
> Fill them up with salt and water.

The doggerel continues through another three verses dealing with other aspects of the diagnosis and treatment of fluid and electrolyte disturbances. Although this particular example deals with medical treatment beyond the stage of primary health care, it illustrates one advantage of considering the usability of the material. Writers who try to make their material memorable, rather than placing the responsibility on the student to remember it, look for design solutions from a perspective not perceived by other writers.

Godwin (1977) has pointed out that the instructions in a manual need to be checked in relation to reality. If a piece of apparatus is meant to have a particular set of colour-coded indicators it is important that the writer checks that it does. Moreover, handling the apparatus makes it less likely that the writer will omit steps considered too obvious to mention. An instruction to "replace the lid" does not imply that the lid should be locked tightly in position. Godwin suggests that one procedure for writing a work manual is to ask repeatedly: "What has to be done next?" The answer can then be given as an explicit procedure to be followed.

Reference and training manuals may also need to indicate how best to make use of them. If ancillary or illustrative material is provided in boxed inserts within the text, an explanation must be given at the outset. It can be hazardous to rely on the chance that the reader will discover that the material is a valuable summary or an expendable frill.

*Finding out if the text is adequate for readers' use*. In spite of the effort made by a writer to find out about his readers and how to present the text, there is still a need to assess the adequacy of the draft document. Wright (1979) has discussed several approaches to pilot-testing a document . These range from critical evaluation of the draft by another experienced writer (here the provision of stated objectives within the manual can be of great assistance to the critic), to a simulation of the situation in which the manual will be used or, indeed, field trials where feasible. The purpose of pretesting a manual is to revise it and any revisions need pre-testing as well.

Pretesting draft documents is a means of discovering if a minimal level of usability has been attained. Fortunately, the need for evaluating health programs is being more often appreciated (Ifekwunigwe, 1977; Jelliffe & Jelliffe, 1977) and evaluating health manuals is one part of this. Even those producing texts on intermediate technology have found pilot testing valuable. For example, a wall chart was included in a booklet on fibre dyeing when its authors found that turning pages was difficult when they were up to their elbows in dye (Canning, Jarman, & Mykoluk 1977). The effectiveness of the illustrations must be tested as well (Sinaiko, 1975). Simulating the health worker's task enables simultaneous evaluation of the effects of the relevant contextual variables. It is easy to overlook the possibility that three hands may be needed to carry out certain procedures. The approach suggested here, of trying to analyse the cognitive activities of the user while he is using the manual, is intended to reduce the number of such oversights.

*Alternatives to usability*

The preceding discussion on achieving usability has illustrated that it is an heuristic rather than a procedural algorithm. It does not provide a sequence of steps for arriving at a design solution but draws attention to the variety of contextual factors which need to be integrated when making decisions for design. The rigour with which these decisions are made and the care with which the necessary classes of information are obtained will vary in relation to the kind of document being produced. It may be unrealistic to think that a single individual designer could be proficient in the diverse skills needed to write well, have a good sense of graphic design, organise projects to collect information about users, examine the research literature, and devise pilot-testing schemes. If so, a team approach should be adopted as, for example, in the work currently being done in the United States on the Document Design Project. There is a growing realisation that designing effective written materials is not an armchair exercise. Nevertheless, to those on limited budgets, design tools such as readability formulae can appear more tractable, quicker, and cheaper than trying to wrestle with a broad concept such as usability.

*Readability formulae.* Since the early 1920s there have been many attempts to devise procedures for estimating if a given text would be understood by a particular group of readers (Lively & Pressey, 1923). These procedures have often incorporated estimates of sentence length (words per sentence) and vocabulary load (frequency of polysyllabic words) into a single readability formula (Flesch, 1948; Gunning, 1952; McLaughlin, 1969). The shortcomings of the formulae have been pointed out by, among others, Bormuth (1966), Klare (1976), Macdonald-Ross (1979), and Rothkopf (1976). Perhaps the most serious defect is that some of the materials which score well may still be difficult to understand. This criticism applies even to formulae which take into account the reading ability of the user, for instance, the cloze test (Taylor, 1953). Modern approaches based on an analysis of the propositional structure of text have a great deal more sophistication (Kintsch, 1976). These approaches tend to be concerned primarily with fictional materials. Consequently they can ignore the many contextual factors so influential for users of non-fiction. It is central to the notion of usability that there is no characterization of the text itself which will predict how easily it can be used.

As one final illustration, consider the work on flow-charts and other alternatives to prose. It has been shown that, although the content and typographic communication of the material may remain constant in different task environments, and although the readers and reading purposes may remain the same, slight changes in the complexity of the task environment can produce great changes in the relative usability of different presentation styles (Wright & Reid, 1973). Therefore, a metric applied only to the written materials cannot possibly provide an adequate assessment of usability.

*Models of the reading process*. Another alternative to the present approach is based on models of "the reading process" (Mackworth, 1971). The two approaches are not incompatible but the reader's interaction with written information is considered from two very different perspectives. In some senses the present approach is scaled larger. Certainly it encompasses more cognitive activity relating to reading than do models which focus on how the meaning of a text is derived from the orthographic characters on the page. There is clearly a need to provide an account of that interpretive process; in addition the notion of usability leads one to ask if the interpretative process is always the same or if it might be qualitatively different on different occasions. For example, it has been suggested above that readers of manuals often maintain a dialogue with the written materials. Teaching students how to ask the questions for such a dialogue has improved their performance using instructional texts (Larkin & Reif, 1976). The implication is that the students are interpreting the text in a qualitatively different way after tuition. The change may occur at the level of attentional selectivity but not all models of the reading process seem to have space for such changes. Even those that do are unlikely to be useful for designing written materials because that was never their purpose. Similar comments have been made about the difficulties of deriving guidelines for teaching reading from models of the reading process (Marcel, 1978).

*Psycholinguistic models*. Clark and Clark (1977) have studied how listeners use the messages they hear and, in addition to the three stages outlined earlier, have put forward three principles. The first is the reality principle: listeners interpret sentences in a way that assumes the speaker is generating a message which is logical, has meaning, and relates to a known world. The second is the co-operative principle, based on the notions of Grice (1967): listeners interpret sentences in a way that assumes the speaker is generating a message which is adequately informative, true, relevant, and clear. The third is the congruence principle: listeners search for information in memory, particularly for target propositions, which matches the message generated by the speaker.

     These three principles in no way conflict with the notion of usability presented here. Indeed, the earlier reference to compatibility between the structure of the message and the requirements of the user can be seen as closely relating to the congruence principle. The co-operative principle explains why readers may be slow to realise that some vital information is missing from the text because, like listeners, they assume that the message is adequately informative.

     However, these three principles were not intended to generate guidelines for designing messages. It is true that they can be used for this but only to a limited extent. Usable messages will be those which conform to the principles. The restriction to speaker-listener interactions inevitably means that presentation factors must be considered separately from the language of the text. This can be a disadvantage because the design for one will often affect that of the other. The analysis of usability enables language and layout to be considered together. Furthermore, by trying to map the cognitive activities of the user through to the general characteristics of human information processing, rather than considering them as related exclusively to language, it is possible to draw on a very wide range of findings in the research literature.

*Advantages of usability*. Two remaining characteristics distinguish the usability approach from many others. One is the ecological validity of the research it generates. Because the objective of a usability analysis is to improve a particular written communication, the starting point for any research is necessarily a real problem with the relevant contextual factors clearly apparent. Other approaches sometimes achieve experimental purity at the cost of practical relevance (Macdonald-Ross, 1979; Pikulski, 1978).

The second distinguishing characteristic of usability is its applicability to a wide variety of written materials. To illustrate what was meant by analysing the cognitive abilities of the user, examples were drawn from materials as diverse as single sentence command instructions and lengthy structures such as manuals and textbooks, from the explicit question-and-answer dialogue of application forms to the implicit linguistic factors determining the usability of numerical tables. Sticht (1978) has argued for the necessity of developing the concept of literacy to encompass a broader range of literacy tasks. Usability may offer a framework within which this is possible. Certainly the notion of a dialogue between user and text is not irrelevant when the user is sitting at a keyboard and the written information is generated via some soft copy display.

It remains to be seen if usability can be sharpened sufficiently to make it both a constructive design tool and a fruitful research approach. Undoubtedly it raises certain kinds of questions about design options. The findings from such applied research may in turn raise issues for those investigating basic psychological processes (Wright, 1978). The findings of basic research may subsequently enable the previous design solutions to be refined and, in this way, usability may promote a two-way interaction between pure and applied researchers.

**Reference notes**
1. Krug, R. E., & Reddish, J. C. *Research planning report No. 1*. American Institute for Research with Carnegie-Mellon and Siegal and Gale, 1978.

2. Waller, R. *Notes on transforming*. Institute of Educational Technology, The Open
   University, Milton Keynes, U.K., 1977-1978.
3. Wason, P. C. *Psychological aspects of negation*. Communications Research Centre,
   University College, London, 1962.
4. Wright, P. Strategy and tactics in designing forms. In R. Easterby & H. Zwaga
   (Eds.), *Visual presentation of information*. London: Wiley, in press.

## References

Aaronson, D., & Scarborough, H. S. Performance theories for sentence coding:
    Some quantitative evidence. *Journal of Experimental Psychology*, 1976, *2*,
    56-70.
Arole, R. S. India: the comprehensive rural health project, Jamkhed. In D. B.
    Jelliffe & E. F. P. Jelliffe (Eds.), *Community action family nutrition pro-
    grammes*. Proceeding of a joint IUNS/UNICEF/ICMR working confer-
    ence at the National Insitute of Nutrition, Hyderabad, India. New Delhi:
    Aruna Printing Press, 1977.
Baddeley, A. D. *The psychology of memory*. New York: Basic Books, 1976.
Baddeley, A. D. The trouble with levels: a re-examination of Craik and Lockhart's
    framework for memory research. *Psychological Review*, 1978, *85*, 139-152.
Barnard, P. J., Morton, J., Long, J., & Ottley, E. A. Planning menus for displays:
    some effects of their structure and content on user performance. In
    *Displays for man machine systems*, Institute of Electrical Engineers Confer-
    ence publication, 1977, *150*, 130-133.
Barnard, P. J., Wright, P., & Wilcox, P. Effects of response instructions and
    question style on the ease of completing forms. *Journal of Occupational
    Psychology*, 1979, *52*, 209-226.
Bever, T. G. The cognitive basis for linguistic structures. In R. J. Hayes (Ed.),
    *Cognition and development of language*. New York: John Wiley & Sons,
    1970.
Blaiwes, A. A. Formats for presenting procedural instructions. *Journal of Applied
    Psychology*, 1974, *59*, 683-686.
Bobrow, D. G., & Norman, D. A. Some principles of memory schemata. In D. G.
    Bobrow and A. M. Collins (Eds.), *Representation and understanding*. New
    York: Academic Press, 1975.
Bormuth, J. Readability: A new approach. *Reading Research Quarterly*, 1966, *1*,
    79-132.
Broadbent, D. E. Language and ergonomics. *Applied Ergonomics*, 1977, *8*, 15-18.
Burnhill, P., Hartley, J., Young, M., & Fraser, S. The typography of college
    prospectuses. In L. Evans and J. Leedham (Eds.), *Aspects of educational
    technology* (Vol. IX). London: Kogan Page, 1975.
Canning, A. J., Jarman, C. G., & Mykoluk, S. Pad-batch dyeing of plant fibres.

Tropical Products Institute, *Rural Technology Guide 2*. London: Her Majesty's Stationery Office, 1977.

Carpenter, M. A., & Just, P. A. Sentence comprehension: a psycholinguistic processing model of verification. *Psychological Review*, 1975, *82*, 45-73.

Chapanis, A. Words, words, words. *Human Factors*, 1965, *7*, 1-17.

Clark, H. H. Linguistic processes in deductive reasoning. *Psychological Review*, 1969, *76*, 387-404.

Clark, H. H., & Chase, W. G. On the process of comparing sentences against pictures. *Cognitive Psychology*, 1972, *3*, 472-517.

Clark, H. H., & Clark, E. V. *Psychology and language*. New York: Harcourt, Brace, Jovanovich, Inc., 1977.

Coke, E. U. The effects of readability on oral and silent reading rates. *Journal of Experimental Psychology*, 1974, *66*, 406-409.

Craik, F. I. M., & Lockhart, R. S. Levels of processing: a framework for memory research. *Journal of Verbal Learning and Verbal Behavior*, 1972, *11*, 671-684.

Drewnowski, A. Detection errors on the word *the*: Evidence for the acquisition of reading levels. *Memory & Cognition*, 1978, *6*, 403-409.

Easterby, R. Tasks, processes, and information display design. In R. Easterby & H. Zwaga (Eds.), *Visual presentation of information*. London: Wiley, in press.

Ellis, K. We shouldn't have to fight to understand our rights. *Good Housekeeping*, 1978, *113*, 57.

Fillenbaum, S. Pragmatic normalization: Further results for some conjunctive and disjunctive sentences. *Journal of Experimental Psychology*, 1974, *102*, 574-578.

Flesch, R. A new readability yardstick. *Journal of Applied Psychology*, 1948, *32*, 221-233.

Foster, J., & Coles, F. An experimental study of typographic cuing in printed text. Ergonomics 1977, *20*, 57-66. *Readability*. London: Hodder and Stoughton, 1972.

Godwin, P. Communication. In D. B. Jelliffe & E. F. P. Jelliffe (Eds.), *Community action family nutrition programmes*. Proceeding of a joint IUNS/UN-ICEF/ICMR working conference at the National Insitute of Nutrition, Hyderabad, India. New Delhi: Aruna Printing Press, 1977.

Grice, H.P. Logic and conversation. In P. Cole & J.L. Morgan (Eds.), *Syntax and semantics Vol. 3: Speech acts*. New York: Seminar Press, 1975.

Gunning, R. *The technique of clear writing*. New York: McGraw Hill, 1952.

Hampson, R. D.H.S.S.'s private language. *New Society*, 1979, 47, 19-20.

Hartley, J. *Designing instructional text*. London: Kogan Page, 1978.

Hartley, J., & Burnhill, P. Exploration in space: a critique of the typography of BPS publications. *Bulletin of the British Psychological Society*, 1976, *29*, 97-107.

Hartley, J., & Burnhill, P. Fifty guidelines for improving instructional text. *Programmed Learning and Educational Technology*, 1977, *14*, 65-73.

Hartley, J., Goldie, M., & Steen, L. The role and position of summaries: Some issues and data. *Educational Review*, 1979, *31*, 59-65.

Hendrickse, R. G. Paediatrics. In D. A. J. Tyrrell, D. P. Burbitt, and W. Henderson (Eds.), *Technologies for rural health*. London: The Royal Society, 1977.

Ifekwunigwe, A. E. Evaluation. In D. B. Jelliffe & E. F. P. Jelliffe (Eds.), *Community action family nutrition programmes*. Proceeding of a joint IUNS/UNICEF/ ICMR working conference at the National Insitute of Nutrition, Hyderabad, India. New Delhi: Aruna Printing Press, 1977.

Jelliffe, D. B., & Jelliffe, E. F. P. (Eds.), *Community action family nutrition programmes*. Proceeding of a joint IUNS/UNICEF/ICMR working conference at the National Insitute of Nutrition, Hyderabad, India. New Delhi: Aruna Printing Press, 1977.

Jenkins, J. *Editing distance teaching texts*. Cambridge, England: International Extension College, 1976.

Jones, S. Instructions, self-instructions and performance. *Quarterly Journal of Experimental Psychology*, 1968, *20*, 74-78.

Kamman, R. The comprehensibility of printed instructions and the flow-chart alternative. *Human Factors*, 1975, *17*, 183-191.

Kieras, D. E. Good and bad structure in simple paragraphs: effects on apparent theme, reading time and recall. *Journal of Verbal Learning and Verbal Behavior*, 1978, *17*, 13-28.

King, M.H., King, F.M.A., & Martopodipoera, S. Health microplanning: a systems approach to appropriate technology. In D.A.J. Tyrrell, D.P. Burkitt, & W. Henderson (Eds.), *Technologies for rural health*. London: The Royal Society, 1977.

Kintsch, W. Memory for prose. In C. N. Cofer (Ed.), *The structure of human memory*. San Francisco: W. H. Freeman, 1976.

Klare, G. R. A second look at the validity of readability formulas. *Journal of Reading Behaviour*, 1976, *8*, 129-152.

Kozminsky, E. Altering comprehension: the effect of biasing titles on text comprehension. *Memory & Cognition*, 1977, *5*, 482-490.

Larkin, J. H., & Reif, F. Analysis and teaching of a general skill for studying scientific text. *Journal of Educational Psychology*, 1976, *68*, 431-440.

Lindsay, P. H., & Norman, D. A. *Human information processing*. London: Academic Press, 1972.

Lively, B. A., & Pressey, S. L. A method for measuring the "vocabulary burden" of textbooks. *Educational Administration and Supervision*, 1923, *9*, 389-398.

Macdonald-Ross, M. Language in texts: a review of research relevant to the design of curricular materials. In L. J. Shulman (Ed.), *Review of Research in Education* (Vol. 6). Itasca, Ill.: Peacock, 1979.

Mackworth, J. F. Some models of the reading process: learners and skilled readers. In F. B. Davis (Ed.), *The literature of research on reading, with emphasis on models*. New Brunswick, N. J.: Rutgers State University, 1971.

Mandler, J. M., & Johnson, N. S. Remembrance of things parsed: story structure and recall. *Cognitive Psychology*, 1977, *9*, 111-151.

Marcel, A. J. Prerequisites for a more applicable psychology of reading. In M. M. Gruneberg, P. E. Morris, & R. N. Sykes (Eds.), *Practical aspects of memory*. London: Academic Press, 1978.

McLaughlin, H. Smog grading—a new readability formula. *Journal of Reading*, 1969, *22*, 639-646.

Morley, D. Organization of paediatric care. In D. A. J. Tyrrell, D. P. Burkitt, & W. Henderson (Eds.), *Technologies for rural health*. London: The Royal Society, 1977.

Pettu, M. Making a match between man and machine. *International Management*, 1979, September, 55-58.

Pinson, G. S. A wooden hand-held maize sheller, Tropical Products Institute, *Rural Technology Guide 1*. London: Her Majesty's Stationery Office, 1977.

Pikulski, J. J. Translating research in perception and reading into practice. In F. B. Murray & J. J. Pikulski (Eds.), *The acquisition of reading*. Baltimore: University Park Press, 1978.

Poulton, E. C. Letter differentiation and rate of comprehension in reading. *Journal of Applied Psychology*, 1965, *49*, 358-362.

Quinton, G., & Fellows, B. Perceptual strategies in the solving of three-term series problems. *British Journal of Psychology*, 1975, *66*, 69-78.

Rothkopf, E. Z. Writing to teach and reading to learn: A perspective on the psychology of written instruction. *Seventy-fifth Yearbook of the National Society for the Study of Education*, 1976, Part 1, 91-129.

Rothkopf, E. Z. On the reciprocal relationship between previous experience and processing in determining learning outcomes. In A. M. Lesgold, J. W. Pellegrino, S. D. Fokkema, & R. Glaser (Eds.) *Cognitive psychology and instruction*. New York and London: Plenum Press, 1978.

Rothkopf, E. Z., & Billington, M. Goal guided learning from text: inferring a descriptive processing model from inspection times and eye movements. *Journal of Educational Psychology* 1979, *71*, 310-327.

Rothkopf, E. Z., & Coatney, R. P., Effects of readability of context passages on subsequent inspection rates. *Journal of Educational Psychology*, 1974, *59*, 679-682.

Samuels, S. J., & Dahl, P. R. Establishing appropriate purpose for reading and its effect on flexibility of reading rate. *Journal of Educational Psychology*, 1975, *67*, 38-43.

Sinaiko, H. W. Verbal factors in human engineering: Some cultural and psychological data. In A. Chapanis (Ed.), *Ethnic variables in human factors engineering*. Baltimore: Johns Hopkins Press, 1975.

Spencer, H. *The visible word*. London: Lund Humphries, 1969.

Srivastava, R. N. *Evaluating communicability in village settings, Part 1*. New Delhi: UNICEF, 1978. (a)

Srivastava, R. N. *Evaluating communicability in village settings, Part 2*. New Delhi: UNICEF, 1978. (b)

Sticht, T. G. Learning by listening. In J. B. Carroll & R. O. Freedle (Eds.), *Language comprehension and the acquisition of knowledge*. New York: Winston & Sons, 1972.

Sticht, T. G. The acquisition of literacy by children and adults. In F. B. Murray & J. J. Pikulski (Eds.), *The acquisition of reading*. Baltimore: University Park Press, 1978.

Taylor, W. L. Cloze procedure: A new tool for measuring readability. *Journalism Quarterly*, 1953, *30*, 415-433.

Tinker, M. A. *Legibility of print*. Iowa State University Press, 1965.

Trabasso, T., Rollins, H., & Shaughnessy, E. Storage and verification stages in processing concepts. *Cognitive Psychology*, 1971, *2*, 239-289.

Wason, P. C. The retention of material presented through precis. *Journal of Communication*, 1962, *12*, 36-43.

Wason, P. C. The contexts of plausible denial. *Journal of Verbal Learning and Verbal Behavior*, 1965, *4*, 7-11.

Wason, P. C. The drafting of rules. *New Law Journal*, 1968, *118*, 548-549.

Whalley, P. C., & Flemming, R. W. An experiment with a simple recorder of reading behaviour. *Programmed Learning and Educational Technology*, 1975, *12*, 120-123.

Wright, P. Transformations and the understanding of sentences. *Language and Speech*, 1969, *12*, 156-166.

Wright, P. Presenting information in tables. *Applied Ergonomics*, 1970, *1*, 234-242.

Wright, P. Decision making as a factor in the case of using numerical tables. *Ergonomics*, 1977, *20*, 91-96.

Wright, P. Feeding the information eaters: Suggestions for integrating pure and applied research on language comprehension. *Instructional Science*, 1978, *7*, 249-312.

Wright, P. Quality control aspects of document design. *Information Design Journal*, 1979, *1*, 33-42.

Wright, P. Is legal jargon a restrictive practice? In S. L. Lloyd-Bostock (Ed.), *Psychology in legal contexts: Applications and limitations*. London: Macmillan, 1980.

Wright, P., Aldrich, A., & Wilcox, P. Research note: Some effects of coding answers for optical mark reading on the accuracy of answering multiple-choice questions. *Human Factors*, 1977, *14*, 83-87.

Wright, P., & Barnard, P. Effects of "more than" and "less than" decisions on the use of numerical tables. *Journal of Applied Psychology*, 1975, *60*, 606-611.

Wright, P., & Barnard, P. Asking multiple questions about several items: The design of matrix structures on application forms. *Applied Ergonomics*, 1978, *9*, 7-14.

Wright, P., & Reid, F. Written information: Some alternatives to prose for expressing the outcomes to complex contingencies. *Journal of Applied Psychology*, 1973, *57*, 160-166.

Wright, P., & Threlfall, M. S. Readers' expectations about format influence the usability of an index. *Journal of Research Communication on Studies*, in press.

Wright, P., & Wilcox, P. When two no's nearly make a yes: A study of conditional imperatives. In P. A. Kolers, M. E. Wrolstad, & H. Bouma (Eds.), *Processing of visible language 1*. New York and London: Plenum Press. 1979.

# Wholistic models of feature analysis in word recognition: a critical examination

Leslie Henderson

*The common assertion that words are perceived "as a whole" is examined. The analysis reveals three independent classes of wholistic theory. These differ in the underlying process that is held to be wholistic. (i) Feature analysis can be characterised as wholistic at either the stage of feature extraction or that of feature interpretation. Both views are united in denying that recognition depends on preliminary letter identification. (ii) The translation of print into sound may be held to be conducted at a lexical rather than an alphabetical level. (iii) A neglected class of theory attributes wholistic effects to preferential recovery in conscious attention of higher levels of code.*

For at least a century there has been a certain amount of loose talk in psychology about *wholes*. It has been asserted that perception is wholistic and that, in particular, words are perceived as a whole. (I have left to the cosmologists the spelling "holism," from the Greek *Holos*, meaning whole, to indicate spiritual states of affairs. "Whole" comes from Old English *hal*, meaning complete, healthy, and gives "wholism" on the grounds of morpheme conservation.) As a theoretical assertion, wholism has been surprisingly persistent and its longevity is itself sufficient reason for subjecting the concept to critical scrutiny. Such an enquiry holds considerable historical interest because we can witness the concept employed in the context of different metatheories. For example, contemporary use of the concept of wholism occurs in the information processing approach to perception. Here we might expect wholism to describe the sort of features extracted from the input signal, the manner of interpreting these features, or, perhaps, the ability of the system to recover the products of earlier encoding stages. In contrast, in the 1920s the notion of wholistic perception occurred in the phenomenological theory exemplified by Gestalt psychology, in which wholism was a statement about the quality of perceptual experience. Earlier, at the beginning of experimental psychology in the nineteenth century both approaches had been combined. Thus, as I shall attempt to show, the proposition that words are perceived as a whole was for Cattell both an assertion about the quality of experience —"the span of apprehension" —and a view of information processing operations — the denial of letter-by-letter processing.

The doctrine of perceptual wholism is not only of interest within the domestic confines of theoretical psychology but has also affected the pedagogy of reading. Early adherents of the *look-say* approach to teaching reading had accepted the demonstrations by experimenters in the nineteenth century that words were perceived as a whole. It seemed to follow then that children should be taught to recognise words by associating the entire visual pattern with its referent, in a non-analytical fashion. Wholism also has implications for the pedagogy of spelling (Henderson & Chard, 1980), because of the common assumption that most spelling is learned incidentally in the course of reading. If perception of words is non-analytic, then so much the worse for spelling. Wholism also has implications for the study of writing systems for, whereas linguists generally distinguish between signs which refer to an entire word (or morpheme), such as the Chinese logograph, and semantically empty signs which refer to elementary speech sounds, such as alphabetic scripts, advocates of the wholistic position assert that alphabetic representations of a word are treated by the reader as logographic, that is, as if they consisted of a single, composite sign. Finally, wholism has implications for the design of ideal typefaces. As Brooks (1977) has noted, if the visual distinctiveness of individual words is the prime objective, the general principle of context independence in the design of letters must be reconsidered. (Brooks does not, I believe, intend us to take this possibility seriously.)

Wholistic theories typically have not been precise in their proposals. Elsewhere I have suggested (Henderson, 1977) that one useful way to proceed towards the clarification of theories of wholism is to demand what exactly they *deny*. As a first approximation, we are told that: "we do not therefore perceive separately the letters of which a word is composed" (Cattell, 1886) or that: "word recognition cannot be analyzed into a set of independent letter recognition processes" (Wheeler, 1970). The shift from the phenomenological language of 1886 ("perceive separately") to the computer language of 1970 ("process independently") is interesting but it is the similarity of these claims which is remarkable. I intend to show, however, that the implication of a single and consistent underlying hypothesis is false. I have given priority to elucidating and contrasting the wide range of theoretical propositions entangled under the umbrella of "wholism." Consequently, the evaluation of the experimental evidence cited has had to take second place.

## Three classes of wholistic theory

Three independent classes of wholistic theories of word recognition are now distinguished, for the moment on purely logical grounds, but later they will be used to categorise particular versions of wholism, or to bring out their ambiguity.

### Wholism in visual feature analysis

The minimum assertion of this class of theory is that word perception, in the sense of visual pattern identification, is not mediated by a processing stage at which individual letter identities are represented. This might be for a variety of reasons. The elementary features extracted from the visual word array might together be adequate to identify the word but inadequate to specify the individual component letters. A variant of this is found in the notion of a "transgraphemic feature"

(Henderson, 1977), in which the visual pattern detected by a primitive feature analyser lies across several letters. The limiting case of this variant is the template theory which asserts that visual patterns are not decomposed at all but are matched in a unitary way against the unitary representations of visual "objects" held in permanent memory.

There is another possible location for wholistic effects in feature analysis. This exists at the stage where the extracted features are compared with the property lists stored in memory. Here we are concerned with what sort of entities we search memory for in the process of perception. We might address our pattern memory with a given set of elementary visual features, matching them to the property lists that define single letters, or which define certain clusters of letters, or those for entire words. (Template theory itself is exceptional in that it does not distinguish between wholism at the feature extraction stage and at the memory access stage.)

*Wholistic orthographic translation*
When we translate patterns into sound by assigning a pronunciation to a word we can again think in terms of a wholistic process. In this case the unit of translation might be the entire word. For example, we might find that the entry in visual memory corresponding to a certain word gives us immediate access to its pronunciation, perhaps because entries in the mental lexicon list together the visual properties of a word and the call signal of the "programme" for articulating it. The translation of print into sound could then be said to be conducted in terms of whole-word units or wholistic translation.

At the other extreme is translation by means of grapheme-phoneme correspondences (GPCs), wherein translation is accomplished by segmenting the visual array into functional graphemic units (Venezky, 1970) and assigning a phonemic value to them by consulting an abstract set of orthographic GPC rules.

At an intermediate point is the view that translation is conducted in terms of units neither maximally analytic (the GPC) nor as large as whole words. This possibility is usually associated with the analogy hypothesis (Glushko, 1979) in which a written word is held to activate an orthographic neighbourhood in the lexicon, consisting of visually similar words. The pronunciation of the stimulus word is synthesised from the sounds listed in the lexicon for the members of the neighbourhood set. By this means even pseudowords that possess no lexical entry can be assigned a pronunciation in a wholistic manner.

It may seem artificial to distinguish between wholism at the level of feature analysis and wholism in orthographic translation. In particular, it might appear that the commitment to a strong version of wholism in visual feature analysis involves accepting a wholistic view of the translation units for assigning pronunciation. But we are making logical distinctions and, furthermore, it is perfectly feasible to deny wholism in visual feature analysis but maintain that, once a lexical representation has been addressed, pronunciation can be assigned at a whole-word level.

*Wholism as an attentional characteristic*

Our final class of wholistic theory is somewhat diffuse because it concerns not so much the nature and layout of the various encoding stages but the ability to recover the products of these stages in awareness. Whereas the previous two classes of theory referred to the nature of the processes for deriving codes, the attentional class of theory is applied to the differences among levels of code in their susceptibility to conscious monitoring. Broadly speaking, this theory asserts that it is the higher-level (less analytic) codes which have preferred access to consciousness. Thus even when a word is presented in fleeting or mutilated form there is a tendency to perceive an entire word, even if it is not what was presented. Furthermore, the negative aspect of this greater *availability to consciousness* of the whole-word level of analysis is a difficulty of selectively attending to components of a word. This can be understood with reference to the well-known Stroop effect in which the name of a word interferes with the attempt to name a component feature, such as the colour of ink in which it is printed.

It is worth noting that this distinction between type 1 and type 3 wholism has not always been neglected: it seems to be implied by Neisser's comment, "I can only think of two indispensible levels of organisation at which 'units' could be said to exist: (a) the *products of figural synthesis*, introspectively available; (b) the *properties of stimulation* which help to determine that synthesis" (Neisser, 1967, pp. 114-115). I identify (b) with type 1 and (a) with type 3, despite the obvious differences in terminology.

**Some history**

Perhaps the earliest formulation of a wholistic view of word recognition is Cattell's (1886). Cattell demonstrated experimentally that a word could be named about as quickly as a single letter and that a display so brief that it only permitted report of 3 or 4 unconnected letters would nevertheless allow report of a least two whole words. This suggested that the processing time required for recognition of a word did not equal the sum of the times taken to identify the component letters. Cattell appears to have assumed that, because a serial, exhaustive letter-processing model was therefore rejected, all that remained was a model in which transgraphemic features are used as the major determinant of word identification. The transgraphemic feature of particular interest to Cattell and his like-minded contemporaries was the word envelope, the gross outline of the entire word. It is now obvious that Cattell's results compelled acceptance neither of a transgraphemic feature theory nor even any member of the general class of wholistic feature analysis theory.

If the subject's actual performance led Cattell to a type 1 wholistic theory, his reports of his perceptual experience of words led Cattell tacitly to accept a type 3 (attentional) theory also. This can best be understood in the context of the historical role of the concept of a "span of apprehension" — that amount experienced in a single act of perception. This concept has been reviewed by Geyer (1970), who makes the following points.

One of the oldest psychological experiments was concerned with the phenomenon now called "subitizing." Early studies (Jevons, 1871) had led to the conclusion that the time required to quantify a random assembly of items was independent of their number, up to about six, increasing linearly with number thereafter. This constant came to be regarded as the limit of simultaneous attention and played a central role in late nineteenth-century psychology. The idea of a quantity of information that could be apprehended in a single, unitary act of perception was attractive at a time when the theory of introspective decomposition of experience into elementary sensations had gone abruptly out of fashion. Wertheimer later developed this theme into what became known as Gestalt psychology (Wertheimer, 1923). In this theoretical context Cattell, and later Erdmann and Dodge, believed they had shown that the span of attention for words was not to be reckoned in letter units. This wholistic property of perceptual experience was also seen as characteristic of the way in which perception breaks down. Thus Huey (1908) wrote that briefly exposed phrases "were either grasped as wholes or else scarcely any of the words or letters were read" and Pillsbury (1897) remarked upon the tendency of the reader to fill in missing data so that even when perception is erroneous it typically consists of whole words.

The fact that these early versions of wholism had no means of distinguishing type 1 from type 3 theories is crucial to an understanding of the development of psychological theory. It is now possible to formulate a distinction between, on one hand, stimulus encoding operations and, on the other, the access that various levels of the resultant codes have to consciousness. The language of information processing allows perception to be described as a large collection of underlying operations and also allows conscious experience to be treated as corresponding to a limited subset of these operations. At the turn of the century, however, there was no theoretical language to express a distinction between perception as information processing and perception as experience. Long after the Structuralists' introspective methods were discarded as impossibly subjective, their successors continued to equate perception with experience. It was, of course, the persistence of this confusion even into the 1950s which resulted in the dismissal of subliminal perception as inherently paradoxical.

The question of the units of translation between print and sound, which concerns type 2 wholistic theory, received little attention in early psychology, perhaps because identifying a visually presented word was often regarded as equivalent to assigning it its spoken form. Huey (1908) makes only a brief reference to the issue, remarking: "It is true that further investigation has not justified

Goldscheider and Müller's conclusion that the letter-sounds are immediately suggested by the visual letter-forms in ordinary reading. The word-sound seems usually to be suggested as a whole" (p. 146). The question of how to teach children to accomplish orthographic translation aroused early interest, however. At the turn of the century teaching was dominated by the "word method" described by Huey (1908), in which "the whole sound of the word is associated with the word's total visual appearance, and is suggested just as the name of any other object comes to mind on seeing the whole object" (p.272).

## Modern wholistic theories
### Feature analysis
As we have noted, wholistic theories of visual feature analysis generally take as their point of departure the assertion that word recognition is not contingent upon a preliminary stage concerned with the detection of individual letters. To the extent that Cattell's had been a type 1 theory this was because he assumed that in rejecting a serial-exhaustive letter processing model he could reject any model in which word recognition was mediated by analysis of individual letters. With the demonstration by Neisser (1967) and others that even random letter arrays could in certain circumstances be processed in parallel the force of this argument was removed. If a parallel process operating at the level of individual letter identities is to be called "wholistic" then the term becomes vacuous. Moreover, in this usage wholistic perception would cease to be a distinctive characteristic of *word* recognition since parallel processing also seems to occur with random letter arrays. The advent of parallel processing models therefore served to clarify and to restrict the conclusions that could be drawn from early word recognition experiments.

*Extraction of wholistic features*. Early type 1 theories asserted that the dominant role in perception was played by transgraphemic features. Of these, the word envelope has received most attention. Yet it cannot be a necessary feature in identification because the ability to recognise upper-case words (which lack a distinctive outline) is only slightly less good than that for lower-case. Furthermore, the availability of this cue cannot even be a necessary condition for superior recognition performance on words than single letters since this effect can be obtained with upper-case stimuli (Wheeler, 1970). There appears to be very little direct evidence in favour of the use of envelope cues (Gibson & Levin, 1975, Chapter 7; Henderson, in press).

　　　　Other transgraphemic-feature theories posit unitary features arising from the conjunction of elements within the word but there seems to be no experimental evidence in support of this view. The most direct test presumably consists of manipulations which disrupt the conjunctions of features across the letters in a word. Several experimenters have done this by means of case AlTeRnAtIoN. It appears that, when a sufficiently sensitive test of performance is used, the overall level of performance is found to decline slightly but the superior perceptibility of words, as compared to pseudowords, survives undiminished (Adams, 1979; McClelland, 1976). These experiments do not, of course, establish that transgraphemic features are never used in word recognition. What they show is that any use of wholistic features does not contribute to the perceptual advantage enjoyed by words. This is not unimportant, however, since the explanation of the word advantage has always played a primary role in motivating wholistic positions.

Despite the force of the preceding argument, case-alternation experiments leave some loose ends. Brooks (1977, pp. 172-175) found that subjects trained to search for first names were slowed when, for instance, what had been lInDa was changed to LiNdA. The claim is disputable for a variety of reasons, one of which is that he fails to exclude the possibility that changing from LINDA to linda produces similar results. Another is that his manipulation confuses changes in the shape of particular letters with changes in the conjunction of shapes between letters. A more problematic finding occurs in the literature on same-different judgments where it is sometimes found that case alternation abolishes the advantage of word (or pseudoword) stimuli over random letter strings (Bruder, 1978). It is not clear if this effect is a peculiarity of same-different judgments and its bearing upon wholistic theory has never been soundly established.

*Comparison of features with wholistic representations in memory.* We turn now to theories which locate wholistic processes at the stage where the extracted features are compared with stored pattern representations in memory. Here wholism asserts that feature bundles, whatever their nature, are used to address directly representations of patterns of a higher order than single letters, such as letter-clusters or words. (It is notable that the distinction between wholism at the extraction and at the interpretation stages has seldom been drawn by proponents of wholism.)

In perhaps the earliest modern formulation of the letter-cluster view Gibson, Pick, Osser, and Hammond (1962) sought what they called "the critical unit of language for the reading process." (Over recent years Gibson's definition of these units has changed somewhat; for the current position, see Gibson and Levin, 1975.) One difficulty is that the units are defined linguistically rather than with reference to a psychological model of the way in which units are used in recognition. As Neisser (1967) states: "the spelling-pattern theory has only shifted the pattern-recognition problem to a new level without disposing of it. How does the subject know a GL- (unit) when he sees one?" (p. 114). The internal consistency of Gibson's definition of units has been criticised by Coltheart (1977) and Henderson (in press).

Another influential adherent of the letter-cluster unit view is E. E. Smith who began with an attempt to distinguish between alternative mechanisms which he calls "unitization" and "inference" (Smith & Haviland, 1972). The inference mechanism is one which computes word identities on a base of letter identities but utilises redundancies in the pattern of letters to effect economies of processing. He describes the unitization mechanism as follows: "when S expects a word to be presented he segments the initial input into perceptual units, which are larger than single letters and correspond to pronounceable English sequences, and then analyses these units" (Smith & Haviland, 1972, p. 59). This description sounds suspiciously like a feature-extraction theory, with clusters acting as gross features that are isolated (extracted) and then analysed (compared with representations in memory). How then can one isolate such a cluster *before* analysing it? (This is a pervasive problem for segmentation of speech and visual objects, as well as words.) Individual letters have physical boundaries, so it is clear how segmentation can precede analysis at that level. But clusters, defined in phonological terms, consist of a highly variable number of letters. The only attempt to show how a parsing process could segment an unidentified string of letters into (quasi-syllabic) cluster units has been that of Hansen and Rogers (1973). However, Coltheart (1978) seems to have demonstrated that for a large number of English words this procedure does not work and it appears doubtful whether such a procedure could, in principle, be made to work.

In later work, Spoehr and Smith (1973) rejected the assumption that clusters were isolated prior to identification of the constituent letters, preferring a "unitization-after-analysis" model in which words are analysed letter-by-letter and then unitized into syllables. This revised model is still vulnerable to Coltheart's criticism of the viability of the unitization procedure, however, and moreover, by virtue of its assumption that initial analysis is into letter identities, seems to have abandoned a wholistic view of feature analysis. We are asked to suppose that word recognition depends upon the following stages: individual letters are identified, then unitized into quasi-syllabic groups which are assigned a phonological value, and the resultant phonological code constitutes "recognition" of the visual input. Exceedingly odd is the implication that visual identification is contingent upon phonological translation of the word. Once the letters in the word have been identified it is difficult to see why we cannot proceed directly to word recognition. In fact, there is overwhelming evidence that the mental word-lexicon can be accessed directly with graphemic information (Henderson, in press). However, if we assume that the subject can proceed directly from the first to the final stage then the intermediate unitization, which is the distinctive attribute of Smith's model, becomes merely an example of type 2 wholism. That is, it ceases to be an assertion about the visual feature analysis of words and becomes instead an assertion about the level at which they are translated into sound.

The hypothesis that the elementary features extracted from the stimulus are used directly to access whole-word pattern representations has been advanced by F. Smith (1971) as part of a general account of word perception. He begins by citing the nineteenth-century literature in support of the thesis that word perception capitalises on the redundancy in words. He considers a wholistic feature extraction account of these effects but rejects it, largely on the grounds that it would require storage of a large vocabulary of specific pattern templates and that it fails to explain indifference of the recognition process to gross variation in the input format. Smith therefore advances a model in which the same set of elementary features is extracted from letters and words but the difference lies in "the categories, and associated feature lists, that the perceiver employs in his analysis of featural information" (p. 128). His formulation provides a clear statement of the locus of the wholistic process, that is, at the stage where the extracted features are used to access memory representations. Unfortunately, although the model is intended to provide a general account of the perceptual advantages enjoyed by words, he does not use it to make any detailed prediction which can be tested, and the nineteenth-century studies which form his empirical base leave a large number of factors uncontrolled in the experimental situation. Johnston (1978) has shown, moreover, that lexical constraint has no effect on letter detectability. That is, the initial S is no more detectable in SNOB, where it is one of only two lexical alternatives, than in SOCK where it is one of many. Johnston was able to show that in this experimental task a letter was more detectable in the context of a word than in isolation. It appears to follow that a letter is more detectable in the context of any familiar word and this has little to do with the predictability imposed by the redundancy in that word. The perceptual advantage enjoyed by words is therefore due to processing stages subsequent to feature analysis where the availability of higher-level codes for words and word-like patterns provides greater resistance to interference from other processing activities (Henderson & Chard, 1979; Johnston, 1978). Thus the formulation of a wholistic theory has passed from a type 1 assertion about the nature of feature analysis to a type 3 assertion about the recoverability of various levels of code.

## Conclusion

The characterisation of perception, and especially of word recognition, as wholistic has been a recurrent theme in experimental psychology. The assertion that processes are wholistic seems to satisfy both those who contemplate the workings of the mind and those who contemplate the workings of the cosmos, as the distinction between wholism and holism indicates.

I have taken as my primary task the translation of wholistic hypotheses into information-processing language. In so doing it was possible to distinguish three general classes of wholistic assertion logically independent one from another.

Having distinguished wholistic visual feature analysis, wholistic translation of print into sound, and wholistic aspects of attentional selection, I then concentrated upon feature analysis. Most wholistic theories of word recognition appear to be of this type. Feature analysis wholism was subdivided into two more basic categories. The first was concerned with the size of visual feature extracted from the stimulus array, wholism here consisting of the postulation of transgraphemic features. The second category was concerned with the comparison of extracted features with the descriptions of entities represented in memory, wholism here consisting of the assertion that features were used directly to access representations of letter-clusters or even whole words.

My evaluation of type 1 wholistic theories is wholly negative. I have been unable to discover any empirical test that selectively favours the theories. For example, feature extraction theories are particularly vulnerable to McClelland's (1976) and Adams' (1979) demonstrations that the perceptual advantage of words survives case alternation, which should surely disrupt transgraphemic features. On the other hand, current formulators of wholistic feature interpretation theories have difficulty with Johnston's (1978) demonstration of the lack of a lexical constraint effect.

In addition, the theories often do not bear logical scrutiny either because the mechanisms they propose are not viable or because the inferences linking them to experimental outcomes are unwarranted (Coltheart, 1978; Henderson, 1975; Henderson & Chard, 1980; Neisser, 1967). Particularly prevalent are failures to distinguish between type 1 wholism and a parallel process that operates on individual letters, and between feature-analytic and attentional wholism. Huey (1908) implied a similar distinction: "We must next consider the mental processes concerned in perceiving what is before us on the page, and the means by which the mind takes note of what is there at such a very rapid rate" (p. 71). It is worth noting his ominous continuation: "This raises, of course, the time-honored question of whether we read by letters or by words; but we shall find that much more is involved than the settlement of this somewhat scholastic query" (p. 71).

This paper was written while I was on sabbatical leave at University College, London. I am grateful to the Social Science Research Council for supporting my work with Personal Research Grant HR5482.

## References

Adams, M. J. Models of word recognition. *Cognitive Psychology*, 1979, *11*, 133-176.

Brooks, L. R. Visual pattern in fluent word identification. In A. Reber & D. Scarborough (Eds.), *Toward a psychology of reading*. Hillsdale, N.J.: Erlbaum, 1977.

Bruder, G. Role of visual familiarity in the word-superiority effects obtained with the simultaneous matching task. *Journal of Experimental Psychology: Human Perception and Performance*, 1978, *4*, 88-100.

Cattell, J. McK. The time it takes to see and name objects. *Mind*, 1886, *11*, 63-65.

Coltheart, M. Critical notice of Gibson, E. J. and Levin, H. The psychology of reading. *Quarterly Journal of Experimental Psychology*, 1977, *29*, 157-167.

Coltheart, M. Lexical access in simple reading tasks. In G. Underwood (Ed.), *Strategies of information processing*. London: Academic Press, 1978.

Geyer, J. J. Models of perceptual processes in reading. In H. Singer & R. B. Ruddell (Eds.), *Theoretical models and processes of reading*. Newark, Del.: International Reading Association, 1970.

Gibson, E. J., & Levin, J. *The psychology of reading*. Cambridge, Mass.: MIT Press, 1975.

Gibson, E. J., Pick, A. D., Osser, H., & Hammond, M. The role of grapheme-phoneme correspondence in the perception of words. *American Journal of Psychology*, 1962, *75*, 554-570.

Glushko, R. J. The organisation and activation of orthographic knowledge in reading aloud. *Journal of Experimental Psychology: Human Perception and Performance*, 1979, *5*, 674-691.

Hansen, D., & Rogers, T. S. An exploration of psycholinguistic units in initial reading. In K. S. Goodman (Ed.), *The psycholinguistic nature of the reading process*. Detroit: Wayne State University Press, 1973.

Henderson, L. Do words conceal their component letters? A critique of Johnson (1975) on the visual perception of words. *Journal of Verbal Learning and Verbal Behavior*, 1975, *14*, 648-650.

Henderson, L. Word recognition. In N. S. Sutherland (Ed.), *Tutorial essays in psychology. Vol. 1*. Hillsdale, N.J.: Erlbaum, 1977.

Henderson, L. *Orthography and word recognition in reading*. London: Academic Press, in press.

Henderson, L., & Chard, M. J. The reader's implicit knowledge of orthographic structure. In U. Frith (Ed.), *Cognitive processes in spelling*. London: Academic Press, 1980.

Huey, E. B. *The psychology and pedagogy of reading*. New York: MacMillan, 1908. Reprinted: Cambridge, Mass: MIT Press, 1968.

Jevons, W. S. The power of numerical discrimination. *Nature*, 1871, *3*, 281-282.

Johnston, J. C. A test of the sophisticated guessing theory of word perception. *Cognitive Psychology*, 1978, *10*, 123-153.

McClelland, R. J. Preliminary letter identification in the perception of words and nonwords. *Journal of Experimental Psychology: Human Perception and Performance*, 1976, *2*, 80-91.

Neisser, U. *Cognitive psychology*, New York: Appleton-Century-Crofts, 1967.

Pillsbury, W. B. A study in apperception. *American Journal of Psychology*, 1897, *8*, 315-393.

Smith, E. E., & Haviland, S. E. Why words are perceived more accurately than nonwords: inference versus unitization. *Journal of Experimental Psychology*, 1972, *92*, 59-64.

Smith, F. *Understanding reading*. New York: Holt, Rinehart & Winston, 1971.

Spoehr, K. T., & Smith, E. E. The role of syllables in perceptual processing. *Cognitive Psychology*, 1973, *5*, 71-89.

Venezky, R. L. *The structure of English orthography*. The Hague: Mouton, 1970.

Wheeler, D. D. Processes in word recognition. *Cognitive Psychology*, 1970, *1*, 59-85.

Wertheimer, M. (1923) On objects as immediately given to consciousness. In R.J. Herrnstein & E.G. Boring (Eds. and trans.) *A source book in the history of psychology*. Cambridge, Mass.: Harvard University Press, 1965.

# Developmental trends in the perception of textual cohesion

L. J. Chapman and Alan Stokes

*The progress of a continuing research programme on the perception of textual cohesion by older children is detailed and the implications of investigating the reading process from a global perspective considered. Data from the performance of 270 children in three age groups is analysed and developmental trends delineated. The growing ability of the children to process some of the textual features of cohesion is discussed.*

In a previous paper on textual cohesion (Chapman, 1979a) mention was made of the work of Halliday and Hasan (1976) who presented a linguistic model which emphasised those global characteristics which distinguish texts from non-texts or haphazard collections of words or sentences. They identified cohesion, which is integrative and gives texts their overall semantic unity, as one such characteristic, the other major factor being register. Cohesion is created by linguistic mechanisms called cohesive ties, which can be placed into five groupings: reference, substitution, ellipsis, conjunction, and textual cohesion. Each of these five categories consists of sub-categories of linguistic elements: reference, for example, is further subdivided into personal, demonstrative, and comparative reference. Cohesion then is said to be created by a variety of linguistic mechanisms which can be grouped as in Figure 1.

In this formulation, the linguistic mechanisms involved are identified in such a way as to enable experimentation and the collection of data. Cohesion and register together define a text and become major new perspectives for processing of visible language. The linguistic specification of the global characteristics of complete texts has been long awaited and some implications of Halliday and Hasan's suggestions (1976) have already been indicated in three papers, one concerned with pedagogy (Chapman, 1979b), one with verbal comprehension (Chapman, 1979c) and one with textlinguistics (Chapman, Note 1).

Linguists have paid great attention to small elements of syntax but little study has been made of larger units of texts which are probably the most important structures for recall and learning (Meyer, 1975, 1977). Using the inventory of cohesive mechanisms provided by Halliday and Hasan, the research reported below attempts to discover how, as they get older, children integrate the smaller units into meaningful larger ones.

*Collection of developmental data*

*Pronouns.* The work reported previously (Chapman, 1979a) left little doubt that the ability to cope with the personal reference group of cohesive ties (as indicated

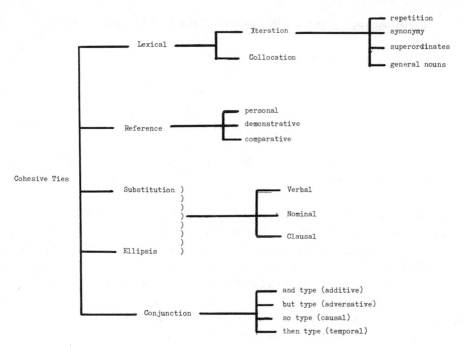

Figure 1. A system of cohesive ties. (Courtesy Halliday & Hasan, 1976.)

by the correct replacement of pronouns in a cloze-type task), is still being acquired by children aged 8 to 9 years. It was decided to extend the age range from 8 to 14 years so that any problems related to immature development, either linguistic or cognitive, might show up when the performances of the age groups were compared. It was also thought that the data might resolve the inconsistencies mentioned by Gurley (1978), who recommended further research, because the work of Lesgold (1972, Note 2) and Richek (1976/77) did not demonstrate clearly whether pronouns facilitated discourse comprehension for children or not. It was decided to make further use of cloze procedure in the investigation. This technique, although inevitably interrupting the reading flow, is as good as any in examining children's performance dynamically (Kingston, 1977).

*Non-pronouns.* There are many mechanisms other than anaphoric pronoun relations at work as tests are processed and it was thought important to match the children's performance on pronoun deletion with that on non-pronoun deletions. A second version of the pronoun texts was prepared in such a way as to avoid deleting words that were part of the anaphoric process and to enable comparisons with the pronoun completion and the connectives in the conjunction tests. The investigation of textual cohesion was thus taken into other areas, as proposed by Halliday and Hasan.

*Conjunctions.* Another important group of cohesive ties is provided by conjunctions and it was decided to investigate children's ability to perceive them by using the same cloze-type techniques. The group of conjunctions can be divided into four: additive, adversative, causal, and temporal connectives. There is some evidence that these connectives are important in the overall comprehension of texts as well. Stoodt (1972), using cloze techniques and working with fourth-grade children in North America, found a significant relationship between reading comprehension and comprehension of conjunctions. Nine single word conjunctions were found to be significantly more difficult and some were found to be easier. It would appear that, unlike pronouns, conjunctions depend on their specific meanings for their cohesive property. They have the function of relating to each other linguistic elements occurring in succession but not related by other structural means. The hypothesis was that these elements would play a significant part in text processing because the mechanism was not only of a different kind but also, because it involved such features as cause and time, would probably make greater cognitive demands than pronoun replacement.

### Subjects

Three age groups were chosen, 90 children in each, with an almost equal representation of boys and girls. The children in the 8-year-old group attended two First schools, those in the 11-year-old group a Middle school, and those in the 14-year-old group an Upper school. The First schools are in the same small town, one in the centre and one in a new housing estate. Both use mixed-ability teaching; the newer school is an open-plan design and uses team teaching. Both schools use the Initial Teaching Alphabet (i.t.a.) for instruction. The children of each school are similar in ability and background but the older school draws from a less mobile population than the newer one.

The Middle school is in a neighbouring, more industrialized area. It has a four class entry and mixed ability class teaching. Its catchment area includes the working class area where the school is but it also draws from new housing estates and outlying villages.

The Upper school is situated in the same area and serves the children of both towns and the outlying villages. In addition, the school has a boarding house accommodating about 40 children. The school is large, taking children at 12 years, and has about 350 children in each year plus a large sixth form. When the children start, they are tested and then assigned to one of three ability bands. Four classes spanning the full range of ability took part in the research.

### Materials

Fourteen short stories were written in a register as close as possible to those found in school readers. The interest level varied to cater as closely as possible to both younger and older children. Two stories were devoted to each of the seven personal pronoun groups according to the paradigm reported previously (Chapman, 1977).

The target pronouns were embedded in the stories so that they did not impede the natural flow of language. After adults had read the stories to confirm their acceptability two versions of the text were prepared. In the first, the embedded pronouns were deleted and, in the second, non-pronouns were deleted to construct a second cloze test. The introductory paragraph had no deletions and the deletions elsewhere were spaced at intervals of approximately seven words. The conjunction stories covered the four connectives (additive, adversative, causal, and temporal) in the same way. The 14 stories were gathered into individual booklets in random order to avoid initial concentration on one story. The same procedure was adopted for the non-pronoun version and the connectives.

### Procedure

All the testing was carried out by the same person with the help of the class teachers involved. The First school children were allowed 45 min to complete the 14 stories and to prevent fatigue a play break was arranged at half-time. The Middle and Upper school children were allowed 45 min to complete the deletions and were not given a break. The same timing was used for the non-pronoun variations of the test and the connective tests.

The order of presentation of the cloze texts was: pronouns, non-pronouns, and conjunctions. To prevent fatigue each task was administered on a different day and there was an interval of seven days between tests.

### Scoring

All the marking was done by the same person for consistency. One mark was allowed for every word correctly inserted and matching the target word. The total possible scores for the pronoun and non-pronoun versions of the tests was 108, and 80 for the conjunctions test. Misspellings were accepted as long as there was no reasonable doublt that the correct word was intended.

### Analysis of results

The mean chronological ages (C.A.) of the children and the mean scores of the three age groups on the three tests were calculated. Correlations were also calculated between chronological ages and the scores for pronouns, non-pronouns, and conjunctions, and between pronoun scores and non-pronoun scores.

### Analysis of correct scores

Table 1 shows the mean chronological ages of the three age groups of children in months and their mean scores on the pronouns, non-pronouns, and conjunction tests.

Table 1. Mean C. A. and mean pronouns, non-pronouns, and connective scores.

| | N | Mean C.A. (months) | Mean Pronoun Score (maximum 108) | Mean Non-Pronoun Score (maximum 108) | Mean Conjunction Score (maximum 80) |
|---|---|---|---|---|---|
| First school | 90 | 90.0 | 32.0 | 40.5 | 4.3 ( 5.8) |
| Middle school | 90 | 127.4 | 64.7 | 72.2 | 13.6 (18.4) |
| Upper school | 90 | 163.3 | 79.1 | 79.7 | 21.9 (28.6) |

Figures in parentheses weighted for comparison (that is, × 1.35).

The mean scores are seen to increase with age, the non-pronouns having the highest mean score, the pronouns next, and the conjunctions the lowest. It should be remembered, however, that the maximum possible score for the pronoun and non-pronoun tests was 108 while that for the conjunction tests was 80. The mean score of the Middle school group on the pronoun test was double that of the First school group, a significant difference. The increase in mean score is not as marked between the Middle and Upper schools. The conjunction mean scores are lower but show an increase with age.

*Correlations*

*C. A. with pronoun scores*. The correlation between chronological age and score on the pronoun test was significant ($r = .69, p < .01$). The scores of the First school group were highly discriminatory, ranging from nil to 86 with a bunching at the lower end of the scale. The Middle school results moved to the upper range but with a tail containing about 15 scores below 50. The Upper school results bunched at the top end of the scale. However, it should be noted that only two of the Upper school children achieved the maximum score of 108. The range of scores in the Middle school group was from 2 to 98 and in the Upper school from 28 to 108.

*C. A. with non-pronoun scores*. The correlation between chronological age and score on the non-pronoun test ($r = .62, p < .01$) showed the same pattern as the pronoun test. The highest score here (108) was achieved by only one 14-year-old pupil.

*C. A. with conjunctions.* In the correlation between chronological age and the conjunctions test ($r = .71, p < .01$) the pattern was different, the First school scores heavily weighted to the lower end and some 15 making no score. Scores of the Middle school children spread out further, from 0 to 35. The older Upper school children's scores ranged from 3 to 44, an appreciable number still being at the lower end.

*Pronoun with non-pronoun* scores. The relationship between pronoun and non-pronoun scores was strong ($r = .94, p < .01$) bunching in the higher range.

### Summary of correlations

Chronological age is more closely related to the conjunction scores and the pronouns and non-pronouns are very highly correlated. The pronoun scores have a higher correlation with the conjunctions than do the non-pronouns.

### Discussion of results

As expected, the analysis of mean correct scores (correct = replacement of actual target word) shows an increase in mean score by age over the three tasks, that is, the completion of pronoun, non-pronoun, and conjunction deletions. A clear developmental pattern of mastery over the three tasks is portrayed.

The data presented in a previous paper (Chapman 1979a) showed that the ability of children to replace pronouns in a cloze-type task was related to their progress in becoming fluent readers. This finding is confirmed by the results obtained here. The present work adds further details, demonstrating that some children are still attaining mastery over pronouns at the age of 14 years. The pronoun mean score of the children in the Upper school was 79.1 which could be taken as satisfactory but nonetheless means that more than 20 percent are still unable to cope with what appears a fairly elementary and straightforward task. The first point to be made is that, if pronoun tasks like this are taken as indicative of children's ability to perform the integrative functions necessary for fluent reading, then the data show that the development of that ability continues well into the Upper school. It would also seem that, in the First school, the task is highly discriminatory, the children's scores being widely spread from 0 to 86, although bunching at the lower end. Moreover, the ability to complete non-pronoun deletions is very closely related to the ability to complete pronoun deletions, the correlation coefficient of pronoun to non-pronoun scores $r = .94$ being highly significant. Although the high correlation was to be expected (the non-pronoun version was the second time the children had read the stories), two points are worth noting. First, the consistency of the results of the two tests indicates that the procedures are very reliable and, second, because many different parts of speech were deleted in the non-pronoun task, it could also be seen as indicating overall text-processing ability because some of the words deleted performed other cohesive functions. (It should be noted that one part of speech not adequately represented was the adjective.) From the research carried out so far, it would appear that the ability to replace pronouns in cloze-type tasks is probably the best indication of the development of fluent reading.

The conjunction test and its results present a variety of problems. The scores are more depressed than those on the other tasks, the youngest group barely able to cope with conjunctions at all and, although some of the Upper school pupils can process some of the features, their performance is still far from acceptable.

It was intimated earlier that there were methodological difficulties with the group of cohesive ties. In many cases the conjunction is composed of a group of words (at the same time) or single words that are infrequent in children's vocabulary (furthermore, nevertheless, finally), and is also dependent on stylistic or register features. To obtain a successful measure on groups of words in a cloze context is a problem because children cannot cope with two, three, or four successive deletions in a text. Other ways of examining the perception of conjunctions during text processing are being sought and a different method of presenting text, using a Visual Display Unit powered by a micro-computer, is being investigated. The experimenter would then be able to control the presentation in various ways to provide further textual details. However, these particular tests did not have $n$-word deletions, instead the key word in a conjunction group was deleted (for example, "hand" from "on the other hand"). It appears that the four types of conjunction used here present even the oldest children with considerable problems and this has far-reaching pedagogical implications. As with the pronoun tasks and early reading, it is possible that the ability to cope with the conjunction cohesive ties will indicate later reading progress.

This research programme is funded by the Department of Education and Science, project no. P1163/07.

## Reference Notes

1. Chapman, L. J. *Some developments in textlinguistics: Implications for the teacher of reading*. Paper presented at the First Anglo-Scandinavian Conference, Leeds Polytechnic, April, 1979. ERIC No. ED 173 767.
2. Lesgold, A. M. *Effects of pronouns on children's memory for sentences*. Pittsburgh, Pa.: University of Pittsburgh. Learning Research and Development Centre, 1972.

## References

Chapman, L. J. Some influences of semantics on reading development. In J. Gilliland (Ed.), *Reading: Research and classroom practices*. London: Ward Lock, 1977.

Chapman, L. J. The perception of language cohesion during fluent reading. In P. A. Kolers, M. E. Wrolstad, & H. Bouma (Eds.), *Processing of visible language 1*. New York and London: Plenum Press, 1979.(a)

Chapman, L. J. Pedagogical strategies for the development of fluent reading. In D. Thackray (Ed.) *Growth in reading*. London: Ward Lock Educational, 1979.(b)

Chapman, L. J. Confirming children's use of cohesive ties in text: Pronouns. *The Reading Teacher*, 1979, *33*, 317-322.

Gurley, J. W. This basal is easy to read—or is it? *The Reading Teacher*, 1978, *32*, 174-182.

Halliday, M. A. K. & Hasan, R. *Cohesion in English*. London: Longmans, 1976.

Kingston, A. J. Towards a psychology of reading and language. In A. J. Kingston (Ed.), *Selected papers of W. W. Weaver*. Athens: University of Georgia Press, 1977.

Lesgold, A. M. Pronominalisation: A device for unifying sentences in memory. *Journal of Verbal Learning and Verbal Behavior*, 1972, *11*, 316-323.

Meyer, B. J. F. The organisation of prose and its effects on memory. In T. A. van Dijk & W. O. Hendricks, *North-Holland Studies in Theoretical Poetics* (Vol. 1). Amsterdam: North-Holland Publishing Co., 1975.

Meyer, B.J.F. The structure of prose, effects on learning and memory and implications for educational practice. In R. C. Henderson & R. J. Spiro (Eds.), *Schooling and the acquisition of knowledge*. Hillsdale, N. J.: Lawrence Erlbaum Associates, 1977.

Richek, M. A. Reading comprehension of anaphoric forms in varying linguistic contexts. *Reading Research Quarterly*, 1976/77, *12*(2), 145-165.

Stoodt, B. D. The relationship between understanding grammatical conjunctions and reading comprehension. *Elementary English*, 1972, *49*, 502-504.

# Structuring an internal representation of text: A basis of literacy

Wayne L. Shebilske

*Most psychological research on literacy focuses upon the recognition operations that map the input from the eyes onto surface structural units such as letters, syllables, and words. Only recently has some research been directed towards the comprehension operations that link surface structural representations with the ideas represented by clauses and weave those ideas into a structured internal representation of the text. This paper will discuss reasons for the emphasis on recognition, present a rationale for studying comprehension in reading, and report results from a project whose goal is to build theoretical and empirical foundations for improving the use of textbooks in mathematics and science instruction. By new modes of analysis this project explores the interrelationships among important variables in the reading process including perceived structure of text and the quality of comprehension.*

The importance of recognition to literacy is obvious. Even though children are able to recognize visual patterns and understand spoken discourse long before they learn to read, their recognition processes must undergo further development before they can begin to recognize linguistic units in print. Children must learn how to discriminate among graphic segmental units and how to map the visual units onto their language. Some preschoolers learn this on their own, but most children require formal instruction before they discover the unique relationship that exists between print and the spoken language. It is the uniqueness of print as a medium of language that has captured the interest of the cognitive psychologists whose research has provided a foundation for improving the teaching of reading and for correcting various kinds of reading deficiencies.

The importance of comprehension to literacy has been less clear to linguists. Confusion has stemmed from the mistaken opinion that written discourse has no unique linguistic status beyond the differences between graphic codes and oral codes. This view was inaugurated by Bloomfield (1933) who summarized his disdain of writing as follows: "Writing is not language, but merely a way of recording language by means of visible marks "(p. 31). Although not unchallenged, this view is still popular. For example, Pearson (1977) in his *Introduction to linguistic concepts* observed, "From the standpoint of the linguist, therefore, language is sound and not print. Writing is a way of representing language, but writing always represents something that could be spoken. Writing is therefore a secondary way of representing language; it is not an alternative way"(pp. 4-5).

This view has an analogue in cognitive psychology. Whereas linguists are concerned with describing the formal structure of language, cognitive psychologists attempt to analyze the mental processes that occur between the initial presentation of a language stimulus and the comprehension of that stimulus. They often use information-processing models to delineate each of the processing stages that leads to the understanding of a language stimulus. These models often include a limited capacity storage structure that functions as an immediate, working, or short-term memory. In Massaro's (1975) model of language processing this structure is called generated abstract memory and it contains units corresponding to words, phrases, and sentences. Most information-processing models assume that written and spoken information gets to this short-term storage structure via different sequences of mental operations, and also that the mental operations required for understanding written and spoken discourse are the same beyond that point. For example, Massaro (1975) said, "Although the meaning of the word is accessed first in this word-by-word recognition process, its meaning can be modified or changed to agree with the overall context of the phrase, sentence, or situational context. At this point, the sequence of operations [for reading] becomes exactly the same to those discussed in speech processing, since they occur at the level of generated abstract memory"(p. 26).

The opinions of the linguists and the cognitive psychologists are related. If cognitive psychologists accept that there are no differences between the structures of spoken and written discourse beyond the different codes for words, then there is no reason to postulate unique mental operations beyond the decoding of words.

## A rationale for focusing on comprehension

The project to be reported in this paper focuses on the mental operations that occur after words and sentences are recognized in textbooks. The rationale for focusing on the higher-order comprehension processes is based on a rejection of Bloomfield's doctrine that writing is merely a secondary representation of speech.

The fallacy of Bloomfield's influential doctrine was clearly exposed by Hirsch (1977) in *The philosophy of composition*, which includes a number of references to other works on the linguistic status of writing. He points out that the structures of written and spoken discourse are fundamentally different because special techniques must be employed to make written discourse more self-contained. "Written discourse has to make up for its lack of intonation, gesture, and facial expression—most of all, for its lack of tacit situational understanding and active feedback between speaker and listener. Transcribed oral speech seems puzzling and elliptical in print because the words alone supply insufficient clues to meaning. On the other side, a written style of oral discourse will seem extremely mannered—highly pedantic and roundabout—in ordinary conversation" (pp. 22-23). Hirsch continues, "This eccentricity of written speech creates problems which cannot be solved by the ablest of native speakers without practice and instruction. That is why one needs to be *taught* composition in one's own language"(p. 31).

Because literacy involves acts of communication between writers and readers, Hirsch's analysis of writing offers insights into reading. Because the chief difficulty for native speakers in learning to write well is in learning to use language in an unaccustomed way, it is plausible that a chief difficulty in learning to read well is in learning to interpret language used in an unaccustomed way.

Educators compensate for this by using story materials in basal readers, thereby reducing the burden on novice readers already familiar with the structure of written stories thanks to teachers and parents who read stories to their children. But, in about the seventh grade, students are asked to learn more and more by reading textbooks that have structures very different from those of stories. In fact, the formal expository structures used in textbooks are different from anything to which students are exposed before they are required to read textbooks. Thus, when students first have to learn from textbooks, they are faced not only with new content, but also with a new kind of discourse. Unfortunately, formal reading instruction often stops at about this time. Some students manage to learn new strategies appropriate to these texts or to adapt old ones to the new discourse, but many students, even some who are fluent story readers, experience difficulty in learning from textbooks (Estes & Vaughan, 1978).

It is common in middle and high schools for teachers to review in class all the ideas introduced in mathematics and science reading assignments. The reason is that many students, even very bright ones who have no trouble learning new concepts when they are presented in class, are unable to pull the same ideas together when they are presented in textbooks. Although some have trouble with the vocabulary used in textbooks, the main problem is not their inability to understand the words or even the sentences in their textbooks but their inability to integrate the ideas into a structured representation of the text. Our research project on comprehension of textbooks grew out of similar classroom observations.

The uniqueness of written discourse extends beyond the uniqueness of print as a means of recording language; people write and speak differently. Written discourse must make up for the lack of many extra-verbal clues to meaning present in spoken discourse. As a result, writers must learn special linguistic devices to make their writing more self-contained than their speaking. These devices give written discourse its unique structure. Conversely, readers must learn to decode these linguistic devices and to use them to structure a representation of the information in the passage. The required cognitive abilities can be learned by reading or, perhaps, by listening to someone else read, but not by listening only to spoken discourse.

## Measuring the perceived structure of texts

The present collaborative research project was initiated to investigate the cognitive processes underlying the comprehension of mathematics and science textbooks (Deese, 1978; Estes & Vaughan, 1978; Rotondo, 1977; Shebilske, 1979). The principal aim is to provide a theoretical and empirical foundation for the development of better textbooks, and better diagnostic and instructional techniques for teaching the kinds of reading demanded by textbooks in mathematics and science. The first step was to develop methods for quantifying relevant aspects of text structure. Two distinctions must be made to explain what has been done so far. One is between the structure given to the text by the author and the structure perceived by the reader, the other is between formal and behavioral measures of text structure.

*The author's structure and the reader's strucuture*

The structure a reader perceives in and remembers about a text is based upon the structure given to the text by the the author, but the perceived and remembered structures are not completely determined by the structure imparted by the author. Iser (1973) expressed this as follows:

> The literary text activates our own faculties, enabling us to recreate the world it presents. The product of this activity is what we might call the virtual dimension of the text, which endows it with its reality. This virtual dimension is not the text itself, nor is it the imagination of the reader: it is the coming together of text and imagination.... Every sentence contains a preview of the next and forms a kind of viewfinder of what is to come; and this in turn changes the "preview" and so becomes a "viewfinder" for what has been read.... whenever the flow is interrupted and we are led off in unexpected directions, the opportunity is given to us to bring into play our own faculty for establishing connections—for filling in the gaps left by the text itself.
>
> These gaps have a different effect on the process of anticipation and retrospection, and thus on the "gestalt" of the virtual dimension, for they may be filled in different ways. For this reason, one text is potentially capable of several different realizations, and no reading can ever exhaust the full potential, for each individual reader will fill in the gaps in his own way, thereby excluding the various other possibilities; and as he reads, he will make his own decisions as to how the gap is to be filled. In this very act the dynamics of reading are revealed.(pp. 284-285)

Iser's notion of "gaps" is useful. Texts sometimes contain gaps which must be filled in by the reader. Filling in also occurs in other kinds of perception. For example, Figure 1 shows a degraded photograph of an intact scene. Once a person recognizes what the picture portrays he or she will have a fairly stable perception of it even though the perception will require considerable filling in. The picture is like a poorly written freshman composition with each black speck representing a sentence. Such a text will finally yield its meaning, but only after considerable filling in by the reader.

Figure 1. Photograph of a Dalmatian dog.

The active contribution of a perceiver is important even when a stimulus is without gaps. For example, Figure 2 contains no gaps, yet what is seen depends upon how the parts are organized. With one perceptual organization, a viewer sees two people standing shoulder to shoulder in front of an archway near the center of the painting. With a different perceptual organization, the features of the two people and the archway can be seen as a bust of Voltaire.

Similarly, to comprehend a text, a reader must combine the ideas expressed in it. An author can select ideas and sequence them in an attempt to lead a reader to a particular combination, but, in the end, the reader must structure a representation of the information in the passage. Sometimes the reader's representation contains much less than the author had intended. For example, suppose a science textbook says "Let the month of September represent the entire age of the earth" and then uses dates in September to indicate the relative times of paleontological events. The text structure is sound, but an internal representation will have a faulty structure if a reader fails to relate the condensed time scale to the actual one, as sometimes happens (Carol Seal, personal communication).

It is not always bad for a reader to construct an internal representation with a structure different from the structure of the text. For example, the internal representation of this statement will be far richer than the structure of the text

Figure 2. Salvador Dali, "The Slave Market with Disappearing Bust of Voltaire."

itself for those readers who can assimilate what is said here with the theories of Piaget (1926), Schank and Abelson (1977), Neisser (1976), and others.

The textbook project at Virginia takes into account the difference between the structure provided by the author and the structure perceived and remembered by the reader. To do this both formal and behavioral measures of text structure are used.

*Formal and behavioral measures of text structure*

The distinction between formal and behavioral measures of text structure is illustrated by the differences between readability formulas and cloze procedures. Readability formulas indicate how information about sentence length and vocabulary difficulty can be combined to yield a measure of text difficulty specified in grade levels (Fry, 1968). They are *formal* in the sense that their measures follow from a specific set of rules applied to the structual characteristics of the text itself. In contrast, cloze procedures indicate grade level by how well readers can fill in words that are removed from the text (Robinson, 1971). Such procedures are *behavioral* in that their measures are based on the performance of subjects on specific tasks.

Readability formulas and the cloze procedures have been useful to teachers and researchers but they are inadequate as the sole means of analyzing the comprehensibility of reading materials because they provide no information about important aspects of a text's macrostructure. For example, they do not indicate how the ideas in one sentence relate to the ideas in another or how the conceptual content of text relates to a specific larger body of knowledge. Measures of both of these factors are being developed but in this paper only the former measures will be reported.

Both formal and behavioral measures are used. The measures are based on work that reduces text to a set of base propositions stated in logical or machine-compatible form (Anderson & Bower, 1973; Frederiksen, 1975a, 1975b, 1975c; Grimes, 1972; Kintsch, 1974; Norman & Rumelhart, 1975; Schank, 1972). Our project makes use of these methods but is developing new ones more appropriate for textbooks.

In addition to the formal methods, behavioral procedures for quantifying important aspects of text structures are under development. For example, one group of subjects segmented passages into "idea units" by marking where they thought one idea ended and another began; a second group rated how important they perceived each idea unit to be with respect to the main ideas the author wished to convey; a third group rated how important they perceived each idea unit to be with respect to a specific task demand (being able to do well on a detailed examination including objective and essay questions); a fourth group recalled the passage in their own words. Like the formal measures, the behavioral measures were based on prior work by other investigators (Brown & Smiley, 1977), but we have refined the experimental procedures and the methods for analyzing the data by taking advantage of advances in partitioning and clustering analysis (Hartigan, 1975) and advances in the analysis of covariance structures in multivariate systems (Rotondo, 1968).

*Selected results*
Some of the results obtained to date can be used to illustrate the importance of formal measures of textual macrostructure and the advantages of behavioral measures over formal measures for some purposes.

*Importance of formal measures.* We have used a formal method being developed by Deese (1978) to analyze the textual macrostructure of chapters from three biology textbooks, one at the seventh grade level, one at the tenth grade level, and one at the college level. We found important differences among the texts which were not reflected in the surface structural aspects usually measured by reading formulas. For example, they differ in the extent to which they demand inferences to be made by the reader, the extent to which information is presented ambiguously, and the extent to which the organization of the presentation follows the organization of the material. The tenth grade chapter for instance begins with a particular example. The general problem of speciation is buried in the text and in the hierarchy describing it. The college text, on the other hand, begins immediately with the general principles so that the topical statement is also the most general statement about species. Another important finding was that the hierarchical structures describing the texts were less elaborate for the lower level texts. These differences probably represent the authors' intuitions about what students at various levels can comprehend. Whether or not these intuitions are correct is now being examined by our research.

*Advantages of behavioral measures.* Formal measures quantify important aspects of the textual structure provided by the author of a passage; behavioral measures reflect text structure as it is perceived and remembered by the reader. The behavioral measure takes into account the active contribution of the reader, which is especially important for research on the comprehension of textbooks. The following results demonstrate the advantage of behavioral measures for studying styles of discourse used in textbooks, task demands made in classrooms, and flexible reading strategies used by superior readers.

*Style of discourse.* A common style of discourse states the most important ideas as topic sentences and less important ideas as subsidiary statements. For this style formal measures of text structures are highly predictive of probability of recall: propositions that are higher in the hierarchy of the discourse are recalled better (Kintsch, 1974; Kintsch, Kozminsky, Streby, McKoon, & Keenan, 1975). However, formal measures are not predictive of recall for other styles occuring frequently in textbooks. For example, Deese (1978) showed that formal measures fail to predict recall for the following paragraph:

> Certain business organizations have as their major task the establishment of credit ratings. Individuals as well as businesses ordinarily need some minimum credit ratings in order to borrow money or open charge accounts. This whole enterprise is based on the simple but critical assumption that there is consistency in man's behavior. If the history of the financial dealings of a man shows that he regularly met his financial obligations, it is assumed that in the future he will continue to respond in the same manner. If, on the contrary, a man's history shows that he has frequently made late payments on his debtors, has often changed his place of residence to avoid being easily contacted, or has had merchandise repossessed, it is assumed that he will be a poor credit risk in the future. Both men have behaved in a consistent manner in the past, and it is presumed that each man's responses in the future will parallel to some extent those of the past; one man will continue to assume only the financial obligations he can handle, the other will not. (Underwood, 1966, p. 1)

On the surface the paragraph is about credit ratings. Correspondingly, formal measures rank the statements about credit ratings high in the hierarchy of the discourse. However, most subjects interpret this paragraph as a kind of parable with the real message being that human behavior is consistent and predictable. As a result their attempts to recall the passage focus on the statements about consistency and predictability, which are low in the hierarchy defined by the formal measures. Karmiohl (1979) has found that the idea expressed in the third sentence, which is about consistency of behavior, was included in paraphrastic recalls more often than the ideas expressed in the first two sentences, which are about credit ratings.

Karmiohl went on to show that behavioral measures succeed in capturing these same recall data. He had separate groups of subjects divide the passage into idea units and rate their importance with respect to the main ideas the author wished to convey. He found that the idea expressed in the third sentence was rated higher than those in the first two sentences, and predicted the recall for this part of the passage. He also found that the importance ratings did well at predicting recall for the rest of the passage and for two other passages which could not be handled by formal measures.

*Task demands*. Another limitation of formal measures is that they are not sensitive to changes in task demands. They yield one and only one structure no matter what the task demands are. This is acceptable when the task demands are straightforward enough that what is important to and emphasized by the author is also important to the reader. However, what is important to the reader can be greatly influenced by the purpose for reading and is not necessarily what is salient in the structure given by the author. For example, some of the author's main ideas are sometimes designated as unimportant with respect to specific learning objectives given to students before they read (Melton, 1978).

Karmiohl has also found that behavioral measures have the advantage of being sensitive to specific task demands. He repeated the rating and recall procedures described above except that subjects were told that they were reading the passage as an assignment for a specific course. The passage from Underwood was read for a business course, an advertisement for Polaroid's SX-70 camera was read for a history of science course, and an editorial on the pros and cons of out-of-state enrolment at the University of Virginia was read for a logic course. He found that the pattern of recall was quite different from those described above. For example, in the passage from Underwood the ideas in sentences 1 and 2 were recalled more frequently than those in sentence 3. The main finding was that the differences in the patterns of recall were predicted quite well by the importance ratings of separate groups of subjects who rated with the specific task demands in mind.

*Flexible reading strategies*. Another advantage of behavioral measures is that they can reflect how the preceived structure of a passage changes during reading. In the procedures described above, subjects read the whole passage before they went back to rate the importance of idea units. This procedure is useful in predicting the structure of what readers will remember about a passage but it cannot reflect how the perceived structure of a passage changes during reading. To measure those changes, Shebilske and Reid (1979) developed a procedure in which idea units are presented one at a time and subjects are asked to rate the importance of each before they have a chance to read the whole passage. In this procedure, the reader must predict, on the basis of the preceding parts of the passage, how an idea fits into the structure of the whole passage.

Using this procedure Karmiohl (1979) found that a reader's perception of textual structure can change during reading. Using the same passages described above, Karmiohl had one group of subjects make predictive ratings of each idea unit before reading the whole passage and another group make final ratings after reading it. He found that the predictive ratings differed significantly from the final ratings in the first part of each passage but that the two kinds of ratings were very similar near the end of each passage. For example, the final ratings of the Underwood paragraph put the importance of the third sentence, about consistency of behavior, above the importance of the first two sentences, about credit ratings; the opposite pattern was indicated by the predictive ratings. However, near the end of the passage both groups rated the importance of statements about consistency or predictability higher than statements about credit. At first, the predictive ratings were consistent with the structure of the text given by the formal measures; near the end, the predictive ratings deviated from the formal measures and reflected the importance of statements with respect to the real message of the passage.

Having measures that reflect moment-to-moment changes in the perceptual organization of text is particularly important for studying how students modulate their rate of and approach to reading with respect to the perceived structure of the text. We are studying this by observing how students modulate their eye movements with respect to units differing in their relationships to the meaning of the passage as a whole (Shebilske & Reid, 1979).

## Implications

The ability of a reader to represent written discourse is a cardinal basis of literacy. Research that explores the comprehension processes underlying the representation of text will have important theoretical and practical implications some of which are already clear in our work with textbooks.

First, the research has provided useful formal and behavioral measures of textual structure. As described above, these measures go beyond readability formulas and cloze procedures in several important ways. These advances are useful not only for quantifying aspects of text for research but also for analyzing text in the classroom and for suggesting how textbooks should be written.

Second, the research has paved the way for describing what readers are doing when they are reading textbooks. Educators agree that an essential part of skilled reading is the ability to modulate one's rate of and approach to reading with respect to changes in conceptual content of texts (Gibson & Levin, 1975; Harris &

Sipay, 1975; McDonald, 1963; Rankin, 1974; Rankin & Hess, 1971; Smith, 1975). This flexibility ought not to be treated as a single strategy but as a compound of component strategies. Our procedures allow us to study these component strategies of flexibility using factor-analytic and experimental approaches in a comprehensive analysis of individual differences in learning from textbooks.

Others have used factor-analytic approaches (Davis, 1968), which have been criticized for isolating component skills that have little or no relevance except in reading tests (Spache & Spache, 1977). In contrast, we give typical classroom reading assignments which are more relevant tasks for identifying important components of reading behavior. We examined reading strategies within passages by observing how students modulate their rate and approach with respect to units differing in their relationship to the meaning of the passage as a whole. This part of our research will have important instructional implications (Cooper & Petrosky, 1975; Goodman, 1967; Schafer, 1978) if it succeeds in describing in detail what readers are doing when they read textbooks. It will also have theoretical implications for theories of comprehension by giving insights into how conceptual representations are constructed *during* reading and for theories of how eye movements are controlled by giving insights into how eye movements are influenced by comprehension processes (Shebilske & Reid, 1979).

Finally, our research has produced some important advances in measures of the quality of comprehension. Both teachers and researchers have long recognized the potential value of asking readers to paraphase what they have read. In the past a disadvantage of this approach has been the inability to evaluate paraphratic recalls. We have made improvements in analyzing this kind of recall by using formal measures and behavioral measures to define propositional structures. We have found our procedures to be useful in analyzing the quality of comprehension, though we are by no means committed to the view that propositional analyses will capture all relations between a text and a student's understanding of it.

Research on recognition processes is important but it can only scratch the surface of literacy. We can approach the heart of the matter by analyzing the interrelationships among text structures, reading strategies, and comprehension with realistic materials and realistic task demands.

# References

Anderson, J. R., & Bower, G. H. *Human associative memory*. Washington, DC: V. H. Winston, 1973.

Bloomfield, L. *Language*. New York: Holt, 1933.

Brown, A. L., & Smiley, S. S. Rating the importance of structural units of prose passages: a problem of metacognitive development. *Child Development*, 1977, *48*, 1-8.

Cooper, C. R., & Petrosky, A. R. A psycholinguistic view of the fluent reading process. *Journal of Reading*, 1976, *20*, 184-207.

Davis, F. R. Research in comprehension in reading. *Reading Research Quarterly*, 1968, *3*, 499-544.

Deese, J. Thought into speech. *American Scientist*, 1978, *66*, 314-321.

Estes, T. H., & Vaughan, J. L., Jr. *Reading and learning in the content classroom: diagnostic and instructional strategies*. Boston: Allyn & Bacon, 1978.

Frederiksen, C. H. Representing logical and semantic structures of knowledge acquired from discourse. *Cognitive Psychology*, 1975, *1*, 371-458. (a)

Frederiksen, C. H. Acquisition of semantic information from discourse: effects of repeated exposures. *Journal of Verbal Learning and Verbal Behavior*, 1975, *14*, 158-169. (b)

Frederiksen, C. H. Effects of context induced processing operations on semantic information acquired from discourse. *Cognitive Psychology*, 1975, *7*, 139-166. (c)

Fry, E. A readability formula that saves time. *Journal of Reading*, 1968, *11*, 513-516.

Gibson, E. J., & Levin, H. *The psychology of reading*. Cambridge, Mass.: MIT Press, 1975.

Goodman, K. S. Reading: A psycholinguistic guessing game. *Journal of the Reading Specialist*, 1967, 126-135.

Grimes, J. F. *The thread of discourse*. The Hague: Mouton, 1972.

Harris, A. J., & Sipay, E. R. *How to increase reading ability*: a *guide to developmental and remedial methods* (6th ed.). New York: David McKay Company Inc., 1975.

Hartigan, J. A. *Clustering algorithms*. New York: Wiley, 1975.

Hirsch, E. D. *The philosophy of composition*. Chicago: University of Chicago Press, 1977.

Iser, W. The reading process: a phenomenological approach. In A. Bradford (Ed.), *Teaching English to speakers of English*. New York; Harcourt, Brace, Jovanovich, 1973.

Karmiohl, C. M. Text-based and reader-based methods of text analysis. Unpublished masters' thesis, University of Virginia, 1979.

Kintsch, W. *The representation of meaning in memory*. New York: Wiley, 1974.

Kintsch, W., Kozminsky, E., Streby, W. J., McKoon, G., & Keenan, J. M. Comprehension and recall of text as a function of content variables. *Journal of Verbal Learning and Verbal Behavior*, 1975, *14*, 196-214.

Massaro, D. W. *Understanding language*. New York: Academic Press, 1975.

McDonald, A. S. Flexibility in reading. *International Reading Association Conference Proceedings*, 1963, *8*, 81-85.

Melton, R. F. Resolution of conflicting claims concerning the effect of behavioral objectives on student learning. *Review of Educational Research*, 1978, *48*, 291-302.

Neisser, U. *Cognition and reality*. San Francisco: Freeman, 1976.

Norman, D. A., & Rumelhart, D. E. *Explorations in cognition*. San Francisco: W. H. Freeman, 1975.

Pearson, B. *Introduction to linguistic concepts*, New York: Academic Press, 1975.

Piaget, J. *The language and thought of the child*. New York: Harcourt, Brace, 1926.

Rankin, E. F. The measurement of reading flexibility: problems and perspectives. *Reading Information Series: Where Do We Go?* International Reading Association, 1974.

Rankin, E. F., & Hess, A. K. The measurement of internal (intra-article) reading flexibility. *Nineteenth Yearbook (Vol. 1)*. *National Reading Conference Milwaukee*: The National Reading Conference, 1971, 254-262.

Robinson, R. D. *An introduction to the cloze procedure*. Newark, Delaware: International Reading Association, 1971.

Rotondo, J. A. Discrete structural models of organization in free recall. *Journal of Mathematical Psychology*, 1977, *16*, 95-120.

Schafer, R. E. Will psycholinguistics change reading in secondary schools? *Journal of Reading*, 1978, *21*, 305-316.

Schank, R. Identification of conceptualizations underlying natural language. In R. Schank & K. Colby (Eds.), *Computer models of thought and language*. San Francisco: W. H. Freeman, 1973.

Schank, R., & Abelson, R. P. *Scripts, plans, goals, and understanding: an inquiry into human knowledge structures*. New York: Halsted, 1977.

Shebilske, W. L., & Reid, S. L. Reading eye movements, macro-structure and comprehension processes. In P. A. Kolers, M. E. Wrolstad, & H. Bouma (Eds.), *Processing of visible language 1*. New York and London: Plenum Press, 1979.

Smith, F. *Comprehension and learning*. New York: Holt, Rinehart, and Winston, 1975.

Spache, G., & Spache, E. *Reading in the elementary school*. Boston: Allyn & Bacon, 1977.

Underwood, B. *Experimental psychology*. New York: Appleton-Century-Crofts, 1966.

# Graphic aspects of complex texts: Typography as macro-punctuation

Robert H. W. Waller

*A case is made for the inclusion of graphic and spatial factors in the linguistic analysis of text, and in common rules and guidelines for clear writing. Some conceptual problems are considered and a parallel is drawn between the roles of punctuation and typography at the micro- and macro-levels of texts. The gradual codification of punctuation, from the original vernacular through an elocutionary or stylistic role to a well-specified syntactic role, is suggested as an indication of a direction for future typographic analysis.*

The study of typography as a functional component of written communication has a relatively short history. Consequently, we have a rather poor armoury of concepts, definitions, metaphors, or frameworks with which to handle a subject area that straddles the critical frontiers between verbal and graphic communication, the writer and the reader, and creative writing and the manufacture of print.

This paper neither reports data nor discusses methodology; rather, it attempts by model and metaphor to establish a background necessary for the formulation of sensible research questions and the design of productive experiments.

Typographic study has suffered from the distinction drawn between two meanings of the word "writing": its literary sense (composing) as distinct from its graphic sense (making meaningful marks). Thus we can "write" (literarily) a speech or a broadcast and we can "write" (graphically) a complex mathematical equation. The one is a transcription of words for which graphic form is simply a recording medium, the other cannot be well encoded verbally and its spatial qualities comprise a syntax.

The majority of printed materials fall into neither of these extreme categories. A typical educational text, for example, consists of a number of verbal sequences, together with illustrative and tabular displays, the organization of which is achieved both by cross-reference and by graphic and spatial arrangement on the page and in the book. The contribution made by typography here is at the "macro" level of text organization, as distinct from the "micro" level that occurs within a linear sequence (such as the mathematical formula).

In the past, typography has been too readily defined in simple operational terms as "what typographers do." Because, for various historical and managerial reasons, the professional activity of typographers is normally confined to the graphic treatment of a (literarily) finished text, we thereby reduce it, in theoretical terms as well, to a largely decorative role. In so doing, we ignore the fact that the "finished" text almost certainly uses many typographic organizational options such as footnotes, headings, captions, lists, and tables. For all these devices, spatial and graphic distinctions are of the essence. However, while rules for the composition of graphically simple verbal sequences exist in usages, and have been described in grammers, the state of typographic theory is relatively primitive. That is, although rules of some kind may exist (and, of course, it is by no means certain that they do) they have not yet been formally codified. Consequently, there is no assurance that writers, or indeed typographers, use typographic options consistently; there is no well-argued and theoretically-sound source of guidance for the composition or evaluation of complex text; and there is no consistent set of rules on which to base the kind of effective-reading instruction that advises students to make sensible use of visually signalled text structure.

For many years linguistics was confined almost exclusively to intra-sentence analysis but recently more attention has been given to the structure of entire texts and discourses. Some of this work has been inspired by the application of computers to language study. Research on machine translation and artificial intelligence has suggested that the interpretation of stories and arguments is governed by grammar-like rules, and that computers must be programmed with these rules, together with contextually relevant background "knowledge," before they can process even the simplest text. The application of computers to practical text-handling (typesetting, editing, and design) may have a similar effect on typography, imposing a similar degree of discipline on our thinking. Text-processing systems offer typographic menus that restrict users to a limited range of options. The quality of such systems will depend on the analysis on which they are based.

A further demand for the codification of a greater part of typographic practice will come from legislators. The "plain English" laws now being passed in a number of states in the U.S.A. are likely the pattern for the future and they will probably encompass graphic as well as linguistic factors of document design.

Such developments will require us to systematize aspects of text presentation that we have previously been content to leave completely to intuition. This is not as great a threat to the graphic designer as it appears. The existence of grammatical rules has not diminished the art of writing and the production of effective documents will always require sophisticated personal skills. The concerned designer will welcome any means whereby the reliability and quality of his products might be assured, and his professional skills might be more fully integrated into our general concept of literacy.


*Text and speech*
The definitional distinction between written and spoken discourse is, plainly, that the first is encoded in graphic marks on a surface or field, while the second is encoded in sound. At the micro-linguistic (word) level the phonic and graphic

media are adequately equivalent but, at the broader level of discourse, significant differences are found. With some exceptions, such as text-like speech (a scripted monologue, for instance) or speech-like text (a spontaneous personal letter), the two forms of discourse, and their sub-varieties, display distinct forms of argument, syntax, and other stylistic variables less easily described. Distinctions of this sort stem not so much from the cognitive differences between reading and listening, or talking and writing, as from the strategic implications of the separation of writer and reader in time and place.

All language is artificial, written language especially so. The degree to which language systems are natural or innate is debatable but there is no doubt that any particular discourse is a constructed affair, derived from the linguistic and cognitive competencies and the social and information needs of its participants. Speech and text relate to the same lexical and syntactic base but an effective performance in either medium requires mastery of contextual and pragmatic factors that lie outside the language and are often peculiar to a particular situation or subject. Competence in speech is acquired more or less naturally, and in normal conversation there are opportunities to query, repeat, or rephrase information. In text, however, clear explanation of complex events (journalism), sciences (schoolbooks), regulations (government documents), or instructions (technical manuals) is an enormously skilled task that few master thoroughly. Studies by Baldwin and Coady (1978) seem to reinforce this view of the artificiality of written language; they found that punctuation—an artificial, non-verbal syntactic aid—had little effect on the comprehension of text by young children but was an acquired and relatively sophisticated skill developed only by older, more experienced readers. There is no lack of evidence that even highly-skilled readers can suffer from the poor standard of writing resulting from a process of education that teaches the established formalities of English grammar to the exclusion of less well-documented communication strategies.

So, while speech is on the whole spontaneous, text is a planned communication and makes a series of assumptions and predictions about the reader. It is, therefore, the product of a design process; and whereas the production of a text involves predictions ranging from the reader's knowledge and purposes to his or her eyesight or the size of the bookshelf, clearly our concept of "design" must refer not only to the visual appearance of the document but to all aspects of information defined in the broadest manner. If "literacy" may be taken to refer to the skilled use of the written word, it is as much a design as a linguistic skill. A fully literate writer, then, is one who has mastered not only conventional grammar (rules for the construction of language that are divorced from either the spoken or the written context) but also the full implications of the "written-ness" of language that is, the constraints and opportunities that result from, first, the separation between the writer and his or her readers and, second, the physical and visual nature of documents and graphic language.

*Writers and readers, speakers and listeners*

Wright (1979) reports that many people prefer to ask someone for information rather than look it up in a book or pamphlet. For example, a person needing information about his or her eligibility for welfare is normally well advised to ask about it rather than attempt to interpret a complex document. The clerk can ask a series of questions about the enquirer's status and quickly give the correct ruling. To rely on the equivalent written information requires careful sifting of the relevant information from a maze of conditional explanations intended to serve many enquirers with a wide range of questions and backgrounds. In face-to-face conversation the expert can eliminate large amounts of irrelevant detail with each question but in the document the individual reader carries the whole burden of search and interpretation.

An appreciation of this type of problem as distinct, for example, from that of purely narrative or descriptive text leads us to treat with caution over-simple models of communication. It is common (for example Guirard, 1968) to find the communication process modelled as a simple one-way transmission of a message from a sender to a receiver, with various embellishments to describe more detailed models of the encoding, transmitting, and decoding mechanisms. Many such models were published (Johnson and Klare, 1961) during the years following the appearance of Shannon and Weaver's (1949) information theory. They were attractive because their mathematical origins gave them a certain scientific status but, although we can identify analogous components in electronic signalling systems and networks of purposive human beings, there is no reason to suppose that they operate in the same way (Waller, 1979).

An inappropriate model can bias the way a subject is researched and taught. In graphic design the prevalence of poorly-posed research questions, with consequently inoperable results, has regrettably turned most practitioners and teachers away from educational psychology as a source of theory and data. A text is not merely a psycholinguistic phenomenon. It is also a physical artefact, the product of writing and publishing processes, and a component in the user's life. A model of textual communication that accounts for all graphically organized text features must relate to these broader, pragmatic issues.

I have argued that because writer and reader are separated in time and place, text plays a role in their relationship quite different from that of speech. Text differs from speech first to compensate for the poverty of prose in comparison with certain aspects of dialogue and second to capitalize on its relative superiority.

The poverty of prose stems from the lack of opportunity for immediate feedback to the communicator about whether or not his or her audience regards the message as relevant, comprehensible, credible, or persuasive. Authors can make fewer accurate assumptions about the pragmatics of communication—the context, purposes, and knowledge of their readers. Explanatory or instructional text therefore contains frequent interpolations in the form of digressions, over-views, conditionals, definitions, and recapitulations, to answer a wide range of anticipated queries from readers. These exist in spoken discourse, too, but they can be tailored to fit a particular audience or to respond to specific feedback cues. Instructional text consists of prose treated graphically and spatially to enable readers to handle its organizational complexity.

The relative superiority of text lies in its physical nature: it provides a permanent organized record that allows analysis, criticism, refinement, reflection, and review, permitting private study and the economical distribution of information.

In direct conversation language is only one element in our recognition and comprehension of another person. A text must completely replace that other, to become a surrogate reader for writer and vice versa. The written-ness of language, its typographic and spatial nature, can be seen from these two perspectives: for the writer it has primarily a rhetorical function, enhancing the available means of expression; for the reader it has an additional access function, enabling the purposive, reflective, and selective use of texts and enhancing the available means of enquiry.

As Table 1 illustrates, some typographically signalled devices are exclusively components of text-as-argument, while others belong to text-as-artefact; many can be placed in both schemas. A typical textbook is, then, a complex system of intermeshed components, some arranged in a simple sequential order, but many displayed in parallel with other components or dispersed throughout the text.

Because this organized complexity of function and structure has no direct equivalent in unscripted spoken discourse, conventions or rules for its display will not be found in natural language. And, because graphic language is thus artificial, such rules must derive from some consideration of the source of that artificiality: the practical aspects of writing and printing systems.

*Codifying rules for graphic language*

The formal codification of English orthography was relatively recent. The development of letterforms was to a large degree frozen by the spread of printing and it was only during the seventeenth and eighteenth centuries after many years of vernacular development in which a wide variety of forms was in use that English spelling and punctuation were standardized. The codification of punctuation suggests an interesting parallel with typography. Punctuation is the single aspect of written language, for which grammatical rules exist, that does not represent words themselves but the spaces between them. It is, then, an organizational system at the micro-text level functioning in much the same way as typographic signals and the use of space at the macro-text level.

Table 1. Some functions of the typographic organization of text.

---

**Rhetorical functions**

---

| | |
|---|---|
| About the argument | summarization (title, summary) |
| | introduction (foreword, preface, introduction) |
| Within the argument | emphasis (underlining, italics, etc.) |
| | transition (headings, space, etc.) |
| | bifurcation (alternative options, parallel texts, interpolation sections) |
| Extra to the argument | substantiation (footnotes, appendices, references) |
| | addenda (apologia, acknowledgements, etc.) |

---

**Access functions**

---

| | |
|---|---|
| About the book | overviews (contents list, abstract) |
| | definitives (glossary, index) |
| | identifiers (title, author, style) |
| Within the book | locators (topical headings, typographic signalling) |
| | descriptors (functional headings, captions) |
| Extra to the book | study guidance (recommended reading, exercises) |

---

Early grammarians regarded punctuation as an elocutionary aid, denoting breathing spaces, pauses for dramatic effect, and cues for special intonations or voices required of the reader (as in exclamation, interrogation, and quotation marks, and the "irony mark" proposed by several early linguists). For many years reading was usually vocalized; silent reading is surprisingly recent

(Pugh, 1975). During the late seventeenth and eighteenth centuries, writers of treatises on grammar began to develop a syntactic function for punctuation distinct from indications of timing, breathing, and voice. The various kinds of period—full point, comma, semi-colon, and colon—rather than denoting relative lengths of pauses, were seen as making syntactically distinct kinds of transitions within and between sentences. Honan (1960) describes how, in the nineteenth century, attempts to inject order and consistency into the use of punctuation led to the complete rejection of elocutionary theories and the description (or, to some, the imposition) of elaborate rules for syntactic punctuation.

At the same time, greater interest was also being shown in purely graphic aspects of text that did not share even the elocutionary link with spoken language: for example, the use of asterisks, matrices, braces, and oblique strokes to organize language spatially and the use of alternative type styles to differentiate text components. This interest was not carried very far, however, and grammarians neither developed rules for these devices nor suggested a place for them in a theory of linguistics.

Cohen (1977) remarks on the attention given to graphic factors by early linguists: "The language texts of the period [1640-1785], reflecting an effort to represent the obvious sense of the written language, include sections on punctuation, capitalization, and often, handwriting and type styles. These sections are significantly prominent" (p. 50). If modern complex instructional texts, maintenance manuals, or government regulations had existed at that time, it seems entirely possible that those linguists would have encompassed in their theories some of the typographic components discussed above.

In contrast, it is hard to find one modern general linguistics textbook that even mentions punctuation. Those linguists who do consider graphic factors are from more recent branches like stylistics (Crystal & Davy, 1969) or text linguistics (Werlich, 1976), although neither develops the topic to any depth. Where modern linguists study language as a key to understanding human thought, early linguists saw it primarily as a representation of reality.

*Typography as macro-punctuation*

Punctuation literally means "pointing," and refers specifically to the use of such marks as the full point, comma, and so on. However, many of the effects achieved by punctuation can also be achieved by other means. For example, a comment that appears in parentheses might just as well appear in a footnote and, indeed, if it is a particularly long comment or quotation it normally is footnoted or may even appear in an appendix. Most other types of punctuation also seem to have equivalents at the macro-text level. Table 2 displays four common functions of punctuation for which there are corresponding devices at the micro- and macro-text levels.

Table 2. Some functions of micro- and macro-punctuation.

|  | Micro-level | Macro-level |
|---|---|---|
| Delineation | initial capital<br>full point<br>comma<br>semi-colon<br>colon | headings<br>title pages<br>space<br>rules |
| Interpolation | parentheses<br>dashes<br>commas | footnotes<br>boxed inserts<br>marginalia<br>indentation |
| Serialization | commas<br>semi-colons<br>oblique strokes<br>bullets<br>numerals | headings, numerals<br>tabular format<br>regular spacing/styling |
| Stylization | quotation marks<br>exclamation marks<br>question marks | size variation<br>style variation<br>layout variation |

Delineation refers to methods of indicating the beginning and end of text segments, ranging from clauses (which can be bounded by commas), through sentences (bounded by initial capitals and full points), paragraphs, chapters, parts, and ultimately, to books (bounded by covers).

Interpolation refers to the insertion or juxtaposition of a short segment into a longer one in such a way that the continuity of the sentence, paragraph, page, chapter, or book is not destroyed.

Serialization refers to the organization of segments into clear structures, sets, or series. For example, this paragraph is one of a set of four that is signalled simply by the linguistic rhythm of the first two words; the set could have been numbered, bulleted, or typographically distinguished from the rest of the text.

Stylization refers to the indication of a mode of discourse differing in voice or genre from the main body of text.

Delineation and stylization have obvious equivalents in spoken language:

delineation similar to the beginning and end of a segment of discourse, stylization having parallels with vocal tone or quality. Complex serialization is less easy to achieve in speech though possible because it refers to sequential aspects of language. Interpolation is particularly interesting because it includes a number of communication strategies that are purely spatial.

Complex text, broadly defined, typically comprises instructions, regulations, classifications, and procedures rather than simple narratives or descriptions; it serves a variety of readers with different needs and purposes; and it is a component of a larger system, industrial, administrative, or educational. Such text rarely has a single author and is often altered or enlarged to reflect new developments in the system, often without an overall review for many years. In effect, then, it contains a large number of embedded conditionals, definitions, digressions, quotations, and other interpolations that, in attempting to solve a wide variety of problems, increase the difficulties for the individual who must separate his or her requirements from those of others.

Because our concept of writing is basically non-graphic, spatial or typographic solutions tend to be used as a last resort: government documents often have boxed inserts containing warnings about the penalties for supplying incorrect information or reminders to sign or read a particular item. Instead of this "lifebelt" approach to the bemused reader, the document, or even the system to which it relates, should be completely redesigned.

A number of fairly radical graphic solutions have been proposed. One of the best known but least used is the ordinary-language algorithm (Lewis, Horabin, & Gane, 1967), which breaks down conditional information (if—then—unless constructions) into simple yes—no questions spatially arrayed in branching sequences. Educational texts frequently contain "concept maps," flow or systems diagrams of the text content that enable readers to see its structure independently of the precise sequence into which the writer has ordered it. Side headings or marginal notes are frequently used to similar effect. They enable the writer, or a commentator, teacher, or editor, to present a viewpoint, structure, or commentary separate from that provided by the author. In this sense, especially if they are so long as almost to rival the main discourse, they can be described as "parallel texts."

Parallel texts, the parallel juxtaposition of two or more texts on the same page, is a technique of language display that has flourished in the past. Medieval books frequently presented classic or sacred texts accompanied by a commentary. There are a number of books which have been overlayed with several generations of commentary, and commentary on the commentary, by a number of different readers. Contemporary parallel texts combine a variety of different text types. For example, texts with an unusually large number of footnotes have occasionally been "legitimized" by a parallel two-column layout; a popular electronics magazine recently published an article in three different but parallel versions that referred to the same concepts and illustrations and were addressed respectively to the beginner, the scientist/expert, and the hobbyist wishing to construct the apparatus. A recent "futures" book interwove several perspectives on the same subject by using colour-coded pages throughout.

Work is still in progress on the analysis of parallel texts (how authors modify their linguistic signals in response to format and typographic options, how parallel texts relate to one another and indicate that relationship) but there is little doubt that exploiting such graphic opportunities for organizing information, displaying relationships and overviewing arguments, communicators can usefully extend the conventions of text beyond the linear form of spoken language.

*Problems of description and analysis*

Although the categories in Table 2 are neither exhaustive in content nor discrete in function, they represent a minimum set of structural concepts with which to handle visually complex text. In addition to the common devices and techniques listed, there are numerous typographic effects that remain unclassified and un-named. For the linguist who wishes to include typographic factors in text analysis there are both simple practical problems of describing and naming typographic variables and interpretative problems of typographic semantics.

The only existing system for describing typography on which there is a large measure of agreement is that of technical specification in the printing industry. Even there it is not always possible for the designer to specify his intentions using only a limited set of proof-correction marks and technical in-structions; he must often provide a drawing for the typesetter. Mountford (per-sonal communication) has identified ten categories of graphic-linguistic devices for inclusion in the linguistic analysis of text, although problems still remain: incorporating those devices in linguistic notation, and describing them in purely linguistic terms to the exclusion of functional factors such as book production and information location. In a personal communication, Twyman notes that he is developing a system that may overcome the notational problem. It is restricted to characters available on a standard typewriter and thus obviates the need for the expensive and difficult reproduction of original documents. It is also content-free and technology-free: it can be used with other systems of linguistic description and is not confined to the limitation of a particular typesetting system.

The problems of typographic semantics have already been implied: there is no agreement about what typographic conventions mean, there is no consistency in their use, and in practical analysis there is even doubt that the phenomenon investigated actually carries a meaning in the ordinary sense of the word.

Table 3 contrasts four sources of graphic effects. Any particular graphic device or example of graphic organization may display a combination of these in a way that defeats a simple analysis of their purpose or function.

Table 3. Semantic confusions in typography.

| Graphic effects | Semantic status |
| --- | --- |
| Conventional | Denotative |
| Representational | Onomatopoetic |
| Associational | Connotative |
| Artefactual | (none) |
| Positional | Syntactic and performative |

Conventional effects are those that have arisen for a number of historical or accidental reasons (including other factors in this table), but which have acquired a meaning about which there is general agreement. In conventional graphic effects there is a visually arbitrary relationship between the graphic symbol, or effect, and its referent. For example, the letters of the alphabet are conventional, bearing no obvious relationship to the sound patterns of speech.

Representational effects are those that have some correspondence with visual experience or some relationship to sounds. For example, the use of bold type for emphasis reflects vocal stress, and musical notation reflects the use of the "up-down" metaphor in the description of music.

Associational effects result from stylization, exploiting graphic motifs originating from one of the other factors in this schema. They are responses to social conventions or aesthetic preferences that become attached to particular graphic effects. For example, the use of copperplate script on items purporting to be valuable (such as guarantee certificates) imitates the original functional use of such lettering in security printing and banknotes.

Artefactual effects result from the fact that a text is a manufactured object. Thus, many of the graphic features of a text that might be mistaken as having some quasi-linguistic intent can be explained in this way. For example, the choice of a typeface may result from the limitations of a printing system: bold type is absent from typewritten material simply because it is not available on a typewriter; and the amount of text or illustrative material that can be placed on a page is limited by the size of that page. Garland (1979) distinguishes between the influence on the form of a diagram of, first, the physical nature of the diagram, its contents, and external constraints of format (its "shape"), and, second, the use of a model, example, or accepted diagram convention (its "pattern").

Positional effects, the relative positions of text components on the page or in a book, can relate to the performative nature of writing and reading. That is, in addition to the syntactic correctness or clarity of a particular sequence of components, their position may relate to an anticipated pattern of the reader in studying or using texts. An index is placed at the end of a book for easy reference; scientific journals frequently place their contents list on the front cover for ease of scanning; and page numbers and other similar reference devices have a purely performative function.

It is because of such potential confusions that successful analysis of typography will never be a simple mechanical process. It requires the same kind of personal skills and sensitivity as linguistic or literary analysis, even if the material examined is less profound. The student of verbal language is alert for metaphor, irony, or idiom, and does not attribute to coughs, grunts, or stutters the same kind of meaning as to words. The typographer also must be aware of the influences of cultural norms, stylistic associations, and technical constraints on the visual form of texts.

## *Conclusion*

A case has been proposed for including typographic and spatial factors in the linguistic analysis of complex text. The problems, though, are numerous. Typography is not simply a linguistic phenomenon but reflects the problems of communicating across time and place through a manufactured medium. Although the difficulties involved in analysing and describing the relationship of discourse to its graphic array are challenging, they are not insurmountable, and the more skilful use of textual communication that might follow from such an effort would lead to considerable social and educational benefits.

## References

Baldwin, R. S., & Coady, J. M. Psycholinguistic approaches to a theory of punctuation. *Journal of Reading Behavior*, 1978, *10*, 363-376.

Cohen, M. *Sensible words: Linguistic practice in England 1640-1785*. Baltimore: The John Hopkins University Press, 1977.

Crystal, D., & Davy, D. *Investigating English style*. London: Longmans, 1969.

Garland, K. Some general characteristics present in diagrams denoting activity, event and relationship. *Information Design Journal*, 1979, *1*, 15-22.

Guiraud, P. *Semiology*. London: Routledge & Kegan Paul, 1971.

Honan, P. Eighteenth and nineteenth century punctuation theory. *English Studies*, 1960, *41*, 92-102.

Johnson, F. C., & Klare, G. R. General models of communication research: A survey of the developments of a decade. *Journal of Communication*, 1961, *11*, 13-26.

Lewis, B. N., Horabin, I. S., & Gane, C. P. *Flow charts, logical trees and algorithms for rules and regulations*. London: Her Majesty's Stationery Office, 1967.

Pugh, A. K. The development of silent reading. In W. Latham (Ed.), *The road to effective reading*. London: Ward Lock, 1975.

Shannon, C.E., & Weaver, W. *The mathematical theory of communication*. Urbana, Ill.: University of Illinois Press, 1949.

Waller, R. H. W. Four aspects of graphic communication. *Instructional Science*, 1979, *8*, 213-222.

Werlich, E. *A text grammar of English*. Heidelberg: Quelle & Meyer, 1976.

Wright, P. The quality control of document design. *Information Design Journal*, 1979, *1*, 33-42.

# Graphic literacy

## Introduction

Paul A. Kolers

It is an old prejudice that we learn to read print but that other forms of symbolic communication are acquired in other ways. Pictures, for example, are said to be acquired as wholes and recognized immediately, whereas words are displayed in space and need tedious examination. Principles of similarity or congruity between the object and its picture are believed by many to constitute the basis on which pictures are immediately perceived and understood.

But pictures of what, and similarity to what? Of course, the more visually similar a picture is to an object in a certain position, perspective, lighting, and so on, the more readily picture and object can be confused. Such confusion is the high point of *trompe l'oeil* painting. Any deviation from that exact resemblance of picture to object pictured creates a different perceptual object from the real thing, however. How is that perceived? Moreover, what shall we say of maps, which convey the relations of space, and of graphs, which also display information using pictorial patterns? Are they apprehended immediately or must one learn how to read them? What role does convention play in their perception? And, irrespective of how they are perceived, are they useful for understanding the text they accompany?

These are some of the concerns that motivate the papers of this section. David Perkins brings his earlier training in topology to his current interest in the perceptual aspects of picture perception. His tutorial paper evaluates the claim that pictures depend for their perception on their resemblance to objects and shows, first, that resemblance to the objects depicted is a characteristic of only a very small number of pictures and, second, that even when resemblance of picture to object is pronounced, conventional and cultural considerations affect perception. Nevertheless, he is able to formulate some rules for making pictures easy to recognize and use as surrogates or informational aids; that is, by heightening resemblance one can aid transfer of skill from recognizing objects to recognizing pictures of them. But that again is small comfort to anyone concerned with picture perception in the large. Hence, the message seems to be that one has to learn how to read pictures much as one has to learn to read other forms of symbol.

Pictures are selective in the features of the world that they depict; a realistic picture tends to select configuration, light, and perspective as the properties of interest. Maps as a form of picture select topographic features for emphasis. Jean Underwood compared the effectiveness of the more visual cue of texture gradient and the more experiential influence of training and expectancy on interpreting maps. It was somewhat surprising to find that convention rather than physical aspects of the cue had the greater influence. Dependence on the interpretive capabilities of the person using the map is emphasized also by Michael Dobson, whose experiments combine the interests of the geographer with the techniques of the experimental psychologist of perception. There too the finding was that interpretive capabilities limit what can be gleaned from a map. As for other cognitive tasks, for map reading too there are limits to the amount of information with which a reader can cope.

The limitations are not restricted to reading maps; Beverly Roller studied the ability of seventh-grade children (aged about 13 years) to interpret simple graphs of the sort found in newspapers and popular magazines. Her findings were that, despite adequacy of literacy and mathematical skills, the students had considerable difficulty in interpreting correctly the information displayed in the graphs. Moreover, the graphs were thought to hinder rather than help comprehension of the accompanying text. Such findings conflict markedly with the results in science where, of course, graphs are relied on extensively. In fact, it is an old finding that many relations are grasped more readily when they are presented graphically than when they are described in words. Reading graphs, like reading maps, thus seems to require specific instruction and seems to tap distinctive skills of interpretation and comprehension that are only moderately related (if related at all) to the skills needed for understanding words.

What some of those special skills might be is a question that motivated the research by Jeanne Sholl and Howard Egeth. Where Underwood and Dobson were interested in the role that particular sorts of symbols played in reading maps, Sholl and Egeth directed their query to ways that people approach the task of getting information from maps and other sorts of spatial displays. Some people are thought to be more verbal, others more pictorial in their cognitive lives. Sholl and Egeth carried the breakdown farther to report differences in the point of view or perspective that people take towards interpreting representations of space. Although the connection is not brought out explicitly, their work is related to classical questions in psychology concerned with the development of spatial representations.

Problems in the design and interpretation of information presented spatially—in picture, map, graph, or the like—challenge all of the fields participating in these conferences. The design of maps and graphs was long left to the convenience of the designer, who usually put the information where room could be found for it. Psychologists concerned with literacy, meanwhile, had concentrated more on textual than on pictorial literacy. The papers presented here suggest that pictorial and linguistic literacy may not be perfectly correlated skills; that the design and layout of information presented spatially taps special procedures for its interpretation. Recent developments in computer technology concerned with spatial and pictorial displays, described in another section of this volume, add still other dimensions to the topic.

# Pictures and the real thing

D. N. Perkins

*What the problems of learning to "read" non-textual symbols might be has been controversial in psychology and education. The reading of realistic pictures is a critical case because many people have maintained that such pictures pose no problems for they resemble what they represent. This article reviews a number of empirical studies to conclude that a "resemblance" view of picturing is only a first order approximation to one which must accomodate custom, invention, and learning in determing how people make and make sense of pictures.*

According to its advertising, Coca-cola may be the "real thing," but a picture of a Coke certainly is not. Notably not cool or refreshing, the picture makes a poor substitute for reality as far as taste is concerned. But as far as appearance is concerned, the picture might do well. The average person's view of pictures and picture perception is that the visual symbol functions as a sort of stand-in for the real thing. We read the symbol for the appearance of an object much as we would the object itself. There is no problem of "pictorial literacy." Pictures are easy to read because they resemble what they represent. The same processes of perception carry over more or less intact. Whatever its truth, this notion is important because it is the obvious way to characterize nontechnically how pictures inform.

J. J. Gibson (1954, p. 14) probably provided the clearest technical version of this position in the following definition: "A faithful picture is a delimited physical surface processed in such a way that it reflects (or transmits) a sheaf of lightrays to a given point which is the same as would be the sheaf of rays from the original to that point." Gibson apparently meant not to single out a rare class of truly "faithful" pictures but to describe what a picture most fundamentally and ideally was. He later was troubled by the stringency of his definition and the way it snubbed pictorial devices like caricature and, in 1971, suggested a second definition designed to accomodate caricature and other less photographic forms of depiction. "A picture is a surface so treated that a delimited optic array to a point of observation is made available which contains the same kind of information that is found in the ambient optic arrays of an ordinary environment" (p. 31). Gibsons's second formulation qualifies the almost total identification between pictures and real scenes in his earlier account. But, as Roupas (1977) pointed out, identity remained central. It was his concept of perception generally rather than his concept of pictures that was new. Gibson considered all perception a matter of picking up information and the appropriate relation between pictures and real scenes thus became one of "same kind of information" rather than identity of light rays.

Of all contemporary writers, perhaps Goodman's (1968) account of picturing contrasts most sharply with Gibson's. Goodman emphasized the arbitrary and conventional characteristics of picturing as follows:

> The plain fact is that a picture, to represent an object, must be a symbol for it, stand for it, refer to it; and that no degree of resemblance is sufficient to establish the requisite relationship of reference. Nor is resemblance *necessary* for reference; almost anything may stand for almost anything else. A picture that represents—like a passage that describes—an object refers to and, more particularly, *denotes* it. Denotation is the core of representation and is independent of resemblance ... the relation between a picture and what it represents is thus assimilated to the relation between a predicate and what it applies to. (p. 5)

Goodman, like Gibson, had an important qualification to make. Although pictures and verbal symbols both depend on denotation as a fundamental symbolic relationship, pictures are not to be identified with verbal symbols. In his theory of notationality, Goodman (1968) carefully delineated a contrast between pictures and text which acknowledges, roughly speaking, the continuous "analog" character of pictures.

There is a standard way of proceeding: a more extended review of the arguments advanced by Gibson, Goodman, and others, a close critique, some effort to choose or synthesize. However, this avenue has been traveled so often lately that, instead, I would like to sample the considerable psychological research on various aspects of picture perception to determine how it informs the issue. The aim is to give the real thing theory its best chance by considering the parts of the issue which really seem *at* issue. Some parts are not. There are obvious psychological reservations about pictures being simple stand-ins for the real thing. For instance, binocular disparity and motion parallax declare the flatness of the picture surface, not the depth of the pictured space. There are also crucial philosophical reservations concerning, for example, how little an appeal to resemblance or similarity explains about picturing or anything else (Goodman, 1968, 1972). Moreover, pictures broadly defined include many sorts of graphic symbolism the reading of which obviously could not involve a straightforward carryover from experience of the real thing: cubist paintings, bar graphs, spectrograms, and topographical maps, for example.

But the real thing theory does not expire completely under these assaults. First of all, if discussion is restricted to more or less realistic pictures ("more or less" includes cartoons and caricatures but excludes cubist paintings, bar graphs, and so on) the theory will have at least a chance. Moreover, most research on picture perception has concerned fairly realistic pictures which, more than any other sort, supplement texts, so that understanding how they inform is of great help in understanding the pervasive relationship between pictures and text.

The arguments concerning stereo viewing, the emptiness of the similarity position, and so on, can simply be granted. However, there remain real empirical issues about whether the roughly projective character of typical realistic pictures helps, hinders, or has no bearing on their informativeness. For example, how readily do people naïve to pictures of familiar things come to understand them? Does more or less realism in picturing relate particularly to more or less informativeness or, if not, what does? Just how does our reading of pictures relate to our perception of the things they depict? Is there a problem of pictorial literacy or not?

*Learning to read pictures: Identification*
Whatever troubles Johnny may have learning to read, no one worries about Johnny learning to read pictures. Clearly, in our culture most people achieve a routine competence in picture perception without formal instruction. This casual observation might seem to indicate that picture perception simply borrows the processes of perceiving the real thing. But matters are more complicated. People do need explicit instruction to learn to read certain kinds of pictures, such as X-rays and satellite photographs, to extract the kinds of information they provide. Moreover, the fact that people do not need explicit instruction for reading the pictures in magazines does not in itself show that no learning is required. Children come to understand and produce speech without formal instruction also but clearly require extended learning.

The question needs reformulating. It is not whether or not pictures are easy to learn to read but how easy and when and for what sorts of pictures inspected for what sorts of information. This section considers one broad and loosely defined way of reading pictures, which might be called "identification." The reading assignment is to identify objects or other elements depicted in the pictures with familiar linguistic labels like "table" or "shoe" or "the head of a cow" or "man running." Psychologists have amassed considerable information on how well people unfamiliar with pictures identify familiar depicted things.

First, consider some studies of children. Hochberg and Brooks (1962) raised their son to an age of nearly two years with minimal exposure to pictures. There were no magazines or picture books about the house. Even the labels on cans were removed. When their son had acquired a substantial vocabulary of the names of everyday objects, the Hochbergs presented him with a series of sparse line drawings, more elaborate line drawings, and photographs of common objects. In almost every case, he identified the objects. Another approach is to study infants, before much exposure to pictures has occurred. Here, of course, the meaning of "identification" becomes altered to transferance of some response other than naming. Results have been mixed in such studies. For example, Bower (1964, 1966) reported that infants did not carry over a trained response from simple objects to pictures of them. On the other hand, Dirks and Gibson (1977) reported some face recognition from color slides. Five-month-old infants were exposed to an actual face until their interest began to wane. Then a slide was substituted, sometimes of the same face and sometimes of a person of different sex, hair color, and hair style. The different face alerted the infants again; the same one did not. Rose (1977) reported a study monitoring which of two displays presented side by side were attended to most by six-month-old infants. He found carryover of habituation between two- and three-dimensional versions of the same patterns.

Cultures with little picturing are another resource. A recent review by Hagen and Jones (1978) began by discussing difficulties with fully colored and detailed photographs and slides. Little systematic work with such stimuli existed but what there was suggested that subjects not familiar with picturing have virtually no difficulty identifying familiar objects pictured in this way. The same was true when subjects were presented with detailed black-and-white pictures, photographs, or shaded drawings. However, an interesting qualification must be made. Often subjects unfamiliar with pictures have to go through a process which might be described as "catching on." Initially, a subject may not realize that the grey splotches on the picture have any significance. The subjects may also need to piece together an interpretation, sometimes failing completely to do so and sometimes making errors of identification. An example of piecing together an interpretation is quoted from Deregowski, Muldrow, and Muldrow (1972, p. 424). Here, a 19-year old woman responds in part to a scene including a man holding a spear.

> (about man) I don't know what this looks like.
>
> (as E outlines the man) It looks like your aeroplane!
>
> (legs) These look like its wings.
>
> (Elephant) I don't know.
>
> (again looks at the man) These (his legs) look like aeroplane wings.
>
> (as E outlines man's head) This looks like a man's head. Those look like his legs. It's a man. His hand is stretched out.

Such episodes are reminiscent of difficulties Western adults sometimes have in interpreting high-contrast photographs in which an array of blotches finally resolves into a meaningful scene (Street, 1931).

As Hagen and Jones (1978) note, by far the greater part of the cross-cultural work has been done with line drawings. A recent study (Kennedy & Ross, 1975), with fairly characteristic findings, reported an investigation of picture identification among the Songe of Papua, New Guinea. The Songe had no indigenous pictorial art and there were no pictorial materials in the village. Those under 20 attended a mission school about six miles away and were, of course, familiar with pictures but school materials were not brought home. The investigators lived with the Songe for a considerable period and, among other studies, tested their abilities to identify pictures. A number of pictures were used representing various familiar and unfamiliar objects and a few scenes. Subjects were asked to name what was depicted as a whole, to identify particular parts pointed to, and to locate others named by the investigator. In general, the subjects performed well. As might be expected, those under 20 almost always responded correctly (meaning that the majority of answers to the several questions about a picture were correct). A group over 40 years of age scored 68 percent and a group aged 20-40 91 percent overall. Although there were clear age differences, even the oldest group did reasonably well, indeed, perfectly on several of the pictures. When subjects did fail to identify a picture, usually naming the thing depicted was enough for them then to identify the parts correctly.

It is, of course, simply not true that subjects unfamiliar with picturing easily identify all aspects of pictures. An interesting qualification appears in a discussion by Friedman and Stevenson (1980) of indications of movement in pictures. They note that certain means of representing motion have commonly been used throughout history and are fairly consistently interpreted even by young subjects. Postures indicating motion, such as a profile of a man leaning forward and with one leg raised, are examples. Other devices seem less readily interpreted, however. For example, Duncan, Gourlay, and Hudson (1973) found that multiple positions of a head, plus path-of-movement lines, rarely conveyed motion of the head to rural Zulus and Tsongas and to about only 30 percent of urban Zulus and Tsongas. White South Africans identified motion 85 percent of the time. Circular marks around a dog's tail to indicate a wagging movement were similarly troublesome. Friedman and Stevenson therefore rejected any simple answer to whether pictures as a whole are conventional or not and argued that different pictorial devices must be scaled for their readability according to the skills of the naïve observers.

Certain special sorts of pictures introduce severe difficulties of interpretation, aerial photography, for example. Considerable research (Cockrell & Sadacca, Note 1; Powers, Brainard, Abram, & Sadacca, Note 2) has been done on the problem of training photo-interpreters to assess the significance of reconnaissance photographs for military purposes. The interpretation of landforms and other terrain characteristics also requires impressive knowledge and skill (Way, 1973). These picture reading activities are troublesome because they require the observer to learn to perceive things displayed from a radically unfamiliar perspective, often, as with military targets, of things deliberately concealed, or as with landforms, of features whose shape and significance may be entirely unfamiliar to the novice photo-interpreter.

Without such problems, the identifications made by people unfamiliar with pictures remains impressive and the evidence appears overwhelming that identification of familiar objects and parts of objects depicted in typical ways poses no major problem for a naïve observer.

*Learning to read pictures: The depth dimension*
Identification aside, viewers can try to judge depicted spatial properties, indicating which objects appear nearer or farther in the pictured space, how much nearer or farther, what orientations in space objects have, and so on. Considerable cross-cultural work has addressed just this issue but the more it is examined, the more disappointing it seems. At first glance, decisive findings appear. Hudson (1960) reported that relatively unschooled African subjects had considerable difficulty in judging depth relationships in a series of scenes employing linear perspective, occlusion, and relative size. Hagen and Jones (1978), reviewing a number of investigations using the same or similar materials, reported that others usually found similar trends. The results suggest that response to the "depth cues" in pictures requires considerable experience with picturing.

A more critical view has disclosed severe methodological lapses in the investigations, however. Jahoda and McGurk (1974) suggested that language difficulties underlie the seemingly less adept picture reading of less acculturated subjects. A revised set of stimuli and procedures modified to avoid language problems revealed little difference between Ghanaian and Scottish schoolchildren. Hagen and Jones (1978) offered another telling criticism: the scenes used in both Hudson's materials and those of Jahoda and McGurk did not offer correct perspective, more distant objects being larger than they should have been. Why then, they asked, should subjects fairly naïve to picturing carry over perfectly successfully perceptual skills adapted to real-world perceiving? Another reservation was that the stimulus materials used elicited a maximum of 69 percent three-dimensional response in Scottish adults. Any fair test of picture-reading for depth ought to receive nearly perfect responses from fully acculturated subjects. There seems little point in demonstrating that less experienced people have somewhat more difficulty with pictures that even fully experienced people cannot interpret.

Findings of some difficulties in less acculturated subjects are probably too persistent to dismiss. Obviously, and unsurprisingly, experience makes a difference. But the cross-cultural research gives no reason to suppose that relatively naïve subjects find pictured depth relationships opaque. On the contrary, the more typical finding is that performance simply falls somewhat below more educated or European groups, in part because of a fault of method.

Several investigations have sought developmental differences between the abilities of children and adults to discern spatial relationships in pictures. In general, such studies have not found marked contrasts. For example, Wohlwill (1965) presented adults and children as young as 5 years with slides showing a model cow, a fence, and a horse placed some distance behind one another on receding planes which were covered with different patterns of large stars to indicate perspective. The subjects were to judge which animal stood nearer to the fence. Some systematic errors appeared but they were not associated with age: the children did as well as the adults. Olson (1975) asked children as young as three which of two drawn houses appeared farther away. The series of pictures manipulated cues of height on the picture plane, occlusion, and size. Even the youngest children performed nearly perfectly with height and occlusion. Response to relative size improved with age but was never strong, even in the oldest subjects. Olson pointed out that, even so, relative size is a problematic cue: one must assume that the two houses are the same size to infer that the one which appears smaller lies farther away.

Olson, Pearl, Mayfield, and Millar (1976) compared the perceptions of five-year-olds and adults of a picture and an equivalent real scene. The subjects saw elongated boxes tipped somewhat towards them, in reality or in photographs. Subjects reported whether the receding axis of a cross on the top of each box appeared longer or shorter than the lateral axis. Again, no developmental differences emerged.

Such results lack the force of Hochberg's demonstration for picture identification, because all the children in these experiments certainly had encountered pictures many times. Also, as Olson (1975) pointed out, ceiling problems account in part for the lack of differences. One could, of course, design a pictorial depth judgment subtle enough so that young children would not perform as well as adults. But the investigations mentioned do indicate at least that children acquire quite early the basic adult competency to make simple spatial judgments from pictures.

These remarks suggest that naïve observers read pictures for spatial information fairly easily. But a crucial qualification needs to be made: we know that, for certain kinds of spatial information, even adult acculturated observers do not read pictures very well. The perception of solid rectangular forms is a case in point. The projection of a rectangular solid contains sufficient information to specify the orientation in space and the proportions of the solid (Attneave & Frost, 1969; Perkins, 1968). The linear perspective of the receding edges provides part of that information, but perspective is unnecessary. The angles between the radiating edges at a corner suffice, even in a projection without perspective.

Furthermore, adult and child perceivers are, in some sense, alert to the geometry. Mathematically, some box-like pictures can be projections of rectangular forms, depending on the angles between the depicted edges, and some cannot. Perkins (1972) reported that adult subjects proved very sensitive to this discrimination and Cooper (1977) showed that young children do nearly as well as adults.

Despite the available information, the demonstration of sensitivity to it, and the addition of redundant information from linear perspective, orientation judgments of the boxes in such pictures usually are faulty. For instance, Olson et al. (1976) discovered substantial differences between two stimulus conditions: subjects' reports were fairly accurate for real boxes but wrong for the pictured boxes. It was as though, at a true slant of 60 deg, they perceived the tops of the boxes to be tilted back only 45 deg. Such regression to the frontal plane occurs commonly in experiments on slant judgment. In one condition (Attneave & Frost, 1969), subjects viewed monocularly from the proper station point perspectively correct depictions of a cube. Their results indicated a regression of about 21 deg at 60 deg. Attneave (1972) later used similar stimulus materials but also used a black light to reduce the phenomenal picture-like quality of the stimuli and found that the regression effect was lessened. Perkins and Cooper (1980) concluded that, to a considerable extent, such regression effects result from the apparent pictoriality of the displays which often appear to induce a perceptual compromise between the flat array of lines and the depicted spatial array. In monocular viewing, when an immobile observer and such devices as fluorescent displays minimize the apparent pictoriality, regression effects dwindle and sometimes disappear. When the frontal picture plane is blatant, as it normally is, regression can be severe.

A related body of work concerns size/distance judgments rather than slant judgments. Hagen (1978) reviewed a number of studies which compared the responses of children and adults to pictures and equivalent real scenes, viewed from correct and incorrect station points and varying other factors like monocular viewing and head motion as well. She found that, despite efforts to equate the available information, judgments of pictures were consistently inferior to judgments of real scenes. In the pictures the subjects expected less perspective shrinkage with distance than perspective specifies, an effect analogous to the regression findings reported above. A second finding was that manipulations to minimize information for the pictorial surface (monocular viewing and so on) made judgments somewhat more accurate.

To summarize, then, all signs are that people naïve to picturing fairly easily read pictures for relationships not requiring metric accuracy, for example, judging simply which object is further when one is much higher on the picture plane. Judgments involving more metric precision are another matter, however. Typically, an adult acculturated perceiver responding to projectively accurate pictures will make incorrect judgments which reflect a pictorial space compressed relative to its real counterpart. In this respect, people generally simply do not learn to read pictures adequately.

*The reading process*

The results presented above hint that people read pictures much as they perceive the world. So readily do those naïve to picturing make sense of pictures, that something like this must be so. However, no one maintains that reading pictures is exactly like perceiving the real thing. The question becomes one of identifying the qualifications needed. Clearly, people have to learn about pictorial devices without analogs like some of the motion indicators examined by Friedman and Stevenson (1980). Equally clearly, the perceiver cannot accept the binocular disparity and motion parallax as representing the depicted scene. He or she must also catch on to what signifies what in what sorts of picture. Line drawings do not represent a wire world, and grey suits in color portraits represent grey suits but grey suits in black and white portraits need not. All these are reasons why the picture reading process *cannot* be exactly like perceiving the real thing. The more interesting qualifications concern when the reading process *could* be, but still is not. For example, we can see correctly objects and scenes rendered in proper perspective, but we do not necessarily, as the studies of slant judgments disclose. The practices of artists and individual preference give further evidence of such a discrepancy. For example, as Pirenne (1970) states, spheres not at the center of projection technically should be rendered as ellipses. But when so rendered, they look wrong because they then appear elliptical. In such cases, of course, artists paint the picture that looks right, not the one that follows the geometric rules.

The perspective shrinking of size with distance also presents some problems. Everyone is familiar with the odd look of a photograph of a person with hand held forward—the hand appears much too large. And who has not been disappointed when a photograph makes an impressive range of mountains into molehills. Again, artists have been quick to cope, adjusting hands and mountains to look right, not to follow the rules. Hagen and Elliott (1976) documented in the laboratory the preference of viewers for pictures with modest front-to-back perspective shrinkage. Using pictures of geometric solids with different degrees of perspective convergence, and soliciting judgments of realism, Hagen found that subjects usually considered little or no convergence most realistic, a degree not at all consonant with their actual station point.

Like metric judgments, these oddities seem due at least in part to the apparent pictoriality of the picture. Pirenne (1970) notes that a very wide-angle photograph of a near object will look odd under normal viewing conditions but normal under illusionistic viewing conditions. The same is true of the oversized hand as is remarkably easy to demonstrate. When one sees such a picture, one need only peer at it through one's fist, screening out the picture boundaries to provide a monocular view. All at once, the hand seems hardly oversize at all but appears appropriately closer. This same trick of peering through a peephole vividly brings out the depth in many sorts of fairly realistic pictures. It seems conceivable that, in normal viewing, a perceptual compromise is made between the blatantly flat picture plane and the depicted spatial arrangement, a compromise compressing the depth dimension and making correct perspective look incorrect. In consequence, pictures have been adapted to the problems of viewers.

However, viewers have adapted to at least one problem of pictures: ambiguity of station point. The problem arises because the viewer does not know where the geometrically correct station point is and often does not even bother to try to find it. Pictures are viewed from various distances and at various angles with no thought given to the proper ones. One argument is that viewers tolerate rather than compensate for variations of viewpoint. An improper viewing point introduces certain distortions which the viewer simply accepts because, as Gombrich (1972) remarked of oblique viewing: "If trees appear taller and narrower, and even persons somewhat slimmer, well there are such trees and such persons" (p. 144).

Recent research has disclosed active processes of compensation for viewing from an incorrect station point, however. Rosinski (Note 3) analyzed mathematically the effects on perspective of magnifying and reducing the image of a tilted lattice. Magnifying should flatten the picture space and induce more frontal judgments of the slant of the lattice. With a few qualifications, Rosinski confirmed this in an experiment where subjects remained at a constant distance from a CRT display and judged lattices of different slants at varying magnifications. Then he conducted a companion experiment: the subjects made a series of judgments involving the same retinal images of the lattices, with magnification accomplished by varying viewer distance from the display. If the subjects were simply responding to the geometry of the display, the results would have been the same. In fact, the different viewing distances influenced the reported slants hardly at all. Clearly, despite the variations in distance, subjects were interpreting the pictures according to a constant station point.

Similar findings obtain for pictures viewed obliquely. These experiments were based on the discrimination between boxes which could or could not be projections of rectangular boxes. Perkins (1972) showed that adult subjects were very sensitive to this discrimination. For some box pictures, viewed obliquely at a considerable angle (41 deg to the plane of the page under one condition), the shapes projected to the eye change status: some boxes rectangular when viewed frontally yield non-rectangular oblique projections and vice versa. However, Perkins (1973) found that, for the most part, subjects classified such cases frontally despite viewing obliquely.

Cooper (1977) conducted a developmental version of Perkins' study. Three groups of children, of mean ages approximately 3, 4.5, and 6, attempted the rectangularity discrimination from frontal and oblique viewpoints. Cooper found that even the youngest group made the rectangularity discrimination reasonably well when viewing frontally but, when viewing obliquely, the youngest group judged predominantly according to projections. The older groups compensated for the oblique view as had the adult subjects. In short, these studies identify a specific adaptation to picture perception not present early in life but developing between 3 and 4.5 years of age.

Hagen (1976) reported an experiment examining the effect of age and station point on size judgments of pictured objects. She confirmed that viewing away from the true station point would reduce the accuracy of children's judgments but enhance that of adults. Apparently, the youngsters made naïve projective judgments, while the adults compensated for the oblique view but found the view from the true station point slightly confusing because pictures are not normally seen in that way.

In summary, the adjustments of perception to the geometry of pictures are oddly mixed. On the one hand, picture perception does not seem to be as selective as it ought to be. Evidence for the frontal pictorial surface, which shall be ignored, induces perception of a flattened picture space, slant judgments regressed towards the frontal plane, preferences for minimal projective shrinkage with distance, and so on. On the other hand, compensations for variations in viewing distance and angle develop, even though the perceiver might manage adequately without them.

It is well to remember above all that the experienced perceiver of pictures will look according to his need for information, sampling the display in ways that satisfy that need. Comparing the reading of text and pictures, Kolers (1977) noted that the scanning of the two runs remarkably parallel. Rather than a linear, word-by-word process, skilled reading of text often proceeds as a flexible process of interrogating the page.

*Realism and informativeness*
Let it be granted that what is identified as realism in pictures involves a curious mix of the practical and the arbitrary: an adjustment of pictures to the quirks of perception and an adjustment of perceivers' expectations to prevailing styles. Nonetheless, broadly speaking, more realistic pictures present more information—color, linear perspective (although modified), texture, and so on—and, in this sense, more realistic pictures are closer to the real thing. Certainly the simplest and most simple-minded hypothesis about realism and information is that more realistic means more informative and not merely more information in the technical sense. For example, Hagen and Jones (1978) note an important result Hudson (1960) did not mention in his cross-cultural work. Subjects in all his groups perceived three-dimensional relationships more poorly in line drawings than in photographed models of similar scenes. Across the groups, the differences

ranged from 12 to 46 in the percentage of subjects classified as perceivers of tri-dimensionality in line drawings versus photographs. The photographs displayed texture gradients receding to the horizon line, extra information which may have allowed the subjects to perform better.

One can easily think of exceptions to the hypothesis that more realism always means more information. Even so, it is not entirely implausible that statistically, over many sorts of pictures and relevant kinds of information, realism and information would be correlated. However, this does not seem to be true, at least not for the range of realism found in normal pictures. Dwyer (1978) has reviewed several of the many studies of the influence of realism on learning. Realism in the sense of detail and photographic quality has not been found to relate consistently to learning, as, for example, when measured by later tests of identification of parts. Color has proved an effective device in some studies but not in others. Learning also is somewhat dependent on interactions between aptitude and manner of depiction.

Such ambiguous findings are hardly surprising. As Dwyer (1978) argues, whether realism helps or not will depend on whether the realism adds information the perceiver needs and what is informative will vary greatly with the task. Uninformative realism may simply confuse and distract. Instead of "more realism," perhaps the following rules would make better sense.

*Rule 1: For more informative pictures, include more information of relevant kinds.* As has been noted, outright departure from realism may help. Examples are numerous: circuit diagrams and other schematic representations which replace the jumble of the real thing with a simplified and clarified display. Ryan and Schwartz (1956) studied the effectiveness of caricature-like drawings, examining not later memory but immediate perception. To determine what mode of representation would best communicate complex spatial arrangements they used four kinds of representations: photographs, shaded drawings, line drawings, and cartoons. The cartoons "distorted the figure to emphasize the essential spatial relationships involved" (p. 61). The pictures showed a hand in various postures, a set of knife switches in several on and off arrangements, and cut-away views of valves in a steam engine at four points in the engine cycle. The pictures were exposed tachistoscopically for longer and longer intervals until the subjects could identify the precise contents adequately—the arrangement of the knife switches and so on. It was found that the cartoon representation produced the most rapid response for the valves and the switches, although only third best for the hand. The averaged results also favored the cartoons.

*Rule 2: For more informative pictures, provide simplified highlighted information of relevant kinds.* Even this further rule does not accomodate another possibility, however. Sometimes apparently relevant, clear, and abundant information can be woefully uninformative. For example, various investigations (Galper, 1970;

Galper & Hochberg, 1971; Phillips, 1972) have demonstrated repeatedly that subjects perform better on face-recognition tasks with photographic positives than with negatives. Likewise, performance is better on upright than on inverted photographs (Goldstein, 1975; Hochberg & Galper, 1967). Obviously, the negatives and inverted photographs contain exactly the same information as the positives and upright photographs. The information is there but is not readily interpreted. A comparison with Harmon's (1973) study illustrates the degree of difficulty. Harmon investigated blurred faces and in one condition used photographs of familiar peers but so badly blurred that eyes and mouth were simply darker regions of fog. Remarkably, the subjects recognized their acquaintances 85 percent of the time. But Goldstein's (1975) study of recognition by peers using sharp, inverted photographs, obtained only about a 60 percent recognition rate from adults (adolescents did much better, perhaps because of less overlearning). Apparently, extreme information loss in blurring reduces face recognition much less than does an inverted image. Such effects of inversion are not limited to pictures; text also presents the same information whether inverted or not, but inversion and other transformations of text produce a substantial decrement in the rate of reading (Kolers & Perkins, 1975).

*Rule 3: For more informative pictures, match the manner of presenting the information to the viewer's habits of information-pickup.* These rules have been listed partly to emphasize the irrelevance of realism but partly to mock the rules themselves. It is too easy to assume that we know what constitutes "more information of relevant kinds" or "simplified highlighted information" or a good "match" between method of depiction and manner of pickup. Research has mapped the broad effects of such important pictorial information sources as texture gradients, linear perspective, and so forth, but the real problems of the practical picture maker typically concern nuances relative to a particular task and context: what properties of the picture will convey precisely *this* information and how can more information be traded off against a simplified, clarified display in *this* situation. As Kennedy (1974) has noted, Gibson's proposed informational account of picturing (1954) is more a promissory note than a developed account and, as Goodman (1971) has noted, information can be encoded in and read out of pictures in a multitude of ways. The somewhat generalized notion of pictorial informing is of little help when the problems get particular.

For example, caricatures presumably highlight the features most relevant to recognition, an idea argued by Gibson (1969) and supported by Perkins (1975) and Goldman and Hagen (1978) in analyses of caricatures of Richard Nixon, and by Ryan and Schwartz' (1956) experimental findings for non-portrait caricatures. It was, therefore, expected that portrait caricatures might inform better about the appearances of faces than photographs, and accordingly an investigation was begun (Perkins & Hagen, 1980). The study used 54 three-quarter-face photographs of individuals unfamiliar to the subjects, 54 profile photographs, and 54 caricatures in three-quarter face, drawn by an artist seemingly of great competence. Fifteen of the persons pictured were chosen arbitrarily to make up a training set. The subjects viewed each picture briefly and then tried to sort the ones depicting persons in the training set out of the full set of 54. Some subjects were trained on the caricatures and sorted the profile photographs, some were trained on caricatures and sorted caricatures, and so on. All possible pairings were investigated.

The findings revealed a clear pattern. Training on caricatures enabled subjects to sort both kinds of photographs correctly at a better than chance level. However, caricatures were less useful as training for sorting either kind of photograph than was training on the other kind of photograph. In short, the investigators' confidence in the general informativeness of caricatures versus realism seemed to be misplaced. The results suggest that the detail and precision of photographs can help the viewer with this particular task more than the supposedly most significant information selected and caricatured by an artist.

Although theories about the informativeness of caricaturing and other pictorial devices are not always reliable, perhaps we can know what informs best simply by looking and seeing. The caricaturist has not failed in this, of course, because his aim is not typically to compete with photographs. Throughout history, artists, draftsmen, and photographers have followed with some success their own ideas about what was needed to deliver the information required. However, there is evidence that visual impressions about what will and what will not inform best are not always reliable. For example, Dwyer (1978) considered several studies where subjects learning from pictures were asked to indicate which depictions seemed most informative: colored drawings versus schematic black-and-white drawings versus photographs, and so on. Very often, either no corresponding differences in learning appeared or differences appeared in the opposite direction. It seems probable, then, that the intuitions of textbook designers and illustrators should not be relied upon too heavily.

This is all evidence of the profoundly heuristic nature of picture-making. No doubt pictures will inform better when they eliminate irrelevant information, provide more relevant information, highlight and clarify it, and present it in an accessible way. However, the implications of these rules taken separately often are not clear, nor do we know how to trade them off against one another when they conflict in many practical circumstances. Neither simple inspection nor theory answer such questions reliably. Practical picture making is more like cooking than like optics, a matter of recipe rather than principle, of tradition and invention rather than law and application.

*What a picture is like*

What is a zebra? A zebra is a horse with stripes. This neat if incorrect answer illustrates a common strategy in human understanding: to understand the nature of one thing, find something familiar which resembles it and then say that the one is like the other, but with certain qualifications. This paper has proceeded very much like that. The issue has been whether pictures are like the real thing in that perceiving pictures proceeds like perceiving the real thing. Do pictures inform by packaging information in essentially the same form as real objects and scenes, the perceiver unwrapping that package in essentially the same way? This was Gibson's position (1954, 1971) although it should be noted that a non-Gibsonian account of perception also could assert the equivalence of perceiving pictures and real scenes.

In a sense, the findings reviewed tend to support this idea. Pictures do prove to be very easy to read in certain basic respects, a result that was hotly debated years ago but is increasingly accepted now. However, to say no more than that would be rather like saying "A zebra is a horse." Instead, crucial qualifications have to be made. Many of these are obvious and accessible to an armchair psychologist. Others are somewhat less straightforward and a quick review of them follows.

Some pictorial devices clearly require experience, for instance, multiple limb or head positions representing motion. Signs of "catching on," rather than effortless understanding, are often apparent in people unfamiliar with pictures. People never learn to read projectively correct, normally viewed pictures for shape and slant information as accurately as they do real scenes: the space of the picture seems compressed and objects appear less slanted than they should. In what might be called pictorial constancy effects, people can compensate somewhat for variations in distance and angle of viewing, rather than simply interpreting the image that strikes the eye. More realism is not, in general, a good indication of more informativeness in pictures, but better formulae fall short of practical demands too: both theory and personal impressions can easily mistake the comparative informativeness of particular sorts of pictures for particular purposes.

Any easy equation between perceiving the real thing and pictures thus is obviously considerably qualified. Then how can the qualifications themselves be characterized? Goodman's (1968) argument for the culture-bound custom-ridden nature of picturing hints at a possible answer. Perhaps pictures are like words, in being conventional and the necessary catching on, the adjustments artists make in principles of perspective, the various more or less realistic manners of depiction, all might be understood as symptoms of convention learning and convention making.

Attractive as this idea sounds initially, it does not take us very far in understanding the nature of the qualifications. The more closely one examines the meaning of convention, the less clearly and straightforwardly it seems to apply to pictures. The standard paradigm of conventionality is the arbitrariness of naming. We do not label dogs "cats," but we could. There are no obvious grounds except custom to prefer "dog" over "cat" as a label for dogs. How well does this formula, "No obvious grounds except custom," apply to picturing?

Consider an artist adjusting an outthrust hand to look normal, either in

systematic accordance with a more distant station point or simply as an ad hoc
modification. To say that this is following a convention is to say that the artist
responds to mere custom; rendered otherwise, the picture would look odd only
because that is not the way we depict. It was suggested earlier, however, that such
adjustments are motivated and maintained partly by the visual rivalry between the
two-dimensional picture surface and the depicted space. This does not mean that
effects of the rivalry absolutely demand an adjustment or even that, with sufficient
exposure to such pictures, what now seems unnatural might not come to look quite
natural. However, it does suggest that accidents of human perception bias the
situation in favor of the adjustment.

For another example, path-of-motion lines are a familiar device in certain kinds of pictures but are not as readily understood as other sorts of motion
indicators (Friedman & Stevenson, 1980). Are they therefore more conventional?
They are not chosen arbitrarily in comparison with other more easily understood
devices or simple marks like asterisks or x's, which might serve just as well as signs
for motion. Lines specify the path of motion as an asterisk would not and, in fact,
suggest a perceptual if not an environmental event: when objects pass rapidly
before the eyes, they do leave fading trails behind them. This is not to suggest that
path-of-motion lines work by simple imitation but it is difficult to see in exactly
what sense they are straightforwardly conventional. The impulse to term them
conventional may come from the mistaken idea that more learning means more
conventionality, an idea which does not hold up under examination. A convention
can be very easy or very hard to learn, depending on its complexity.

It is annoying not to be able to explain pictures simply as like the real
thing, and, furthermore, not to be able to explain the qualifications simply as
conventions. However, the evidence forces the conclusion that we can do nothing
to explain exactly what pictures are like. There is no reason to hope for a neat,
parsimonious account of what pictures are or ought to be because they result from
diverse contrary influences. The situation might be summarized as follows.

A first order rule for making a more or less realistic picture of a thing is to
make something like a projection. It can follow optics or not, but should preserve
at least crudely the relative layout of the thing. The pictorial marks meaning eyes
should occur with the mark meaning head and not off to one side as do the
linguistic marks meaning eyes in this sentence. Beyond the first-order rule, picturing becomes radically heuristic in response to diverse influences: the rivalry
effects, difficulties in discerning exactly what properties of natural objects do the
perceptual informing, differing purposes, and so on. Learning becomes a requisite and pictorial literacy a problem. Gibson's view (1954, 1971) is apt so far as the
first-order rule is concerned but Goodman's (1968) view is apt so far as the second
order effects are concerned, where matters become, if not precisely matters of
convention, at least matters of custom and invention. Furthermore, the deliberate
restriction in this paper to more or less realistic pictures should be remembered.

The more one departs from that, the more custom and invention displace the first order projective rule as well as describing the second order circumstances.

This is one reason why picture making has a complicated history, although throughout time and across cultures nearly all pictures can be read easily for their simpler messages: man versus dog versus building, and so on. Gombrich (1960) recounts admirably the development of Western realism as the evolution of a technology of depiction where certain people at certain times invented pictorial devices which were then assimilated and extended by others. His lesson is equally applicable to picturing of all sorts. Simply knowing the real thing helps. But there is no single rule which covers the various ways of depicting things effectively for various informative and expressive purposes. Each different way had to be discovered and indeed, in computer graphics and image enhancement and holograms, as well as in superrealism and other explorations of contemporary art, new ways are still being discovered.

This article was prepared at Project Zero, Harvard Graduate School of Education, operating with support from the Spencer Foundation and National Institute of Education Grant No. G-78-0031. The opinions expressed here do not necessarily reflect the positions or policies of the supporting agencies.

## Reference notes

1. Cockrell, J. T., & Sadacca, R. *Training individual image interpreters using team consensus feedback* (Technical Research Report 1171). Arlington, Va.: U.S. Army Behavior and Systems Research Laboratory, 1971.
2. Powers, J. R. III, Brainard, R. W., Abram, R. E., & Sadacca, R. *Training techniques for rapid target detection* (Technical Paper 242). Arlington, Va.: U.S. Army Research Institute for the Behavioral and Social Sciences, 1973.
3. Rosinski, R. R. *Effects of optical magnification on the perception of displayed orientation*. Department of Information Science, University of Pittsburgh, 1979.

## References

Attneave, F. Representation of physical space. In A. Melton & E. Martin (Eds.), *Coding processes in human memory*. Washington, D.C.: V. W. Winston & Sons, 1972.
Attneave, F., & Frost, R. The determination of perceived tridimensional orientation by minimum criteria. *Perception & Psychophysics*, 1969, *6*, 391-396.
Bower, T. G. R. Discrimination of depth in premotor infants. *Psychonomic Science*, 1964, *1*, 368.

Bower, T. G. R. Slant perception and shape constancy in infants. *Science*, 1966, *151*, 832-834.

Cooper, B. Development of sensitivity to geometric information for viewing shapes and sizes in pictures. In R. N. Haber (Ed.), *Proceedings of the tenth symposium of the center for visual sciences*, Rochester, N.Y.: University of Rochester, 1977.

Deregowski, J. B., Muldrow, E. S., & Muldrow, W. F. Pictorial recognition in a remote Ethiopian population. *Perception*, 1972, *1*, 417-425.

Dirks, J., & Gibson, E. Infants' perception of similarity between live people and their photographs. *Child Development*, 1977, *48*, 124-130.

Duncan, H. F., Gourlay, N., & Hudson, W. *A study of pictorial perception among Bantu and White primary school children in South Africa*. Johannesberg: Witwatersrand University Press, 1973.

Dwyer, F. M. *Strategies for improving visual learning*. State College, Pa.: Learning Services, 1978.

Friedman, S., & Stevenson, M. Perception of movement in pictures. In M. Hagen (Ed.), *The perception of pictures, Vol. I. Alberti's window: The projective model of pictorial information*. New York: Academic Press, 1980.

Galper, R. E. Recognition of faces in photographic negative. *Psychonomic Science*, 1970, *19*, 207-208.

Galper, R. E., & Hochberg, J. Recognition memory for photographs of faces. *American Journal of Psychology*, 1971, *84*, 351-354.

Gibson, E. J. *Principles of perceptual learning and development*. New York: Appleton-Century-Crofts, 1969.

Gibson, J. J. A theory of pictorial perception. *Audio-Visual Communications Review*, 1954, *1*, 3-23.

Gibson, J. J. The information available in pictures. *Leonardo*, 1971, *4*, 27-35.

Goldman, M., & Hagen, M. A. The forms of caricature: Physiognomy and political bias. *Studies in the Anthropology of Visual Communication*, 1978, *5*, 30-36.

Goldstein, A. G. Recognition of inverted photographs of faces by children and adults. *Journal of Genetic Psychology*, 1975, *127*, 109-123.

Gombrich, E. H. *Art and illusion*. Princeton: Princeton University Press, 1960.

Gombrich, E. H. The "what" and the "how": Perspective representation and the phenomenal world. In R. Rudner & I. Scheffler (Eds.), *Logic and art: Essays in honor of Nelson Goodman*. Indianapolis: Bobbs-Merrill, 1972.

Goodman, N. *Languages of art: An approach to a theory of symbols*. Indianapolis: Bobbs-Merrill, 1968.

Goodman, N. On J. J. Gibson's new perspective. *Leonardo*, 1971, *4*, 359-360.

Goodman, N. Seven strictures on similarity. In *Problems and Projects*. Indianapolis: Bobbs-Merrill, 1972.

Hagen, M. A. The influence of picture surface and station point on the ability to compensate for oblique view in pictorial perception. *Developmental Psychology*, 1976, *12*, 57-63.

Hagen, M. A. An outline of an investigation into the special character of pictures. In H. Pick & E. Saltsman (Eds.), *Modes of perceiving and processing information*. Hillsdale, N.J.: Lawrence Erlbaum Associates, 1978.

Hagen, M. A., & Elliot, H. B. An investigation of the relationship between viewing condition and preference for true and modified linear perspective with adults. *Journal of Experimental Psychology*, 1976, *2*, 479-490.

Hagen, M. A. & Jones, R. Cultural effects on pictorial perception: How many words is one picture really worth? In R. Walk & H. Pick (Eds.), *Perception and experience*, New York: Plenum Press, 1978.

Harmon, L. D. The recognition of faces. *Scientific American*, 1973, *229* (5), 70-84.

Hochberg, J. E., & Brooks, V. Pictorial recognition as an unlearned ability. *American Journal of Psychology*, 1962, *75*, 624-628.

Hochberg, J., & Galper, R. E. Recognition of faces: I. An exploratory study. *Psychonomic Science*, 1967, *9*, 619-620.

Hudson, W. Pictorial depth perception in sub-cultural groups in Africa. *Journal of Social Psychology*, 1960, *52*, 183-208.

Jahoda, G., & McGurk, H. Pictorial depth perception in Scotish and Ghanaian children: A critique of some findings with the Hudson test. *International Journal of Psychology*, 1974, *9*, 225-267.

Kennedy, J. M. *A psychology of picture perception*. San Francisco: Jossey-Bass, 1974.

Kennedy, J. M., & Ross, A. S. Outline picture perception by the Songe of Papua. *Perception*, 1975, *4*, 391-406.

Kolers, P. A. Reading pictures and reading text. In D. Perkins & B. Leondar (Eds.), *The arts and cognition*. Baltimore: Johns Hopkins University Press, 1977.

Kolers, P. A., & Perkins, D. N. Spatial and ordinal components of form perception and literacy. *Cognitive Psychology*, 1975, *7*, 228-267.

Olson, R. K. Children's sensitivity to pictorial depth information. *Perception & Psychophysics*, 1975, *17*, 59-64.

Olson, R. K., Pearl, M., Mayfield, N., & Millar, D. Sensitivity to pictorial shape perspective in 5-year old children and adults. *Perception & Psychophysics*, 1976, *20*, 173-178.

Perkins, D. N. Cubic corners. MIT Research Laboratory of Electronics, *Quarterly Progress Report*. Cambridge, Mass.: 1968, *89*, 207-214.

Perkins, D. N. Visual discrimination between rectangular and nonrectangular parallelopipeds. *Perception & Psychophysics*, 1972, *12*, 396-400.

Perkins, D. N. Compensating for distortion in viewing pictures obliquely. *Perception & Psychophysics*, 1973, *14*, 13-18.

Perkins, D. N. Caricature and recognition. *Studies in the Anthropology of Visual Communication*, 1975, *2*, 10-24.

Perkins, D. N., & Cooper, R. How the eye makes up what the light leaves out. In M. Hagen (Ed.), *The perception of pictures, Vol. II. Dürer's devices: Beyond the projective model*. New York: Academic Press, 1980.

Perkins, D. N., & Hagen, M. Convention, context and caricature. In M. Hagen (Ed.), *The perception of pictures, Vol. I. Alberti's window: The projective model of pictorial information*. New York: Academic Press, 1980.

Phillips, R. J. Why are faces hard to recognize in photographic negative? *Perception & Psychophysics*, 1972, *12*, 425-426.

Pirenne, M. *Optics, painting and photography*. Cambridge: Cambridge University Press, 1970.

Rose, S. A. Infants' transfer of response between two-dimensional and three-dimensional stimuli. *Child Development*, 1977, *48*, 1086-1091.

Roupas, T. G. Information and pictorial representation. In D. Perkins & B. Leondar (Eds.), *The arts and cognition*. Baltimore: Johns Hopkins University Press, 1977.

Ryan, T. A., & Schwartz, C. B. Speed of perception as a function of mode of representation. *American Journal of Psychology*, 1956, *69*, 60-69.

Street, R. F. *A Gestalt completion test*. New York: Teachers College, 1931.

Way, D. S. *Terrain analysis: A guide to site selection using aerial photographic interpretation*. Stroudsberg, Pa.: Dowden, Hutchinson & Ross, Inc., 1973.

Wohlwill, J. F. Texture of the stimulus field and age as variables in the perception of relative distance in photographic slides. *Journal of Experimental Child Psychology*, 1965, *2*, 166.

# The influence of texture gradients on relief interpretation from isopleth maps

Jean D. M. Underwood

*Two experiments are reported in which adult subjects were required to interpret the direction of depth in isopleth patterns. The perceptual and cognitive factors considered important in that judgment are the texture gradient effect of the increasing spatial frequency, a characteristic of some isopleth features, and the expectancy or prior set which the perceiver employs on the basis of previous experience. If isopleths are seen as texture gradients, then an increasing frequency of lines should be seen to indicate descent, whereas expectancy might identify "steep" as "leading upwards." The two experiments found expectancy and experience more influential than the texture gradient effect.*

Both Balasubramanyan (1971) and Koeman (1971) have emphasized the unique importance of maps in an age of information overload. Kolacny (1971) suggested that modern man cannot fully understand his world without acquiring appropriate map-reading skills and Ferro (1971) stated that maps, once auxiliary, have now become basic to geographical study. Maps constitute the first element of geographical research by fixing on paper the striking characteristics of a land area, by promoting comparison with other known land areas, and by facilitating formation of cognitive syntheses based on the localisation of different phenomena.

Koeman (1971) and Kolacny (1971) emphasized that the main role of a map is to communicate information to the map user. It should be pointed out that the cartographer, in selecting both the data and the mode of presentation, is more than a data presenter: he becomes a data processor (Keates, 1972; Koeman, 1971; Kolacny, 1971). It has long been assumed that the map user will interpret the finished map in the way the cartographer intended, that is, the cartographer's perception of reality will become the map user's perception as well. Doubts have been raised about that assumption: witness the work on choropleth maps and the perception of colour by the map user (Cuff, 1973; Keates, 1962). The map maker now realizes that he cannot ignore the map user and that new awareness has been reflected in many recent maps. In compiling the new city plan for Edinburgh, Bartholomew and Kinniburgh (1973) stated that: "Our aim has been to attempt to create a mental image in the mind of the user of what he can expect to find when he arrives at a particular point" (p. 62).

The cartographer has always tried to produce maps which give the maximum of information in the shortest possible time but he has frequently been foiled by a failure in the communication system. Much work has been done to strengthen the communication system, particularly in those fields directly impinging on cartography. Cartographers have developed new skills and techniques for both data collection and data representation and have been increasingly concerned about the function of any map they produce. As far as accuracy goes, however, Keates (1972, p. 168) stated that: "The emphasis on this aspect [of maps] seems at times to be so great that it can be inferred that this is the only aspect for which exact information is required.... But now that we are in a position to produce a variety of maps which are 'accurate' in this sense, it is perhaps desirable to consider whether accuracy for the map user does not have a wider meaning." His statement was a plea for an investigation into the map user's interpretation of maps which has, in part, been answered. There has been an increased interest in the two-way relationship between the map and the perception of the map user, particularly for thematic maps. Thematic maps have always lacked the accuracy of plans and topographic maps and have, therefore, lacked the traditional measure of whether a map is good or bad (Koeman, 1971). In this study perceptual processes were considered as important a variable in the comprehension of non-thematic maps as in thematic maps.

*The significance of isopleth maps*
An analysis of non-thematic maps showed that isopleths are one of the most frequently used methods of symbolic representation. These lines on the map, joining all points with equivalent quantitative and qualitative values, are used in a wide variety of maps but are probably most familiar on topographic maps (contours) and weather maps (isobars). Isopleths are popular because the data can be displayed both accurately and highly descriptively, allowing interpolation. Contours represent two basic but separate concepts of relief, slope and elevation. Elevation can be interpolated directly by eye but accurate slope data can be recovered only by measurement and calculation. Miller and Summerson (1960) pointed out that contours give a three-dimensional effect, allowing the map user to construct a mental image of the landscape. Similarly, on charts of barometric pressure, closely packed isobars indicate a rapid change in pressure and, consequently, weather of greater variability.

Isopleths grouped as patterns also form a texture gradient and therefore closely spaced contours give an illusion of depth. The map reader views the map as if from some aerial vantage point above the landscape and the denser the texture the further away it should appear from the observer. Gibson (1950) stated that, in the absence of other cues, the perception of the degree of slant of a surface was dependent on the observed rate of change of the texture density. The texture gradient effect, which encourages the map reader to equate closely spaced contours with depth or distance, was, therefore, considered important to the map reader's perception of isopleth patterns.

The influence of expectancy based on previous experience and knowledge was also considered to be highly significant in perception. Keates (1972) stated that, given a map whose symbols were both legible and discriminable, perception proceeded either by recognition or by identification, or possibly by both. With recognition, the symbol on the map is matched or compared with known possibilities by consulting either the map legend or the memory of that legend, the vocabulary of the map. In identification, the map reader matches the symbol with his or her own set of possibilities and alternatives, that is, against his or her own mental concept of the nature of the object for which he or she is looking. For example, blue symbols are associated with water. Whereas the ultimate aim of recognition is the construction of a complete dictionary, identification allows the construction of a grammar or set of rules for interpretation. Obviously, experience speeds recognition of symbols but it is even more important in identifying the information given by them because identification is controlled by individual expectancy.

Dember (1960) considered that expectancy was the context provided by cognitive rather than simple stimulus conditions. For the map reader cognitive context could be acquired from two sources: experience provided by the general environment (uncontrolled) and experience provided by direct teaching (controlled). Uncontrolled experience was considered to be the sum of nonspecific environmental influences acquired from reading, watching television, travelling, socializing, and so on.

Experiment 1 investigated the relationship between the texture gradient effect and expectancy. Expectancy was varied using two groups of subjects, each of which was considered to have a different degree of controlled experience. It was varied in order to assess whether the relationship between expectancy and the texture gradient effect was constant or whether it changed with changing expectancy. Experiment 2 attempted to change the expectancy of subjects to alter the results predicted by the unprimed Experiment 1 and thus assess the influence of controlled experience.

*Perceptual and cognitive factors in contour interpretations: Experiment 1*
Experiment 1 was designed to investigate the relationship between the texture gradient effect and individual expectancy.

The texture gradient effect was assumed to be a constant influence on all subjects, encouraging them to perceive more closely spaced stimuli (the isopleths) as farther away and more sparsely spaced stimuli as closer. An individual examining a map has a "bird's-eye view" and "closer" is thus equated with high points or features while "farther" is equated with low points or features. Subjects were encouraged to consider any isopleth patterns as contour lines because topographic maps are the most commonly used isopleth maps. It was considered that, for topographic maps, the texture gradient effect would encourage a subject to perceive closely spaced contours as descending into the map and representing lower land while sparsely spaced contours would stand out as higher land. It was argued that expectancy, based on uncontrolled experience, would encourage the reverse perception and more densely spaced contours, representing steeper slopes would be seen as higher land while widely spaced contours, representing gentler slopes, would be seen as lower land. Expectancy was considered to be a variable not only among subjects but also for each individual.

Two groups of subjects were tested, each judged to have significantly different degrees of controlled experience with topographic maps. To assess the influence of the two factors on the perception of isopleths, subjects were presented with a series of contour patterns and asked to indicate their interpretation of each pattern by drawing a cross-section of the land represented. Because the experiment was an investigation into the perception and interpretation of isopleth patterns, the contours were not given numerical values.

*Method*. Ten simplified isopleth patterns were generated, four of which had two slope elements only (simple patterns) and six with more than two slope elements (complex patterns), each pattern mounted on a separate sheet of paper (Figure 1). Subjects were given instruction sheets which included a completed example and the 10 isopleth patterns randomly ordered. Because no numerical values were placed on the individual isopleths, at least two correct interpretations of the patterns were possible. Two possible interpretations were given for the completed example, and 50 percent of the subjects in each group were given one interpretation and 50 percent the other. Subjects were assigned to one of the two groups on the basis of the amount of controlled experience with topographic maps and landforms they were judged to have had. Familiarity with landforms and topographic maps were considered adequate criteria for judging experience because the subjects were actively encouraged to consider the isopleth patterns as representing a piece of terrain.

*Subjects*. Sixty-seven undergraduates were tested, 29 first year and 38 third and fourth year students at the University of Waterloo, Canada. The first year students were taking an introductory human geography course but otherwise had little experience of topographic maps and landforms. The third and fourth year students were taking advanced studies in geomorphology and were considered to have a high degree of experience with topographic maps and landforms. Subjects were tested in groups.

*Material*. The 10 simplified isopleth patterns were drawn by hand, reproduced individually on ditto paper, assembled in random order, and had the following characteristics:
1) four of the patterns were simple, six were complex;
2) two simple and two complex patterns were formed of straight lines, two simple and four complex patterns of curved lines;
3) the direction of curvature in any one pattern was consistent;

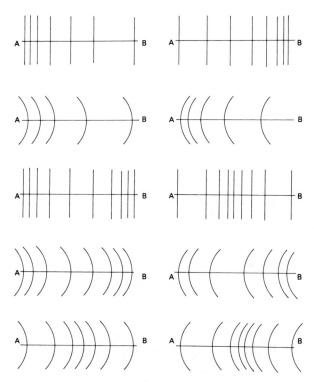

Figure 1. The 10 isopleth patterns used in Experiments 1 and 2. The task for each subject was to interpret the isopleth pattern by drawing a cross-section along the line AB. Examples of cross-sections drawn in response to the instructions are presented in Figure 3 and 4.

4) cure was taken to draw all the isopleths at a constant length to avoid presenting an added visual stimulus to the subjects;
5) a line AB was drawn through each pattern to indicate the section of terrain the subject was to interpret;
6) a line, equal in length to AB, was drawn on each page to act as a base line for the subjects' interpretive cross-sections.

*Procedure*. The following instructions were read to and by the subjects:
1) Please state the academic level to which you have studied geography.
2) This experiment requires you to draw the shape of a section of landscape shown by a number of contours. It is not necessary to have worked with contours before. The contour diagrams shown indicate the relative heights of different sections of landscape. It is your task to show the shapes of these sections—it is not necessary to give specific heights, only the relationship between them. Remember—the closer the contour lines the steeper the slope; gentle slopes and flatter lands are shown by widely spaced contour lines.

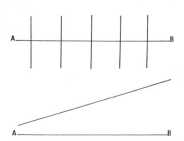

Figure 2. One cross-sectional profile of an even or uniform slope.

3) An example of an even or uniform slope (shown in Figure 2). The subjects were
   told to work quickly through the booklet in order and without turning back to
   sections already completed. The task took approximately 10 min.

*Scoring technique.* The data were scored by counting the number of times a subject
drew steeper land rising from gentler slopes (ups) as Figure 3a, and the number of
times steeper land fell away from gentler highland areas (downs) as in Figure 3b.
For each simple cross-section a subject scored one "up" or one "down" and for
each complex cross-section it was possible to score two "ups" and no "downs," one
"up" and one "down," or no "ups" and two "downs." Difficulty in scoring arose
with those complex sections which had a combination of sparsely spaced contours
at A, more closely spaced contours in the centre, and more sparsely spaced
contours again towards B (Figure 4). If the subject saw the tract of land either
descending into a steep valley (Figure 4a) or rising up to a sharp peak (Figure 4b)
there was no difficulty in scoring the data. Many of the subjects, however, drew a
cross-section representing an escarpment (Figure 4c). They had seen the closely
spaced contours as representing one slope element and the gentler slopes as
forming higher land, a plateau or slope surface, and lower land at the base of the
scarp face, a score of one "up" and one "down" was recorded for each subject. One
score was omitted from the third and fourth year complex scores because the
subject had failed to complete the test.

*Results.* The data from the simple cross-sections and the complex cross-sections
were analysed separately. A chi-square ($\chi^2$) test was used to test the null hypothesis
of equal frequencies of "up" and "down" responses.
      The less experienced group scored reliably more "ups" than "downs"
when drawing both simple (65 percent "ups"; $\chi^2(1) = 11.17, p < .01$) and complex
cross-sections (63 percent "ups"; $\chi^2(1) = 25.39, p < .01$). Thus the less experienced subjects dominantly perceived steeper as being the highest land within any
one tract of country. The more experienced ones showed no reliable preference
between "ups" and "downs" on the simple cross-sections (56 percent "ups"; $\chi^2(1)$
$= 2.63, p > .05$), but scored significantly more "ups" than "downs" on the complex

Scoring technique

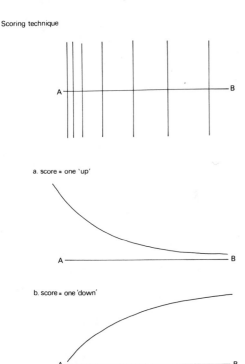

a. score = one 'up'

b. score = one 'down'

Figure 3. The scoring of cross-sections of simple isopleth patterns. In these patterns only one area of steep land is indicated, and this may be interpreted as being adjacent to high or low land.

cross-sections (65 percent "up"; $\chi^2(1) = 4.77, p < .05$). In interpreting the simple contour patterns, therefore, the more experienced subjects were equally able to see steeper slopes as hillsides rising up from lowland plains or as cliffs or scarps descending from plateau surfaces. On the complex sections there was a small trend to interpret steep slopes as being synonymous with upland or higher land.

*Discussion.* The results suggested that expectancy was the dominant factor influencing less experienced subjects in their perception of two-dimensional contour patterns. The more experienced subjects showed less tendency to equate steeper slopes with higher land. The shift in emphasis of scores from dominantly "ups" to fewer "ups" suggested that the influence of texture gradient may have become a more important factor in the perception of the more experienced subjects. That shift in emphasis was considered to be a result of their changed expectancy because they were more familiar with topographic maps and landforms. The experienced subjects were more aware that steeper slopes might not be the highest land because controlled experience had repeatedly shown that the reverse was often true. The less experienced subjects had great difficulty in

Scoring technique

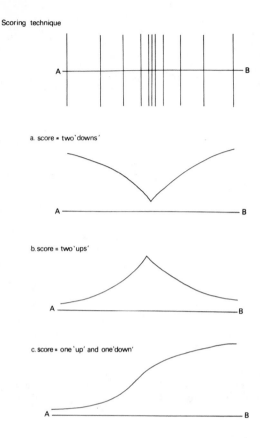

a. score = two 'downs'

b. score = two 'ups'

c. score = one 'up' and one 'down'

Figure 4. The scoring of cross-sections of complex isopleth patterns. In the pattern shown here, the steep land at the centre of the section line AB may be interpreted in one of three ways. In section *a* it has been represented as a valley, and in *b* as a ridge. In *c* the steep area represents a gradient in a single direction and is perceived as being higher than one part of the surrounding area and lower than another part.

equating steeper slopes with lower land. More experienced subjects gave a greater number of valid interpretations of the contour patterns, that is, they were less biased to one interpretation of a pattern. It was concluded that the increased freedom resulting from a wider choice of interpretations meant that the more experienced subjects were possibly more influenced by the texture gradient effect; that is, as the influence of expectancy decreased, the influence of the texture gradient effect increased for the more experienced subjects.

*Experiment 2*
The results of Experiment 1 suggested that less experienced subjects tended to equate steeper slopes with higher land. Experiment 2 was designed to prime or encourage subjects to interpret a series of isopleth patterns in one specific way.

Subjects were all judged "less experienced" and were primed to perceive higher land as having steeper slopes or as flat or gently sloping.

*Method*. Subjects were presented with individual booklets consisting of a short descriptive passage, an instruction sheet with a completed example, and 10 iso-pleth patterns randomly ordered. They were required to read the passage provided and then to interpret the isopleth patterns as in Experiment 1.

*Subjects*. The subjects were 53 first year undergraduates taking the same introductory human geography course as the less experienced subjects in Experiment 1. They were divided into two approximately equal groups on a random basis. The groups were tested concurrently.

*Material*. Two descriptive passages were selected, each a few hundred words long. Passage "A" described a descent from the Pyrenees to the Meseta Plateau. At no point was the term "plateau" used and it was judged that the passage suggested that steeper slopes were synonymous with higher land. Passage "B" described a journey up to the plateaux of Asia and was judged to suggest that steeper slopes often form the lower land in any one tract of country. The passages were duplicated as separate pages and attached to the booklets used in Experiment 1. The booklets were divided into two sets. Booklet IIA contained the passage equating higher land with steeper slopes and IIB that equating lower land with steeper slopes.

*Procedure*. The subjects were asked to read the descriptive passage in their booklet twice. They were told to read slowly and when finished to await further instructions. They were given one minute to study the passage and the importance of not perusing the task booklet was emphasised. When all the subjects had read the passage provided they were asked to turn to the instruction sheet, read it, and complete the task as in Experiment 1. The data were scored by counting the number of times a subject drew steeper land rising up from gentler slopes ("ups") and the number of times steeper land fell away from gentler highland areas, as in Experiment 1.

*Results*. The subjects primed to perceive steeper land as higher scored reliably more "ups" than "downs" when drawing both simple (63 percent "ups"; $\chi^2(1) = 8.04, p < .01$) and complex cross-sections (59 percent "ups"; $\chi^2(1) = 11.21, p < .01$). They dominantly perceived steeper land as being the highest land within an area. The subjects primed to perceive steeper land as lower showed no reliable difference in scores between "ups" and "downs" in both the simple (57 percent "ups", $\chi^2(1) = p > .05$) and complex cross-sections (52 percent "ups"; $\chi^2(1) = 0.89$, $p > .05$). Thus the latter subjects were able to see steeper slopes as descending from gentle highlands or as hills rising up from lowland plains.

*Discussion*. It is difficult to assess the influence of passage "A" on the subjects primed to equate steep slopes and higher land. The scores recorded were very similar to those of the less experienced subjects in Experiment 1. It is suggested that the expectations of most subjects in group IIa, and also in group Ia, were so heavily biased towards a perception of steeper slopes equating with higher land, that passage "A" was largely redundant.

The results may possibly indicate that there was a ceiling effect beyond which no further "ups" were scored because the texture gradient effect could not be nullified completely.

The subjects primed to equate steep slopes with lower land produced results very similar to those of the more experienced third year group in Experiment 1. It was concluded that passage "B" had a considerable effect on their expectancy, making them aware of the possibility of gentle slopes forming the highest land and they produced a greater number of geographical interpretations of the contour patterns, and were possibly more influenced by the texture gradient effect. The result was not seen as an experimenter-demand effect (Rosenthal, 1966) because in both conditions subjects expressed considerable bewilderment about the relevance of the two passages to the task.

In summary, Experiment 2 indicated that, although expectancy was the dominant factor influencing perceptions of isopleth patterns, it could be changed, at least for a short time. Passages "A" and "B" provided a context for the isopleth patterns. That provided by passage "A" was no different from that provided by the personal experience of most of the subjects but passage "B" provided a new context which had considerable effect upon the expectancy and perception of subjects in group IIb who had been encouraged to equate gentle slopes with higher land.

Although texture gradients provide vital cues for the perception of horizontal distances and depth, it was shown that individual expectancy was far more important in interpreting isopleth patterns.

Texture gradients formed by isopleths have been shown to have a relatively small influence on the interpretation of those isopleths (Experiment 1). They do influence our perception, however, by providing cues for the size of objects. Artists and draughtsmen simulate this gradient in depicting three dimensions in two. If the texture gradient is manipulated, however, an illusion of size is created. For instance, it is probable that, if two equal areas of woodland were depicted on a map by using the contour method of relief representation, the woodland located on the steeper slope (closely spaced contours) would appear to have a greater area than that located on the gentler slope. It is hypothesised that isopleth patterns will distort non-terrain information and handicap the map-reader to some extent. This may prove a significant avenue for further research.

The implications of the study are that the cartographer must provide stronger cues for the map reader to compensate for expectancy. Expectancy based on uncontrolled experience strongly prejudices the map reader and the information on the isopleth map can thus be misinterpreted. Many cartographers have tried to find adequate methods of compensation (Baldock, 1968; Philips, DeLucia, & Skelton, 1975; Magee, 1968; Tanaka, 1950). Cartographers face a second problem, however, because the addition of cues, such as relief shading, may impair the map reader's ability to extract non-terrain information from the map (DeLucia, 1972).

Thanks to Dr. J. Gardiner for comments on an earlier draft of this paper and to Dr. G. Underwood for assistance during its final preparation.

# References

Balasubramanyan, V. Application of information theory to maps. *Internationales Jahrbuch für Kartographie* 1971, *11*, 177-181.

Baldock, E. D. Cartographic relief portrayal. *Internationales Jahrbuch für Kartographie* 1968, *8*, 75-78.

Bartholomew, J. C., & Kinniburgh, I. A. G. The factor of awareness. *The Cartographic Journal*, 1973, *10*, 59-62.

Cuff, D. J. Colour on temperature maps. *The Cartographic Journal*, 1973, *10*(1), 17-21.

DeLucia, A. The effect of shaded relief on map information accessibility. *The Cartographic Journal*, 1972, *9*, 14-18.

Dember, W. N. *The psychology of perception*. New York: Holt, Rinehart & Winston, 1960.

Ferro, G. Valeurs expressives et fonction formative de la cartographie dans les livres de texte et dans les atlas, selon la moderne didactique. *Internationales Jahrbuch für Kartographie*, 1971, *11*, 189-193.

Gibson, J. J. The perception of visual surfaces. *American Journal of Psychology* 1950, *63*, 367-384.

Keates, J. S. Symbols and meaning in topographic maps. *Internationales Jahrbuch für Kartographie*, 1972, *12*, 169-176.

Koeman, C. The principle of communication in cartography. *Internationales Jahrbuch für Kartographie*, 1971, *11*, 169-176.

Kolacny, A. The importance of cartographic information for the comprehending of messages spread by the mass communication media. *Internationales Jahrbuch für Kartographie*, 1971, *11*, 216-223.

Magee, G. A. The Admiralty chart: Trends in content and design. *The Cartographic Journal*, 1968, *5*(1), 28-33.

Miller, O. M., & Summerson, C. H. Slope-zone maps. *Geographical Review*, 1960, *50*, 194-202.

Phillips, R. J., DeLucia, A., & Skelton, N. Some objective tests of the legibility of relief maps. *The Cartographic Journal*, 1975, *12*, 39-46.

Rosenthal, R. *Experimenter effects in behavioral research*. New York: Appleton-Century-Crofts, 1966.

Tanaka, K. The relief contour method of representing topography on maps. *Geographical Review*, 1950, *40*, 444-456.

# The acquisition and processing of cartographic information: Some preliminary experimentation

Michael W. Dobson

*Two studies are presented that probed map readers' abilities to isolate and process cartographic information visually. The first study describes a limited investigation of the relationship between three fixation-related variables and the informational characteristics of a map. The results indicated that map reading was typified by intelligent scanning. The second study followed from the first and describes six experiments investigating the relationship between the amount of graphic information and the accuracy of processing during a map-like visual choice task. The results of these experiments indicated that increasing the amount of graphic information decreased the accuracy of response when a basic level of information was presented.*

One of the most persistent themes in recent cartographic literature concerns the role of the map as a communications device. Research has been aimed at clarifying, enhancing, and refining the visual aspects of cartographic displays in order to increase the efficiency of performance in terms of accuracy and speed. This objective, in turn, has made it necessary to understand the factors influencing the relationship between performance and graphic symbolism in using maps.

This paper describes two studies of processing of visual information for maps. The first study examines fixation selectivity during map reading and probes the relationship between the informativeness of display elements and intelligent scanning. The second study deals specifically with the relationship of information, visual acuity, and the ability to process symbols during fixation.

## Visual selectivity during map reading

A recent cartographic experiment (Dobson, 1979a) examined Mackworth and Morandi's (1967) eye-movement oriented, subjective information metric in an attempt to determine the relationship between fixation localization and displayed graphic information during map reading. The experiment preserved the general outline of Mackworth and Morandi's investigation in that the study was based, in part, on a comparison between the locations fixated by subjects looking at an entire map (Figure 1) and estimates by other subjects of the relative importance of the individual squares comprising the same map.

The latter differed from Mackworth and Morandi's study in several ways, however. First, the subjects estimating the informativeness of the 143 cells comprising the map were allowed to see the entire display and marked estimates of each cell's informativeness on a clear plastic grid overlaying the display. Second, unlike the 10-sec constraint imposed by Mackworth and Morandi, the viewing

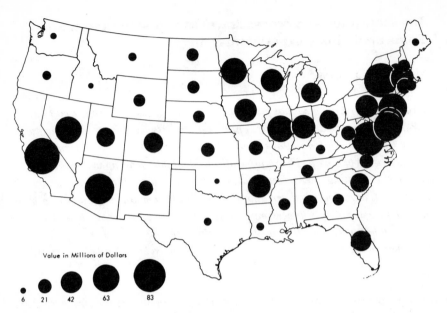

Figure 1. The stimulus display. The distribution on the stimulus is fictitious and the title deliberately vague.

time for the subjects whose eye movements were recorded was not limited. Third, besides the number of fixations (the measure used by Mackworth and Morandi), the number of refixations and average fixation time were calculated for each cell on the display. Finally, all three of these variables were compared with the subjective information measure.

## Results
The results of the experiment were highly supportive of Mackworth and Morandi's study. The association between subjective information and eye movement variables was determined with Spearman rank correlations. The relationship between the subjective information content of the display and the group fixation matrix indicated that the information measure was a sensitive predictor of fixation localization ($r_s = .76, p < .01$). The number of refixations per cell and the average time of fixation per cell were also highly correlated with the subjective information matrix ($r_s = .72$ and $.70, p < .01$). Hence, the amount of time spent looking at a region, and the number of times a region was looked at increased linearly with its measured informativeness.

## Discussion
The subjective information measure appeared to make plausible estimates of the key visual regions on the stimulus even though the subjects were allowed to view the display for an unlimited amount of time. This point is considered very

important because the temporal limitation imposed in Mackworth and Morandi's study could have been responsible for the trends in fixation locatization reported. That is, because of the time limit, the subjects may have inspected the obvious global features of the display and ignored local features but there was no indication that the local features would continue to be ignored during an extended scan. The results of the present experiment suggest that the map readers hierarchically distributed their visual attention in a manner that localized display areas of high information content and that they selected visual inputs by operating efficient and discriminative search strategies.

Besides fixation localization, refixation and average fixation time per cell were used to evaluate the concept of key regions. During a viewing period regulated by the reader, refixations are relatively common. These redundant fixations are generally conceded to be attempts either to clarify or to reappraise the utility of display information previously fixated. Interestingly, the results suggest that the intensity of refixation showed a positive trend in conjunction with the subjective information rankings. The selectivity indicated by analysis of the fixation and refixation variables appears to provide evidence that particular portions of the display attracted more visual attention than others. Because this selectivity apparently reflects variability in the information content of cells, it would be expected that visual processing, as measured by fixation, would require a variable duration with respect to the levels of information displayed. Consequently, it is not surprising that the general trend of the average fixation time analysis was localized with longer values at the areas of the display with high subjective information rankings. We may assume, then, that the subjects examined and reexamined high information locations more frequently and for a longer time than less informative locations.

The evidence that the eye movement variables covaried reliably with the subjectively estimated informativeness of portions of the map provides some indication that the readers were able visually to isolate the important data used in the construction of the map. It may also suggest, however, that performance of this type of task is not uniform over a display surface.

The relationship between the average fixation time per cell and the information ratings for those cells indicates that variable amounts of time were required to process different levels of informativeness. The fact that fixations and refixations tended to localize in areas of high estimated informativeness may also indicate that variable amounts of effort are required to target and visually isolate display elements of varying informativeness.

An additional analysis was, therefore, performed. A photographically produced positive of the achromatic stimulus was placed on an evenly illuminated light table and the reflectivity of each of the 143 cells read twice. The reflectometer used had a circular aperture approximately the same size as the cells but to insure independence of the readings each cell was measured through an aperture corresponding exactly to the cell size. The aperture sheet was sufficiently large and dense so that the readings were influenced only by the amount of light passing through the apertured cell. The reflectometer was calibrated so that a cell without information (clear and no symbols) read 50 and a solid black cell read 0. Before analysis the average value of the two readings for the cell were subtracted from 50 (the maximum value) so that the scale would provide a measure of increasing blackness.

The linear relationship between the subjectively derived information content of the display and the reflectivity data indicated that blackness per cell may have been a prime variable influencing the subjective rankings ($r_s = .87, p < .01$).

We may consider that the informativeness ratings were responses to the density of information per cell. The analysis further suggests that as the density of information increased there was a higher probability of increased fixation, refixation, and average fixation time. In this sense, the relationship between eye movement and displayed information may be regarded as an indication of the difficulty of extracting information at the various display locations.

The ease with which graphic information is processed is an area of extreme interest to cartographers who are continually debating "how much is too much" in the symbolic content of maps. Although the cartographic side of this issue is well understood, there is little knowledge of the perceptual consequences of the amount of graphic information on performance. A further analysis of the relationship between the amount of graphic information and the ease of processing was, therefore, undertaken.

*Amount of information and the ease of processing*
In order to examine the relationship between the amount of information presented and the ability to process visually, an experimental situation was devised that approximated visual fixation, provided data on the processing of foveal and peripheral information, simulated a realistic map reading task, and incorporated a response to increasing information (Dobson, 1980).

The subject was required to determine if two symbols at the ends of a row were of the same size as or a different size from the circle at the center of the row. The targets (the symbol at each end of the row) were to be assessed during the fixation as well. Fixation time (the time that the stimulus was illuminated on the tachistoscope) was limited to 100 msec so that it was impossible to move the eyes to either end target if the subject first observed the center.

The task, then, required a distribution of attention across the visual field and simulated the processing of information during normal fixation, except that the relative location of all targets was stipulated. In terms of map reading, the task is comparable to determining, while looking at a specific size of circle, the location of symbols of the same size in surrounding areas.

The relationship between the amount of graphic information and processing was probed on displays of three different widths, which subtended three specific angles on the retina. These angles subtended 2.5 deg, 5 deg, and 7.5 deg. Presentation at the 2.5 deg angle positioned the image mainly in the fovea. The retinal position of the 5 deg presentation was both foveal and extra-foveal although still within the area of the retina with good resolving power. The 7.5 deg angle extended somewhat outside the fovea.

Each of six circle sizes was used as the standard circle (center) in a four-question set. Each set consisted of two presentations in which the center and the ends matched and two presentations in which the center and ends did not match, both ends being either larger or smaller than the center. The circles which did not match were the two sizes (one larger and one smaller) closest in diameter to the circle used for the center in a particular presentation. When the smallest and largest of the six circles were the centers, however, the symbols used in the two mismatched trials were always larger than the center for the former and smaller than the center for the latter. Each question set was prepared in widths corresponding to the three visual angles, generating 72 images (six sizes of circles × four questions per center × three widths of presentation). This was termed the *no noise* condition and constituted the first experiment (Figure 2).

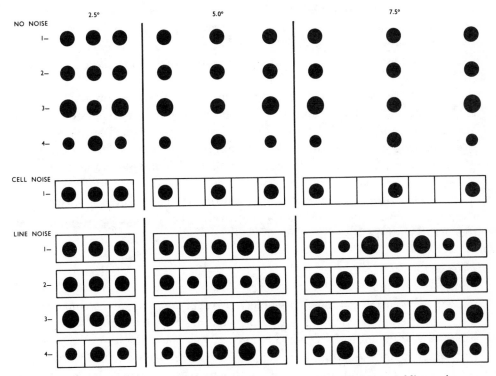

Figure 2. Examples of the four-question sets for the no noise, cell noise, and line noise experiments. There were four-question sets at each angle for every target in all experiments. All questions use same stimuli as *no noise* but are enclosed in cells.

The second condition was approximately the same except that the circles were placed inside of cells 1.7 cm square. At the 5 deg angle there was one empty box between the standard and each end target. At the 7.5 deg angle there were two empty boxes between the standard and each end. This was termed *cell noise* (Figure 2).

The third condition, termed *line noise*, differed in that the empty cells were filled with the mismatched circle sizes for that specific question set. At the 5 deg angle, when the ends matched the center both noise circles were smaller than the center or ends on one question and larger on the other question. When the mismatched end was larger than the center, the noise circle was smaller and in the reverse case it was larger (Figure 2). At the 7.5 deg angle the situation was somewhat more complicated because there were four empty boxes to fill. Here both the smaller and the larger noise circles were used although their position varied with respect to the size of the end target (Figure 2).

In the fourth condition (*map noise*) the central row of each stimulus was identical to one of the rows generated for the previous condition. Each central row, however, was centered in a matrix 3 cells wide × 5 cells high at the 2.5 deg angle, 5×5 at the 5 deg angle, or 7×5 at the 7.5 deg angle. The cells surrounding the central row were indicated with the two circles that were mismatched to the center in each four-question set. These noise symbols were keyed to the central row and the adjacent vertical circle was the inverse of the symbol in the central row. Each additional row varied similarly in respect to the preceding row (Figure 3).

The six sizes of circles used as stimuli in the experiment ranged from .48 cm to 1.6 cm in diameter (Table 1). The sizes of circles used were judged to be suitably discriminable from one another. It should be noted that the difference in diameter between circle 6 and circle 5 was approximately three times the other gradations, an aberration resulting from the limited choice of suitable circle sizes available. Rather than use an inter-stimulus dimension that was minimally discriminable when the circles were arranged in order, the larger size was selected. Its use was not considered problematical, however, but advantageous with respect to the task the subject would perform.

*The experimental session*

Eighty college students with various levels of experience with maps volunteered to participate in the experiment. The subjects were randomly assigned to take one of the four experiments, twenty subjects participating in each experiment. Each subject was tested individually and performed only one of the four experiments. During the first few minutes of the session, data were gathered concerning the subject's age, sex, vision, and experience with map use. Instructions and explanation were then provided concerning the task, the stimuli, the form of response (same-different), the limitation on eye movement, and the structure of the session.

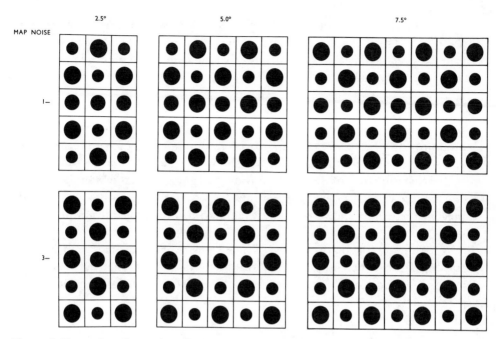

Figure 3. Examples of a portion of the four-question set for the map noise experiment.

      The subject saw each presentation in a specific sequence. A blank white field lasted for 5000 msec; the fixation point then appeared in the center of a white background for 1500 msec, followed by a black field for 50 msec; next, the stimulus field, centered on the fixation point, appeared for 100 msec. Finally, the white field reappeared signaling the end of a trial.

Table 1. Size characteristics of the stimuli.

| Circle No. | Diameter | | Visual angle on retina (degrees) | Difference: 6-5, 5-4, etc. |
|---|---|---|---|---|
| | Inches | Centimeters | | |
| 6 | .64 | 1.62 | 1.18 | .38 |
| 5 | .45 | 1.14 | .83 | .11 |
| 4 | .39 | .99 | .72 | .13 |
| 3 | .32 | .81 | .59 | .13 |
| 2 | .25 | .63 | .46 | .11 |
| 1 | .19 | .78 | .35 | |

The 72 images required for each experiment were blocked into three sets of 24 trials and the blocks were separated by 3-min periods. The cards were shuffled for each subject but structured so that the same size center did not appear on two successive trials.

*Results*

The data for the experiment (5760 responses) were 1440 responses for each condition and 480 responses per angle within conditions. These responses were used to calculate the performance curves shown in Figure 4. Analysis of variance revealed that the effect of the displays, the visual angles, and the interaction between these variables were all significant (all $p < .01$). Analysis of age, sex, and experience with maps showed that these factors did not significantly influence the results.

Although the main concern of the experiment was to analyze the relationship between increased information and the task, rather than between circle size estimates and visual angle, Figure 5 is of interest nevertheless. Variability of

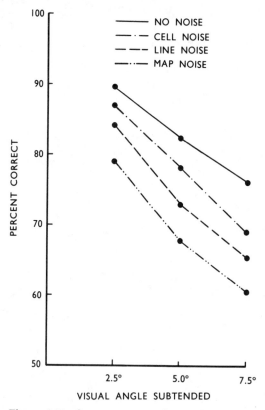

Figure 4. Performance curves by condition and angle of presentation.

the data in respect to the angle of presentation is lessened, yet the superiority of the larger symbols for the task remains obvious.

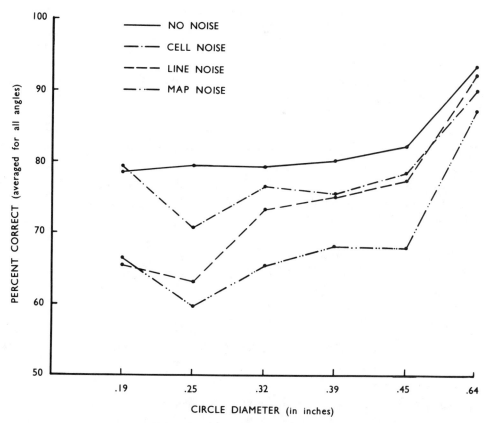

Figure 5. Performance curves by condition and size of targets, averaged for all angles.

It should be noted that the flexures on the curves between sizes 1 and 2 and between sizes 5 and 6 reflect the unique matches comprising the question sets when the smallest and largest circles were the center targets. (Size 1 was mismatched against sizes 2 and 3, and size 6 was mismatched against sizes 5 and 4.) Responses to the largest circle should also be elevated because the difference in visual angle between it and the next closest size was approximately three times the difference in angle between any other pair.

*Discussion*
The "no noise" experiment must be considered to be primarily an acuity task providing a context for the remaining experiments. It should be noted that the

accuracy of response to it was not perfect and also that foveal processing (2.5 deg) was superior to extra-foveal processing (5 deg and 7.5 deg). These relations held in the three subsequent experiments. It is apparent, however, that each successive increase of information decreased the accuracy of response at all angles of presentation.

The results of the experiment suggest that the additional information on the displays impaired matching even though the subjects were told that this information was irrelevant to the task. In this sense, increasing graphic information must demand increased processing.

*A further step*
The first set of experiments was based on symbols uniformly spaced across the visual field. Because most maps have uneven densities of information across the display, a second set of experiments was devised to simulate processing when the fixated target is surrounded by a high density of graphic information.

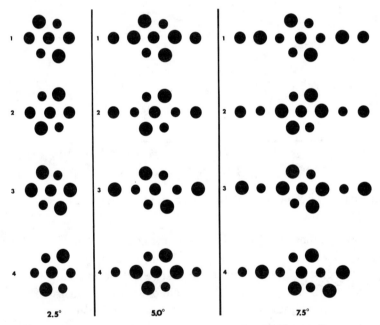

Figure 6. Examples of the four-question sets for the clustered experiments. There were four-question sets at each angle for every target in both experiments.

These experiments retained the basic format of the first four, the main difference being that circles were loaded into the foveal field rather than distributed regularly across the display. The format of the display followed from the *line noise* experiment (Figure 2) except that the cells were omitted. Four circles were added to each display and surrounded the central target with one circle located at each of four azimuths (30, 150, 210, and 330 deg) measured from the central target. Two of the additional circles were one size larger than the target and the other two circles were one size smaller. The circles were presented either standing alone (Figure 6) or surrounded by an island-like shape with internal boundaries separating all circles (Figure 7). All other aspects of the presentation were the same as in the first experiments.

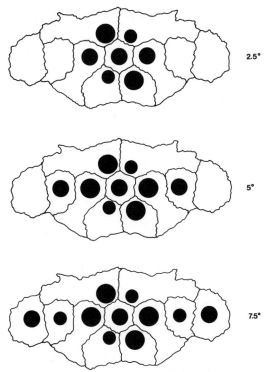

Figure 7. An example of the use of the island in the second clustered experiment.

*Results*
The results are shown in Figure 8 where they are compared with the results of the *map noise* experiment (which produced the lowest accuracies in the first experiments). Analysis of variance revealed that accuracy of response was influenced by the angle of presentation but not by the nature of the displays ($p < .01$).

*Discussion*
The results of the second set of experiments clearly suggest that increasing the density of foveal information decreased the accuracy and extent of processing across the visual field. Positioning four circles around the central target produced results comparable to those of the map noise experiment, which utilized 8 more circles at 2.5 deg, 17 more at 5 deg, and 24 more circles at 7.5 deg.

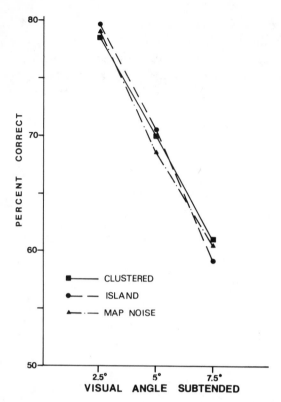

Figure 8. Performance curves by condition and angle of presentation.

The use of the island shape surrounding the circles did not have any significant effect; this experiment produced the same levels of performance recorded when the circles were shown alone. It would appear that the subjects were able to ignore the borders and concentrate solely on the symbols. The subjects in the earlier cell noise experiment did not seem able to ignore the cell shape; this would bear further investigation. It is possible that the pattern of symbols in the latter experiment was superior to the pattern of symbols in the cell noise experiment and allowed the surrounding shapes to be ignored more easily.

The influence of the clustered symbols is clear: loading the fovea with a high density of information produces the same results as uniformly loading the visual field.

*General Discussion*

The experiments were designed to evaluate visual search and visual information processing of maps. Although the results indicated that maps are selectively and intelligently scanned, ability to process fixated information lagged far behind the ability to isolate it.

Results of altering the visual field are unclear. It could be argued that increases in accuracy might result if fixation time were increased, but there is some evidence that increasing time to process does not yield this outcome (Dobson, 1979b). The arrangement of the curves (Figures 4 and 8) suggest that each increase in information requires an increased amount of time to process, however. Hence, more study is required for, if a simple task and relatively simple stimuli induce these results, it would be reasonable to suspect that the demands of processing an actual map are severe.

The artificial restriction on fixation during the experiment also influenced the accuracy of processing, especially in the normal situation where multiple fixation occurs. Unfortunately, increasing the number of fixations to compensate for a decreased ability to process during a fixation simply increased the total amount of processing required for reading the map. In addition, the research suggests that the usefulness of peripherally sensed information decreases as the amount of graphic information increases, leading one to suspect that this information would be of limited value for targeting subsequent fixations. The strategy of allocating fixations should reflect the limited value of these peripheral cues and a subsequent decrease in the efficiency of search.

Three other discrepancies between the experiment and normal search should be noted. First, it is generally not the case that a reader will have specific pre-search knowledge about the location of surrounding targets. Second, a reader will not be able to discard targets as potential matches because they are not in a specific location. Finally, during normal viewing a reader will have to attend to fields of view much larger than the limited ones used in this experiment.

Although the specific influence of these three factors during visual search is unknown, it is hypothesized that the result would be further decreases in the accuracy of matching. If this is the case, then map reading tasks using the map as an areal storehouse (Jenks, Note 1) may be laborious for information processing.

The cartographer's solution to this problem should not be the production of simplistic maps, however, because processing demands can be lightened by using alternative or innovative symbols. It is possible that unique symbols may provide stimuli of such visual consequence that processing is facilitated even when targets are positioned in dense contexts.

A human factors approach to map design could be of value for the development and testing of effective symbol systems. For example, it seems likely that the accuracy of matching in the visual field experiments could be improved by using other symbols as the stimuli. The research on coding by Williams (1967) is particularly applicable here. It is probable that symbolizing two variable dimensions (such as size and value) would be superior to symbolizing only size, as in the present experiment. This sort of manipulation would increase symbol visibility and perhaps speed symbol discrimination during processing.

In any event, continued analysis of performance factors is needed for developing an understanding of the success of cartographic communication. Questions concerning the appropriateness of symbol system to task ability must be asked and analyzed.

## Reference note

1. Jenks, G. F. Conceptual and perceptual error in thematic mapping. *Technical Papers from the 30th Annual Meeting, American Congress on Surveying and Mapping*, 1970, 174-188.

## References

Dobson, M. W. The influence of map information on fixation localization. *The American Cartographer*, 1979, *6*(1), 51-65. (a)

Dobson, M. W. Visual information processing during cartographic communication. *The Cartographic Journal*, 1979, *16*(1), 14-20. (b)

Dobson, M. W. The influence of amount of information on visual matching. *The Cartographic Journal*, 1980, in press.

Mackworth, N. H., & Morandi, A. J. The gaze selects the informative details within pictures. *Perception & Psychophysics*, 1967, *2*, 547-552.

Williams, L. G. The effects of target specification on objects fixated during visual search. *Acta Psychologica*, 1967, *27*, 355-360.

# Graph reading abilities of thirteen-year-olds

Beverly V. Roller

*To determine how well graph reading skills are applied in social studies, science, and consumer mathematics, seventh grade students were asked to answer multiple-choice graph reading, interpretation, and summarization questions when graphs were embedded in a text and when they were seen in isolation. Results favored isolated presentation of graphs for reading and interpretation items, but no differences were found for summarization items. Reading comprehension and mathematics computation scores were correlated with responses to the three types of questions and revealed weak relationships. High and low scorers and two randomly selected groups were interviewed and asked to explain how answers were obtained. They were also asked to identify graphs as easy or difficult and to indicate where they had learned about graphs, if they liked graphs, and if they ignored them or paid attention to them when reading a textbook. The students identified a number of graph readability and difficulty factors affecting their understanding of graphs. They also reported that graphs increase the difficulty of reading and many depend upon their teachers to explain the graphs.*

Graphs are one of the multidisciplinary devices of the secondary curriculum, a visual method of presenting large amounts of information illustrating relationships and comparisons. Graph reading is usually classed as a study skill with initial instruction assigned to the elementary school subjects of reading and mathematics. Within the secondary curriculum, science and social studies require the application of graph reading skills. By ninth grade, readers encounter many graphs in functional and consumer mathematics situations.

From about the sixth grade, readers are expected to integrate information contained in graphs with a surrounding text, an expectation explored and defined by Vernon. Vernon (1946, 1950, 1951, 1953, 1954) reported a series of experiments with subjects of differing age groups and the effects of presenting information in a variety of media (pictorial charts, graphs, tables of figures, pictures and narrative, expository text) on isolated fact recall and general argument recall. Vernon (1951) observed that a text with graphs is more difficult than a text without graphs.

In direct contrast, the testing methods commonly used to assess graph reading abilities of students seldom require the integration of graph and text information. Usually, isolated graphs (without a supporting and surrounding text) are used in conjunction with questions in a multiple-choice answer format. Typical examples of assessment procedures may be found in the National Assessment of Educational Progress (Reading, 1973, 1978; Social Studies, 1975; Mathematics, 1975a, 1975b; Science, 1970, 1975, 1978).

Vernon's work influenced the design of a number of subsequent studies which tended to center on the question of whether or not a graphic aid contributes to the comprehension of the text (Turner, 1974). However, the study by Eggen, Kauchak, and Kirk (1978) produced results which seemed to run counter to previous expectations and research, leading them to suspect that textual cues interfered with comprehension of information on graphs. Their study hinted that text and graphs may be "incompatible" in the minds of readers, perhaps causing readers to avoid graphs in textbooks.

*Purposes of the study*

One purpose of the study was to determine how well seventh grade students can apply the skills of graph reading, graph interpretation, and graph summarization in social studies, science, and consumer mathematics, with and without a supporting text. A second purpose was to study the relationship of achievement in reading comprehension and mathematics computation to graph response skills. Because none of the researchers had reported how the subjects thought or felt about the graph reading task, a third purpose was to determine those feelings and perceptions.

*Procedure*

Two testing procedures, using a multiple-choice item format, were developed and informally named Text Graphs and Isolated Graphs. The reliability coefficients were .60 and .72 respectively, determined by Cronbach's Alpha, a test of internal consistency. Text Graphs consisted of two selections from social studies and science textbooks, containing approximately 2420 words, two sets of two circle graphs and one simple line graph, accompanied by 15 items. Isolated Graphs consisted of eight graphs, the three used in Text Graphs plus five additional simple and complex bar and line graphs taken from the business section of a popular periodical. These eight graphs were accompanied by 38 items. Three graphs and 10 items on the two tests were identical and were used to compare the effects of graph presentation within a text and in isolation.

The multiple-choice items, called graph items, required subjects to use skills defined as reading, interpretation, and summarization. *Reading* required use of directly stated information and included estimating amounts between grid lines on bar and line graphs and relative size on circle graphs. *Interpretation* required use of computation (limited to addition or subtraction) to achieve interpolated information, or two comparisons of areas as on circle graphs. *Summarization* required recognition of the statement which best described the total graphic presentation. Some items were classified as non-defined and were not used in the statistical analyses.

Two hundred sixty-eight seventh graders, 136 boys and 132 girls, in three junior high schools, in different areas of a school system of 80,000 students were tested, 119 taking Text Graphs and 149 taking Isolated Graphs. Four groups of 15 subjects each were identified as random group administration, random individual administration, high scorers, and low scorers on Isolated Graphs. These subjects were interviewed on how their answers had been obtained. They were also asked to identify graphs as being easy or difficult, and to indicate if they liked graphs, where they had learned about them, and if they ignored or paid attention to graphs when reading a textbook.

Following identification of subjects in the study, reading comprehension and mathematics computation scale scores were located and used in the Analysis of Covariance. The subtests of the *Comprehensive Test of Basic Skills* (1977) had been administered to most of the subjects half-way through grade 6.

*Results*

*Textual and isolated graph presentation.* To compare the effects of graph presentation with and without a supporting text, the reading comprehension and mathematics computation scores of all subjects were entered into the Analysis of Covariance as covariates. Responses to four reading, three interpretation, and three summarization items on the two tests were the dependent variables. Analysis of Covariance revealed significant differences of a little more than 20 percent favoring *isolated* presentation of graphs for the item clusters identified as reading and interpretation (mean of .56 vs. .69 for reading, and .38 vs. .48 for interpretation). No significant differences were seen for summarization items, .59 and .63.

These findings support the hypothesis that text and graph information are not commonly merged in the mind of the reader. Vernon (1951) found that a text with graphs is more difficult than a text without graphs; in addition, our finding shows that graphs presented in text are more difficult than graphs presented in isolation. The magnitude of the differences between the two groups on reading and interpretation items is notable. The lack of differences on summarization items appears to repeat a similar finding of Eggen et al. (1978).

*Correlations.* The grade equivalent means for all subjects in the study were 8.8 for reading comprehension and 7.8 for mathematics computation. To determine if the reading comprehension and mathematics computation scores would predict how subjects would respond to graph items, a Pearson product moment correlation was computed. Although it would appear that reading comprehension and mathematics computation scores (CTBS) are related to graph items of reading, interpretation, and summarization, the relationships are weak (see Table 1). This finding suggests that standardized achievement test data should not be used to group students for instructional or research purposes, and may explain Turner's (1974) findings. Although the correlation was statistically significant, the relationship appears too weak to be significant for education.

Table 1. Correlation of reading comprehension and mathematics computation scores (CTBS) and item categories for 268 subjects.

| | Comprehension | |
| --- | --- | --- |
| Reading | .30 | .14 |
| Interpretation | .22 | .14 |
| Summarization | .30 | .12[a] |

Note. All $p < .01$ except as noted.
[a]$p < .02$.

*Instructional background.* To define the instructional background of the subjects, particularly for graphs, they were asked where they had learned about graphs (Table 2). Note that, in the school district where this study was done, "study skills" is one of the areas in which instruction must be given and records must be kept at the elementary level. Although considered one of the objectives of the reading program of the district, seventh graders did not consider study skills a part of their definition of reading. (See Otto, Kamm, & Weible, Note 1.)

Table 2. Percent of subjects reporting content setting of graph instruction, by interview groups.

| Categorized responses | Low scorers $N=15$ | High scorers $N=15$ | Random groups $N=30$ |
| --- | --- | --- | --- |
| Mathematics | 27 | 27 | 30 |
| Study skills | 27 | 33 | 60 |
| Reading | — | 7 | 3 |
| Language arts | — | 13 | 7 |
| Social studies | 13 | 20 | — |
| Don't know | 7 | — | — |
| Non-defined answers | 27 | — | — |

The prominence of the two categories, mathematics and study skills, suggests that the subjects had studied graphs isolated from text.

*Feelings about graphs.* The students were asked if they liked graphs and their responses were categorized yes, no, and ambivalent. The last category was created because a fair number of subjects hedged on answering this question. (The students seemed somewhat concerned about the interviewer's attitude: "If you are interviewing me about my answers and about graphs, you must like graphs.") Much of the ambivalence was expressed verbally by comments such as: "Sometimes yes, sometimes no" and "It depends." Nonverbal behavior included shrugs of the shoulders, eye contact and a searching of the interviewer's face for cues, or a refusal of eye contact accompanied by vague answers. As can be seen in Table 3, low scorers were likely to say "no" and high scorers "yes."

Table 3. Percent of subjects reporting positive, negative, and ambivalent feelings about graphs, by interview groups.

| Categorized responses | Low scorers $N=15$ | High scorers $N=15$ | Random groups $N=30$ |
|---|---|---|---|
| No | 47 | 7 | 30 |
| Ambivalent | 27 | 40 | 20 |
| Yes | 27 | 53 | 50 |

*Ignoring or paying attention to graphs.* Subjects were asked two questions: "Do you ignore graphs when reading a textbook?" and "When do you stop and pay attention to a graph?" The questions may appear to be positive and negative versions of the same inquiry, but the categories of responses to each are somewhat different. The most surprising finding was in the identification of the categories teacher directed and text directed. Subjects described teacher direction in the form of classroom assignments, quizzes and tests, and direct instruction. Many said that if a teacher told them that a graph was important and likely to be on a test then they would study it. Some few students, generally high scorers, volunteered that they paid attention to graphs either because of a direction in the textbook to "look at the graph" or because study questions in the text required extracting information from the graph.

Table 4. Percent of subjects who say they ignore or pay attention to graphs, by interview groups.

|  | Ignore | | | Pay Attention | | |
|---|---|---|---|---|---|---|
|  | Low scorers | High scorers | Random groups | Low scorers | High scorers | Random groups |
| Categorized responses | $N=15$ | $N=15$ | $N=30$ | $N=15$ | $N=15$ | $N=30$ |
| Always | 33 | — | 20 | 7 | 7 | 3 |
| Sometimes | 13 | 60 | 70 | — | — | — |
|    Teacher directed | — | — | — | 47 | 33 | 33 |
|    Text directed | — | — | — | — | 20 | 10 |
| Never | 40 | 40 | 7 | — | — | — |
| Don't know | 13 | — | — | — | 33 | 20 |
| Non-defined answers | — | — | 3 | 47 | 7 | 33 |

*Difficulty of graphs used in this study.* Subjects were asked to identify the easiest and hardest of the eight graphs used in the investigation. This elicited information about the readability and understandability of the graphs bore little relation to how the subjects answered the multiple-choice items which accompanied the graphs. The ranking tended to support the logical principle that the more things compared and displayed on a graph, the more difficult the graph becomes. This can be affected, however, by a number of factors in the way the graph is drawn, especially in the labeling of the comparisons and additions to graphs (perhaps assumed by the illustrator to be "eye-catching"). Generally, seventh grade students saw graphs as difficult where the illustrator had tried to put "too much" into a compact space. Two of the graphs used in the investigation are reproduced (Figures 1 and 2) to illustrate the perceptions of the subjects.

Subjects saw the simple bar graph in Figure 1 as the easiest and best understood. Contributing factors were the "flat-top" bars, clear vertical scale of twos, and non-interference from horizontal grid lines. The graphic design of the title (featuring large, bold print for the first part) appeared to be visually compelling, thus causing some subjects to disregard the last two words. The abbreviation, "Proj.," at the base of the 1976 bar tended to be noticed by high scorers and not by low scorers.

Subjects saw the complex line graph in Figure 2 as the most difficult, one subject saying, "It's going up and down, all over it." Subjects talked about a

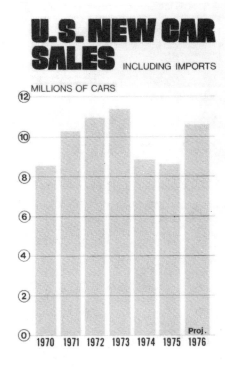

Figure 1. Reprinted by permission from *Time*, The Weekly News Magazine, ©*Time*, Inc., June 14, 1976.

number of features of the graph including calendar markers, four graphs in one, interference of grid line and information line labeling, and title information running counter to the trend of upward prices.

*Item analysis*. Although an attempt had been made to define each item in the study in terms of what was expected of the reader (reading, interpretation, summarization), the interviews revealed that readers' reactions to each item were distinctive. Two items utilized the information in the graph in Figure 2. One asked if the cost of a pound of round steak in June 1975 was almost $1.00, 60 cents, over $2.00, or $1.50. Sixty-two percent of 149 subjects answered over $2.00 and 31 percent answered $1.50. During interviews it was revealed that most of the latter seemed to focus on the words "round steak" in the question, which they then located on the graph. The label, "1 lb. round steak" was extremely close to the $1.50 grid line, causing confusion of the grid line with the information line. By contrast, those who answered correctly (over $2.00) were paying attention to the date (1975) given in the question. They located 1975 on the horizontal scale and moved up to above the $2.00 grid line to the information line.

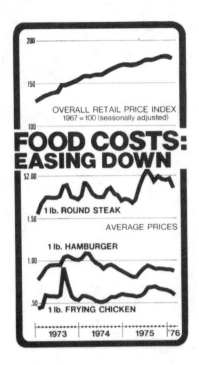

Figure 2. Reprinted by permission from *Time*, The Weekly News Magazine, ©*Time*, Inc., April 19, 1976.


The graph summarization item read as follows:

The graph shows:

(a) meat prices have stayed the same since January, 1975
(b) high meat prices appear to be going even higher
(c) prices of three meats
(d) meat prices compared with the retail price index

The two most popular choices for low scorers were (b) and (c), those answering (c) apparently confident of their answers and not looking at the top of the graph. The two most popular choices for high scorers were (c) and (d). As with low scorers, the high scorers answering (c) were confident in that answer and disregarded the top of the graph.

*Conclusions and implications*
One of the most remarkable aspects of the study is that all of the subjects interviewed could "read" and no interviews were terminated because of an inability to

cope with the test. At the same time, these seventh graders were very similar to first graders learning to read. They exhibited much of the behavior usually associated with beginning reading or frustration including reading aloud, whispering, subvocalization, following lines of print with a forefinger, following grid and information lines with fingers, and relying on fingers as measurement devices. (Only two of 59 subjects used straight-edge devices such as rulers.)

In explaining their answers, subjects seemed to fall into four major groups, apart from the designation of high or low scorers. The first group did not have a strategy for achieving an answer saying, "I don't know" or "I guessed." The second group exhibited attraction to, and distraction by, isolated words and phrases, reducing the task to what was known in much the same way a first grader will say "big" for "pig" because the word looks like one he knows. This group was susceptible to perceptions of size and height (bigger is better, higher is better). The third group, also susceptible to perceptions of size and height, had a strategy and expressed confidence in their answers. They exhibited a restricted, limited use of available information and did not confirm their answers. The last group applied a strategy accurately, were direct and coherent in their explanations, and were likely to have a method for confirming answers.

The *members* of the above groups changed with each item in the study, low scorers applying strategies with confidence on certain items and high scorers saying, "I don't know." Each individual, then, might fall into any one of the four groups described for any one item.

There was a stability, a repetitive, "stuck" quality to the way in which a particular subject dealt with a particular item. For example, if he or she first gave an answer which, in the judgment of the interviewer indicated attraction to or distraction by isolated words and phrases, and then wished to change it, the change appeared to have been made on the same basis. The procedures during the interviews were intended to inhibit the investigator from introducing the instructional variable and apparently were effective.

However, focusing the subject's attention upon a disregarded or ignored piece of information very likely would have been helpful. Attention should be called to ignored or disregarded information on the graph and students should be urged to incorporate that information into their thinking to achieve accurate answers.

## Reference note

1. Otto, W., Kamm, K., Weibel, E. *Wisconsin design for reading skill development: Rationale and objectives for the study skills element, Working Paper no. 84.* Madison: Wisconsin Research and Development Center for Cognitive Learning, February 1972.

# References

*Comprehensive Test of Basic Skills, All Levels, Expanded Edition, Technical Bulletin, No. 2*. Monterey: CTB/McGraw-Hill, 1977.

Cronbach, L. J. *Essentials of psychological testing*. New York: Harper & Brothers, 1960.

Eggen, P., Kauchak, D., & Kirk, S. The effects of generalizations as cues on the learning of information from graphs. *Journal of Educational Research*, 1978, *72*, 211-213.

Guenther, W. C. *Analysis of variance*. Englewood Cliffs: Prentice-Hall, Inc., 1964.

National Assessment of Educational Progress. *Report I, 1969-70: National results and illustrations of comparisons* (Science). Washington, D.C.: U.S. Government Printing Office, 1970.

National Assessment of Educational Progress. *Reading: graphic materials (Theme 2)*. Washington, D.C.: U.S. Government Printing Office, 1973.

National Assessment of Educational Progress. *Consumer mathematics*. Washington D.C.: U.S. Government Printing Office, 1975. (a)

National Assessment of Educational Progress. *The first national assessment of mathematics: An overview*. Washington, D.C.: U.S. Government Printing Office, 1975. (b)

National Assessment of Educational Progress. *Changes in science performance, 1969-73*. Washington, D.C.: U.S. Government Printing Office, 1975.

National Assessment of Educational Progress. *Social studies technical report: Exercise volume*. Washington, D.C.: U.S. Government Printing Office, 1975.

National Assessment of Educational Progress. *Three national assessments of science: Changes in achievement, 1969-77*. Washington, D.C.: U.S. Government Printing Office, 1978.

National Assessment of Educational Progress. *Reading change; 1970-75; Summary volume*. Washington, D.C.: U.S. Government Printing Office, 1978.

Roller, B. V. *Graph reading abilities of seventh grade students*. Unpublished doctoral dissertation, State University of New York at Buffalo, 1979.

Turner, B. *The extent to which selected sixth grade students' use of graphic aids enhances their comprehension of content materials*. Unpublished doctoral dissertation, University of Northern Colorado, 1974.

Vernon, M. D. Learning from graphical material. *British Journal of Psychology*, 1946, *36*, 145-158.

Vernon, M. D. The visual presentation of factual data. *British Journal of Educational Psychology*, 1950, *20*, 174-185.

Vernon, M. D. Learning and understanding. *Quarterly Journal of Experimental Psychology*, 1951, *3*, 19-23.

Vernon, M. C. The value of pictorial illustration. *British Journal of Educational Psychology*, 1953, *23*, 180-187.

Vernon, M. D. The instruction of children by pictorial illustration. *British Journal of Educational Psychology*, 1954, *23*, 171-179.

# Interpreting direction from graphic displays: Spatial frames of reference

M. Jeanne Sholl and Howard E. Egeth

*Spatial frames of reference are integral to knowing where objects are located in space. Spatial location may be described verbally or graphically. When the cardinal points are used as verbal descriptions, north and south judgments are faster than east and west judgments. This phenomenon is investigated in the first study reported. In a second study, spatial frames of reference are inferred from individual graphic descriptions of macrospace. Subjective and objective measures of spatial ability are found to be correlated with individual differences in cognitive mapping.*

Map reading is a topic of both theoretical and practical interest. It is, moreover, a topic that appears to be generating a great deal of interest at present.

Much of the existing research on map reading deals with what might be called the human engineering of maps. For example, work has been done on the effects of visual clutter on map legibility, on the optimal coding of map symbols, and on the efficacy of various systems for indicating altitude. Robinson and Petchenik (1976) discuss some of these issues from the geographers' point of view. Recent reviews of selected aspects of map design from the psychologists' point of view have been prepared by Potash (1977) and Phillips (1979).

The research done by cartographers, graphic designers, and human factors experts to improve the design of maps is of great importance. However, some of the *cognitive* problems involved in reading and understanding maps have not been addressed. In this paper we present the results of the first of a series of investigations undertaken on cognitive factors affecting map reading.

To use a map effectively, the user must accomodate knowledge of space to the information conveyed by the map. It was, therefore, of interest to ascertain how adults commonly represent knowledge of large-scale physical space. Spatial knowledge presumably is organized according to some system of reference that functions as a framework for localizing objects in what we shall call macrospace, the space that stretches beyond the fingertips of the individual and can extend outward indefinitely across the surface of the earth. As Downs and Stea (1973) describe it, a reference system "spatially orients the individual in some systematic manner to the environment" (p. 275). Because we are concerned with the reference systems adopted by adults when conceptualizing macrospace, we assume that we are dealing with *coordinate* frames of reference, that is, Euclidean reference systems defined by coordinate axes. This assumption concurs with Piaget's premise that a coordinate frame of reference is the culmination of ontogenetic development of macrospatial representations (Piaget & Inhelder, 1967).

A reference system is integral to locating objects in macrospace. A prototypical Euclidean reference system is the geometrical construct of three-dimensional space delineated by $x, y$, and $z$ coordinate axes. A point can be localized uniquely within this abstract system by determining its rectangular or polar coordinates. Two examples of reference systems that might be used in everyday situations are the topographic or conventional map reference system and the egocentric reference system. At present we consider these to be the two primary systems of reference utilized by adults, although variants of them have been observed.

The cardinal points, north, south, east, and west, define the reference system used in locating the position of an object on a map and its corresponding position on the surface of the earth. When locating position on the surface of the earth north and south are objectively defined, that is, by the magnetic deflection of the compass needle. In physical space geographical location is defined absolutely in terms of degrees of longitude east or west of the Greenwich meridian and degrees of latitude north or south of the equator, after correcting for the magnetic declination of the compass needle (Bowditch, 1939). When locating position on a map the cardinal points are defined with respect to a reference system intrinsic to the map. A map has a top and a bottom, irrespective of whether it is hanging on a wall or lying flat on a table. Typically, north is at the top of the map, south at the bottom, east to the right, and west to the left. We shall call this type of orientation a conventional or topographic frame of reference.

The cardinal reference system is abstract in that it defines location independently of the position of the map user. To use the cardinal coordinate system to aid navigation in physical space, the map user must cognitively "map" the cardinal coordinates onto his body coordinates. The coordinates defined by the three major anatomical axes of the human body delineate an egocentric frame of reference. The sagittal plane passes through the body vertically from front to back, dividing the body symmetrically into right and left halves. The frontal plane passes vertically through the body at right angles to the sagittal plane, asymmetrically dividing the front of the body from the back. The transverse plane passes horizontally through the body at the waist, parallel to ground level, dividing the top of the body from the bottom (Groves & Camaione, 1975). Thus, the egocentric reference system is characterized by the directional terms *right-left, front-back, up-down* which, in turn, are coordinate to the sagittal, frontal, and transverse anatomical planes respectively.

It should be noted that the terminology in this area is contradictory and hence confusing. Claparède (cited in Howard & Templeton, 1966) identifies an egocentric type of reference system which corresponds to our conventional or topographic reference system and his realistic type of reference system is analogous to our egocentric type.

The particular system of reference adopted by an individual in describing spatial location can be observed by the way location is *verbally* described, or inferred from an individual's *graphic* representation of objects in his geographical surround. In the first investigation to be reported we have focussed on verbal descriptions of relative location characteristic of the cardinal reference system. By taking a process-oriented approach we were able to determine the locus of what we have called the north-south superiority effect, that is, the well-documented phenomenon that judgments of relative location are more accurate along the north-south axis than along the east-west axis. In the second investigation we proceeded at a more molar level of analysis, inferring frame of reference from the individual's graphic models of macrospace. We were particularly interested in substantiating reports of individual differences in the frame of reference adults adopt when locating objects in space and the implications of frame of reference for geographical orientation ability.

*North-south superiority*

The general nature of the experimental paradigm employed in the initial study is as follows. On a trial a circle is shown that contains 2 digits and a letter representing one of the directions north, east, south or west (Figure 1). The letter is a query. For example, the stimulus array at the lower left-hand corner of Figure 1 is to be interpreted as a question: which is to the west of the center of the circle, 1 or 2?

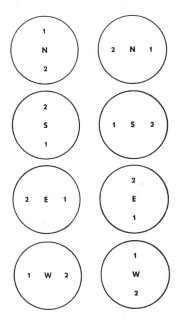

Figure 1. Example of stimulus arrays. The four arrays on the left are from the 0 deg orientation condition and the four arrays on the right from the 90 deg orientation condition.

With such a paradigm it is easy to show that judgments about north and south are faster than judgments about east and west and the same effect is demonstrated readily in other paradigms as well (Loftus, 1978).

Analysis of performance of such a task is modeled after Clark and Chase's (1972) application of Sternberg's stage analysis of reaction time. We considered the task of determining relative position or direction to be similar to the task of sentence-picture verification studied by Clark and Chase. Their model, developed to account for the pattern of reaction time, consisted of four stages. In the first, a mental representation of the sentence or word is formed. This "verbal code" is posited to be propositional in nature. In the second stage, perceptual attributes of the picture, such as the relative locations of the pictured objects, are encoded. The "perceptual code" is presumed to be translated into an abstract propositional format compatible with the verbal code. The third stage determines by comparison whether or not the perceptual and verbal codes match. The fourth stage generates a response based upon the outcome of the comparison.

Given this conception of the information processing stages underlying task performance, the next step is to try to ascertain if the locus of the north-south superiority effect is in one or more of them. There is some precedent in the literature for ascribing north-south superiority to perceptual encoding (Farrell, 1979) or to verbal labeling (Maki, Grandy, & Hague, 1979). Let us suppose that people are told to imagine a new orientation of the map axes. Specifically, suppose that, instead of the usual axes shown in Figure 2(a), the axes shown in 2(b) are in force. To see how these axes would be interpreted, examine the two sets of stimulus arrays in Figure 1. The displays on the right are examples appropriate when the compass points have been rotated 90 deg clockwise. In each, the correct response is *1*. (Of course, in the experiments, there are just as many displays in which the correct answer is *2*.)

One hypothesis of how such a set of stimuli might tease apart the alternative explanations of the north-south superiority effect holds that the effect is localized in the perceptual encoding stage. More specifically, the difference may be attributed directly to two things: the virtual symmetry of the human perceiver about the sagittal plane, and the striking asymmetry about the transverse plane. The argument accepts Ernst Mach's (1897) claim that right-left mirror image discrimination is very difficult for bilaterally symmetric organisms. One might therefore expect that, after rotating the coordinates of the map, judgments in the vertical dimension might still be superior. However, those judgments now refer to east and west and should yield an east-west superiority effect. In other words, the hypothesis that north-south superiority reflects the ease with which objects can be localized in the vertical dimension predicts an effect of spatial axis.

Alternatively, the north-south superiority effect may reside in the verbal labeling process in which case one might expect a north-south superiority effect even with axes tilted by 90 deg. Response to north and south should be faster than

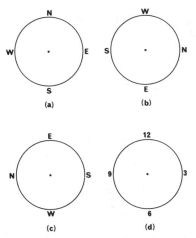

Figure 2. Representations of schematic maps defining the orientation of compass directions in the (a) 0 deg orientation condition, (b) 90 deg orientation condition, (c) 270 deg orientation condition, and (d) schematic clock defining direction in Experiment 3.

response to east and west, even though the former terms describe location on the horizontal axis while the latter describe vertical location.

The experiments were straightforward. Experiment 1 presented the two conditions already described: the 0 deg or normal condition and the 90 deg or rotated condition, explained to subjects by means of schematic maps (a) and (b) in Figure 2. Subjects served in both conditions but on different days about a week apart. Within each condition the first 32 trials were practice ones. Reaction times were collected only from the last 96 trials. All cardinal directions were tested equally often and in a random order. The exposures were brief (200 msec) to eliminate eye movements. Experiment 2 was a replication of Experiment 1 except that the map axes were rotated 270 deg as shown in Figure 2(c).

Overall, subjects were slower when the compass coordinates were rotated from their normal orientation with north at the top. By combining the data from Experiments 1 and 2 it was possible to estimate the increment in response time attributable to map rotation. When response time was plotted as a function of spatial axis and compass points, with the effect of map rotation subtracted from the 90 deg and 270 deg data points, a clear pattern emerged. The results are shown in Figure 3 in which mean reaction times are averaged for north and south and for east and west, after the adjustments noted above had been made. Note that north-south judgments are faster than east-west judgments and objects on the horizontal axis were located slightly faster than those on the vertical axis.

We may conclude from the first two experiments that there is little difference between the horizontal and vertical spatial axes, and that north and south are superior to east and west even when axes are rotated 90 deg or 270 deg. It seems that the usual north-south superiority effect is due more to the presence

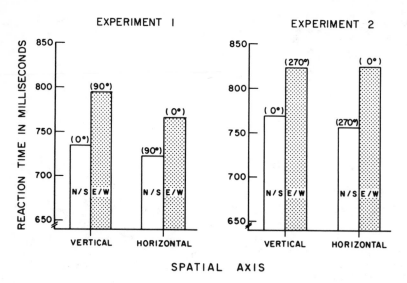

Figure 3. Mean reaction time with estimated 25 msec rotation time subtracted from 90 deg and 270 deg data points, as a function of compass points and spatial axis for Experiments 1 and 2.

of the verbal labels *north* and *south* than to any superiority of judgment in the vertical dimension. If this conclusion is correct, there should be no analog of the north-south superiority effect if a schematic system with neutral labels is used. In Experiment 3, circular displays were used again, but the circles represented a schematic clock as shown in Figure 2(d). The subject's task was to identify the letter (*x* or *o*) lying in the "direction" specified by the numeral, a task which does not require any overt encoding of spatial labels. Twelve new subjects were tested in a single session. Note that there was no rotation condition. The major result was that there was no analog of a north-south or up-down superiority effect. On the contrary, reaction times for 3:00 and 9:00 averaged a nonsignificant 14 msec faster than for 12:00 and 6:00.

The results of these experiments seem clear. There appears to be no difference in perceptual codability between the vertical and horizontal spatial axes, but the effect of the verbal factor is substantial: when the words *north* and *south* are used, processing is easier than when *east* and *west* are. It is interesting to speculate about *why* there should be a north-south superiority effect. Our results may support the notion of a semantic feature or marker underlying the lexical entries denoting relative spatial location. Clark and Chase (1972) have proposed that human performance data substantiate the reality of a polar marker for representing contrastive relationships within a spatial coordinate (that is, up versus down). In much the same way, our data may demonstrate the reality of a marker that denotes the coordinates themselves (that is, vertical versus horizontal).

Direction referred to by verbal labels may initially be learned by mapping the spatial terms onto the body coordinates. Faster processing of terms represented by a marker denoting the vertical dimension may have a direct parallel in the head-to-toe asymmetry of the human body. This anatomical asymmetry may facilitate mapping the terms *up* and *down* onto body coordinates, whereas the bilateral symmetry of the human body may impede mapping of the labels *left* and *right* onto their body referents. In fact, right-left discrimination may not be feasible until development of handedness produces a response asymmetry about the sagittal plane. Thus, anatomical organization may be represented at an abstract semantic level, enhancing discrimination when the referent spatial coordinate can be tied directly to an anatomically asymmetric body coordinate.

Within the topographic reference system north, south, east, and west are the analogues of up, down, right, and left. The demonstrated primacy of the north-south referent axis may be the result of a "second-order" mapping of the labels *north* and *south* onto the asymmetric up-down body axis (a case can also be made for mapping north and south onto the asymmetric front-back body axis when describing location in physical space). Suggesting that the words, perhaps at the semantic level, are responsible for the north-south superiority effect does not elucidate an underlying mechanism, however. Tentatively we propose that the words *north* and *south* facilitate the direction of attention to spatial location. Presumably such an attentional mechanism operates independently of eye movements and absolute referent location.

*Graphic models of macrospace*
Trowbridge (1913) provides one of the few accounts linking spatial frame of reference to individual ability to maintain georgraphical orientation. His subjects were asked to pinpoint the location of distant places on a circular piece of paper given that the center of the paper represented New York City. Although his methodology is unclear, Trowbridge apparently was able to identify a variety of idiosyncratic frames of reference. He reported that individuals with a good sense of direction draw "realistic maps," localizing objects in space as they are in reality given the orientation of the body. According to our terminology such a subject is using an egocentric reference system. To produce a realistic map, at least for distant places, it is necessary to have the ability to align the cardinal directions with the body axes, thus maintaining a constant awareness of the body's transitory orientation with respect to the cardinal reference system. Those individuals who did not adopt an egocentric reference system produced what Trowbridge called "imaginary maps" and were afflicted with varying degrees of geographical disorientation. A common type of imaginary map was produced by people who seemed to think of north as directly in front of them and south as behind them irrespective of their body's actual orientation in space. This kind of framework for localizing objects is analogous to what we have termed a conventional or topographic reference system. The "errors" made by people who produced imaginary maps varied according to the direction in which they were facing. (Note that if, by

chance, they were facing north their imaginary map would coincide with a realistic map.)

The implication of Trowbridge's paper is that people who adopt an egocentric reference system when localizing distant places have a better sense of direction than those who adopt a conventional map system of reference. Perhaps the most definitive conclusion that can be drawn from Trowbridge's paper is that there are individual differences in how adults conceptualize the relative location of objects in macrospace. Howard and Templeton (1966) drew the same conclusion after reviewing several studies in which subjects either drew maps, pointed out the direction of unseen localities, or placed maps in their most "natural" orientation.

Although they did not examine spatial reference systems directly, Kozlowski and Bryant (1977) related individual self-ratings of sense of direction to various performance measures of orientation skill. Their subjects were told to assume an egocentric frame of reference, for example: "imagine you are standing on the stone platform behind the library facing directly at the white domed part of the astronomy observatory" (p. 591). Kozlowski and Bryant then measured both angular error and distance error in the subjects' localization of campus buildings. They also assessed the subjects' ability to draw an arrow pointing north. Interestingly, sense of direction was correlated with angular error in localizing campus buildings ($r = -.49$), but there was no relationship between sense of direction and distance estimation or the ability to point to the north. The former result demonstrated that people who report a good sense of direction determined the bearing of local buildings more accurately. People's self-assessment of their sense of direction is apparently a valid indicator of their orientation ability. A good sense of direction does not seem to be related to ability to estimate distance, however. Perhaps this lack of correlation is due to a ceiling effect for all subjects estimated distance fairly accurately. Surprisingly, sense of direction was not related to ability to orient to the compass coordinates ($r = .01$). This suggests that sense of direction has less to do with orientation of the body to the cardinal reference system than with an ability to orient oneself with respect to objects in the immediate environment.

Lord (1941) tested the orientation skills of 317 children in grades 5 through 8. One of the tasks assessed the child's orientation with respect to cities within a 40-mile radius of the testing location. The child located the cities by arranging dots on a circular piece of paper with respect to a central reference point which was a city familiar to all the children. Lord distinguished two types of response. Some children arranged the cities by adopting a conventional map frame of reference, that is, locating the cities as they would be located on a map with north corresponding to the top of the circle. Lord called these map answers. Other children located the cities in physical space, that is, they adopted an egocentric frame of reference and located the cities in relation to the position of their bodies in space. Lord called these space answers. The ratio of space answers to map answers was approximately 2:1, a majority of the children adopting an egocentric frame but a substantial proportion utilizing a conventional map frame of reference. Lord also pointed out that children were more likely to adopt a conventional map system for locating distant cities and an egocentric system for locating nearby cities, leading him to conclude that a child's knowledge of distant places is learned from maps and primarily reflects knowledge of geography.

We have carried out an exploratory study designed to address some of the following issues. First what type of reference frame do adults spontaneously adopt when localizing objects in the environment, that is how do adults organize their representations of macrospace? Second, what is the effect of the scale of space on the way object location is conceptualized? From Lord's (1941) observations we thought there might be a tendency for adults to respond egocentrically when visualizing the location of nearby objects and topographically when localizing distant ones. Accordingly, we increased the area of space to be represented in the map and subjects were asked to make pointilistic maps of the Johns Hopkins campus, of Baltimore, and of the United States. Our third question was what are the relationships between self-assessed sense of direction and individual differences in representing macrospatial information? Is sense of direction related to spatial frame of reference (Trowbridge, 1913) or to the magnitude of error made when locating objects in physical space (Kozlowski & Bryant, 1977)? Finally, what is the relationship between individual differences in macrospatial representations and spatial ability assessed by an objective test?

A task was set up which discriminated between egocentric and conventional frames of reference. Subjects were seated facing south in a room with large windows so that cues were available for determining body orientation. (We have no doubt that if a subject were isolated from all environmental cues he or she would be forced to use a conventional frame of reference for localizing objects in macrospace.) The subject was seated at a desk on the surface of which was taped a set of three circles stapled together at the top. A dot was printed at the center of each circle and functioned as a reference point, that is, the origin of the system. Subjects drew separate pointilistic maps for the Johns Hopkins campus, Baltimore, and the United States on each circle. Instructions for each map were provided on separate pages in a test booklet. For the campus map the subject was instructed to consider the dot at the center of the circle to be Ames Hall (the building in which the experiment was conducted) and to locate within the circle ten specific campus landmarks where he or she imagined or visualized them to be. After the experiment was over the experimenter placed a tick at the top of the circle corresponding to straight ahead for the subject, so that vertical and horizontal coordinate axes could be superimposed on the map prior to experimental analysis.

A subject utilizing an egocentric reference system visualizes the campus buildings at distances and directions with respect to his own body. For example, one of the landmarks, Garland Hall, was located directly in front of the subject and slightly to the right. If the subject located Garland Hall directly above the reference point and slightly to the right he or she would be responding as if the reference point at the center of the circle were his or her body. We infer then that the vertical axis of the map is analogous to the front-back axis of the subject's body and the horizontal axis to the right-left axis of the subject's body.

A subject utilizing a conventional reference system visualizes north as corresponding to the top of the circle, and thus the vertical axis of the map corresponds to the north-south axis of the cardinal reference system and the horizontal axis to the east-west axis. One likely strategy that would enable a subject to respond as if north were at the top of the circle would be to think of the reference point objectively, that is, as Ames Hall. These subjects would localize Garland Hall in relation to Ames Hall as on a conventional map, below the reference point and to the left. In order to bring the coordinate axes of the conventional map into congruence with the realistic space map, the axes of the former would have to be rotated 180 deg.

A total of 30 male and female subjects were tested. Twenty-two subjects were Johns Hopkins University students and were tested during the academic year. The remaining eight subjects were tested early in the summer and were drawn from summer courses. They were not regular students, but reported that they were familiar with the buildings on campus. All subjects received either research credit or pay for their participation in the experiment.

Subjects were tested in groups, sitting facing south in the experimental room through whose large windows one campus building could be seen. That building was not a test item. Each test booklet contained the following sequence of paper and pencil tests: the Revised Minnesota Paper Form Board Test, a separate page of instructions for each of the three maps, a rating scale with items measuring the subject's assessment of his orientation abilities, and some "style of thinking" items adopted from Zenhausern's scale (1978). The mapping task always appeared at the same place in the sequence, but the order in which the three maps were given was counterbalanced across subjects. Three maps can be ordered in six ways so five subjects were randomly assigned to each sequence.

The instructions for each topographic map were printed at the top of a separate page. The 10 objects to be localized were listed after the instructions. Next to each object there was a space for the subject to rate his confidence in his response from 1 (just guessing) to 9 (absolutely certain). The instructions for the campus (Baltimore, United States) map were as follows: "Consider the dot at the center of the circle to be Ames Hall (Johns Hopkins University, Baltimore). We want you to localize each of the buildings (landmarks, cities) listed below as you imagine or visualize them to be." Subjects were instructed to locate each object with a dot and to number the dot with its corresponding number from the instruction sheet. They were also instructed that the interrelationships and relative distances between all pairs of points should be as accurate as they could make them. The distance between the first object and the reference point was to serve as a standard and was the longest distance within each map. Subjects were told that, although this distance was arbitrary, all other objects were to be localized at distances proportional to the standard.

Subjects were instructed to leave all test materials on the desk when they were finished. Before removing the circles from the desk the experimenter marked a tick at the top of the circle. The Revised Minnesota Paper Form Board Test was timed by the experimenter and subjects were allowed 15 min to work on it. None of the other tests was timed and subjects worked at their own pace. The entire session lasted approximately 50 min.

The following analysis was carried out separately on each map. A rectangular coordinate system was superimposed on each map. A vertical ($y$) axis was drawn through the tick, which represented subjective straight ahead, and the reference point. A horizontal ($x$) axis was drawn at right angles to the vertical axis. The reference point corresponded to the origin of the system. Polar coordinates were obtained for each point on each map. Distance was measured to the nearest millimeter and angle to the nearest degree in standard position. Because each subject scaled distance differently across maps, the distances were standardized within maps so that the average squared distance of each point from the reference point was equal to one. Each distance within a map was multiplied by a constant $c$, where $c = \sqrt{N} / \sum d_i^2$, for $i = 1, 2, ... N$, and $N$ equals the number of points localized on a map. (We thank Tim Satalich and Warren Torgerson for pointing this out.) A conversion from polar to rectangular coordinates was carried out using the normalized distances. At this stage we had a set of normalized $x$ and $y$ coordinate points for each subject's map. This set of coordinates we call the observed matrix. Each observed matrix was entered into a congruence progam which rotated the observed matrix a maximum of 180 deg clockwise or counterclockwise into congruence with a reference matrix.

There was a reference matrix for each map scale: campus, Baltimore, and the United States. Each reference matrix contained the normalized coordinates of the points as they actually were in physical space given the orientation of the subjects. The $y$ axis corresponded to the front-back anatomical axis of the subject ($+y$ = front and $-y$ = back) and the $x$ axis corresponded to the right-left anatomical axis ($+x$ = right and $-x$ = left). Polar coordinates for the campus and Baltimore were obtained by applying the method outlined for subjects' maps to professionally prepared maps. The polar coordinates for the cities were obtained geometrically by assuming the earth's surface to be flat and applying plane sailing navigation equations for distance and heading. This procedure introduces some distortion because it ignores the curvature of the earth, but we chose it in preference to the great circle distances and headings because it corresponded more closely with the interrelationships among cities typically portrayed on flat maps. Polar coordinates within each map were normalized and transformed to rectangular coordinates by the same method used for the subjects' maps.

The congruence program rotates the subject's map to the angle that maximizes congruence with the reference map. The criterion for congruence is minimization of the mean squared Euclidean distance between the two sets of points after rotation. The angle of rotation provided a measure of frame of reference. If the subject had adopted an egocentric frame of reference when localizing the points, his or her map would have to be rotated 0 deg to bring it into congruence with the reference map; if the subject had responded on the basis of a conventional map frame of reference, that is, with north at the top of the map or in the straight ahead position, his or her map would have to be rotated 180 deg to bring it into congruence with the reference map. (Remember that in the reference map south corresponded to straight ahead or analogously to the top of the map.) It was not possible to calculate a rotation angle for four of the 90 maps (one campus map and three Baltimore maps) because in them, in order to bring the subject's map into congruence with the reference map, the program carried out an improper rotation, that is, a rotation followed by a reflection. It is unclear to us how to represent the reflection which is in effect a 180 deg rotation through the third dimension. The mean Euclidean distance between the two sets of points after rotation provided us with an error measure, that is, a measure of the discrepancy between how the subject visualized the relationships among the sets of points and how the points are actually related in physical space. If a subject failed to locate any points on a map, the same analysis used for complete maps was carried out on the incomplete map with appropriate modifications.

Correlations of error and rotation angle were determined across maps and with each of the other measures of spatial ability included in the test battery. Surprisingly, campus error was uncorrelated with campus orientation, Baltimore error with Baltimore orientation, and United States error with United States orientation.

This result indicates that, when conceptualizing the relative location of objects within an area of macrospace, the frame of reference assumed by the subject is independent of his or her error in locating the objects.

Campus orientation was positively correlated with Baltimore orientation, $r = .48$, $p < .01$, while United States orientation was correlated only marginally with Baltimore orientation and was uncorrelated with campus orientation. Apparently there is some relationship between the frame of reference adopted for the campus map and the frame of reference adopted for the Baltimore map. This correlation reflects the fact that all subjects who adopted a conventional map reference frame for the campus map adopted a conventional reference frame for the Baltimore map. However, the reverse relationship did not hold, that is, not all subjects who adopted a conventional reference frame for the Baltimore map did so for the campus map.

The correlation of United States error with campus error, $r = .44$, $p < .01$, perhaps reflects some underlying ability to visualize the interrelationships among a set of points. Such an interpretation is perhaps feasible given that the Revised Minnesota Paper Form Board Test, a test of spatial orientation and visualization, was substantially correlated with both campus error, $r = -.51$ and United States error, $r = -.61$, both $p < .01$. It is not clear why United States error correlates with campus orientation, $r = .42$, $p < .05$.

Table 1. Proportion of subjects assuming an egocentric, topographic, nonstandard, or improper frame of reference as a function of the scale of space.

| Scale of Space | | Frame of Reference | | |
|---|---|---|---|---|
| | Egocentric | Topographic | Nonstandard | Improper* |
| Campus | .53 | .20 | .23 | .03 |
| Baltimore | .27 | .43 | .20 | .10 |
| United States | .00 | .93 | .07 | .00 |

*Improper refers to maps that were rotated and then reflected to bring them into congruence with the reference map.

The two typical frames of reference adopted in spatial localization were the conventional map and the egocentric reference frames. We operationally defined a conventional map reference frame as analogous to $180 \pm 20$ deg rotation angle. In like manner we inferred that a subject adopted an egocentric reference system if rotation angle was from $0 \pm 20$ deg. As shown in Table 1, the proportion of subjects assuming an egocentric reference frame decreases as the area of space encompassed by the map increases. Conversely, the proportion of subjects adopting a topographic reference system increases as area increases. The column headed "nonstandard," lists the proportion of subjects with rotation angles between 20 deg and 160 deg for each map. There were, therefore, frames of reference within each spatial scale which did not conform to the norms. In general, our data substantiate Lord's (1941) observations. As the places to be located become more distant, the possibility that the observer will adopt a conventional map reference frame becomes greater. This may reveal simply that our knowledge of the interrelationships among distant cities reflects geographical knowledge gained from maps. However, it is not clear if people who assume a topographic frame of reference commonly think of north as corresponding to the top of a circle, as if visualizing location on a conventional map, or as directly in front of them (Trowbridge, 1913).

One of Zenhausern's (1978) items requires subjects to assess the degree to which they think in words or pictures (1 = words to 9 = pictures). This item was positively correlated with campus orientation, $r = .54$, and Baltimore orientation, $r = .47, p < .01$. Those who adopted a conventional map reference frame when locating objects on campus or in Baltimore tended to report that they think in pictures, whereas those who egocentrically localize objects reported that they are more likely to think in words. This relationship may indicate that those who think in pictures are more likely to generate a mental image of the interrelationships among landmarks on campus and in Baltimore independent to their own position in space. It is not clear why this should be the case. Because there was very little variability in United States orientation, it is not surprising that it did not correlate with this item.

The frame of reference adopted by the subject was not correlated with any of the sense of direction questions which included such items as: (1) Are you ever disoriented when walking out of an unfamiliar room or exiting from an unfamiliar building (for example, a theater or large department store)? (1 = always to 9 = never). (2) How good is your sense of direction? (1 = very poor to 9 = excellent). The lack of relationship between map orientation and self-assessed sense of direction held across all three levels of spatial area. Given Trowbridge's (1913) data we would have expected a negative correlation between sense of direction and frame of reference. Those subjects egocentrically locating objects in macrospace with map rotation angles close to 0 deg should have reported a good sense of direction but that was not the case. It is interesting to note that Trowbridge found individual differences in conceptual orientation when the space being mapped circumscribed a very large area. However, when our subjects localized cities in the United States all but two located them as if north were at the top of the "map"; the deviant rotation angles were 98 deg and 155 deg.

Overall error, the average Euclidean distance between the observed matrix and the reference matrix after rotation, was correlated with both subjective and objective measures of spatial ability. Campus error was negatively correlated with each question in our set of sense of direction questions. Correlations ranged from $r - .49$ to $r = -.64$. All were significant $p < .01$. There was no relationship between overall error in the Baltimore and United States maps and self-assessed sense of direction. These results are consistent with Kozlowski and Bryant's (1977) finding of a relationship between error in locating campus buildings and sense of direction, and with their suggestion that sense of direction may be tied to the individual's interaction with his immediate environment.

The results of this study raise some intriguing questions. There appear to be two independent components underlying macrospatial representations of the immediate environment: spatial frame of reference which is related to the subject's reported tendency to think in pictures and accuracy in abstracting the interrelationships among a set of localities in the environment which is related to sense of direction and visuospatial ability. Adults seem to organize their cognitive representations of macrospace either egocentrically or topographically, the egocentric model of representation becoming less viable as the area of space increases. We are currently attempting a more comprehensive analysis of the factor structure underlying spatial orientation ability, the long-range goal being to develop processing models for map-related tasks (Sternberg, 1977).

This research was supported in part by a grant from the Army Research Institute (DDSW-MDW-903-79-G-002) to Howard Egeth. The authors thank Ronald Cammarata and Lauren Mardell for their help in testing subjects and acknowledge especially the contribution of Peter Lewis, who tested subjects and helped analyze the cognitive map data.

### References

Bowditch, N. *American practical navigator*. Washington: United States Government Printing Office, 1939.

Clark, H. H., & Chase, W. G. On the process of comparing sentences against pictures. *Cognitive Psychology*, 1972, *3*, 472-517.

Downs, R. M., & Stea, D. *Image and environment*. Chicago: Aldine Publishing Co., 1973.

Farrell, W. S. Coding left and right. *Journal of Experimental Psychology: Human Perception and Performance*, 1979, *5*, 42-51.

Groves, R., & Camaione, D. N. *Concepts in kinesiology*. Philadelphia: W. B. Saunders Co., 1975.

Howard, I. P., & Templeton, W. B. *Human spatial orientation*. London: John Wiley & Sons, 1966.

Kozlowski, L. T., & Bryant, K. J. Sense of direction, spatial orientation, and cognitive maps. *Journal of Experimental Psychology: Human Perception and Performance*, 1977, *3*, 590-598.

Loftus, G. R. Comprehending compass directions. *Memory & Cognition*, 1978, *6*, 416-422.

Lord, F. E. A study of spatial orientation of children. *Journal of Educational Research*, 1941, *34*, 481-505.

Mach, E. *The analysis of sensations*. Chicago: Open Court, 1897.

Maki, R. H., Grandy, C. A., & Hauge, G. Why is telling right from left more difficult than telling above from below? *Journal of Experimental Psychology: Human Perception and Performance*, 1979, *5*, 602-612.

Piaget, J., & Inhelder, B. *The child's conception of space*. New York: W. W. Norton & Co., 1967.

Phillips, R. J. Making maps easy to read—a summary of research. In P. A. Kolers, M.E. Wrolstad, H. Bouma (Eds.), *Processing of visible language 1*. New York and London: Plenum Press, 1979.

Potash, L. M. Design of maps and map-related research. *Human Factors*, 1977, *19*, 139-150.

Robinson, A. H., & Petchenick, B. B. *The nature of maps*. Chicago: University of Chicago Press, 1976.

Sternberg, R. J. *Intelligence, information processing, and analogical reasoning*: *The componential analysis of human abilities*. Hillsdale: John Wiley & Sons, 1977.

Trowbridge, C. C. On fundamental methods of orientation and "imaginary maps." *Science*, 1913, *28*, 888-897.

Zenhausern, R. Imagery, cerebral dominance, and style of thinking: A unified field model. *Bulletin of the Psychonomic Society*, 1978, *12*, 381-384.

# Textual technology

# Introduction

H. Bouma

Both in quality and in quantity, textual technology is advancing rapidly. Electronic displays (soft copy) that generate light are called active displays, a familiar one being the cathode ray tube (CRT) display, which is an offspring of commercial television tubes and professional oscilloscopes. Passive displays, such as liquid crystal displays (LCD) change only their reflecting properties; they require outside illumination and have recently increased in text capacity. Printed sheets (hard copies) are reproduced by techniques which are already approaching large-scale magazine printing machines. Myers' tutorial paper provides a comprehensive account of present-day devices for producing soft and hard copies and is a tribute to the technical creativity directed at rapid, flexible, high-quality, low-cost displays.

Both soft and hard copy displays derive from the computing and storage power of present micro-electronics. Individual data bases can now be made available to any user. The user either types appropriate key words or selects from a limited list of alternatives by pressing a button or by pointing with a light-pen or finger to the relevant portions of the screen. Such systems have been used by computer specialists for a number of years and are now increasing rapidly. In the public sector a number of systems have been designed which send information along with regular broadcast television for display on regular TV screens or via the regular telephone network to special visual display units (VDU).

Other options allow for sharing information among a restricted set of users who may be either local or spread out over vast distances. By distributing printed messages or extended papers, such facilities make possible so-called computer conferencing, fully electronic scientific journals, and the like. As a final example, the "text-processor" has begun to surpass the classic typewriter through its editing facilities, essentially by separating keying from printing functions and allowing the user access to the keyed, stored and displayed, but not yet printed text.

From a purely technological point of view, the storing and sorting power of present micro-electronics is the motor behind such developments, which have been remarkable both as to reduction of cost and increase of speed. Consequently, textual technology is spreading quickly and printing, displaying, storing and retrieving technology is ready to become commonplace. One implementation of this capability is realized in Moray's note describing his experience with an electronic journal.

Such fascinating developments would indeed be a remarkable advance if only we paid attention to the problem of how to use them properly, something that technology cannot teach us. What is needed for proper applications is insight into human needs and human capabilities of absorbing, processing, and retrieving information. This will also lead to a proper definition of the very concept of information itself. Only by insight into the psychology of human information processing can we design the interface between the human user and textual technology with the same superior control as exists in the technology itself.

The poor quality of font, format, and use of colour in texts on many display screens bears witness to the sharp contrast between the options of technical sophistication and the actual results. Research psychologists and designers must become involved to work out the value of creative intuitions and to eliminate the trial-and-error methods which now dominate developments. The single road to a human future for textual technology seems to lie in understanding how humans deal with textual information.

An account of human reading processes as straightforward as Myers' paper on textual technology cannot as yet be given. Nevertheless, there is a substantial body of reliable psychological research. Here we touch on a few relevant issues. To begin with technology, the text has to be focussed on the retina, an automatic process but the focussing capabilities of the eyes decrease with age and frequent shifts in focus, such as when two reading distances are involved (in typing from a draft, for example), are fatiguing. Leaving retinal adaptation to prevailing illumination conditions aside, we consider the technical quality of the text close to the centre of vision, the notion of legibility. Legibility includes both the quality of the symbols proper (sharpness, type, font, size, luminous contrast with background) and such layout factors as distances between lines. Proper guidance of the eye along and between the lines requires suitable margins, vertically aligned line beginnings, and interline distances more than 3-4 percent of line length. Legibility factors are sufficiently known both in graphic design and in psychology: what seems lacking are thorough checks on such information and a translation in terms of rules of thumb and quick standard experiments to make the proper notions generally applicable. Treurniet's contribution is in this area and, although it is unlikely that the results of the letter search task can be generalized to the reading of words and text, his work is a good beginning and can perhaps be used in the reading of codes.

The quality of the content of a text is usually referred to as "readability" and includes ease of comprehension. Here, knowledge of the language and of the subject matter are important and naturally differ for different users and for different languages, natural or artificial. Consequently, it is difficult to translate in terms of practical situations. Nevertheless, the contribution by Pynte and Noizet neatly isolates a problem in this area, the optimal segmentation of sentences given relatively short lines of print, and they give an example of how the body of research can be brought to bear on problems posed by textual technology.

Interestingly, rules of thumb exist for establishing readability on the basis of some external text parameters which generally correlate positively with reading difficulty—word length and sentence length, for instance. An objective test used for establishing readability is the cloze test, where every fifth word is omitted and has to be filled in. These tests and formulas may well be of use, pending increased insight into readability proper.

Reading in daily life is certainly not restricted to neat sentences and paragraphs absorbed from beginning to end. Another category of textual literacy is scanning, either in search of something special or merely skimming through newspaper headlines or ads. The general notion of perceptual selection reflects the fact that the amount of perceptual input almost always exceeds the amount of information that we can adequately handle.

In perceptual selection, two factors may be distinguished: first, in the outside world, certain perceptual stimulations stand out against their background more clearly than others and consequently are seen more easily and attract more eye fixations (visual conspicuity); second, the momentary inner world of the subject makes the perceptual system accept certain kinds of information more easily than others (directed attention). Clearly, when looking for certain information on a display, both factors play a part. The format of the displayed information should help rather than distract the selection process by a proper and modest use of colour, typefonts, and so on, and one should make sure that the user is aware of their purpose and code. The user looking for certain information has to read all kinds of things in which he or she is *not* interested until the desired item is found. In that process the user may easily be distracted, a serious difficulty of menu selection. The situation becomes worse when the menu is hierarchically organized in a tree structure and the subject is supposed, though often fails, to keep track of his or her precise positions in the tree. The theory of information dialogues between man and machine has now been identified as an important area of research, needed for all new interactive technology.

New interactive systems such as in text processors or computer conferencing may well turn out to be counterproductive because they suppose either too much or too little knowledge of the system by the user who is then confronted with distracting questions. The computer conferencing system described by Baer and Turoff is valuable in part because such underlying problems are exposed. In addition, Moray describes his experiences with a learned journal, produced electronically and run as an experimental project for a period of about a year. The system was often found to interfere with thinking, reflecting, and formulating. The paper by Frase, Keenan, and Dever helps to open this field for research. As so often is the case, practical problems may lead to new research areas.

Advances in textual technology should be turned to advances in the human access to useful information and communication by gearing such systems to the capabilities and limitations of human users. This is a new, rich and attractive area for much needed creative research and design.

# The presentation of text and graphics

R. A. Myers

*This paper reviews the concepts used in describing the functions performed by printing and display devices, some of their most important operational parameters, and the technology of some of the most important displays and printers. Its purpose is to place current technology in proper perspective in order to appreciate the capabilities and limitations of the devices available.*

The primary function of information handling systems is to extend the power of the people who use them. The ultimate result of "data processing" or "word processing" is in most cases an image of some sort, presented in a form most suited for the human operator's use. This image is presented either as a *display* or printed out on paper (or a reasonable facsimile). These two modes of image presentation are referred to as *hard copy* and *soft copy* display. When information is presented in a form most suited to the operator's use, it is assumed that the presentation means are within the limits determined by the technology and cost of the devices available. In this paper, I will review the concepts used in describing the functions performed by printing and display devices, and the technology of some of the most important displays and printers. I begin with the definition of some terms.

## Concepts and terms

*Presentation modes*

The most important distinction drawn is that between *text* and *image* modes of presentation. Text covers the alphanumeric character set and special symbols on a typewriter or computer terminal keyboard. However, it is important to remember that the size of such a character set is not fixed. A display or printer, for example, usually can produce 128 or 256 different characters, 256 being the maximum number of different things that can be described with an 8-bit (1 Byte) code. This limitation is a problem for some important tasks. For example, the APL programming language has a complete set of special characters. Mathematicians and scientists often use both upper and lower case Greek characters. Many documents can be greatly enhanced by the use of multiple *fonts*. The ability to change or expand a character set is, for display devices, primarily an electronics problem, but in many kinds of printer it is a mechanical one. Most familiar perhaps is the concept of interchangeable print elements (Selectric ball, or daisy wheel, for example). The operation of a textual display or printing device is obviously easy to describe, except for the logographic writing systems which may require as many as

10,000 different characters. They constitute a special case which will be referred to only briefly.

In contrast to the textual mode of presentation, an image device offers the information handling system the power to determine what intensity is displayed or printed at every point of the screen or page. The number of these points, technically known as "picture elements" and usually shortened to *pixels* or *pels*, is a characteristic of the particular physical hardware used. A device which operates in the image mode, as defined here, is said to have "all-points-addressable" or "all-points-available" capability (APA). A particular device technology may have APA capability in principle but the capability not be used by the system in which the device is contained. For example, a printer might be capable of putting a spot anywhere on a sheet of paper but its control unit be designed so that only characters of a specified font can be printed at specified positions. Often, too, no programming is available for handling the much more complex problems associated with the use of an image device.

Some image devices can provide only two levels of intensity, usually black and white. Other devices and media can display varying levels of intensity, known as *gray scale*. A photograph, which has the capability of portraying any level of intensity from 100 per cent white to 100 per cent black, is said to have *continuous tone* capability. Many devices, particularly at the electronic control level, are limited to quantized gray levels. Research suggests that 64 gray levels (6 bits of information) are generally enough to provide a good picture, the eye rarely being capable of discriminating more, even though under ideal conditions it can distinguish between 500 and 1000.

The vast majority of gray scale pictures (apart from photographs) are reproduced by the *half-tone* process. This traditional graphic arts technique divides the picture into regions by use of a screen about $40 \times 40$ picture elements per square centimeter and displays a black spot at each point of the screen, the diameter of the spot increasing as the desired blackness increases. For those devices incapable of producing a half-tone image, including nearly all current computer output printers, alternate methods must be used to show varying intensity levels. In the most common, *digital half-toning*, a desired intensity level is approximated by the density of black spots of uniform size which are presented in a unit area (which is, of necessity, larger than the size of the smallest spot the device can print or display).

There are two intermediate modes of presentation, each offering more power than a simple text mode without going as far as a complete image capability. One is often called *character graphics*, that is, the use of a non-alphanumeric font in an otherwise text-oriented device. For example, the font might consist of elements allowing simple line drawings to be generated. The "characters" in the font would then include diagonal line elements, shaded elements, and so forth. A rudimentary form is the Selectric typewriter: very rough graphs are sometimes printed using the asterisk character, for example, but there are also special plotting print elements which allow a picture of considerably higher quality to be made.

 *Graphics* refers to a different intermediate state, in which the system, usually a display terminal, can draw arbitrary line segments. Usually they are straight line segments, often specified by both endpoints, or by one endpoint, a direction, and a length. Graphic elements which are not straight line segments can also be defined and generated directly on a display screen by means of electronic circuits. This is then another form not only of character graphics but of image device as well, in that such a device can address all of the available points. However, this is prevented in practice by other limits, such as the size of the memory needed to hold data for all the points in a display when they are described in this inefficient way.

*Color*
Existing information handling technologies have accustomed users to a monochrome type of presentation which has, of course, been satisfactory, but human perception usually deals with information presented in *color*. Most people see colors, most familiar media present their message in color, and color appears to be a very powerful means for improving the communication between a machine and a user.

 The most basic distinction in color technology is between a *full fidelity* color image and a *multi-color* image. The former implies that all the colors of the visible spectrum can be presented in a continuum of intensity levels. As we know, this is possible with only three colors, either additive (light) or subtractive (dyes or inks). At the other extreme, there are applications (and devices) which call for only one color in addition to black: accountants need only red, and there are two-color typewriter and printer ribbons to accommodate them. Most presentations of color information fall in between; although a continuous tone-continuous hue picture is not presented, the picture does contain several different colors. The advantage of such a presentation is most evident in a complex picture such as a utility map. In black and white, the picture looks like a mass of meaningless lines but, when coded by color, the pertinent information is easily seen and understood. Note that the distinctions between the various degrees of color presentation apply both to text and to image modes.

*Dimensionality*
There is, as well, the possiblity of presenting information in *three dimensions*, the technology for which, at least, has been available for many years. Note that there are several different kinds of 3-D display. The most familiar is one in which the stereoscopic nature of human vision is approximated by presenting two different images, each of which is viewed by one eye. This is called an approximation because a particular stereoscopic pair presents the image only as viewed from one

point. A line "hidden" from view is not simply hidden in a stereoscopic display: it is not there at all.

The alternative is a true three-dimensional image, in which (again, within some technical limit) a particular scene is presented and, by moving one's head slightly, a formerly hidden line can be examined. This type of display can be obtained from holograms. A hologram captures the electromagnetic field radiated by a scene and stores it on film; it can be regenerated by illumination with a laser. Until now this technology has been limited to film-like media; electronically generated and modified holograms, although feasible in principle, have not been found useful in practical systems. Thus, although one knows how to generate a hologram or similar artificial source of an electromagnetic field with a computer, the amount of information needed to generate a useful three-dimensional picture is so great that neither the computer nor the output display device has enough power to do it.

There are intermediate stages of display for three-dimensional images as well. Between a pure stereoscopic display and a full holographic display, for example, are displays which give many discrete views which when viewed together give the illusion of full, solid objects. The most effective is to generate a succession of two-dimensional images on a vibrating surface (a display surface which oscillates rapidly). If the oscillation frequency is high enough, then the eye perceives a three-dimensional scene. Some spectacular effects can be generated by this technique, but the demands placed on the back-up computer make it impractical.

*Interactivity*

*Interactivity* refers to the ease with which a specified character or field can be changed, or to the time taken to rewrite the whole display screen. Some technologies, by their very nature, are suited to interactive use. The refresh cathode ray tube (CRT), for example, paints the entire screen some 60 times per sec; any change, therefore, can be displayed in the next "frame" considerably faster than the eye can perceive. Other technologies require seconds to paint an entire screen and are not as well suited for interactive use.

A variety of physical means is available for interacting with a display. The most direct, of course, is with a *keyboard*. For greater ease in interacting with a picture, however, many current graphics devices use a *light pen*, a device which allows one to access a particular spot on a display screen by sensing its emitted light (in the most common technology). Other devices permit pointing to the screen by means of transparent overlays which are sensitive to some physical signal such as pressure or sound. Another approach is by means of a *tablet*, which is also sensitive to some physical effect, often electrostatic induction, but which is addressed by a "pencil" writing on paper rather than by a screen overlay. Each approach has advantages and drawbacks, depending upon the speed with which it accepts input, the accuracy of the device, the number of available points, the ease of use by an operator, and the cost.

## Operational properties

*Resolution*

One of the fundamental characteristics of all information display is the minimum spacing achievable between points. This spacing is the inverse of the resolution, ordinarily measured in terms of pels or pixels per inch or per centimeter. Resolution is frequently determined by the *Rayleigh criterion* which, for spots with a gaussian intensity distribution, gives a mathematical formula for the resolution. This criterion, originated to determine when two stellar images can be resolved in a telescope, is only approximately useful in printing and display. For example, in wire matrix printers, the spot-intensity contour is closer to a step function than a smoothly varying gaussian, and the Rayleigh criterion is not appropriate.

A more general concept is the *Modulation Transfer Function (MTF)*, a two-dimensional function appropriate to imaging systems in general. One determines the MTF by choosing as the object to be imaged a sinusoidal grating of variable frequency and measuring the contrast of the grating, as imaged through the system, as a function of the spatial frequency for both $x$ and $y$ orientations. Given the MTF for a system, an equivalent resolution is often defined as the (inverse) spatial frequency at which the value of the contrast has fallen either by 50 per cent or to $1/e$ of its maximum value.

A related concept, often confused with the resolution, is the *addressability*: the number of points in the field that the device is capable of writing on. For a continuous system, such as photographic film, the addressability is the inverse of the resolution. However, most devices of interest here are limited either to writing points on a fixed grid (in one or both dimensions), or because of electronic driving considerations only to activating a discrete number of addressable points. For example, a display utilizing light emitting diodes (LED's) may generate a character with an array of very small spots but only 35 non-overlapping spots will be available for creating any character. With such a device the "resolution" can be much higher than the inverse addressability. There are also devices (such as the CRT) whose physical limits are such that only relatively large spots can be created but the electronic control circuits are such that many different "addressable" (but unresolvable) spots may be written very close together.

It is usually sufficient to know the resolution and the addressability for printing devices. For display devices, however, an additional parameter relating to the resolution must be specified: the number of addressable elements in the field. There are several display devices (of which the LED example given above is an extreme) in which a major practical limit affects only the number of spots, not the number which may be written or addressed per unit area. Another way of stating this parameter is to give the size of the display surface and possibly its form factor if there should be limits on that.

*Matrices*

The resolution, addressability, and size of a display device provide a measure of the number of binary points that can be displayed. Thus, for the presentation of *pictorial information*, little further information is needed except as qualified above. However, the display of text introduces a further means of characterising a device: the number of pels used to display a character, sometimes called the *character box*. It is obvious that a box with only seven spots (which could be either black or white) suffices to "display" or "print" unambiguously a font with $2^7 = 128$ different characters. However, to reproduce upper case characters which can be read by a person, a box at least 3 pels wide by 4 pels high is needed. In industry the lowest number of pels in a box is now 5 wide × 7 high. This box allows both upper and lower case characters, although the descenders in "p" and "q" cannot be provided. Usually an additional horizontal row is added to the box to provide underscored characters.

Considerably better quality is provided with a 7×9 pel box, and recent products use a 12×16 box; with a 35 cm (diagonal) cathode ray tube, and 27 spots per cm, some 3400 characters can be displayed at a time. The 12×16 box, it should be noted, also includes the underscore and permits fairly complex characters to be displayed. At the other extreme is the IBM 6640, a high quality non-impact ink jet printer which has a character box 26 pels wide × 40 high, corresponding to a printing resolution of 96 pel per cm (240 pel per inch). Note that not all display technologies need build up characters from spots. As has been noted, CRT hardware can make straight and curved lines by means of special purpose hardware; when these capabilities are used to form characters, the technique is called *stroke* character generation. A very high quality font can be displayed from a set of some 40 elementary strokes (as in the IBM 2265); of course, there is always a basic relationship between the stroke font and an equivalent point font. Because the resolution/addressability of the display device limits performance, the choice between strokes or points is typically determined by electronic rather than electro-optic criteria.

The significance of the character box is most explicit in conjunction with a quantitative measure of the text to be displayed or printed. Printers usually speak of *points* and *pitch* in this context: a point is 1/72 in (.035 cm) and pitch is the number of characters per vertical or horizontal inch (or the number of lines per vertical inch). Traditional computer printers print six lines to the vertical inch and ten to the horizontal (12 point, 10 pitch). However, considerably denser printing is common, fifteen characters to the horizontal inch being available, as well as eight, ten, or twelve to the vertical.

For a display, the capability to present text is usually given simply as the number of characters per line and the number of lines displayable on the screen. A *full page display* corresponds to the characters that can be typed on a standard 8.5×11 in (21.6×27.9 cm) sheet of paper: approximately 80 characters per line and, at 8 lines per vertical inch on the paper, approximately 72 lines in the display, for a total of nearly 6000 characters. Such a large screen capacity is expensive, and many devices are available with 1000, 2000, 3400, or more characters per screen. Often, to be compatible with line printers that print 132 characters per line, displays are provided with the same 132 characters per line, although with as few as 20 or 30 lines of characters at a time.

The display and printing of Chinese and Japanese is a special case. Although it is possible, for example, to display and print (mostly) unambiguous Kanji ("Han characters") in a 16×16 pel box, reasonable quality, particularly for printing, requires at least a 32×32 box. Quality printing can be provided but even a 40×40 box is not considered a limit.

A variety of factors influence the resolution which can be achieved with a particular display or printing technology. Many are the result of electronics limitations but others are intrinsic to the technologies themselves. For example, the CRT-based displays paint a picture with a beam of electrons, and it is difficult and expensive (and, ultimately, impossible) to make this beam arbitrarily small. Similarly, in printing technologies where, for example, one uses fluid ink (as in ink jet printers), what is a well-defined spot when the ink strikes the paper later is seen to be a larger, ill-defined spot because the ink has been drawn along the paper fibers by capillary action. This is known as *feathering* and varies with the quality of paper: coarse, recycled paper, for example, shows much more feathering than high quality, coated bond paper. In impact printing, the structure of the ribbon is important: a carbon film ribbon (a thin film of plastic, such as Mylar, with ink bonded to it) produces a very sharp, clear spot with a resolution corresponding to perhaps 200 pels per cm. A reusable fabric ribbon, however, has fine structure of its own in the form of the woven fibers which are easily seen with very little magnification and limit fabric ribbon resolution to about 100 pels per cm. The nominal printing resolution range is set out in Table 1.

Table 1. Nominal printing resolution range (pels per cm).

| | |
|---|---|
| Fabric ribbon typewriter | 100 |
| Film ribbon typewriter | 200 |
| | |
| Wire matrix | 25-50 |
| Thermal | 40-80 |
| Electrostatic | 40-100 |
| Ink jet | 50-150 |
| Xerographic | 100-150 |
| Silver halide | 300-600 |

Wire matrix printers typically print about 35 spots per cm, with the spot size approximately .03 cm. Some electrostatic ink jet printers (like the IBM 6640) print 100 spots per cm, with a spot size of approximately .015 cm. The IBM 3800 laser printer has a resolution of 72 spots per cm horizontally and 57.6 spots per cm vertically, and the Xerox 9700 laser printer has a resolution of 120 spots per cm. A well adjusted electrophotographic copying machine can reproduce an image with a resolution of close to 200 spots per cm, and photocomposers can achieve 320 spots per cm. This resolution is the lower limit of what might be called "graphic arts quality": a quality magazine, printed on fine paper (such as National Geographic), might require a process with twice this resolution. Low resolution photographic film can resolve between 200 and 400 spots per cm but almost any reasonably good film can resolve well over 2000 spots per cm.

A CRT of the type used in home television sets has a field of approximately 320 horizontal spots by 256 horizontal lines per frame. Alternate frames are *interlaced*, however, giving an effective display of 320×512 pels, a total of 164,000. In the interlace mode of display, text seems to flicker because some of the displayed spots appear only in alternate frames and have a refresh rate of only 30 per sec. Many people perceive flicker at refresh rates of about 40 per sec. Careful font design can minimize this effect. A high quality display of text usually does not employ interlace, however. The highest quality CRT's readily available today can display a field of 1000×1200 pels or a total of 1.2 million points (using gray scale; the highest density color displays available are limited to approximately 1 million points). The other most common electron beam-based display technology is often called the *direct view storage tube* (*DVST*). It cannot display color but can produce a half-tone effect by modulating the size of the displayed spots. It is limited in its interactivity and can be obtained with a field of over 12 million points on a screen with a diagonal of approximately 62 cm. Other techniques, notably the liquid crystal projection display, appear capable of displaying still more points in a field. Table 2 compares the number of pels typically displayed with these devices.

*Speed*
The concept of *speed* of a printer appears reasonably unambiguous: it measures

Table 2. Typical display sizes in pels.

| | |
|---|---|
| Entertainment grade CRT | 150,000 |
| Plasma panel | 250,000 |
| Monitor CRT | 1,000,000 |
| Laser liquid crystal | 4,000,000 |
| Storage CRT | 12,000,000 |

the throughput of the machine in characters, lines, pages, reports, and so on per unit of time. Although display devices do not have a throughput that can be evaluated in the same fashion, they too can be characterized by the number of dots, characters, lines, or frames displayed in some unit of time. For a soft copy device, one can also state the time needed to change a specific character, an important distinction because of the desirability of interactivity. Some display technologies can write a frame at the rate of several thousand characters per second but cannot alter any point on the screen without rewriting the entire display, a process that could easily take several seconds.

The speed of a device has another implication relating to communication between the display or printer and some other node in an information handling system, particulary when that node (usually a computer system) is the source of the information being presented on the device. A 15 character per sec printer communicates only at the rate of 120 bits per sec (assuming 1 Byte per character), a rate that can easily be handled by very low cost electronic devices on almost any communications medium. On the other hand, a 1.2 million pel display, refreshed at 60 frames per second with neither gray scale nor colors must be fed 72 million bits per sec simply to maintain the display. (This assumes a refresh rather than a storage display. Ordinarily the refresh function is co-located with the display, so the distance over which the data must flow can be short. Even so, such a high data rate poses serious technical problems.) Even assuming local refresh, that same display with six bits per pel of gray scale information must receive 7.2 million bits of data to paint a full screen.

Printers have traditionally been compared in terms of printing speed, as was natural in an era when their major function was to produce as quickly as possible a hard copy of some data generated by the computer. The performance of those early computers was limited in that they were unable to print out results fast enough; the purchaser or developer of a printer was, therefore, almost exclusively concerned with throughput.

The measure of printing speed for *serial* printers has been the number of characters per second printed, and for *parallel* (or line) printers, the measure has been lines per minute. Each of these terms requires considerable amplification. Measuring the number of characters per second printed is not done simply by turning on the printer, starting a stop watch, and counting characters. The first question must be which characters are printed. In a data set, for example, blanks (spaces) and carriage returns are well-defined characters, the former being relatively easy to print, the latter, for most serial printers, not. The question is even more complex, and involves which character set is to be printed. If we look at a disk printer, for example, it is clear that a whole line of a *single* character can be printed more readily than a whole line in which the characters come from opposite sides of the disk. (In some printers the disk always returns to a "home" position between impacts.) Thus, the time taken to access a character must be considered, as well as the time taken to generate that character once it has been found. Note that there are a limited number of positions on the print element so that, if a particular character appears more than once on the disk, it can be printed more quickly than if it appeared only once. Examples of special character sets are all-numeric, and upper case only.

Yet another factor plays a key role in printer throughput, called tabbing (after the traditional typewriter function). Much text, and even more tabular material, consists of lines with many consecutive blanks. It is possible to design printer mechanisms in which the print element (or platen) can skip over these blank areas much more quickly than if the hammer were actuated at every print position. This tabbing speed might be ten times faster than the normal printing speed. Carriage return is one obvious example of a situation in which tabbing pays big dividends. In this case, the carrier tabs all the way to the left margin.

Tabbing can be monodirectional or bidirectional, as can printing. The interplay between forward and reverse tabbing and bidirectionality has a complicated effect on actual throughput; it is not possible to state easily the actual throughput enhancement conferred by bidirectionality.

One last relevant factor for serial printers concerns the number of copies that are to be printed of each data set, that is, in printing terminology, *the number of parts per form*.

Nearly all of the above considerations apply to line or parallel printers. Throughput was originally measured in lines per minute because of the technology of early printers. A bank of print hammers was used in those devices, as in their successors, typically one per print position. The output was generated a line at a time, the paper incrementing the required line spacing between print times. Even for this apparently simple operation, however, stating print speed requires an additional parameter, the number of print positions in the line. The importance of this factor can be seen by comparing a printer on a small calculator, printing a line with only 10 positions, with one having the usual 132 print position line.

With line printers, too, it is necessary to know how many parts per form are to be printed and with what character set. Tabbing may or may not be relevant because some machines that are called "line" printers actually print characters in sequence and, therefore, could benefit from fast tabbing, fast carriage return, and bidirectionality. In addition, these machines have the very important ability to *skip*. Skipping refers to the ability of printer hardware to move paper extremely rapidly if no marks are being made on the paper. For example, a line printer which normally moves paper at about 17 cm per sec (about 2400 lines per min when the lines are spaced 2.5 per cm, that is, 6 per in) might be able to skip over blank lines at speeds approaching 250 cm per sec, corresponding to 36,000 lines per min. Clearly, the determination of a printer's rated throughput depends on a detailed definition of the specifications of both the printer and the data to be printed. In recent years, advancing technology has led to the development of printers for which neither characters per second nor lines per minute is the best measure of performance. These are *page* printers in which the motion of the paper is synchronous, and at constant velocity, regardless of what is to be printed on the page. This is the case, for example, in printers which use xerographic technology. The process requires a series of steps following in the correct order and timing. In these machines, a line or even a page requires a fixed amount of time to be printed, even if it is entirely blank. For such machines, tabbing and skipping are not possible; as a rule the characters are electronically generated, so the character set is not a concern (even the vertical and horizontal pitch of the characters can be controlled), and the only relevant attributes of the data set are the physical size of the page and the number of parts per form.

Table 3. Typical burst speed, impact printers.

| | | |
|---|---|---|
| Selectric ball | 15 | characters per sec |
| Daisy wheel | 50 | |
| Metal belt | 6000 | |
| Metal belt | 2500 | lines per min |

One parameter of printing speed that is often used is called *burst* speed or the number of characters that can be printed in a fixed time interval, exclusive of tabbing, skipping, carriage return, and so on. When technologies, rather than printers, are being compared, burst speed becomes a most useful concept, as long as the qualifications and constraints summarized above are kept in mind (particularly technology-related constraints, as in laser printers).

In Tables 3 and 4 some quantitative relations and parameters are listed to provide a frame of reference for future discussions.

Table 4. Typical printing speed, matrix printers (spots per sec per transducer).

| | |
|---|---|
| Thermal | 500-2000 |
| Wire matrix | 1000-2000 |
| Electrostatic | 100,000 |
| Ink jet | 100,000 |
| Xerographic/laser | 20,000,000 |

A Selectric typewriter prints approximately 15 characters per sec. There are either 10 or 12 characters per in, so the print element moves at approximately 3.75 cm per sec. There are approximately 80 print positions per line, so this type of machine can print at approximately .2 lines per sec, or 12 lines per min, for dense text. At a vertical pitch of 2.5 lines per cm, there are about 50 lines of printing on a page, and a page is printed in about four minutes. Daisy wheel printers have a burst speed in the range of 25 to 60 characters per sec; wire matrix printers have a burst speed of from 40 to over 600 characters per sec. The most common line printers print 1200 lines per min, or a maximum rate of about 2700 characters per sec (10 pitch horizontally, 6 pitch vertically), and a fast laser printer moves the paper at nearly 80 cm per sec, that is, nearly 12,000 lines per min, or 27,000 characters per sec, for 10 pitch horizontally, 6 pitch vertically. At maximum vertical pitch (4 lines per cm), the speed is approximately 18,000 lines per min.

## Display technology

Although image display technologies are ubiquitous in our society in the form of home TV sets, the technology of image display is relatively complex, and offers a variety of alternatives. For example, displays may either be *beam addressed* or *matrix addressed*. In the former, a single scanning beam (usually of electrons, but more recently of lasers also) is directed to each different picture element of the display, where light is either generated or controlled. If the light is controlled, the device is known as a *light valve*. The light may either sweep out the display in a point-by-point, line-by-line mode, a *raster scan*, or successively draw the line elements making up the picture. The latter is known as a *beam directed*, or vector display. For a picture which is not too dense, the vector mode allows the picture to be drawn much more quickly and, therefore, to be refreshed more frequently if the display is without intrinsic memory.

A matrix addressed display functions much like a memory: a point which is to be written is identified by an $x, y$ address, and both an $x$ and a $y$ drive circuit must be energized in order to display the point. There is a degenerate form of matrix display, a one-dimensional addressing scheme, in which a separate circuit is needed for every display point. This is required by some electrochromic and liquid crystal displays.

Both beam addressed and matrix addressed displays can be *storage* or nonstorage types. In a display with intrinsic storage a picture element once written will be displayed until erased. Display technologies which lack this capability (the normal cathode ray tube, for example) require some form of *refresh memory* to store the information contained in the picture and thus enable the transducer continuously to repaint it.

*The cathode ray tube (CRT)*

Almost everyone is familiar with the electro-optic transducer in the home TV set, the cathode-ray tube (CRT) (Figure 1). In a CRT, a beam of electrons is generated by an electron gun and accelerated by a voltage between 15 and 25 thousand volts, so that it strikes a phosphor-coated faceplate. (Phosphors are materials which give off light when struck by energetic electrons.) The electron beam is positioned on the target by electrostatic or magnetic deflection fields and is turned off by a control signal applied to an electronic grid, located at the gun.

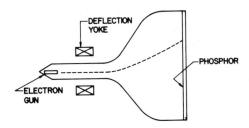

Figure 1. A cathode ray tube (CRT).

The home TV set is a raster-scanned CRT capable of displaying a field of 525 lines with about 325 resolvable spots per line; the odd and even lines are displayed alternately 30 times per sec in the interlace mode. The effective refresh rate of the display is 60 frames per sec, provided that an image point occupies pels in both odd and even frames.

The CRT is, of course, capable of displaying gray scale by varying the intensity of the beam; no more than five or six bits of intensity information are resolvable, however, corresponding to 32 to 64 intensity levels. There are several different means of providing color on the CRT: the most direct is to have three different electron guns and to have each picture element divided into a triad of different color phosphors, each point being masked from the other two electron guns by a precise "shadow mask." This is a refresh device in that there is no intrinsic storage in the tube; it is a raster device in that the picture is written one horizontal line at a time and the electron beam covers every spot.

Conventional CRT technology is capable of modest extensions in performance at somewhat immodest increases in cost. A monochrome television monitor, for example, can display nearly 1.25 million spots and refresh a full frame at a rate of 50 per sec. High resolution color CRT's are currently limited to about 350,000 color triads (although tubes with finer shadow masks capable of displaying about one million triads are available at high prices). An important limitation on the performance of all these devices is the quality of the electron optics and the cost of correcting for aberrations. However, at the higher resolution, higher refresh rate limit, the required speeds themselves create expensive problems. A one million pel display, refreshed 60 times per sec, for example, requires a refresh memory capable of putting out 60 million bits per sec, without allowing for multiple intensity levels. The performance can easily be limited by the bandwidth of the grid on which the information signal is placed.

It is clear that a refresh display requires a memory which stores enough information to paint a display completely. In character coded systems the refresh memory is a recirculating coded memory, containing the code (EBCDIC, for example) for the character to be written in every character block on the screen. The actual bit pattern is generated only between the refresh memory and the grid and is called *on-the-fly* character generation. This approach can also be used if the picture is stored in *bit coded*, *compressed* format. Data compression is the process of coding a picture, say, in such a way that some of the redundancy in the data is removed. Compression may be lossless, as when the exact compressed image can be retrieved by applying an inverse algorithm and decompressing the bits, or the compression can be lossy, as when some of the information may be irretrievably lost. Thus, if a picture has been compressed according to an algorithm, the compressed bits might be stored in the refresh buffer and decompression carried out on the fly. One difficulty is that not all images compress the same amount, so extra constraints are necessary to ensure that every picture can in some way be put in the memory. Another difficulty is the hardware problem of decompression at the high speeds required. A third alternative for a refresh memory is simply to have a *bit buffer*, a map of the intensity that is to be written on the screen. This is less trivial than it seems: a half-tone display, for example, might have five bits per spot, and a color display would have at least three more. A common design approach to the bit buffer for a color display device is to have a separate memory, called a *memory plane*, for each color. Thus, in a three-gun CRT, each gun receives its information from a different memory plane.

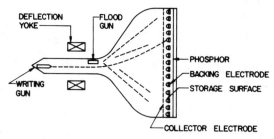

Figure 2. A type of direct view storage tube (DVST).

*Direct view storage tube (DVST)*

A popular form of electron beam addressed display is the *direct view storage tube* (*DVST*) (Figure 2) which consists of an electron gun, grid, and deflection means similar to those in a conventional CRT, but with a different target. Instead of a simple phosphor, a complex structure stores the charges deposited by the electron beam in such a way that, once a pattern has been written on the target, it is regenerated each time the beam sweeps over the screen (for periods as long as several hours). In one such tube, for example, the phosphor is screened by a mesh which has initially been given a negative potential and on which there is a material with high secondary emission of electrons. Such a material gives off more charge than the amount striking it so that the negative electron beam induces a positive charge. Thus, the next time the beam returns to a spot written in this manner, the electrons can pass through the mesh and strike the phosphor. The remainder of the mesh is maintained at the uniform negative potential so that the electrons are unable to penetrate it and strike the phosphor. The different modes of operation (writing, storing, erasing) are controlled by a combination of variable acceleration voltages and variable voltages on different parts of the target.

There are several different varieties of these tubes but, for all, a spot once written need not be refreshed. In theory, spots can be erased individually but, in practice, an entire screen must be erased (by another electron gun, called a flood gun), usually creating a green flash, which is somewhat objectionable. These tubes are all monochrome and are restricted for technical reasons to a single intensity (on/off operation). The number of spots which can be displayed in a DVST is very high, as many as 12 million in some tubes. Some DVST's also have a "write-through" capability in which a stored image can be overwritten in nonstorage mode by the scanning beam. An evident advantage is that a light pen may be used.

*Laser liquid crystal display*

The most interesting laser addressed display is the *laser liquid crystal display* (Figure

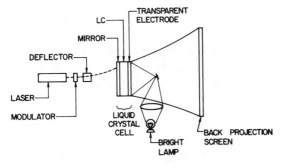

Figure 3. A laser liquid crystal display (LLCD).

3). In this device, a small (2 cm square) liquid crystal cell is used as a light valve; spots are switched from clear to scattering by a scanning gallium arsenide laser beam, and the liquid crystal cell then works like a photographic slide to control light projected from a high-intensity lamp onto a screen. This device can readily write 4 million or more spots but a significant limitation is the time needed to deflect the laser light to enough spots to write a full screen: some working models require a few seconds to write a 4 million pel display. The device has storage but is not easily used with selective erase or conventional light pens. Color is possible, although difficult to achieve.

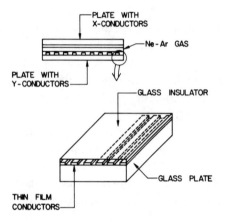

Figure 4. A plasma display panel assembled from two identical plates rotated so that two sets of thin film conductors are orthogonal.

*Plasma display panel*
One matrix display technology which appears promising for textual display is the *plasma display panel* (Figure 4) in which a neon-argon gas mixture is sandwiched between two glass plates on which orthogonal lines of fine electrical conductors are photolithographically formed. Simultaneous excitation of $x$ and $y$ conductors lights the intersecting spot. The panel has memory in that a spot which has been written with a high writing pulse may later be lit with a lower sustaining pulse. Thus, the entire panel is sustained but only spots which have been intentionally written light up. Panels with the same number of addressable spots as an entertainment grade CRT have been made by several manufacturers. Gas panels are monochrome with excellent visual appearance. Technical challenges involve improving the resolution and increasing the size of the viewing area.

## Printing technology
In traditional printing, the page to be printed was set by a compositor using different sizes and shapes (fonts) of the characters of the alphabet. The type was

then inked and pressed against successive sheets of paper, making any number of identical images. Thus, a fully formed image of a character is brought into contact with a sheet of paper or with a ribbon which in turn contacts the paper, a form of what is known as impact printing.

In the past 30 years the printing of information has been transformed by three important advances. First, families of printers have been developed in which the character to be printed is selected *dynamically* rather than being part of a fixed matrix which reproduces many copies of a single page. Second, new printing technologies have been developed in which the marks are formed by *nonimpact* phenomena. Finally, many printers, both impact and nonimpact, print dots in an All-Points-Addressable *matrix* mode.

There is one further trend that should be noted. This is the widening use of printers in which the marks are made on *special paper*. Plain paper is nearly always less expensive but, by building a more complex paper, it is usually possible to effect savings in some other part of the printer. That is, because a specific characteristic has been added to the paper, it can take over some part of the marking process. At the present time, almost all special paper printers are nonimpact.

*Character printers*
In dynamic printing, each successive impression can be different, a necessity for

Figure 5. A wheel printer. In the original version of this printer each wheel was independently rotatable and also functioned as a hammer. This figure shows separate hammers.

computer applications. A mechanism similar to modern computer printers was invented in the 1850s and made dynamic printing possible but, because there was no need for it, it did not become practical until the 1950s (Figure 5). In that early invention, the characters to be printed were engraved on the outer rim of a disk, one disk to a print position in the line and a full set of letters (a complete font) on each disk. Each disk could be rotated independently to place any desired letter against the paper. The inked disk was driven into the paper, printing the letter. The process was capable of high speeds but the gearing required was very complicated. In the 1950s, however, when advances in electronic computers had generated a requirement for printing speeds of over 1000 lines per min, the process was reinvented and developed commercially.

In the earliest mechanical typewriters a fully formed character image was driven into a ribbon which in turn marked the paper by a mechanical device linked to a keyboard (Figure 6), a process that has changed little even in present electric type-bar machines. Another early typewriter, the first *single element* typewriter, had all the letters on a single hammer, spread around the periphery of a disk (Figure 7). The disk was rotated to the proper letter and then driven into the paper, in combination either with a ribbon or some other means of inking the disk to mark the paper. Following the printing of one letter, an escapement moved the disk (or the paper carriage) into place for printing the next. This is the basis for a modern printer, the *daisy wheel* (Figure 8), which prints at speeds of from 25 to 60 characters per sec.

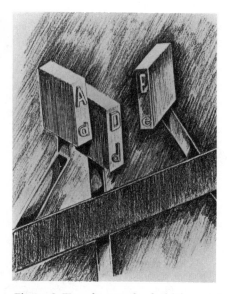

Figure 6. Type bars each of which contains two characters. Many different configurations are possible.

Figure 7. A character disk and hammer.

Figure 8. "Petals" on daisy wheel.

The most successful single element character printing mechanism has been a sphere, the Selectric ball (and other related mechanisms), on the surface of which are raised characters (Figure 9). By aligning the ball in two axes, a specific character can be selected, driven into the ribbon, and printed. Almost all of these ball-type mechanisms operate at about 15 characters per sec. Only slightly less successful, and until recently the most satisfactory means for obtaining high speed computer output printing, is a parallel printing technology variously called *chain*, *train*, *band*, or *belt* printing. The characters to be printed are placed on a metal belt, interconnected to form a train of characters or otherwise arranged so that they may rapidly be moved past a bank of hammers (Figure 10). There may be as many as 132 hammers (one hammer per print position), and the belt often moves at speeds of 10 meters per sec. An electronic record of the line to be printed is stored in a memory, a *line buffer*, and when the letter to be printed at any position passes the proper hammer, that hammer is energized. Many hammers may be fired simultaneously, and there are ordinarily several copies of a font per belt; printing speeds as fast as 3800 lines per minute (about a page per sec) are well within the capability of these machines.

*Matrix printing*
Movable type revolutionized printing by allowing a printer to compose a complex

Figure 9. A spherical element (Selectric ball).

Figure 10. A band printer.

page by assembling individual characters rather than by carving a woodblock of the entire page; matrix printing allows each letter to be composed from an array of dots and to be changed virtually instantaneously. The first and still most common matrix printer makes each character from a selection of 35 dots (in a $5 \times 7$ pattern) which are printed 25 per cm; the print head itself usually contains seven or eight wires (each about .33 mm thick) which are themselves the hammers (Figure 11). One end of the wire is magnetically coupled to a solenoid so that, when the coil is energized, the wire is driven into a ribbon and the paper at rates between one and two thousand times per sec. By this method more than 200 characters per sec can be printed. One can make a line printer by positioning wires across the full page width; as many as 1000 wires are needed. Many other variations have also been developed.

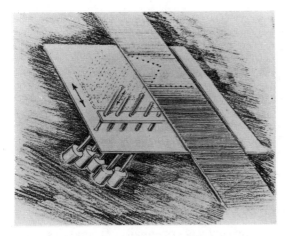

Figure 11. A type of wire matrix print head.

*Nonimpact printing*

Printing technology has recently moved in the direction of *nonimpact* marking phenomena in an effort to increase the function of a machine while reducing service costs and acoustic noise. The nonimpact printing technologies are too numerous to discuss in detail but several are particularly important for printing text and pictures: electrophotographic (xerographic), ink jet, electrostatic, and thermal technologies. The first two are primarily plain paper technologies and the latter two require treated papers. Other nonimpact technologies include silver halide, dry silver, diazo, and other light-sensitive films, electro-erosion printing, and magnetic printing.

Office copying machines use the best known of the nonimpact printing technologies. Known as *xerography* or *electrophotography*, it is actually a form of photography: an object, usually a document, is placed so that it may be imaged onto a photosensitive surface which is then treated so that a permanent replica of the original is created. This type of camera can be converted to a printer by substituting a controllable light source such as a laser or a CRT for the document (Figure 12).

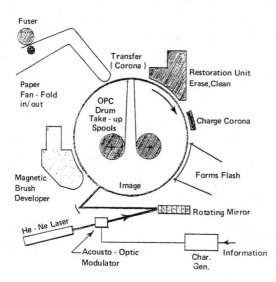

Figure 12. The elements of a laser printer (the IBM 3800).

The photosensitive surface may be an alloy of materials like selenium and arsenic or an organic photoconductor. The surface is originally charged to some voltage in the dark and the object discharges it where the light falls. The *electrostatic latent image* produced is then developed by cascading over it a mixture of black thermoplastic material (toner) and beads of material (carrier) which provide the toner particles with an electrostatic charge of the proper sign to make them stick to the black areas in the image. The toner is then transferred to a piece of paper and fixed by the application of heat or pressure.

Copier technology has been modified in several different ways to function as a printer. Typically, a helium-neon laser beam is modulated at a very high frequency to control its intensity, and deflected across the photoconductor surface by a rotating mirror assembly. Printing process speeds of 80 cm per sec, corresponding to printing rates of over 18,000 lines per min, can be achieved. Resolution of 120 points per cm in the vertical and horizontal directions is the highest specification for an available product. It should be noted that the throughput of this type of printer is somewhat limited because it is not only a single part printer but also a synchronous machine incapable of skipping.

Although in principle the scanning light beam can write an arbitrary pattern, some of the available printers limit their output to characters and character graphics; special forms may be achieved by imaging the form onto the drum each time a new page is printed or the forms may be generated electronically. Color can be provided by using different pigments in the toner; the machines commercially available use this approach and get multiple colors by repeating the entire imaging process for each different color desired.

In *ink jet printers*, a stream of ink droplets is directed onto the paper from one nozzle or from an array of nozzles. A drop may be ejected only when a spot is to be printed, known as *drop-on-demand* ink jet, or there may be a continuous stream of droplets, the *synchronous drop stream*, in which some modulation means selects from the drop stream only those droplets desired. Both the nozzle and the paper may be stationary or move. There may be a single color ink or several diffferent inks to produce color printing. Some ink jet printers deflect the droplets either by electrostatic or magnetic forces to a desired print position in the character box. Others simply modulate the stream in an on-off binary mode, all deflec-

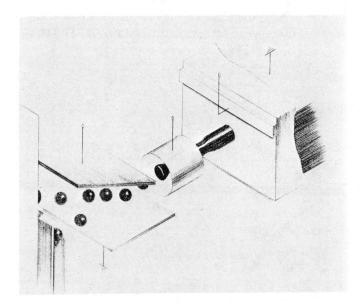

Figure 13. The print head of a synchronous electrostatic ink jet printer The drops usually travel two to five centimeters before hitting the paper.

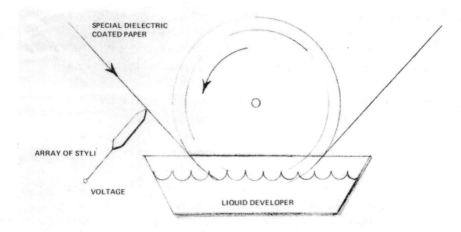

Figure 14. An electrostatic printer.

tion being obtained from the relative motion between the nozzle(s) and the paper.

A typical nozzle can generate 100,000 drops per sec; if all drops are used, and the resolution is 80 spots per cm, then the printing rate is about 16 sq cm per sec but, because of current physical limitations, it is possible to achieve a maximum rate of only half this. The speed can be increased by increasing the number of nozzles; at least one printer has 600 spread across a width of 12.5 cm. The IBM

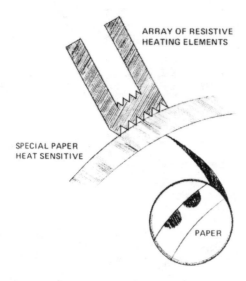

Figure 15. The functioning of a thermal print head.

6640 ink jet printer (Figure 13) has a nozzle approximately 30 micrometers in diameter which prints 100 spots per cm, each with a diameter of approximately .15 mm. Color could be provided by having a different color ink for each different primary color needed and by successively printing the different colors to generate the document.

Another nonimpact printer is the *electrostatic* printer (Figure 14). It requires a special paper, coated so that electrostatic charges may be deposited directly on it without decaying. The electrostatic latent image is written with an array of styli which ordinarily extend the full width of the page and are spaced 80 or more per cm. The latent image can be developed with a solid toner but it is more common to use a liquid developer, which does not require thermal fusing. The speed of these printers can be as high as approximately 20,000 lines per min. However, because of the higher cost of the special paper, most of the electrostatic printers in use operate at much lower speeds. Color printing is also available.

*Thermal* printers (Figure 15) also require a special paper, one in which the application of heat changes the color of the paper (usually turning it blue or black). The most common means for achieving this is to build into the paper a combination of chemicals which enter into a dye-forming reaction when exposed to heat. The source of the heat is typically an array of semiconductor or thin film heating elements. The speed at which spots can be written is limited by the time taken for a heater to cool off after writing a spot; typical speeds are 500 to 2000 spots per sec for a single element, although speeds some ten times faster have been demonstrated. Thus, if an array of heaters extends the full width of the page, it is possible to print as fast as 20 lines per sec with relatively coarse matrices. Another limitation is the difficulty of writing very small spots: 200 per in (80 per cm) is the best resolution people generally achieve.

## Conclusions

There are many aspects to be considered in analyzing the printing or display of text and image information, and one has a variety of technology choices available in order to offer some function to a user. The details of the different technical options point to a more useful observation. One has available today a variety of different display and printing technologies. Each of these has characteristics which favor its use in some set of the functions but, at this time, there appears to be no single display or printer which does everything equally well. Thus, the user of a system must make a series of trade-offs to select the devices which best suit his needs. Perhaps, in the future, research will lead us to a single best approach, but that seems unlikely today.

Julia Petrishin's help in preparing this manuscript for publication is gratefully acknowledged.
"Selectric" is a registered trademark of the IBM Corporation.

## References

*IEEE Transactions on Communications*, 1977, *25*. (Special issue on data compression)

*IBM Journal of Research and Development*, 1977, *21*, 1-96. (Special issue on ink jet printing)

*IBM Journal of Research and Development*, 1978, *22*, 2-49. (Special issue on the IBM 3800)

Kazan, B., & Knoll, M. *Electronic image storage*. New York: Academic Press, 1968.

Kuhn, L., & Myers, R. A. Ink jet printing. *Scientific American*, 1979, *240* (*4*), 162-176.

Pearson, D. E. *Transmission and display of pictorial information*. New York: Wiley, 1975.

Poole, H. H. *Fundamentals of display systems*. Washington: Spartan, 1966.

Sherr, S. *Electronic displays*. New York: Wiley, 1979.

Society for Information Display, International Symposium, *Digest of Technical Papers*, 1970-1979, vols. I-X.

Woolridge, S. *Computer output design*. New York: Petrocelli/Charter, 1975.

## Appendix

Different presentation media offer the viewer different esthetic experiences. Although it is simply not possible to simulate on paper the differences between the many display devices discussed, there is at least a hope of doing so for different printing technologies. Examples of the output of some common printers are shown in the figures. The basic problem is that what the reader of this volume sees is copy that has, at a minimum, been photographically processed at least once in the course of being converted to a master suitable for mass reproduction. The process of creating a master is nonlinear; contrast differences are greatly reduced, edges are sharpened, background may be cleaned up, and so forth. In addition, the copy seen by the reader is not printed by a typewriter, or a line printer, or whatever, but on a press. Moreover, there is no (economical) way to show the differences between the many special papers since, of course, this book is printed on "plain" paper. Nonetheless, as the figures show, one can see many of the gross differences in the output of different printing devices.

*Selectric Typewriter*

The original for this sentence was prepared on a Selectric typewriter on bond paper using a film ribbon -- generally accepted as the highest quality ordinarily seen in an office environment.

The original for this sentence was prepared on a Selectric machine using a fabric ribbon; the somewhat lower quality is accepted because the ribbon can be reused.

*Train Printer*

This was originally printed on an Ibm 3211 train printer. The machine has a fabric ribbon, and the paper was conventional "fan-fold" computer paper. In normal use this printer goes at about 2000 lines/minute.

*Wire Matrix Printer*

This was printed on an IBM 3286 wire matrix printer. The machine has eight wires (one is used for underscores) and a fabric ribbon. The various models of this printer have speeds ranging up to 120 characters/second.

*Laser Printer*

This was printed on the IBM 3800 laser printer, on conventional (roll-fed) office stock-type paper.

*Ink Jet Printer*

This was printed on the IBM 6640 printer, running in the "quality" mode, on bond paper.

*Electrostatic Printer*

This was printed on a Versatec electrostatic printer, having a resolution of 80 pel/cm. The original, of course, was on treated paper, and the processing has significantly altered the appearance.

*Thermal Printer*

THE ORIGINAL FOR THIS WAS PRINTED ON THE TEXAS INSTRUMENTS "SILENT 700" COMPUTER TERMINAL PRINTER. THE ORIGINAL, OF COURSE, WAS PRINTED ON SPECIAL HEAT SENSITIVE PAPER, AND THE REPRODUCTION HERE IS GREATLY CHANGED.

*Photocomposer*

The original for this is the output of an experimental photocomposer with a resolution of 320 pel/cm; the medium is a photographic film (silver halide) which has been chemically processed.

*Dry Silver*

The original for this was created by the Tektronix Display Hard Copy Unit Model 4610. The medium is a different photographic paper, known as dry silver which is processed, by heat, without wet chemicals.

Figure A1. Reproductions of text generated by different printing technologies. The difficulties associated with comparing these are discussed in the text.

# Spacing of characters on a television display

William C. Treurniet

*The legibility of text presented on a television display can be influenced by the density of the text. An experiment using a search task and a 5 ×7 character set suggested minimum values for spacing between characters for good legibility. On the basis of the experimental results, a horizontal space of two pixels and a vertical space of three pixels were recommended. In addition, descender characters should extend below the line by at least one pixel. The data indicate that no more than 20 lines of text per page with approximately 40 characters per line should be displayed on televisions employing the National Television System Committee (NTSC) television standards.*

Several countries, including Canada, are introducing a type of videotex service to the public which permits a user, either at home or at work, to view information received from a data base on a raster television display. Some information might be pictorial but most will likely be text. Because communication often crosses national boundaries, a common standard must be agreed upon for the display of text pages. That is, when a page containing text is created in one country, the format should appear the same when that page is displayed in another country. An international standard should, therefore, define horizontal character spacing, spacing between successive lines, and the degree to which descender characters extend below the line. Appropriate values for these parameters are suggested based on behavioural measures obtained in the laboratory.

  The most appropriate measure appears at first to be the viewer's reading rate or comprehension. Tinker (1965) reviewed a number of studies that used speed of reading as the dependent measure to evaluate various characteristics of the printed page. His experiments typically employed large numbers of subjects to compare such characteristics as type font, page colour, and ambient lighting. The Tinker Speed of Reading Test (1955) demanded little in terms of comprehension and was, therefore, thought to be sensitive to changes in perceptual input. More recently, Snyder and Maddox (Note 1) used a modified form of the test to demonstrate the effect on reading performance of variations in the appearance of dot matrix characters drawn on a cathode-ray tube (CRT) display. Specifically, a larger size matrix element increased reading time, a square shape element reduced reading time compared to elongated shapes, and increases in the space/element size ratio increased reading time. However, our laboratory studies have found the speed of reading test to be insensitive to whether text is in upper or lower case, on paper or on a television display. Previous work comparing the effect of case on reading rate found that lower case text was read more quickly than upper case at normal reading distances (Breland & Breland, 1944; Paterson & Tinker, 1946; Warren, Note 2). Our failure to find the effect raises questions about the appropriateness of the test for use on video displays and also casts some doubt on its reliability. At least some of the early work, as well as the Snyder and Maddox (Note 1) study, employed between-subject designs whereas we used within-subject designs. Our results may, therefore, have been influenced by carry-over effects. If the test is reliable only when used in a between-subject design, it is not efficient with respect to the number of subjects required and alternate methods should be considered when many experimental conditions are to be tested.

Another method used to evaluate display quality employs a search task. The dependent measures here are the time taken to locate a specified target following presentation of the display, and the frequency of incorrect target identifications. The validity of search time as a measure of display quality for reading text deserves serious consideration. Snyder and Maddox (Note 1) show that manipulations of independent variables affecting character size result in opposing effects on menu search time and on reading time. Specifically, larger characters are identified more quickly than smaller ones when contextual aids are minimal but are read less quickly in a semantic context. Snyder and Maddox (Note 1) suggest that reading time is increased when characters are larger because more eye fixations are required to cover the larger area. On the other hand, search time is decreased when characters are larger because larger characters are more easily detected in the visual periphery. These findings question the appropriateness of using a menu search task to study reading performance.

Although the search measure reflects the legibility of individual characters, its relation to reading performance depends on how well the search task approximates the mechanics of reading and on how important individual letters are as aids to reading. Other features at the word, syntactic, and semantic levels, are available to experienced readers and may facilitate the understanding of print. Manipulations such as alternating the case of component letters or filling or removing spaces between words detrimentally affect both reading and search rate when the search target is a particular word (Fisher, 1975; Fisher & Lefton, 1976; Spragins, Lefton, & Fisher, 1976). Further, Malt and Seaman (1978) demonstrated that improvements in reading performance when a particular filler was used to eliminate word boundaries was specific for that filler. That is, when a filler was replaced with one of a different shape, performance fell drastically, indicating that a letter-by-letter strategy is used when reading text without word boundaries. However, the result does not prove that a letter-by-letter strategy is used when reading normal text. In fact, Wheeler (1970) suggests that "higher level" features such as those found in digrams and trigrams probably aid in word recognition. Similarly, Dunn-Rankin (1978) reports that "letter combinations, either adjacent or separated in the word, are important visual cues used in word recognition," a conclusion reached by analyses of word groups categorized in terms of similarity. However, the most dominant visual characteristic in comparing words was found to be the initial letter.

Mason (1975) studied the effect of spatial redundancy in identifying letter symbols. Spatial redundancy was defined as "a correlation between distinctive features of letters and the positions they most frequently occupy in printed English words." Good readers were more sensitive than poor ones to the spatial redundancy of single letters in nonword letter strings. Further, good readers searched word anagrams for targets faster than they searched the words themselves if the anagrams were more spatially redundant. The confounding effect of sequential redundancy was removed in another experiment (Mason & Katz, 1976) that used non-alphabetic symbols instead of letters. In this experiment, spatial redundancy was affected by controlling the probability of occurrence of a symbol at a particular location in a six-symbol string. Here also, spatial redundancy was of more assistance to good readers than to poor readers although both groups were equal when there was no redundancy. Thus, good readers seem to have positional expectancies for letters in addition to discriminating their visual features. It appears that single letter identification is a component skill in reading; that is, a letter must be identified before its location can be of some use.

The preceding discussion does not include all of the literature that may be relevant. However, it presents enough to show that reading skill includes the ability to obtain information from individual letters as well as from combinations of letters in a familiar context. Thus, if character and line spacing significantly affect letter discrimination, they should also influence the reading process. An appropriate task may be selected by considering, first, why spacing may have differential effects on perception and, second, the mechanics of reading.

There is some psychophysical evidence that foveal sensitivity is not independent of events occurring in the visual periphery. For example, Breitmeyer and Valberg (1979) found that sensitivity to a test flash is reduced in the foveal region when the periphery is stimulated by an oscillating square-wave grating. Further, Mackworth (1965) reports that the addition of extraneous letters to a display severely affected a subject's ability to compare accurately a letter at the fovea with two letters presented in the periphery. Mackworth used the concept of the "useful field of view" to interpret his finding. According to that concept, the useful field of view is centered at the fixation point. When too much information is present, the useful field contracts to prevent overloading the visual system. Therefore, when spacing between characters and lines is reduced, the size of the useful field should contract, resulting in a slower scanning rate during reading. The slower rate would be a consequence of both reduced peripheral information and reduced foveal sensitivity. However, the increased number of characters within a given area would likely compensate for reduced peripheral information.

A task suitable for studying character spacing on a page of text should be analogous to a reading task where multiple lines of characters are present. The normal mechanics of reading English suggest that the task should involve left to right movements of fixation along the line of characters. If a search task employed such a display, it would be possible to show variations in scanning rate along a single line in terms of both distance traversed and characters read. Characters may be processed more slowly when they are farther apart because a greater distance must be scanned. However, scanning rate in terms of distance per unit time should increase as character spacing increases in order to maintain the rate of character processing. The distance scanned per unit time should increase until the trade-off between horizontal character spacing and speed of eye movement gives the maximum amount of accurate information with the least amount of effort. This point should, by definition, be correlated with the lowest error score.

*The experiment*

The displays presented to each of the ten subjects participating in the experiment were similar to that shown in Figure 1. The figure is a photograph of a television screen and shows the 5×7 character set employed. The letters in the display were selected randomly by a computer algorithm from the entire lower case alphabet. The critical line to which the subject was required to attend was marked in the left margin by a plus symbol. Because the length of the descender on the letters $g, j, p,$ $q,$ and $y$ was a variable of interest, these five letters were selected as the search targets. The first letter in the critical line was always one of these five letters and indicated the target to the subject at the beginning of each trial. The subject's task was to scan the critical line for the next occurrence of the target letter, and to name the next letter after it. (In Figure 1, the target letter is $q,$ and the letter to be named is $v$). The subject was requested to scan the line only once. If he reached the end of the line without identifying the target letter, he gave the end letter as his response. The target letter occurred only once on the critical line, following the initial cue, as did each of the two indicated response letters. The subject was further instructed to attempt to regulate his scanning rate so that targets were missed on no more than 10 percent of the trials. Onset of the display was almost instantaneous and activation of a voice switch by the response erased it. Response time was measured to the nearest msec and the experimenter entered the actual response at the computer console during the three-second inter-trial interval.

The 5×7 character matrix spanned ten picture elements (pixels) horizontally and was displayed vertically on 14 television scan lines to minimize the flicker that would result from displaying each dot of the matrix on only one field of the television frame. During the experiment, a Conrac Model RHN 19/C 19-inch colour television monitor was employed. This monitor has circular phosphor elements arranged in the usual triangular pattern. The letters were always displayed in white on an unilluminated background. The white had a colour temperature of 6500 deg Kelvin and the display intensity at full illumination was 48 Nit. Ambient room lighting was approximately 366 Lux.

Figure 1. A representative sample of the displays presented on each trial of the experiment.

The subject was seated approximately 4 ft from the monitor. A page was displayed to help the experimenter explain the task and then 10 trials were presented for practice. The experiment itself was a $3\times3\times3$ repeated measures design with length of descender, horizontal spacing, and vertical spacing as the three factors. The length of descender, the amount a letter extended below the line, was 0, 1, or 2 pixels. Both vertical and horizontal spacing were 1, 2, or 3 pixels. Each of the five target letters was presented twice in each experimental condition. The $3\times3\times3 = 27$ test conditions were randomly ordered within each of 10 blocks of trials. Thus, the total number of trials for a subject was 270. The session lasted about 35 min and a short pause was permitted after the 135th trial.

A repeated measures analysis of variance was performed on each of the three dependent variables: frequency of misses, scanning rate in characters per sec, and scanning rate in pixels per sec. Analysis of frequency of misses showed a significant effect due to horizontal spacing ($F(2,18)=5.59, p<.05$), and an effect due to length of descender ($F(2,18)=15.94, p<.01$). No interactions were significant. Analysis of scanning rate in characters per sec showed a significant effect due to vertical spacing ($F(2,18)=5.37, p<.05$), horizontal spacing ($F(2,18)=42.72, p<.01$), and length of descender ($F(2,18)=15.74, p<.01$). No interactions were significant. Analysis of scanning rate in pixels per sec showed a significant effect due to vertical spacing ($F(2,18)=5.60, p<.05$), horizontal spacing ($F(2,18)=205.32, p<.01$), and length of descender ($F(2,18)=18.32, p<.01$). Figures 2, 3, and 4 show the means corresponding to the above effects. Table 1

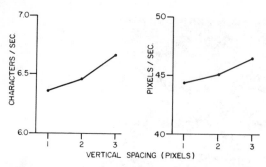

Figure 2. The relation between spacing between rows of characters and scanning rate while searching for the target letter.

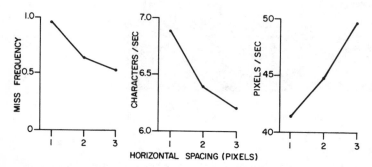

Figure 3. Frequency of missing the target and scanning rate while searching for it as a function of spacing between characters on a row.

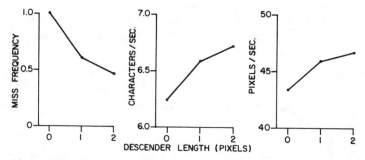

Figure 4. Frequency of missing the target, and scanning rate while searching for it as a function of the number of pixels by which descender characters extend below the line.

shows the proportion of the total variance explained by each of the significant effects.

The statistical significance of differences among the means was tested using the Newman-Keuls procedure (Winer, 1962). Descender lengths of zero resulted in significantly more misses than descender lengths of one or two pixels. There was, however, no significant difference between the latter two descender lengths. Similarly, the lack of a descender was related to a significantly slower scanning rate than were descender lengths of one or two pixels. Again, there was no significant difference between the latter two descender lengths. These findings suggest that the descender should extend below the line by at least one pixel if it is to be readily noticed.

Table 1. Percentage of total variance of each measure explained by each independent variable.

| Independent variable | Dependent variable | | |
|---|---|---|---|
| | Miss Frequency | Character per sec | Pixels per sec |
| Vertical spacing | —— | 1.3 | 1.1 |
| Horizontal spacing | 4.3 | 6.6 | 16.6 |
| Descender length | 7.2 | 3.2 | 3.2 |

The reason for the effect of descender length is probably straightforward: a descender that extends below the line by even one pixel is a cue distinctive enough to aid detecting that character accurately.

The amount of space between lines of characters did not appear to affect the frequency of missed targets. However, the rate of scanning the line was affected. A vertical spacing of three pixels resulted in significantly faster scanning than did spacings of one or two pixels. There was no significant difference between the latter spacings. These findings permit some leeway in determing the minimum spacing. If scanning speed is not a requirement, the minimum spacing of one pixel appears to be adequate. However, if faster scanning is required, spacing of at least three pixels should be maintained between lines. If faster scanning occurred because less effort was necessary to identify letter features, it may be that lines of text separated by at least three pixels are less fatiguing to read than lines separated by only one or two pixels.

It is not immediately obvious why the spacing between lines should affect the rate of horizontal scanning. It is possible that the reduction in the density of visual noise, obtained in the periphery by increasing the spacing between lines, enlarges Mackworth's (1965) "useful field of view." If the useful field of view is enlarged, at least horizontally, increased use of peripheral information in the direction of scanning might result in faster scanning rates.

A space of one pixel between characters on a line (horizontal spacing) resulted in significantly more misses than did spaces of two or three pixels. There was no significant difference between the latter two spacings. Analyses of the two rate measures showed that all three spacings were significantly different, however. The number of characters scanned per second decreased with increasing spacing, the number of pixels scanned per second increased with increasing spacing. Presumably, the highest character input rate occurred at the smallest spacing because a maximum number of characters was squeezed into a unit distance. This high density is probably responsible also for the concurrent higher miss frequency, accuracy declining slightly but significantly when characters were processed at the highest rate.

An increase in the spacing between characters was accompanied by sensitivity to a wider visual field in a given time period. This, too, may have resulted from a larger "useful field of view" because of decreased letter density. On the other hand, processing a wider visual field per unit time could have resulted from more frequent eye movements and shorter fixation durations. However, spatial apprehension did not increase enough to maintain the rate at which characters were processed at the smallest spacing.

All three dependent measures must be considered to determine the best horizontal spacing. The miss frequency and rate measures suggest that a space of at least two pixels should separate characters to permit the fastest, most accurate letter identification. A further increase in spacing would significantly increase the rate of spatial apprehension but would reduce the rate of input of characters, an important point for it is characters, not distance, that yield information in reading.

The effect of horizontal spacing on the rate of scanning characters can be attributed to change in the density of characters with varying horizontal spacing. Although the high density with the shortest spacing appeared to demand an undesirably high processing rate, as was indicated by the accompanying higher miss frequency, the density with intermediate spacing did not. If it did, the significant increase in the rate of spatial apprehension would not have occurred. Further, the miss frequency began to asymptote around the intermediate horizontal spacing employed. Therefore, a minimum horizontal spacing of two pixels is recommended because of human limitations on the rate of information transmission. However, caution must be exercised in applying this recommendation to a page of text with all its redundancies and higher order features. Analysis during reading uses information varying from the single letter to the word or phrase level. Given these additional cues, the effect on reading errors of a space of only one pixel between characters may be undetectable.

*Conclusions*

Recommendations for the minimum required spacing between characters and between lines and the minimum distance a character should extend below the line can be made from the speed and accuracy data obtained in this experiment. The recommendations are relevant for the presentation of text on a television display when the reading distance is approximately four feet, the characters are designed on a $5 \times 7$ dot matrix, the character matrix spans 14 television scan lines, and the phosphor elements are round rather than oblong. It is assumed that the differences in miss frequencies have practical as well as statistical significance, and that letter identification is a significant component of reading skill. The recommendations follow.

*Vertical spacing.* The results indicate that the space between lines, even when it is as little as one pixel, does not influence accuracy. However, speed of letter recognition and possibly ease of reading, can be improved significantly by increasing the space to three pixels. Therefore, the recommended space between lines is either one or three pixels depending on whether or not reading speed is an important criterion. This recommendation is independent of the length of descender. An additional advantage in using a separation of three pixels between lines is that space is provided for accent marks in a language such as French.

*Horizontal spacing.* A space of two pixels between successive characters on a line is recommended. Less than two pixels results in significantly more errors in letter identification, and more than two pixels causes an unnecessary reduction in the rate of information input.

*Descender length.* It is recommended that a descender should extend below the line by at least one pixel. Descender characters that do not descend below the line are missed significantly more often and are identified more slowly. A descender length of more than one pixel does not improve performance significantly.

### Reference notes

1. Snyder, H. L., & Maddox, M. E. *Information transfer from computer-generated dot-matrix displays* (Report HFL-78-3/ARO-78-1). Research Triangle Park, N.C.: U.S. Army Research Office, 1978.
2. Warren, A. L. *The perceptibility of lower case and all capitals newspaper headlines.* Unpublished master's thesis, 1942. Abstracted in Cornog, D. Y., & Rose, F. C. *Legibility of alphanumeric characters and other symbols: II. A reference handbook.* Washington: U.S. Government Printing Office, National Bureau of Standards Miscellaneous Publication 262-2, 1967.

### References

Breitmeyer, B. G., & Valberg, A. Local foveal inhibitory effects of global peripheral excitation. *Science*, 1979, *203*, 463-464.

Breland, K., & Breland, M. K. Legibility of newspaper headlines printed in capitals and in lower case. *Journal of Applied Psychology*, 1944, *28*, 117-120.

Dunn-Rankin, P. The visual characteristics of words. *Scientific American*, 1978, *238*, 122-130.

Fisher, D. F. Reading and visual search. *Memory & Cognition*, 1975, *3*, 188-196.

Fisher, D. F., & Lefton, L. A. Peripheral information extraction: a developmental examination of reading processes. *Journal of Experimental Child Psychology*, 1976, *21*, 77-93.

Mackworth, N. H. Visual noise causes tunnel vision. *Psychonomic Science*, 1965, *3*, 67-68.

Malt, B. C., & Seaman, J. G. Peripheral and cognitive components of eye guidance in filled-space reading. *Perception & Psychophysics*, 1978, *23*, 399-402.

Mason, M. Reading ability and letter search time: effects of orthographic structure defined by single-letter positional frequency. *Journal of Experimental Psychology: General*, 1975, *104*, 146-166.

Mason, M., & Katz, L. Visual processing of nonlinguistic strings: redundancy effects and reading ability. *Journal of Experimental Psychology: General*, 1976, *105*, 338-348.

Paterson, D. G., & Tinker, M. A. Readability of newspaper headlines printed in capitals and lower case. *Journal of Applied Psychology*, 1946, *30*, 161-168.

Spragins, A. B., Lefton, L. A., & Fisher, D. F. Eye movements while reading and searching spatially transformed text: a developmental examination. *Memory & Cognition*, 1976, *4*, 36-42.

Tinker, M. A. *Examiner's manual for Tinker Speed of Reading Test*. Minneapolis: University of Minnesota Press, 1955.

Tinker, M. A. *Bases for effective reading*. Minneapolis: University of Minnesota Press, 1965.

Wheeler, D. D. Processes in word recognition. *Cognitive Psychology*, 1970, *1*, 59-85.

Winer, B. J. *Statistical principles in experimental design*. New York: McGraw-Hill, 1962.

# Optimal segmentation for sentences displayed on a video screen

Joël Pynte and Georges Noizet

*Sentences composed of either short or long words were presented on a video screen connected to a computer, using various levels of segmentation. For sentences with short words, the fastest reading times were obtained with segmentation level which divided sentences into Noun Phrase and Verb Phrase. For sentences with long words, the optimal presentation was almost word for word. The significance of these results is discussed in the light of various models of psycholinguistic processing.*

The strategies used in the perception and comprehension of language are no doubt based on an accumulation of linguistic and extra-linguistic knowledge difficult to evaluate. They are also determined by certain well-known constraints of the perceptual system. In reading, for example, it is known that the span of an eye-fixation rarely exceeds eight to nine letters (Paterson & Tinker, 1947). It is possible that other types of units are constituted during later stages of processing, in particular of the short-term storage capacity.

The interactions between perceptual mechanisms and psycholinguistic processing has until now been investigated primarily in the auditory domain. Abrams and Bever (1969) and Bever and Hurtig (1975) showed, for example, that the level of attention does not remain stable during the perception of a complex sentence. A click is less well perceived at the end of clauses. The authors concluded that this decline in performance indicates that the subject's attention is directed "inwards." This would imply the existence of two types of mechanisms used alternately: at the beginning of a clause the subject's first concern is with the external properties of the signal and the processing is passive; "at the end of a clause [he] is actively organizing an internal representation of what [he] has just heard" (Bever & Hurtig, 1975, p. 6).

Jarvella (1971), Jarvella and Herman (1972), and Caplan (1972) have, moreover, insisted that processing clauses must be accompanied by memorization. At the end of a clause, however, when a more abstract representation has been elaborated, the contents of immediate memory can be erased in order to leave room for the next unit.

In the visual domain, the results obtained by Aaronson and Scarborough (1976) can be compared with those of Abrams and Bever (1969) and Bever and Hurtig (1975). Their technique was to ask the subject to control the successive appearance of the words of the sentence to be read by pressing a bar. In this situation the subject tends to segment the sentence into clauses and the longest presentation times are usually observed on the last word of each clause. These "pauses" introduced into the sequence of presentations are similar to the drops of attention observed in auditory experiments. Like them, they can signify that other types of mechanisms are being used. It should be noted, however, that in this experiment the subjects were required to report the presented sentences immediately after they had been read. In a control situation when the subjects were required simply to read the stimuli, no comparable effect was observed.

It is worth noting some paradoxical aspects of the model devised by Bever and Hurtig (1975). In order to mark the boundaries between clauses, the subject would need to have processed at least part of the relations. Bever, Garrett, and Hurtig (1973), however, have formulated a more satisfactory theory: "during a clause a listener projects potential organizations for the underlying semantic relations in it. At the end of each clause a definitive structure is assigned" (p. 278).

An even more flexible system would be one in which all the different levels operate in parallel (Marslen-Wilson & Welsh, 1978). Supporting arguments come mainly from experiments on shadowing. Marslen-Wilson (1973, 1975) showed, for example, that subjects capable of repeating an utterance with a delay of about one syllable are nonetheless affected by such factors as the syntactic regularity or semantic coherence of what they hear. What is particularly important, as far as we are concerned, is that in such a model the constraints linked to the sequential nature of the intake of information during reading or listening lose their importance. In particular, the subject does not have to memorize the information and so it is futile to search for some sort of unit defined on the peripheral level.

The question is whether operations carried out during psycholinguistic processing can effectively be studied through certain observed aspects of the activity of reading. In particular, it can be asked whether units elaborated during the different stages of the process (eye-exploration, short-term storage) are really linked to carrying out these operations. There is a possibility that they are determined entirely by perceptual or mnemonic constraints. In the experiments described here we attempted to approach the problem from a different direction. By means of a technique derived from that used by Aaronson and Scarborough (1976), the subject was obliged to take into account different types of units of varying length. The aim was to discover an optimal segmentation which would accelerate comprehension. The idea of using such a procedure was suggested by results obtained during a preliminary experiment. These results are presented in Experiment 1. Experiment 2 was designed to confirm and develop some of them. The significance of the results is then discussed in the light of the foregoing and of a new model presented by Frazier and Fodor (1978).

## Experiment 1

*Method*

The sentences the subject was to read (silently) appeared on a video screen connected to a computer. The subjects controlled the appearance of each section (and the disappearance of the last one) by pressing a bar. Furthermore, in order to simulate natural reading more closely each section appeared to the right of the position where the last one had been rather than in the same place. The subjects were not disturbed by this presentation but seemed to be capable easily of synchronising their eye movements with those of the hand controlling the appearance of the stimulus.

Five segmentation types were compared. In addition to word-by-word presentation and single-block presentation (no segmentation), three intermediary levels were chosen according to the constituent structure of the sentences. The material comprised sentences of types (1) and (2) which were composed of a single clause and those of types (3) and (4) with two. The lines of dashes, in which solidus strokes represent the different segmentation levels, are differentiated by lower case letters for the first types and upper case letters for the second.


1.      Le python féroce dévore voracement le pygmée
(a)     /—— ——————— ——————— ——————— ——————————— —— ———————/
(b)     /—— ——————— ———————/——————— ——————————— —— ———————/
(c)     /—— ——————— ———————/——————— ——————————/——— ———————/
(d)     /——/——————— ———————/——————— ——————————/——/———————/
(e)     /——/———————/———————/——————— ——————————/——/———————/

2.      La pythie livide évoque le combat du centaure
(a)     /—— ——————— ——————— ——————— —— ——————— —— ———————/
(b)     /—— ——————— ———————/——————— —— ——————— —— ———————/
(c)     /—— ——————— ———————/———————/—— ——————— —— ———————/
(d)     /——/——————— ———————/———————/——/——————— —— ———————/
(e)     /——/———————/———————/———————/——/———————/——/———————/

3.      Le taureau qui fascine la baronne culbute le picador
(A)     /—— ———————— ——— ———————— —— ——————— ———————— —— ————————/
(B)     /—— ————————/——— ———————— —— ————————/———————— —— ————————/
(C)     /—— ————————/———/———————— —— ————————/———————— —— ————————/
(D)     /—— ————————/———/————————/—— ————————/————————/—— ————————/
(E)     /——/————————/———/————————/——/————————/————————/——/————————/

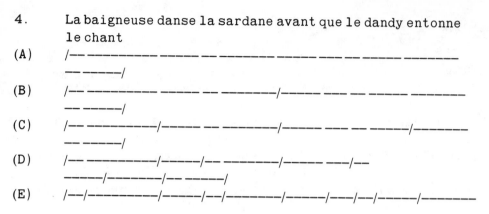

4.      La baigneuse danse la sardane avant que le dandy entonne
        le chant

(A)     /—— ————————— ————— —— ———————— ———— —— ————— ————————
        —— —————/

(B)     /—— ————————— ————— —— ————————/————— ———— —— ————— ————————
        —— —————/

(C)     /—— ——————————/————— —— ————————/————— ———— —— —————/————————
        —— —————/

(D)     /—— ——————————/—————/—— ————————/————— ———/——
        ——————/————————/—— —————/

(E)      /——/—————————/—————/——/————————/—————/———/——/—————/————————

      Ten psychology students, divided into five groups, took part in five experimental sessions. During each session a different segmentation type was used. The order of the five presentations was different for each group.

      The stimulus sentences (two or three of each type for each session) were mixed with "noise" sentences of varied structure and length. Both were presented by section using comparable segmentation rules to avoid a systematic strategy which would give the subject an automatic cue for the end of the sentence.

### Results

The total reading-time (TRT), that is, the sum of the time measured for each section, was calculated for each stimulus sentence. We would expect a regular increase in the values as the number of sections increased because the motor reaction times of the subjects were included in the TRT and they, of course, increased as the number of sections increased.

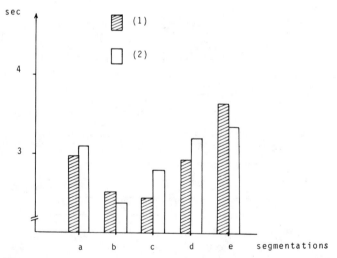

Figure 1. Experiment 1. Mean TRTs for each type of segmentation, sentences (1) and (2) (one clause).

The mean TRT for each segmentation type is given in Figure 1 for sentences with a single clause and in Figure 2 for those with two clauses. The means represented in the figures correspond to data smoothed to eliminate aberrant values (± 3 standard deviations from the mean).

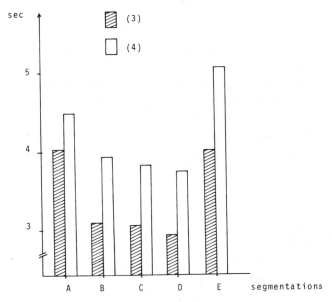

Figure 2. Experiment 1. Mean TRTs for each type of segmentation, sentences (3) and (4) (two clauses).

It is immediately apparent that the best performance was not obtained through single-block presentation (as would be expected from the motor reaction times mentioned above). Furthermore, in sentences of types 3 and 4, the successive presentation of two sections corresponding to the two clauses (segmentation level (B)) is not better than certain finer segmentations ((C) or (D)) corresponding respectively to four and six or seven sections. Finally, the similarity between the results for one and two clauses should be noted. Segmentations (b) and (c), optimal for sentences of types 1 and 2 should be compared with (C) and (D), optimal for sentences of types 3 and 4. The units isolated were for (b) and (C), Noun Phrase + Verb Phrase, and for (c) and (D), Noun Phrase subject + verb + Noun Phrase object.

The reading rate expressed as a number of words per minute was similar to that obtained by Baker, Dounton, and Newell (this volume) with self-presentation of slides. For single-block presentation, the range was from 140 words per min (wpm) for seven-word sentences to 180 wpm for twelve-word sentences. For optimal segmentation, the range was from 180 wpm for seven-word sentences to 240 wpm for twelve-word sentences.

## Experiment 2

*Method*

In order to study the interactions between perceptual mechanisms and psycholinguistic processing to try to explain certain effects observed in Experiment 1, in
Experiment 2 the length of the words constituting the stimulus sentences was
varied while the syntactic structure was maintained. Thus certain sentences
(example 5) contained 35 or 36 letters while others (example 6) contained 65 to 66.
The syntactic structure was the same in each case and the segmentations used are
given for one example only. The segmentations (a) to (e) correspond to those in
Experiment 1. Two extra segmentations were used. In one (b'), there were two
sections as in (b), but they did not have the same syntactic relevance because the
verb was grouped with NP subject instead of with NP object (as in (b)). The other
segmentation (d'), like (d), corresponded to the presentation of five sections, but
the articles were grouped with the nouns and the adjectives and adverbs were
separated from the word they modified.

```
5.        La bête effarée gagna alors un abri
(a)       /-- ---- -------- ----- ----- -- ----/
(b)       /-- ---- --------/----- ----- -- ----/
(b')      /-- ---- -------- ----- -----/-- ----/
(c)       /-- ---- --------/----- -----/-- ----/
(d)       /--/---- --------/----- -----/--/----/
(d')      /-- ----/--------/-----/-----/-- ----/
(e)       /--/----/--------/-----/-----/--/----/
```

```
6.        Une tubulure alambiquée assure continuellement le re-
          froidissement (Segmentation levels the same as for 5.)
```

The procedure was identical to that for Experiment 1. Fourteen
psychology students, divided into seven groups, took part in seven experimental
sessions. A different segmentation was used in each session. Three different
sentences of each length were presented among noise sentences presented with
the same type of segmentation. The order in which a subject participated in the
different sessions varied according to the group to which he belonged.

## Results

The data, smoothed as in Experiment 1, are given in Figure 3. The curve corresponding to short sentences is remarkably similar to that obtained in Experiment 1
for equivalent syntactic structures (Figure 1). The optimal segmentation seems,
once again, to be that separating the Noun Phrase and the Verb Phrase (b)
although the differences between this segmentation and single-block presentation
seem less marked than in Experiment 1.

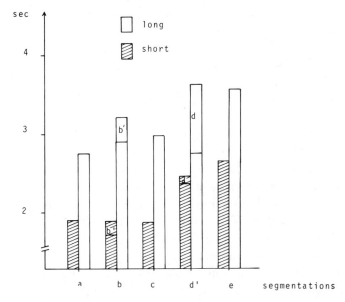

Figure 3. Experiment 2. Mean TRTs for seven types of segmentation as a function of syntactic relevance ((b) and (d) vs. (b') and (d')) and word length (short vs. long).

   In the long sentences, reading for both (b) and (b') is slower than for (a). Consequently, the effect observed in Experiment 1 is not reproduced. Nonetheless, segmentation (d'), corresponding to word-by-word presentation (except that articles were grouped with nouns), allows a performance equivalent to that obtained with single-block presentation.

   Two interesting effects are to be noted in comparing the segmentations which divide the stimuli into the same number of sections: (b) and (b') on the one hand, (d) and (d') on the other. There is a noticeable drop in performance from (b) to (b'), the verb being grouped with the object in (b) and with the subject in (b'), and an improvement in performance (more marked for long sentences than for short ones) from (d) to (d'), the noun being grouped with the adjective in (d) and with the article in (d').

   When the segmentation isolates two words which syntactically are closely linked (the article and the noun for example) while grouping two words less closely linked (noun and adjective or verb and adverb) performance drops drastically, as between (d) and (d'). The difference between (b') and (b) can be interpreted similarly. The node on the phrase-marker is higher (the relations less narrow) between the subject and the verb in (b') than between verb and object in (b). The differences can be explained by another factor: the respective lengths of the different segments which were approximately equal for (b) and (d') but differed considerably for (b') and (d). Further experiments would be necessary to determine the importance of this factor. Analysis of variance for these four segmentations gives a value of $F(1,13) = 4.16, p > .05$ for the difference between (b) and (b') and $F(1,13) = 10.79, p < .01$ for the difference between (d') and (d).

If segmentations (b') and (d) are excluded from the data and only those which respect the immediate constituent analysis of the stimuli ((a), (b), (c), (d') and (e)) included, we find the trivial effect mentioned earlier: the greater the number of sections, and thus the greater the role of the motor reaction time, the higher the TRT. There are two exceptions, however: (b) which appears optimal for short sentences and (d') which appears optimal for long sentences. An analysis of variance taking into account only the five segmentations mentioned above gives a value of $F(4,52) = 7.99, p < .01$ for the interaction between the length and the segmentation type. For the main effects, $F(1,13) = 96.88, p < .01$ for the length factor and $F(4,52) = 11.10, p < .01$ for the segmentation factor.

The fact that the optimal segmentation is finer for long sentences than for short suggests that certain perceptual or mnemonic constraints have an effect on the type of units elaborated during reading. These constraints, however, are not strong enough to impose an invariant effect which can be expressed as a number of letters or syllables. The units corresponding to segmentation (b) for short sentences are longer for example, than those corresponding to segmentation (d') for long.

It might be asked if other factors intervene to determine the overall processing load associated with a given unit. One possibility is the relative frequency of the lexical items because, of course, more frequent words tend to be shorter than less frequent ones. It is also possible that lexical access is less immediate for words composed of more letters than the perceptual span. The fact that the optimal units can include up to four words (for short sentences), however, suggests that mnemonic constraints play an important role at another level as well.

Again a great deal of variability was observed between subjects, some being fast with most segmentations, others being slow for all. Eight subjects stood out from the others, four being consistently faster, four consistently slower.

It might be thought that the two groups of subjects had understood the task completely differently and had, therefore, adopted entirely different strategies. Analyzing their data separately yielded surprisingly parallel results, however (Figure 4), suggesting a good deal of internal coherence in the data. It should also be noted that rapid subjects process long sentences in less time than slow subjects process short ones, the sentences varying in length by as much as twice.

Analysis of variance was carried out on the two groups of subjects. The interaction between the segmentation type and length gives $F(4,24) = 9.29 p < .01$. The performances obtained with the optimal segmentation and with the next less fine segmentation were also compared for both types of sentences. The comparison between (b) and (a), short sentences, gives $F(1,6) = 5.81, p < .06$. That between

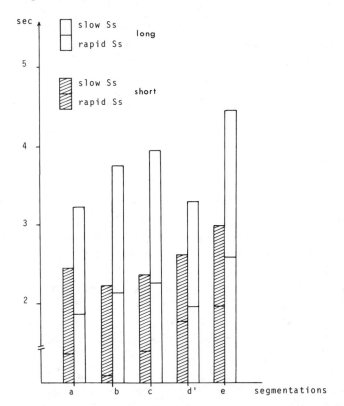

Figure 4. Experiment 2. Mean TRTs for five types of segmentation, opposing two groups of subjects according to speed.

(d') and (c) gives $F(1,6) = 31.08, p < .01$. The effect is the same for both groups of subjects and the interaction is non-significant in both cases: $F < 1$ for short sentences and $F(1,6) = 4.02, p > .05$, for long ones.

## Conclusion

One of the initial strategies involved in the perception of sentences might be the isolation of complete syntactic units, such as clauses. This could be achieved through a crude lexical analysis. The full semantic interpretation, however, would take place only at the end of the syntactic units. According to another interpretation, semantic processing would take place from the beginning of the clause, interactively with visual, lexical, and syntactic analysis. In the framework of online processing, the context should resolve syntactic difficulties as fast as they occur and "perceptual" or mnemonic units are of no help.

The two experiments reported above suggest that it is possible to accelerate the comprehension of a sentence by presenting it in sections. The optimal segmentation depends on whether the sentence comprises short or long words. For the former, it corresponds to the division between Noun Phrase and Verb Phrase. Moreover, the visual and lexical levels seem to interact with the other levels of processing to determine the overall processing load for a given unit.

These results seem incompatible with both types of models outlined above. On one hand, clauses seem to have less importance during reading than has sometimes been suggested. In the framework of a continuous model, on the other hand, it is hard to explain why reading seems to be accelerated by isolating units composed of several words. Such units are probably greater than the perceptual span. If they are effectively processed during reading, it would then seem that certain syntactic relations cannot be assigned on the basis of a purely continuous procedure.

It is not known if optimal units are actually formed during normal reading, however. Perhaps by presenting sentences with optimal segmentation, we are merely encouraging mechanisms which intervene naturally. The improved performance might well be due to the fact that the subject bypasses the normal processes necessary to isolate these units. It is, however, possible that in continuous text the role of context is determining. If so, the correct model would then be the continuous one. Furthermore, in our experiments, the subjects were required to give the overall meaning of each sentence as soon as it had been read. Although verbatim reports were not specifically required, most reports were in fact of this nature. Reading may thus have been accompanied by an act of memorisation which may not normally occur.

Frazier and Fodor (1978) have recently proposed a model of a syntactic parser which could help us to understand these results. Their conceptions avoid, in an original way, the dichotomy between "sequential" and "parallel" models. According to them sentence-processing occurs in two successive stages but syntactic processing occurs on both the first and second levels, the main difference being in the rules employed. The proximity of words, in particular, can have an effect only on the first level. Furthermore, the passage from the first level to the second is not determined by the syntactic form of the units elaborated in the model devised by Bever, Garrett, and Hurtig (1973). The determining factor in this model is simply the number of words encountered. This model makes possible an explanation of certain factors of perceptual complexity, for example, the length of constituents. A number of segmentation errors which occur with short constituents can often be avoided with long ones. Frazier and Fodor postulate that the analysis could be carried out entirely on the first level for short constituents and the principal relations processed on the second level for long ones.

It is possible that a segmental presentation, which respects the syntactic structure of the stimuli, assists processing because of a distinction between the two levels. In single-block presentation the syntactic relations between the constituents, which seldom comprised more than three or four words, have probably been processed on the first level. In the optimal presentation, because segmentation introduced time-lags between the sections, relations may have been processed directly on the second level.

We are not able to give a unitary explanation of the effects observed. In a first interpretation we assumed that the units corresponding to the optimal segmentation are also formed in natural reading, the only effect of the presentation technique being to simplify the subject's task. According to this point of view, however, these units are not normally processed. The acceleration of reading in our experiments would have been caused artificially by bypassing the natural processing mechanisms. In future experiments it will perhaps be possible to find empirical evidence for one or other of these interpretations by varying (as Frazier and Fodor suggest) the length of the constituents and not merely the length of the words.

# References

Aaronson, D., & Scarborough, M. S. Performance theories for sentence coding: some quantitative evidence. *Journal of Experimental Psychology: Human Perception and Performance*, 1976, *2*, 56-70.

Abrams, K., & Bever, T. G. Syntactic structure modifies attention during speech perception and recognition. *Quarterly Journal of Experimental Psychology*, 1969, *21*, 280-290.

Baker, R., Downton, A., & Newell, A. Simultaneous speech transcription and TV captions for the deaf. In P. A. Kolers, M. E. Wrolstad & H. Bouma (Eds.), *Processing of visible language 2*, New York and London: Plenum Press, 1980.

Bever, T. G., Garrett, M. F. & Hurtig, R. The interaction of perceptual processes and ambiguous sentences. *Memory & Cognition*, 1973, *1*, 277-286.

Bever, T. G., & Hurtig, R. Detection of a non-linguistic stimulus is poorest at the end of a clause. *Journal of Psycholinguistic Research*, 1975, *4*, 1-7.

Caplan, D. Clause boundaries and recognition latencies for words in sentences. *Perception & Psychophysics*, 1972, *12*, 73-76.

Frazier, L., & Fodor, J. D. The sausage machine: a new two-stage parsing model. *Cognition*, 1978, *6*, 291-325.

Jarvella, R. J. Syntactic processing of connected speech. *Journal of Verbal Learning and Verbal Behavior*, 1971, *10*, 409-416.

Jarvella, R. J., & Herman, S. J. Clause structure of sentences and speech processing. *Perception & Psychophysics*, 1972, *11*, 381-383.

Marslen-Wilson, W. D. Linguistic structures and speech shadowing at very short latencies. *Nature*, 1973, *244*, 522-523.

Marslen-Wilson, W. D. Sentence perception as an interactive parallel process. *Science*, 1975, *189*, 226-228.

Marslen-Wilson, W. D., & Welsh, A. Processing interactions and lexical access during word recognition in continuous speech. *Cognitive Psychology*, 1978, *10*, 29-63.

Paterson, D. G., & Tinker, M. A. The effect of typography upon the perceptual span in reading. *American Journal of Psychology*, 1947, *60*, 388-396.

# Text enhancement and structuring in computer conferencing

A. Baer and M. Turoff

*This paper summarizes preliminary efforts to integrate graphics enhancement and structuring techniques in a computer conferencing system (EIES). The facilities presented serve the creation and display of schematic graphics where editing is possible on both dimensionless and dimensional descriptions. This separation encourages interactive development of figures, facilitates multiple authorship, and allows independent device display as alphanumeric or linegraphics. In addition, the use of the EIES programming facility permits hierarchical figure composition, easy creation of powerful higher level operations, and embedding in text, message, and conference processes. Significant improvement is expected from these features in the representation and comprehension of complex information exchanges in co-operating participant groups.*

Computerized conferencing uses a computer to aid groups in structuring their communication exchanges. It rests on the premise that appropriate communication structures, protocols, and aids can improve the effectiveness or efficiency of a particular group endeavor. The design of such systems permits the "correct" structures to be dependent upon both the nature of the task or objective and the makeup of the group involved (Hiltz & Turoff, 1978).

The Electronic Information Exchange System (EIES) centered at the New Jersey Institute of Technology was designed as a research vehicle emphasizing interaction between humans and humans as well as between humans and a computer system. Features of gradual familiarization (learning by trial-and-error) were considered as important as scope or generality of functions. At the lowest level EIES may be used exclusively through its menu system, then with online documentation, and finally (if appropriate) as a proficient general purpose programmer. Consequently there are considerable capabilities within the general EIES environment to develop and evaluate new structures and tools. The kernel of EIES encompasses the messaging, conferencing, and personal notebook features as well as extensive word processing and text organization capabilities. Through the availability of a general purpose interactive computer language, which can operate on any transactions between any user and the basic EIES system, it is possible to tailor unique subsystems and capabilities for individual users, groups, or the system as a whole. This language is called INTERACT (Hiltz, Turoff, & Whitescarver, 1977) and is highly oriented towards string processing and interface control. Any text item on EIES may contain an executable INTERACT program and INTERACT may act on any EIES text item.

Currently EIES has 500 users, mostly professional and scientific groups representing informal networks. A number of them have evolved their own specialized communication structures as self-contained subsystems of the general

EIES system. An example is the Inquiry-Response structure for the *Legitech* network of science advisors (Lenz & Lenz, 1979) or the *Electronic Journal of the Mental Workload* group (Moray, 1980). The evolution of EIES has been integrated with an evaluation program (Hiltz, 1978) in which it has been observed that this medium of communication leads to unique psychological and sociological characteristics differing from those associated with other modes of human communication. Most significantly it was found that, in text communication over an asynchronous process, time lag made responses sparse and trivial. As a result, more experienced users attempt to enforce critical response from other members via a wide use of EIES structuring techniques: keys, indexing, and graphical schemata. Because of this and the restricted suitability of standard text-editing facilities in EIES, the current graphical capabilities summarized in this paper were developed. Various approaches to graphics have been taken in computer conferencing (Gardan, 1979; Spangler, Lipinski, & Plummer, 1979). These systems, however, are oriented towards modelling explicit tasks such as flowgraphs, organigrams, and networks. Correspondingly, the user has no access to the immediate graphics features and, moreover, cannot build higher level features from given capabilities.

*Problem*

In the remote exchange of visual data a user works in one of the following modes: figure creation, figure instantiation, figure modification, or figure reading or display. The first three modes involve the user as originator, the fourth as consumer. Graphics capabilities in a computerized environment suggest two objectives in figure origination: first, a minimum of command syntax must be required from the individual user to define a figure and, second, a minimal effort should permit extensive modification on a whole composition of figures.

Multi-user joint authorship, one of the primary functions of a conferencing system, must be facilitated in time-reference, segment identification, and authorship. Figure display requires review of entire figures, simple as well as composed and plain as well as annotated.

In view of the given text generation and exchange environment of EIES, as well as the programming capability available, an experimental facility was designed to manage a set of universal graphics capabilities consisting of figure creating as well as figure editing operations to be used to structure and enhance conference-related texts. For figure overlay, storage, retrieval, hierarchy, and conventional editing, general purpose EIES features were used. Creation of a figure includes the specification of an ad hoc line drawing, possibly irregular, as used for symbols, diagrams, maps, and so on. The specification for a figure needs to be useful either as a single instance or as a basis for repeated use, frequently with altered dimensions. It has to be easily edited, using both special graphics and general purpose editing features. Editing includes the capability to redimension a figure once created (varying size and proportions), repeat it at varying locations (copying), and add text for labelling and arrows. If unsatisfied with a design, a user may move, erase, or copy parts of a figure.

In a computerized environment where raster-generated images are used, there are essentially two ways to create graphics. One is by calling primitive graphics commands, for example, to generate a line segment, to produce a character image on the storage medium. The generating function is subsequently lost. The other method defines a larger figure composition by a file consisting of such commands, together with merging calls for character images already inter-preted. Editing is performed differently on each of these representations. The direct modification of a character image (direct editing) is distinct from editing the generating commands (indirect editing). Character images do not need to be re-interpreted for each change but overlaying features such as two intersecting lines can no longer easily be edited separately in a character image. EIES includes both methods of figure descriptions, plus a third, interpretive, method for cases where the dimensions of an orthogonal line drawing change more often than its composition. Text pages in EIES may be used to store graphics features expressed as character image, graphics commands, or data related to the interpretation of special graphics commands. In the approach taken for EIES, primitive operations were devised as a set of building blocks which could be shared by different graphics editing functions and be combined into higher level facilities. The objective was both to reduce actual program efforts, that is, run-time require-ments on a time-sharing system, and to facilitate experimentation in user interface and application. For reasons of internal representation and the processing of text in EIES, these building blocks include four separate features: creating orthogonal figures, creating non-orthogonal figures, moving figure sections, and enhancing by text-strings (Figure 1). Each feature consists of one or more system procedures which may be called by the user and become embedded in user programs (forming command pages) by means of the INTERACT programming language. One particular high level feature, provided as a set of standard functions, allows a user to define a hierarchy of picture descriptions. Often only the dimensions of a line drawing are modified, the shape (the way in which line segments are connected) being retained. It was, therefore, considered practical to have a user define a figure shape as a distinct set of data and derive various dimensional instances as desired. Typical shapes (for instance, a box) can then be kept in a library of shapes and identified by name. Composition of a page of figures or a text enhanced with figures is interactively performed in a typical scratchpad page of 57 lines of text. A shape description consists of a symbolic, abreviated notation stored as text in user pages (personal notebook pages or shared conference pages) called data pages. When a dimensional instance is created, the symbols are interpreted by a call to a procedure and the resulting pattern merges with the contents of the scratch page to form a feature page. Any text enhancement, figure-moving, or regular text-string editing can then be performed on either shape definition or interpreted figure.

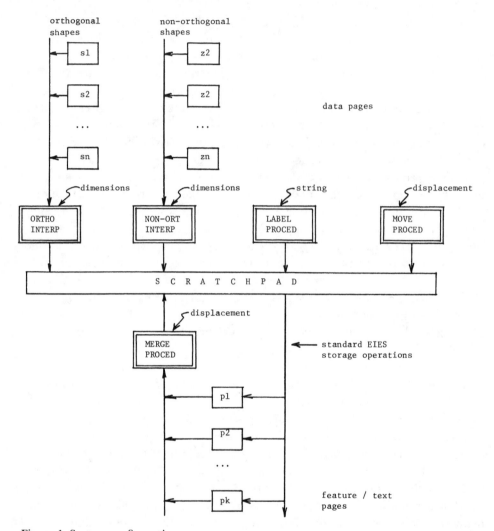

Figure 1. System configuration.

*Figure structure and instances*

A line drawing is defined by both the way in which its line segments are related (a dimensionless property) and the actual position and length of each segment. The dimensionless relationships can be represented by a graph by placing each of the vertices into a page. The links, if they are linear, will then be dimensioned by their vertices.

　　　　In order to facilitate adjustment of dimensions during a figure design, a (dimensionless) shape decription should contain those features least likely to change. In a figure consisting of a combination of orthogonal lines these would be the number and connection of line segments, for example, in a grid or a business form. The actual length of each line segment is more likely to change over instances. The implication for orthogonal figures is that fields between line intersections change.

　　　　In non-orthogonal figures (meant to include both orthogonal and non-orthogonal lines) less likely to change is the sequence of line segments as opposed to the change of a particular endpoint of a line segment. Because non-orthogonal shapes need to represent only a single connection from one line segment to another, the most general representation is by a list of point co-ordinates (for example, for the triangle in Figure 2a). Interpretation of the line segments would produce the traingle in Figure 2b.

```
2,3,8,1
2,3,8,12
8,1,8,12
END

    (a)                    (b)
```

Figure 2. The non-orthogonal figure interpreter.

　　　　Orthogonal figures have from 0 to 4 line segments meeting in a point. Such shapes will need to use symbols to identify explicitly not only points but also connecting lines. If each text line in the sketchpad which will contain a line of the figure is specified by a symbolic string, and each column specified as well, a separate identifying symbol is needed for each column, to be repeated for each line where a column-incidence appears, as for the rectangle in Figure 3. Dimensioning the fields horizontally with 6,10 and vertically with 8,15 will derive an instance of the rectangle. A corresponding interactive command sequence will put the interpreted figure into the scratchpad. In general, a shape definition consists of a column list (in the function of a declaration) and a set of line definitions. Each line definition consists of either endpoint of a vertical or a horizontal line (Figure 4a). Their combination may be used to describe a typical line, for example, line 10 in Figure 4b where lines 9 and 11 show the connecting vertical segments in the final picture. The symbolic description underneath defines seven columns, A through G, and the formal descriptions for line 10. Note that no explicit dimensions are given yet. Dimensions are associated with column as well as row fields so that the first value defines the distance from the left margin or from the top. Thus a box with shape A,B; A.-B.; A-B, when dimensioned with 6,10; 8,1, will result in the polygon in Figure 3. When figures are merged with the contents of the

```
NP14:

        A,B
        A.-B.
        A-B


       6         10
       |          |  |
  8    |          |  |
       |          |  |
  _____*********|
       *         *
 15    *         *
       *         *
  _____*********
```

```
+ORTO
COLUMN SPACING?6,10
ROW SPACING?8,15
SOURCE OF PICTURE DESCRIPTION?NP14
POINT-,HLINE-,VLINE-CHARACTER (or cr)?***

or, as a command string:

+ORTO;6,10;8,15;NP14;***
```

Figure 3. The orthogonal figure interpreter.

scratchpad, the new characters will override existing ones, unless blank. The result is an impression of overpainting. Instances of the same shape may be placed on top of each other. Figures may be transmitted either by sending an interpreted set of instances, for example, the contents of scratchpad (feature page), or by sending merely the generating symbolic description (command page), possibly with some sample dimensions (data page).

*Figure editing*

Although a user is given some flexibility in defining a composition of figures, for example, by re-using a shape definition, the composition may fail to satisfy some objectives. There are two basic forms of figure editing: modification of the generating description, which has been discussed above, and modification of the interpreted figure in the scratchpad which creates special problems. Editing of small fragments of a complex figure by conventional text editing becomes unsatisfactory particularly if changes along rows have to be made. For this type of editing, EIES text structuring and enhancement features a Move procedure. The scratchpad area may be enclosed by a rectangular window of appropriate size and then moved to another location in the figure. The windowed subfigure at the source of the move may be left there or be erased, that is, replaced with blanks. At the

```
                    (a) Syntax
                                             +
shape-def     ::=  column-list cr {line-def} cr

                               +
column-list   ::=  {letter},

                                      +
line-def      ::=  {line-seg | col-incid},

                           +
line-seg      ::=  {col-incid}-

col-incid     ::=  letter | letter .

              +
        where {} means one or more repetitions, separated
        by the subscript and | means "or"

            (b) Example of an Incidence Line

 9:           |               |
10:+---+--+      +--+     +       +
11:           |               |

    A,B,C,D,E,F,G
    ...
    A-B.-C,D-E,F,G.
    ...
```

Figure 4. The symbolic description of orthogonal figures.

destination, the new figure may be merged with the underlying characters, be dropped altogether, blank the source window only, replace the entire underlying window with the moved window, or be inserted into a page, beginning at a given line (Figure 5).

Adding labels to existing figures in a scratchpad can be tedious if general purpose line-editing features have to be employed. Problems of column alignment with a fast rate, fully cursor-controlled CRT terminal are only tolerable. For this reason, a labelling procedure has been provided which allows defining and moving text-strings to any desired location in a page, again merging with the underlying characters. This feature has proved practical for writing and drawing both horizontal and vertical enhancements. For the latter, a top-down character sequence is supplied by the user in left-to-right order (Figure 6).

*Figure composition*

In figure transmission between various conference participants, annotation must be used, as, for example, where a non-monitoring member picks up a contribution and suggests change through highlighting. Such a change should neither affect the original figure directly nor should it use excessive space. It should be possible to edit such an annotation directly into a given figure, after consensus, or autonomously by the monitor. Thus a view can be structured via an overlay operation which, in effect, dynamically merges the figures for output. Partial figures can be contributed by any number of conference participants. Any conference member may compose either a comprehensive image of all the information already in the conference or special views of that material. The key to composition is the PICTURE function which calls a subfigure, subject to a translation along

```
AAAAAAAAAAAAAAAAAAAA
AAAAAAAAAAA┌──────┐AA        ˆ  drop
AAAAAAAAAA │      │AA        │
AAAAAAAAAA └──────┘AA────── erase
AAAAAAAAAAAAAAAAAAAA
```

```
AAAAAAAAAAAAAAAAAAAA
AAAAAAAAAAAAAAAAAAAA<───── replace
          ┌─────┐          │
          │AAAAA│          │
          │AAAAA└──┐       │
          │     │  │───  leave
AAAAAAAAAAAAAAAAAA│AAAA│
          └──────┘
```

```
AAAAAAAAAAAAAAAAAAAA
AAAAAAAAAAAAAAAAAAAA
AAAAAAAAAAA┌AAAAAA..│A<───── merge
AAAAAAAAAAA│AAAAAA..│A      │·
AAAAAAAAAAA│...┌───.│A..  ─── leave
AAAAAAAAAAAAAA│AAAAAA..
          └───┤........│
              └────────┘
```

```
AAAAAAAAAAAAAAAAAAAA
AAAAAAAAAAA AAAAAAAAAA
          ┌─────┐
          │AAAAA│  <───── insert
          │AAAAA│          │
          │     │          │
AAAAAAAAAAAAAAAAAAAA        │
AAAAAAAAAAAAAAAAAAAA        │
AAAAAAAAAAAAAA┌─────┐───  erase
AAAAAAAAAAAAAA│     │
              └─────┘
```

Figure 5. Examples of the move procedure.

```
+HLABEL;<---START;2,3

1:
2:    <---START
3:
```

```
+VLABEL;2,4;ˆ│││

1:
2:    ˆ
3:    │
4:    │
5:    │
6:
```

Figure 6. Labeling procedures.

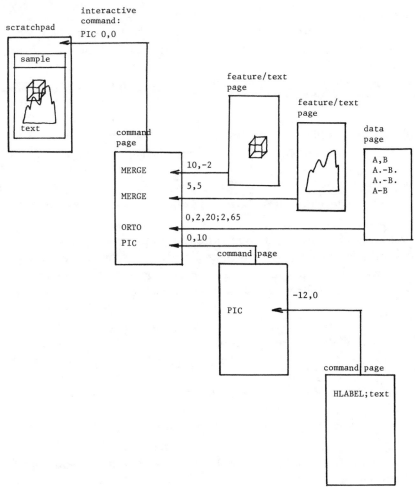

Figure 7. Hierarchical figure composition.

lines and columns. Because this command may also be included in a command page, figures may call the command description of others, in hierarchical fashion, when their commands are interpreted. In order to blend an interpreted character image into a page, a MERGE function is embedded in a figure command description (Figure 7). Finally, in a conferencing system a large variety of terminals having different graphics capabilities and intelligence is used. Efforts are under way at EIES to improve the use of graphics in conferencing by speeding up the display process and interactive editing. Such improvements will be particularly helped by the symbolic description that can be sent in less time than a full page of characters and then be locally interpreted by the microprocessor of an intelligent terminal. A similar technique will allow interpretation of alphanumeric symbols or line drawings, depending on the type of terminal.

*Multiple authorship*

For several persons to originate a figure the parts of that figure must be identified. This is necessary partly because each person takes a different view of a subfigure and partly because of the fitting of the detail. For example, in the joint design of a human face a mouth may be seen as a single line, curved up or down, and it may also include teeth. Keyed references to subfigures need to be written and, finally, a user needs to be able to review a particular alternative composition. Although the current implementation still lacks some features of convenience, the hierarchical picture interpretation functions of EIES accomodate such applications.

*Higher level applications*

Every user will in time develop certain favourite standard constructs which, for him, constitute primitives on a higher level. They should be easily available and have very few parameters and only a single procedure call. For these EIES provides the application programmer and occasionally the programming end-user with an interactive, interpreting, programming language. This language, INTERACT, includes the following features: conditional program execution control, reference to any text-page, execution of text-pages as INTERACT commands, command substitution and answer-ahead capability, and user-function definition capability. By these means, multiple uses of the text-structuring and enhancement primitives may be embedded in programs. For example, an upward arrow may be constructed by one call to VLABEL (Figure 8a) for the tail and another for the head. A program may be written containing these calls which is then placed into a notebook page. The execution of this page may be associated with a user-defined name, such as UPARROW (Figure 8b), and answer-ahead features may be used to construct appropriate calls to the primitives. Figures 9, 10, and 11 illustrate figures constructed by a variety of the EIES graphic features in pure and embedded form.

*The future*

It is clear that the extensive use of computerized conferencing provides new styles of verbal communication. To date our work in graphics has emphasized graphical aids in the composition of individual items and the portrayal of concepts within a text item. However, text items taken as a set often represent highly non-linear compilations because of a number of factors. First, within a given conference the discussion leads to the interweaving of many discussion threads within a single sequence of items. Because text can be executable programs, and programs can call upon text in alternative manners and key the presentation to the readers' inputs, it is possible to have situations where no two readers will read the same sequence or the same items within a given text structure. A good example is a program developed by Robert Theobald and Peter and Trudy Johnson-Lenz on EIES where a reader can take a guided TOUR OF THE FUTURE and may

```
(a)   +VLABEL;3,6,5;¦
      +VLABEL;3,5;^


(b)   DEFINE UPARROW=
      +INPUT Q$,'L1,L2,COL',';'
      +LET Q#:=NMB(Q$)
      +VLABEL;@(Q#(1))+','+@(Q#(2))+','+@(Q#(3));¦
      +VLABEL;@(Q#(1))+','+@(Q#(3));^


      +UPARROW;3,6,5

      1:
      2:
      3:        ^
      4:        ¦
      5:        ¦
      6:        ¦
      7:
```

Figure 8. Control of enhancement routines by the Interact language.

```
A,B,C,D,E,F,G,H,I,K,L
A.-C.-E.-G.
A-B.-C-D.-E-F.-G-H.
B-C.-D-E:-F-G.-H-I.
B.-C-D.-E-F.-G-H.-I-J.-K.-L.
B-D-F-H-J-K-L
```

```
+----------+---------+----------+
!MOVE-AWAY!TILT-AWAY!MOVE-RIGHT!
!    6    !    7    !    8     !
+----+----+----+----+----+-----+-----+
     !TURN-LEFT!MOVE-UP !TURN-RIGHT !
     !    Y    !   U    !    I      !
     +----+----+----+----+-----+------+-----+
          !TILT-LEFT!MOVE-DOWN !TILT-RIGHT !
          !    H    !    J     !    K      !
     +----+----+----+----+-----+------+------+-----+--------+--------+
     !SCALEDOWN!MOVE-LEFT!TILT-TOWARD!MOVE-TOWARD!SCALE-UP!CAM/OBJ !
     !    B    !    N    !    M      !           !        !        !
     +---------+---------+-----------+-----------+--------+--------+
```

Figure 9. Example of ORTO and HLABEL.

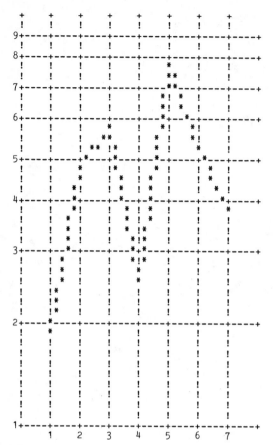

Figure 10. Example with ORTO and NONORT.

choose his own path through a labyrinth of alternative futures and add new scenarios for subsequent readers.

As users evolve structures that relate fragments of text within some framework and as their number increases, it is necessary to find ways to clarify and represent the multi-directed and multi-valued relationships among a large set of text items. Both analytical and graphical techniques are necessary to represent the concept structures (gestalt) of a discourse collectively evolved by a group. Part of the problem of how individuals reorganize material along the lines most appropriate to their concerns is, of course, the dynamic nature of the data base resulting from a continuing process of communication and the evolution of the material in time. The time dependence can be a significant factor in the representation of the material.

Individual users can now impose their own index structure on all the text items they can read by utilizing a feature called COLLECTIONS which is a dynamic outline under which the user can vary and catalogue items. One possi-

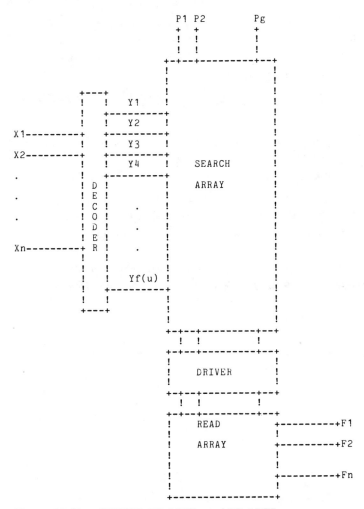

Figure 11. Use of ORTO, VLABEL, and HLABEL.

bility is to examine text items common to different collections to see if they can serve as links for collective analyses of these collections. The result is a process that would typically lend itself to graphical representation.

This work was funded by the Division of Computer Science of the National Science Foundation under Grant MCS 78-00519.

## References

Gardan, R. CONGRÈS: a computer assisted conference system allowing sketch transmission. In M. Boutmy & S. Danthine (Eds.), *Proceedings Teleinformatics 79.* IFIP, The Hague: North Holland Publ. Co., 1979.

Hiltz, S. R. Electronic information exchange: Findings. *Telecommunications Policy,*
    1978, *3*(2), 156-161.

Hiltz, S. R., & Turoff, M. *The network nation: Human communication via computer.*
    Reading, Mass.: Addison-Wesley, 1978.

Hiltz, S. R., Turoff, M., & Whitescarver, J. The human-machine interface in a
    computerized conferencing environment, *Proceedings IEEE Systems, Man
    and Cybernetics.* New York: IEEE, 1977.

Lenz, P., & Lenz, T. *LEGITECH /EIES* : Information exchange and collective
    knowledge building among state legislative researchers. In M. M. Hen-
    derson & M.H. McNaughton (Eds.), *Electronic communication: Technology
    and impacts.* Boulder, Col.: Westview Press, 1979.

Moray, N. Towards an electronic journal. In P.A. Kolers, M.E. Wrolstad, & H.
    Bouma (Eds.), *Processing of visible language 2.* New York, Plenum
    Press, 1980.

Spangler, K., Lipinski, H., & Plummer, R. Interactive monitoring of computer-
    based group communication. *Proceedings National Computer Conference*
    (Vol. 48). Washington: AFIPS Press, 1979.

# Towards an electronic journal

Neville Moray

*With the increasing cost of conventional publishing and libraries and the decreasing cost of electronic media, a case can be made that journals would be more cheaply and efficiently used to store and disseminate information if they were not printed but held as data bases in computers. This paper decribes some of the problems encountered in an experiment in producing an electronic journal during 1978-80. The process is certainly practical, given current technology, but certain legal problems concerning international telecommunications must be solved.*

Because of the rising cost of paper, buildings, printing, and libraries, and the falling costs of electronic equipment, information storage, and transmission, a case can be made that it would be cheaper to publish scientific journals electronically rather than by conventional means. The National Science Foundation is at present funding an experiment to evaluate the problems and advantages of such a system. This paper briefly describes what has been discovered.

A group has been formed of approximately 30 participants with a common interest in the topics covered by the broad title "mental workload." Each participant has access to a computer terminal which can be linked via the telephone system and Telenet to the New Jersey Institute of Technology Electronic Information Exchange System (EIES), a description of which appears in another paper in this volume (Baer & Turoff, 1980). Only a brief account of the features most directly related to the electronic journal will be given here.

A member wishing to submit a paper to the journal prepares it by typing it on his terminal in his Notebook, a storage space allocated to him by EIES and private to him and to those whom he admits to it. Each page of the Notebook contains roughly the amount of material which can be typed onto a standard 8 1/2"×11" page. Either upper case only or upper and lower case may be used. When the paper has been written the author may compose pages of the notebook into a single continuous message using a command SUBMIT. This allows him to concatenate pages in any order and sets up a title and abstract page. Full editing facilities are available when writing in the Notebook.

The command SUBMIT sends a message to the (human) editor of the journal in his Message space, and when he next logs on to the system he will be told that there is a message waiting for him. When he says that he wishes to see it he will be shown the title and abstract page and asked if he wishes to see the rest. The editor has the option of reading the rest of the paper and of printing it either as hard copy or as the output to a VDU, depending on his terminal.

It has been suggested that with the virtually infinite memory of computer data bases there will be no need for refereeing. Instead, all papers would be stored, and a program written to tally the number of times a paper is read and the mark for quality, perhaps on a 10 point scale, given by each reader. We believe that traditional refereeing will still be required. Otherwise an appalling amount of material would enter a system. Readers would have to read everything submitted to decide if any articles were valuable and relevant. Therefore, the filtering function of refereeing must be retained but other arrangements can easily be implemented, of course.

In order to send the paper to a referee the editor uses a RESUBMIT command which sends a message to the designated referee, which he will find when next he logs on to the system. The paper is not actually rewritten. SUBMIT and RESUBMIT merely make it more accessible. The referee, having written his comments, SUBMITs them to the editor who RESUBMITs them to the author. RESUBMIT messages appear to originate from the editor unless they are signed deliberately by the referee.

The parts of the paper which need to be changed or enlarged can be processed using the edit commands of EIES without rewriting the paper, the SUBMIT and RESUBMIT cycle being repeated as required.

When the paper is finally accepted, it is SUBMITted to a Conference, a collection of accepted papers. The first few pages of Conference comments are used as author, title, and topic indexes. Once in the Conference the paper is available to all readers.

Thus far the process is fairly conventional, except that no bound journals appear in a library. It is at this stage, however, that some exciting possibilities arise. A second set of Conference comments can be set up, to which those who have read the paper can submit material. The editor of the journal can append information about where to access reader's comments to each paper. Thus the impact of readers' criticism can be immediate, the original author can reply, and there is the possibility of an evolving body of knowledge associated with each paper. The comments can be rearranged and edited by the journal editor at any time for the convenience of readers.

The fact that publication is asynchronous should accelerate it, although a possible problem may lie in the fact that a referee would know a task awaited him only when he logged onto the system.

Costs to readers should be less than for conventional journals because there is no reason why they should not be levied per article rather than for the whole journal.

Some serious problems arise in using the EIES system to produce the journal. Some belong merely to EIES, others have more general import. A specific problem is that messages in EIES cannot be entered by block transfer. Each line of text must be typed in in real time at 300 baud and after the carriage return is executed the writer must await a prompt from the system before entering the next line. This may not be too inconvenient for teleconferencing, although it is annoying when the system is very busy, but it is devastatingly inefficient for entering long messages such as papers. Users become unwilling to spend the time necessary and it is clear that even secretarial time would be grossly wasted; whereas 300 baud is not too slow for entry at the keyboard the pause of between two and 20 or more sec between lines is found completely unacceptable. Obviously, as the cost of intelligent terminals decreases, this feature can readily be altered (and indeed other systems exist which feature block transfer), but it is clear that block transfer following local text production is absolutely essential for an electronic journal. Moreover, although telephone costs are negligible if the terminal uses an acoustic coupler and only local calls are needed to connect to the network, some subscribers will have to use long distance to reach a port and, unless fast block transfer is available at rates substantially higher than 300 baud, phone charges will be prohibitive.

A further specific problem, which again can be avoided by new terminals, is that no graphics are available in a convenient form on EIES, restricting users to tabulated data.

A more general problem is the optimal power of the commands available to the user. Clearly text editing is mandatory, and a good editor (in the sense of a computer language for editing programs) is required. But it must be kept simple and transparent. The EIES system has a very powerful menu of commands designed to cover almost any imaginable eventuality in teleconferencing. It is, in fact, too powerful, for the complexities of the user's manual are so intimidating that a number of people have found it almost impossible to overcome their timidity to get on the system. Any system for the general user should have the smallest possible set of instructions, and logging on, submitting, and logging off should be as nearly single statements as possible. Terminals and languages still need considerable development to simplify human interactions.

It is apparent that most of the above problems can either be solved simply or have already been solved on other systems. Two others are not so easy. One is that unless a user logs on to the system he will not know that there is a message for him. In refereeing long delays in handling papers might result. It is hoped that most users will fall into the habit of accessing the system daily or arrange that their secretaries do so, much as they now deal with mail.

The other problem is much more severe, and is beyond the control of those running the system. At present there exist international agreements between government and commercial telecommunication companies which restrict the passage of information between computers. These agreements date from the era of telegraphic transmission but the various authorities show a marked reluctance to give up the monopolies involved. We had intended that a dozen British users would be involved in our experimental journal but although funds had been provided by the British Library, the Post Office flatly refused permission for message transmission over Telenet and were completely obstructive about the experiment. It may be some time before such resistance is overcome and, until then, electronic journals are viable only inside certain geographical boundaries, North America, for example. Furthermore, although most people in North America will normally be within reach of a Telenet port, or whatever system may be used, for the cost of a local call, those in other countries may not. For example, in the United Kingdom all local calls, as well as long distance calls, are costed by time, not by a flat rate per month. If one is connected for an hour, even on a local call, the cost is considerable. Because the number of ports to international computer networks is very limited (in the U.K. at the time of the experiment the only Telenet port was in London), all connections would be at long distance rates and except for those living within a few miles of London, the cost of using the system would be prohibitive.

Finally, there are a large number of problems involving copyright, "copyright libraries," payments to authors, ownership of the "manuscript," and so on, all of which will have to be solved as the new technologies develop. Predominant is the question of scientific ethics. If a medium is used to publish a journal which is inaccessible in many countries because of the state of technology or telecommunications systems, that information is actually reserved to a small subset of scholars. Should that medium then be used for the dissemination of general scientific information?

Despite these problems, our own experience has been favourable. The EIES system at present is not suited for producing an electronic journal but it is possible in principle and I, for one, would welcome it as long as the funds were provided to participate!

# Human performance in computer aided writing and documentation

L. T. Frase, S. A. Keenan, and J. J. Dever

*This paper outlines problems in the design and management of technical documentation. We focus on four areas: document writers, document users, document translation, and mechanized documentation systems. Based on interviews with technical writers and translators, models of writing and translation activities are described. Stages in these activities demonstrate how computers might be used to support reading and writing in technical environments. Although we have completed detailed research and developmental activities related to the problems, our paper concentrates on providing a framework for further work rather than on offering solutions.*

Current documentation methods are challenged by increasing needs for technical information and the need to communicate that information to diverse populations. It is within the context of these challenges, and the potential use of computer systems to meet them, that this paper was written. In it we examine the problems that complex systems create for the design and management of technical documentation, concentrating on four major areas: document writers, document users, document translation, and mechanized documentation systems.

Our approach is technological. Growth in the number and complexity of technical documents has aroused concern in the military, in industry, and in government about computer ability to deliver usable documents efficiently. The problem will become more acute as the information necessary to engineer, operate, and maintain technical innovations continues to be highly complex and the level and amount of detail required to document new systems increases. In addition, readers will probably interact more with documents on-line and documentation and training will increasingly occur in a mechanized enviroment. Therefore, in this paper, we have emphasized the human engineering aspects of documentation and the ways in which computers can be used to meet documentation challenges.

Documentation comprises a complex information system. Thus it has been necessary to explore not only the elements of documentation but also the ways in which those elements affect each other, for example, how the words and sentences used by a writer influence the translation of a document into a foreign language, or how a computer-based editing-writing system might facilitate planning a documentation project. In short, our paper presents a systems perspective on documentation.

Table 1. Stages in technical documentation.

| Stage | Objective | Stimulus | Response | Data Source |
|---|---|---|---|---|
| 1 | define documentation needs | new product; specific request | conferences | system requirements; administrative guides |
| 2 | assemble relevant information | need for content | assemble sources; conferences and travel | technical staff; records |
| 3 | produce draft | scheduled writing | compose | Stages 1 and 2 |
| 4 | assess draft | completed draft | distribute; field trial | Stage 3 output |
| 5 | edit draft | Stage 4 output | revise | reviews; field data |
| 6 | produce document | scheduled production | production process | writer output |
| 7 | deliver document | production output | distribution | standing and new orders |
| 8 | update document | field comments | possibly modify document | nature of comments |

## Document writers

In this section we concentrate on the writer and on the different activities involved in documentation. Text-editing systems provide a unique resource for writers not only because they facilitate the routine activities of writing, such as editing (for instance, changing lines, checking for typographical errors), but also because they make possible immediate access to information from other writers that can support the creation of new documents. Easy access to source documents facilitates technical writing for parts of early documents can be incorporated directly into new ones.

The effective use of these new editing facilities requires additional training for writers. Furthermore, composing in disciplined ways, compatible with a planned data base, may exert unusual controls over their writing. The psychological consequences of these constraints on writers are little understood. It is a common characteristic of the projects which we have reviewed, that disciplined writing requires more time than writing done without strong data base constraints. In ordinary writing more than 70 percent of a writer's time is devoted to planning. Disciplined writing increases that time. In addition, new demands arise if writers have to produce text which is to be delivered by an interactive device. Creating response alternatives, for instance, would be a new requirement for most writers.

The following review of the stages in documentation defines, in part, what is meant by a documentation system. A variety of areas is suggested in which computer-based systems can support documentation activities. If these supports were suitably implemented, they would comprise a system extending beyond text writing, editing, and production into the realm of information exchange in general.

### Stages in technical documentation

The process of preparing a technical document entails a great deal more than putting words on paper and involves many more people than the writers. Producing a draft is only one of several stages in technical documentation. Based on interviews with telecommunication writers (Schwartz, Fisher, & Frase, Note 3), we have subdivided this process into eight stages, in six of which the writer is actively involved. Our conceptual scheme is not a model of the writer's job only but provides an overview of all phases involved in issuing a document.

The eight stages, categorized by their objectives, are: define documentation needs, assemble relevant information, produce draft, assess draft, edit draft, produce document, deliver document, and update document. These stages constitute a cycle and the last stage may require repetition of the entire cycle.

*Define documentation needs.* The need for new documentation originates concurrently with the need for and design of new equipment or other technology. Alternatively, a need might arise for reissue of an existing document owing to changes in equipment or requests for more detailed information. Writers must attend conferences of various groups to define the type and quantity of documentation needed.

*Assemble relevant information.* Once the precise needs of a project have been determined, the appropriate source information must be assembled. This stage can be time consuming if source information is not coordinated. A writer may have to travel to various places to consult with engineers and designers and to obtain the preliminary information that provides the source information for final documents. The writer must arrange to be informed of any design changes. The frequency of such changes makes writers reluctant to begin too soon because, if they do, their work will have to be revised after design changes have been made. A data base in which all relevant source documents were stored and updated would be of great value for conserving writers' time at this stage.

*Produce draft.* Using the information obtained in the previous stages, the writer begins. "Writing" includes converting the information contained in the highly technical source documents into a format compatible with both document type and users. Individual methods of producing a draft vary among writers of differing experience and ability. Further study of writing processes is necessary to determine optimal aids for writers at this stage.

*Assess draft.* Completion of the preliminary draft prompts the fourth stage, which is to distribute the document to various people qualified to comment on it: engineers, designers, and document users. Feedback both verifies technical information and evaluates relevance for the user.

      A significant problem may arise at this stage if there is a long time-lag between circulation of the draft and receipt of feedback. When production schedules are fixed, feedback must be immediate for changes to be incorporated. Yet reviews sometimes take a month. A computer system in which documents could be stored, made available for comment, and reviewed could save time.

      Current work includes the development of a variety of computer assessments for prose and procedural documents. These programs, based on pattern matching and language analysis, summarize the frequency of parts of speech, evaluate document readability, and provide other editorial comments in ordinary language.

*Edit draft.* Feedback on the first draft must be evaluated and incorporated into the document. The editing process could be aided by computer facilities. In addition to cut-and-paste operations, editing might include detecting spelling errors, measuring readability, and checking for redundancy.

*Produce document.* At this stage the document is out of the writer's hands. Although the technology for document production is highly developed, delays at this stage are common.

*Deliver document.* After a document is produced it must be delivered to users before the technology to which it pertains becomes outmoded. Documentation systems may have various distribution schemes. For instance, documents may be issued in a standard form for each category of user and distributed with the new technology. An ideal system would shape documents according to the individual needs and requests of a user and then deliver them via computer links to remote stations.

*Update document.* Writers continue to be involved with a document after production and distribution. Feedback from users often provides a basis for revision. Here again, on-line comments from users could speed document modification.

## Document users

In this section we explore human factors relevant to document use and especially how foreign users affect document design. User response is the test of any documentation system. It is difficult within one society to adapt documents to the requirements of particular users. In foreign contexts new design constraints emerge. For instance, a procedural document that requires left-to-right scanning might have to be reversed for cultures accustomed to reading right-to-left or top-to-bottom.

### Variety of users

The broad model of technical documentation outlined in the previous section implies a variety of users for text editing-writing systems: writers, editors, administrators, and others. In this section the focus is on individuals who are not technical writers in a formal sense but who are using a documentation system as a resource for their work. The following discussion implies two different classes of users of a documentation system: *immediate* and *remote*. Immediate users are those who interact directly with a documentation system, entering and retrieving data at a terminal and possibly responsible for supplying documents to other workers. Remote users are recipients of documentation products, either delivered to them in hard copy or displayed at a terminal as a result of the actions of an immediate user.

### User problems

Hiltz and Turoff (1978) cite the following common problems met in using computer system documentation. These problems reflect such features of human information processing as selective attention, constraints of previously acquired knowledge, and memory limitations, all too detailed to be included here. The most common problems are:

(1)     Users will fail to observe even the most explicit instructions.
(2)     There is no single way of describing anything that will satisfy
        every user.
(3)     Users will disregard or forget instructions.
(4)     Users will formulate opinions based on inadequate knowledge.

These problems suggest that flexible, interactive types of document systems designed to be used on-line must be simple to use, have the confidence of the user, and be introduced in a way that ensures early and frequent success. A useful review of man-machine system experiments, covering many of these issues, can be found in Parsons (1972).

*Cross-cultural differences*
Differences among specific cognitive and perceptual abilities in document design may have a cultural basis. Arends (1975), reviewing the results of selection tests in various countries, states that "there exists, at least in South American countries, a lack of experience in working with symbols, characters, and digits that influences test results." He also cites examples from leaders of training courses for repair workers in Africa and goes on to claim that spatial and abstract topics are difficult to communicate, that written materials are ineffective for communicating instructions, and that three-dimensional representations are especially difficult to comprehend. In general, it appears that cultural differences affect documentation systems primarily in the use of symbolic representational systems.

Given these differences, special steps must be taken to ensure that documents are compatible with the concepts and skills of the target population. Not all cultural differences affect the use of documents, but studies are needed to determine which differences are relevant. Furthermore, if such differences affect the success of training programs as well as job performance, then training must be adjusted to personnel whose skills and abilities differ from those for whom present documents and training are designed.

It may be that new document forms are needed. The use of flowcharts and simplified text representations has become common in our technological society. If it is true that these forms of representation, including the use of three-dimensional drawings, conflict with concepts learned in other cultures, then new forms of representation will have to be developed. Audio presentation of materials might be useful.

**Document translation**
Translation is a complex process which may be studied from various theoretical perspectives, including linguistics, ethnology, psychology, logic, philosophy, and communication theory. Technical translation shares many fundamental goals and inherent problems with other types of translation. In this section, the problems of

translating technical documents are examined. Human translation processes are discussed in terms of a general stage model and means of facilitating translation are reviewed.

*Stages in translation*

The process of translation has received little empirical study. After interviewing translators in the telecommunications area, we developed a preliminary model of translation activities. The segmentation of the model into its conceptual components suggests points at which translations might be facilitated and also provides a basis for a more complete and detailed empirical analysis.

Eight stages emerged from our analysis. These, categorized by their objectives, are: determine if a translation already exists, specify the requester's requirements, specify the text requirements, expand the translator's knowledge of the subject matter, assemble relevant aids, prepare a draft translation, obtain feedback from the requester, and produce a finished translation. These stages are described briefly below in terms of the event that triggers a translator's action, the action taken, and the data that support that action. A full summary of the events in the translation process is presented in Table 2.

*Determine availability.* An external request triggers a search through available translations to determine if the document has already been translated. The translator's knowledge of sources and the availability of library facilities determine the efficiency of the search. Freelance translators often do not have convenient library facilities. Such resources, therefore, are an unreliable or at least a potentially costly source of translation skills because considerable time may be devoted in seeking access to them. This particular stage of the process affects the translation of English documents into other languages required for new documentation. For instance, a writer might find that relevant portions of the description of a new type of equipment have already been translated into some target language. The activities of writers and translators must therefore be coordinated if previous translations are to be utilized.

*Specify request requirements.* Given that a translation does not exist, the needs of the requester are determined. In some cases a brief summary may be sufficient and can be done on the spot. Just as one might provide documents at varying levels of detail, so one might provide translations at varying levels of detail. In many cases detailed translations are required and further information must be gathered. At this stage of the translation process, however, the translator's knowledge provides the primary data.

*Specify text requirements.* Not only does the need of the requester determine the task constraints, but the nature of the document may require special actions as well. By

Table 2. Stages in the translation process.

| Stage | Objective | Stimulus | Response | Data Source |
|-------|-----------|----------|----------|-------------|
| 1 | determine availability | external request | search | library |
| 2 | specify requirements | external request | query requester | experience |
| 3 | specify requirements | external request | read text | experience |
| 4 | expand understanding | complex requirements | query requester; study texts | people; books |
| 5 | assemble aids | acceptable understanding | collect references; glossaries | library; own shelf; experience |
| 6 | produce draft | sources collected | translate | glossaries; dictionaries |
| 7 | feedback | completed draft | send to requester | draft |
| 8 | final version | requester | final edit | requester feedback |

becoming familiar with the subject matter, the translator soon determines how much work will be needed to prepare for the translation.

*Expand understanding.* Complex task requirements are a stimulus for the collection of a variety of data. The requester may be queried about the subject matter, books may be consulted to obtain a clear understanding of the area, and so forth. The purpose is to develop an appropriate vocabulary for and to facilitate comprehension of the material to be translated. The writers of documents become expert in their fields; translators must develop correspondingly appropriate knowledge of their subject matter. It may be an expensive and time-consuming task. Given that few translators have the expertise to deal with specific technical content, it might be useful to establish translation services for them.

*Assemble aids*. The next stage is to assemble the aids required for translation, including glossaries and references of various kinds. Translators external to a particular group of translators are not always available but within the group information may be exchanged. When sufficient resources have been gathered translation can begin.

If better glossaries of terms used in specific content areas were produced, they could form a base for translation glossaries. To do so would require assessment of the vocabularies of various kinds of technical documents. Because many documents are now stored in computer-readable form, the assessment could be done automatically. It would be useful if the translation aids included not only word equivalents but also synonyms, definitions, meaningful contexts, examples, and perhaps brief discussion of a word.

*Draft product*. With sufficient aids, a draft translation is produced which is usually a close approximation of the final version. Theoretical models of the procedures translators actually or should follow and what rules they should obey exist (Newmark 1974, 1976; Nida, 1975). However, the translators we interviewed were unable to verbalize the mental processes which occur when they translate a document.

*Requester feedback*. The next stage is to send the draft translation to the requester for comment. Usually the requester contributes little to the revision of the document.

*Final version*. Once the requester has had an opportunity to make comments and suggestions a clerk can polish the final document.

It is clear that translation, like writing, is a multidimensional activity involving comprehension of the subject matter as well as translation from one language to another and even some detailed editing. It is unfortunate that, in view of the growing need for it, technical translation is not supported strongly in our academic institutions. On the other hand, the expertise needed to translate technical documents may require more specific training than that offered by a general course of studies in translation.

### Facilitation of translation

There are many ways of facilitating translation. Improvements in document preparation, aids to translation, reviews to maintain quality standards, and use of a constructed or intermediate language are some of the proposals.

Careful document preparation in both writing and formatting can help to overcome some of the basic problems of translation. Brislin (1972), on the basis of several studies, drew up a list of rules for writing translatable English as follows:

(1)   Use short, simple sentences of less than 16 words.

(2)   Employ the active rather than the passive voice.

(3)   Repeat nouns instead of using pronouns.

(4)   Avoid metaphor and colloquialisms.

(5)   Avoid the subjunctive mood (could, would).

(6)   Add sentences that provide context for key ideas. Reword key phrases to create redundancy.

(7)   Use specific rather than general terms.

(8)   Avoid words indicating uncertainty about an event or thing (probably, frequently).

(9)   Use wording familiar to the translators where possible.

(10)  Avoid sentences with two different verbs if the verbs suggest different actions.

Translators cite poorly written documents as being extremely difficult if not impossible to translate.

## Mechanized documentation systems

In this section we review, from our perspective as users of computer systems, current computer documentation systems and discuss critical data base and interface problems. The treatment of computer documentation systems identifies resources that might be pursued further but our major focus is on system features relevant to human information processing.

### Current systems

A number of writing-editing computer-based systems already exist that can serve as models. These systems (or relevant companies) include the Honeywell Information System, the Raytheon Service Company, the Jet Propulsion Laboratory, United Air Lines, the TRUMP (Technical Review and Update of Manuals and Publications) system of the United States Navy, Lawrence Livermore Laboratories, and Stanford Research Institute. To our knowledge only one review of these systems exists (Berman, Note 1) and it does not evaluate them.

### User interface

We have already mentioned some factors relevant to the ways in which humans relate to a computerized document system. Hiltz and Turoff (1978) list a set of "short items of wisdom" which summarize our major points including:

(1)   The most efficient structures for computers are not necessarily efficient for users.

(2) Effectiveness of an interface design is measured by the interface.

(3) Users should not have to cope with details extraneous to their tasks.

(4) Error messages should be informative.

(5) Every designer assumes the system is easy to use.

(6) The user should be involved in the evolution of the system.

(7) Users learn best by doing—trial and error.

(8) Users should have convenient access to a system.

(9) Users who have spent years learning their jobs should not be expected to spend years learning about computers.

Guidelines exist for construction of human/machine interfaces (Engel & Granda, Note 2). Among the areas to consider are display formats, frame content, command language, recovery procedures, user entry techniques, and machine response time. *The command language is of particular importance to a computerized documentation system*. If users are to interact directly with the system and perhaps compile their own documents, that is, if they are to be immediate rather than remote users of the system, then the command language must be simple and as close to English as possible. A menu system that presents response alternatives to the user might be best for non-typist users. Menus have the additional advantage of presenting possible actions to the user and to some extent they eliminate the need to learn a special command language.

## Conclusion

Although their paper is based largely on interviews with a restricted sample of writers, technical translators, and others involved in technical documentation, it provides a tentative model for documentation, the elements of which clarify points at which human engineering and computer technology might facilitate this complex process. The goal has been to provide an outline of critical areas which require deeper analysis and empirical work, to establish a framework for further work rather than to offer solutions.

## Reference notes

1. Berman, P. I. *Survey of computer-assisted writing and editing systems*. Advisory Group for Aerospace Research and Development (AGARD), Report No. AGARD-AG-229, AGARDograph AD A045010, Neuilly-sur-Seine, France, July, 1977.

2. Engel, S. E., & Granda, R. E. Guidelines for man/display interfaces. IBM Technical Report, TR 00.2720. Poughkeepsie, N.Y., 1975.

3. Schwartz, B. J., Fisher, D. L., & Frase, L. T. *Empirical analysis of technical documents*. Paper presented at the Annual Meeting of the American Educational Research Association, New York, April 1977.

## References

Arends, G. Experience with selection tests in various countries. In A. Chapanis (Ed.), *Ethnic variables in human factors engineering*. Baltimore: The Johns Hopkins University Press, 1975.

Brislin, R. W. Translation issues: multilanguage versions and writing translatable English. *Proceedings of the 80th Annual Convention*, American Psychological Association, 1972.

Hiltz, S. R., & Turoff, M. *The network nation: human communication via computer*. Reading, Mass: Addison-Wesley Publishing Co., 1978.

Newmark, P. Further propositions on translation, Parts I & II. *The Incorporated Linguist*, 1974, *13*, 34-42;62-72.

Newmark, P. The theory and the craft of translation. *Language Teaching and Linguistics: Abstracts*, 1976, *9*, 5-26.

Nida, E. A. *Language structure and translation*. Stanford, Cal.: Stanford University Press, 1975.

Parsons, H. M. *Man machine system experiments*. Baltimore: The Johns Hopkins Press, 1972.

# Graphic technology

## Introduction

H. Bouma

At first sight, there is something contradictory in having a section on "non-textual media" in a symposium book on the processing of visible language. Visible language can be taken to refer to visible manifestations of natural language. The wider term "visual language" may then be used for all visual symbol systems, the term "symbol" indicating that meaning rests on conventions agreed among users rather than on a natural relation between visual features and meaning as such. Examples can be found in many graphical representations and in direction-finding systems.

Baecker's tutorial review covers the even wider area of all types of interfaces by which humans can communicate with logic circuitry, in both directions. Many interfaces other than displayed text and keyboards can communicate the required information and for a user-directed technology the choice between text, graphs, speech, and music as computer-output precedes any choice between various print options. Moreover, the choice is not stable over time, because advances in technology are not the same in the various media. For example, in machine speech output economic voice response units have recently become available which provide immediate access to any of a series of prerecorded utterances. The technology of automatic word recognition is probably about to advance rapidly as well.

Once problems of technology have been solved, the choices between text, speech, and text+ speech have to rest on their characteristics in human information processing. For example, text is permanent and an effective medium for deliberate selection of information (search), but it requires the user to watch the display closely. Speech is quick and volatile and offers fewer options for selection but it leaves eyes and hands free for other tasks. In the section on textual technology several user-related issues have already been mentioned.

For other information media, human characteristics are equally important, and with bold strokes, Baecker sketches the wider field to which the technology of visible language belongs.

This wider field is of immediate interest to people with certain perceptual and motor deficiencies for whom the new technology offers great promise in diminishing or compensating for their handicaps. Information may be presented adapted to the lower degree of perceptual functioning. Those with poor vision may benefit from magnified text of sufficient contrast at their optimal level of light adaptation and functional field of view. For the hard of hearing, speech should have a high signal-to-noise ratio and sometimes a higher sound level. Individual differences are substantial and control of the various parameters should be left to the user.

An alternative sense may be used as well to supply the information required. Blind persons may benefit from a Braille or other tactile display and voice response units can provide them with much of the information available to sighted persons, such as scale readings and typewriter feedback. A "reading machine for the blind" is gradually being developed. Deaf persons need displayed text which corresponds in some way to the speech that they cannot hear in television broadcasts, telephone services, or personal "conversation." People with motor handicaps can use voice commands to get machines to print the messages they cannot, and to carry out all kinds of distant actions. Through their extensive adaptability humans can compensate for their handicaps by a proper application of technology.

Clearly, the scope of the solutions is as wide as that of Baecker's tutorial paper. The two contributions on the handicapped in this section have to be considered primarily as reminders of the much wider problem of finding proper interfaces and software for the various types of handicap. Baker, Downton, and Newell describe their heroic effort to convert speeches to text on line for a deaf MP. They combine a human transcription of speech into very roughly spelled text with a clever restoration algorithm which removes many errors, the reading done by the MP compensating for the remaining difficulties. The results have much wider implications than merely as an aid for one particular handicapped person. In fact, there seems no obvious reasion why human text production should be slower than speech; perhaps the proper method or aid has simply not yet been invented. In a different field, Vincent shows that with a proper aid blind persons can produce certain drawings in geometric perspective which they themselves can feel from special relief-producing sheets. Until now, it had generally been assumed that congenitally blind persons lack the notion of perspective.

In a different domain and with a different emphasis are the contributions of Bown, O'Brien, Sawchuk, Storey and Treurniet, and by Çakir. Bown et al. are deeply involved in, not a one-way, but an interactive communication net, trying to develop for TV the informational capabilities of newspaper, reference work, and journal. Their contribution conveys both their approach to the problem and their open attitude to communication with researchers from other disciplines.

As such techniques develop, problems develop with them. Çakir reports on his extensive field investigation into problems met by operators of visual display terminals. Complaints are frequent and often involve headache, neckache, and visual strain. A number of ergonomic improvements seem mandatory and it is sad that feedback to the designers responsible has been so slow that thousands of persons suffer unnecessarily. Field trials prior to large scale introduction of new models appear indispensible.

For aids especially for the handicapped, the road from laboratory prototype via industrial prototype to available product is a difficult one. Regular channels of development for mass-produced products are found to be closed to restricted production for a scattered market: this alone is sufficient reason why so many proudly announced laboratory prototypes never become marketed products. Nevertheless, the continuous and enthusiastic effort in this area is in itself a demonstration of an essential characteristic of technology, that of serving humans.

# Human-computer interactive systems: A state-of-the-art review

Ronald Baecker

*This paper surveys the state-of-the-art in the design and implementation of human-computer interactive systems. Such systems are based on the technologies of computer processing and storage, of information display, and of interactive input to a computer. Examples of the use of display and input devices in person-machine dialogues are presented as well as examples of human-computer interactive systems that are dynamic media for human creativity and problem solving. The paper concludes with several formulations of principles for the design of user interfaces to such systems.*

Information displays of the future will be profoundly different from those of the past. Printed pages, sketches and diagrams, and photographs are *passive*—they do not respond to the reactions of their viewers. Information displays of the future will incorporate microelectronic technology, that is, computers. Computer-based information displays are *interactive*—they respond and behave in relation to the reactions of their viewers and to the modes of possible behavior with which they have been programmed.

The purpose of this paper is to survey the state-of-the-art in the design and implementation of human-computer interactive systems. Such systems are based on the technologies of computer processing and storage, of information display, and of interactive input to a computer.

I will begin with the technology of computer-based information displays and be concerned with the presentation of soft copy, rather than the production of hard copy, of displays which may consist of text, line art, or graphics, and grey scale or photographic images. Examples are included to illustrate the quality of image that may be produced with modern technology.

I will continue with a discussion of computer input devices, instruments with which those viewing computer-mediated displays can interact as part of a human-computer system to change the display. In considering both output and input we will not, as is done conventionally, restrict ourselves to visual modalities but consider as well the domains of sound, speech, touch, and music.

It must be stressed that the properties of the interaction between a computer-based information display system and a "user" are most relevant to those concerned with enhancing information display and with building the "office of the future," the "library of the future," and the "videotext system of the future." This paper presents a number of simple techniques for coupling information display technology and interactive input devices into effective mechanisms for dialogue between person and machine. Such techniques are employed in the design of human-computer interactive systems. The nature of such systems is illustrated with examples drawn from computer-aided animation, newspaper page layout, and especially musical composition. These examples show how such dialogues can enhance and alter the creativity of the person, providing a new medium for expression.

It will be argued that the construction of appropriate interactive dialogues and media for computer-aided creation is an art that is poorly understood. It requires contributions from graphic design, from the arts of dynamic presentation (including film and theatre), and from the sciences of human perception, cognition, and information processing. It is hoped that this paper will help stimulate communication and collaboration among representatives of these disciplines.

## Information display technology

The purpose of information display technology is to present information in a vivid and intelligible form to the viewer. Almost all recent work has focussed on the synthesis of visual displays. I will concentrate on this area but take a somewhat broader view.

*Fundamental concepts*

A user of a computer-based information display system requests in some manner the construction of a new image which is then presented electronically as *soft copy* on a display screen. It is called soft copy because the screen is reused repeatedly to display new images as they are produced. At certain times a *hard copy* of the contents of the screen may be requested, that is, a permanent unchangeable record on some physical medium, usually paper.

Screens which present displays have certain attributes which determine the utility and attractiveness of the displays. *Addressability* is a measure of the fineness of detail which can be presented to the display screen. *Resolution* is a measure of the fineness of detail which can be distinguished (resolved) when it appears on that screen. *Linearity* is a measure of the degree to which straight lines presented anywhere on the screen will appear straight or, more generally, the degree to which images will appear undistorted. *Repeatability*, which is usually not a problem for soft copy, is a measure of the degree to which an image written on the screen repeatedly will appear the same. *Clarity* is a measure of the readability of the display and is usually a problem not only because points presented to the display appear as fuzzy dots but also because we attempt to display text that is finer than that which the display can resolve adequately. *Brightness* of the display is an obvious consideration, particularly for viewing by a group. *Image variability* of the display includes the ability to present levels of intensity and a variety of colors. Finally, the *speed* of the display determines how quickly new images can be written onto the screen.

A fundamental distinction among soft copy displays deals with the order in which parts of the image are transmitted to the screen. A *random scan* display is one in which the image, usually limited to line art, is created by tracing it out line by line, in a connect-the-dots fashion. The alternative is that of the *raster scan* display, in which the image, which may contain shaded areas and levels of tone, is created with a picture-independent, left-to-right, top-to-bottom, scanning pattern like that of a television set.

A second distinction deals with the method of storage or regeneration of the information which produces the picture. A *storage* display keeps internally all the information required to maintain a picture on the screen. Thus the image, once generated, is maintained without any further action from the computer which transmitted the information. A *refreshed* display is one in which the picture is constantly being read and regenerated from a representation within a controlling digital memory. The memory is called a *display buffer*, the representation is called a *display file*, and the circuitry that performs the reading and image regeneration, itself a computer, is called a *display processor* (Myer, 1968).

Thus it is possible to distinguish displays according to whether they are random scan or raster scan and storage or refresh. Randon scan, refreshed devices using a cathode ray tube (CRT) allow the most dynamic form of inter-action because the picture can be changed in significant ways very rapidly. (Such devices are also known as calligraphic, line drawing, stroke writing, or vector displays.) The most common line-drawing storage device is the ubiquitous Direct View Storage Tube manufactured by Tektronix (Preiss, 1978). It significantly limits interaction style because the screen is not selectively erasable, that is, the picture can be changed only by removing it entirely (with a green flash), waiting half a second, and rewriting it totally. The only mildly successful raster scan storage device has been the Plasma Panel (Slottow, 1976), but its slow speed, limited resolution, and lack of color resulted in its recent demise at the birth of the digital video display. The digital video display system, a raster scan refresh device, will become the dominant technology for soft copy information display in the 1980s because it is relatively inexpensive, can be selectively erased, is capable of showing grey scale and color, can be given adequate resolution, and can (with effort) be made highly dynamic (Baecker, 1979).

*Digital video display systems*
A *digital video display system* is one in which the final image is displayed on a raster scan CRT (television type terminal) and there is an underlying digital representation which is stored in a controlling computer memory and from which the image is refreshed.

The raster scanning signal may but need not conform to an international TV standard which determines characteristics of the signal, such as its frame rate, the number of lines per frame, and the method of colour encoding (Pearson,

1975). The digital representation may be a *frame buffer*, in which contiguous chunks of memory (such as bits or bytes) represent contiguous *pixels* (discrete element of the final picture), or it may be an encoded representation of the picture in which case it must be transformed into video format (*scan converted*) by a video display processor on its way to the cathode-ray tube.

Digital video systems emerged in the late 1960s and came into their own in the mid-1970s as an alternative to random scan displays. Initially, digital video displays were attractive because they were clustered systems which shared expensive image generators and allowed additional workstations to be added at low incremental cost. The universality of television meant that digital video workstations based on TV monitors could take advantage of their low cost and readily available maintenance expertise. The communication of images from site to site could also be facilitated by the use of the established technology of television transmission.

Other aspects of television gave raster scan displays an advantage over random scan terminals. Lines could easily be thickened; areas could be shaded. Grey scale, colour and black-and-white reversal could be employed. The computer-generated images could easily be mixed with live television images, either still or moving.

Raster scan displays, however, have had some significant problems to overcome. Most have been limited to resolutions such as $256 \times 256$, $240 \times 320$, $512 \times 512$, or $480 \times 640$, although 1000-line resolutions are now available. Raster scan displays have been expensive because of the cost of randon access memory sufficient for a frame buffer, although progress in large scale integrated (LSI) circuitry has made this less of a problem. Raster scan displays have been slow because of the difficulty of the processing required for scan conversion, although this problem is being solved through advances in our understanding of scan conversion algorithms. There are now close to 50 manufacturers supplying digital video display terminals at costs ranging from a thousand to several tens of thousands of dollars.

*Image creation with computer graphics*
The recent widespread availability of moderately priced high quality raster scan displays has encouraged the development of sophisticated techniques for computer image creation. The most dramatic are methods that produce richly colored and textured computer-based paintings or highly realistic images of simulated three-dimensional environments. Sample images and the programming techniques used to produce them have been described elsewhere (Newman, Note 13; SIGGRAPH, 1978, 1979).

*Audio output: Sound, music, and speech*
Until now computers have displayed information only to the eyes; for various

reasons, the other senses have been ignored. For example, computers have been too slow and too expensive to allow the incorporation of sound generators in information display terminals. Touch and smell are relatively insensitive media for conveying detailed information. For vision, on the other hand, a picture could be generated at whatever speed was technologically and economically feasible, and the eye could observe the image during its formation and for as long as it could be maintained on the screen.

Recent technological advances, however, allow the cost-effective incorporation of sound, speech, and music as integral parts of an information display system. Accordingly, the three families of techniques commonly used in the computer synthesis of speech (Sherwood, 1979) will be reviewed before outlining the two most important techniques used in the computer synthesis of music (Moorer, 1977, 1978).

The oldest set of techniques is based on the analog recording of words or messages which are then retrieved and played back under computer control. The storage of entire messages gives the highest quality of any of the techniques but is the least flexible because each response must be anticipated in advance and recorded. Storing words gives greater flexibility at the cost of a significant deterioration in quality.

The second set of techniques is based on recording and encoding into compressed form digitized speech and resynthesis by a parametric synthesizer. Most designs are based on models of the human vocal tract; parameters for each sound typically include the pitch and amplitude of a periodic excitation, the formant frequencies of a simulated vocal tract, and the amplitude of a noise source. Parametric synthesizers require the storage of significantly less data than do analog recordings and are now available in a number of solid state realizations at prices ranging from a few to tens of thousands of dollars.

The most ambitious set of techniques synthesizes speech directly from character strings, either symbols from the source language itself, or symbolic representations of the fundamental sounds of that language, known as *phonemes*. Typically such devices accept strings of phonemes and a few other bits representing volume, rate, and pitch, and produce from these strings sequences of parameters which can drive a parametric synthesizer. When supported by hardware or software which can translate words to phonemes, such a synthesizer provides a speech output device of remarkable power and flexibility.

The most common set of techniques for the production of music is based on the concept of additive synthesis. The music signal is obtained by summing the outputs of a number of signal generating units, usually oscillators, each characterized by a particular waveform, amplitude (which may be time-varying), and frequency (which may also be time-varying). The well-known method of Fourier synthesis, in which the waveforms are all sinusoids whose frequencies are multiples of a particular fundamental frequency, is a special case of this technique.

A recent technique which has proved both powerful and computationally efficient is Chowning's (1977) *frequency modulation* technique. The frequency of a carrier signal is varied by a modulating signal which is itself varying at some frequency. By controlling the relationship among the carrier frequency, the modulating frequency, and the amplitude of the modulating signal, one can generate complex audio spectra corresponding to a rich set of musical sounds.

Understandably, these advances are important to the development of effective human-computer interactive systems. First, of course, because sound is everywhere. Second, sound has depth, and people can localize its source effectively. And finally, sound enriches images: consider how much more effective video games are with their pings and bleeps, how much more secure one feels with a calculator that gives acoustic feedback with each keystroke, how much richer the communication of sound is over silent films.

## Interactive input technology

For a computerized information display to be meaningful, it must respond to commands and instructions from the viewer. Many computer systems force all user input to be typed through a keyboard. Yet richer and far more expressive methods have been developed. Some of the devices that make such methods possible (Ohlson, 1978) will now be examined.

### Discrete input devices

The computer terminal keyboard is similar only superficially to a typewriter. A typewriter accepts key strokes and immediately "echoes" them as hard copy on paper. (Modern electronic typewriters relax this restriction.) In a computer terminal the keystrokes are input to the computer and are echoed back to the terminal by the computer. This means that keys may assume different functions at different times, and keystrokes may be echoed in different ways. For example, in some systems the first few characters of a word are recognized and the remainder is completed automatically.

The purpose of keystrokes is twofold. First of all, the user is signalling to the computer, "Do it *now*. Begin." The action signalled usually consists of a command that has been typed, with some *arguments*, or *parameters*, of the command. If there is only a small set of command alternatives, then typing is cumbersome and prone to error. A variety of devices are more appropriate for such input.

Perhaps the most common is a set of *function keys*, a miniature keyboard which usually consists of a small (typically, $3 \times 5$ or $4 \times 6$) rectangular array of keys on a pad. The keys may be named permanently, or they may be named with plastic overlays which can be changed so that the keys can assume different functions at different times. If the keys contain no *state* information, depressing them simply activates a function; if they do contain state information, depressing them changes some parameter from "on" to "off" or vice versa. Keys that manipulate state information are best implemented with lights inside them so the user can tell at a glance the value of the parameter.

Other devices in less common use serve similar functions. Push buttons are similar to keys on a keypad in that they may either activate functions or set state variables. Toggle switches or rotary switches are most naturally suited for setting state variables; foot pedals are best suited for activating functions.

### Continuous input devices

Often we want to input a number or select a position along a continuum rather than choose from among a discrete set of alternatives. A variety of devices allow us to do this in either one or two dimensions.

The simplest such device is known as a *shaft-angle encoder*, or simply a knob. Rotating it turns a potentiometer, whose value is sampled and fed to the computer; in effect we are dialing the value we desire. An alternative is known as a *slider* (developed by Guy Fedorkow in our laboratory from a mechanism produced by Allison Research) which is a continuous belt of clear plastic ruled with opaque black markings at short intervals. When it is moved, the black markings pass over a tiny light source and photocell. Reflections from the markings entering the photocell produce pulses which are amplified and provide a measure of the motion of the plastic relative to its housing. The slider is thus a *motion-sensitive* instrument, whereas the knob is a *position-sensitive* instrument.

Users of interactive systems often need to point to something on the screen. To do so requires specifying a point along the $x$ axis and a point along the $y$ axis. The simplest method is to use two shaft-angle encoders, usually mounted perpendicularly as a pair of *thumb wheels*. A more common method is to use a lever known as a *joy stick* which can be pushed front to back and side to side. Yet another technique is to use a ball, called a *track ball*, which is set in a housing capable of turning in two dimensions.

### Drawing devices

Some devices capable of continuous two-dimensional input can be used for sketching or drawing. The earliest such device is known as the *light pen*. It contains a photocell which is activated by a pulse from a point on the screen. When the computer receives the pulse, it determines that the user is pointing at the portion of the screen being refreshed at that instant. By tracking or following a special image known as a *tracking cross*, the user can input rough sketches into the machine.

A more recent invention, originally developed at Stanford Research Institute, is known as the *mouse*. It is a small device on the bottom of which are mounted two wheels with shaft-angle encoders mounted perpendicularly. When the mouse is placed on a surface and rolled, the motion of the wheels is transmitted to the computer. The mouse is thus a motion-sensitive device. One of its advantages is that it can be used on many surfaces including cluttered desks and books.

The best of the drawing devices is the *tablet*. Although there are a variety of different realizations based on different physical principles, all share a common logical structure. The surface of the tablet, which may range in size from 11 × 11 in to 36× 48 in or even larger, is ruled typically at 100 lines to the inch. Signals propagating in the surface of the tablet are coded in such a way that a receiver above the surface will pick up a signal, indicating where it is located. The receiver is usually contained in the tip of a *stylus* or in a flat puck often known as a *cursor*. Tablets can be used for pointing and sketching, or even for tracing because the signals can usually be detected through thin sheets of paper.

*Touch sensitive displays and panels*
The use of the finger as a pointing device has a number of advantages over a stylus or a cursor, being cheap, not connected to the computer, and lifting it is natural and requires no learning. Furthermore, one typically has ten.

A number of methods have been devised to allow using the finger as an input device. The *touch-sensitive display* contains a mechanism like an electric eye in the surface of the display which senses where the finger is pointing by means of an array of light sources and photocells, or by detecting reflections of ultrasonic waves from the finger transmitted along the surface. A number of *touch pads* have also been constructed, small horizontally mounted tablets designed to sense motions of the finger. Areas for research include the detection of pressure, orientation, and torque (Herot, 1978); the more accurate measurement of finger positions and the sensing of multiple finger positions simultaneously.

*Speech input technology*
The voice too can be used as an input device. Active research on automatic recognition of human speech over the past decade has led to a number of devices now in day-to-day use. These devices are capable of being trained to recognize with perhaps 98 or 99 percent accuracy a very limited vocabulary of a single individual. Such performance is often adequate where the recognized word can be echoed by the computer and corrected if wrong.

*Input via other parts of the body*
Other parts of the body have been proposed as input devices for interactive computer systems. The prime use of such techniques would be by handicapped people. One example is automatic tracking of eye movements; another is the use of mechanisms capable of harnessing movements or twitches from almost any point of the body. There is even current interest in the use of body harnesses or total body sensors.

## Interactive techniques using a refreshed display and a tablet

Display technology and input technology can be coupled into a dialogue between human and machine as in a system with a refreshed display and a tablet. Figure 1 depicts such a system, one which also includes a keyboard, switches, and sliders for input.

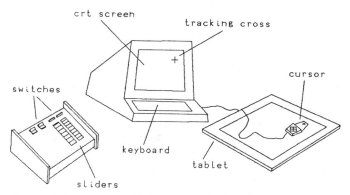

Figure 1. A system combining a refreshed display and a tablet.

  The user moves a stylus or cursor on the tablet, but the user must keep his or her attention on the display screen. To accomplish this, a tracking symbol, or visual cursor, is displayed in precise synchronization with the hand movement. It takes only a few minutes for a new user to develop the hand-eye coordination to point or sketch as desired without looking at his or her hand.

*Tracking and dragging*

For historical reasons, based on the technology of the light pen, the tracking symbol in common use has been a cross. Lately we have begun to use multiple tracking symbols, designing them to have iconic significance and alternating them as a means of conveying information to the user. In our laboratory we conventionally use a thumbs-down or question-mark symbol to indicate that the user has done something illegal, a keyboard symbol to indicate that typing is expected, a symbol consisting of a series of notes to indicate that the synthesizer is about to play some music, and a smiling-Buddha symbol to encourage patience on the part of the user.

  Tracking symbols are not the only pictures that can be moved across the screen of refreshed displays. Arbitrary pictures can be dragged across the screen and repositioned within the image as a whole. This can be done without *constraints*, so that motion anywhere is legal, or with constraints, so that, for example, the picture does not go off the screen or overlap some other picture.

*Light buttons and paint pots*

Another common technique in systems using tablets is to display an array of command names in some portion of the screen. Pointing at one of these names is then interpreted as a signal to carry out the associated command. Because of the similarity of this technique to the use of a function box or button box, these command names are known as *light buttons*.

Typically one activates a command with a light button and then inputs the arguments, or parameters, required to complete the command. For example, one could designate the "Delete Component" command in a computer-aided circuit design system and then point to the component which is to be removed. There is, however, another way of accomplishing the same task, based on the metaphor of "painting" recently developed in digital color video systems for creating images. In such systems, the user is presented with a palette of colors and a palette of "brushes" from which to choose. By "dipping" the pen into a particular "pot" of paint, and dabbing it onto a particular brush, the pen takes on the qualities of that brush and that color of paint. When the user begins to sketch, he or she deposits that paint on the "canvas" with a style of line that depends upon the chosen brush.

If we generalize the concept of the paint pot to allow the stylus to take on any abstract quality, then we can apply that quality to multiple pictures in the image by dabbing them in turn with the stylus. Thus, we can make the stylus into an eraser which removes every picture it touches, or into a squaring-off instrument which makes every line it touches horizontal or vertical, or into a resistor drawing instrument which deposits a resistor on a circuit diagram every time a button is depressed.

*The trainable character recognizer*

A more formal view of light buttons and paint pots is in terms of sequences of command names and command arguments. With the light button, we first specify which command is to be executed and then which picture or part of a picture is to be the argument of the command. With the paint pot, we specify a command which changes the mode of behavior of the pen and then wield the pen in that mode until we change its mode again. With both techniques, it takes separate actions to specify *what* is to be changed and *how* it is to be changed. These specifications can be combined into a single action through the use of a *trainable character recognizer*.

To delete a circuit symbol by using the character recognition technique, we would sketch a symbol representing "delete" on top of the symbol to be deleted. The computer would recognize the symbol's meaning and would know which symbol was to be deleted by comparing the position of the sketch to the position of every circuit symbol. Thus a single action has indicated both the command and its argument.

The problem with the character recognition technique is that the computer must be trained to recognize the handwriting of the user, and the user must employ the same style of handwriting consistently. Furthermore, the recognition algorithm must operate not only accurately but rapidly as well.

## Interactive dialogues and systems

There are a number of technologies, the digital video display system dominant among them, for presenting information through a computer to a viewer and an even greater variety of technologies that allow the viewer to initiate, control, and mediate this information display through direct input to the computer system. These technologies are important to students of visible language because they let us construct human-computer interactive systems that enable us to be more creative across a great variety of areas and disciplines. Some concrete examples illustrate this point.

### Some sample interactive systems

Late in 1966, I began work on the use of interactive computer graphics in the production of animated movies. I built a system named GENESYS which allowed a computer-naïve animator to sketch crude outline static images called *cels* and to sketch and mimic movements, or *motion descriptions*, into the computer (Baecker, Note 1, 1969, 1974; Baecker, Smith, & Martin, Note 2). GENESYS applied the motions to the images to produce and immediately display a movie on a CRT. The animator could explore with speed and fluidity alternative realizations of his or her ideas about movement. In a later system called SHAZAM (Baecker, 1976), developed as part of the Xerox Dynabook project, I showed how the same ideas could be applied to images with shading and tone on a digital video display.

In 1975, Tilbrook (Note 17) began to apply interactive computer graphics to the process of newspaper page layout. Page layout is a design problem very different from animation, requiring decisions based on quantitative measures of the fit of text or graphics to allocated space, and also on qualitative judgments about the attractiveness and impact of these decisions. With his NEWSWHOLE system Tilbrook demonstrated the feasibility of rapid and responsive editorial page makeup using a CRT, cursor, and tablet (Tilbrook, Note 17; Baecker, Tilbrook, Tuori, & McFarland, Note 3). With only a few strokes one could reconfigure the stories, pictures, and ads on a page; the electronic dummy was shown to be vastly different from the paper dummy of old.

Since 1977 an interdisciplinary project known as the Structured Sound Synthesiss Project (SSSP) (Buxton, Note 1; Buxton & Fedorkow, Note 7; Buxton, Fedorkow, Baecker, Reeves, Smith, Ciamaga, & Mezei, Note 8) has been under way. Its purpose is to conduct research into the problems and benefits arising from the use of computers in musical composition and performance. The research consists of the investigation of new representations of musical data and process

(Buxton, Reeves, Baecker, & Mezei, 1978) and the study of human-machine communication as it relates to music. A computerized environment which could be termed a "composer's assistant" has been developed which includes a powerful and flexible digital sound synthesizer (Buxton, Fogels, Fedorkow, Sasaki, & Smith, 1978) and a variety of congenial interactive graphic interfaces to allow its use in composition and performance (Reeves, Buxton, Pike, & Baecker, Note 14; Baecker, Buxton, & Reeves, 1979; Buxton, Reeves, Fedorkow, Smith, & Baecker, 1979).

*Snapshots from some sample interactive dialogues*
Some examples of the kind of interactive dialogue provided by these systems and, specifically, the interactive graphics system developed by the SSSP for the input and editing of musical scores (Reeves, et al., Note 14; Baecker, et al., 1979; Buxton, et al., 1979) are illustrated below.

Figure 2. A snapshot from the musical score editor.

Figure 2 is a snapshot from the most recent version of the musical score editor. The score being worked on is depicted in conventional music notation on the screen. Below the score are some light buttons, which are used to command the system, and some status displays which tell the user about the state of the system. Above the score is a thick bar, which can be read as signifying that the first 40 percent of the score is currently visible on the screen. The user can drag, stretch, or shrink this bar by means of gestures with the cursor or stylus and thereby navigate through a lengthy score.

A score can be represented to the composer in different ways at different times. Figure 3 is a snapshot which shows a portion of the same score depicted in some of the many different representations available through the system. The

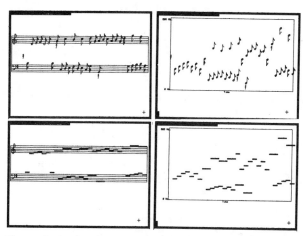

Figure 3. A snapshot showing four representations of the same score.

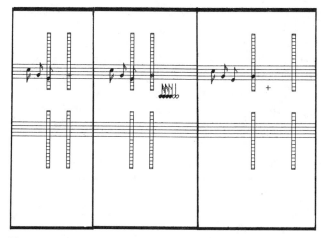

Figure 4. One of the tools for the input of notes

notes are drawn with conventional music notation or in "piano-roll" form; they are drawn on a conventional staff or in a pure frequency-time space. The user can change representations at the flick of a light button.

Figure 4 shows one of the many tools for the input of notes with which we have experimented. Two ladders are displayed to indicate allowable positions for a new note. Use of the ladder on the left would turn the most recently entered note into a chord. Use of the ladder on the right allows entry of a note to follow the last note directly. The composer first places the tracking symbol (shown as a cross) over the desired note g4. When he pushes a button on the cursor, a "marker" note appears over g4 (center panel), and the tracking symbol becomes a series of notes. He then places the quarter-note symbol over the "marker" note, and pushes a button on the cursor, causing the quarter-note g4 to be entered. Notice that the original tracking cross is restored.

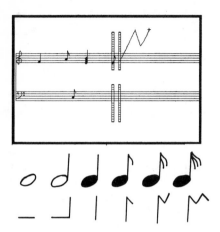

Figure 5. Another method of note entry.

Figure 5 shows another method using a trainable character recognizer. The composer draws the jagged three-line symbol directly over the score. The symbol indicates the desired duration of the note (in this case, a sixteenth-note) according to the correspondences shown at the bottom of the figure. The starting position of the first line indicates the desired note, in this case, g4, and the desired relationship to the last note, in this case, starting a new note.

Figure 6 shows another use of freehand sketching as an input tool. The composer is trying to specify the scope (or set of notes) to which some later operation (such as orchestration) will be applied. He draws two closed curves

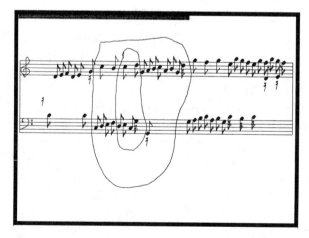

Figure 6. Use of freehand sketching as an input tool.

around a part of the score which signify that he wants later operations to be
applied to all notes inside the outer curve but outside the inner curve.

*Implications*
The above systems and dialogues have been chosen from among many that would
have illustrated recent achievements in the design and implementation of
human-computer interactive systems. A number of important features characterize all such systems:

1. Human-computer interactive systems are new media for creative expression
   offering new styles and possibilities in addition to the automation of
   routine functions.

2. Critical to the success of each system is the appropriate design of what Newman
   and Sproull (1979) have termed the *user's model*, "the conceptual model
   formed by the user of the information he manipulates and of the procedures he applies to this information" (p. 445). The user's model underlying GENESYS consisted of cels and motion descriptions which could be
   defined and manipulated in various ways. The user's model underlying
   NEWSWHOLE consisted of rectangular regions of the page which could
   be manipulated in various ways in relation to the newspaper items that
   were to fill those regions, to certain vertical lines on the page known as
   column rules, and to each other. The user's model underlying the SSSP
   system views musical composition as consisting of four main subtasks:
   *musical object definition*, which is analogous to the choosing of instruments;
   *score definition*; *orchestration* of the score using the repertoire of musical
   objects; and *performance* of the composition.

3. The information manipulated by the user in an interactive computer system
   consists as we have seen of families of objects: cels, motion descriptions,
   and movies; stories, pictures, and pages; musical objects, scores, and
   compositions. These entities all have *internal structure*. They do not consist merely of the lines and character strings with which they are drawn
   on the screen. In fact, their pictures are but one external manifestation of
   their structure. Thus, movies (pages, compositions) in GENESYS
   (NEWSWHOLE, the SSSP) consist of cels and motion descriptions
   (stories and pictures, musical objects and scores) linked together in
   various ways by internal relationships, associations, and hierarchies.

4. The structure of the information manipulated by the user can be made visible in
   various ways. New means of graphical representation are developed to
   reflect in an external tangible form the relationships, associations, and
   hierarchies which characterize the entities internally. These entities and
   their internal structure can be viewed in terms of different *levels of
   representation*. Means can be provided for displaying these levels and for
   moving from display to display.

5. Finally, in some recent human-computer interactive systems, such as SHAZAM
   and others implemented in the Smalltalk language (Goldberg & Kay,
   Note 9), objects not only have internal structure but also are represented
   and can be viewed as *active processes* capable of behavior in response to
   messages from the user and from other entities. In such a formalism,
   each movie, page, or composition has certain modes of behavior which it
   exhibits in response to these messages. Entities may be created or destroyed at any time; they are viewed anthropomorphically as being
   capable of responses and patterns of interaction as sophisticated as can be
   programmed into them by their creators. Such formalisms, known gen-
   erically as *object-oriented* or *actor* formalisms, provide a rich avenue for
   current and future explorations.

## The design of interactive dialogues and systems

No one knows how we design good interactive dialogues and systems. It is an art
form. Our current understanding (or lack thereof) can be summarized by quoting
three articulate and cogent, yet nonetheless inadequate, recent formulations.
Foley and Wallace (1974) specified that:

> A designer of conversational graphics systems should be concerned with:
> guaranteeing *complete* and *efficient* discourse, reducing the psychological
> distance by avoiding unnecessary *trauma*, improving the naturalness of
> the discourse by imposing syntactic regularity on the action language
> (notably, *sentence structuring* and *continuity*), using the *logical equivalences*
> among action devices to exploit their *psychological differences*, and choos-
> ing *implementation* of action language constructs to suit the context. (p.
> 462)

Newman (Note 13) suggested that interactive user interfaces require four components:

1. A *user's model*, i.e. the user's conceptual model of the information he
   manipulates and of the processes he applies to this information;
2. A *command language* in which the user expresses his commands to
   the program;
3. *Feedback* provided by the computer to assist the user in operating
   the program;
4. *Information display* showing the user the state of the information he
   is manipulating.

Thus we can use the set of four components as a "check-list" against
which to test the user interface. We can ask ourselves whether the user's
model is complex and consistent; whether the command language is

simple and convenient; whether feedback provides adequate confirmation to the user's commands; and whether information is clearly displayed.

My colleagues and I (Baecker et al., 1979) have suggested a number of principles which seem to apply to the design of good interactive dialogues:

1.  The nomenclature used is oriented towards and appropriate for the application.
2.  The techniques are refined through careful observation of their use by real users, that is, the intended users of the ultimate system.
3.  Screen layouts are very carefully designed and refined.
4.  A small but effective set of input transducers is used. Too many can lead to wasted actions; too few can lead to cumbersome interactions.
5.  The techniques are natural, easy to learn, not cumbersome.
6.  The feedback given in response to user input is iconic and is appropriate for the task at hand.
7.  The feedback occurs rapidly. One must use different techniques if the system cannot respond instantaneously to user input.
8.  The feedback occurs predictably. Unpredictable response is even worse than predictably slow response, leading to frustration, tension, and anxiety.
9.  The technique implemented is a powerful one, giving the user many degrees of freedom and control.
10. The technique allows the user to focus his attention, avoiding wasted hand and eye movements.
11. The proper visual ground or context is presented.
12. It is easy to escape from or abort the action.
13. It is difficult to make mistakes, and the system is robust enough to minimize the damage from mistakes that are made.
14. As few demands as possible are made on the user's memory.
15. The various techniques embedded in the system share a unity of protocol—a common syntax, set of visual conventions, and interactive style. This, along with some of the other characteristics listed above, allows the user to focus on the applications, not the communication.

## Historical review and notes

I include a brief review of some of the landmark achievements in the conception, design, and implementation of human-computer interactive systems. A more detailed technical presentation of some of this material may be found in Newman and Sproull (1979) and Booth (Note 5). Further discussions of human-computer interaction may be found in Martin (1973), Foley (1974), Nickerson (cited in Treu, 1976), Treu (1976), Baecker (Note 4), and Seillac (Note 15).

In a remarkably prescient paper Bush (1945) envisioned how a computer-based system that he termed the Memex could augment the information handling and processing capabilities of a scholar. As computer technology progressed through the next 15 years, there was little direct progress towards the construction of a Memex. However, a vision of the potentialities of "man-computer symbiosis," and some of the first steps towards its realization, were described by Licklider (1960, 1962).

The first vivid realization and demonstration of these ideas was carried out by Sutherland (Note 16, 1963). The SKETCHPAD system showed dramatically how graphics with a computer was different from graphics with pencil and paper. At the same time, there were equally impressive demonstrations of the potentialities of computer-aided design (Ross and Rodriguez, 1963) and of interactive computing (Shaw, 1964).

The possibilities of the MEMEX were revived in the work of Engelbart (1968) and Nelson (Note 12). Both were concerned with the processes of document creation and the enhancement of intellect in scholarly pursuits. Whereas Nelson's dream is primarily that of individual worlds for flights of fancy and · exploration, however, Engelbart is more concerned with improving cooperative creativity and problem solving.

In terms of both far-reaching vision and significant technical achievement, the landmark work of the 1970s has been carried out by Kay (Note 10; Learning Research Group, Note 11) and Negroponte (1970, 1975). Kay has pursued his vision of a personal computer for "children of all ages," striving to build a device that is portable and that interacts with its user through a variety of sensory modalities. Negroponte has stressed that interactive computer systems should behave intelligently in response to the working habits and cognitive styles of their users, a goal that we are still striving to achieve.

## Reference notes

1. Baecker, R. M. *Interactive computer-mediated animation* Project MAC Tech. Rep. 61, Massachusetts Institute of Technology, 1969.
2. Baecker, R. M., Smith, L., & Martin E. GENESYS: An interactive computer-mediated animation system. 16 mm color sound film, Lexington, Mass.: MIT Lincoln Laboratory, 1970.

3. Baecker, R. M., Tilbrook, D. M., Tuori, M. I., & McFarland, D. NEWSWHOLE. 3/4 in black-and-white sound video cartridge, University of Toronto, Dynamic Graphics Project, Computer Systems Research Group, 1976.

4. Baecker, R. M. *Towards an effective characterization of graphical interaction*. Paper presented at the IFIP W. G. 5.2 Workshop on the Methodology of Interaction. Seillac, France, May 1979.

5. Booth, K. S. (Ed). *Tutorial: Computer graphics*, IEEE Computer Society, 1979.

6. Buxton, W. A. S. *Design issues in the foundation of a computer-based tool for music composition*. (Tech. Rep. CSRG-97). Toronto: University of Toronto Computer Systems Research Group, 1978.

7. Buxton, W. A. S., & Fedorkow, G. *The structured sound synthesis project (SSSP): An introduction* (Tech. Rep. CSRG-92). Toronto: University of Toronto, Computer Systems Research Group, 1978.

8. Buxton, W., Fedorkow, G., Baecker, R., Reeves, W., Smith, K. C., Ciamaga, G., & Mezei, L. *An overview of the structured sound synthesis project*. Paper presented at the Third International Conference on Computer Music, Northwestern University, Evanston, Illinois, 1978.

9. Goldberg, A., & Kay, A. (Eds.). *Smalltalk-72 instruction manual*, Xerox Palo Alto Research Center Rep. SSL 76-6, 1976.

10. Kay, A. Presentation at the First Annual Conference on Computer Graphics and Interactive Techniques, Boulder, Colorado, July 1974.

11. Learning Research Group. *Personal dynamic media*. Xerox Palo Alto Research Center Report SSL 76-1, 1976.

12. Nelson, T. H. *Computer lib/dream machines*. South Bend, Indiana: The Distributors, 1976.

13. Newman, W. M. Some notes on user interface design. Paper presented at the IFIP W. G. 5.2 Workshop on the Methodology of Interaction. Seillac, France, May 1979.

14. Reeves, W., Buxton, W., Pike, R., & Baecker, R. *Ludwig: An example of interactive computer graphics in a score editor*. Paper presented at the Third International Conference on Computer Music, Northwestern University, Evanston, Illinois, 1978.

15. Seillac II Workshop on Man-Machine Interaction Position Papers, Stichting Mathematisch Centrum, Amsterdam, January 1979.

16. Sutherland, I. E., SKETCHPAD: A man-machine graphical communication system (Tech. Rep. 296). Cambridge, Mass.: MIT Lincoln Laboratory, May 1963.

17. Tilbrook, D. A newspaper pagination system. Unpublished manuscript, Department of Computer Science, University of Toronto, 1977.

## References

Baecker, R. M., Picture-driven animation. *Proceeding of the Spring Joint Computer Conference*, 1969, *34*, 273-288.

Baecker, R. M. GENESYS—Interactive computer-mediated animation. In J. Halas (Ed.), *Computer animation*. New York: Hastings House, 1974.

Baecker, R. M. A conversational extensible system for the animation of shaded images. *Computer Graphics*, 1976, *10*, 32-39.

Baecker, R. M. Digital video display systems and dynamic graphics. *Computer Graphics*, 1979, *13*(2), 48-56.

Baecker, M., Buxton, W. A. S., & Reeves, W. Towards facilitating graphical interaction: Some examples from computer-aided musical composition. *Proceedings of the Sixth Man-Computer Communications Conference*, Ottawa, 1979.

Bush, V. As we may think. *Atlantic Monthly*, 1945, *176*(7), 101-108.

Buxton, W., Fogels, A., Fedorkow, G., Sasaki, L., & Smith, K. C. An introduction to the SSSP digital synthesizer. *The Computer Music Journal*, 1978, *2*(4), 28-38.

Buxton, W., Reeves, W., Baecker, R. M., & Mezei, L. The use of hierarchy and instance in a data structure for computer music. *The Computer Music Journal*, 1978, *2*(4), 10-20.

Buxton, W., Reeves, W., Fedorkow, G., Smith, K. C., & Baecker, R. M. A computer-based system for the performance of electroacoustic music. *Audio Engineering Society Preprints*, November 1979.

Chowning, J. M. The synthesis of complex audio spectra by means of frequency modulation. *Journal of the Audio Engineering Society*, 1973, *21*(7), also appears in *Computer Music Journal*, 1977, *1*(2), 46-54.

Engelbart, D. C., & English, W. K. A research center for augmenting human intellect. *Proceedings of the Fall Joint Computer Conference*. Washington, D.C.: Thompson Books, 1968.

Foley, J. D., & Wallace, V. L., The art of natural graphic man-machine conversation. *Proceedings of the IEEE*, 1974, *62*(4), 462-471.

Herot, C., & Weinzapfel, G. One-point touch input of vector information for computer displays. *Computer Graphics*, 1978, *12*(3), 210-216.

Licklider, J. C. R. Man-computer symbiosis. *Transactions of the IRE*, Vol. HFE-1, 1960.

Licklider, J. C. R., & Clark, W. E. On-line man-computer communication. *Proceedings of the Spring Joint Computer Conference*, National Press, 1962.

Martin, J. *Design of man-computer dialogues*. New York: Prentice-Hall, 1973.

Moorer, J. A. Signal processing aspects of computer music—A survey. *The Computer Music Journal*, 1977, *1*, 4-37.

Moorer, J. A. How does a computer make music? *The Computer Music Journal*, 1978, *2*, 32-37.

Myer, T. H., & Sutherland, I. E., On the design of display processors. *Communications of the ACM*, 1968, *11*(6), 410-416.

Negroponte, N. *The architecture machine*. Cambridge, Mass.: MIT Press, 1970.

Negroponte, N. *Soft architecture machines*. Cambridge, Mass.: MIT Press, 1975.

Newman, W. M., & Sproull, R. F. *Principles of interactive computer graphics* (2nd ed.). New York: McGraw-Hill, 1979.

Ohlson, M. System design considerations for graphics input devices. *Computer*, 1978, *11*(11), 9-18.

Pearson, D. E. *Transmission and display of pictorial information*. New York: Halsted Press, 1975.

Preiss, B. *Storage CRT display terminals: Evolution and trends. Computer*, 1978, *11*(11), 20-26.

Ross, D. T., & Rodriguez, J. E. Theoretical foundations for the computer-aided design system, *Proceedings of the Spring Joint Computer Conference*. Baltimore, Md.: Spartan Books, 1963.

Shaw, J. C. JOSS: A designer's view of an experimental on-line computing system, *Proceedings of the Fall Joint Computer Conference*. Baltimore Md.: Spartan Books, 1964.

Sherwood, Bruce A. The computer speaks. *IEEE Spectrum*, 1979, *16*, 18-25.

SIGGRAPH-ACM, *Computer graphics*. Quarterly Report of the Special Interest Group on Graphics of the Association for Computing Machinery, 1978, *12*, (3).

SIGGRAPH-ACM, *Computer graphics*. Quarterly Report of the Special Interest Group on Graphics of the Association for Computing Machinery, 1979, *13*, (2).

Slottow, H. G. Plasma displays. *IEEE Transactions on Electronic Devices*, 1976, ED-23, *No* (7).

Sutherland, I. E., SKETCHPAD: A man-machine graphical communication system. *Proceedings of the Spring Joint Computer Conference*. Baltimore, Md.: Spartan Books, 1963.

Sutherland, I. E., Computer inputs and outputs. *Scientific American*, 1966, *215*(3), 86-96.

Sutherland, I. E., Computer displays. *Scientific American* 1970, *222*(6), 56-81.

Treu, S. (Ed.). User-oriented design of interactive graphics systems. *Proceedings of the ACM/SIGGRAPH Workshop*, Pittsburgh, Pa., October 1976.

# Simultaneous speech transcription and TV captions for the deaf

Robert G. Baker, Andrew C. Downton, and Alan F. Newell

*This paper is concerned with two related areas of research; one is the development of a portable speech transcription system for those whose hearing is impaired. A pilot study of the readability of the system's output is reported. The second part of the paper deals with the application of this system within a television subtitling service and outlines some of the broader problems of subtitling television. An experiment comparing two styles of subtitle text is described.*

There is a clear need for a visual communication aid for the hearing-impaired in certain circumstances where conventional communication strategies are inefficient or inappropriate. Table 1 illustrates the main receptive communication skills employed by the hearing-impaired. As can be seen, it is necessary to make a clear distinction between people who suffer hearing loss before the acquisition of language, the prelingually deaf, and those whose hearing has been lost at a later stage, the postlingually deaf. There are a number of situations in which mixed groups of hearing-impaired and people with normal hearing may wish to participate: in particular, lectures, conferences, and meetings. In such cases, sign language is rarely used because of its continuing low social status and the few people with normal hearing who use sign language. Furthermore, the already limited usefulness of lipreading skills and residual hearing will be further restricted by the presence of several speakers. The Southampton University Speech Transcription System, designed to provide a written display of speech, was developed initially for the postlingually deaf and, in particular, for the person who, because of illness or accident, loses his or her hearing in mid-career. The resulting occupational and social disability can be dramatic and traumatic. An aid was designed to allow such people to resume work by providing a simultaneous visual display of spoken English.

Although automatic machine recognition of speech would clearly be desirable in such a visual aid, a review of the literature (Underwood, 1977) indicates that, at least in the foreseeable future, there is little chance of speech recognition machines being used in this way. The system was, therefore, based on a human operator of a mechanical shorthand machine known as the Palantype machine. This device, used in the United Kingdom for transcribing law-court proceedings, and analogous to the American Stenograph machine, can be operated at speeds up to about 200 words per minute, and can thus adequately cover the normal range of human speech rates. The Palantype machine has 29 keys which are pressed in combinations to produce "chords," each chord representing a spoken syllable. Syllables are coded in a phonetic form based on arbitrary and semi-arbitrary conventions justified by operator experience. Because there are

Table 1. Receptive communications skills of the hearing-impaired.

|  | Sign Language | Lipreading and Use of Residual Hearing | Reading |
|---|---|---|---|
| Prelingually deaf | Common: often first language | Less useful because hearing lost before attainment of normal language skills | Generally low level of literacy |
| Postlingually deaf | Rare: always second language | More useful | Normal range of literacy |

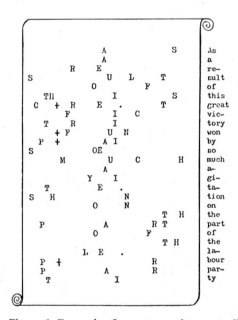

Figure 1. Example of unprocessed paper-roll output from a Palantype machine.

more English speech sounds than there are keys on the keyboard, some individual sounds are produced by key-combinations, P+ = B, for example.

The raw output of the machine (Figure 1) is not immediately readable except by the operator. It is, therefore, connected to a microprocessor system which carries out a number of translation processes on the coded "chords." The complete system is shown in schematic form in Figure 2. Each Palantyped syllable is stored on input as four 8-bit words. Syllables are then passed on to a small dictionary where words are recognised by longest match algorithms. For reasons of portability, the dictionary is kept as small as possible. The current system uses approximately 1200 English words plus their Palantype translations and requires 20 kilobytes of store. In fact, statistical studies have shown that the most frequent 1200 words will account for at least 80 percent of normal English discourse (French, Carter, & Koenig, 1930).

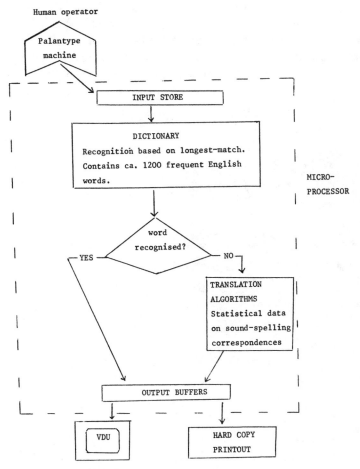

Figure 2. Southampton University Speech Transcription System.

Syllables which are not matched in the dictionary are processed by a set of sound-spelling correspondence algorithms which use statistical frequency data to provide the most probable spelling representation for each phonetic syllable.

Thus the chord TAIP will be transformed into TIPE. The output of these two processes is converted to ASCII code characters, formatted, and displayed on a visual display unit, or VDU, or printed out as a permanent record. Figure 3 shows what is virtually a simultaneous display of speech as it is being spoken. It can be seen that approximately 70 percent of the words are spelt correctly and the greater part of the remainder is in recognisable semi-phonetic form. The high speed of operation necessary for conversational speech rates results in a significant number (5 to 15 percent) of operator keying errors. Improvements in keyboard design are reducing this rate, however. It would be possible to reduce it still further, at the expense of increased computing capacity, by coding common keying errors into the dictionary or the sound spelling algorithms. Another source of error occurs when a word is incorrectly recognised by the dictionary. Such errors are of two types: homophones, for example, SEEM for SEAM, and incorrect longest matches, for example, THERE MUST BEFORE for THERE MUST BE FOUR. Such errors occur rarely (3 or 4 percent of the output at most). The majority of these types of errors and the operator keying errors can be resolved by the reader making normal use of contextual information, however.

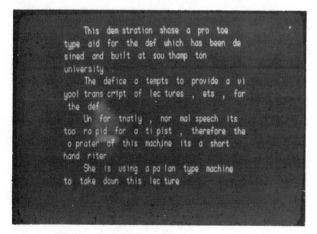

Figure 3. VDU screen showing output of Southampton University Speech Transcription System (processed Palantype).

Such statements must be supported by objective evidence. The basic system is undergoing two long-term field trials. The first, using a less advanced version of the equipment based solely on sound-spelling correspondence algorithms, has been running for three years. The user, a British Member of Parliament who became profoundly deaf several years before the equipment was made available, states that it took him 20 hours to learn to read the output with ease. However, he has now been able to resume a full and active part in the proceedings of parliament. The second field trial, using a later version of the equipment, is being carried out by a businessman who became deaf three years before receiving the equipment and has now been using it for one year. He states that he was able to gain full advantage from the system after approximately three hours' experience.

Neither of these earlier versions contained a dictionary but relied exclusively on phonetic spellings of syllables. One significant disadvantage of this type of output was the lack of word boundaries. The addition of the dictionary thus represents two major improvements: a significant improvement in spelling, and improved readability because dictionary recognition allows the insertion of most of the appropriate word boundaries.

More extensive experimental tests of readability are planned. However, it has already been shown that such a system is useful as a personal communication aid for highly motivated hearing-impaired people of above average cognitive ability. Further applications are being explored. One such application could be as part of a television subtitling service for the deaf and hard of hearing.

*Teletext subtitling with Palantype*
The development of Teletext in the U.K. offers considerable potential benefit to the hearing-impaired. The Teletext systems, developed in parallel by Independent Television and the British Broadcasting Corporation, involve the insertion of digitally coded data into two of the empty lines of the field-blanking interval of the television signal. These data are not normally visible but may be displayed, by means of a special decoder, over all or part of the TV screen, either instead of or mixed with the normal video signal. Teletext is already being used to provide pages of textual and graphic information ranging from up-to-date weather forecasts, news and sports reports, and stock market figures to recipes, horoscopes, and quiz games. Pages are selected by the viewer by means of a push-button control. The particular advantage of this system for hearing-impaired viewers is that it allows Teletext subtitles to be transmitted with ordinary television broadcasts. These subtitles can be decoded and displayed on the screen as and when the viewer wishes. In this way, television broadcasting can be far more meaningful to the hearing-impaired viewer without inconvenience to the rest of the population. The special relevance of Palantype in this context is that it would permit television to be subtitled in "real-time." Verbatim subtitles could be inserted into the TV signal while a programme was running. For the majority of pre-recorded programmes the need to reduce preparation time is purely economic. Research (Torr, Note 2) indicates that it takes approximately 30 man hours to prepare conventional subtitles for a single hour of television. Conventional subtitling is, therefore, an expensive process. However, there may well be other factors counteracting the economic advantages of using a Palantype subtitling system exclusively. It is conceded that Palantype is less easily readable than conventional

English, a problem increased for the prelingually deaf whose level of literacy is generally low (Conrad, 1977). Indeed, in some circumstances there may be a strong case against attempting to provide a verbatim transcript of television sound at all. The extent of this problem is currently under investigation. There may also be pedagogical objections to the use of unconventional spelling in the mass media.

On the other hand, there remains a class of programmes for which time is at a premium. Most news bulletins and sporting events are broadcast live with little or no preparation or rehearsal. The immediate and central role envisaged for Palantype subtitling is in dealing with such programmes. Palantype subtitling of live programmes is currently being evaluated at Southampton.

*A study of the readability of Palantype subtitles*
A pilot study has been conducted in order to obtain some preliminary data on the usability of Palantype subtitles in comparison with conventional English subtitles. A four-minute sequence from a daily news bulletin was subtitled live using the Southampton University Speech Transcription System. The bulletin concerned a railway journey to the Far East and was Palantyped "unseen" by a highly skilled and experienced Palantypist. It must be emphasized that reporting news is very different from reporting normal conversation. The pace of news is relentless and there are few pauses. The average speech rate of this sequence was 153 words per min. Although this rate is comparable to the upper limits of the range of normal conversational speech rates (generally given as $140 \pm 20$ wpm), such speeds usually only occur in short bursts and there are frequent pauses. News also has a high information content with very few redundant words and thus there is little possibility of omitting occasional words as is the practice in conventional Palantype reporting. The Palantypist had had virtually no experience of news reporting and as a result her error rate was considerably higher than would be expected under normal reporting conditions. (We are confident that an operator's performance would improve after he or she became accustomed to the particular rhythm and rate of news broadcasts.)

A total of 428 words was spoken in the news sequence. The Palantype output contained 355 words (73 words were omitted) and 247 (69.6 percent) of these were spelt correctly. An example of a Palantype subtitle taken from the sequence is shown in Figure 4. The same sequence was subtitled verbatim by conventional means. The sequences were videotaped and shown without sound to two separate groups of nine subjects with normal hearing (hearing-impaired subjects were deliberately excluded from this first exploratory study). There were two control groups of nine subjects each. The first control group viewed the sequence under normal conditions, with sound but not subtitles. The second control group received neither sound nor subtitles (the usual situation for the profoundly deaf).

After the viewing session, a 14-item questionnaire containing three types

Figure 4. Example of a real-time Palantype subtitle taken from the Subtitled News Experiment.

of comprehension questions was given. Type A questions could be answered either from the soundtrack, or from one of the two different types of subtitles, or from the original video alone, that is, under all four viewing conditions. One question was, "What is the destination of the journey?" (The destination was stated in the audio and was clearly marked in animated graphics on the original video.) Type B questions could be answered from soundtrack or subtitles but not from the video alone ("How much will the trip cost?"). Type C questions could be answered only by attending to the original video ("How many people did the reporter interview at the station?"). The experimental design and mean percentage correct responses are shown in Table 2.

An analysis of variance for a split-plot design was applied to arcsine transformations of the percentage scores for each subject. There was a significant effect of question type ($F(2,64) = 10.4, p < .01$), and of viewing condition ($F(3,24) = 3.55, p < .05$), and a significant interaction between them ($F(6,64) = 4.69, p < .01$).

It is clear that the question types were not comparable in content. Therefore, the main comparisons of interest are those between different viewing conditions. Duncan's New Multiple Range test was applied to the relevant means. For Type A questions both Normal viewing and No Sound viewing were significantly superior to Palantype subtitles at the .01 and .05 levels respectively. Neither was significantly superior to Conventional subtitles, and Conventional subtitles were not significantly superior to Palantype subtitles. For Type B questions, Normal viewing, Conventional subtitles, and Palantype subtitles do not differ significantly from one another but all three are superior to No Sound viewing. (The fact that any scores above zero were obtained in the latter condition is a measure of the effectiveness of guesswork.) For Type C questions, the only significant difference

Table 2. Subtitled news experiment. Responses in comprehension test to three types of question under four viewing conditions (percent correct).

| Viewing conditions | Question Types | | |
| --- | --- | --- | --- |
| | A Soundtrack, subtitles, or original video | B Soundtrack or subtitles only | C Original video only |
| Palantype subtitles | 30 | 43 | 11 |
| Conventional subtitles | 48 | 57 | 11 |
| Normal viewing (with sound) | 61 | 65 | 44 |
| No sound viewing | 59 | 16 | 22 |

Note: Nine subjects were tested in each condition.

was between Normal viewing and the two subtitle conditions. The fact that scores in No Sound viewing were comparatively worse than those in Normal viewing, even when the information required was available only in the video, suggests that the removal of sound effectively places subjects with normal hearing under stress. It is also clear that the addition of subtitles distracts from full appreciation of the visual action. This effect is likewise apparent in the results for Question Type A. For these particular questions, the information which could be retrieved from soundtrack, subtitles, or video appears to be retrieved more readily from the video than from the subtitles.

   The results are encouraging for Palantype subtitles but perhaps less so for subtitles in general. In this admittedly small-scale experiment, we were unable to demonstrate any statistically significant inferiority of Palantype subtitles to conventionally prepared subtitles in conveying the information required by the questionnaire. This was true of all three question conditions and, for Type B questions, even Normal viewing conditions showed no statistically significant advantage. Although the results for Palantype were consistently numerically inferior to Normal viewing conditions and Conventional subtitles, it is clear that they were successful in conveying a significant amount of the soundtrack information (Palantype significantly superior to No Sound viewing for Type B questions). A more disturbing finding is that both types of subtitles interfered with full appreciation of the purely visual content of the programme.

*Towards a theory of subtitling*

The results from the Subtitled News Experiment suggest that reading even carefully prepared and correctly spelt subtitles requires considerable effort. The amount of effort required may well decrease with practice and with continual exposure to subtitled television. However, the experiment highlights the fact that subtitle reading is not a process exactly analogous to listening to a soundtrack. With subtitled video only one sense is being used rather than two as in audio-visual presentation; indeed, the two visual information components are in physical conflict because one is superimposed on the other. Data on the reading ability of the deaf (Conrad, 1977; Bonvillian, Charrow, & Nelson, 1973) suggest that they are unlikely to represent an ideal population for subtitle reading. For these reasons a full-time investigation of television subtitling is being conducted in conjunction with the Palantype work, the aim being to provide a service which will fulfill the needs of as wide a section of the hearing-impaired public as possible.

Audience research (Baker, Note 1) indicates that the TV viewing habits and preferences of the hearing-impaired are generally indistinguishable from those with normal hearing and it is legitimate to assume that their requirements from television will be essentially similar. However, it does not necessarily follow that subtitles should simply and directly duplicate the spoken soundtrack of the television programme. Many aspects of spoken language cannot be directly reflected in written language. One thinks immediately of the information carried by intonation and stress which the resources of written language are severely limited in conveying (having only punctuation and italics). Differences of voice quality give important cues to the identity of speakers in group conversation because camera cuts do not necessarily correspond to changes in speakers and, indeed, speakers may not be on screen at all. The structure of informal conversation (in talk shows, for example), with false starts, hesitations, and incomplete syntax cannot be felicitously transferred directly into written language. Furthermore, many special sound effects, which may be integral to a plot, cannot easily be represented in written language, the howling of the wind, for instance.

Nonetheless, the role of soundtrack information in different types of TV programmes is not fully understood. For example, it is likely to be more central in a news bulletin than in a sports commentary, where one of the main functions of speech seems to be to generate excitement. In the Palantype study reported above it seemed reasonable to ask subjects questions about the content of the news programme because the transmission of information is purportedly the main function of news broadcasts. This function is much less important in many other types of programmes and different types of programmes may call for different strategies of subtitling. The general requirement for maximum economy of text will be subject to various provisos in terms of the way in which the role of the soundtrack is construed. Some types of soundtrack may inherently be more amenable to editing than others. There are many different types of editing: scripts may be "tidied up" by deleting "redundant" features, syntax or vocabulary may be normalized or simplified, or the precise wording of scripts may be ignored and a narrative of the action supplied instead.

It is generally true that television conventions are validated by television ratings, ranging from matters of programme content to the acceptable limits of glamour in newscasters or of partisanship in sports commentators. Similar forces are likely to operate in the case of TV subtitles once the service is on air. So little is known about the subject, however, that a schedule of preference studies is being undertaken. Experimental videotapes are being compiled in which different types of television programmes are subtitled in various alternative styles and viewed by groups of hearing-impaired people. Responses are gauged by questionnaires. A preliminary study is described below.

*An exploratory study of subtitling styles*

It was decided to compare two fundamentally different approaches to subtitling a popular British soap opera: first, an almost verbatim representation of the shooting script, deleting in an impressionistic fashion features (such as "wells," "ums," and "ahs") deemed to be redundant to the dialogue and normalizing syntax and dialect to a certain extent and, second, a commentary on the action, ignoring the dialogue and supplying the story-line only. Two short extracts from the same episode of "Coronation Street" were subtitled in this way. Some deaf viewers have more trouble than others in keeping up with the semi-verbatim subtitle which changes every few seconds (Figure 5). The "commentary" subtitle (for example, "Ken is advising Eddie on his Social Security problem") changes far less often, giving the viewer more time to read it and more time to watch the action on the screen. It is also possible that commentaries will support lipreading skills and the use of residual hearing in an appropriate context. It is possible, however, that such ancillary strategies may be supported better by a perfect match between spoken dialogue and subtitles.

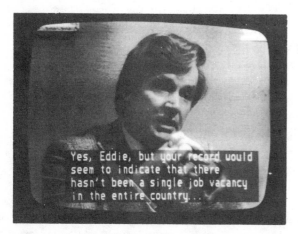

Figure 5. A semi-verbatim teletext subtitle from an episode of "Coronation Street."

The semi-verbatim subtitles were presented at between 120 and 160 wpm and the commentaries at between 30 and 60 wpm. The extracts were viewed by a group of prelingually deaf adults ($n = 20$) and a group of postlingually deaf adults ($n = 14$). The viewing sessions were followed by a short questionnaire containing the following questions:

Did you enjoy the films?
Were the films easy to understand?
Did you have enough time to read the subtitles?
Did you think the subtitles fitted the action well?
Did the subtitles give you enough information?
Were the subtitles pleasant to look at?
Was it tiring to watch the subtitles?
Did the subtitles distract you from the action?

Results from the questionnaire are shown in Figure 6.

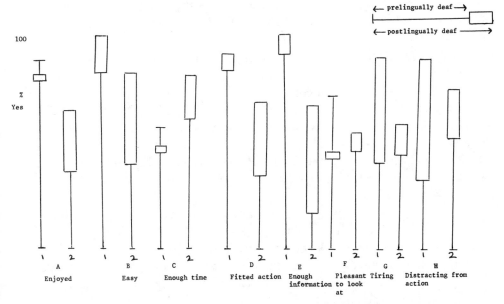

Figure 6. Percent "yes" responses from prelingually and postlingually deaf adults to questions asked about two different subtitle styles (style 1: semi-verbatim; style 2: commentary).

Both groups found the semi-verbatim subtitles more enjoyable, easier, more appropriate to the action, and more adequate in information content than the commentary subtitles. It is interesting, however, that all of these responses are much stronger in the prelingually deaf than in the postlingually deaf. There is clearly more time available to read the commentaries than the semi-verbatim subtitles but the prelingually deaf seemed to be less aware of this advantage. The most interesting responses are those which are reversed in the two subject groups. The prelingually deaf reported that they found the commentaries less pleasant to look at, more tiring, and more distracting than the semi-verbatim subtitles. The postlingually deaf reported exactly the converse.

There are a number of possible interpretations of this difference. First, it may reflect a difference of attitude. It is possible that the considerable amount of editing in the commentaries was seen as "simplification" and deemed condescending by the prelingually deaf. Alternatively, this group may be less aware of the possibilities for editing and transforming text than are those with normal experience of language and, therefore, find any "meddling" unacceptable. Finally, they may indeed find the mismatch between text and visually perceived verbal action unpleasant, tiring, and distracting. Intuitively, however, one would expect such a reaction to be stronger in the postlingually deaf.

Many of the subjects in both groups volunteered that the commentaries were boring and oversimplified and, perhaps more seriously, that they could not convey the humour of the programme. It is noteworthy that it was only elderly individuals who found the commentaries preferable to the semi-verbatim subtitles.

The semi-verbatim text is clearly preferred for this type of programme. It would appear that the essence of this programme's appeal lies not in the plot but in the dialogue itself, and that people are prepared to perform an arduous reading task to comprehend it. A stronger test of this hypothesis would be to offer a fully verbatim representation of the script. It would also be possible to produce more elaborate, less condescending commentaries while still retaining a moderate rate of text presentation. It is expected that the application of such heuristic strategies to this and other types of programmes will result in a set of guidelines for subtitling television.

It is essential that the needs of the hearing-impaired be given full consideration in setting up a television subtitling service. A close examination of the nature of television soundtrack and of the various ways of dealing with it is also called for. The responses of hearing-impaired viewers will provide the validation for such work. It is already clear from the data presented here that it is rash to jump to conclusions about what types of subtitles would be preferred. In particular, assumptions based on a superficial understanding of the functions of television programmes and on known characteristics of the intended users (such as reading speeds of the hearing-impaired) may be unjustified. Teletext offers to bring a very powerful technology to the aid of the deaf but there is a great deal more to learn about its most effective application. It is expected that extensive preference studies will also clarify the role of Palantype within a television subtitling service. More generally, it is expected that such studies will contribute to the establishment of a service which is fully sensitive to the needs of its users.

The developmental work on Palantype was supported by the Science Research Council; the work on television subtitling is being supported jointly by the Independent Broadcasting Authority and the Independent Television Companies Association. We also acknowledge the help of Isla Beard in preparing the Palantyped experimental materials, and thank Jacques Bertin for advice on preparing Figure 6.

## Reference note
1. Baker, R. G. TV viewing habits and preferences of the deaf and hard of hearing. In preparation.
2. Torr, D. V. *Captioning project evaluation—final report*. Washington D.C.: Public Broadcasting Service, 1974.

## References
Bonvillian, J. D., Charrow, V. R., & Nelson, K. E. Psycholinguistic and educational implications of deafness. *Human Development*, 1973, *16*, 321-345.

Conrad, R. Reading abilities of deaf school leavers. *British Journal of Educational Psychology*, 1977, *47*, 138-148.

French, N. R., Carter, C. W. Jr., & Koenig, W., Jr. The words and sounds of telephone conversations. *Bell Systems Technical Journal*, 1930, *9*, 290.

Underwood, M. J. Machines that understand speech. *The Radio and Electronic Engineer*, 1977, *47*, 368-376.

# Pictorial recognition and teaching the blind to draw

Christopher N. Vincent

*The author wished to discover how the blind mentally envisage three-dimensional form and if any connection existed between their conceptions and those of sighted persons. One question was if conventional orthographic presentations conveyed anything to the blind, or would three-dimensional representations be more meaningful? If the latter, to what extent could this system of drawing be utilised and would new doors be opened for the blind? In the long term, it was realised that many human factors were involved in promoting an entirely new concept in drawing technique.*

Through tests and experiments psychologists have long endeavoured to define blind persons' powers of visualisation. It is well known that through touch, vibrations, textures, sounds, and smells, blind persons can develop extraordinary skill in recognising shapes, surfaces, planes, and direction, both in solid form and in space.

By comparison with the sighted, the blind can achieve only limited mental configurations in a pictorial sense; greater accuracy is observed when they are in a familiar situation or when objects can be encompassed by touch.

Without having seen three-dimensional objects depicted in two-dimensional picture form, mental conceptions vary enormously according to individual imagination and power of retention. Transposing mental impressions into visual form by drawing usually presents problems.

Allowing for the lack of dexterity in the handling of pens, pencils, and the like, the blind invariably attempt to produce drawings in much the same way as do very young sighted children. Objects are usually depicted in a single frontal plane, with horizontal surfaces placed above in a vertical position (Figure 1). Verbal descriptions relate to three-dimensional concepts as, indeed, do descriptions of their dreams.

## Picture book for the blind

Numerous tactile maps, charts, and line illustrations have been produced as aids in the construction of mental pictures. In tests with three-dimensional line illustrations of common objects, it was found that by tracing contours by touch and using an element of elimination combined with simple clues (used outside the house, for example), recognition was possible. Repeating this exercise at intervals, using a number of illustrations in picture book form (Figure 2), increased powers of comprehension and retention.

Further research established that it would be futile to institute a method of drawing which would be alien to the blind persons' mental approach to the subject. All possible methods of drawing were examined to arrive at one which had

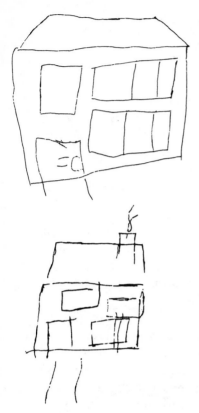

Figure 1. Comparison of childrens' drawings (top sighted; below blind).

Figure 2. Examples from raised line picture book.

some affinity with their powers of conceptualisation and, indeed, their way of life. It was assumed that any method beyond their comprehension of a three-dimensional image would prove limited.

Personal conceptions of objects always vary; it was considered advisable, therefore, to evolve some standard format as a matrix upon which drawings could be constructed.

*Perspective grids*

It was decided to adapt a three-point perspective grid, used extensively in the field of visual communication, as a basis for constructing a special drawing board for the blind. The author designed these grids specifically as drawing aids for producing perspective illustrations. In effect they duplicate the perspective of the camera and preserve the original proportions of objects. Perspective scales calibrated in centimetres cross the centre of the grid which represent centre lines in orthographic drawings of the length, breadth, and height of an object.

By rotating the grid it is possible to produce 24 basic views, 12 from above an object and 12 from below (Figures 3 and 4).

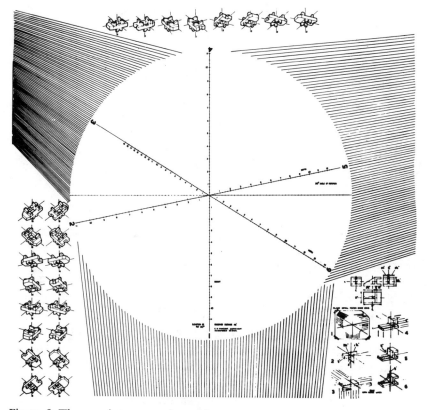

Figure 3. Three-point perspective grid.

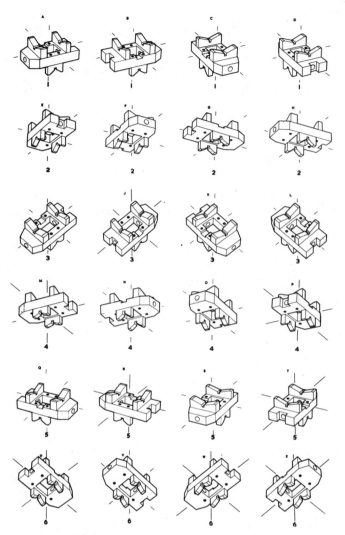

Figure 4. Symbol drawings (24 basic views).

*Special drawing board for the blind*
The transposition from a perspective grid to a specially constructed drawing
board for the blind can be seen in Figure 5. Two T-squares run on arcs derived
from respective vanishing points taken from the original grid layout. Each arc is
graduated with raised perspective marks in centimetres, the equivalent of scales
crossing the surface of the grid. These marks can easily be felt by blind people.

Elongated marks on each scale act as an equivalent centreline. Lines
projected from these marks meet at a centre point which effectively establishes the
centre or core of an illustration, from which all measurements are taken. Finding
distances from this point going to left and right, that is, finding the length and

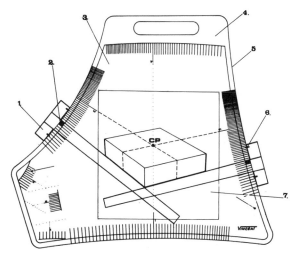

Figure 5. Mark II drawing board for the blind.

1. T-square (two);
2. clicking device (two);
3. rubber surface;
4. plastic backing;

5. metal insert on edge;
6. magnetic studs;
7. MELINEX in position.

breadth of an object, is made easier by the addition of spring-loaded clicking devices positioned on the T-squares. When moved along the arcs, the T-squares engage with indentations on the backing board which correspond to the raised centimetre marks.

The material found most suitable for drawing on was a very thin plastic sheet which is smooth on one side and known by the trade name of "MELINEX." It adheres to the resilient rubber surface of the board simply by wetting the rubber before placing the MELINEX smooth side down and excluding all air. A ball-point pen is used, which when drawn across the surface, leaves a raised ridged line which can be both seen and touched.

*Drawing technique*
Once the principles of perspective were integrated in the design of the board it was possible, after some practice and provided the equipment was used correctly, for blind people to produce reasonable line drawings.

Connecting lines from one point to another along a T-square is simplified by rotating the pen to form depression dots in the MELINEX surface at the beginning and end of each line measurement. Light pressure is applied on the pen when first connecting the dots, positive location being made when the pen drops into the depressions; by traversing backwards using more pressure a good raised line is obtained.

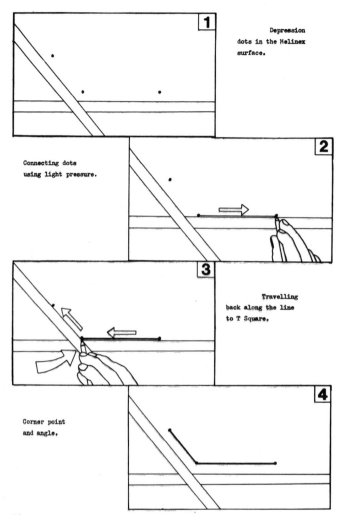

Figure 6. Connecting lines and corners.

Corners can be correctly located by the simple procedure of holding the pen at the end of a line and bringing a T-square into contact, forming another angle (Figure 6).

Initial attempts at drawing were of blocks of wood in various shapes and sizes. Given instruction in Braille and on tape recordings, blind people were encouraged to use their imaginations in defining the shapes of common objects, analysing the construction and form before beginning. By slowly co-ordinating the step-by-step breakdown of their mental pictures with their physical reproduction, blind persons could draw. For many the psychological effect of developing these techniques was tremendous. In this field, at least, they were almost on equal terms with sighted people. Some examples of blind students' drawings are given in Figure 7.

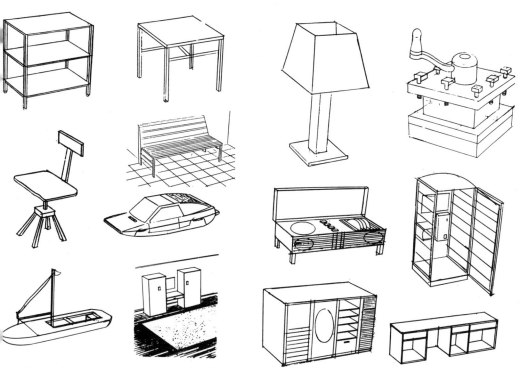

Figure 7. Examples of drawings by blind students.

Throughout the various experiments, many children became obsessed with the idea of drawing objects with wheels. ("If I can manage to draw a box, can I put wheels on it and turn it into a truck?") It became obvious that a simple means had to be found to achieve this. Using centres of ellipse guides which could be outlined appeared logical but, in practice, this method of drawing wheels had to be aligned with correct positioning to be successful.

Accordingly, several sheets of raised ellipses were prepared showing positions relative to the centre of vision and to the top of the board. Braille numbers were added to each ellipse, defining the width of the minor axis. The sheets were then thermoformed on plastic to serve as guide positioning charts. Examples are shown in Figure 8.

The children were taught to relate the positioning of wheels on their own drawings in correlation with the charts by measuring with a raised ruler or by the finger method of spacing, all measurements being taken from the centre of vision. Of necessity the ellipse centres had to be of a size easily handled, any size less than 1 in across the major axis being difficult to hold. These centres, ranging from 20 to 70 deg, were produced on thin plastic and arranged in order of degree sizes in separate containers.

The centres of wheels were established making depression dots on the

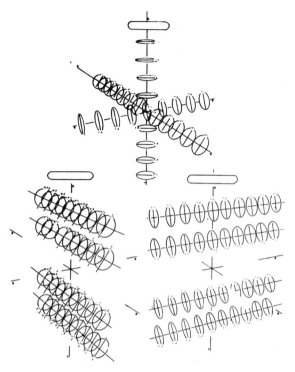

Figure 8. Ellipse positioning charts.

MELINEX surface. The correct ellipse centres to use is given on the guide positioning chart (Figure 9).

The manipulation of ellipse centres proved difficult for some younger children but older ones between 14 and 16 were fascinated with the idea and developed considerable skill and dexterity in the technique involved. Many reasoned that by placing ellipse centres in appropriate positions they could then proportion the remainder of their drawings accordingly (Figure 10).

Surprisingly, no blind person asked why ellipse centres should be used as representative of wheels in perspective. Presumably they realised that, if complete circles, devoid of any thickness, were put onto a three-quarter-view illustration of a truck or car, they would be positioned in opposing directions. The use of ellipse centres as a solution was accepted without question.

Examples shown give a clear indication of what is possible when clear visualisation and a progressive step-by-step thought process are employed. (The same is true of the blind learning to walk.) Deliberate ordering of their thoughts appeared to be the crux of the matter; thinking out a series of moves and connecting measuring points on a drawing bore a distinct relation to their motivation and mental perception of objects.

Evaluating the significance of these observations in comparison with

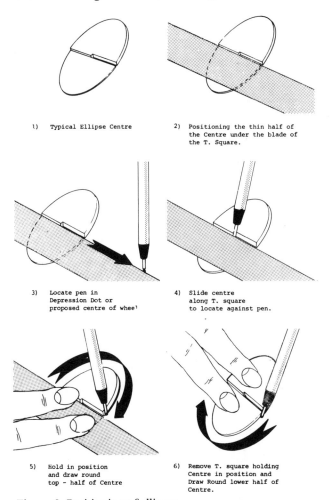

1) Typical Ellipse Centre

2) Positioning the thin half of the Centre under the blade of the T. Square.

3) Locate pen in Depression Dot or proposed centre of wheel

4) Slide centre along T. square to locate against pen.

5) Hold in position and draw round top - half of Centre

6) Remove T. square holding Centre in position and Draw Round lower half of Centre.

Figure 9. Positioning of ellipses.

how sighted persons approach drawing could occupy psychologists for many years.

It is estimated that over 5000 drawings were made by various groups of blind people from the beginning of the private research project in 1967 until 1975. Though a great many were experiments or trial efforts, a fair proportion of really remarkable line illustrations were produced. From 1975 until 1977 another 3000 drawings were produced by blind and partially sighted people at various schools and institutions both in England and on the continent. The number shown in Table 1 applies only to drawings in our possession: many were spirited away to the homes of very proud children, others were displayed in exhibitions. The most significant feature shown in Table 1 is that a large percentage of drawings were completed unaided. One can gather from this that blind people genuinely in-

Figure 10. Ellipse centres placed in the correct positions.

terested in the subject of drawing and well trained in the use of the board
described can apply their powers of visualisation and retention in a very practical
way.

The drawing board and the methods of instruction used have been
widely tested.

At the Birmingham Royal Institution for the Blind in England, experiments were conducted to see how far blind people could convey their powers of
visualisation and drawing techniques to others by step-by-step tape-recorded
instruction. A team of five students, three boys and two girls, average age 15,
undertook the experiment. Two of the boys were completely blind from birth and
the other three members were only partially sighted and had little light percep-

Table 1. Results of the instructional program.

| Type | Approximate number |
|---|---|
| Initial exercises in drawing blocks of wood, boxes, etc. | 900 |
| Drawings produced from Braille and typewritten instructions | 100 |
| Drawings of students' own designs completely unaided | 950 |
| Drawings produced from tape-recorded instructions devised by students and teachers | 200 |
| Drawings of a variety of homework projects completely unaided | 750 |
| Drawings produced from verbal instructions dictated by teachers | 120 |

tion. One blind boy performed the role of designer and visualiser while the others acted as final testers of the system. The partially sighted students recorded the drawing instructions and it was noted that the voices of the girls came over particularly well.

Very little assistance was necessary in the production of the tapes: one could only advise students not to rush through verbal instructions but to allow time for slow learners to assimilate the information. The group decided for themselves that drawing instruction tapes produced by blind children would be more readily accepted than those produced by teachers and they are probably correct.

The experiment was successful largely because the blind visualiser selected simple objects to draw and gradually progressed to more complicated ones. Great enthusiasm for this type of teamwork was soon forthcoming, for it was realised that the tapes could benefit other blind people throughout the world. It was envisaged that future programmes devised by the team would not necessarily require any teacher participation and might conceivably provide a new form of employment (depending on the scheme being accepted in its entirety by teachers and educational establishments.

It was feared that some teachers of the blind would not be able to deal with children capable of producing accurate drawings unaided unless they too could visualise in depth to the same degree. This is especially difficult when coping with several children at once, each making his own individual effort; it takes practice, understanding, and, indeed, a capacity almost akin to thought transference. The more advanced children are usually several steps ahead in thinking out the breakdown of their mental pictures into line illustrations. In this area of study blind children do not need guidance or any interference in their train of thought.

Working from tape-recordings, many children forged ahead of instructions to complete their drawing; others deviated somewhat, giving the impression that they were quite capable of designing for themselves. It has been decided to pursue an idea instigated by the students and, by establishing a competitive spirit, try to determine how far tape-recorded drawing instructions produced by young blind people could benefit mankind. Consideration is being given to establishing competitions among those who have the Vincent drawing board in Canada, New Zealand, and Germany; if they can be arranged the results should be most interesting. Table 2 gives a time scale for the tapes available.

Table 2. A time scale for the tapes available, from conception of the idea to final recording.

| Drawing | Tape Time in Hours |
|---|---|
| Block of wood | 1.75 |
| Bed | 1.25 |
| Portable radio | 2 |
| Dressing table and wardrobe | 3 |
| Toy boat | 3 |
| Toy boat in different position | 3 |

A film entitled "Drawing Board," dealing with teaching the blind to draw, has been made; it summarizes graphically the principles of three-point perspective.

The perspective methods described here have been tried and tested over many years, yet it has been very difficult to comprehend why blind children can adapt so well to this system of drawing.

Grateful acknowledgement is made to Herr Bätz, Herr Bender, Gerhard Lund, M. Neuhauser, and T. L. Rogerson, all of whom collaborated in the research programme. Some of the work was supported by a grant from NATO Scientific Affairs Division and from Birmingham Polytechnic.

## References

Vincent, C. N. Illustration for instruction. *Industrial Training International*, 1967, *2* (4), 167-174.

Vincent, C. N. A mechanical aid to 3-dimensional drawing. *Machine Design Engineering*, 1967, *5*, 56-58.

Vincent, C. N. Pictorial recognition and teaching the blind to draw. *The Institute of Scientific and Technical Communicators*, 1977, *31*, 8-15.

Vincent, C. N. Training without words. *The Institute of Scientific and Technical Communicators*, 1978, *36*, 13-19.

Vincent, C. N. Step-by-step assembly in visual form. *Plant Engineering and Maintenance*, 1979, *3* (4), 23-25.

# Telidon Videotex and user-related issues

H. Bown, C. D. O'Brien, W. Sawchuk, J. R. Storey, and W. C. Treurniet

*Videotex systems are interactive visual communication systems intended initially to permit public access to computer-based information sources. Pages of information from a data base can be selected by commands issued by the user via a keypad. The page is then displayed on the screen of a domestic television receiver. This paper discusses the problem of system flexibility with respect to picture description and describes one solution which is the basis of the Canadian Telidon system. Various user-related issues concerned with requirements for the display of information and for the software interface are also presented.*

Videotex is the generic name for information retrieval services that use suitably modified television receivers as the terminal display. Users of a Videotex system will be able to use a keypad or keyboard to instruct a data base computer at a distant location to send a particular image to the display. With current technology, the image must be mainly static and may contain textual information, geometric drawings, or more complex photographic objects. Communication with the data base computer will be mediated by telephone lines or other interactive networks. The Videotex concept is revolutionary in that the user will have much more control than at present over what appears on his television screen.

Pages of information are created for the data base by using more sophisticated terminal equipment. An individual using such a terminal can make information available for profit or as a means of advertising. In the first instance, an author may wish to use the service as an inexpensive publication medium. In the second, a store may wish to advertise its wares. Eventually, if barriers to electronic funds transfer can be overcome, sales may even be concluded remotely.

As technology progresses, terminals may be able to communicate directly without mediation by a host computer. When the two displays respond identically to instructions given at either terminal, they may be used as an "electronic blackboard" or as a means for playing a game such as chess at a distance.

The service can improve the convenience and immediacy of such activities as reading newspapers, writing letters, advertising, banking, and playing games. Public access to information will be one of the first applications of a Videotex service because many daily activities are directed at discovering the state of the world around us. The technology required for this application is well understood and, because an information retrieval service can satisfy many special requirements, it has the potential for attracting a sufficiently large market.

The method of choice for accessing Videotex information is a tree-structured search technique, an approach initially proposed and implemented by the British Post Office (Fedida, Note 3). Its primary advantage is that it consumes the fewest computing resources while servicing a request for information, an important consideration when thousands of users are connected to the computer at one time. The more the computer is required to do to service requests, the longer a person may have to wait to receive the desired page, and the less interactive the system appears to the user. As an example of a search through a tree structure, a user might select "real estate" from one menu page, which is then followed immediately by another menu listing the areas within the city. Selection of any one of these results in display of another page with categories of real estate such as "business" or "residential." Selections of items on this and subsequent menus may lead eventually to a description of a house at a particular address. This information could have been entered initially either by a real estate company or by an individual wishing to sell his own property. Either could be contacted further by individuals interested in the description so conveniently discovered.

*The problem of image description*

Two different approaches to Videotex systems have evolved in Europe and North America. They differ mainly in how the images are coded for storage in the data base and for subsequent transmission to the terminal display. The European systems are character-oriented, which restricts the displays to fixed format textual messages and rudimentary graphic images. If that approach is adopted extensively, it will be difficult, if not impossible, to change to new communication methods which would allow the display of higher quality images.

The adaptability of character-oriented systems to new requirements is constrained mainly by the way an image is described. Images are transmitted as sequential pieces of a picture consisting of 24 rows of 40 characters each. Graphic images are similarly constructed from specially identified, coded graphic characters fitted together in a mosaic of picture components. This technique requires that the stored information include information about the display terminal resolution. Thus, information banks would have to store multiple versions of an image to transmit to terminals with differing display resolutions.

A Videotex system suitable for today's technology should be designed to incorporate future modifications easily. To achieve this, images need to be described in the data base in such a way that they are completely independent of the data access procedure, of the characteristics of the communication medium, and of the display terminal construction. These criteria are met by the Picture Description Instructions (PDIs) incorporated in the Telidon Videotex system (Bown, O'Brien, Sawchuk & Storey, Note 1). Graphic images are described by PDIs in terms of the geometric shapes they contain. Only seven basic instructions, each followed by high resolution data, are needed to describe virtually all graphic images. Four of the instructions define objects geometrically in terms of primitives consisting of lines, circular arcs, rectangular areas, or polygons. A fifth instruction indicates that the following data are in "bit" form, or photographic mode, for images where the structure cannot be defined by using the four geometric primitives. A sixth instruction defines the position of the object on the display. The seventh instruction is used for control and usually sets a status register before other instructions are sent. For example, one function of the control instruction is to define the colour of an object. These seven instructions can describe all graphic images in a compact form for transmission to a terminal designed to interpret them.

Another command is required to change from graphic to alphanumeric mode when text is to be transmitted and back to graphic mode for transmission of non-textual information. The alphanumeric mode is the default mode and so a subset of the PDI set can be used with simple terminals which respond only to alphanumeric information.

The proposed PDI codes can be of use only if the receiving terminal can interpret them and fill the display memory with the appropriate contents. For this reason, the terminal must contain a microprocessor to perform the interpretation and generate the display memory code. The display memory itself may be either character- or bit-oriented. The European approach was to design character-oriented terminals. The Canadian Telidon terminal, however, uses the bit-map display memory which means that every pixel on the display has a corresponding location in the display memory. The colour and brightness of a pixel depends on the contents of its corresponding memory location. The result of this approach is a need for considerably more memory than is required by the character-oriented approach. There is, of course, an accompanying increase in cost but that must be weighed against the benefits of a much higher resolution display. Further, memory costs continue to decrease with advances in integrated circuit techniques. Figure 1 demonstrates the quality of graphics possible on the Telidon system using a display resolution of 240×320 pixels.

The PDI code, which is the basis of the Telidon system, is extensible. As different uses for Videotex terminals are conceived, the code can be extended to incorporate new instructions that will facilitate such activities as generation of pictures and person-to-person communication with textual messages and graphic images.

Picture Manipulation Instructions (PMIs) are already envisaged for use by information suppliers which will allow a user of a Telidon-like terminal to create pictures on his television screen and store the picture descriptors in a data file. Selective erasures will be permitted as well as additions and modifications to images created previously. Further instructions can be included to permit rotation, scaling, and transposition of portions of a displayed image. Instructions may even be developed to code basic speech patterns so that speech can be synthesized to accompany displayed images.

Graphic communication between individuals continues to be a subject of our research (Bown, O'Brien, Warburton, & Thorgeirson, Note 2). Person-to-

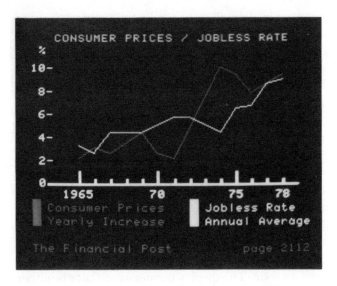

Figure 1. An example of the quality of graphics possible on the Telidon Videotex system.

person image communication would be useful to any individuals discussing the merits of some kind of spatial organization. An example might be an architect discussing the plans of a building with a client. Applications to entertainment may also appear as games are adapted or developed to take advantage of the visual interaction capability. As long as the picture description technique is independent of the hardware employed, future technological developments need not threaten the data base with obsolescence.

*User-related issues*
Advances in consumer technology inevitably raise questions of what design is most appropriate for human use. Implementation of Videotex services requires consideration of issues related both to display of information and to interaction protocol, as well as identification of the most appropriate services for the medium.

Information display issues need to be addressed because the home television will be used to show static images rather than the dynamic images for which it was designed. Most human factors data related to the display issues are not directly applicable to matrix television displays. Either analogue television technology was employed or an electronic display was not employed at all. There is no question that digital television displays have new and different characteristics that need to be studied in their own right. Further, the new technology provides the capability to do experiments that previously were difficult. It also permits economical use of some features such as colour. Because colour is expensive to manipulate in print, for example, study of its full potential for coding information was not always feasible.

A number of countries are negotiating international standards that will affect how information such as text is formatted on the display and this in turn will influence the acceptability of the medium. Standards proposed by any country should be supported by relevant empirical evidence. Accordingly, we are currently studying how legibility of text is affected by various display parameters related to the density of characters on a page. Our experiments will provide a basis for a proposal regarding the maximum number of both characters on a row and lines on a page suitable for North American television. Such a standard may be applicable only under well defined conditions, however. For example, the optimum character density may be different for monochrome and polychrome television displays, for composite (RF) and red-green-blue (RGB) video input, and for dot-matrix and in-line picture tubes. It may be different when proportional character spacing is used from when such spacing is not used. Other environmental factors such as ambient lighting, viewing distance, image contrast (both luminance and colour contrast), and screen size may also influence the optimum character density with respect to readability of text. There is also evidence that the dependent measure employed can drastically influence the conclusion of an experiment on display characteristics. Specifically, speed of reading has been shown to improve as character size decreases, and search time for a target character randomly located in two-dimensional space has been shown to decrease as character size increases (Snyder & Maddox, Note 4). Thus, it may be that one character size is most appropriate for continuous text and another for graphic annotation. What appeared at first to be a simple question about the optimum number of characters per line and lines on a page has become much more complex because various other factors must be considered simultaneously.

There are other display issues not directly relevant to implementation of international standards for Videotex but important for user acceptance of the medium. Specifically, the relative merits of low versus high resolution displays should be examined considering the cost differential involved. There may well be a point above which further increases in resolution are inconsequential for most applications. Again very little work has been done on the optimization of a lower case character set for dot-matrix displays. A number of upper and lower case fonts differing in size and shape need to be designed and evaluated for use by information providers. Design principles need to be established so that information providers can create comprehensible and pleasing pages of information. Readability can be facilitated by appropriate use of colour and spatial organization on a page. Rules for speed of presentation need to be made explicit so that an idea does not remain suspended when five to ten seconds elapse before a new page appears. The utility of various ways of scrolling text also requires examination.

Interaction protocol for information retrieval is another complex issue because it relates to data base structure, querying language and mode, input devices, and the organization of information in the mind. From a technical point of view, data stored in a hierarchical or tree structure are retrieved more efficiently in that the fewest computing resources are consumed. This is an important consideration because too slow a response by the host computer can destroy the interactive feature intended for Videotex services. The usefulness of a fast response is debatable when the information content of such a response is minimal, however. Advancing through a long series of menu pages may be analagous to conversing with a person who answers quickly but who has a very limited vocabulary. Eliciting the desired message then becomes laborious. The tree structure is efficient technically but it may be very inefficient for the user who wishes to retrieve information that has multiple attributes. Research in this area should be governed by either of two assumptions: the hierarchical approach is the only approach that is technically feasible or more sophisticated network structures are possible.

Under the first assumption, the research should attempt to identify rules for organizing information hierarchically with the least ambiguity about the correct path to take to receive the information desired. That is, do individuals' cognitive maps appear more congruent with some hierarchical arrangements than with others? Under the second assumption, an interdisciplinary effort is required to define the characteristics of a system designed for the fastest possible reponse to requests for information searches. Here also, the structure of individual cognitive maps needs to be studied in a general way. This kind of information may aid other specialists such as systems analysts to design the most efficient means of information retrieval for the user.

The language and mode (selective versus generative) of querying and the design of the most appropriate input device are other relevant issues that are interdependent and influenced heavily by the logical structure of the information in the data base. It is probable that a considerable proportion of potential users is unfamiliar with computers and, in fact, does not wish to learn a complex procedure for accessing information. If this is true, it is the system designers, and possibly the information suppliers as well, who must simplify access to information while minimizing the time to produce the desired information.

Finally, an issue which may ultimately determine the viability of Videotex services in a market controlled economy is the way in which the medium is used. It has several characteristics that make it unique, being interactive, network-based, and providing easy access to colour. These characteristics need to be exploited so that the medium can be seen to provide useful services as well as services that are not easily available by other means.

## Reference notes

1. Bown, H. G., O'Brien, C. D., Sawchuk, W., & Storey, J. R. *A general description of Telidon: A Canadian proposal for Videotex systems* (CRC Technical Note No. 697-E). Ottawa: Dept. of Communications, Canada, 1978.

2. Bown, H. G., O'Brien, C. D., Warburton, R. E., & Thorgeirson, G. W. *System independence for interactive computer graphics application programs*. Proceedings of the 4th Man-Computer Communications Conference, Ottawa, May 1975.

3. Fedida, S. *Viewdata: An interactive information service for the general public*. Proceedings of the European Computing Conference on Communications Networks, 1975.

4. Snyder, H. L., & Maddox, M. E. *Information transfer from computer-generated dot-matrix displays* (Report No. HFL-78-3/ARO-78-1). Research Triangle Park, N. C.: U.S. Army Research Office, 1978.

# Human factors and VDT design

A. E. Çakir

*Visual strain is one of the most significant problems in working with VDTs. Field studies involving more than 1000 subjects have shown that both the optical properties of displays and the paper documents used are highly correlated with visual strain experienced by the operators. Somatic symptoms of discomfort, such as backaches, neckaches, or headaches, are significantly correlated to them and to visual strain. A VDT should be designed for a bright office. There are at least three relevant visual objects (keyboard, visual display unit, paper documents). The most relevant recommendations are to avoid specular reflections both on keys and on display and to provide an adjustable contrast, as much as 10:1. The use of filters cannot be recommended for all environments. Their use depends on the luminance distribution and the characteristics of ambient light in the environment.*

Visual display terminals (VDTs) are the principal means by which people communicate with computers. An investigation concerning the extent to which VDT workplaces are adapted to the working needs of VDT operators was completed recently at the Institute of Ergonomics of the Technical University of Berlin. It was designed mainly as a series of field studies and involved more than 1000 subjects in 30 sites, representative of a wide range of industrial and administrative activities. The results show that visual strain is one of the most significant problems in working with VDTs but that there is no means by which it can be measured objectively. On the basis of subjective responses, it was found that the incidence of visual strain among VDT operators is highly correlated not only with the optical properties of CRT displays but also with the optical properties of paper documents and especially keyboards, even when the operators are skilled typists.

The term "visual strain" is used to describe the following responses of the subjects:

I experience excessive eye strain while working with the VDT.

My eyes burn while working with the VDT.

My eyelids twitch while working with the VDT.

The response to these and many other items was evaluated by means of factor analysis which was carried out after more than 800 VDT users had been questioned. This analysis allows us to distinguish clearly between the incidence of visual discomfort caused by the illumination of the workplace (glare, for example) and visual strain caused by the nature of the task itself.

*Correlation between visual strain and somatic symptoms*
When working with a VDT, the individual operator must compensate for such

unfavourable effects as defective or inadequate vision, inadequate visual conditions of the CRT display, documents, keyboard, and so on. Because it is seldom possible to move the main visual elements towards the eyes, the operator must keep changing posture.

When reading paper documents, the viewing distance is normally 30 to 40 cm if the reader is holding the documents. At most VDT workplaces, however, documents often rest on the desk, usually to the left of the keyboard, and the reading distance is then most often between 50 and 60 cm or even more. To read the document, the person has also to direct his or her eyes at an angle of about 60 deg below the horizontal and between 45 and 75 deg to one side. Moreover, when the keyboard is used, the operator's line of sight is about 60 deg below the horizontal plane.

Both skilled and unskilled typists look at the keyboard when keying (Figure 1). Thus the usual posture of VDT operators is not upright but leaning forward or bending. While reading the text on documents, the upper part of the spine is bent forward and twisted to one side, mostly to the left. Matters are made even worse if the operator wears glasses which are adjusted to a reading distance of between 30 and 33 cm.

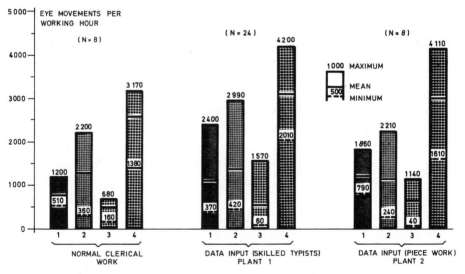

Figure 1. Eye movements as a function of task, place, and worker. Movements between documents and display (1), document and keyboard (2), display and keyboard (3), and their sum (4 = 1+2+3).

In the course of these studies, we registered the following symptoms of discomfort: backaches, neckaches, and, in significant correlation with both of them, headaches. The longer a VDT operator works, the greater is the likelihood of these somatic symptoms.

Computer programmmers, whose work requires only a low keying rate and relatively small amounts of information to be taken from paper documents, very seldom complained of headaches (6 percent). Data typists, on the other hand, often complained of headaches (45 percent) as is shown in Figure 2. The correlation between the incidence of somatic symptoms and visual strain was $r = .59$.

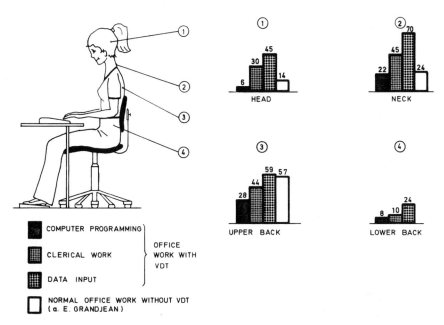

Figure 2. Parts of the human body strained by office work whether using a VDT or not.

Subjects who frequently experienced somatic discomfort often visited an orthopaedist. It was found that 32 percent of the subjects with normal eyesight and 49 percent of those wearing glasses appropriate for a reading distance of about 30 cm had sought orthopaedic treatment. Obviously, avoiding visual strain not only achieves higher performance or more accuracy in reading but is also an important aspect of health and safety. Because visual strain can be avoided or at least decreased by improving the optical quality of visual objects, it is necessary to examine the relevance of those objects to find the most effective way of reducing visual strain.

*Relevance of visual objects*
In most investigations of the visual conditions at VDT workplaces, the aim has been to find the optimum visual environment for a given display. Inevitably the incidence of visual strain was attributed to the poor quality of character images in the display, reflections, and so forth, and there is no doubt that these are factors. That does not necessarily mean, however, that using a VDT causes the most strain.

One aim of our investigations was to determine the relevant visual objects at a given VDT workplace and then evaluate their importance in relation to visual strain.

Figure 3 shows comparisons by 784 VDT operators of the optical quality of the CRT displays and paper documents. Surprisingly, the users themselves fault not the VDTs but the paper documents. Although of secondary importance for most workplaces the quality of VDTs can be improved, as laboratory measurements of the luminance distributions of characters on CRT displays and paper documents have proved. It should also be borne in mind that VDTs are normally more favourably placed for reading than are paper documents.

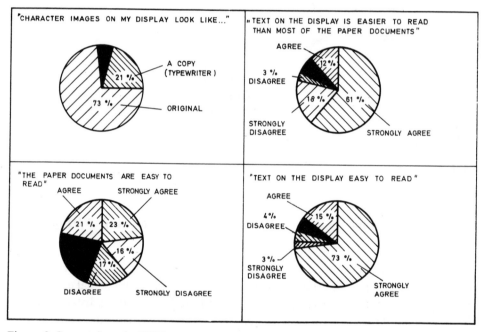

Figure 3. Comparisons by VDT operators of the optical quality of CRT displays and paper documents.

Working with a VDT normally requires manipulation of a keyboard which, as can be seen in Figure 1, is an important visual object for the user of a VDT as far as frequency of viewing is concerned. Figure 4 demonstrates the effects of the reflection characteristics of the keyboard on visual strain, somatic symptoms, and fatigue experienced by the subjects.

There are, therefore, at least three relevant visual objects at a VDT workplace, the most important being the paper document which is used by about 80 percent of VDT operators. For several reasons, however, the quality of paper documents cannot be improved easily and so the optimum visual environment should be

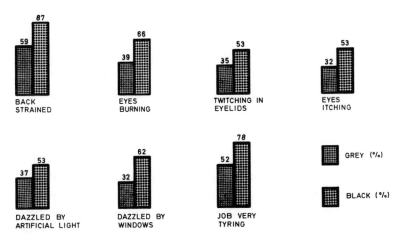

Figure 4. Responses of VDT operators using grey and black keyboards to some relevant items.

chosen by considering the ease with which poor quality print can be read. The next step is to find which VDTs are most suitable.

*Designing a VDT for a bright environment*
In designing a VDT for use in a bright environment, the following points should be carefully considered:

To avoid contrast glare, the display background should not be too dark (minimum luminance 10 cd/m²).

The optimum contrast lies between 8:1 and 10:1. The minimum character luminance should, therefore, exceed 80 to 100 cd/m². At this luminance the character images should not merge but remain distinct.

The minimum character size should be 18 minarc at a viewing distance of 50 cm. If a high resolution CRT is not used, the character size should be at least 3 mm. (This recommendation does not apply to make-up displays, and the like.)

Specular reflections should be avoided as much as possible ($\delta_0 < 0.5$ percent) without diffusing the character images, as spray coatings tend to do, for example, because both reflected glare and blurred characters impair legibility and increase visual strain.

The character images should be sharp and stable, that is, no flicker or jitter.

The keytops should be bright and have a matt finish; reflection about 40 to 60 percent.

The function keys should be coded with different colours to reduce search time.

These are some of the minimum specifications recommended for VDT work-places (Çakir, 1978, 1979).

*Subjective evaluation of visual strain*

In one experiment we were able to compare the visual strain experienced by subjects using the same VDT model in two different rooms by day and by night. The keyboard was grey and the background luminance of the display was about 20 cd/m². The character luminance on the VDT could be adjusted up to 150 cd/m² giving an average character contrast of about 7:1. One room contained a large mural illuminated with 1000 lux, the other room had 500 lux artificial light. Under these conditions and using a VDT with a maximum character luminance of 150 cd/m² the artificial illumination should not exceed 500 lux. By increasing it from 500 to 1000 lux, the legibility of paper documents is slightly improved, but the contrast on the display is decreased to about half with the result that visual strain is significantly increased. If the character luminance had been much less the optimum luminance might have been around 100 lux and, in that case, we would recommend the use of another display. The lower limit for the illumination of a daylight room with artificial light is about 300 lux.

*Specular reflections*

Most CRT terminals have a large screen which usually has a diagonal measure of 28 cm or more and a curved glass surface which tends to reflect some light. In addition, VDTs are often used in brightly-lit offices and frequently are close to windows or other bright surfaces. Reflections on the display screen are a major source of distraction and complaints of visual discomfort at work can often be traced to them. Two kinds of reflection are characteristic of visual display screens: the *direct* reflectance, which provides a measure of the luminance of the image that can be seen directly reflected on the surface of the screen, and the indirect or *diffuse* reflectance, which provides a measure of the luminance of the screen when light falls on it. (Direct surface or mirror-image reflections are sometimes referred to as "glossy.") These two kinds of reflection are not necessarily related. The appropriate choice of the reflectance properties of the equipment, materials, job aids, and other surfaces in the working environment can usually free visual displays from disturbing reflections.

*The disturbing effects of specular reflections*

Specular reflections on the VDT screen are a major source of distraction and discomfort first, because the brightness contrast of the display is reduced, making the displayed character images more difficult to read and, second, because the reflected images obscure the visual display. Moreover, it has often been suggested that screen reflections can also be a source of glare and increase the likelihood of visual discomfort.

*Reflection "glare."* In offices, the highest levels of luminance from room lighting usually fall between 5000 and 8000 cd/m². Because the direct reflectance of an untreated VDT screen is typically less than 4 percent, the luminance of the images reflected on it would be expected to fall in the range of 200 to 300 cd/m². In comparison, the luminances of paper copy, desks, and so on, fall typically between 150 and 250 cd/m². Therefore, because paper documents and other light reflecting surfaces represent the greater and, in many tasks such as text and data copy entry, the more frequently referred to parts of the visual field, screen "glare" cannot be considered a major factor in visual discomfort.

*Reflections and accomodation difficulty.* Reflections on the VDT screen represent an additional image which comes between the eye of the operator and the plane on which the character images are displayed. That is, the focal plane of the reflected images is closer to the eyes than that on which the character images are displayed. The consequences are shown in Figure 5 which illustrates the reflection of a light source L on the display screen B on which a character Z is displayed. In order to see the character Z clearly, both eyes accommodate according to the distance between the eyes and the character, that is, to avoid a double image, the visual axes through both eyes intersect at Z. However, the reflection is seen by the left eye to be in the position L", and by the right eye in position L' and so the viewer sees a double image of the reflection. When this happens, the eyes tend to reaccommodate to bring the points L" and L' together. In this position, however, the character Z is now perceived as a double and unclear image and the accommodation process is repeated. In the long run, therefore, accommodation oscillates between the plane of the character Z and that of the reflected image L.

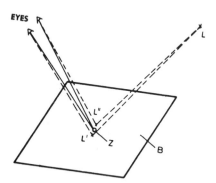

Figure 5. Reflection of a light source L on the display screen B on which the character Z is displayed.

This type of disturbance increases as: the luminance of the reflected image increases; the direct reflectance of the screen surface increases; the form of the reflected image becomes more sharply defined; the horizontal extent of the reflected image decreases; the distances L' and L" decrease; and the distance between Z and L', L" decreases.

In general, an unstructured source of reflections, that is, one without a clearly defined shape, gives a more diffuse reflected image which is less disturbing than mirror-image reflections. The consequences for design of VDT workrooms are important: lights should be shaded to avoid their direct reflection on the display screens and windows shaded by pattern-free curtains or roller rather than by venetian blinds, louvres, or similar blinds that might cause a pattern of stripes of light. Neither character brightness nor colour plays a particularly important role in the disturbing effect of reflections. The most important display feature is the uniformity of the background luminance. As a general rule, reflections with sharp contours and high luminance should be avoided even when the contrast between the character and background luminances on the visual display is sufficient.

*Contrast reduction.* In the absense of reflections, the percentage luminance contrast on the display screen can be calculated as follows:

$$C = \frac{L_Z - L_U}{L_U} \times 100.$$

If $L_D$ is the luminance of a directly reflected image, $L_Z$ the character luminance, and $L_U$ the background luminance of the screen, the percentage contrast is reduced to a value that can be calculated from:

$$C = \frac{(L_Z + L_D) - (L_U + L_D)}{L_U + L_D} \times 100.$$

Consider the following example. The character and background luminances on VDT displays are typically $L_Z = 140 \text{ cd/m}^2$ and $L_U = 20 \text{ cd/m}^2$ respectively, giving a contrast C = 600 percent. With an ambient luminance of 8000 cd/m² and a screen with a direct reflectance of 3 percent, the luminance of the reflected image would be $L_D = 240 \text{ cd/m}^2$ in which case the contrast is reduced to 46 percent.

Because the reflected images are not distributed uniformly over the face of the screen, the characters are, or at least appear to be, more readable in the higher contrast regions of the display than in the lower. Most VDT operators try to overcome this by adjusting the character luminance to a higher level: this is one reason why character luminance control is usually regarded as an essential feature of visual display equipment. One way of reducing the effects of screen reflections is to make use of a screen filter. The most effective, obvious, and least costly way of avoiding the problem, however, is to adjust the position of the terminal so that reflections are no longer present. Under constant artificial lighting with an illuminance of 500 lux in a room with a depth of 4 metres or more, daylight has relatively little effect on reflections provided the screen is at right angles to the windows.

*The use of screen filters*
Screen filters, of one type or another, are often used by manufacturers and operators in an attempt to combat screen reflections and thereby improve the visual quality of the display. However, a filter placed between the eye and the visual display cannot improve all of the characteristics that affect the quality of the display. An appropriate filter can reduce reflections but at the expense of reduced character brightness and resolution.

The use of screen filters, therefore, should be approached with caution. If its use is being considered it is important that the operator clearly understands the characteristics of the various types of filter available.

*Reflectance from the untreated CRT glass surface.* The luminance of the characters of an untreated CRT display is usually in the range 100 to 300 cd/m². The smooth glass surface of the CRT screen typically reflects about 4 percent of the light which falls on it or about 3 percent if the surface is less smooth or is dusty. This is enough to produce clearly visible and sharply defined reflections on the screen. Even with low ambient illumination, the operator can usually see his or her own image clearly reflected on the screen.

When the phosphor is bonded directly onto the inner surface of the screen, that is, without any intermediate filter substrate, the diffuse reflectance of the screen is typically in the range of 22 to 27 percent and the screen usually appears milky-grey in colour.

The untreated display has the highest character and background luminances under ambient illumination. However, some of the incident light is transmitted through the phosphor; the result is that reflections can occur within the CRT which tends to reduce the luminance contrast on the screen.

*Filter panels.* There are several kinds of glass or plexiglass panels which can be installed in front of the display to provide some measure of filtering. In some cases, the panels are used to change the apparent colour of the display. Individual VDT operators often use colour filters to produce a preferred screen colour; no problems arise unless the terminal is used by several operators who disagree about what is not a pleasing colour!

Less justifiable is the use of coloured filters to produce a "less tiring" colour. There is a great deal of confusion about colour and visual fatigue. It is often claimed, for example, that green is a good colour for visual displays because the spectral sensitivity of the eye is greatest in the green part of the spectrum and hence green is less tiring. Provided that the luminances and luminance contrast of the display are sufficient to ensure good readability, however, there is no evidence to suggest that any one colour is less tiring than any other. In fact, although they are sometimes used in the belief that the resulting effect is less tiring, colour filters and most other types of glass or plastic panel usually have a smooth, glossy surface which is less uniform than the surface of the screen glass and results in a highly reflective surface. A further disadvantage is that the filter material usually absorbs between 30 and 70 percent of the character luminance, and the background luminance is also reduced. Altogether, filter panels reduce the legibility of the display and tend to increase the visibility of screen reflections.

*Polarization filters.* The only type of panel filter which can sometimes be used to advantage is the *polarization* filter in which the incident light is polarized and then dispersed from the surface of the screen. Polarization filters reduce both direct and diffuse reflections but are usually glossy and reflective, sometimes to the extent that the images reflected may be even clearer than those on the untreated screen. Figure 6 gives an example of the reflections produced by a polarization filter. Because the filter material is usually plexiglass, it is not possible to reduce specular reflections on the surface of the filter by vapour depositing an anti-reflection coating. A thin glass layer can be suitably treated and bonded to the surface of the panel, however. Polarization filters are most effective on small display surfaces, such as meter displays, but are not widely used for larger displays because of the practical difficulties and costs involved in overcoming the problems they present.

Figure 6. An example of reflections produced by the front surface of a polarization filter.

*Micromesh filters.* Meshes or *micromesh* filters placed directly on the surface or a short distance in front of the display screen are often used to help reduce reflections. Filters of this kind usually give the screen a black appearance, and the mesh acts as a large number of very small tubes, as is illustrated in Figure 7. Micromesh filters effectively reduce reflections but some of the disadvantages outweigh the advantages to such an extent that their use is often questionable. The main drawbacks are that, depending on the coarseness of the mesh, the display is obscured by the mesh when viewed from certain oblique angles, some of the light passing through the mesh is scattered, and the characters appear less bright because some of the light emitted from each is absorbed by the filter, in some cases up to 70 percent. Provided that the terminal is used by one operator only, and that sitting position and height of the display screen are adjusted to permit direct viewing, the directional readability of the display is not a problem.

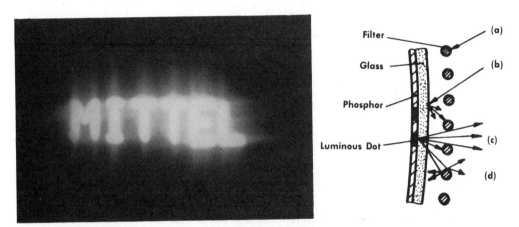

Figure 7. Micromesh filters for the prevention of screen reflections. (a) the reflectance of the surface is very low, the incident light is scattered with a diffuse reflectance typically about 5 percent; (b) that part of the incident light which passes through the filter is mainly reflected directly from the screen surface; (c) the character luminance is reduced; (d) part of the light emitted from the characters is scattered. With black filter materials the scattered light has a low luminance, about 3 to five percent of the character luminance.

Figure 8 shows a diffusing surface used to reduce specular reflections. When light rays from outside sources strike the first surface they are scattered and the reflected image is diffused and out of focus. The same thing happens to the light rays coming from a character or point generated in the display. The effectiveness of the filter in scattering and absorbing some of the light which passes through it depends on the coarseness of the mesh and if the filter is bonded to, laid

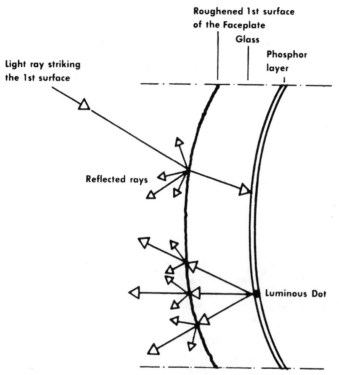

Figure 8. A diffusing surface used to reduce specular reflections.

on, or placed a short distance in front of the screen surface, in a frame, for instance.

If the mesh is placed in front of but not in contact with the screen, direct reflections can almost be avoided, the direct reflectance of the surface being reduced from about 4 percent to less than 1 percent. The diffuse reflectance is also reduced, however, from about 25 percent to about 3 to 5 percent.

The reduction in character brightness is a more serious problem. Depending upon the coarseness of the mesh, the character luminance can be reduced by between 30 and 70 percent because of light reflection and absorption within the mesh. If the mesh is free from dust and the screen glass is uniformly smooth, the reduction in sharpness of character image because of light scattering in the mesh is usually less of a problem. If the glass is not smooth, however, other optical effects can occur, such as Newton rings, and the character luminance is usually reduced by more than 50 and sometimes by as much as 80 percent.

Many of these problems can be overcome by adhesively bonding the mesh to the glass surface, giving a diffuse reflectance of seldom more than 3 percent. The effectiveness of the filter depends on how the mesh is bonded to the glass, however, and it is important to use an adhesive which does not, itself, produce a glossy surface.

Micromesh filters can be used to advantage only if the ambient illuminance exceeds about 500 lux. The filter helps to reduce reflections from other
bright surfaces in the room, as well, and its effectiveness may in some cases be
determined by the luminance of the reflecting surfaces. Reflections may be reduced by micromesh filters but only at the expense of readability. The display
contrast is often reduced to such an extent that the display looks "flat" and may, in
extreme cases, be more difficult to read than handwritten copy.

*Etching the screen surface.* Direct reflections can also be reduced by roughening the
surface of the glass screen by etching or by installing a roughened glass panel in
front of the screen. This can be effective but there are drawbacks. Only the outer
surface of the glass screen can be treated in this way; it is not possible to roughen
the phosphor side. The sharpness of the character images is greatly reduced
because of light scattering. Moreover, the greater the distance between the visual
display and the roughened surface, the greater the light scattering effect will be. It
will be greater still if a roughened panel is placed in front of the display screen.

An etched glass surface can reduce the direct reflectance from about 4
percent to about 2 to 2.5 percent, but only at the expense of reduced image clarity.
The problem of light scattering might not, in itself, be so important were it not for
the additional problem of reduced character brightness. Etching the glass surface
can reduce character brightness by as much as 80 percent and the reduction may
be greater still if an etched panel is placed in front of the screen glass.

Effectiveness depends on how the surface is etched. The result can vary
from a very coarse, highly diffusing surface to a fine surface finish where the
scattering effect on the character images is very small. If one is either unable or
unwilling to etch the screen glass directly, a separate panel can be etched and then
bonded to the screen. Providing an etched, unbonded panel in front of the display
does not reduce reflections and does reduce the quality of the character images
(Figure 9).

*Spray-on anti-reflection coatings.* The main drawback in spraying coatings on the
external surface of the display screen is that light is scattered as it passes through
the coating, reducing the sharpness of the character images, sometimes so much
that the characters appear to be surrounded by a halo, particularly if the grain of
the coating is too coarse or if the coating thickness is uneven.

*Vapour-deposited screen coatings.* It is technically possible, though more costly, to
overcome some of the disadvantages of spray-on coatings by vapour depositing a
thin layer of a suitable material onto the glass surface of the screen. The main
advantage is that the structure of the surface is less coarse and the resolution of the
characters at a normal reading distance not appreciably reduced.

*Thin-film layers.* A very effective method of treating the glass surface with an

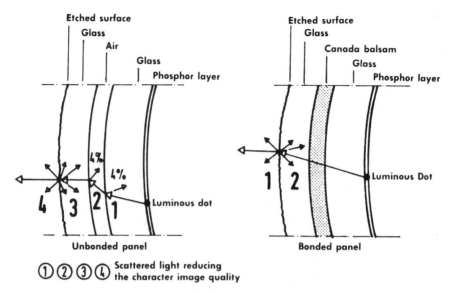

Figure 9. Because of reflection from the air/glass and glass/air surfaces between an unbonded filter panel and the screen glass, light is scattered, reducing the quality of the character images. This effect is minimized by bonding the panel onto the screen glass.

anti-reflection coating without diffusing the character images is vapour depositing a thin-film layer whose thickness is one-quarter the wavelength of light, usually called a "quarter wavelength" or $\lambda$ /4 layer. Other techniques are also available. Using this type of filter, the luminance of the reflected images can be reduced by a factor of about 10 without reducing the luminance of the character images. Thus, the perceived quality of the character images is greatly improved.

The method is not without some drawbacks, however. One is the relatively high cost of the filter which cannot be applied directly to the screen glass but must be applied to a glass panel which must then be bonded to the glass screen. If the CRT is replaced, a new filter is required. A second disadvantage is the sensitivity of the filter to dust and finger touch. If the filter surface is not regularly and carefully cleaned, the character images look smeared.

*Tube shields*. It is possible to reduce reflections by fitting a tubular shield around the display screen. The idea itself is not new, shields of this kind having been used since the invention of CRT, but its use in offices is. Tube shields are often fitted as a visor on CRT oscilloscopes where the information content is not very great (certainly much less than on a VDT screen) and the display screen is consulted much less frequently. If a tube shield is to be fitted to a VDT, care must be taken that it is not fitted in such a way that the operator must sit in an awkward position to read the display.

*Subjective evaluation of screen filters*

No clear correlation has been found between the surface characteristics of the display and any visual discomfort suffered by VDT operators, in part because there are other, more important variables. As might have been expected, however, a very clear correlation has been found between the surface characteristics of the display and legibility.

CRT displays with fine-grained anti-reflection coatings, so-called anti-glare displays, or with a high-quality etched surface are more highly ranked by VDT operators than other types of filter both for effectiveness in reducing reflections and for legibility of the display. Micromesh filters have been judged to be equally effective in reducing reflections alone.

Subjective evaluation of untreated visual display screens depends greatly on the visual environment. In using CRT displays, careful attention must be paid to the height and inclination of the display screen in relation to both the viewing angle of the operator and the position of lights and reflecting surfaces in the room. As a general rule, however, the anti-glare displays are preferable to displays on untreated screens.

Displays with glass or polarization filters were judged less favourably, especially for display legibility which, under typical office conditions, is greatly inferior to that obtained with other types of display. Until the optical quality of this type of filter is improved, its use cannot be recommended.

Black micromesh filters were also judged to be poor by most VDT operators, again because they reduced display legibility. They can be used to advantage only when the ambient illuminance exceeds 500 lux and the problem of reflections cannot otherwise be resolved, for example, in some VDT workplaces close to windows or in environments without favourable illumination such as shops, warehouses, booking halls, and so on.

## References

Çakir, A., Reuter, H. J., van Schmude, L., & Armbruster, A. *Untersuchungen zur Anpassung von Bildschirmarbeitsplätzen an die physische und psychische Arbeitsweise des Menschen.* Bonn, F. R. G.: Bundesministerium für Arbeit und Sozialordnung, 1978.

Çakir, A., Hart, D. J., & Stewart, T. F. M. *The VDT manual.* Darmstadt, F. R. G.: IFRA (1979).

# Theory of representation

# Introduction

Paul A. Kolers

Psychologists, despite their deep concern for them, seem to lack coherent theories of performance. The theories that do exist tend to be theories of phenomena—theories of word recognition, or theories of sentence interpretation, and the like; but large-scale theories of performance are lacking. Alternatives to microtheories are sometimes proposed as the underlying "pre-theoretical assumptions" guiding an investigation. The experimenter's biases and assumptions, however, if not incorporated into an explicit theory, are nevertheless not pre-theoretical; they express the biases of theories held implicitly and guide and direct investigations as strongly as (or even more strongly than, if one believes in unconscious direction of thought) the theories that can be explicated. Theory surrounds us; we are immersed in it, and better to make it explicit than keep it tucked away in unspoken and sometimes unrecognized assumptions.

The word representation has quite different meanings in different disciplines, however. Among philosophers it has usually meant a picture of some sort, a meaning familiar to designers and others working in pictorial media. Some philosophers use the term a little more broadly to mean not only pictures but any inscription that "carries information"—picture, word, number, and so on. Psychologists have come to use the word in yet another way, referring to how knowledge is expressed within the nervous system or the mind. Among philosophers, then, representations are symbols that refer or inscriptions that are members of some system used to express knowledge, but for psychologists they are often the mental embodiment of knowledge. With all this confusion, it is not remarkable that theoretical discussion of the notion of representation has not been found much in psychology; the confusion suggests, however, that a clear understanding of the issues involved in and invoked by the term is needed.

Vernon Howard, trained in philosophy of science and interested in questions of knowledge, performance, and skill, discusses aspects of representation. His paper draws some distinctions among uses of the word representation in everyday talk, and distinguishes also between the representations we all may see and the representations that we only infer; between inscriptions as conveyors of meanings, and internalized states or dispositions that guide and control behavior. Discussing inscriptions, he tells of some ways that symbols may inform.

Howard is diffident about the notion and points out that he offers only *a* but not *the* theory of representation. Patricia Wright directs her analysis at an outline or schema for a theory of reading, and amplifies aspects of the discussion she brought forward in her paper on usability. The format here is somewhat different and constitutes almost a catechetical approach of question and response in respect to issues related to reading and writing.

Julia Dutka surveys research and raises questions regarding the role of distant reference in understanding text. Richard Venezky, Nathan Relles and Lynne Price talk on a theorectical level of some issues concerning how best to implement the interaction of person and computer and make some very practical suggestions. At a different level of discourse and with a different concern for representation, Gay Snodgrass reviews some of the data collected in an information processing approach to picture-word comparisons. Her paper exemplifies some of the issues Howard talks of as far as the notion of representation of knowledge is concerned. Snodgrass is working within the tradition that holds that knowledge, if not structurally localized in the nervous system, is certainly functionally localized in the mind, and she takes as her task finding a good way to describe it.

A different sort of concern with pictorial representation is found in Jacques Bertin's paper. A leading figure in the developing field of optimizing graphical representations, Bertin illustrates some ways in which spatial representation of data can equally conceal or clarify relations to be found in the data. This theoretical approach to representing data is of the greatest interest to empirical investigators who are concerned to present their own findings as effectively as possible on the printed page.

# Theory of representation: Three questions

V. A. Howard

*This paper focusses on the phrase, "theory of representation," and what it means or might mean for researchers on visible or, indeed, any kind of language. Hence, the absence of the definite or indefinite article in the title: a theory of representation is not being offered, still less the theory of representation: only a few cautious, clarifying observations on the very idea of theory of representation, but without technical artifice or the detail of supporting argument they deserve.*

The idea of theory of representation would appear to encompass at least the following three questions. First, what are the varieties of representation or "language" in the broadest sense of a communicative medium, and how are they to be distinguished? Second, how is knowledge in general represented, that is, in what form? And third, how do we represent knowledge of skills, of intelligent, trained procedures?

*The varieties of representation*
To give an idea of the varieties of representation, consider the following statements.

> Jones represents (that is, "speaks for") Biddulph Township in the Provincial Parliament.
> That portrait represents ("depicts") the elderly Rembrandt.
> *War and Peace* represents ("describes") events of the Napoleonic War.
> The whale in *Moby Dick* represents ("symbolizes") Evil.
> *Punch* represents ("caricatures") Churchill as a bulldog.
> *La Mer* represents ("expresses") moods of the sea.
> Ghandi represents ("exemplifies") the spirit of nonviolent protest.
> Let *a* represent ("substitute" or "stand for") *b*.

We must also consider how maps of various kinds represent geographical areas, how scores represent music, how blueprints represent buildings, how codes represent messages, and so on. With the possible exception of political/legal representation (given above in the first example), all the examples of representation fall within our purview.

First, note that the same verb, "represents," refers to an impressive array of different *functions* that symbols may perform: depiction, description, expression, and the like. Note too that a given type of representation, language, for example, may perform several such functions (description, expression, exemplification), while a function like expression is possible in many different representational forms.

The term "representation" is employed in a way roughly equivalent to current social science usage. On one hand, the noun appears to refer to what would otherwise be called a "medium" or "symbol"; on the other, the verb designates the various functions that the media can perform. Thus, the linguistic medium may describe or express (and much else), whereas the pictorial medium, though it cannot, strictly, describe, may depict or express.

Some confusions surround the notion of a medium, chief among which is the tendency to equate the notions of *medium* and *symbol*. Reflection reveals that they have different, though complementary, uses. Except where otherwise defined, a medium usually involves a stimulation of one or more senses or has a particular material composition *plus* informational content (Gardner, Howard, & Perkins, 1974, p. 30). For example, a school bell announces to the ear that classes are about to start, or traffic lights signal to the eye "stop," "caution," or "go." Similarly, we often speak of print, or paint, or clay as being the medium, emphasizing their physical differences.

As thus construed, the same medium, radio, for example, may be the vehicle for different forms of symbolization: language or music, for instance. By the same token, natural language considered as a form of symbolization may occur in different media such as radio or print. Obviously, then, a theory of representation based on the notion of "medium" would obscure important differences between language and other types of symbolization by stressing differences in sense appeal or material composition over more fundamental syntactic and semantic features. Such features are *systemic* rather than sensory, and some discussion of them is required for a theoretical understanding of media.

If a medium is the sensory manifestation of a representation, then we should know something about the logical form and usual semantic functions of that particular kind of representation or symbol to explain its affinity for one or other medium. Clearly, pictures are no good for radio; language is, but not because radio is inherently "verbal" (even though auditory) any more than it is musical or than language is inherently auditory. (Radio, the medium, *is* inherently auditory, whereas language is not.) We do not get any closer to the essential differences between pictures and language by classifying the one a "visual" medium and the other "verbal" if only because so-called verbal materials can be visual as well as auditory, and visual materials verbal or non-verbal. "Visual versus verbal" seems a particularly untenable dichotomy.

The words "representation," "language," and "symbol" are virtually interchangeable on their broadest usages, though it is not difficult to find distinctions drawn among them. Some cognitive psychologists, for instance, divide their "inner representations" or "schemas" into enactions, icons, and symbols or, more simply, actions, images, and language (Bruner, Olver, & Greenfield, 1966).

Similarly, the American father of semiotics, C. S. Peirce, in his famous trichotomy of "signs" divided them into indexes (pointers), icons, and symbols, the latter comprising language, mathematics, and other complex forms of symbolization (Peirce, 1960, pp. 2.274-2.308). The growth of taxonomies among semioticians verges on the ridiculous but, among Anglo-American symbol theorists of philosophical ilk, the term "symbol" is used very broadly to indicate diverse materials used referentially, that is, to stand for or refer to something else. Thus symbol systems divide into many different kinds: representational, linguistic, diagrammatic, or notational, some symbol functions like expression or exemplification cutting across the different special types of symbol system (Goodman, 1976). Terminology proliferates in aesthetics, art history, linguistics, anthropology, communication studies, psychology, and every nook and cranny of social science.

To bring order to this chaos we might begin by recognizing one of the fundamental ambiguities that helped create it. On the one hand, there is a widespread use of the *nouns* "representation" or "symbol" roughly synonymous with anything that carries meaning in any of a variety of ways: descriptions literal and metaphoric, paintings realistic and abstract, portraits, gestures, codes, maps, music, and silhouettes on lavatory doors, to mention only a few. On the other hand, a much narrower use, particularly of the *verbs* "represents" and "symbolizes," tends to restrict them to the metaphorical and allegorical, the esoteric, hidden, latent, deeper, more general, or recondite significance of things. It is the difference between the word "blue" used to denote a colour in the spectrum and the colour blue used to express melancholy or as a "cool" hue.

Again, *Moby Dick* is symbolic in the narrow sense when read as an allegory of the struggle with Evil but not so when read as a simple sea story, a difference that would hardly matter were it not for the fact that language, especially complex, descriptive language, however literal, must be placed very near the apex of human symbolic achievements. So too must be the number system, perspectival drawings, blueprints, codes, and music notation. In effect, a special plea for the broader usage for theoretical purposes is made, the implication being that logical distinction be drawn among the various types of symbols (or representations) in ordinary and extraordinary use. Such deliberate adoption of the exoteric, subfusc sense of "symbol" gives little offence to science or to the vernacular but does gain some clarity.

For example, on the recommended broader usage, things classed as symbolic on the narrower usage turn out to be symbols of symbols: a description ($S^1$) of a whale ($S^2$) expressing the essence of Evil; a picture of a bulldog representing Churchill; a war narrative exemplifying heroism, endurance, or human fraility. That one simple distinction (a choice, really, of one side of an ambiguity) explicitly allows for the varieties of function possible for a given mode of symbolization: for a literal description of one thing (a whale) metaphorically to describe another (Evil); for pictures to represent while expressing much about things undepicted; for fictional narratives to exemplify truths about the human condition. The ultimate task, then, of a theory of symbolism (or representation) can at least be stated if only dimly perceived. It is to give an account in the form of a logical plot of the varieties of *reference*, of symbolic functions both exoteric and esoteric, inclusive of description, depiction, representation (in a sense applicable to language, music, and gestures, as well as pictures), expression, exemplification, and the like.

Besides indicating that a theory of representation involves types of reference or symbolic functions mention was made of giving them a "logical plot," using that expression to distinguish a logical analysis from others with which it might be (and often is) easily confused. It is well to note the differences among three perspectives on the study of symbols, two of which reflect the aforementioned ambiguity in our ordinary use of the term. First and closely allied to the narrow usage of "symbol" is what might be called the *lexical* perspective which involves the meaning of a particular symbol or array of symbols: their levels of meaning, specific and general, literal and metaphorical, their etymology, and, where appropriate, their ethnographic variations. The quest for the meaning of symbols may range from learning to use a particular form of symbolization, say, language or music notation, to questions of style and interpretation in art or of the nature of artistic, scientific, historical, or religious understanding. One might think of the *Oxford English Dictionary* and Cassirer's monumental exercise in cultural epistemology, *The Philosophy of Symbolic Forms* (brilliantly digested in his last book [Cassirer, 1944]), as representing extremes in the quest for the meaning of symbols. Included under this heading, then, would be aspects of the work of lexicographers, art critics, cultural anthropologists, epistemologists, and historians but primarily the efforts of Everyman to understand and communicate about his world.

Corresponding to the broader colloquial view of symbolism as anything that can carry meaning is what will be called the *functional* perspective. It concerns how particular items—gestures, utterances, inscriptions, objects—acquire their symbolic functions to describe, name, express, depict, and so forth. In other words, what are the relations that sustain a particular symbolic function and its contribution to meaning? Such relations form a system consisting of a symbol scheme (the items or inscriptions used to symbolize) correlated with a field of reference (Goodman, 1976, pp. 143 ff). The logical analysis or plotting of specific differences and kinships among linguistic, logico-mathematical, pictorial, diagrammatic, gestural, musical, and other sorts of symbol systems construed as different ways of using one thing to refer to another delimits that branch of the theory of representation known as semiotics. The question here, in contrast with the lexical perspective, is not so much what are the various meanings of symbols as what does it mean to be a symbol and how do they variously provide their meaning? Immediately the names of de Saussure and Peirce come to mind as the linguistic and philosophical originators, respectively, of modern semiotics. To their names must now be added that of Goodman whose *Languages of Art* (1976) stands out as the single most elegant and rigorous effort in the area in nearly 70 years. (Though subtitled, "An approach to a theory of symbols," it might well have been subtitled, "An approach to a theory of reference," inasmuch as it provides a comprehensive taxonomy of the forms of reference.)

The key to Goodman's theory of symbols is his theory of notation (Goodman, 1976, chap. 4) which, besides stipulating the logical requirements for a strict notation is also used to measure the similarities and contrasts among different systems of symbols in terms of their conformity or nonconformity to any one or combination of the requirements for notationality. There are five such requirements, two syntactic and three semantic. To give the barest impression of how they work, visualize the theory of notation as a map-like grid with the five logically independent conditions running down the left-hand column. Across the top of the grid, from left to right, would be listed various symbol systems in common and extraordinary use, beginning at the top left corner with notations and moving on to language, maps, diagrams, pictures, and so on.

Reading down the grid for a particular symbol system, language, for example, and across from notationality, one discovers that notations and language alike are "syntactically disjoint" and "finitely differentiated" (Goodman, 1976, pp. 133-137). That is, they consist of segregated characters in a symbol scheme to which various inscriptions may be assigned without confusion or overlap. In a word, they are alphabetical implying criteria for determining "sameness of spelling" (Goodman, 1976, pp. 115-117). Beyond that, the two kinds of symbol system begin to diverge. Notations are also semantically disjoint and differentiated which means that the members of their compliance classes correspond to at most one symbol in the scheme, like books in a library catalogue, for instance. Although applied notations, like standard music notation, are sometimes redundant (c#, d♭) or even ambiguous, a strict notation is neither and thus ensures the "mutual recoverability" of symbol and referent so useful to codes, naming, or other sorts of retrieval systems. Language, by contrast, allows for class inclusion and intersection, for different ways of saying the same thing, for saying subtly different things in nearly the same way, or widely different things in exactly the same way. Though syntactically notational, language is, in Goodman's phrase, semantically "dense" (Goodman, 1976, pp. 152-54). Far to the right on the grid, in the vicinity of pictures or aesthetically expressive symbols of one kind or other, one would encounter systems that are both syntactically *and* semantically dense, lacking an alphabet or literal vocabulary, in which the slightest differences in configuration may correspond to differences of meaning: analogue systems of measurement or paintings, for example. And ranging between the extremes of notational and dense systems are all the other "routes of reference" (Goodman, 1980) characteristic of the varieties of symbol system common or uncommon, natural or fabricated.

The principal relevance of Goodman's approach to symbolism as far as visible language is concerned is first, that different ways of presenting information on a surface can imply different ways of relating to those marks and inscriptions, because, second, what differentiates descriptions, depictions, graphs, maps, and so on, are not so much the visible marks on a surface (though, of course, they will also differ) as the different sets of rules for their construction and interpretation.

Beyond the lexical and functional perspectives on symbolism is the *cognitive* perspective concerned with the role of symbols in the growth of knowledge and perception in the individual, in communication, and in culture, raising such questions as, How do symbols of different kinds mediate thought and perception? Do symbols emerge in regular sequences and through some sensory channels rather than others? How does information (on some proper analysis of that puzzling notion) admit of multiple symbolic manifestations and which ones are more economical for certain educational purposes or levels of learning? In short, what are the psychological, cultural, or communication processes required or most frequently involved in the acquisition and mature use of many sorts of symbols in both thought and action? Here we enter the realms of social science, graphics, and engineering, perhaps less concerned with questions of interpretation, meaning, or logic, as with facts and hypotheses about the acquisition and use of symbols in virtually every aspect of life. Certainly, lexical and functional issues are involved in such inquiries, not as they pertain to language only but to whatever enables us to understand and function in the world.

That is why this perspective is termed "cognitive" rather than "scientific" or "experimental"; to emphasize that the object of investigation is the mediating power of symbols as instruments primarily of cognition and secondarily of communication. This is not to underrate the importance of communication for cognition but rather to underscore the logically prior purpose of symbolization to facilitate understanding in the widest sense of the term. Without understanding communication would not merely fail: it would not exist.

Clearly, then, the aforementioned perspectives on theory of representation are complementary and, to a degree, intersecting rather than exclusive realms of inquiry. It is as fruitful to distinguish what something means from how it means from how we learn or communicate what it means as it is folly to separate them. It is the confusion of interpretive, logical, and empirical matters that creates problems, especially when the questions we ask run them together indiscriminately. Obviously, questions about theory of representation raised here are mainly functional/cognitive and perhaps weighted more evenly between the functional and the cognitive than one might at first suspect. Certainly that appears to be true of the first question raised about the varieties of representation and will be shown to be equally true of the second and third about the representation of knowledge and skills.

*The representation of knowledge*

Philosophers tend to be concerned with what knowledge *is*; how we define or otherwise characterize the basic kinds of knowledge there are. Cognitive psychologists appear to be concerned with how we *have* knowledge; how it is encapsulated, "stored away" even, *in* representations or symbols. To the extent that this is so, the question of how we represent knowledge generally is a psychological one of evident philosophical dimensions. We should like to know what is being stored by what means where.

Philosophers are accustomed to distinguish two broad categories of knowledge, propositional, "knowing that," and procedural, "knowing how" (Ryle, 1949, chap. 2), roughly corresponding to the kinds of representation in question: of knowledge and of skills. Propositional knowledge observes canons of belief, evidence, and truth whereas procedural knowledge refers mainly to abilities like riding a bicycle, acquired through practice. As Polanyi (1958, pp. 49-50) has observed, it is not much help in trying to balance a bicycle to be told to adjust the rate of curvature of the bicycle's path proportional to the ratio of the angle of unbalance over the square of the speed. Nor do we finally come to know that the earth is roughly spherical by repeating to ourselves: "it is round," "it is round." It is quite possible to know (or learn) *how* without knowing *that*, and conversely. Though logically independent, propositional and procedural knowledge are, of course, contingently related in innumerable ways, particularly in the exercise of critical judgment, and often in ways that are quite recondite, as when one senses the mood of a room full of people. Indeed, a third category of "understanding" might be added: that of critical judgment in the deployment of sundry bits of information and skill as in any virtuoso performance by artist, artisan, or athlete. Such judgment is learned, perhaps nudged along at intervals by helpful "tips" or "cues," but remains ever irreducible to stereotypical rules and routines. Wittgenstein (1968, p. 227) broaches a similar idea.

However one chooses to divide epistemology, the question of how we have such knowledge raises several possibilities. One such, of perennial appeal to social scientists, is the notion that knowledge is stored away, encapsulated in templates, engrams, or inner representations. A further suggestion is that "away" has a locale, perhaps in the neurons or inner space of the mind depending upon one's predilection for physicalistic or mentalistic models of explanation. It is a bit like looking after knowledge capsules in a cranial cupboard, a search for the ontic location of the "inner" versus the "outer" representations of knowledge.

What engenders this odd quest? A subtle twist of logic called psychologism: the dual tendencies to view meaning as well as knowledge as mental processes or events so that the meaning of a symbol is taken to exist temporally in the mind, while knowledge is identified as a cognitive state, task, or activity. Ironically, psychologism afflicts certain areas of psychology more than linguistics or philosophy and the reification *in mens* of schemas, images, enactions, and so on (a virtual commitment to an out-moded theory of ideas) has not gone unnoticed by critics of cognitive psychology, especially Schwartz (1968).

Psychologism is perhaps natural enough, common sense in fact. For example, when we read, we (presumably) understand what we read; and the process of understanding does indeed consist of a series of conscious states. But to leap from that observation to the conclusion that the meaning understood is a mental event is to confuse acts of understanding (which can be highly variable from one individual to another) with the meaning understood. Furthermore, if meaning were a mental event, it would exist only so long as and vary with each different state of consciousness evoked by a symbol, varying both from one individual to another and from one occasion to another for the same individual. It would then be impossible to speak of words, sentences, or any symbol as having the same meaning for more than one individual on more than one occasion; with that sacrifice of the publicity of meaning would go all possibility of communication as well (Greenlee, 1973). The consequences thus far exceed the usual complaints of the empirical elusiveness of meanings that are interior events.

The same point can be made about knowledge in general which, no less than meaning, is irreducible to peculiar mental states dredged up by an effort of introspection. We should not find it strange to say, "I am now thinking about the proof for the Pythagorean theorem," whereas to say, "I am now knowing the proof for the Pythagorean theorem" is strange precisely because it suggests that knowing is a kind of mental performance detachable from the external world of proof, evidence, and fact. To be justified in saying, "Now I understand the proof for the Pythagorean theorem," requires not introspection but demonstration.

Psychologism is a classic instance of the confusion of the functional and cognitive perspectives mentioned above, a running together of the logical and psychological conditions of meaning, knowledge, and symbolization. They are complementary, contiguous, and yet distinguishable views of the same landscape. Ideally, we should like to have a reasonably clear generic picture of the landscape of knowledge before inquiring into its genetic origins. In lieu of that, we can at least remind ourselves that our theories are bifocal.

The value of that reminder for the representation of knowledge is very simply that, because on the functional approach meaning and knowledge are not *events*, the obfuscating consequences of psychologism are avoided and the way is cleared for inquiry into the true processes involved in their *achievement*. Moreover, to inquire how a representation or symbol functions relative to other symbols of that kind in a system of symbols (which system is logical, not mental or physical), be it a word, image, map, or graph, eliminates much, though not all, of the mystery of and lack of access to so-called inner representations, difficulties which accrue as well, though perhaps less obviously, to symbols outside the head. Moreover, there is no information contained in the symbols by which we represent knowledge beyond that which results from their functioning within a particular system of symbols. Examples are pictures drawn in reverse perspective or, more simply, the different meanings of the word "son" spelt in English and in French. As Goodman (1971) has observed, "The amount and kind of information derived from an optic array or anything else is usually no constant function of what is encountered but varies with the processing. A symbol may inform in as many different ways as there are contexts and systems of interpretation" (p. 360).

A further theoretical caution concerns "having" knowledge which, if not a mental event, is not "stored away" anywhere. Indeed, storage and retrieval metaphors are seriously misleading if one forgets that they are only metaphors. When we get to know something, we do not really store the knowledge away. Rather, we learn certain habits, tricks, or rules (educators prefer "strategies") for dealing with circumstances as they arise. Those tricks may leave neural or mnemonic traces but that is not at all the same as storing knowledge.

To reformulate, "having" knowledge is a complicated philosophical issue. It is possible to begin by noting that one knows in logically the same way that glass is brittle, which is, *dispositionally*. Thus, to say that something made of glass is brittle is to say that it will shatter if struck sharply with a hard object. Similarly, to say that I know that the earth is round is to say that I can give evidence for my belief, argue the case, and so forth—all the things a parrot, however talkative, cannot do. Having knowledge is thus a question of what I can produce when prompted and of the criteria used to judge my performance, not of *where* the ability is stored when unused and of how we retrieve it in a rush. By construing the possession of knowledge dispositionally we are also reminded that knowledge, though not itself a mental event, nonetheless involves skills, trainable ways of doing things, of solving problems, in short, of responding to circumstances intelligently or not as the case may be. That brings us to the third and final question, the representation of skills.

*The representation of skills*
How do we represent skills? First of all, how should we present the question? If the question is: How do we *represent* skills? we seem to be asking what are the mnemonic, symbolic, and schematic devices that mediate the acquisition and execution of a skill or, in other words, the role of symbolism *in* skills. If, on the other hand, the question is: How do we represent *skills*? attention is directed to how we might explain or characterize skills as a kind of human action, to the conditions of knowing how to do something, to use language, to sing, or to play tennis, for example. Moreover, we talk a great deal *about* skills in the course of learning them, often in language specially tailored to the purposes at hand.

Most of the actions involved in skilled procedures are what philosophers from Wittgenstein (1968) onwards describe as "rule-governed" or "rule-following." Certainly, one characteristic use of the language particular to established skills is to formulate rules and procedures to follow. What it means to follow a rule is the subject of much philosophical discussion most of which centers around moral principles or casuistry and is, therefore, somewhat irrelevant to present concerns. An exception is Black's (1967) four-part classification of actions following rules which cuts across our two questions in a way that illuminates the different roles played by technical jargon.

According to Black, an action is *rule-invoking* if it follows a set of explicit, fully articulated procedures or steps any one of which could be invoked to explain or justify what one is doing at any given moment while following them. In such cases, one is fully aware of the rules just as they are given in a cookbook or handbook of qualitative analysis, for example. Exercises, recipes, and regulations intended to build muscles or make fruit cake, to control traffic or run a committee come readily to mind. A set of directions and the will to follow them are the only requirements.

An action is *rule-accepting* if a rule can be formulated to describe exactly what a person is doing even if he or she is not consciously following it. A person counting "*one*, two; *one*, two . . .," might be told that he is counting a passage in 2/4 meter: two beats to the measure, one to each quarter note. That is true, of course, unless that person happened to be counting in 2/2 time. Though Black does not say so, it is crucial to accepting a rule properly that the conditions of its rejection also be clear. By the same token, it is possible to reject the action once the "rule" is made clear in a diagnostic comment such as: "It is as if you try to compensate for lack of pleasing timbre with sheer volume." Or, more simply, "You took your eye off the ball." That is no rule but an explanation of failure via an announcement of a violation of a rule. One accepts the explanation because one accepts the rule.

*Rule-covered* action is where an explanation is given in terms that could not be followed. It seems that rule-accepting and rule-covered actions are not necessarily distinct: a covering rule exactly describing an action is also rule-accepting. However, the idea of a rule that "could be followed" is ambiguous between one that the actor could appeal to as sufficient to *direct* or *control* performance (rule-accepting) and one that properly *describes* or *explains* his performance (rule-covered). Clearly, one rule does not entail the other. If it is enough to distinguish the two categories of rule-following action, in practice a particular rule may fall into either or both categories, varying from time to time and from person to person for any given rule. In short, the categories appear to be disjoint but not differentiated.

Polanyi's example of an explanation of how one maintains balance on a bicycle using terms like rate of curvature and angle of unbalance cites a rule that covers without directing action. Kinesiological explanations of athletic movements, physiological accounts of singing, and so on, would fall into this category. At best its influence is indirect, resulting, perhaps, in revisions of practical directives or confirmation of others but of no immediate self-critical value to the agent.

Finally, there is *rule-guided* action, virtually synonymous with the kind of understanding mentioned above where, in lieu of an explicit list, one finds only tips and cues as well as various images affecting a kind of "phenomenological compression" of vast amounts of detail (Black, 1967, p. 100). A distinguishing feature of this "assimilated" level of action is an ease and fluency of execution conspicuously absent when rules are consulted one by one. The private, synoptic shorthand devised for guidance and reduced to essentials is "appropriately articulated by non-verbal symbolism" (Black, 1967, p. 101). Though intuitively transformed and idiosyncratic, such condensations, Black urges, are "not 'private' in the philosopher's technical sense of unintelligibility in principle to another" (Black, 1967, p. 100). Indeed, they are not; it is just such mnemonic, controlling devices as constitute the tips and cues that one may offer another to aid the exercise of high skill. Wittgenstein places such subtle hints beyond the reach of rules and formulae, whereas Black views them as simplified, though amazingly versatile, summaries of rules, the means whereby "the rule" becomes "my rule" in a fluid performance (Black, 1967, p. 101). Both acknowledge, while I should stress, their role in communicating about the subtleties of skill. A properly balanced view acknowledges all these possibilities.

Between the extremes of blind mastery (rule-covered behaviour) and slavish adherence to precept (rule-invoking behaviour) Black discerns the relative ease of implicit conformity to rule (rule-accepting behaviour) and the "free-flowing" action without apparent calculation of trained virtuosity (rule-guided behaviour). Arranged thus on a continuum, Black's types of rule-governed action suggest that there are limitations on the articulation of rules beyond those arising from an inability to put things into words or the initial obscurity of complicated jargon.

Consider the following situation. A standard tax form instructs us to enter all taxable income and supplies rules for determining taxable income. It is easy to imagine further rules for interpreting the rules for determining taxable income, and so on indefinitely. What stops the regress of rules is, in a word, unintelligibility. "The chain of rules will quickly terminate, for want of an adequate vocabulary. The nearer we come to what is readily *seen* by an apt learner, the harder it becomes to articulate the governing rule and a point is soon reached at which the effort of attending to the verbal formula positively interferes with the primary performance."(Black, 1967, p. 101.) This is not the unintelligibility of misuse, mistiming, or the first encounter with a new terminology but of distraction. Language exceeds its descriptive usefulness almost to the point of trying to reproduce the prescribed behaviour. "Of course," Black (1967, p. 102) remarks, "sensible men soon abandon *saying* in favor of *showing*." However, it is germane to note that abandoning descriptions and rules for demonstrations and samples (which do selectively reproduce the behaviour in question) is less a matter of jettisoning symbols than shifting their emphasis or direction, from labeling by words to showing by actions.

Because one must learn how to follow rules and make sense of demonstrations, a "foundation of primitive habits of response" (rule-covered behaviour) is presupposed, so that "The ideal cycle, indefinitely repeated, will be from 'rule-covering behaviour' to 'rule-guided behaviour'" (Black, 1967, p. 102). Thus the full development from novice to virtuoso takes the form of training that is symbolically mediated even if, as must happen, there comes a time when explicit rules are cast aside.

Conspicuous by its absence from Black's account of rule-governed action in procedural contexts is an examination of how we reason using such rules. As suggested earlier (when discussing violations), we are accustomed not merely to accepting or obeying rules but to utilizing them critically as well. We resort to rules to compare and contrast our successes with our failures in terms of what we believe to be the underlying causes (if we have confidence in the rules). Black approaches the topic twice: once when he observes that the "credentials" of rules ultimately are cognitive, even if momentarily backed by personal authority; they are rooted in the nature of things so that the difference between a rule and a principle is largely a matter of grammatical mood (p. 96). Again, in a footnote, he avers that "Verbal articulation will *change* the performance, in subtle or massive ways. Indeed its main point will often be to correct and to improve the performance" (p. 104). If the rules are often mini-principles, however, the matter is not merely one of following orders but of understanding the criticism implied in their violation and of making inferences from causes to their effects and back again.

A simple example like, "You took your eye off the ball," is an instance of diagnostic reasoning by reference to a procedural rule but it fails to express the interrelationships among many such rules communicated in a jargon that has achieved technical status. A more comprehensive example is the way in which singers talk about exercises and technique designed to build and maintain a singing voice equal to the demands of the classical repertoire. Vocal exercises, construed as rules, are intended to strengthen organic responses, perfect vocal registration, and train the ear (Reid, 1970, pp. 231-249; 1971, pp. 36-64). The mature integration of these elements in action is singing skill, while knowledge of what will and how to strengthen, perfect, and train, is the craft of voice building. For a singer devoid of such knowledge, exercises are useless, the proper execution, aims, effects, and so on remaining obscure. The technical language of singing spans these practical, as well as artistic, considerations, emphasizing generally vocal registers and breaks, tonal quality (timbre), resonance, and respiration (support) and specifically the functional effects of certain pitch and intensity patterns that the student of singing learns to discriminate and correlate with certain physical sensations.

Though initially seeming metaphysical, such terms are actually perceptual, phenomenal, and subphysical in the sense of preceding any physical (rule-
covering) explanation. Except for explicit (rule-invoking) exercises, most are of
the rule-accepting kind whereby one sensation is evoked to "explain" another. If
(a) that sound, then (b) that feeling (physical sensation), and (c) that physiological
function. For example, we know what the falsetto voice sounds and feels like in
contrast to the full-throated chest voice and that it results from the independent
vibration of the outer longitudinal lining of the vocal folds. We also know (in the
rule-covering sense) that it is only as the outer lining and *vocalis* muscles or tensors
are brought into synchronous vibration that the break between falsetto and chest
voices, typical of the yodeller, for instance, can be eliminated.

While knowing (c) may aid a broader understanding of the voice, we
apply the rules (exercises) and give advice in terms of the covariance of (a) and (b).
The language, though not the inductive correlations represented in (a) and (b),
may be rather loose, expecially at first. Indeed, it must remain versatile and
suggestive to have effect. ("Round the back of the throat" or "Place the tone
forward," or "Make the tone 'brighter' or 'darker.' ")

Nearly any complex skill or craft has a similar domain of sensation,
perception, and special effects included in its jargon, however variable, fragmentary, or confusing its descriptions may at first appear. The prime value of such
language lies in its utility in directing and communicating rather than in any strict
consistency, coherence, or capacity for extended arguments and explanations.
Like descriptions, explanations that exceed useful limits quickly become unintel-
ligible or, at best, irrelevant. Nonetheless, the utility and communicative power of
any language, however much action-oriented or intuitively suggestive, requires
that *some* standards of coherence, of consistent use of terms, imagery, and inference be observed if its explanations and directives are to be of any pedagogic or
critical value. Certainly, the organization and structure sought is in the activity
itself, so that, paradoxically, the language or imagery employed while learning a
skill may become more fragmentary as it becomes more literal and synoptic at
higher levels of rule-guided action.

When explanation stops demonstration begins but showing is not merely
doing: it is representational action, each step a sample-action that makes a point
about itself and all others of its kind. Indeed, much telling takes the form of
indicating when to look for what in a demonstration or sample. The descriptive
cue need not be complete in every detail (in truth it could not be); it need properly
apply only enough to select the sample or aspect thereof which in turn supplies the
relevant detail. Further talk may or may not obscure matters depending upon the
circumstances, for example, if something important has been missed in the demonstration. A demonstration thus is worth a thousand words, provided it is clear
in principle what the thousand words would be about, the point, in short, that the
demonstration seeks to demonstrate. In passing, therefore, from telling to showing we do not leave the realm of representation but rather enter another dimen-

sion of it, that is, exemplification (Goodman, 1976, pp. 57-67), closely allied to language though distinguishable from it. Logically, sample-actions cannot simply be said to "speak for themselves" if only because the nature of such speaking would have to be contrasted with all the talk that has gone before. And here we return to the original question about the varieties of representation, that is, all existing forms of reference.

This is not the place to go into detail about the differences among descriptive and other functions of language, exemplification in its many forms, depiction, and so on, or the perceptual capacities required to master the varieties of representation in the first instance or their conceptual dominion over intellectual and motor skills. Rather, the intention has been merely to draw attention to the delicate conceptual and logical as well as psychological and technological questions broached by the very idea of theory of representation. To that end three major questions have been distinguished as fairly delineating the domain of such a theory and centering, appropriately, on the varieties of representation (or symbolization) though encompassing the representation of knowledge and of skills. We are at least somewhat clearer about the questions themselves and what is in the nature of the asking, if not, regrettably, in the answering.

### Reference note
1. Goodman, N. Routes of reference. Paper presented at the 2nd Congress of the International Association for Semiotic Studies, Vienna, July 1979.

### References
Black, M. Rules and routines. In R. S. Peters (Ed.), *The concept of education*. London: Routledge & Kegan Paul, 1967.

Bruner, J. S., Olver, R. R., & Greenfield, P. M. *Studies in cognitive growth*. New York: Wiley, 1966.

Cassirer, E. *An essay on man*. New Haven: Yale University Press, 1944.

Gardner, H., Howard, V. A., & Perkins, D. N. Symbol systems: A philosophical, psychological, and educational investigation. In D. E. Olson (Ed.), *Media and symbols: The forms of expression, communication, and education*. Chicago: University of Chicago Press, 1974.

Goodman, N. On J. J. Gibson's new perspective. *Leonardo*, 1971, *4*, 359-360.

Goodman, N. *Languages of art, an approach to a theory of symbols* (2nd ed.) Indianapolis: Hackett, 1976.

Greenlee, D. *Peirce's concept of sign*. The Hague: Mouton, 1973.

Peirce, C. S. The icon, index, and symbol (1902.) *Collected Papers* (Vol. II). Cambridge, Mass.: Harvard University Press, 1960.

Polanyi, M. *Personal knowledge: Towards a post-critical philosophy*. London: Routledge & Kegan Paul, 1958.

Reid, C. L. Functional vocal training. *Journal of Orgonomy*, 1970, *4*, 231-249, 1971, *5*, 36-64.

Ryle, G. *The concept of mind*. London: Hutchinson, 1949.

Schwartz, R. Review of *Studies in cognitive growth*. *The Journal of Philosophy*, 1968, *65*, 172-179.

Wittgenstein, L. *Philosophical investigations* (G.E.M. Anscombe, trans.). Oxford: Blackwell, 1968.

# Textual literacy: An outline sketch of psychological research on reading and writing

Patricia Wright

*This paper outlines the major emphases within psychological research on reading and writing. It is divided into four sections. Section 1 examines the notion of literacy and suggests that much everyday reading differs from that studied in the experimental laboratory. In sections 2 and 3 the research on reading and writing is reviewed and it becomes apparent that there are virtually no points of contact between the two fields of research. Section 4 discusses some implications of broadening the concept of reading to include a wide range of cognitive processes. The value of increased interaction among different researchers is pointed out and it is suggested that a slight shift in the focus of the research makes it easier to apply our understanding of the processes of comprehension to the practical problems of helping readers acquire the skills necessary for literacy and of creating materials adequate for the various domains of textual literacy.*

## What is literacy?

Literacy means more than the ability to understand the words and sentences on a page. For example, Sticht (1978) pointed out that, "a large part of learning to be literate, and perhaps the most important part for acquiring higher levels of literacy, is learning how to perform the many tasks made possible by the unique characteristics of printed displays, their permanence and spatiality" (p. 152). Readers have a wide range of options in dealing with written information: they can sample paragraphs and reject them as irrelevant; they can start at the end or in the middle of a text; they can read smoothly on or hop backwards and forwards. Indeed, it can be advantageous to teach readers that there are merits in departing from the linear sequence provided by the writer (Pugh, 1978).

Characteristics of the visual presentation of a message may determine how easily it is understood (Hartley, 1978). The importance of suprasegmental cues such as pausing and intonation have been clearly demonstrated for spoken language (Cruttenden, 1974) but the corresponding visual cues for written language have seldom been explored. Such cues might well be helpful in acquiring reading skills (Cromer, 1970).

Sticht (1978) distinguished between "reading to do" and "reading to learn" and there are probably variants within each of these categories. For example, Samuels and Dahl (1975) found that people read a passage faster for general content than for specific facts. The notion of the reader as an active participant in the interaction with written materials was expanded by Olshavsky (1976-77) who reported 10 different reading strategies used by 24 people who were reading short stories which varied in their degree of abstractness. When interpreting experimental studies of reading, it is important, then, to specify the reading of what, by whom, and for what purpose.

A quite different question from "What is literacy?" is "What do people want to read and write?" Williams (1976) reported that newly literate adults, asked what they found most advantageous about their new skills, replied variously: "Reading means that I can look at the cereal packets and send away for special offers." "Reading means being able to go shopping on your own and write a list and compare things." "Reading means being able to look up bus times." "Reading is knowing what you're signing when you write your name."

Given the diversity of materials read, it may be helpful to subdivide the field of literacy into domains of different kinds of written materials. Williams (1976) suggests it might be useful to consider a domain of "domestic literacy" (the reading skills needed in private life) in addition to the existing notion of functional literacy (Gray, 1956). Examples of the kinds of written materials likely to be found in each domain include:

Domestic literacy (private life)
    a) instructions: cooking, using appliances, and so on
    b) highway information, route directions, timetables
    c) completing forms and leaving messages
Functional literacy (job related)
    a) warning notices
    b) manuals and assembly instructions
    c) work sheets and pay slips
Advanced literacy (entertainment and self instruction)
    a) magazine articles
    b) textbooks
    c) novels and other fiction

## Research on reading

The following list illustrates the kinds of issues addressed by researchers in different disciplines.

| *Field* | *Questions* |
| --- | --- |
| Pedagogy | How should reading be taught? |
| Psychometrics | What reading skills will the average child have? |
| Social-personality | Who reads what and how well? |
| Curriculum development | What reading skills are needed for different subject matters? |
| Experimental psychology | What cognitive processes underlie reading skills? |
| Neuro-psychology | What are the functional substrates and anatomical correlates of reading impairments? |

The present overview will concentrate on the field of experimental psychology. The experimental research falls roughly into four domains: the reading of letters, words, sentences, and paragraphs. For each domain a sketch will be given of the main questions asked and answers given together with some aspects of the issue which seem to have been overlooked.

*The perception of letters*

*Questions*. How do we identify letters? What is the role of letter identification in reading? What are the relationships among eye movements, visual span, and reading comprehension?

*Answers*. Haber (1978) has estimated that 20 features may be needed to differentiate both upper and lower case letters, punctuation, and other common typographic symbols. Kolers (1975) has shown that the ability to process orthographic features has much in common with the acquisition of a skill. For example, once people have learned to read text printed upside down, or mirror reversed, they retain this skill for a year without practice (Kolers, 1976). Posner and Mitchell (1967) have shown that there are many levels at which people "identify" a letter. It is possible to identify much more rapidly that two familiar graphemes have the same shape (*a* and *a*) than that they have the same name (*a* and *A*). Such variation is what is meant by saying that letter identification creates problems for researchers. The psychological processes responsible for letter identification are, for the most part, unconscious (Marcel, 1978a; 1980). Therefore tasks requiring conscious letter identification (whether naming or matching) may distort the very processes being examined. Similar distortions can arise in research on the perception of words, sentences, and paragraphs.

The role of letter identification in reading is unclear. Our ability to read degraded and mutilated texts is evidence that there is often no need to identify all the letters before the word itself can be recognized. Indeed, it has long been known that people can detect a letter faster in a word than when it is presented alone or in a nonsense string (Cattell, 1886). Johnson (1978) suggests that this may be due to memory rather than perceptual process, but other studies have shown effects that are unambiguously perceptual. For example, when proof-reading, people are more likely to overlook mistakes at the end of words (Corcoran, 1966; Smith and Groat, 1979). Readers apparently use their knowledge of the orthographic patterns of English spelling to assist in word identification (Frith, 1979). Haber (1978) has suggested that this knowledge enables readers to broaden their visual span.

Good readers can also name letters faster (Jackson and McClelland, 1979) and pronounce nonsense words more quickly (Firth, Note 1; Venezky, 1976). However, it does not follow that phonological coding is important for word identification although it may well play some other role in reading (McClelland & Jackson, 1978), being most critical perhaps in tasks dependant on the reader's short-term, or working, memory (Baddeley, 1979).

There are several reviews of eye-movement studies (Levy-Schoen & O'Regan, 1979; Rayner, 1978). In brief, it has been found that although only six or seven letters surrounding the fixation point are seen clearly, some information is received from 21 characters on either side of the fixation point (Schiepers, 1976). Readers make larger saccades near short words (Rayner & McConkie, 1976) and are more likely to skip a three-letter function word such as *the*, than a three-letter verb such as *was* (O'Regan, 1979). Such studies emphasize the multiplicity of control processes in reading. It is not an activity controlled solely by the graphic marks on the page.

*Issues overlooked*. The use of white space is rarely considered. Research has shown that longer lines require more space between them if they are to be equally legible (Tinker, 1965) but it is not yet known why this is so. Similarly, it could not be predicted from the psychology of letter identification that, when text is printed on paper so thin that the reverse side shows through, people can read it more easily when the lines of print on both sides of the page are aligned, so maintaining the clear white space between them (Spencer, Reynolds & Coe, Note 7).

The interference of surrounding contours is not well understood. It has been shown that legibility is reduced when the answers to questions on forms are written with each letter in a separate box (Barnard & Wright, 1976; Barnard, Wright, & Wilcox, 1978). Dobson (1980) has reported similar problems in carto-graphic displays. The literature predicts nothing about how the proximity or salience of these surrounds affects identification.

Electronic displays raise many questions which are difficult to answer from our present knowledge of letter identification. For example, at what speed should a text "walk" from right to left, or scroll upwards? Is a static text that is overwritten preferable to a rolling text?

Generalizations from legibility research have often seemed hazardous (Wright, 1978). The results of studies using large signboard displays differ from those using typewritten displays viewed at normal reading distance or presented briefly in a tachistoscope. Possibly, various psychological processes, both active (hypothesis testing) and passive (driven by sensory data), are recruited in different proportions by different reading tasks (Broadbent & Broadbent, 1975, 1980).

*The reading of words*
A useful review is given by Allport (1979).

*Questions*. What is the processing sequence that enables readers to move from the graphemic marks on the page to the identification of a particular word? How are the meanings of words represented and inter-related within memory?

*Answers*. There appear to be at least two routes, one a "direct" word identification, the other a grapheme to phoneme conversion (Marcel & Patterson, 1978). Some models of the reading process appear to go no further than the identification of words (Mackworth, 1971) and tend to assume that the starting point for word identification is the graphic marks on the page. Other approaches (Kolers, 1969) have emphasized the roles played by context and the reader's expectations. For example, grammatical errors are automatically corrected by the reader (Kolers, 1966). Such "misreadings" of words are the basis for a model developed by Goodman (1973) which likens reading to a "psycholinguistic guessing game."

There is currently no consensus on the way meanings are represented within memory. Models range from the rigidly hierarchical (Collins & Quillian, 1969), through the fuzzy set notions of family resemblances (Rosch, 1975), to the random network proposed by Landauer (1975). The use of heterarchies and their contribution to individual differences in semantic organization are also being explored (Broadbent, Cooper & Broadbent, 1978).

*Issues overlooked*. Single words often represent entire sentences (for example, STOP, NAME). In children's speech these one-word utterances are termed holophrases (Bloom, 1973) but little attention seems to have been paid to their role in adult reading.

It is possible that Sticht (1972) might consider the interpretation of holophrases as not being particularly difficult for readers because they are part of oral language competence. Yet when the clerk behind the desk says "Name?" the query is denoted by a rising intonation. Such cues are completely missing for readers. Instead, they must learn how to interpret variations in typography and in spatial presentation.

Blakar (1979) has pointed out that words have not only a referential function and an associative component but also an emotive aspect. This is well illustrated by mock conjugations of the kind: I stick to principles, you are insistent, he is stubborn. Psychologists have developed techniques such as the semantic differential for measuring the emotive aspects of words (Osgood, Suci, & Tannenbaum, 1957) but the emotive aspect is often omitted from models of how readers interpret a text. The emotive force of an expression may well change when it is written. Those providing television commentaries for the deaf (Baker, Downton, & Newall, 1980) have found that strong language, acceptable to the viewing audience as part of a dialogue, could become offensive when written on the screen.

*Reading sentences*
A useful summary is given by Levelt (1978).

*Questions*. How are sentences represented in abstract form? What further operations are needed to answer questions or carry out instructions successfully?

*Answers*. The most powerful models of sentence representation are those based on augmented transition networks (Wanner, Kaplan, & Shiner, Note 9). Central to such networks is the concept that tests are applied to incoming stimuli and, from their results, the processing system is able to move from one state of the network to another. The strength of this approach lies in the fact that the tests applied can be of any sort and there is no necessity for making sharp distinctions between syntax, semantics, and pragmatics.

The operations carried out upon these internal representations can be specified in the process-oriented framework of artificial intelligence (Olson & Filby, 1972; Carpenter & Just, 1975). However, it is not clear if these operations are applicable beyond a particular range of experimental tasks in which people assess whether a sentence is a correct description of a picture (Glushko & Cooper, 1978).

Research on sentence comprehension is gradually being extended to include the drawing of inferences (Clark, 1978, 1979). This could be particularly relevant to the development of literacy skills, for a mini-evaluation of functional literacy carried out in 1974 found that all groups were best at word-naming but had most difficulty with drawing inferences (Kirsch & Guthrie, 1977-78).

*Issues overlooked*. What the writer omits is often as informative as what is said, as Winograd (1977) has pointed out and as referees' comments on job applicants demonstrate. Even simple notices for the general public may mean something rather different from what they say. In Britain escalator signs may request, "Stand on the right" when they mean, "Do not stand still on the left."

Differences between reading and listening must be considered as well. Olson (1977) has pointed out that the written word facilitates certain reasoning and inferential thinking and, consequently, in some tasks people do better when reading than when listening (Walker, 1977). This implies that readers need to be taught how to use written text to aid thinking.

### Reading paragraphs
A useful collection of the many psychological studies is provided by Just and Carpenter (1977). One of the most influential texts has been that by Halliday and Hasan (1976).

*Questions*. How are the meanings of paragraphs represented in abstract form? What factors contribute to the thematic unity of a text?

*Answers*. Although many models have been proposed (Anderson, 1976; Kintsch, 1974; Mandler and Johnson, 1977). Most relevant to literacy skills have been the findings that readers expect specific episodic structures within a text (van Dijk, 1977). Perfetti and Lesgold (1977) have suggested that there may be ways in which the skilled reader resembles a chess grand master in that the skill consists in recognizing a great many macrostructures and responding appropriately. Readers certainly anticipate where certain kinds of information will be located in a document. Sticht (1977) found that, rather than use an index, 90 percent of his readers (military personnel) preferred to leaf through the document.

Macrostructures also influence the reader's eye movements (Shebilske & Reid, 1979). It is not clear to what extent the macrostructures are generated by readers on the basis of the text itself or are brought to the reading task by the reader on the basis of experience. Certainly, expectations influence the strategy for reading a text and also memory both for theme and detail.

Frederiksen (1977) has suggested that there are at least four interactive levels at which the coherence or unity of a text must be maintained. One level concerns the objectives of the communication and it is here that decisions are made about including or omitting certain points that embellish or support the theme. A second level concerns the sequential organization of the information and use is made of linguistic devices (for example, the order of mention and assignment of definite or indefinite articles—*the/a*) for differentiating between the information assumed to be known to the reader and the new information given by the text (Chafe, 1972). A third level is the explicit linking of particular sentences with other parts of the text (by the use of pronouns, conjunctions, or phrases referring to material elsewhere in the text). Frederiksen's fourth level is concerned with the unity of the sentence itself. Research is being done at all these levels but we are still some way from understanding how these factors which contribute to the unity of prose interact to provide readers with the perception of a coherent paragraph.

*Issues overlooked*. Studies of paragraph comprehension have used a limited range of texts, mostly fictional narratives which are very different from the material found in the categories of domestic and functional literacy. The cohesive structure of a story obviously differs from that of a procedural sequence like a recipe. In particular, typographic factors and details of design may play a more important role in domestic and functional literacy than in advanced literacy. Both at home and at work, words and pictures are often combined and each influences the interpretation of the other.

Related to the limited range of materials studied is the fact that psychologists have also restricted the range of reading tasks chosen. Retention has been emphasized in spite of the evidence that by doing so the view of the language processing can easily be distorted (Fillenbaum, 1970). Little attention seems to have been given to Kolers' (1973) remark that readers are skilled practitioners with a hierarchy of processing options from which to choose. Anzai and Simon (1979) suggest that strategy selection is an important consideration in all cognitively complex "problem-solving" tasks. What appears to be lacking is any account of the determinants of strategy selection in reading. The limitations of reading materials and reading tasks make it particularly difficult to move from research on the psychology of reading to guidelines for designing written material.

## Research on writing

One of the curious aspects of research on writing is that there is so little of it. There is a considerable amount of research on comprehension (reading) but very little on production (writing). It might be interesting to speculate why. Perhaps there has been a tacit assumption that if one knows how language is produced (speech) and how people deal with graphic symbols (reading) then nothing more needs to be known about writing.

Certainly there is some evidence that writing is related to speech. Slips of the pen are often substitutes of phonologically similar items (Frith, 1979). Nevertheless, Olson (1975) has pointed out that the literature of a culture is expressed in a language that is not spoken by any member of that culture. For example, we tend to shift register when we write and at the same time curtail the ideas we express (Horowitz and Berkowitz, 1967).

The following outline of research on the design of written information will divide "writing" into three subfields: the writer's conceptual approach to communicating, the writer's selection among presentation options, and the writer's evaluation of the communication. Within each of these subdivisions there will again be a brief sketch of questions, answers, and issues overlooked.

### Conceptual approach

One of the few overviews of research in this area is found in Gregg and Steinberg (1980).

*Questions.* Why do writers have problems saying what they mean? What strategies do writers have?

*Answers.* Flower (1979) has systematically analysed some of the problems of writing, suggesting that writing has more in common with Vygotsky's notion of inner speech than with the characteristics of oral speech. The implication is that writing is a mode of expression having its own characteristics including its elliptical nature (that is, many references are deleted because the writer knows the topic and has no need to refer to them), its private use of words (terms used in an idiosyncratically narrow sense without explanation), and its omission of causal relations because much inner speech follows associative rather than logical paths. Walker (Note 8) suggests that writers may adopt a "stream of consciousness" technique whereby only the sentence to sentence transitions are planned rather than higher order development of the argument. In this respect, there is a contrast between the processes of reading and writing. Readers may use well-developed macrostructures. It is less obvious that writers do.

Rommetveit (1972), on the other hand, suggests that ellipsis is a normal characteristic of human communication: "Ellipsis is the normal case under conditions of love, trust and a shared social world. A request for full sentences stems from linguists and pedantic schoolmasters who believe that man is alienated from his fellow man." (p. 25.) Communicating at a distance instead of face-to-face may involve just such alienation. It is interesting to note that Davies (1978) has suggested that reading should be considered "a long range conversation" with its own specialized constraints for which writers need to acquire special skills.

Given the likelihood of problems in creating the first draft there is, obviously, a need to develop editing skills. Good readers seem to be better editors because they are better at discriminating the material central to the theme of a passage (Eamon 1978-79). Hayes and Flower (Note 4) have distinguished between an editing facility, which writers use while writing, and a rewriting skill used to amend and improve the draft version of a text. Suggestions for developing such skills can be found in Flower and Hayes (1977).

Sometimes the writer's sequence of ideas is not in the order most easily grasped by readers and the medium of communication may change the nature of the information provided. Typewritten messages were found to be shorter and less informative than handwritten ones which, in turn, were terser than spoken messages (Chapanis, Parrish, Ochsman, and Weeks, 1977). The ways in which the choice of display medium affects both writers and readers has received little examination.

*Issues overlooked*. Studies have contrasted the writing abilities of different authors (Funkhouser and Maccoby, 1971), but seldom focussed on the process of writing as distinct from the product. Yet of these processes the writer's presuppositions can be crucial because if these are wrong then the entire conceptual approach of the text can sometimes be flawed. An example is a booklet on how to make a corn-sheller (Pinson, Note 5) where technical diagrams, including detailed measurements, are given in a text intended for use at the village level in the Third World. Scientists writing for a lay readership often encounter similar difficulties. It has been suggested that authors should empirically determine the relevant characteristics of their audience (Wright, 1979).

It is difficult to find research studies on the training and acquisition of communication skills in a broader sense than that of writing a letter or an essay. Guides to good writing have been widely available for years (Flesch, 1946) but have apparently had little effect on some authors (Redish, Note 6). Perhaps, like many other skills, practice may be indispensable in the realm of functional literacy. Interactive computer facilities have led to innovations in teaching technical writing (Frase, 1980; Frase, Keenan and Dever, 1980) although software can provide writers only with certain kinds of support (Frase, Note 3). It can detect long words, long sentences, and so on, but this may not be most useful when dealing with extended passages of prose.

Training programs might be developed to help writers select not only the appropriate registers of expression but also the appropriate display medium and format for the communication. Many kinds of domestic and functional literacy require integrating a wide variety of modes of expression. At the moment we seem to know very little about how such integration is achieved either by writers or by readers.

*Selection among presentation options*
A useful starting point for exploring this literature is Hartley (1978).

*Questions*. What aspects of typographic presentation can make prose more comprehensible? When is prose alone inadequate for communication?

*Answers*. Foster (cited in Wright, Note 10) coined the phrase "format exposes structure," that is, the way in which information is presented on the printed page should make clear how the various sections of the material relate to each other, as in the use of space, headings, and subheadings. Waller (1979) discussed the need to provide readers with adequate "access structures" for locating specific information within documents. Design factors can easily affect the accuracy of the information collected on the form (Wright, 1980a) or the accuracy with which a numerical table is used (Wright, 1977).

There have been very few investigations of the relative advantages of alternatives to prose for communicating either different kinds of subject matter or to different kinds of reader, although these options have been clearly indicated by Twyman (1979). It has been shown that, for a given content, audience, and reading purpose, the most effective presentation of the information depends on the context in which the information is used (Wright & Reid, 1973). The numerous problems of generalizing from studies of text comprehension have been discussed by Macdonald - Ross (1979).

*Issues overlooked*. Seldom do researchers feel obliged to point out the financial implications of their results but without such information it can be difficult to know what to make of the finding that people using version A were $x$ seconds faster than those using version B. Whether or not these few seconds matter depends on various factors such as how the information is used and how large a proportion of such usage is contributed by the factors examined experimentally. Another practical difficulty is that of locating research on information design. The writer of an insurance contract cannot look up "insurance contract" in the psychological abstracts. The issues which researchers address are much smaller. Yet how can the writer know what these issues are? By heightening the awareness of presentation options it may be possible to improve the writing skills of some writers and also provide them with conceptual facilitate locating and interpreting the research literature.

*Evaluation of the communication*
An outline of how the notions of quality control might apply to document design can be found in Wright (1979). The usefulness of readability formulae has been discussed by Klare (1976).

*Questions*. What are the characteristics of the audience? Is the information in the text adequate?

*Answers*. Writers need to know what vocabulary will be suitable for their readers, also what preconceptions those readers may have about the subject matter and its presentation. Knowing how frequently different portions of the text will be used may have implications for sequencing the material. A wide range of techniques is available for exploring aspects of a text's content. These include field studies, surveys, in-depth interviews, and laboratory experiments.

There is also a range of techniques for determining if the information provided by the document is adequate, both in the sense of being sufficient and in the sense of being usable by the reader (Wright, 1980b). The development of sophisticated word-processing systems can help writers detect several kinds of problems with the wording of a text but ambiguities arise all too easily. So an empirical check that a document can be understood by its audience is the only way of ensuring a minimal level of communicative adequacy.

*Issues overlooked*. Although there exist a variety of ways for finding out if something crucial is missing from the text, it is much more difficult to find out if unnecessary information is being given. Within the domains of domestic and functional literacy, providing too much information may decrease the chances of any of it being read.

There is a tendency for text evaluation to concentrate on the reader's "comprehension" but, for materials in the realm of domestic and functional literacy, this may not be adequate. A discussion of the value of designing written information to achieve "usability" as well as "comprehensibility" is provided by Wright (1980b).


## An alternative approach to the psychology of reading and writing

The preceding discussion implies that there is no relation between the research questions asked about reading and those asked about writing. Marcel (1978b) is equally pessimistic about the relation between research on reading and the teaching of literacy skills. By taking a much broader approach to reading, however, it may be possible to forge closer links between the two fields. By focussing on the cognitive components of reading and writing it may be possible to develop an overlapping middle group between the study of comprehension and research on information design. It has been argued that such an approach to reading, in terms of cognitive components, can highlight both research issues and design options (Wright, 1980b).

| *Kinds of reading* | *Cognitive components* | *Design options* |
|---|---|---|
| reading to do | perception | confirmation— list or prose |
| reading to learn facts | attention | representation— verbal or pictorial |
| reading to learn concepts | language | thematic structure— linear or hierarchical |
| searching | decisions | sectional demarcation— sub-headings |
| browsing | memory | amplification— notes and examples |
| reading for pleasure | response generation | signposts— indices, contents etc. |

If there is to be real progress in information design, much more interaction should be fostered among different kinds of researchers. Three overlapping kinds of enquiry exist: tactical, applied, and basic. The tactical researcher is looking for a total solution to a communication problem within the constraints of available time and finances. For tacticians concerned with writing, the final product is a document; for those concerned with reading, the final product is usually a group of pupils who have attained a particular level of mastery of the required reading skills. Both face recurrent decision points which they treat on an ad hoc basis. Applied researchers, presented with these problems, however, might be able to establish a body of findings that would reduce the ad hoc nature of tactical decisions. Similarly, if applied research establishes that version A is more effective than version B, an explanation in terms of the underlying psychological processes is required. At the moment, however, psychologists are busy building comprehension models of materials read by only a small number of people (the advanced literacy domain) and the tacticians firmly believe that psychology is irrelevant in solving practical problems.

## General conclusions

This outline of research relating to textual literacy has tried to show that there are various kinds of reading and consequently, that literacy comprises many different skills associated with both reading and writing. It has been suggested that one of the deficiencies in research is the general assumption that the meaning is *within* the text whereas, in reality, readers go far beyond the text in deriving their interpretation. Knowing what the words mean or how to deal with particular syntactic structures is seldom adequate within the domains of domestic and functional literacy. But writers sometimes lack the skill to provide adequate cues to the correct interpretation of their texts, just as they may be unaware of factors which can contribute to misunderstandings. One way to avoid miscommunications might be to develop an integrated approach to the study of reading and writing, focussing on the cognitive components of both. It may then be easier to apply the findings from research on comprehension to the practical problems of designing written communications for the many varieties of textual literacy.

## Reference notes

1. Firth, I. Components of reading disability. Unpublished manuscript, University of New South Wales, Kensington N.S.W., Australia, 1972.
2. Flower, L. S. & Hayes, J. R. (Eds.), *A process model of composition* (Document Design Project, Tech. Rep. 1). Pittsburgh, Pa.: Carnegie Mellon University, 1979.
3. Frase, L. T. *The problem of multiple markets and evolving product lines for Bell System Documentation*. Unpublished manuscript, 1979. (Available from the author at Bell Laboratories, Piscataway, N.J.).
4. Hayes, J. R., & Flower, L. S. Identifying the organization of writing processes. In L. S. Flower and J. R. Hayes (Eds.), *A process model of composition* (Document Design Project, Tech. Rep. 1). Pittsburgh, Pa.: Carnegie Mellon University, 1979.
5. Pinson, G. S. *A wooden hand-held maize sheller*. Tropical Products Institute, Rural Technology Guide 1, 1977.
6. Redish, J. C. *Research planning report No. 1., the Document Design Project*. Unpublished manuscript, 1978. Available from the author at the American Institute for Research, 1055 Thomas Jefferson Street, N.W. Washington, D. C., 20007, U.S.A).
7. Spencer, H., Reynolds, L., & Coe, B. *The effects of show-through on the legibility of printed text*. (Rep. 9). London: Royal College of Art, Readability of Print Research Unit, 1977.
8. Walker, J. H. Collection of thoughts about writing. Unpublished manuscript, 1979. (Available from the author at Bolt, Beranek & Newman, Inc., Cambridge, Mass.)
9. Wanner, E., Kaplan, R., & Shiner, S. Garden paths in relative clauses. Unpublished manuscript, 1975. (Available from the authors at Harvard University, Cambridge, Mass.)

10. Wright, P. Designing information: Some approaches, some problems and some suggestions. London: British Library Research and Development Department, 1979.

## References

Allport, A. Word recognition in reading. In P. A. Kolers, M. E. Wrolstad, & H. Bouma (Eds.), *Processing of visible language, 1*. New York and London: Plenum Press, 1979.

Anderson, J. R. *Language, memory, and thought*. Hillsdale, N.J.: Lawrence Erlbaum Associates, 1976.

Anzai, Y., & Simon, H. A. The theory of learning by doing. *Psychological Review*, 1979, *86*, 124-140.

Baddeley, A. D. Working memory and reading. In P. A. Kolers, M. E. Wrolstad, & H. Bouma (Eds.), *Processing of visible language, 1*. New York and London: Plenum Press, 1979.

Baker, R., Downton, A., & Newell, A. Simultaneous speech transcription and TV captions for the deaf. In P. A. Kolers, M. E. Wrolstad, & H. Bouma (Eds.), *Processing of visible language, 2*. New York and London: Plenum Press, 1980.

Barnard, P., & Wright, P. The effects of spaced character formats on the production and legibility of handwritten names. *Ergonomics*, 1976, *19*, 81-92.

Barnard, P., Wright, P., & Wilcox, P. The effects of spatial constraints on the legibility of handwritten alphanumeric codes. *Ergonomics*, 1978, *21*, 73-78.

Blakar, R. M. Language as a means of social power. In R. Rommetveit & R. M. Blakar (Eds.), *Studies of language, thought and verbal communication*. London: Academic Press, 1979.

Bloom, L. M. *One word at a time: The use of single word utterances before syntax*. The Hague: Mouton Publishers, 1973.

Broadbent, D. E., & Broadbent, M. H. P. Some further data concerning the word frequency effect. *Journal of Experimental Psychology*, 1975, *104*, 297-308.

Broadbent, D. E. & Broadbent, M.H.P. Priming and the passive/active model of word recognition. In R. Nickerson (Ed.), *Attention and performance VIII*. Hillsdale, N.J.: Lawrence Erlbaum Associates, 1980.

Broadbent, D. E., Cooper, P. J., & Broadbent, M.H.P. A comparison of hierarchical and matrix retrieval schemes in recall. *Journal of Experimental Psychology: Human Learning and Memory*, 1978, *4*, 486-497.

Carpenter, P. A. & Just, M. A. Sentence comprehension: A psycholinguistic processing model of verification. *Psychological Review*, 1975, *82*, 45-73.

Cattell, J. M. The time taken up by cerebral operations. *Mind*, 1886, *11*, 220-242.

Chafe, W. Discourse structure and human knowledge. In R. Freedle and J.B. Carroll (Eds.), *Language comprehension and the acquisition of knowledge*. Washington, D.C.: V. H. Winston, 1972.

Chapanis, A., Parrish, R. N., Ochsman, R. B., & Weeks, G. D. Studies in interactive communication: II. The effects of four communication modes on the linguistic performance of teams during cooperative problem solving. *Human Factors*, 1977, *19*, 101-126.

Clark, H. H. Inferring what is meant. In W. J. M. Levelt & G. B. Flores d'Arcais (Eds.), *Studies in the perception of language*. Chichester: John Wiley & Sons, 1978.

Clark, H. H. Responding to indirect speech acts. *Cognitive Psychology*, 1979, *11*, 430-477.

Collins, A. M., and Quillian, M. R. Retrieval time from semantic memory. *Journal of Verbal Learning and Verbal Behavior*, 1969, *8*, 240-247.

Corcoran, D. W. J. An acoustic factor in letter cancellation. *Nature*, 1966, *210*, 658.

Cromer, W. The difference model: A new explanation for some reading difficulties. *Journal of Educational Psychology*, 1970, *61*, 471-483.

Cruttenden, A. An experiment involving comprehension of intonation in children from 7 to 10. *Journal of Child Language*, 1974, *1*, 221-231.

Davies, A. Review of E. J. Gibson and H. Levin (1975), The psychology of reading. *Journal of Research in Reading*, 1978, *1*, 145-149.

Dobson, M. The acquisition and processing of cartographic information: Some preliminary experimentation. In P. A. Kolers, M. E. Wrolstad, & H. Bouma (Eds.), *Processing of visible language*, *2*. New York and London: Plenum Press, 1980.

Eamon, D. B. Selection and recall of topical information in prose by better and poorer readers. *Reading Research Quarterly*, 1978-1979, *14*, 244-257.

Fillenbaum, S. On the use of memorial techniques to assess syntactic structure. *Psychological Bulletin*, 1970, *73*, 231-237.

Flesch, R. *How to write, speak and think more effectively*. New York: Harper & Row, 1946. (Reprinted in Signet books.)

Flower, L. Writer-based prose: a cognitive basis for problems in writing. *College English*, 1979, *41*, 19-37.

Frase, L. T. Writing, text and the reader. In C. Frederiksen, M. Whiteman, & J. Dominic (Eds.), *Writing: The nature, development and teaching of written communications*. Hillsdale, N.J.: Lawrence Erlbaum Assoicates, 1980.

Frase, L. T., Keenan, S., & Dever, J. Human performance in computer aided writing and documentation. In P. A. Kolers, M. E. Wrolstad, & H. Bouma (Eds.), *Processing of Visible Language*, *2*. New York and London: Plenum Press, 1980.

Frederiksen, C. H. Structure and process in discourse production and comprehension. In M. A. Just & P. A. Carpenter (Eds.), *Cognitive processes in comprehension*. Hillsdale, N.J.: Lawrence Erlbaum Associates, 1977.

Frith, U. Reading by eye and writing by ear. In P. A. Kolers, M. E. Wrolstad, & H. Bouma (Eds.), *Processing of visible language, 1*. New York and London: Plenum Press, 1979.

Funkhouser, G. R., & Maccoby, N. Communicating specialised science to a lay audience. *Journal of Communication*, 1971, *21*, 58-71.

Gibson, E. J., & Levin, H. *The psychology of reading*. Cambridge, Mass.: MIT Press, 1975.

Glushko, R. J., & Cooper, L. A. Spatial comprehension and comparison processes in verification tasks. *Cognitive Psychology*, 1978, *10*, 391-421.

Goodman, K. S. Analysis of oral reading miscues: Applied psycholinguistics. In F. Smith (Ed.), *Psycholinguistics and reading*. New York: Holt, Rinehart, & Winston, Inc., 1973.

Gray, W. S. *The teaching of reading and writing*. Chicago: UNESCO and Scott Foresman, 1956.

Gregg, L. W., & E. R. Steinberg (Eds.) *Cognitive processes in writing*. Hillsdale, N.J.: Lawrence Erlbaum Associates, 1980.

Haber, R. N. Visual perception. *Annual Review of Psychology*, 1978, *29*, 31-59.

Halliday, M. A. K., & Hasan, R. Cohesion in English. London: Longmans, 1976.

Hartley, J. *Designing instructional text*. London: Kogan Page, 1978.

Horowitz, M. W., & Berkowitz, A. Listening and reading, speaking and writing: An experimental investigation of differential acquisition and reproduction of memory. *Perceptual and Motor Skills*, 1967, *24*, 207-215.

Jackson, M. D., & McClelland, J. L. Processing determinants of reading speed. *Journal of Experimental Psychology: General*, 1979, *108*, 151-181.

Johnson, J. C. A test of the sophisticated guessing theory of word perception. *Cognitive Psychology*, 1978, *10*, 123-153.

Just, M. A., & P. A. Carpenter (Eds.), *Cognitive processes in comprehension*. Hillsdale, N.J.: Lawrence Erlbaum Associates, 1977.

Kintsch, W. *The representation of meaning in memory*. Hillsdale, N.J.: Lawrence Erlbaum Associates, 1974.

Kirsch, I., & Guthrie, J. T. The concept and measurement of functional literacy. *Reading Research Quarterly*, 1977-78, *13*, 485-507.

Klare, G. R. A second look at the validity of readability formulas. *Journal of Reading Behaviour*, 1976, *8*, 129-152.

Kolers, P. A. Reading and talking bilingually. *American Journal of Psychology*, 1966, *79*, 357-376.

Kolers, P. A. Reading is only incidentally visual. In K. Goodman & J. Fleming (Eds.), *Psycholinguistics and the teaching of reading*. Newark, Del.: International Reading Association, 1969.

Kolers, P. A. Three stages of reading. In F. Smith (Ed), *Psycholinguistics and reading*. New York: Holt, Rinehart, & Winston, Inc., 1973.

Kolers, P. A. Memorial consequences of automatized encoding. *Journal of Experimental Psychology: Human Learning and Memory*, 1975, *1*, 689-701.

Kolers, P. A. Reading a year later. *Journal of Experimental Psychology: Human Learning and Memory*, 1976, *2*, 554-565.

Landauer, T. K. Memory without organization: Properties of a model with random storage and undirected retrieval. *Cognitive Psychology*, 1975, *7*, 495-531.

Levelt, W. J. M. A survey of studies in sentence perception: 1970-1976. In W. J. M. Levelt & G. B. Flores d'Arcais (Eds.), *Studies in the perception of language*. Chichester: John Wiley & Sons, 1978.

Levy-Schoen, A., & O'Regan, K. The control of eye movements in reading. In P. A. Kolers, M. E. Wrolstad, & H. Bouma (Eds.), *Processing of visible language 1*. New York and London: Plenum Press, 1979.

Macdonald-Ross, M. Language in texts: A review of research relevant to the design of curricular materials. In L. S. Shulman (Ed.), *Review of research in education* (Vol. 6). Itasca, Ill.: Peacock, 1979.

Mackworth, J. F. Some models of the reading process: Learners and skilled readers. In F. B. Davis (Ed.), *The literature of research in reading, with emphasis on models*. New Brunswick, N.J.: Rutgers State University, Graduate School of Education, 1971.

McClelland, J. L., & Jackson, M. D. Studying individual differences in reading. In A. Lesgold, J. Pellegrino, S. Fokkema, & R. Glaser (Eds.), *Cognitive psychology and instruction*. New York and London: Plenum Press, 1978.

Mandler, J. M., & Johnson, N. S. Remembrance of things parsed: Story structure and recall. *Cognitive Psychology*, 1977, *9*, 111-151.

Marcel, A. J. Unconscious reading: Experiments on people who do not know that they are reading. *Visible Language*, 1978, *12*, 391-404. (a)

Marcel, A. J. Prerequisites for a more applicable psychology of reading. In M. M. Gruneberg, P. E. Morris, & R. N. Sykes (Eds.), *Practical aspects of memory*. London: Academic Press, 1978. (b)

Marcel, A. J. Conscious and unconscious perception: The effects of visual masking on word processing. *Cognitive Psychology*, 1980, in press.

Marcel, A. J., & Patterson, K. E. Word recognition and production: reciprocity in clinical and normal studies. In J. Requin (Ed.), *Attention and performance VII*. Hillsdale, N.J.: Lawrence Erlbaum Associates, 1978.

Olshavsky, J. E. Reading as problem solving: An investigation of strategies. *Reading Research Quarterly*, 1976-1977, *12* 654-674.

Olson, D. R. The languages of experience—on natural language and formal education. *Bulletin of the British Psychological Society*, 1975, *28*, 368-373.

Olson, D. R. From utterance to text: The bias of language in speech and writing. *Harvard Educational Review,* 1977, *47*, 257-281.

Olson, D. R. and Filby, N. On the comprehension of active and passive sentences. *Cognitive Psychology,* 1972, *3*, 361-381.

O'Regan, K. Saccade size control in reading: Evidence for the linguistic control hypothesis. *Perception & Psychophysics,* 1979, *25*, 501-509.

Osgood, C. E., Suci, G. J., & Tannenbaum, P. H. *The measurement of meaning.* Urbana: University of Illinois Press, 1957.

Perfetti, C. A., & Lesgold, A. M. Discourse comprehension and sources of individual differences. In M. A. Just & P. A. Carpenter (Eds.), *Cognitive processes in comprehension.* Hillsdale, N. J.: Lawrence Erlbaum Associates, 1977.

Posner, M. I., & Mitchell, R. F. Chronometric analysis of classification. *Psychological Review,* 1967, *74*, 392-409.

Pugh, A. K. *The study and teaching of silent reading.* London: Heinemann, 1978.

Rayner, K. Eye movements in reading and information processing. *Psychological Bulletin,* 1978, *85*, 618-660.

Rayner, K., & McConkie, G. W. What guides a reader's eye movements? *Vision Research,* 1976, *16*, 829-837.

Rommetveit, R. Deep structure of sentences versus message structure. *Norwegian Journal of Linguistics,* 1972, *26*, 3-22. Reprinted in R. Rommetveit & R. M. Blakar (Eds.), *Studies of language, thought and verbal communication.* London: Academic Press, 1979.

Rosch, E. Cognitive representations of semantic categories. *Journal of Experimental Psychology: General,* 1975, *104*, 192-233.

Samuels, S. J., & Dahl, P. R. Establishing appropriate purpose for reading and its effect on flexibility of reading rate. *Journal of Educational Psychology,* 1975, *67*, 38-43.

Schiepers, C. W. J. Global attributes in visual word recognition. Part 1. Length perception of letter strings. *Vision Research,* 1976, *16*, 1343-1349.

Shebilske, W. L., & Reid, L. S. Reading eye movements, macro-structures and comprehension processes. In P. A. Kolers, M. E. Wrolstad, & H. Bouma (Eds.), *Processing of visible language 1.* New York and London: Plenum Press, 1979.

Smith, P. T., & Groat, A. Spelling patterns, letter cancellation and the processing of text. In P. A. Kolers, M. E. Wrolstad, & H. Bouma (Eds.), *Processing of visible language, 1.* New York and London: Plenum Press, 1979.

Sticht, T. G. Learning by listening. In J. B. Carroll & R. O. Freedle (Eds.), *Language comprehension and the acquisition of knowledge.* Washington D. C.: V. H. Winston & Sons, 1972.

Sticht, T. G. Comprehending reading at work. In M. A. Just & P. A. Carpenter

(Eds.), *Cognitive processes in comprehension*. Hillsdale, N.J.: Lawrence Erlbaum Associates, 1977.

Sticht, T. G. The acquisition of literacy by children and adults. In F. B. Murray and J. J. Pikulski (Eds.), *The acquisition of reading: Cognitive, linguistic and perceptual prerequisites*. Baltimore, Md.: University Park Press, 1978.

Tinker, M. A. *Legibility of print*. Iowa: State University Press, 1965.

Twyman, M. A schema for the study of graphic language. In P. A. Kolers, M. E. Wrolstad, & H. Bouma (Eds.), *Processing of visible language, 1*. New York and London: Plenum Press, 1979.

van Dijk, T. Semantic macro-structures and knowledge frames in discourse comprehension. In M. A. Just & P. A. Carpenter (Eds.), *Cognitive processes in comprehension*. Hillsdale, N.J.: Lawrence Erlbaum Associates, 1977.

Venezky, R. L. *Theoretical and experimental base for teaching reading*. The Hague: Mouton, 1976.

Walker, L. Comprehension of writing and spontaneous speech. *Visible Language*, 1977, *11*, 37-51.

Waller, R. Typographic access structures for educational texts. In P. A. Kolers, M. E. Wrolstad, & H. Bouma (Eds.), *Processing of visible language, 1*. New York and London: Plenum Press, 1979.

Williams, A. *Reading and the consumer*. London: Hodder & Stoughton (in association with the United Kingdom Reading Association), 1976.

Winograd, T. A framework for understanding discourse. In M. A. Just & P. A. Carpenter (Eds.), *Cognitive processes in comprehension*. Hillsdale, N.J.: Lawrence Erlbaum Associates, 1977.

Wright, P. Decision making as a factor in the ease of using numerical tables. *Ergonomics*, 1977, *20*, 91-96.

Wright, P. Feeding the information eaters: Suggestions for integrating pure and applied research on language comprehension. *Instructional Science*, 1978, 249-312.

Wright, P. Quality control aspects of document design. *Information Design Journal*, 1979, *1*, 33-42.

Wright, P. Strategy and tactics in form design. In R. S. Easterby & H. Zwaga (Eds.), *Visual presentation of information*. London: Wiley, 1980. (a)

Wright, P. Usability: The criterion for designing written information. In P. A. Kolers, M. E. Wrolstad, & H. Bouma (Eds.), *Processing visible language, 2*. New York and London: Plenum Press, 1980. (b)

Wright, P. & Reid, F. Written information: Some alternatives to prose for expressing the outcomes of complex contingencies. *Journal of Applied Psychology*, 1973, *57*, 160-166.

# Anaphoric relations, comprehension and readability

Julia To Dutka

*This paper explores the role of anaphoric relations in the processing of visible language. It was found that anaphor-resolution is a highly complex skill and is a factor in reading comprehension. The distance that a reader has to backtrack to locate the antecedent and the amount of information represented by the substitute were found to be good predictors of the amount of difficulty encountered in performing this referencing task. Because readability measures do not incoporate anaphoric relations, the author recommends a framework for examining the comprehensibility of text as a more valid alternative in evaluating and selecting materials for specific readers.*

Using a single sentence as the basic unit of analysis has been a well-established tradition within linguistics. This tradition is evident in work by Bloomfield (1933), Fries (1952), and Chomsky (1957). Although the analysis of syntactic relationships among linguistic units on the sentence level has served these linguists well in theory building, it is inadequate in advancing our understanding of the way people process and, more importantly, comprehend language. In comprehending text, it is necessary to go beyond individual sentences and see how the entire structure develops in a given discourse. In shifting from single sentences to connected text, one important question emerges: what binds the sentences together in a text? This question can be explored in the context of the recent advances made in discourse analysis.

Grimes (1975) proposed that the semantic structure of discourse has three components: content, cohesion, and staging. Cohesion is what binds the text together by relating what is being said to what already has been said. On the surface level, cohesion can be realized through the use of various ties such as lexical cohesion, reference, substitution, ellipsis, and conjunction (Halliday & Hasan, 1976). One such cohesive device is anaphora.

The concept of anaphora can best be introduced by considering the following two passages.

In the past years people had been thrown into prison at the whim of the government—a custom which persists in some countries to the present day. A person so imprisoned could be kept there indefinitely, without any charges being brought against him. Perhaps he had committed no crimes; who could say, since he had been charged with none? Perhaps he was merely a political opponent of the government, or had for some other reasons incurred someone's ill will. The American colonists would have none of *this*. (Felder, 1970, p. 54)

A great majority of those who commit crimes do so impulsively, giving little if any thought to their actions. Perhaps a crime is committed in a fit of anger or as the result of unbearable economic pressure. *This* of course does not lessen the seriousness of the act, nor does *it* relieve society of the responsibility to punish the offender. (Felder, 1970, p. 172)

The pronominals, which are italicized, refer back to, or are anaphoric to, certain elements already expressed in the text. On the semantic level, the pronominal *this* in the first passage refers to the ideas expressed in the preceding context whereas, on the syntactic level, it replaces the construction which could be used instead in the same position. The pronominal *this* in the second passage refers to the ideas expressed in the preceding sentences but can replace only the nominalized form of the ideas to which it refers because of its position in the sentence. The pronominal *it* in the second passage functions in a similar manner. Cohesion is achieved neither by the pronominal alone nor by reference to the item. What binds the text together is the relationship between the two. This relationship seems to lie on the borderline between reference and substitution.

There are other kinds of anaphoric relations such as proverbs and ellipses but pronominals occur most often in the language. It is, indeed, difficult to read even a few lines of text without encountering one. Despite the frequency with which anaphora occur, this linguistic phenomenon is little studied and poorly understood. Menzel (1970, p. 97) explained that "one reason for our ignorance in this area is that anaphora are partly syntactic and partly semantic, so that grammarians feel that any solution of the problem must await a systematization of semantics, which today is far from being realized." Although our understanding of semantics is still far from complete, recent advances in text linguistics and text comprehension (van Dijk, 1977; Kintsch & van Dijk, 1978; Meyer, 1975, 1977; Norman & Rumelhart, 1975) and computer-based models for handling anaphora (Burton, Note 1, Levin, Note 3; Rieger, 1974; Rosenberg, Note 4; Wilks, 1975; Winograd, 1972) have generated much interest in this area. In the following section, some current attempts in studying anaphora will be reviewed in the hope that some structure will thus be imposed on the bits and pieces of observation in linguistics and psychology.

*Anaphoric relations: An overview*
Although repeated attempts were made in linguistics to further understanding of the theoretical basis upon which pronouns or, more precisely, pronominals were to be analyzed (Jespersen, 1909-1949; Kruisinga, 1932; Poutsma, 1904-1926; Sweet, 1891 & 1898/1955 & 1958), the real breakthrough did not come until Bloomfield (1933) introduced the notion of substitution. He defined a substitute

as "a linguistic form or grammatical feature which, under certain conventional circumstances, replaces any one of a class of linguistic forms" (p. 247). According to Bloomfield, a pronominal is an anaphoric substitute in that it is dependent on its antecedent for meaning. Bloomfield commented that despite this reliance on prior information, pronominals work more accurately than noun forms because they refine the specific meaning of the noun forms which they replace. For example, *who* and *what* subdivide English substantive expressions into animate and inanimate, and *he* and *she* further divide the animate substantives into masculine and feminine. Bloomfield's theory emphasizes the utility of substitutes in promoting accuracy and clarity as well as economy in the use of language.

Bloomfield's postulation has delineated two important aspects of pronominalization. One is the replacement function of a pronominal and the other is its function in redefining the meaning of the noun form it replaces. Both Allen (1961) and Crymes (1968) supported Bloomfield's use of the term "replace" in defining a substitue. They argued that in pronominalization, although a pronominal refers to an antecedent for its meaning, it actually replaces a construction which could occur in the position occupied by the pronominal in the sentence. A pronominal therefore has a referential and a substitution function. The former signifies a semantic relationship between the pronominal and what it refers to. The latter signifies a syntactic correlation within the text. Crymes (1968) extended her investigation of anaphoric relations beyond the pronominals. Her findings confirmed Bloomfield's position that substitutes signal meaning which the replaced constructions do not. Givón (1976) further proposed that the pronominal system in a text represents the reduced semantic form of its nominal system. All the pronominal agreement features which characterize the nominal universe in the lexicon, such as plurality, gender, and animateness, represent only the more general features which underlie this universe. Because pronominals are used in contexts where their antecedents have already been mentioned, it is redundant to be more specific than to describe the general properties of the referent nominal. In a given discourse context, the more specific characterization of the coreferent nominal should easily be recoverable.

The ease with which readers do this has been investigated in several studies (Bormuth, Manning, Carr, & Pearson, 1970; Chai, Note 2; Lesgold, 1972, 1974; Richek, 1976-77). These studies yielded variant results, depending on the anaphoric relations examined and the measure of comprehension used. However, one finding common to all is that intermediate grade students appear to have difficulty in identifying the antecedents for various anaphoric substitutes, a skill which is assumed to have been mastered early in life. There are great variations among subjects and among anaphoric relations in terms of performance. The feasibility of viewing anaphoric relations as an ordered set of hierarchical skills is, therefore, questionable.

In explaining the results of these studies, Lesgold (1974) argued that grammatical rules for nine-year-olds are not abstract structures that apply mechanically but are inextricably bound with semantics. Children at that age may know the grammatical rules but not the interpretive rules required to understand the structure in a particular semantic context. Lesgold further pointed out that, because children's memory span is limited, they may not be able to process units of information which are long and, therefore, the extent to which a given item exceeds or stays within their capacity may be a determinative factor in their performance. The length of an antecedent may present varying degrees of difficulty for children as far as identification is concerned. Lesgold's position is supported by Richek's (1976-77) study. She found her subjects' comprehension best when the noun forms instead of the substitutes were used. She explained that the amount of information immediately available to the reader can be an important factor in reading comprehension. These proposals led Chafe (1974, 1976) to claim that only terms which are assumed to be in the consciousness of the reader can be referred to pronominally. The stretch of text which separates a substitute from its antecedent may perhaps signal the availability and accessibility of information.

The purpose of the present study was to examine the relationship between anaphoric nominal substitution and reading comprehension. Specifically, two theoretical questions were formulated:

1. Is there a relationship between readers' ability to reproduce constructions which are replaced by anaphoric nominal substitutes in discourse and the readers' reading comprehension?

2. Which of the following variables, or combinations of variables, best predicts item difficulty in anaphoric nominal substitution?

(a) A change in the grammatical form of the antecedent when the construction is reproduced in the position occupied by the substitute.

(b) A discrepancy between the position of the substitute on one layer of a sentence and the position of its antecedent on another layer.

(c) The distance between the substitute and its antecedent.

(d) The length of the construction replaced by the substitute.

*The study*

*Method.* One sample for the study was composed of juniors, seniors, and graduate students enroled in a teacher certification course. The other consisted of college freshmen who had sought assistance in improving their reading skills. Altogether, 172 subjects were tested, 80 in the first sample and 92 in the second.

Reading scores of the subjects were obtained by applying the Diagnostic Reading Tests: Upper Level, Survey Section. Total substitution scores were collected by administering a substitution test made up of two continuous texts. Seventy-nine instances of anaphoric nominal substitution were identified and subjects were asked to write down what they thought had been replaced by the substitute in each instance. The responses were scored according to semantic and syntactic appropriateness. Thirty sets of protocols from each sample were scored independently by a second judge.

*Results*. Positive and significant relationships were found between total substitution scores and reading scores for both samples, the highest being that between total substitution and reading comprehension in the combined sample ($r = .78$), followed by that between total substitution and total reading ($r = .77$), and, finally, that between total substitution and reading vocabulary ($r = .68$), all $p < .01$.

      Using four item characteristics—change, discrepancy, distance, and length—as independent variables and item mean as the dependent variable, length consistently predicted item difficulty best, yielding a correlation of $-.51$ across the samples. When a stepwise multiple regression procedure was employed, length and distance combined best predicted item difficulty. Tables 1 and 2 summarize the data for these analyses. The statistical indices obtained were almost identical regardless of whether the analysis was done on the subjects in the first sample, the second sample, or the two combined.

*Discussion*. This study has yielded four findings in relation to anaphoric relations. First, the ability to determine what is replaced by a substitute is an important factor in reading comprehension. Second, the process of antecedent-substitute resolution is not simply a matter of recovering the information from the context as Bloomfield (1933) and Givón (1976) suggest. This process may involve sophisticated syntactic, semantic, inferential, and evaluative skills. Third, difficulty in

Table 1. Pearson product-moment correlations between item characteristics for the combined sample.

|  | Change | Discrepancy | Distance | Length |
|---|---|---|---|---|
| Item mean | -.32* | -.27* | -.44* | -.51* |
| Change |  | .35* | .15 | .10 |
| Discrepancy |  |  | .21 | .17 |
| Distance |  |  |  | .17 |

$*p < .01.$          $N = 79$ items

Table 2. Multiple regression data for item characteristics and item means for the combined sample.

|                                        | Multiple R | F       |
| -------------------------------------- | ---------- | ------- |
| Length                                 | .51        | 26.64*  |
| Length, distance                       | .62        | 24.11*  |
| Length, distance, change               | .66        | 19.31*  |
| Length, distance, change, discrepancy  | .66        | 14.41*  |

*$p < .01$.                     $N = 79$ items

handling anaphoric relations is not restricted to children alone. The performance of the college students in this study points to Flavell's (1977) production-mediation deficiency hypothesis. Some may not have used the strategy because they were unaware of it. Others may have known the strategy but did not have the skill to apply it independently. Fourth, of the four item characteristics investigated, the syntactic variables (change and discrepancy) were not as powerful as the semantic variables (length and distance) in explaining item difficulty. Although anaphoric relations are in some sense governed by grammatical constraints, being realized through sentences, such constraints may become insignificant when the relationship between the antecedent and its substitute extends beyond sentence boundaries as is frequent in continuous text. Semantic considerations may thus possibly be more crucial than grammatical relations to an understanding of discourse structure, and reference rather than substitution be a factor in comprehension.

The semantic variables, length and distance, were the best combination in predicting item difficulty. The distance between an antecedent and its substitute in a text can be interpreted as a semantic tie between the two. The antecedent, acting as the referent, determines how far back the reader has to go in order to recover the meaning of the substitute from its linguistic context. The negative correlation between distance and item mean suggests that the farther away the antecedent, the more difficult the item. This finding may perhaps be related to the information processing in operation in memory (Kintsch, 1974, 1976). An antecedent far distant from its substitute may not be present in the working memory of the reader as the substitute is read; therefore, what is being referred to may not be available for immediate retrieval when its meaning is called for. A reader may have to backtrack over sizable stretches of text to locate the antecedent to determine the meaning embodied by the substitute. Such backtracking, in regressive eye movements or turning the pages backwards, may signal a parallel process of mental search. When the information needed to supply the missing links is not available, comprehension stops.

Length alone best predicted item difficulty. The negative correlation between length and item mean indicated that the longer the construction replaced, the more difficult the item. In the present study, the length of a construction was measured by the number of words used. The assumption was that longer constructions contain more information than shorter ones. Although using this procedure to measure information load is at best inadequate, the amount of information represented by a substitute is seen to be a factor in comprehending anaphoric relations. The difficulty in processing substitutes which carry a high information load may, like the distance factor, be related to the way our memory system works (Chafe, 1974, 1976; Lesgold, 1974). It is also possible, especially given the common notion of a pronoun being a word that "takes the place of a noun," that the subjects were simply unaware of the capacity of these nominal substitutes.

In a society where knowledge is acquired mainly through the printed word, one important goal of education is to help students develop more efficient strategies in acquiring information from reading. Educators have long recognized that reading comprehension involves "the ability to follow the organization of a passage and to identify antecedents and find references in the passages" (Davis, 1941, p. 23). The literature reviewed and this study all support this observation. If readers do not recognize a substitute as anaphoric, or are unable to determine its meaning, the likelihood that they can make sense of what they are reading is slim. Some samples of responses from the poorer readers in the study (Figures 1 and 2) illustrate this point. The responses suggested that these readers' perception of linguistic units was a function of the physical layout of the text.

As shown in Figure 3, these readers were able to locate the antecedents but were unable to pinpoint what was being referred to. In extreme cases, such a failure in referent resolution can result in a total loss of comprehension.

*Anaphoric relations, readability and comprehensibility of text*
Based on the foregoing observations, a systematic analysis of anaphoric relations is likely to improve our understanding of aspects of text comprehension. Conversely, any model of text comprehension is incomplete if anaphoric relations are not accounted for. In order to understand the role of anaphoric relations in this context, an examination of anaphors in relation to readability and text comprehension is necessary.

For many years, "readability" has been associated almost exclusively with assessing reading levels of tests and instructional materials for school children. As a result, communicative efficiency in prose often supersedes any discussion of readability. In theory, the major purpose of readability research is to ascertain the

*Left*      *Right*

| Left | | Right | |
|---|---|---|---|
| 1 | Over three and a half centuries ago | 1 | |
| 2 | Sir Francis Bacon, a brilliant but | 2 | |
| 3 | unscrupulous statesman in the court of | 3 | |
| 4 | King James, let *his* nimble mind wander | 4 | King James, let *King James'* nimble mind wander |
| 5 | through a great number of subjects. So wide | 5 | |

Figure 1. An example of subjects' response indicating a reliance on the physical layout of the text in anaphor-resolution.

| Left | | Right | |
|---|---|---|---|
| 78 | than every word. Knowing when and how to | 78 | |
| 79 | do *these things* will give you a greater | 79 | do ——————— will give you a greater |
| 80 | understanding of general informational | 80 | |
| 81 | material, a greater appreciation of | 81 | |
| 82 | literature and a greater speed in reading | 82 | *understanding of general informational material, a greater appreciation of literature and a greater speed in reading* |
| 83 | *both.* | 83 | |

Figure 2. An example of subjects' response indicating a reliance on the physical layout of the text in anaphor-resolution.

| Left | | Right | |
|---|---|---|---|
| 90 | conclusion. The nature of the material may | 90 | |
| 91 | determine whether you mainly study *it* for | 91 | determine whether you mainly study *the nature of the material* for |
| 92 | details, analyze *it* to get the author's | 92 | details, analyze *the nature of the material* to get the author's |
| 93 | main ideas, or examine *it* critically to | 93 | main ideas, or examine *the nature of the material* critically to |
| 94 | draw your own inferences. Materials to be | 94 | |

Figure 3. An example of subjects' responses indicating difficulty in anaphor-resolution.

factors which affect comprehension of the written language, incorporating them into a theory of how people read and understand text (Klare, 1963, 1974-75). In practice, however, constant effort has been directed to developing faster, easier, more reliable, and more valid procedures for readability assessment (MacDonald-Ross, 1979). These procedures have generally incorporated sentence length (in terms of the number of words per sentence), and vocabulary load (in terms of frequency of occurrence or polysyllabic count) into a formula which is to apply. The discrepancy between what these formulas are supposed to do and what they are equipped to do has resulted in great confusion and a number of unfortunate practices.

First, readability formulas are often used as the sole measure of reading levels of text materials, resulting in serious mismatches between the reader and the text (Bormuth, 1966). Second, these formulas are often called upon to perform functions beyond their capabilities. Users of these formulas seldom know that the formulas are designed to estimate reading levels on the basis of sentence length and vocabulary load, but not to predict how difficult or easy a particular reader or well-defined class of readers will find a particular piece. Third, text features, such as cohesion, subject content, content structure, and aspects of readability pertaining to the physical layout of a text are rarely, if ever, taken into consideration in such assessment. These practices have further compounded the confusion already existing between readability, which is text-based, and the level of reading ease, which is reader-based. The reading level designation given by a particular formula yields precisely what is being fed into the formula to obtain such a measure. To stretch the predictive power of such a designation beyond the limits as imposed by the input data is inappropriate.

If the purpose in estimating reading levels is to lessen the mismatch between the reader and what is read and to foster the acquisition of knowledge through the written language, what is needed is not an index of the readability of a piece of writing, but an index of its comprehensibility for a specific reader or a well-defined class of readers. The concept of comprehensibility of text differs from that of readability in that comprehensibility encompasses more than merely what is in the text itself. The degree to which a reader will find a text comprehensible is dependent upon the interaction of three sets of variables—the reader's assets, text features, and pragmatic factors. The conceptual framework of the comprehensibility of text is represented schematically in Figure 4. It is beyond the scope of this paper to discuss this conceptual framework in full, but from the figure it is possible to see how anaphoric relations are related to readability and comprehension. To comprehend a piece of writing, a reader has to apply affective, cognitive, and language abilities. Comprehension will be easier if the text features and the pragmatic factors support these efforts. When one of these variables imposes excessive demands on the reader comprehension is likely to be drastically reduced.

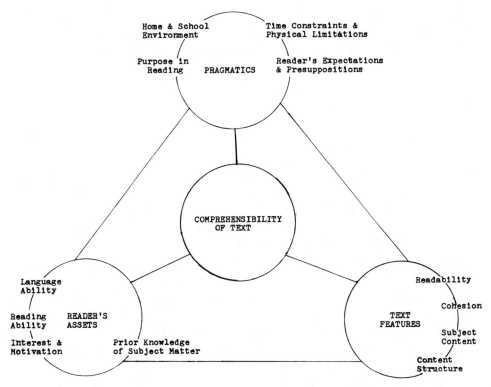

Figure 4. A schematic representation of the comprehensibility of text.

As a system of meaning representation, anaphoric relations exist in every piece of writing and their potential for creating barriers in comprehension cannot be ignored. As a cohesive device, these relations can provide links for transferring meaning between the reader and the text as well as between segments within the text. The key to efficient comprehension may not lie merely in an awareness of how this device can be used in writing but in the ability to use it. To know that current readability assessments do not incorporate anaphoric relations as a factor may help those involved with any aspects of textual literacy to evaluate and select materials for their users.

### Reference notes

1. Burton, R. *Semantic grammar: An engineering technique for constructing natural language understanding systems* (BBN Report No. 3433). Cambridge, MA: Bolt, Beranek, & Newman Inc., 1976.
2. Chai, D. T. *Communication of pronominal referents in ambiguous English sentences for children and adults*. Ann Arbor: University of Michigan, Center for Human Growth Report No. 13, 1967. (ERIC Document Reproduction Service No. ED 012 889.)

3. Levin, J. A. *Proteus: An activation framework for cognitive process models* (Working paper WP-2). Marina del Ray, CA: Information Sciences Institute, 1976.
4. Rosenberg, S. *Discourse structure.* (Working paper 130.) Cambridge, Mass: MIT Artificial Intelligence Laboratory, 1976.

## References

Allen, R. L. The classification of English substitute words. *General Linguistics*, 1961, *5*, 7-20.

Bloomfield, L. *Language*. New York: Henry Holt & Co., 1933.

Bormuth, J. R. Readability: A new approach. *Reading Research Quarterly*, 1966, *1*, 79-132.

Bormuth, J. R., Manning, J., Carr, J., & Pearson, P. D. Children's comprehension of between and within sentence syntactic structures. *Journal of Educational Psychology*, 1970, *61*, 349-57.

Chafe, W. Language and consciousness. *Language*, 1974, *50*, 111-133.

Chafe, W. Givenness, contrastiveness, definiteness, subjects, topics and points of view. In C. N. Li (Ed.), *Subject and topic*. New York: Academic Press, 1976.

Chomsky, N. *Syntactic structures*. The Hague: Mouton, 1957.

Crymes, R. *Some systems of substitution correlations in modern American English*. The Hague: Mouton, 1968.

Davis, F. B. *Fundamental factors of comprehension in reading*. Unpublished doctoral dissertation, Harvard University, 1941.

van Dijk, T. A. *Text and context. Explorations in the semantics and pragmatics of discourse*. London: Longmans, 1977.

Felder, D. *The challenge of American democracy*. Boston: Allyn & Bacon, 1970.

Flavell, J. H. *Cognitive development*. Englewood Cliffs, N.J.: Prentice-Hall, 1977.

Fries, C. C. *The structure of English*. New York: Harcourt, Brace & Co., 1952.

Givón, T. Topic, pronoun, and grammatical agreement. In C. N. Li (Ed.), *Subject and topic*. New York: Academic Press Inc., 1976.

Grimes, J. *The thread of discourse*. The Hague: Mouton, 1975.

Halliday, M. A. K., & Hasan, R. *Cohesion in English*. London: Longmans, 1976.

Jespersen, O. *A modern English grammar on historical principles*. 7 vols. Copenhagen: Ejnar Munksgaard, 1909-1949.

Klare, G. R. *The measurement of readability*. Ames, Iowa: Iowa State University Press, 1963.

Klare, G. R. Assessing readability. *Reading Research Quarterly*, 1974-75, *10*, 62-102.

Kintsch, W. *The representation of meaning in memory*. New York: John Wiley & Sons, 1974.

Kintsch, W. Memory for prose. In C. N. Cofer (Ed.), *The structure of human memory*. San Francisco: W. H. Freeman, 1976.

Kintsch, W., & van Dijk, T. A. Toward a model of text comprehension and production. *Psychological Review*, 1978, *85*, 363-394.

Kruisinga, E. *A handbook of present-day English* (5th ed.), 4 vols. Groningen: P. Noordhoff, 1932.

Lesgold, A. M. Pronominalization: A device for unifying sentences in memory. *Journal of Verbal Learning and Verbal Behavior*, 1972, *11*, 316-323.

Lesgold, A. M. Variability in children's comprehension of syntactic structures. *Journal of Educational Psychology*, 1974, *66*, 339-47.

MacDonald-Ross, M. Language in texts. In L. S. Shulman (Ed.), *Review of research in education 6*. Itasca, Ill.: F. E. Peacock, 1979.

Menzel, P. The linguistic bases of the theory of writing items for instruction stated in natural language. Appendix to Bormuth, J. R. *On the theory of achievement test items*. Chicago: University of Chicago Press, 1970.

Meyer, B. J. F. *The organization of prose and its effect on recall*. Amsterdam: North Holland Publishers, 1975.

Meyer, B. J. F. The structure of prose, effects on learning and memory, and implications for educational practice. In R. C. Anderson, R. J. Spiro, & W. E. Montague (Eds.), *Schooling and the acquisition of knowledge*. Hillsdale, N.J.: Lawrence Erlbaum Associates, 1977.

Norman, D., & Rumelhart, D. *Explorations in cognition*. San Francisco: W. H. Freeman & Co., 1975.

Poutsma, H. *A grammar of late modern English for the use of continental, especially Dutch, students*. 5 vols. Groningen: P.Noordhoff, 1904-1926.

Richek, M. A. Reading comprehension of anaphoric forms in varying linguistic contexts. *Reading Research Quarterly*, 1976-77, *12*, 145-165.

Rieger, C. J. *Conceptual memory*. Unpublished doctoral dissertation, Stanford University, Department of Computer Science, 1974.

Sweet, H. *A new English grammar, logical and historical*. 2 vols. Oxford: The Clarendon Press, 1955 & 1958. (First printed, 1891 & 1898.)

Wilks, Y. A preferential, pattern-seeking semantics for natural language. *Artificial Intelligence*, 1975, *6*, 53-74.

Winograd, T. *Understanding natural language*. New York: Academic Press, 1972.

# Communicating with computers

Richard L. Venezky, Nathan Relles, and Lynne A. Price

*As the major expenses for computing have shifted from machines to people, the need to improve user effectiveness has become more obvious. Almost all online systems today are advertised as "user oriented"; few of them, however, are fully integrated systems with consistent protocols for all subsystems, convenient command procedures, context-sensitive online aids, or any of the other features that have been shown to facilitate user interaction. Interaction techniques utilized in several experimental systems could be adapted to improve existing commercial systems. In addition, computers could be programmed to exhibit intelligent behavior in adapting to user characteristics.*

## Part 1: From Ur of the Chaldees to Silicon Valley

On ENIAC, the first electronic calculating machine, the programmer communicated with the machine via switches and dials. For the EDSAC, an electronic computer developed just after ENIAC for the Cavendish Laboratory in Cambridge, England, programmers were not required to perform so much hardware manipulation but communications were limited, as the following description shows:

> When a program tape [paper tape] is ready to be put on the machine, the programmer writes out a ticket saying what he expects the machine to print and giving any other information which the operator may need. He then hangs the tape with its ticket from a clip running on a horizontal wire. The various tapes hanging from the wire form a queue and the machine operator puts them through the EDSAC in order.... If the machine prints what is expected, the output sheet is placed in a rack ready for collection by the programmer. If the machine stops unexpectedly the operator notes on the ticket the place at which it has stopped... and then proceeds to the next tape in the queue. (Wilkes, Wheeler, & Gill, 1951, p. 43.)

On this side of the Atlantic, punched cards were used instead of paper tape and the card drawer substituted for the overhead wire but, this excepted, the procedures described above typified programmer-machine communication until the advent of online computing. Few developments have had as profound an effect on man-machine communication as the online revolution. In batch processing, the user's relationship with the computer during job execution is passive and remote. The totality of communication from programmer to machine is derived from the submitted job deck, with limited mediation by the operator. The computer's response is generally a series of staccato error messages with a few post hoc comments on the nature of the job's termination. The operating system must do the best job possible with the information contained in the job deck and then move on as quickly as possible to the next job. With the exception of a few instructional systems like CORC (Conway & Maxwell, 1967), deviations from rigidly prescribed behavior are grounds for job termination.

From the user's viewpoint, batch computing is a cycle of discrete steps involving preparation, testing, output evaluation, and revision. The only assistance that the computer provides (besides job execution) is additional information for output evaluation: for example, traces, postmortem dumps, and snapshot dumps. Detailed documentation is external to the computing system because the user is not a participant in job execution.

## Part 2: Mechanical metamorphosis

With online computing, the user became an active and immediate participant in job execution and the entire nature of computing changed. The discrete steps required in batch computing became a continuum in which computer resources could be used to monitor, test, and revise a job. A text editor and file management system became requisite support elements. On timesharing systems, users could obtain assistance by communicating through the system with one another or with an operator or consultant.

Early online systems were basically extensions of batch systems, using line images entered at a terminal rather than cards and retaining all of the syntactic rigidities and abbreviated command forms of the batch systems, yet making little attempt beyond the interactive text editor to simplify the user's work. The major manufacturers moved gradually towards what the industry has labeled "user-oriented systems" by introducing superficial aids, primarily of the single-statement variety (for example, HELP, LIST FILES). All too often, however, such features are added after an implementation is otherwise complete. The insensitivity of some programmers to users' needs is shown in the following response to a user's request for help on a commercially available system.

> First, if you know the value of the system error (errno), you can either look up a description of it in INTRO(II), or execute "help err<number>" (e.g., if the error number is 1 execute "help errl"). If you don't know the error number, or you don't understand what's going on, try the following, in order:
> 1. Make sure the answer isn't in the documentation. We get upset if you call us and it is.
> 2. Try to write (I) to anyone logged in as "pw" or "pw < name>."
> 3. Contact your PWB counsellor.

4. File an MR (see PIB-75-02).

5. Go on to something else.

6. Take a nap (after hanging up).

   When you awake go to step 1.

 

With increased experience, however, and with wider applications of online computing, designers have begun to recognize the new relationship between users and computing systems. On many current systems, online aids include inventories of available programs, brief explanations of commands, lists of current online users, and descriptions of operating schedules and policies. Furthermore, universities, non-profit research groups, and computer service organizations have continued to experiment with innovations to facilitate online computing. The remainder of this paper is concerned with these innovations with particular emphasis on two systems developed at the University of Wisconsin for helping the online user.

### Augmented human intellect

One of the earliest studies of human factors in on-line computing was done by the Augmented Human Intellect Project at Stanford Research Institute which began experimenting in the 1960s with computer conferencing and with alternatives to keyboard input (Englebart & English, 1968). From a number of different cursor-locating techniques tested, a device called a "mouse" was developed. The mouse, about the size of a small toy car, could be rolled on any surface to move a cursor about the screen. The Augment project also tested text-editing techniques, document preparation, and hierarchical structures of data entities for user files. Many of the design principles (Meyer, Note 2) are similar to those of the LEXICO system described below. Augment is now available from Tymshare, Inc.

Kay (1977) adapted the mouse at Xerox Palo Alto Research Center for an experimental personal computer system which also uses display frames ("windows") and menu selections to provide more information to the user. By moving the cursor to a particular window and pressing a function key, the information or selections in that window are activated and other windows pushed into the background. Through extensive use of menu-selection techniques, the user is able to communicate with the system without learning a command language. The window approach to online communication was also used by Teitelman (1977) in the Programmer's Apprentice, an online system for programming support, particularly for Interlisp.

### PLATO

In PLATO, a computer-aided instruction system developed at the University of Illinois (Bitzer, 1973) and currently marketed by Control Data Corporation, the hardware and software have been integrated and have a consistent set of protocols for all user communications. The PLATO operating system offers all users online documentation through a sequence of 150 AIDS lessons, comprising more than 250,000 words of text. The lessons evolved, as did the modern dictionary, from explanations of only the most difficult concepts; gradually more and more material was incorporated until AIDS contained a complete set of explanations. Today it is the primary documentation medium not only for the current capabilities of the system but also for new language (TUTOR) features and for changes to system policies (Kraatz, Note 1).

AIDS may be requested from the lesson editor via a user-supplied term or concept, or from the display of condenser (compiler) errors as part of the system error diagnostics, or as a lesson. In the last case, the user is routed first to the Main Aids Index from which he selects the topic that will provide a more detailed explanation. Requests for terms or concepts that are not recognized by the system are automatically recorded and periodically monitored by the programming staff.

The PLATO system also facilitates online interaction through the use of function keys (for instance, HELP, DATA, TERM) that can be programmed within lessons for whatever type of interaction a lesson designer wants. Menu selection is used extensively throughout the PLATO system for routing users to lessons. Additional aids include a mail system for forwarding stored messages to other users and a communication mode that allows immediate, non-stored message transmission between users or between a user and an online consultant.

## ZOG and TOPS-20

Menu-selection techniques similar to those used in PLATO and in the various systems derived from the Augmented Human Intellect Project are also used in ZOG, an interface for man-machine interaction developed at Carnegie-Mellon University (Robertson, Newell, & Ramakrishna, Note 3). ZOG is intended to be a general-purpose interactive programming language, with potential application in a variety of systems including data base retrieval, computer-aided instruction, and question answering.

The TOPS-20 operating system for the DEC System 20 computer combines menu selection with a command-completion facility. (Augment and other TENEX-based systems provide similar features.) When interacting with the command interpreter, users can enter a question mark to obtain an alphabetical list of possiblities for the next keyword. All keywords may be abbreviated by any unique prefix. If a user is not sure whether the initial characters uniquely identify a keyword, he can press the ESCAPE key and the system responds by displaying the remainder of the keyword. Despite the convenience of these features for interacting with the operating system's command language, application programs cannot provide them without a special purpose assembly language interface.

*LEXICO*

A different set of user-related problems was addressed by the LEXICO system developed at the University of Wisconsin to assist lexicographers in word studies and in dictionary development (Venezky, Relles & Price, 1978). LEXICO supports a diverse set of tasks performed on natural language texts: storage, editing, concording, headword classification, and respelling. Nevertheless, to the user the system appears as a unified entity with a consistent means of communication. The user does not need to know about the internal structures of any of his records or files, nor does he need to learn the operating system protocols for creating, updating, and removing files. Tasks are specified in the user's vocabulary (for example, EDIT, CONCORD, UPDATE) through a combination of statements and replies to prompts. These specifications were developed experimentally to provide flexibility for the user while minimizing the chances for specification errors.

Expensive tasks like concording can be performed either online while the user enters the same task specifications. However, at the end of specification user enters the same task specifications. However, at the end of specification blocks for potentially expensive processing, LEXICO asks the user how soon he needs the results. For the user who is not sure what all this means, the system helps by giving the relationship between waiting time and cost. Users may then specify the priority they wish or request information on the costs of specific tasks.

Task specifications have been further simplified through an hierarchical default structure. The user's data are arranged in collections of texts. For each parameter that the user can specify (for example, word delimiters, stop words, text-identifier type) the system originates and maintains a default value. These values are applied automatically to every collection of texts and to every text in a collection. The user can reset the values as he desires, either for an entire collection or selectively for texts within a collection, or temporarily for a particular task on a specified text or group of texts.

Once set, these values need not be included in task specifications other than to override temporarily an existing default value. If the system does not find a value for a relevant parameter in a task specification, it extracts the default value for that parameter from the text file. The default values that the system initially sets are those found through experience to be most often specified by users.

During an interaction with the system, whether to set default values or to specify processing tasks, the user can obtain online explanations of error messages, system prompts, and available features. Explanations are typically multilevel so that the first response is brief; however, by repeating the same request for information (ideally through a single-function key), the user can obtain successively longer and more detailed explanations, terminated by a reference to the relevant sections in the printed documentation.

LEXICO also contains features for simplifying debugging, for expanding system capabilities, and for collecting user protocols. User protocols were used extensively in developing and improving interaction techniques and in debugging error messages. LEXICO is now running on a Univac 1110 at the University of Wisconsin, and is accessed by users throughout North America via EDUNET.

*Generalized user aids*

LEXICO's user aids have been generalized in a utility package that can be accessed by any program to handle error messages, prompts, and online documentation. These routines have been implemented for the UNIVAC 1100 series computers and for UNIX. the UNIVAC version has been incorporated into three systems at the University of Wisconsin: a database management system pertaining to state elections, a software distribution system used by the computing center, and an experimental bank account management system. The UNIX implementation has been used by NASA at its Ames Research Center and by BNR INC., in a program for analyzing text structure, a file inspection utility program, and a program for partitioning files.

The utility package provides programmers with a simple method of incorporating online assistance into a program. Separation of the coding and message-composition processes encourages the programmer to consider possible error conditions carefully. Each multi-level message (or *script*) is edited as a separate file with any text editor available under the operating system. This technique allows messages to be revised, as a result of user feedback or system monitoring, without recompilation or relinking of program modules.

The programmer can provide several different types of aids whose characteristics can be tailored to particular applications or users. Some examples of the types of aids that can be provided are shown below.

| *user enters* | *to obtain* |
|---|---|
| ?ERROR | successively more detailed explanations of a displayed error message |
| ?QUESTION | successively more detailed explanations of a displayed question or prompt |
| ?EXAMPLE | successive examples of correct input or valid commands |
| ?DEFINE *term* | explanation or definition of a specified term |
| ?FORMAT *command* | a description of the format of a specified command |

| *user enters* | *to obtain* |
|---|---|
| ?MENU | a list of allowable commands |
| ?DOC *section#* | a display of a specified section of documentation |
| ?INSTRUCT | instruction on the use of the system |
| ?NEWS | news of interest to users of the system |
| ?HELP | a list of available user aids |

Although the aids are represented by special commands (preceded by a question mark in this case), they could be invoked by pressing special function keys or pointing to part of a screen, when such hardware is available. Interaction using the aids is illustrated below, user input being capitalized.

```
ready for next command: DELETE MYFILE
*** 'myfile' is read-only; cannot be deleted. ***
ready for next command: ?ERROR
*** file 'myfile' cannot be deleted or written
            on unless a write-key is specified. (?ERROR
            for more information)
ready for next command: ?ERROR
*** If you want to delete 'myfile' you must
            specify its write-key. If you are trying
            to write into 'myfile' you should interrupt your
            current task, re-open 'myfile' and then
            resume the current task.
ready for next command: ?DEFINE WRITE-KEY
            a write-key is a sequence of up to ten (10)
            characters that can be associated with a file
            by its creator. Subsequent attempts to write
            on the file are possible only if this key is
            specified.
ready for next command: ?FORMAT DELETE
the format of the delete command is
    delete file-name//write-key
            (?FORMAT for more explanation)
ready for next command: DELETE MYFILE//sesame
file 'sesame' deleted
ready for next command:
```

The characteristics of the aids worth noting are that their invocation does not disturb the task at hand, successive explanations (*levels*) are obtainable by repeatedly invoking an aid, and the user can choose from several aids the one that best suits his immediate needs.

Of course, the provision of online aids does not guarantee an easy-to-use system. The effectiveness of the aids is highly dependent on the content of the messages. Through the experience gained with developing and testing messages for LEXICO and the early versions of the Aids Package, a number of guidelines for writing messages were developed.

First, messages should be specific. The increasing display speed of terminals should not be used as an excuse to inundate the user with entire screenfuls of information; the reader should not have to search through several paragraphs for a single needed fact. However, user aids should not be an opportunity to make messages as short as possible. Even when an initial message must be brief, it can contain useful information (for example, FILE NAME MORE THAN 14 CHARACTERS rather than LONG FILE NAME); messages should indicate when input is ignored (for example, INVALID FIELD NAME; COMMAND IGNORED instead of INVALID FIELD NAME), and should indicate the form of the expected response (for example, DELETE? (Y or N) rather than DELETE?).

Second, whenever possible, a message should end with an indication of what the user may do next. If a question was asked, the question should be repeated. Messages should indicate when additional messages in a script are available. For example, all but the last item in a series might end with ENTER *eg FOR ADDITIONAL EXAMPLES.

Third, the user aid routines should be designed to provide several different aids simultaneously rather than individually. Such a design includes the ability to associate a script with more than one aid. There may be situations, for example, when a request for EXPLAIN ERROR, EXPLAIN QUESTION, and FORMAT can be satisfied by the same information. It also includes having a command that explains the function and use of all the other user aids. In particular, the sign-on message for a system should explain how assistance can be obtained. For example,

> SYSTEM X VERSION Y
> For available user aids, enter HELP.

Fourth, messages should be polite, but not anthropomorphized (MY MEMORY BANKS ARE OVERLOADED). Whenever possible, error messages should reflect system limitations rather than the user's inadequacy (FILE XYZ CANNOT BE FOUND not NON-EXISTENT FILE: XYZ).

To assist the programmer evaluate both his system and its messages, the user aids package records the identity and number of levels used for each message displayed. The resulting statistics file keeps the programmer informed about errors that occur frequently and messages that do not contain sufficient information. An interface to the statistics file allows other information (such as frequency of use of different program features, utilization of system resources) to be logged in the same place.

## Part 3: As Armageddon approaches

The need to improve man-machine communication is not based solely on humanistic concerns but on economic grounds as well. Hardware costs, which depend upon microelectronic technology and manufacturing quantity, continue to decline while software development, which is labor-intensive, continues to become more expensive. Indeed, at the Madison Academic Computing Center software maintenance costs are now pro-rated among the users of each software system.

Training is becoming more expensive and the savings from using a well-designed online system can no longer be ignored. With the techniques mentioned above, man-machine communication techniques could be vastly improved in online computing systems.

First, communication protocols could be consistent throughout an operating system. The user of a present-day $n$th generation system must deal with several disparate systems to complete even simple tasks. Each of these systems typically has its own statement protocols, error-handling procedures, and documentation standards. Computing systems of the future could follow the PLATO example, where programs that differ in function are nonetheless similar in input conventions, display techniques, and forms of interactive assistance. This high degree of consistency is achieved in large part through a common and suitably general implementation language.

Second, documentation could be available online, supplemented by extensively annotated error messages and reminders. In the midst of interaction, an online user profits more from the immediate and unobtrusive display of required information than from a lengthy search through printed materials. As more documents are prepared with word-processing systems, the duplication of effort required to write different online and offline versions of the same information should be eliminated. The THUMB system (Price, 1978), under development at BNR INC., suggests how such integration can be achieved.

With THUMB, an author enters the unformatted text corresponding to each of the finest divisions of an outline. These passages can be concatenated by the THUMB processor and run through a document formatter to produce a printed copy of the document. In addition, the passages can be individually processed and retrieved by an online documentation system. Retrieval is based on a generalization of a heavily cross-referenced index, with multiple synonyms, also prepared by the author. This data structure shows non-adjacent passages where semantic interaction of different concepts occurs. The user can sequentially inspect successive index entries for a term and can automatically trace references to other sections. Because retrieval is based on semantic units rather than on page numbers, the user is spared the skimming often necessitated by conventional indexing methods.

Third, user-defined default conditions could be available in all systems and particularly in those in which similar requests are made over and over.

Fourth, bookkeeping facilities could be available to tell the user what has been done recently, what files are online and what their characteristics are, how much has been spent lately, and so on.

Some form of voice communication will probably be available in the next five years, along with extensive access from a home terminal to data banks and networks. The value of this increased access will depend heavily, however, upon the empirical development of convenient communication protocols. In the past, human factors research has investigated physiological aspects of the man-machine environment (fatigue, stress, the effects of different knob positions and sizes, and so on). In computer sciences, human performance was studied until recently only in terms of programming, debugging, and language selection (Grant & Sackman, 1967; Shneiderman, Note 4; Weismann, 1974). Only recently have studies begun to look at the human factors peculiar to online computing (Miller, 1977; Reisner, 1977; Walther & O'Neill, 1974). In an experiment conducted at the University of Wisconsin, the effectiveness of online aids (in particular, those that grew out of LEXICO's aids) was evaluated empirically, with both experienced and inexperienced subjects (Relles, 1979). Significant differences in user performance were observed between users who had access to online aids and those who did not. The effectiveness of online aids was found to depend on the manner in which they were provided as well as on user experience. The experiment provided some evidence that, for extremely inexperienced users, online aids can actually have a detrimental effect on self-confidence and on performance. For users with a few hours of interactive practice, however, the provision of online aids improved their performance and increased their confidence in their ability to use the system. More studies like these need to be done to resolve other issues related to man-machine communication.

Yet even without further informtion on user performance, the techniques described above could be implemented with existing hardware and software. However, because they are specified totally by the user, they are passive as far as the computer is concerned. A higher level of utility might be obtained by programming computers to adapt to the particular needs and characteristics of users.

By monitoring and saving task specifications of users, for example, a system could itself determine which values for system parameters occurred most frequently. Then, through appropriate algorithms and with the user's approval, a system could decide which of these values to establish as user default values. Various levels of complexity of algorithms could be used, from independent parameter counts to user and context-sensitive counts.

A second type of intelligent behavior might be obtained by collecting data about user errors. Through continual analysis of these errors, the system might decide to provide brief training to the user, or alternate specification procedures, or (wherever possible) conversion of what the user said to what the user meant. For example, the user might repeatedly type DELETE rather than REMOVE for removing files from his directory. The system might, after several recurrences of this error, offer the user the opportunity to redefine the term DELETE. Systems would be required to monitor user behavior and make the information so gathered available for decision-making procedures, a minimum requirement for any user-oriented system, whether or not intelligent machine behavior is incorporated into its design. There is an axiom in industry that it is inefficient to develop a production process without building into that process the collection of information for its improvement. The same is true of interactive systems. Designers need real performance data to determine whether language constructs are understood, whether error messages are resulting in correct input, and whether users are performing tasks in the manner originally desired. Dependence upon post hoc reports and personal experience alone is inadequate.

Monitoring user performance and deciding on changes in system interaction techniques all require memory and CPU resources. These commodities are declining in cost even as programmer and user time are increasing. Indeed, we have probably already reached the point where computing resources can profitably be traded for increased user effectiveness. The challenge now is not only to implement and test passive user aids but also to search for techniques to enable computers to act intelligently for their users' benefit.

## Glossary

CORC  -  Cornell Compiler. A FORTRAN-like compiler developed at Cornell University for introducing students to computer programming.

EDSAC  -  Electronic Delay Storage Automatic Calculator. The first general-purpose electronic calculator built in England. It was designed by Maurice Wilkes and placed in service on May 6, 1949.

EDUNET  -  Educational Network. A consortium of college and university computing centers that provides access by telephone networks to various computing resources.

ENIAC  -  Electronic Numerical Integrator and Computer. The first general purpose electronic calculator built anywhere. Designed by J. Presper Eckert, Jr., and John W. Mauchly at the Moore School of Electrical

Engineering (University of Pennsylvania) and dedicated in February, 1946.

INTERLISP - Interactive LISP. A version of the LISP language developed for interactive computing by Warren Teitelman. LISP is a list processing language designed by John McCarthy in 1959. It uses conditional expressions and mathematical functional notation.

LEXICO - An online system developed by the present authors for aiding in language studies and lexicographic work.

PLATO - Programmed Logic for Automatic Teaching Operations. A computer-based system for instruction, utilizing completely integrated hardware and software. PLATO was developed over the last 20 years at the University of Illinois under the direction of Donald Bitzer and is now distributed by Control Data Corporation.

TENEX - A computer operating system built around the DEC-10 computer.

THUMB - Text Heuristics for Using Manuals Better. An online documentation system developed by Lynne Price and now being implemented at BNR, Inc. in San Jose, California.

TOPS-20 - A computer operating system built around the DEC-20 computer.

TUTOR - An author language for writing lessons on the PLATO system.

UNIX - An operating system developed at Bell Laboratories, originally for the PDP-7 and PDP-9 computers. UNIX now runs on the PDP-11 computer series.

ZOG - A software interface for man-machine interaction, developed at Carnegie-Mellon University.

## Reference notes

1. Kraatz, J. *AIDS: the user's guide to PLATO*. Unpublished manuscript, Computer-based Education Research Laboratory, University of Illinois, n.d.

2. Meyer, N. D. *Executive information tools*. Stanford Research Institute (Tech. Rep. ARC 34111), 1975.

3. Robertson, G., Newell, A., & Ramakrishna, K. *ZOG: a man-machine communication philosophy* (Tech. Rep.). Carnegie-Mellon University, August 4, 1977.

4. Shneiderman, B. *Exploratory experiments in programmer behavior* (Tech. Rep. 17). Indiana University, 1975.

## References

Bitzer, D. L. Computer-assisted education. *Yearbook of science and technology*. New York: McGraw-Hill, 1973.

Conway, R. W., & Maxwell, W. L. CORC: The Cornell computing language. *Communications of the Association for Computing Machinery,* 1963, *6*, 317-321.

Engelbart, D. C., & English, W. K. A research center for augmenting human intellect. *Proceedings of the Fall Joint Computer Conference,* 1968, *33* (1), 395-410.

Grant, E. E., & Sackman, H. An exploratory investigation of programmer performance under on-line and off-line conditions, *IEEE Transactions on Human Factors in Electronics,* *8,* 33-48.

Kay, A. C. Microelectronics and the personal computer. *Scientific American,* 1977, *237* (3), 230-244.

Miller, L. H. A study in man-machine interaction. *Proceedings of the National Computer Conference,* 1977, *46,* 409-421.

Price, L. A. *Representing text structure for automatic processing.* Unpublished Ph. D. thesis, University of Wisconsin, 1978. (University microfilms no. 78-15, 065)

Reisner, P. Psychological experimentation as an aid to development of a query language. *IEEE Transactions on Software Engineering,* 1977, *3* (3), 218-229.

Relles, N. *The design and implementation of user-oriented systems.* Unpublished Ph. D. thesis, University of Wisconsin, 1979.

Teitelman, W. A display oriented programmer's assistant. *Proceedings of the Fifth International Joint Conference on Artificial Intelligence,* 1977. Pittsburgh, PA: Department of Computer Science, Carnegie-Mellon University.

Venezky, R. L., Relles, N., & Price, L. A. LEXICO: A system for lexicographic processing. *Computers and the Humanities,* 1977, *11,* 127-137.

Walther, G., & O'Neill, H. On-line user-computer interface, *Proceedings of the National Computer Conference,* 1974, *43,* 379-384.

Weismann, L. Psychological complexity of computer programmes. Unpublished Ph. D. thesis, University of Toronto, 1974.

Wilkes, M. V., Wheeler, D. J., & Gill, S. *The preparation of programs for an electronic digital computer.* Cambridge, Mass.: Addison-Wesley, 1951.

# Towards a model for picture and word processing

Joan Gay Snodgrass

*A model is proposed to account for similarities and differences between picture and word processing in a variety of semantic and episodic memory tasks. The model contains three levels of processing: the most superficial concerned with low-level processing of the physical characteristics of externally presented pictures and words; an intermediate level in which the results of the low-level processer make contact with prototypical information about how objects (or the pictures which represent them) look and how words sound; and the deepest (propositional) level in which meaning is analyzed. The interlingua between pictures and their names (or between their visual and acoustic images) can take place either directly, with connections between the two image stores, or indirectly, via the propositional level to which both image stores have access. Two differences emerge between pictures and their names: first, greater variability in the way objects or pictures appear compared to the way names appear or sound, which leads to greater variability in prototypical visual images than in prototypical acoustic images; and second, less ambiguity of reference for pictures than for their names, with correspondingly fewer propositional memory nodes accessed by pictures than by words. These differences are shown to be consistent with a large body of literature on picture-word processing differences.*

Processing of pictures and words has been compared in many different tasks and for many different reasons. In order to systematize this literature somewhat, the tasks are grouped into two broad categories: those studying semantic memory and those studying episodic memory. Semantic memory is assumed to be a store of general knowledge representing a systematic and organized set of information about the world which is shared by members of the same cultural group. In contrast, episodic memory is autobiographical and idiosyncratic, and represents information about the occurrence of events in time and space for that individual (Tulving, 1972).

Examples of semantic memory tasks are naming pictures and words, generating images to words, categorizing pictures or their names, and making symbolic comparison judgments about whether $X$ has more of some property than $Y$. In all of these tasks, people must base their judgments on their own knowledge of the world, including information about how words are pronounced, by what name or names pictures are called, and whether a particular stimulus is a member of category $X$ or $Y$.

Episodic memory tasks, on the other hand, require that people first learn a set of materials in the laboratory before being tested on it. When pictures of known objects or their names are used, people need note only that they occurred in a particular context at a particular time and place. Episodic memory tests include the standard verbal learning and memory paradigms such as free and serial recall, paired-associate recall, yes/no or forced-choice recognition, and serial and spatial reconstruction and recognition.

In order to relate this body of literature to the proposed model for picture-word processing, the model will first be presented, then its relation to other models in the literature will be explored, and finally the empirical data on picture-word processing differences will be reviewed within the context of the proposed model.

Figure 1. Exemplary picture-word pairs considered by the proposed model (Snodgrass & Vanderwart, 1980).

The model was developed to account for processing differences between the type of pictures and words shown in Figure 1, that is, relatively simple line drawings of common objects, and the names most commonly used to identify them. Other possible picture-word pairs of items not considered are abstract paintings and their names, faces and their names, and complex scenes and their descriptions. Attention is confined to this relatively simple set of stimuli primarily because most of the experimental data about picture-word processing differences are based upon similar types of materials.

## A model for picture and word processing

Figure 2 presents a schematic representation of the model. We first consider its operation from an external-to-internal (top-to-bottom) sequence.

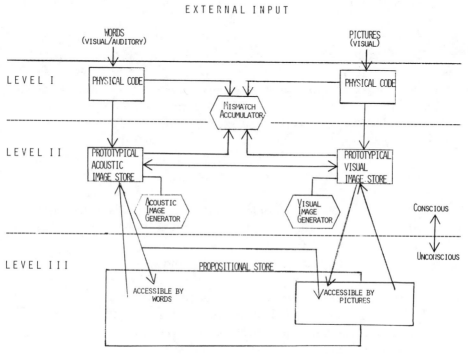

Figure 2. A schematic diagram of a model for picture and word processing.

External input may be in the form of either visually or auditorily presented words, and visually presented pictures. The first level of processing consists of the raw verbal or visual codes resulting from some relatively low-level processing of the external stimulus. Level I includes such physical characteristics as voice and intonation or typeface and color for auditorily and visually presented words, respectively, and orientation, amount of detail, and any peculiar characteristic not an integral part of an object's characteristics for pictures.

Level II consists of prototypical information about acoustic and visual images. Specifically, it contains information about how words sound, for the acoustic image store, and how objects (or the pictures that represent them) look, for the visual image store. Such information is acquired by experience in speaking and listening to language, and in seeing objects and pictures and, sometimes, drawing them. The acoustic image prototype store corresponds to the products of inner speech, and is assumed to be the same store accessed in verbal thinking, while the visual image prototype store is assumed to be accessed in visual thinking or imaging.

The image stores are prototypical in the sense that they contain features which represent the basic characteristics of acoustic and visual images but leave out nonessential or idiosyncratic detail which sometimes accompanies instances of words and objects or pictures. They represent the average way the word "apple" sounds or the average way the object "apple" looks.

Each image in the store can be in a potential or a generated form. A potential image consists of a set of features, with a probability distribution across the possible values each feature can be assigned. Generating an image consists of picking a value for each feature and then using these values to generate the image. This generated image is then available to introspection. Thus, a string of generated acoustic images represents "internal speech" and a set of generated visual images represents "visual or mental imagery." It seems likely that the acoustic and visual image generators are of limited capacity, perhaps limited to producing a single acoustic or visual image at a time, although the two types of generators may work in parallel. Thus, it may be possible to have simultaneous acoustic and visual images but not two simultaneous acoustic images or two simultaneous visual images. On the other hand, the potential image store is of unlimited capacity.

The features of the potential acoustic images might consist of lists of phonemes, number of syllables, sequencing rules, and so on, along with pitch period, formant frequencies, and intonation; the features for visual images might consist of shape, orientation, size, detail, color, and so on. Some features of the potential image might have a default character: for example, pitch period and formant frequencies similar in value to the speaker's own voice in the acoustic case, and a standard orientation and size in the visual case.

It seems plausible that there is more inter- and intra-subject consistency in the values assigned to features for acoustic images than for visual images (that is, the probability distributions for each feature are less variable in the former than in the latter). That is, there are more ways to image a concept than to name it. For example, subjects rate the degree of agreement between their internally generated name to a picture and the picture's name higher than between their internally generated image to a word and the word's picture (Snodgrass, Wasser, Finkelstein, & Goldberg, 1974).

Products of both Level I, physical analysis, and Level II, image generation, are available to introspection. In addition, it seems likely that subjects can also access information in potential image stores without necessarily generating the image. We assume this because of such phenomena as "tip-of-the-tongue" states, in which subjects seem to be aware of some, but not all, of the features of a potential acoustic image, and what we might call "tip-of-the-mind's eye" states, in which subjects cannot generate an image of a concept even though they know its meaning and some of its visual characteristics.

The potential image stores also serve as the pattern recognition systems. A pictorial or verbal pattern is recognized as being of a known picture, object, or word if enough of its features correspond to the feature lists in one of the image stores. When the potential image is used for recognition, the recognition system acts like a feature-analysis system and probably operates in parallel, as in "Pandemonium" (Neisser, 1967). When generated images are used, the recognition system acts like a template-matching system and, given the limited capacity of the image generation system, probably operates in serial. It seems likely that subjects may need to resort to generation for ambiguous or noisy pictorial and verbal stimuli.

In the process of recognizing speech or written language and pictorial input, subjects also accumulate information about the degree of mismatch between Level I, the physical image store, and Level II, the prototypical image store. We assume that the mismatch processer will accumulate more mismatch information if a spoken word differs from the observer's internal voice, if a visually-presented word has a peculiar or unexpected typescript or color, or if a picture does not correspond closely to the prototypical image.

Level III is the propositional store, which is accessible by both acoustic and visual image prototypes. The propositional store is viewed as an abstract set of nodes and of interconnections among nodes which differ qualitatively and could be labeled by such relationships as "is a coordinate of," "is a member of the category," "has the property," and so on. Although we use language to talk about the nodes in propositional memory and their interrelationships, propositional memory has no language (or for that matter visual images) and its operations are not accessible to introspection (hence it is labeled as being at the unconscious level). Rather, relationships and nodes are connected to the acoustic image store on the one hand, and to the visual image store on the other, but in the latter case only for concepts and relationships which are picturable.

Although particular visual and acoustic images can access common nodes in propositional memory, many acoustic images will access nodes not accessible by visual images. Thus, the two are shown as having only partial overlap, with words shown as accessing more propositional "space" than pictures. The nature of many tasks may limit the number of propositional nodes a word will access: for example, when subjects are told to form visual images of words in a memory experiment, they may only access nodes in propositional memory which are also connected to the visual image store. However, many words have several picturable senses, for example, "pipe," "nut," "bat," and "top." Thus, access to one node may lead to one visual image (for example, a baseball bat) while access to another may lead to a different image (for example, a flying rodent). Thus a single acoustic image may access more than one node in Level III.

Figure 2 shows direct connections between the acoustic and visual image prototype stores. This direct matching mode allows for the possibility that picture-name matches may be made without accessing the semantic memory store although this mode does not seem to be used often, for reasons we consider in a moment.

The operation of the schema from a bottom-up or internal to external way is analogous to its top-down operation. Thinking, for example, is the activation of propositional memory nodes which in turn activate either acoustic image prototypes (in verbal thinking), visual image prototypes (in visual thinking), or both. We have assumed that propositional memory is unconscious because it seems difficult, on the basis of introspection, to know what we will think, say, or dream next until we have thought, said, or dreamt it. On the other hand, input from propositional memory can be used to clarify the "meaning" of thoughts. For example, if I think, "tomorrow I will buy a *top*," the acoustic image prototype is identical whether I mean a toy, a blouse, or a coffee pot lid, yet there is no ambiguity in my understanding of my thought. This might be because the propositional node from which the acoustic image *top* is generated can be known to me, or because the same propositional node also activates the relevant potential or generated visual image, or both. Thus, although the operation and activation of propositional memory is not available to introspection, the input nodes from which images are generated may be. This problem of the potential ambiguity of verbal thoughts suggests that adults may use input from propositional memory to clarify the meaning of thoughts (either through direct access to the node from which input is coming or by awareness of accompanying visual imagery). In tasks where propositional activation is not necessary (such as picture-naming or picture-word matching) subjects may continue to access the propositional store because in the past it has been useful.

### Relationship of the proposed model to other memory models

All three levels of the proposed model depicted in Figure 2 may be considered parts of semantic memory. Level I must include knowledge about how to clarify and categorize the products of perception, Level II must include knowledge about the appearance of words and things, and Level III must include knowledge about types of associations among concepts.

Level III, the propositional store, most closely resembles the concept of semantic memory as it has been used in the literature, and the acoustic image store of Level II most closely resembles the concept of the internal lexicon. The lexicon is usually assumed to include information about graphemic as well as phonemic and acoustic features of words. In the present model, the graphemic part has been omitted for simplicity, although a complete model clearly would require it. Emphasis has been placed upon the acoustic image because of the large amount of evidence that phonemic encoding of visually-presented words occurs at least some of the time (Nelson 1979). In any case, the model does not require that an acoustic image be *generated* during visual word recognition (a step implied by the phonemic recoding hypothesis), only that its potential image code be accessed.

Both the acoustic and the visual image stores of Level II resemble feature analysis models of pattern perception in their potential form, and template-matching models in their generated form. Finally, Level I analysis includes iconic and echoic perceptual processes, and the residue of the pattern recognition process accumulated in the mismatch processer.

An important aspect of the model is its multipurpose use of stores and their processes for analyzing incoming information, carrying on internal processes such as thinking, and generating external responses. For example, the visual image store can be used to clarify visual pictures and scenes, to generate visual images during thinking, and to generate a visual image to a spoken word for comparison with a picture.

Because aspects of the model embrace almost all of cognitive psychology, only those which are of particular importance in picture-word processing differences will be discussed—the operation of the two image stores and their relation both to each other and to the propositional store. Within this limited domain, some crucial issues to be considered are: the nature of the propositional store, including its unconscious status; the level of abstractness at which concepts are represented in the visual image store; whether a given surface form of a word or picture (or its corresponding image) has multiple representations in the propositional store; the relationship of the model to dual-code versus propositional models; and the relationship between episodic and semantic memory.

*Theories of semantic memory.*
As Smith (1978) pointed out, models of semantic memory can range from very broad views which include both "semantic" and "episodic" memory events (Anderson & Bower, 1973; Kintsch, 1974; Norman & Rumelhart, 1975); through somewhat narrower views encompassing only information in what I have called semantic memory, but including forms of knowledge other than linguistic (such as the present model); to, finally, the most restricted view which considers only words, their meanings, and the rules governing their use.

Most models of semantic memory fall into this last category. These models correspond roughly to propositional memory and its connections to the acoustic image store in the present model. Within this restricted domain, theories of semantic memory can be classified into network models (Collins & Loftus, 1975; Collins & Quillian, 1972a, 1972b; Quillian, 1967; Wickelgren, 1979) and feature-comparison models (Rips, Shoben & Smith, 1973; Smith, Shoben & Rips, 1974).

The propositional component of the proposed model most closely resembles a network model with labeled associations, although the visually and acoustically representable properties of both nodes and associations are retrieved from the visual and acoustic image stores. The meaning of a concept is defined as the sum of a node's associations with other nodes in the network, although the present model does not propose a particular structure for the network (in particular, no hierarchical structure is assumed).

A basic problem in the present model is to decide at what level of abstractness visual images are stored. At the most general level, the visual image store might consist of a single vector the selection of whose values could generate any possible visual image. At the most specific level, a vast array of entries might correspond to each and every possible appearance of each and every object. In the model the assumption is made that images are stored at an intermediate level of abstractness, corresponding to what semantic memory theorists identify as examplars of categories (for example, dog, canary, chicken, tomato). However, these exemplars in turn can be considered categories for such subordinate concepts as collie, pullet, plum tomato, and so on. Rosch and her colleagues (Rosch, 1975, 1978; Rosch, Mervis, Gray, Johnson, & Boyes-Braem, 1976) have proposed that a basic conceptual level for most tasks occurs at a level of categorization called the basic level, defined by a variety of criteria, including similarity of appearance, function, and motor involvement. In accordance with this principle, the model assumes that the visual image store consists of separate entries for basic level categories, and that concepts subordinate to the basic level are generated by selecting particular (and unusual) values for the features. For example, the image of a plum tomato would be generated by selecting the less probable value on the shape feature of oblong rather than round.

Perhaps the most straightforward criterion for determining if a concept is at the basic level is if it can be drawn so that most subjects identify it by the same name (Snodgrass & Vanderwart, 1980). This would mean that they had a separate entry for it in their image stores. Snodgrass and Vanderwart (1980) found, in agreement with Rosch et al. (1976), that basic level categories include some which are usually considered to be superordinates, such as bird, tree, fish, and flower, and some which are usually considered to be atypical subordinates, such as chicken, duck, ostrich, and penguin. Thus, although most semantic memory theorists look to formal class inclusion relationships to define examplars and close and distant superordinates, the present model relies on pragmatic considerations for their definitions.

*Multiple entries in propositional memory*
The question of whether or not the same surface form of a word has multiple representations in semantic or propositional memory has been investigated in a number of different processing tasks. Usually this issue has centered around the difference between homographs (words with two clearly different meanings, such as "bank") and nonhomographs. However, homography is probably best viewed

as a continuous rather than as an all-or-none characteristic of words.

The multiple representation question has taken two forms. The first is whether or not multiple entries for homographs exist, and the answer seems to be a clear Yes. The second is whether subjects can be simultaneously aware of more than one of the meanings of a homograph, and the answer seems to be a clear No with, however, an interesting exception.

Both questions have been investigated using the lexical decision task in which subjects must decide if a string of letters is a word or a nonword. Several investigators have found that homographs are responded to faster than nonhomographs (Jastrzembski & Stanners, 1975; Rubenstein, Garfield, & Milliken, 1970; Rubenstein, Lewis, & Rubenstein, 1971). Furthermore, semantic priming of a word, by presenting a related word prior to the target word, speeds word classification (Meyer & Schvaneveldt, 1971; Schvaneveldt & Meyer, 1973). These results suggest that semantic activation of one node in semantic memory spreads to other semantically related nodes. This is known as the spreading-activation hypothesis.

The same method was used to investigate the second question: whether subjects can be aware of more than one meaning of a word at a time. Schvaneveldt, Meyer, and Becker (1976) found that when one meaning of a homograph was primed, it facilitated lexical decisions only for words related in meaning to the primed meaning, not to words related to the unprimed meaning (for example, priming "bank" for its "river" sense speeds the classification of "river," but not of "money," and vice versa). This suggests that only one meaning of a word can be active in semantic memory at any one time.

In an interesting variation, Marcel (1979) used a pattern mask to make the homograph unavailable to consciousness and found facilitation for words related to both primed and unprimed meanings of the homograph. This suggests that when propositional memory is activated at an unconscious level, all meanings and their related concepts are activated.

The concept of multiple access and representation in semantic memory has also been used as a principle to account for the encoding specificity results obtained by Tulving and his associates (Tulving & Thomson, 1971). Those results show that changing the context in which a word is embedded between study and test produces a decrease in recognition memory. Tulving argues from those results that recognition, contrary to popular belief, *does* involve a retrieval operation, and that an episodic memory store is established, during episodic memory tasks, separately from the semantic store.

Critics of the encoding specificity principle argue that most words are homographic to some degree, even though they might not be classified as such with an all-or-none criterion. The node accessed in semantic memory for a word occurring in one context will be different from the node accessed when the same surface form occurs in a second context, thereby accounting for the decrease in recognition memory with changed-context tests (Anderson & Bower, 1974; Martin, 1975; Reder, Anderson, & Bjork, 1974).

The principle of multiple access is represented in the model by assuming that a given entry in the acoustic image store may have more than one entry in propositional memory (for instance, "top," "well," "bank"), and also, when picturable, more than one entry in the visual image store. When the particular meaning of a word is clarified (either spontaneously by the subject or by experimenter-imposed context), a single node in propositional memory is activated which in turn may activate a single entry in the visual image store.

*Dual-coding versus propositional memory models*
The dual-code model, most widely associated with the work of Paivio and his colleagues (Paivio, 1969, 1971; Paivio & Csapo, 1973), proposes that two qualitatively different memory stores exist: one, the visual image system, in which information about picture or object appearance is stored in an analog form, having spatial and configural properties similar to the picture (or its object), and the second, verbal system, in which both phonemic/acoustic and symbolic information are stored. The two systems differ in neural locus and in their specialization for different tasks but are richly interconnected. In Paivio's system, meaning is provided by associations between and within each store.

Both pictures and words may be encoded into both systems. Pictures will probably be encoded into the image system and words into the verbal system; pictures are less likely to be encoded into the verbal system and concrete words even less likely to be encoded into the image system. The two memory systems are assumed to be independent and thus registration in either one or both of the stores may provide a basis for recognition or recall.

Pictures are better remembered than words in most tasks because, in the first place, pictures are more likely to be dually-coded than words, that is, registered in both the image and the verbal stores; and, secondly, the image code, which is more likely to be stored to a picture than to a word, is the more effective code (Paivio & Csapo, 1973).

Evidence that naming of pictures is more likely than imaging of concrete words was obtained by Snodgrass and McClure (1975) in an item recognition task, and evidence that the image code is more effective than the verbal code was obtained by Paivio and Csapo (1973) in a recall task, and Snodgrass, Burns, and Pirone (1978) in an item and order recognition task. However, Paivio found that when recall was the memory test the image code was equally effective when generated either to a picture or to a word, whereas Snodgrass et al. (1978) found that when recognition was the memory test the image code was more effective when generated to a picture than to a word.

A second model which accounts for the superiority of pictures over words in episodic memory is the superior sensory code hypothesis, proposed by

Nelson and his colleagues (Nelson, Reed, & McEvoy, 1977; Nelson, Reed, & Walling, 1976). Their model is similar to the present one in proposing that both pictures and words access a common semantic representation. However, their model differs in proposing that the sole advantage of pictures over words is the more elaborate sensory codes of pictures as compared to words. They showed that when the visual similarity of a set of pictures which served as stimulus items in a paired-associate recall task was increased, pictures showed no advantage over words as stimulus items and in some cases a word advantage was obtained.

The most persuasive critics of the dual-code hypothesis have been the propositional theorists (Anderson & Bower, 1973; Pylyshyn, 1973, 1978) who argue that both pictures and words are encoded in a common format as a system of abstract propositions and relationships. The propositionalists do not deny the introspective reality of mental imagery or of verbal thinking but regard them simply as epiphenomena which do not in themselves constitute evidence for two types of memory storage.

The present model includes aspects of both the dual-coding and the propositional models. The dual-coding system is represented by the two image systems at Level II. In contrast to Paivio's model, however, interconnections between the two systems typically are made via the propositional system rather than directly. Comparisons among entries in the two image systems are made only on the basis of shared feature values; thus, phonemic and visual similarity judgments can be made within Level II but conceptual similiarity judgments must be made by accessing Level III.

The propositional level of the proposed model corresponds, of course, to the propositional memory of the propositional theorists, including the assumption made by Pylyshyn (1973) that the operation of the propositional system is not available to consciousness.

## Relationship of empirical data to the model

In this review of empirical evidence for processing differences between pictures and words, we consider two issues: first, how pictures and words differ in their access to semantic memory and, second, how they differ in their registration in episodic memory.

*Evidence from semantic memory tasks*
Semantic memory tasks may be divided into those which require translation from one internal image code to the other, such as naming pictures and imaging words, and those which require access to propositional information such as categorization and symbolic comparison judgments.

*Naming and imaging compared.* In the model, naming a word or picture involved accessing the acoustic image store and imaging a picture or word involved accessing the visual image store.

Naming latencies, as measured by voice key activation, are faster for words than for pictures (Cattell, 1886; Fraisse, 1960; Potter & Faulconer, 1975). Each of the following variables has been shown to affect picture-naming latencies: the frequency in print of a picture's name (Oldfield & Wingfield, 1965); age of acquisition of the concept name (Carroll & White, 1973); and the codability, or degree of naming agreement, of the picture as measured by the information statistic $H$ (Lachman, 1973).

Although direct comparisons between naming and imaging latencies are hard to make because different responses have been used, available evidence suggests that imaging a word takes longer than naming a picture. Imaging latencies have been measured in single key-press tasks, in which subjects press a key as soon as the image has been generated (Paivio, 1966; Kosslyn, 1975), or in two-choice tasks, in which subjects press a key as soon as they have identified as present or absent a particular aspect of an image (Kosslyn, 1973, 1978). Single key-press latencies have proved sensitive to variables related to the image. For example, Paivio (1966) found that images could be generated to concrete words faster than to abstract words, and Kosslyn (1978) found that forming images of complex pictures took longer than for simple pictures of the same concepts. Furthermore, identifying a detail in a small image took longer than in a large image (Kosslyn, 1975).

In a two-key response, Kosslyn and his collaborators found that scanning a larger distance in an image takes more time than scanning a small distance (Kosslyn, Ball, & Reiser, 1978). In addition, Kosslyn and Shwartz (1977) have implemented a computer program of image generation which shows many of the properties shown by their human subjects. Their program is similar to the proposed model in that potential (stored) image values are distinguished from generated images (formed on a cathode ray tube) and default values are given for certain values such as size. Their program differs in having both a "literal representation," a rough drawing whose visual features are stored in a spatial grid, and propositional features which can be called to elaborate and enrich the image.

Within the model, naming words is faster than naming pictures because direct access between physical analysis and the acoustic image code is possible for words whereas pictures must first access their visual image code and then either find direct access to the acoustic image code or access it via the propositional system.

The variables of frequency and age of acquisition have much larger effects on picture-naming latencies than on word-naming latencies, suggesting that the effect may take place at the propositional level: because pictures are more likely to require propositional access than words, they will show correspondingly larger effects. In contrast, picture codability would appear to have its effect in the access route from the propositional to the acoustic image code. If a picture has more than one name, a particular propositional node may access more than one acoustic image code. These multiple representations then might be expected to slow naming for pictures though not for their names.

That imaging words takes longer than naming pictures can be accounted for in at least two ways. First, because words are semantically ambiguous, nodes may be accessed which have no corresponding visual image code (the adverbial form of "well," for example) or several which compete (such as the various possible images of "bat" and "top"). Second, because visual images have more variable feature values than acoustic images, visual images may take longer to generate than acoustic images.

*Categorizing names versus pictures.* It seems clear that words can be named faster than pictures, and that pictures can be imaged faster than words. We turn now to the speed with which pictures and words can be understood. While understanding the meaning of pictures and words can take various forms (for example, the symbolic comparison judgment [Banks, 1978]), this review will concentrate on the categorization task.

The available evidence on categorization times suggests that pictures are categorized more quickly than words. For example, in a yes/no task in which the category is given ahead of time, pictures are either categorized faster than words (Potter & Faulconer, 1975) or with the same speed (Smith & Magee, 1980). When two instances of pictures or words in the same or different categories are presented simultaneously in a same-different task, pictures result in faster match or mismatch decisions than words (Pellegrino, Rosinski, Chiesi & Siegel, 1977). Furthermore, in a yes/no categorization task in which pictures and words are presented simultaneously, incongruous pictures have a larger interference effect on word categorization than incongruous words have on picture categorization (Smith & Magee, 1980).

Characteristics of the category exemplars and the similarity of the items within categories have also been shown to affect categorization times. Rosch (1975) showed that prototypical members were categorized faster than non-prototypical members, and Klatsky and Ryan (1978) and Klatsky and Stoy (1974) showed that the physical similarity of items within a category affected both category matches and identity matches.

Within the context of the model, categorization superiority of pictures over words is puzzling. A possible basis for it might be, again, the greater semantic ambiguity of words over pictures. However, because the context provided by the categorization task would appear to bias the meaning of homographic words towards their intended meaning, and because the evidence suggests that only one meaning of a word is activated in propositional memory, this explanation is tenuous at best.

Another alternative is that objects and their pictorial representations within a category may appear more similar visually than those between categories, whereas the names of the objects show no such graphemic similarity. Some judgments might then be made on the basis of feature similarity (that is, at Level II) and propositional memory would not be accessed. This interpretation is consistent with the results found by Klatsky and her collaborators for articifically defined categories.

Alternatively, it may be that subjects in a categorization task verbally rehearse the name of the category when they are carrying out the yes/no or matching task, thereby causing verbal interference with the naming of words (required before they can access semantic memory) but not the recognition (imaging) of pictures.

*Evidence from episodic memory tasks*

The model makes no distinctions between episodic and semantic memory. Rather, it assumes that an item presented in the study phase of an episodic memory experiment may be registered in three stores: the mismatch accumulator store which registers the degree and type of discrepancy between the physical input and the prototypical image, the prototypical image store, and the propositional store.

Consistent with the notion of levels of processing (Craik & Lockhart, 1972; Craik & Tulving, 1975), the registration is assumed to be hierarchical, with registration in the deepest, propositional store dependent upon registration in the shallower stores. The rate at which registration information decays over time is assumed to be fastest for the shallowest levels and slowest for the deepest level. Thus, the typeface or voice in which a word is presented is available for a shorter amount of time than a concept presented as a picture or a word, which in turn is available for a shorter amount of time than the meaning of the concept.

During the memorization phase of an episodic memory task, subjects may store information at all three levels of memory. The importance of each level in performance depends upon at least two variables: the delay between study and test and the type of test.

We consider results from three types of test procedures: same-form recognition, same-concept recognition, and recall. In same-form recognition, recognition memory for a picture is assessed by presenting the same picture, and recognition memory for a word is assessed by presenting the same word. In same-concept recognition, recognition memory for a picture is assessed by presenting the name of the picture and recognition memory for a name is assessed by presenting the picture of the name.

It seems reasonable that same-form recognition tests should be more effective in accessing all three levels of memory than opposite-form recognition tests but, to the extent that information is still available at the two shallower levels, subjects in opposite-form test conditions should be able to decide, with fair accuracy, in which form the original concept was presented.

Studies which have compared performance on same-form versus opposite-form recognition have shown that same-form performance is either superior to or equal to opposite-form. For example, Jenkins, Neale, and Deno (1976) found a decrease in opposite-form compared to same-form recognition tests, whereas Paivio (1976), Snodgrass and McClure (1975), and Snodgrass and Asiaghi (1977) found no such decrease. In addition, Snodgrass and McClure (1975) found that memory for the form in which a concept was studied was remarkably good, even when the concept was tested in its opposite form. In fact, when a signal detection model was used to analyze memory for both concept and form, there was no significant difference between the $d'$ estimates for concept memory and for form memory.

These results appear, at first glance, to cast some doubt on the present model's assumption that registration occurs at all three levels. If this were the case, subjects should have been more uncertain about which form the original stimulus was in (form memory), than which concept had been presented (concept memory), because form memory is retrievable only from the shallower levels, whereas concept memory is retrievable from all three levels.

It must be noted, however, that subjects in this experiment were warned that recognition tests would be in either form and thus they knew that they would need to remember both the surface and the propositional form of the concept. Moreover, because the picture stimuli comprised some inherently ambiguous stimuli, all picture-name pairs were presented to the subjects prior to the experiment. In this way subjects may have been provided with ways in which to distinguish images stored to pictures from those stored to words. (This illustrates the desirability of having available a large set of picture stimuli which do not suffer from either name or image ambiguity, like that recently published by Snodgrass and Vanderwart [1979].)

Recall, relying as heavily as it does on retrieval operations, may differ from recognition in the importance which the various levels have in determining performance. Available evidence suggests that the meaning, rather than the appearance, of concepts is more important in recall than in recognition, and thus that registration at the propositional level plays a much larger role than registration at the shallower levels. For example, Frost (1972) showed that when pictorial stimuli varied on both semantic similarity (category membership) and visual similarity (shape and orientation of the drawing), subjects expecting a recall task clustered by semantic category in their (expected) recall test, whereas subjects expecting a recognition test clustered by both dimensions in their (unexpected) recall test. Furthermore, a large verbal learning literature shows that semantic organizational factors play a much larger role in recall than in recognition, where their effect is either absent or minimal (Klatzky, 1975). This evidence leads to two conclusions: first, that recall is much more dependent upon retrieval from propositional memory than from the shallower stores based on appearance and, second, that subjects can vary their encoding strategies to take advantage of this fact.

These conclusions are consistent with the recall and recognition differences between dually-encoded pictures and words reviewed earlier. According to the model, dually-encoded pictures and words are assumed to be registered in both image stores as well as in propositional memory. In addition, dually-encoded pictures have an advantage over dually-encoded words in accumulating more mismatch information. However, mismatch information may be effective only in a recognition test and not in recall. This would account for the finding that imaged words do not differ from pictures in recall (Paivio & Csapo, 1973) but are inferior in recognition (Snodgrass & McClure, 1975; Snodgrass, Burns, & Pirone 1978).

If a picture and its name both access the same propositional node, it should be possible to show some confusion between the two surface forms. Just such an effect was observed by Snodgrass, Wasser, Finkelstein, and Goldberg (1974), who found that when subjects were forced to choose between two surface representations of the same concept in a two alternative forced-choice recognition test, they showed more confusions than would be expected from control conditions. These confusions were especially large for unambiguously nameable studied pictures paired with their names and were nonexistent for studied words paired with their pictures. The lack of confusion for words was attributed either to the absence of stored images for words, or, if images had been stored, the greater variability of image codes, leading to the greater liklihood of a mismatch between the generated image to a name and the picture of that name.

This has been a selective review of the episodic memory literature on picture-word differences. The results are understandable, if not predictable, within the context of the proposed model. It is clear that more sensitive tests of the model will have to be devised before either accepting it, modifying it, or rejecting it.

## References

Anderson, J. R., & Bower, G. H. *Human associative memory*. Washington, D.C.: V. H. Winston, 1973.

Anderson, J. R., & Bower, G. H. A propositional theory of recognition memory. *Memory & Cognition*, 1974, *2*, 406-412.

Banks, W. P. Encoding and processing of symbolic information in comparative judgments. In G. H. Bower (Ed.), *The psychology of learning and motivation* (*Vol. 2*). New York: Academic Press, 1977.

Carroll, J. B., & White, M. N. Word frequency and age of acquisition as determiners of picture-naming latency. *Quarterly Journal of Experimental Psychology*, 1973, *25*, 85-95.

Cattell, J. M. The time it takes to see and name objects. *Mind*, 1886, *11*, 63-65.

Collins, A. M., & Loftus, E. F. A spreading-activation theory of semantic processing. *Psychological Review*, 1975, *82*, 407-428.

Collins, A. M., & Quillian, M. R. Experiments on semantic memory and language comprehension. In L. W. Gregg (Ed.), *Cognition in learning and memory*. New York: John Wiley, 1972. (a)

Collins, A. M., & Quillian, M. R. How to make a language user. In E. Tulving & W. Donaldson (Eds.), *Organization of memory*. New York: Academic Press, 1972. (b)

Craik, F. I. M., & Lockhart, R. S. Levels of processing: A framework for memory research. *Journal of Verbal Learning and Verbal Behavior*, 1972, *11*, 671-684.

Craik, F. I. M., & Tulving, E. Depth of processing and the retention of words in episodic memory. *Journal of Experimental Psychology: General*, 1975, *104*, 268-294.

Fraisse, P. Recognition time measured by verbal reaction to figures and words. *Perceptual & Motor Skills*, 1960, *11*, 204.

Frost, N. Encoding and retrieval in visual memory tasks. *Journal of Experimental Psychology*, 1972, *95*, 317-326.

Jastrzembski, J. E., & Stanners, R. F. Multiple word meanings and lexical search speed. *Journal of Verbal Learning and Verbal Behavior*, 1975, *14*, 534-537.

Jenkins, J. R., Neale, D. C., & Deno, S. L. Differential memory for picture and word stimuli. *Journal of Educational Psychology*, 1967, *58*, 303-307.

Kintsch, W. *The representation of meaning in memory*. Hillsdale, N. J.: Lawrence Erlbaum Associates, 1974.

Klatzky, R. L. *Human memory: Structures and processes*. San Francisco: Freeman, 1975.

Klatzky, R. L., & Ryan, A. S. Category-structure effects in picture comparisons. *Perception & Psychophysics*, 1978, *23*, 193-204.

Klatzky, R. L., & Stoy, A. M. Using visual codes for comparisons of pictures. *Memory & Cognition*, 1974, *2*, 727-736.

Kosslyn, S. M. Scanning visual images: Some structural implications, *Perception & Psychophysics*, 1973, *14*, 90-94.

Kosslyn, S. M. Information representation in visual images. *Cognitive Psychology*, 1975, *7*, 341-370.

Kosslyn, S. M. Imagery and internal representation. In E. Rosch & B. B. Lloyd (Eds.), *Cognition and categorization*. Hillsdale, N. J.: Lawrence Erlbaum Associates, 1978.

Kosslyn, S. M., Ball, T. M., & Reiser, B. J. Visual images preserve metric spatial information: Evidence from studies of image scanning. *Journal of Experimental Psychology: Human Perception and Performance*, 1978, *4*, 47-60.

Kosslyn, S. M., & Shwartz, S. P. A data-driven simulation of visual imagery. *Cognitive Science*, 1977, *1*, 265-296.

Lachman, R. Uncertainty effects on time to access the internal lexicon. *Journal of Experimental Psychology*, 1973, *99*, 199-208.

Marcel, A. J. Conscious and preconscious recognition of polysemous words: Locating the selective effects of prior verbal context. In R. S. Nickerson (Ed.), *Attention and Performance VIII*. Hillsdale, N.J.: Lawrence Erlbaum Associates, 1979.

Martin, E. Generation-recognition theory and the encoding specificity principle. *Psychological Review*, 1975, *82*, 150-153.

Meyer, D. E., & Schvaneveldt, R. W. Facilitation in recognizing words: Evidence of a dependence between retrieval operations. *Journal of Experimental Psychology*, 1971, *90*, 227-234.

Neisser, U. *Cognitive psychology*. New York: Appleton-Century-Crofts, 1967.

Nelson, D. L. Remembering pictures and words: Appearance, significance, & name. In F. I. M. Craik & L. Cermak (Eds.), *Levels of processing*. Hillsdale, N.J.: Lawrence Erlbaum Associates, 1979.

Nelson, D. L., Reed, V. S., & McEvoy, C. L. Learning to order pictures and words: A model of sensory and semantic encoding. *Journal of Experimental Psychology: Human Learning and Memory*, 1977, *3*, 485-497.

Nelson, D. L., Reed, V. S., & Walling, J. R. Pictorial superiority effect. *Journal of Experimental Psychology: Human Learning and Memory*, 1976, *2*, 523-528.

Norman, D. A., & Rumelhart, D. E. *Explorations in cognition*. San Francisco: Freeman, 1975.

Oldfield, R. C., & Wingfield, A. Response latencies in naming objects. *Quarterly Journal of Experimental Psychology*, 1965, *17*, 273-281.

Paivio, A. Latency of verbal associations and imagery to noun stimuli as a function of abstractness and generality. *Canadian Journal of Psychology*, 1966, *20*, 378-387.

Paivio, A. Mental imagery in associative learning and memory. *Psychological Review*, 1969, *76*, 241-263.

Paivio, A. *Imagery and verbal processes*. New York: Holt, Rinehart, & Winston, 1971.

Paivio, A. Imagery in recall and recognition. In J. Brown (Ed.), *Recall and recognition*. New York: Wiley, 1976.

Paivio, A., & Csapo, K. Picture superiority in free recall: Imagery or dual coding? *Cognitive Psychology*, 1973, *5*, 176-206.

Pellegrino, J. W., Rosinski, R. R., Chiesi, H. L., & Siegel, A. Picture-word differences in decision latency: An analysis of single and dual memory models. *Memory & Cognition*, 1977, *5*, 383-396.

Potter, M. C., & Faulconer, B. A. Time to understand pictures and words. *Nature*, 1975, *253*, 437-438.

Pylyshyn, Z. W. What the mind's eye tells the mind's brain: A critique of mental ✓ imagery. *Psychological Bulletin*, 1973, *80*, 1-24.

Pylyshyn, Z. W. Imagery and artificial intelligence. In W. Savage (Ed.), *Perception and cognition: Issues in the foundations of psychology*. Minneapolis: University of Minnesota Press, 1978.

Quillian, M. R. Word concepts: A theory and simulation of some basic semantic capabilities. *Behavioral Science*, 1967, *12*, 410-430.

Reder, L. M., Anderson, J. R., & Bjork, R. A. A semantic interpretation of encoding specificity. *Journal of Experimental Psychology*, 1974, *102*, 648-656.

Rips, L. J., Shoben, E. J., & Smith, E. E. Semantic distance and the verification of semantic relations. *Journal of Verbal Learning and Verbal Behavior*, 1973, *12*, 1-20.

Rosch, E. Cognitive representations of semantic categories. *Journal of Experimental Psychology: General*, 1975, *104*, 192-233.

Rosch, E. Principles of categorization. In E. Rosch & B. B. Lloyd (Eds.), *Cognition and categorization*. Hillsdale, N.J.: Lawrence Erlbaum Associates, 1978.

Rosch, E., Mervis, C. B., Gray, W. D., Johnson, D. M., & Boyes-Braem, P. Basic objects in natural categories. *Cognitive Psychology*, 1976, *8*, 382-439.

Rubenstein, H., Garfield, L., & Milliken, J. A. Homographic entries in the internal lexicon. *Journal of Verbal Learning and Verbal Behavior*, 1970, *9*, 487-494.

Rubenstein, H., Lewis, S. S., & Rubenstein, M. A. Evidence for phonemic recoding in visual word recognition. *Journal of Verbal Learning and Verbal Behavior*, 1971, *10*, 645-657.

Schvaneveldt, R. W., & Meyer, D. E. Retrieval and comparison processes in semantic memory. In S. Kornblum (Ed.), *Attention and performance IV*. New York: Academic Press, 1973.

Schvaneveldt, R. W., Meyer, D. E., & Becker, C. A. Lexical ambiguity, semantic context, and visual word recognition. *Journal of Experimental Psychology: Human Perception and Performance*, 1976, *2*, 243-256.

Smith, E. E. Theories of semantic memory. In W. K. Estes (Ed.), *Handbook of learning and cognitive processes* (Vol. 5). Hillsdale, N.J.: Lawrence Erlbaum Associates, 1978.

Smith, E. E., Shoben, E. K., & Rips, L. J. Structure and process in semantic memory: A featural model for semantic decisions. *Psychological Review*, 1974, *81*, 214-241.

Smith, M. C., & Magee, L. E. Tracing the time course of picture-word processing. *Journal of Experimental Psychology: General*, 1980 (in press).

Snodgrass, J. G., & Asiaghi, A. The pictorial superiority effect in recognition memory. *Bulletin of the Psychonomic Society*, 1977, *10*, 1-4.

Snodgrass, J. G., Burns, P. M., & Pirone, G. V. Pictures and words and space and ∨

time: In search of the elusive interaction. *Journal of Experimental Psychology: General*, 1978, *107*, 206-230.

Snodgrass, J. G., & McClure, P. Storage and retrieval properties of dual codes for pictures and words in recognition memory. *Journal of Experimental Psychology: Human Learning and Memory*, 1975, *1*, 521-529.

Snodgrass, J. G., & Vanderwart, M. A standardized set of 260 pictures: Norms for name agreement, image agreement, familiarity, and visual complexity. *Journal of Experimental Psychology: Human Learning and Memory*, 1980 (in press).

Snodgrass, J. G., Wasser, B., Finkelstein, M., & Goldberg, L. B. On the fate of visual and verbal memory codes for pictures and words: Evidence for a dual coding mechanism in recognition memory. *Journal of Verbal Learning and Verbal Behavior*, 1974, *13*, 27-37.

Tulving, E. Episodic and semantic memory. In E. Tulving & W. Donaldson (Eds.), *Organization of memory*. New York: Academic Press, 1972.

Tulving, E., & Thomson, D. M. Retrieval processes in recognition memory: Effects of associative context. *Journal of Experimental Psychology*, 1971, *87*, 116-124.

Wickelgren, W. A. Chunking and consolidation: A theoretical synthesis of semantic networks, configuring in conditioning, *S-R* versus cognitive learning, normal forgetting, the amnesic syndrome, and the hippocampal arousal system. *Psychological Review*, 1979, *86*, 44-60.

# The basic test of the graph: A matrix theory of graph construction and cartography

Jacques Bertin

*The value of a diagram or map is defined by the service it provides. The question is how to define this service. It is shown here that the service is complete when the figure provides an immediate visual answer to the two questions: 1. What are the x and the y components in the table of data? 2. What are the groups in x and the groups in y that the data construct? When there is no visual answer to these questions, the figure is useless. Above all, then, all users of diagrams or of maps must learn to pose these two questions.*

All disciplines use the graph to greater or lesser extent and in all cases the problem is: how to depict the data? Although I tried to solve this problem by outlining the principles of the graph and its semiology useless maps and diagrams still abound. To avoid errors a simpler test has been devised that is easy to apply and is intended particularly for those involved in research or publishing and for every user or reader of diagrams and maps.

Two observations are basic to this test: every diagram and every map is the transcription of a two-dimensional table of data—the objective of a graphic transcription is comprehension, that is, the reduction of a multiplicity of elementary data to the groupings that the set of data generates.

Consequently, a diagram or a map must furnish a visual answer to these two questions: 1. What are the $x$ and $y$ components of the table of data? 2. What are the groups of elements in $x$ and the groups of elements in $y$ that the data generate?

These two questions constitute what may be called the basic test of the graph. The test affords a solution to the problem of how to depict by a preliminary analysis of why depict, using the notion of relevant questions and their hierarchical arrangement, from elementary questions to essential questions. The test shows that the latter questions have only one graphic solution.

There are no good or poor diagrams or good or poor maps. Rather, some constructions answer the questions that one is entitled to ask and others do not. By making the hierarchy of possible questions apparent, the test underlines the fact that one cannot look at a graph or a map as one looks at a painting or a traffic signal. One does not passively "read" a graph: one queries it. And one must know how to ask useful questions.

This test defines the essential questions and, presented with any graphic construction, it provides an immediate and indisputable verdict and often reveals incredible errors. Moreover, it allows us to avoid irrelevant questions. Besides underlining the two phases of graph perception, the two questions of the test demonstrate that communication theory is not relevant to graph perception and that such tests as "What do you see?" "What do you prefer?" bear no relation to the objective of the graph and become instead a source of confusion and error. By its simplicity and by the developments that it fosters, this test seems to enjoy a hitherto unequalled efficiency not only to the benefit of graph construction but also to logic and its language. The justification for the two preliminary observations and their applications will now be discussed.

*Two preliminary observations*
Every "graph" is the transcription of a table of data. A "datum" is the relation between two elements. For example, the assertion that "Mr. M is 25 years old" establishes a relation between the element *M* of a set of individuals and the element *25* of a set of ages.

A *set of data* generates the relations that exist between a set of elements called "objects" and another set of elements called "characteristics," attributed to these objects. Every set of data can be arranged in the form of a table that places the component called objects in the *x* dimension and the component called characteristics in the *y* dimension or vice versa. Usually, however, the objects can be enumerated while the characteristics must be defined. These definitions are more legible when they are horizontal, that is, when the characteristics are in *y*. The cells of the table so constructed show the relation observed between each of the elements in *x* and each of the elements in *y*. This notation is the *z* dimension of the image. This analysis imposes an absolute condition: the relations can only be expressed by *yes* or *no* (1 or 0), by order (1st, 2nd, 3rd...), by quantities, by *?* (absence of data), or by *not applicable*. All other notation is excluded.

One enters data into a computer with the aid of a two-dimensional table. Cartography begins with the topographer who establishes a set of points, that is, a two-dimensional table. Every network of relations can be constructed in the form of a two-dimensional table. If one grants that the *x* and *y* entries of the table are unlimited in terms of the number of their elements, one can conceive of every problem in terms of a matrix of data. Thus, every graph and every map, no matter how large, is the transcription of a two-dimensional table.

*Every graph has as its object the reduction of the entries of the table of data.* Data, that is, the observations that one can make, are always multitudinous. To decide is to choose, yet at the moment of decision we cannot possibly retain and organize this multiplicity with the necessary rigor. It is necessary to reduce this multiplicity, that is, to discover similar elements and then group and classify them. In effect, "To understand is to categorize" and, more precisely, to understand is to reduce the complete set of relevant data to the groupings that the relations generate. Consequently, to understand is to demonstrate in the table of data:

the groups of objects,
the groups of characteristics,

generated by the z relations. In graphic matrices, the z relations are the variations from white to black corresponding to these entries.

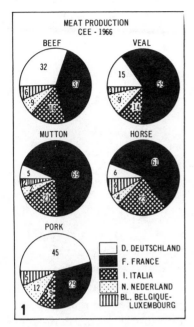

Figure 1. Diagram constructed by the E.E.C.

A deliberately simple example illustrates. In 1966, the five Ministers of the European Economic Community (the Common Market), met to discuss problems about the sale of meat. They issued numerous statistics. To facilitate their use, the administration of the EEC had some diagrams constructed (Figures 1 and 2). Figure 1 gives very little visual information and, in fact, the participants themselves preferred the table of numbers in Figure 2. Undoubtedly, they perceived the uninteresting nature of the answers furnished by Figure 1. One sees

| | | | | | |
|---|---|---|---|---|---|
| 6 | 3 | 2 | 6 | 5 | BELGIQUE LUXEMBOURG |
| 32 | 15 | 5 | 6 | 45 | DEUTSCHLD |
| 37 | 59 | 69 | 61 | 29 | FRANCE |
| 16 | 14 | 21 | 23 | 9 | ITALIA |
| 9 | 9 | 3 | 4 | 12 | NEDERLAND |
| 100 | 100 | 100 | 100 | 100 | |
| BEEF | VEAL | MUTTON | HORSE | PORK | |
| | | MEAT PRODUCTION | | | 2 |

Figure 2. Alternative diagram constructed by the E.E.C.

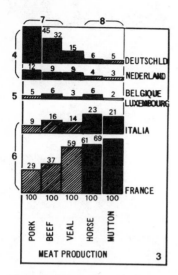

Figure 3. Normal construction of the same data.

that 69 percent of the sheep are in France and only 2 percent in Belgium or, alternately, that France produces more than Belgium but it does not seem necessary to have a figure in order to show that France is larger than Belgium!

The normal construction (Figure 3), by contrast, makes the real content of the table of data more apparent, which is of some importance: Germany and the Netherlands have the same relative production based on pork and beef. These two countries thus form a group (Section 4) opposed to another group, France and Italy, which is characterized by an inverse relation (Section 6). Finally, the relative production of the Belgo-Luxemburg Union (Section 5) is different from the two preceding ones. It turns out that the policies of the first two groups within the framework of these data can only be opposed or complementary and, if the vote of each country carries equal weight, the decision will rest with the Belgo-Luxemburg Union!

By revealing the fact that ($5 \times 5 =$) 25 elementary data reduced the countries to three groups, defined by two groups of products as in sections 4, 5, and 6, the table of data, Sections 7 and 8, has furnished essential information with which every elementary datum can be seen to be either consistent or inconsistent. Moreover, the problem remains the same whether it involves a $5 \times 5$ table comprising 25 elementary data, or a $1000 \times 1000$ table comprising a million data. It is known that man cannot integrate more than seven combinative concepts concerning a given problem and thus every table, every set of information, must be reduced to about this number. It is, in fact, a matter of reducing the table to the groupings or to the orders, in $x$ and $y$, that the $z$ relations generate. This is the object of statistical analyses, particularly of multivariate analysis, and, indeed, of every graphic transcription.

*Application to diagrams*

The foregoing very simple example clarifies the basic principles of graph perception and construction. The essential information takes the form defined by the second question: What are the groupings in $x$? The answer is: Sections 4, 5, and 6 (Figure 3). What are the groupings in $y$? The answer is Sections 7 and 8. Consequently, *familiarity with the $x$'s and $y$'s is the prime requisite.*

Obviously, every useful reading of a graph begins with familiarity with the nature of the $x$ and $y$ entries of the table of data. Why, then, as in Figure 4 disrupt these entries graphically? How long will the reader require to define the $x$ and $y$ entries of the table that served to construct this figure? How can the reader, in these circumstances, see the information contained in these data? Why, as happens in too many instances, write these entries in letters less than one millimeter in size or even omit them? The written definition of these entries is the first phase of graphic perception and is the true heading of a diagram.

The first rule of construction of diagrams is to write the definition of the objects and of the characteristics in a highly visible fashion. Every useful graph must spontaneously answer the first test question. By asking this question, the reader can make an initial evaluation of any diagram; unfortunately, this evaluation all too often runs the risk of being negative.

*Know how to define the relevant questions and to arrange them hierarchically.* Once the reader has been able to familiarize himself with the entries of the table of data, he must know how to define the complete set of relevant questions and to arrange them hierarchically. ("Hypotheses" simply represent a choice of relevant questions and, in principle, precede the table of data and thus allow for its conception.) There are two types of questions: those introduced by $x$ (for instance, such a country, how much?) and those introduced by $y$ (for instance, such a product, how much?). The full significance of this observation will be seen in cartography. Each type can be applied to the individual elements or to a sub-set or to the complete set of elements and, consequently, three levels of questions can be posed: elementary (for example, such a country, such a product, how much?), intermediate (for example, such a country, what are its characteristics?), and global (for example, how do the countries regroup themselves?). This analysis by type and by level defines the complete set of relevant questions and constructions such as Figure 1 are obviously useless because they answer only the elementary questions: such a section of the circle, that is, such a product, such a country, how much? These elementary questions are multitudinous and the object of the graph, like that of mathematics, is not to represent this unmemorizable multiplicity but, on the contrary, to collate it to reveal the global relations that can be remembered. The useful graph must thus furnish a visual answer to the global question, that is, it must answer the second test question.

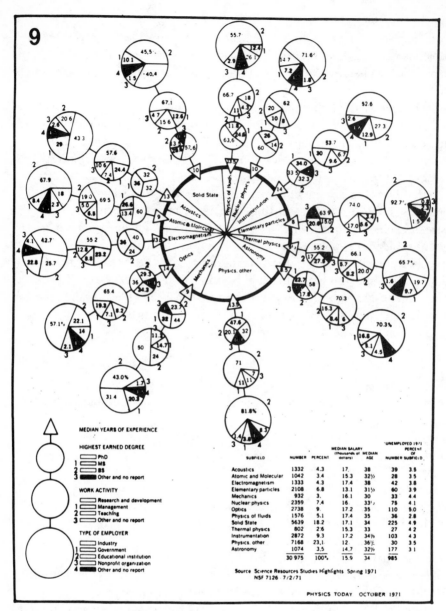

Figure 4. Incoherent presentation of data.

*Know how to define the useful construction, that is, the normal construction.* Yet how is one to answer the second test question and discover the groupings in $x$ and in $y$ when the figure disrupts the entries of the table as in Figure 1 or Figure 4? The groupings can be made apparent only under two conditions which define the normal construction. The normal construction preserves the matrix structure of the table of data, placing the $x$ and $y$ entries of the table on the $x$ and $y$ axes of the paper and transcribes the $z$'s (yes-no relations, order or quantity) by a variation from white to black given by the value or the size of the markings on the page. This is the second rule of construction of diagrams. The normal construction rearranges the rows or columns of the matrix in order to show the groups clearly. This is the third rule of diagrams. In fact, the rows and columns of Figure 3 are not in the same order as those in Figure 2.

It is by permuting the rows and combining similar ones and by permuting the columns (if appropriate) and combining similar ones that one discovers the groups, the global information. These permutations are simple. A child performs them naturally (Gimeno, 1977), sometimes surprising adults who have, in the course of a schooling based on the element, the word, the number, the sign, gradually lost the habit of seeing wholes. The problem of permutations is primarily a practical one which can be performed simply by cutting up the figure. When the data are numerous, specialized materials allow one to proceed easily with the permutations (Bertin, 1977, p. 35).

The properties of the normal construction must all be exploited. The normal construction answers all relevant questions, that is, it simultaneously answers global questions and elementary questions, making every piece of elementary information useful because one can see immediately if it is representative of the general trend or, on the contrary, an exception. Thus the graph is the only "language" that allows one to move instantly from the whole to the part and from the part to the whole as well as to evaluate every element. This is true only for the normal construction, however. No other construction allows one to move to the whole (for example, those in Figure 5 which represent the same facts as Figures 1 and 2). Such constructions answer only the elementary questions and without them we could still evaluate the individual elements of information. In short, the classical constructions are useless. And they are no more useful when they are distributed on a map (cartograms) because the minimum order remaining in the diagrams is disrupted on a map. If graph construction has been brought into disrepute, it is principally because of the uselessness of these constructions.

The normal construction avoids irrelevant questions. The frequent observation that, if one had chosen other characteristics, the groupings would have been different, is probably correct. However, it involves the completely different problem of what table of data to construct, a problem extrinsic and irrelevant to the table. It is important not to confuse two distinct phases of the thought process: the choice of data and the analysis of data. This is an essential rule of logic made particularly evident by the normal construction.

Such an observation could not have been made in connection with Figure 1. It is the result of the analysis, that is, the groupings, that allow these observations and permit the initiation of research into new characteristics. The graph can aid in determining what table of data should be constructed. This is called the matrix analysis of the problem and is an operation of a very different nature (Bertin, 1977, p. 233).

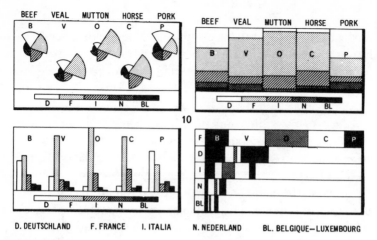

Figure 5. Other representations of the data in Figure 1. The four constructions "represent" the data in Figure 2.

The normal construction demystifies the computer. "I have fed my data into the computer!" we hear. But what questions has the computer been asked? How many researchers could answer precisely and simply? Because every investigation and every study is in reality simply the resolution of one and only one table of data (that obviously must be conceivable), the two test questions and the list of relevant questions allow one to give a precise answer and to define clearly all the means of analysis. The graph thus gives a visual form to what is called data analysis. It always involves the discovery of the groupings in $x$ and $y$ that the $z$ relations of a given table generate. Graphic analyses and multivariate mathematical analyses thus complement classical statistics which calculate a correlation coefficient or a law of correspondence between two rows of a table.

*Going from spectator to actor*

To become involved in a problem and to understand it is to shift from an elementary reading to a global reading. Graph construction aims to promote this transition. It is not an art but, unlike "graphics," a language that is rigorously finite in its means of expression (it is alone in this respect) and operates on rigorously defined sets. Thus it is characterized neither by communication theory nor by psychology. To perceive a poster, a traffic signal, a word, requires only one phase of perception: what is it about? To perceive a graph requires, as we have just seen, two distinct phases of perception:

    1. What components are involved?

    2. What are the relations among them?

The first phase is conventional. It involves the identification of a few concepts from among the unlimited number of imaginable ones, for example, discerning that, in Figure 1, five *countries* and five types of *meat* are involved. Given the infinity of possible states, the verbal or figurative conventions with which one must deal always lend themselves to diverse possibilities of interpretation. The first phase is thus characterized by the classic schema of polysemic communication: Sender $\leftrightarrow$ Code $\leftrightarrow$ Receiver.

The second phase is not conventional. We are now no longer dealing with an unlimited number of concepts, but with only three: the three fundamental relations to which every observation must be reduced: the relations of resemblance or difference ($=$); the relations of order ($O$); and the relations of proportionality ($Q$). The graph is not conventional because it transcribes a relation by the same relation. It transcribes a *resemblance* between things by a visual resemblance between signs or positions (they are close). It transcribes an *order* between things by a visual order between signs or positions. It transcribes a *proportion* between things by a visual proportion between signs or positions.

In the second phase the eye does not consider the significance of a single sign (which is always disputable). Instead, it considers the variations from one sign to another. It makes use only of the visual variation between signs (which is indisputable). Consequently, to transcribe an order by a resemblance is not simply to make use of a convention. It is to generate false groupings and consequently to create a falsehood. Graphic transcription is thus not free. But it is for this reason that it is universal. Sender and Receiver are united by the table of data and are in exactly the same situation. They are the "actors" who ask the second test question: what are the proportions and the orders in the table and, finally, what are the groups (resemblances) generated by the data?

In the second phase of perception, the author and the reader follow the monosemic schema: actor $\leftrightarrow$ three relations ($Q, O, =$). This schema underlines the fact that classical tests which ask what is seen in a diagram, a map, which color is preferred, assume that one looks at a graph as one looks at a painting. The applications of communication theory are concerned only with the first phase of graph perception and do not furnish precise and concise means for the indisputable definition of the *why* and consequently the *how* of a diagram or map.

The schema of monosemic transcription is in a sense the canonical form of the two test questions and, with them, provides an instrument of analysis that allows one to discover and avoid the principal errors.

The principal errors in graph construction are given in the following paragraphs.

1. Failing to highlight the $x$ and $y$ entries of the table. The entries of the table are the only means of knowing what it is about. They must thus appear instantly, in their place in a highly visible script with the entries of the graphic matrix.

2. Disrupting the entries of the table. The normal construction preserves the $x, y, z$ structure of the table of data. Every other construction disrupts the entries and answers only elementary questions or certain intermediate questions.

3. Failing to make the groupings obvious. It does not suffice to preserve the structure of the table. One must make the similarities apparent, that is, one must adjoin similar rows and, if appropriate, similar columns. It is these permutations that cause the groups in $x$ and the groups in $y$ to appear clearly.

4. To make use of a convention and transcribe an order by a disorder. In the $x, y$ plane, this simply means to commit errors 2 and 3 above. In the third or $z$ dimension of the image, this means (say) to transcribe a continuum by a disorder of values, as often happens with color. The eye then perceives false visual groupings. This error is particularly frequent with maps of a single characteristic. The maps furnished on a cathode-ray tube to the President of the United States may have marvellous colors but the levels of the values do not coincide with quantitative levels in the data and thus the President may see false groupings, false geographies.

5. To make use of a convention and transcribe an order by a difference. For example, in transcribing an order by a variation in shape the groupings disappear. There are only four ordered visual variables: the two dimensions of the plane, size, and value. A proportion ($Q$) can be transcribed only by the plane and size. An order ($0$) can be transcribed only by the plane, size, and value. Other variables such as texture, color, orientation, and shape are not ordered. They do not generate groups but segregate only pieces of elementary information. They can sometimes underline the groupings, but only when the distribution in the plane is extremely simple or, in other words, when the elements are already grouped in the plane.

6. To draw solely for publication. A graphic construction is not made to be published. It is above all a product of personal labor that permits one to analyse information and to discover the groupings contained in the data. Publication comes later and only what is necessary and sufficient is published.

7. To multiply partial diagrams. This is the basic error. It disrupts the global view of the problem under consideration. A study is a whole and a single table must be conceivable; it alone can justify separately analyzed sub-sets.

*Application to cartography*

*Every map is the transcription of a two-dimensional table*. In Figure 6, Map 12 is the transcription of Table 11. On the map, the *départements* are scattered across the plane. In the table, these same *départements* are aligned in $x$ and the characteristics are aligned in $y$. Whatever the number of elements on the map containing information, 90 *départements* or 90 million points, one can imagine them aligned in $x$ in a table that transcribes the observed characteristics in $y$. Every cartographic problem can thus be conceived from the outset as the transcription of a table comprising geographic points in $x$ and characteristics in $y$. Consequently, the set of questions relevant to a map corresponds to the set of questions relevant to the table of data of which it is the transcription. What applies to diagrams applies also to every cartographic problem. The two test questions allow one to define *how* to make the map by analyzing *why* make the map, that is, by the precise analysis of the relevant questions and of their visual answers.

*First test question: What are the x's and the y's of the table of data?* $x$ is the definition of the space under consideration in the map. The geographic shape or the context can be sufficient to define the space under consideration: Argentina, U.S.A., London, a neighbourhood, a house, or an object. This is not necessarily always the case, however, and when this information is missing, the map loses all meaning (for example, partial enlargements that are not identified in a master table). Graphically, or verbally, the space must be clearly identifiable for every consultant.

$x$ is also the scale and the partition of the space when necessary. It is important to define the level of information: *département*, community, one kilometer squares, plots of land, and so on.

$y$ is the definition of the characteristics. In a map of a single characteristic, that characteristic is the heading. In maps of several characteristics, why should the same heading generally be written in microscopic letters opposite the boxes of the legend? The legend is simply the $y$ entry of the table of data, the second part of the heading and the indispensable means for entering the map. The same is true of the boxes of the legend. Yet they are often so small that one cannot distinguish which "green" or which "brown" is involved. The legend, the true heading of the map, must be clearly visible and the necessary space provided for it.

Economies of space or labor effected by some lay-out artists or graphists, for whom the usefulness of the map is the least concern, cost very dearly. To be unable automatically to recognize the $x$'s and the $y$'s of the table, that is, the space being represented and the characteristics being distributed, is the best reason for the reader to turn the page.

*Second test-question: What are the groupings in x and the groupings in y?* This question raises the specific problem of cartography, that is, a map of several characteristics cannot simultaneously answer both elementary and global questions unless it is simplified. To construct a map is thus to proceed, consciously or not, with two choices:

the choice of a level of response: elementary or global;
the choice between a simplified or an unsimplified (exhaustive) map.

*The level of response*
If we ask, in Map 12 (Figure 6), what are the groupings in $y$ (that is, what characteristics have the same geography?) we find that there is no visual answer. If we ask, what are the groupings in $x$ (that is, what homogeneous regions do the data generate?) again there is no visual answer. The superposition map, 12, which

corresponds to section 13 in the table of data, answers elementary questions (at such a location, what is there?) but it does not answer global questions. This is easily explained. Can one superpose numerous photographs on the same film and see each one separately? Obviously, the superposition of several images disrupts each particular image and the superposition map is one to be read piecemeal. In section 14 there are four maps. What are the groupings in y? The answer is immediate: maps II, III, and T resemble one another and are different from I. What are the groupings in x? The answer is that the data generate two geographies: a "rural" France (I) and an "urban" France, (II, III, T). The collection of maps in Section 14 answers the global questions posed in Section 16 by asking: "such a characteristic, where is it?" (Section 15). Each map is one to be seen instantly, permitting one to discover the resemblances and the differences. Obviously, however, the collection does not provide instant answers to elementary questions of the type posed in section 13.

To construct a map of several characteristics always involves the choice between two levels of information: the elementary level (*at such a location, what is there?*) as in Section 13 or the global level (*such a characteristic, where is it?*) as in Section 15. By asking these two questions, every reader of a map can immediately evaluate the level of the perceptible information. Similarly, one who wants to can define the useful level of information and the corresponding graphic formula: the elementary level is furnished by the superposition map. The global level is furnished by the collection of maps of a single characteristic. The most common error is to overlook these two levels of information and to construct superposition maps when it is the global information that is relevant.

*Case 1: The global questions.* These are the most important. The map must furnish an immediate answer to the question: such a characteristic, where is it? The following study provides a typical example. A large and very advanced country has undertaken a remarkable ethnological study involving more than 2000 investigation sites, more than 800 types of folklore manifestations, multiplied by three possible dates, giving 2400 characteristics × 2000 points or 4,800,000 yes/no responses. Unfortunately, the test questions were not asked. The usual strategies were followed and the characteristics were superposed on the map. But, because the superpositions were limited, the problem was divided. Twenty-five maps were constructed, each of about 32 characteristics, differentiated by shape, and multiplied by three colors for dates.

Numerous researchers were then invited to make use of these maps. They were not asked, "at such a location, what is there?" On the contrary, they were asked if there were relations between the types of manifestations, between the types and the dates, whether certain groupings characterized some regions and, if so, what groupings and what regions? In other words, how to regroup the x's and the y's of the table of data. To answer accurately, they had to redraw the 800 maps by characteristic; otherwise all commentary would have been only anecdotal. It is easy to calculate the cost of this error of analysis.

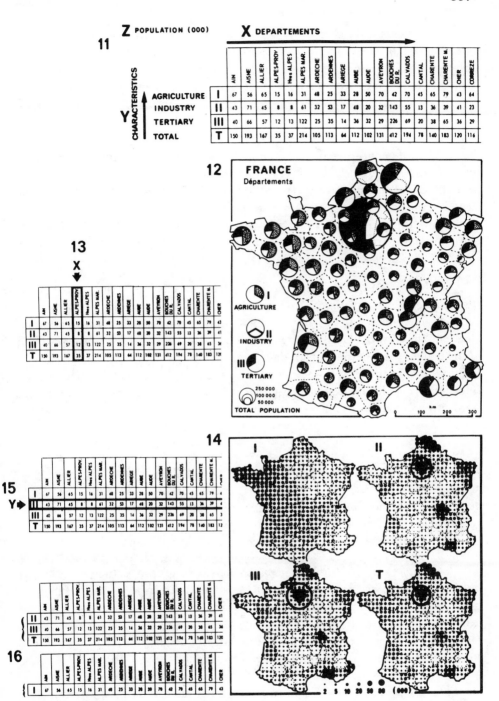

Figure 6. Cartographic representations of data.

Obviously, the characteristics should not have been superposed. A two-dimensional table should have been constructed and the groups made apparent, with the aid of the computer which can furnish groups and also sub-groups and their geography, and can even answer elementary questions.

If one does not have a computer there are two types of solution. One is to allow a loss of information, proceed by sampling, and reduce either the 800 characteristics or the 2000 points to a smaller number. It is preferable to reduce the number of geographic points. An image file preserves the groups and allows one to return later to the exhaustive information. The other solution is to preserve the exhaustive information and, from the start, make a map for each characteristic denoting the dates by a variation in size. This solution is less costly because it does away with the infernal work of isolating each characteristic on the superposition maps and doing this 800 times! It is thus more useful than the 25 maps that were undoubtedly spectacular but totally useless.

*Legibility*. Complex superpositions become "illegible." And yet the authors of the 25 ethnographic maps made use of the best arrangement in order that each sign be "legible," that is, in order that it not be confused either with another characteristic or with neighbouring signs. The cartographer resolved the problem of the legibility in $x$ in the table of data by answering the question: "at such a location, what is there?" However, he forgot the legibility in $y$ (such a characteristic, where is it?), the only legibility capable of answering the second test question. It is still often forgotten in classical cartography that there are two types of questions and thus two problems of legibility that cannot be resolved at once.

*Construct a working instrument*. When the second test question must be answered, and when the number of characteristics is large, one should not begin with superposition maps. One should construct a working instrument that will make the correlations and the groups apparent. Cartography then can reveal the geographic distribution generated by the groupings. The working instruments are multivariate analysis, graphic matrices, or the collection of maps.

*Cartography is independent of publication*. Cartography is, first, a working instrument and it is very important to understand that a large number of illustrated maps are never published. Those involved in cartography must know how to differentiate between laboratory documents necessary to define what there is to say about a problem but not usually published, and documents for publication constructed for a given public and chosen from among the working documents as justification. It must be emphasized that one does not draft the text first and illustrate it afterwards. On the contrary, like mathematical analyses, diagrams and maps are the points of departure for the text and the text is simply the justification of the analysis and the interpretation of the groupings discovered by the researcher.

*Case 2: The elementary questions.* These are the most relevant. Only elementary topographic relations are useful. For example, an architect's plan shows the mason the precise location where he must construct a wall and the plumber where he must put a tap. The plan defines the points and the lines in relation to small identifiable sub-sets. The users do not need to see the overall picture of each characteristic but must find a precise and complete answer to the question: "at such a location, what is there?" It is thus necessary to superpose on the map all the useful characteristics. These are reference maps. It is the domain—and the only domain—of conventional signs: one sign means "tap," another means "house," another means "contour-line." It suffices first, that the information be exhaustive, that is, that the map contains all the elements required by a well-defined user; and, second, that the elements are not confused with respect either to position or to meaning. This is the problem of the visual segregation of elements and is not easy to resolve because it depends essentially on the complexity of the distribution. The matrix view allows one to analyze the principal parameters of this complexity which increase with the number of characteristics (the $y$ of the table of data), the number of topographic elements (the $x$ of the table), and their heterogeneity of size, the number of levels of each characteristic (the $z$ of the table), and, finally, from the juxtaposition to the superposition (inclusions and the distinctness of the segregations in $x$). The visual separation of the characteristics is a delicate problem and one that is rarely resolved as any collection of tourist guides shows. It is not, however, the only problem of cartography. More important is to know whether this problem needs to be posed or not, whether superposition is necessary or not.

The first error is to regard every map as reference map and to superpose several characteristics on the same map when global information is required. We have seen the cost of such errors. They become serious when superposition maps are the only guide to decisions. Only some pieces of elementary information can be seen and it is impossible to see whether they are exceptions to the general trend or not. Certain official documents contain only cartograms (superposition of $n$ characteristics on a map by means of diagrams such as in Sections 1, 10, 12, 18, and so on scattered across the map). A cartogram excludes the global information and one therefore asks with disquiet the bases on which the decisions have been made.

The second error is to forget to construct reference maps when they are required. How many history, geography, archaeology, and science texts do not provide a map, indispensable in order to follow the author in his text! There are numerous types, however (topography, road maps, maps of vegetation, geology, climate, morphology, and so on) which do respond to an elementary and some-times to a global reading when the zonal characteristics simply serve to divide the plane (as in geology, for example).

The necessity to introduce numerous characteristics into a problem calls into question some cartographic types and one turns more willingly towards a cartography of regional intervention capable of including all the desired characteristics by utilizing multivariate mathematical or graphic analyses and a collection of maps.

*Case 3*: *Both levels of questions*. In many cases, for example, with national or regional geographic atlases whose users are numerous, both levels of questions are relevant and the only cartographic solution is to make several maps: 1. the superposition map, to answer the question, "at such a location...," 2. a map by characteristic, to answer the question, "such a characteristic...." The latter can be much smaller than the superposition map and do not require the use of color. They must, however, comprise a reference system that is spatially discrete (checkered, for instance), and sufficiently compact to facilitate precise comparisons.

*Simplified map or an unsimplified (exhaustive) map?* The schematic map often encountered not only in textbooks but also in information documents is useful but it must be noted that it cannot replace the original information. Map 20 (Figure 7) does not allow one to reconstruct the exhaustive facts given in section 19. When the latter are useful for other comparisons, the simplified map is inadequate. Moreover, there is always dispute either in the choice of groupings to be indicated or in the choice of the level of simplification.

The schematic map corresponds to the simplification of the table of data. It transcribes geographically the groupings in $x$ (regions) defined by the groupings in $y$ (characteristics) that the $z$ data generate. The discovery of these groupings can be made by means of a collection of maps or by means of matrix manipulations.

For example, take the classic map of the pyramidal distribution of age (Figure 7, Section 18) which transcribes the table in Section 17. Like every cartogram it disrupts the "geographies." In order to see them it is necessary to construct either a collection (as in Section 19) that leads to the simplified maps (Section 20) or a matrix (Figure 8, Section 22) that is easily grouped (Section 24) and furnishes the simplified map (Section 23). But Section 20 of Figure 7 and Section 23 of Figure 8 do not permit reconstruction of the original data which are lost if they are not furnished as in Sections 18 and 19 of Figure 7 or Section 24 of Figure 8.

A simplification is always disputable. Map 20 of Figure 7, for example, is disputable. That is, why not maps 23, 25, 26, or 28 of Figure 8? Map 23 defines seven categories of regions, from the youngest to the oldest, plus an exceptional category defined by the simultaneous presence of young and old. Map 25 defines only three regions and the exceptional category. Map 26 defines two "systems": young or old regions in five categories and regions of extreme or central classes in three categories. Map 28 defines the same systems but with only two categories in each system.

Every simplification represents a particular interpretation. Should it be imposed on the user without justification or provision of the means for possible criticism? It can be useful to know what differentiates two regions regrouped in the schematic map. Scientific rigor thus requires provision of the exhaustive

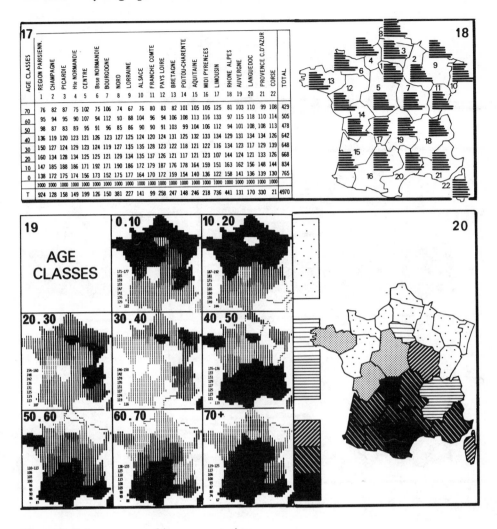

Figure 7. Other cartographic representations.

information in addition to the schema, that is, to provide either Map 23 and Section 24 of Figure 8 or Map 20 and Section 19 of Figure 7. Sections 24 or 27 of Figure 8, like Section 19 of Figure 7, contain all the elements of other possible interpretations, adapted to the specific problem of each user. This example is easily transposed into every problem of cartographic simplification.

"Cartographic generalization" is a matrix operation. "Generalization" is the required simplification, particularly when the scale of the map is reduced. It leads to the elimination of some characteristics or to their regrouping. The matrix transformation shows that generalization is of the same nature as simplification, that is, it involves permutations and regroupings of the table of data corresponding to the map. This observation indicates numerous perspectives: the preserva-

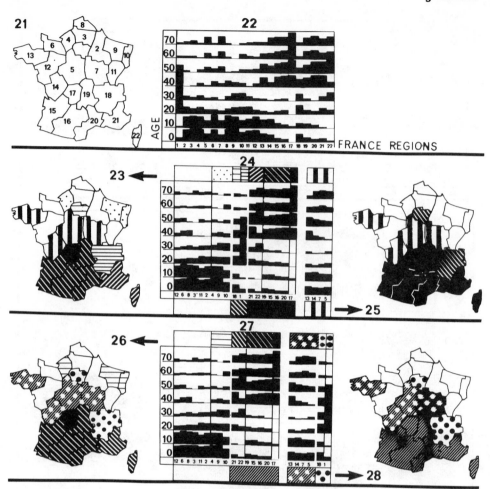

Figure 8. Further cartographic representations.

tion or elimination of an indentation in a contour-line, for example, does not depend solely on the size of the indentation. The decision depends above all on the variation of the values of all the points (x) that surround it, for all the characteristics (y) chosen. Each person can now defend his or her own list of characteristics! Generalization is thus a problem of choice of characteristics rather than a problem of method. Once the characteristics have been chosen, the matrix conception of the problem allows one to conceive an automatic system of generalization.

In sum, in cartography, each characteristic occupies the whole image. Conesequently, the two test questions complement one another: 1. What are the x's and the y's of the table of data and, in addition, is the map unsimplified (transcribing all the data of the table) or simplified? 2. How do the x's and the y's of the table of data regroup themselves? In addition, is the relevant question the question in $y$ (such a characteristic, where is it, that is, geography of the whole) or the question in $x$ (at such a location, what is there, that is, point information)? Every reader can make use of these two alternatives to evaluate the answers given by a map or to avoid the three principal errors. 1. Failing to highlight the $x$'s and the $y$'s of the table. The reader must easily recognize the space being represented and also recognize instantly the distributed characteristics. 2. Superposing several characteristics when a global reading is useful. This is the error of all cartograms, the folklore maps, for example. The information is not simplified but complete. However, it is impossible to see the "geography" of the characteristics. The question, "such a characteristic, where is it?" has no answer. 3. Making a simplified map when exhaustiveness is necessary. This is the error of schematic maps unaccompanied by their justification. Every simplification is arguable. For errors 2 and 3 the general solution is to provide, in addition, the separate map for each characteristic. These maps can be smaller, monochromatic, and, if need be, the corresponding mathematical or graphic analysis can be furnished. But the basic information is furnished only by the matrix of data.

*Conclusion*

Every problem can be posed in terms of a network of relations or in terms of a matrix of relations. But a network quickly becomes illegible while the visual matrix allows one to move spontaneously from the part to the whole and from the whole to the part while accommodating a significant number of data. The graph has as its aim the use of this property of visual perception to undertand the problem better and to make better decisions. The use of this property in cartography and *the conception of every map as the transformation of a matrix of data* allows one to approach the general theory of cartography in a precise and concise manner. The transformation underlines the fact that the map, like every network, easily becomes illegible. Detail disrupts the whole and the need to choose between the two is inevitable. The transformation clarifies the choice by providing a complete analysis of the *why*? (relevant questions) which allows one to define the *how*? It shows that one does not read a map any more than one reads a diagram: one queries it. These questions are at three levels and every user must learn to ask the relevant questions and to arrange them hierarchically. Finally, the transformation avoids analyses that confuse the choice of data and the transcription of data. There is no "real" world and its transcription more or less problematic. There is a finite table of $x, y$ data to be transcribed cartographically. The choice of $x, y$ data will always be perfectly free; this choice, as well as the interpretation of the results of the analysis, are problems for the geologist, the historian, the geographer, the pedagogue, the doctor, and so on. Choice is not the problem for the cartographer. On the other hand, the transcription and the analyses of the data will always be dependent on the laws of logic and visual perception. These are problems for the mathematician, the graphist, and the cartographer. Let each play his role. And if the same individual plays two roles, he must be able to separate them and to learn two scripts. He must know his domain and he must also know the visual bases of logic to which the two test questions are the essential introduction.

This paper was translated from the French by Paul G. Allen.

## References

Bertin, J. *Sémiologie graphique* (2nd ed.). Paris: Mouton, Gauthier Villars, 1967.
Bertin, J. *La graphique et le traitement graphique de l'information*. Paris: Flammarion, 1977.
Bonin, S. *Initiation à la graphique*. Paris: L'Epi, 1975.
Gimeno, R. L'enseignement par la graphique. *Les Cahiers de la graphique*, Laboratoire de Graphique de L'E.H.E.S.S., 1977.

# Subject Index

Abbreviations, 25, 26, 33, 34, 37-9
*Abdjad*, 157, 173
Allah, 157, 159, 163, 164, 165, 167, 168, 175
Alphabet, 67-73, 75, 80; packaged symbols of, 75-7. *See also* Reading, Writing
Analysis, levels of, 114, 115, 116
Anaphora, 537-47 passim; nominal substitution and, 540; overview of, 538
Animal communication, 7, 16
Arabic calligraphy: styles of, 158, 160-1, 171-2; symbolism of, 161-5, 168, 172-6
Artificial intelligence, 114

Body motion, 8, 10
Boutique graphics, 129

Captions. *See* Subtitles
Cartography, 152, 291-305 passim, 315-29 passim, 585-604 passim. *See also* Maps
Causal relationships: representation of, 121-2
Characters, 365-73 passim; brightness of, 485, 488; on CRT, 366; density of, 372; distribution of, 482; luminance of, 484, 486, 487; Videotex approach to, 474
Chartjunk, 131, 132, 137, 140
Clauses, 377
Cloze, 220, 221, 222, 224
Coating, optical, 493
Coding of images, 474, 475, 476. *See also* Image
Cognition, 186, 506; and design, 191, 194; and linguistic processes, 188; and maps, 315, 329; and text restraints, 184
Cohesion, 219, 220, 537, 538; and text processing, 224
Color, 12, 15; and display, 476-7; nonverbal, 100
Communication: exchange of, 387; and language, 186, 194; protocols of, 555, 559, 560; systems of, 279; theories of, 592; and typography, 186, 197; and Videotex, 474, 475. *See also* Comprehension, Language, Reading, Writing
Complexity: of illustration, 148, 149; of text, 243, 244, 245, 249. *See also* Text
Comprehension, 538, 539, 540

Data-ink ratio, 140
Data processing, and graphs, 592. *See also* Computers
Data table, 586-8, 603; matrix analysis of, 591; matrix operation of, 601; matrix structure of, 586, 590
Deaf, 445-57 passim; prelingually, 445, 449, 454-5; postlingually, 445, 454-5
Default values, 555
Demonstrations and samples, in representation, 511
Demotic, 43, 53, 61, 62
Depth perception, 279, 288
Descenders of characters, 368, 369, 373
Design, 89, 186, 187, 190, 191-6, 199, 528. *See also* Graphics, Typography

Digital Video Display Systems, 425-6, 433
Display, 337-63, 365-73, 423-40; CRT and, 425, 482; graphics design and, 424; and gray scale, 338; and international standard, 477; memory and, 475, 476; plasma panel of, 352; and resolution, 341, 349, 361; searches of, 366, 368; with screen, 340; technology of, 348; and users, 477
Documents, 405-15 passim; cross-cultural differences in, 410; and readability, 196; stages in, 407; users of, 409, 554
Drawing board for the blind, 462, 469, 470
Drawing technique, 463-70 passim; psychological effect of, 464
Dual coding, 574-5, 580

Editing, 401-4 passim, 525; of character image, 389; and computers, 414; of documents, 407-8; of figures, 388; interactive, 392-3, 395. *See also* Writing
Egypt, 43-64 passim; and language, 48, 49, 52
EIES, 401-4; graphics and, 403. *See also* Computers, Electronic journal
Electronic displays, 520. *See also* Display
Electronic journal, 401-4 passim; British bureaucracy and, 40; copyright and, 404; costs and, 402, 404
Etching, 493
Expectancy in perception, 279, 280, 281, 285, 286, 288
Eye movement, 291, 293, 520, 523; fixation and, 291-2, 293, 294, 297, 301, 303, 520; limitations on, 296; refixation and, 292, 293; regression and, 266-7; units of, 376

Feature extraction, 208-10, 212, 214; and representation in memory, 213
Filters: micromesh, 491; screen, 489
Frame of reference, 315, 316, 317, 322-3, 326-9; in spatial terms, 321

Geographical orientation, 317-21
Gesture language, 9
Graphics, 337-63 passim, 588; analysis of, 592; commands in, 389, 396; constructions in, 395; definition of, 339; information and, 291, 294, 303; and publication, 594; semiology of, 585
Graphs: design of, 589; difficulty of, 310; feelings about, 309; interpretation of, 306; permutations of, 591; reading of, 305-13 passim; reference system of, 315-17, 321-9; summarization of, 306; without text, 307

Hearing impaired. *See* Deaf
Hierarchy: of figure composition, 387, 388; multiple authorship and, 398; of picture description, 395
Hieroglyphs, 43, 45, 57-64; historical development of, 50-3; symbolic interpretation of, 46. *See also* Orthography

# Author Index